Languages and Children—Making the Match

Languages and Children— Making the Match

New Languages for Young Learners, Grades K–8

●FOURTH EDITION

Helena Curtain

University of Wisconsin–Milwaukee, Emerita

Carol Ann Dahlberg

Concordia College, Emerita

Boston ● New York ● San Francisco
Mexico City ● Montreal ● Toronto ● London ● Madrid ● Munich ● Paris
Hong Kong ● Singapore ● Tokyo ● Cape Town ● Sydney

Editor-in-Chief: Aurora Martínez Ramos
Editorial Assistant: Amy Foley
Vice President, Marketing and Sales Strategies: Emily Williams Knight
Vice President, Director of Marketing: Quinn Perkson
Executive Marketing Manager: Krista Clark
Production Editor: Annette Joseph

Editorial Production Service: Lynda Griffiths
Composition Buyer: Linda Cox
Manufacturing Buyer: Megan Cochran
Electronic Composition: Publishers' Design and Production Services, Inc.
Interior Design: Denise Hoffman
Cover Designer: Elena Sidorova

For related titles and support materials, visit our online catalog at www.pearsonhighered.com.

Between the time website information is gathered and then published, it is not unusual for some sites to have closed. Also, the transcription of URLs can result in typographical errors. The publisher would appreciate notification where these errors occur so that they may be corrected in subsequent editions.

Library of Congress Cataloging-in-Publication Data
Curtain, Helena.
Languages and children : making the match : new languages for young
learners, grades K/8 / Helena Curtain, Carol Ann Dahlberg.—4th ed.
    p. cm.
  Includes bibliographical references and index.
  ISBN-13: 978-0-205-53548-4 (alk. paper)
  ISBN-10: 0-205-53548-8 (alk. paper)
  1. Languages, Modern--Study and teaching (Elementary)—United States. I. Dahlberg, Carol
Ann. II. Title.
  LB1578.C86 2010
  372.65—dc22
                                                                          2009028492

Printed in the United States of America
10 9 8 7 6 5 4 3 2 1   RRD   13 12 11 10 09

Permission Acknowledgments:

Standards from *Standards for Foreign Language Learning* reprinted by permission of ACTFL.

Page 5: List from Teacher Partnership at National K–12 Foreign Language Resource Center reprinted by permission from Foreign Language Resource Center, Iowa State University, Ames, IA.

Pages 18–28: Dialogue reprinted by permission of all participants.

Continued on page 543, which constitutes a continuation of the copyright page.

PEARSON

www.pearsonhighered.com

ISBN-10: 0-205-53548-8
ISBN-13: 978-0-205-53548-4

about the authors

Helena Curtain has a wealth of experience as a language educator and has taught at elementary school through university levels. She served as Foreign Language Curriculum Specialist for the Milwaukee Public Schools for many years and in that capacity coordinated and supervised K–12 foreign language and ESOL programs. She served as associate professor at the University of Wisconsin–Milwaukee and directed the Foreign Language and ESOL teacher preparation programs. She is the author of various articles dealing with language instruction. Helena is active professionally and has received both state and national awards for her service to the language teaching profession. She is an internationally known expert on second-language teaching methodology and curriculum development, bilingual education, immersion programs, and two-way immersion programs, especially at the elementary school level. She has also served as speaker, consultant, and visiting professor both nationally and internationally in 25 countries.

Carol Ann Dahlberg is Professor Emerita in Education at Concordia College, Moorhead, Minnesota, where she taught methods courses for secondary and elementary school teachers of foreign languages. She has also taught German K–12 and at the college level. She has authored and coauthored numerous articles and has received national awards from ACTFL and AATG. A founding member of the National Network for Language Learning, Carol Ann served as its first president. She works nationally and internationally as a consultant, curriculum developer, and workshop leader for early language learning.

contents

● PART ONE **The Learner**

● PART TWO **Communication**

● PART EIGHT **Teachers**

18 Developing Professional Teachers for Early Language Programs   502

preface

Languages and Children—Making the Match is designed both as a methods text and as a practical guide for school districts and teachers. It is intended for those preparing to teach languages at the elementary and middle school level (grades K–8); for practitioners already involved with languages for children; and for teachers, parents, and administrators engaged in the planning or in the evaluation process.

The book has been written by practitioners primarily for practitioners. We have included the historical and theoretical elements that have been important to us in our own classroom practice and that we regularly share with our students and in workshop and professional development sessions. Although we have not placed the teaching of world languages at the elementary and middle school in a comprehensive theoretical or historical framework, we believe strongly that classroom practice must be built on a basic understanding of theoretical and historical issues. An understanding of theoretical issues can help teachers know why certain strategies are successful; it can empower them to be effective planners of curricula and interpreters of the program and its methodology to fellow teachers, administrators, parents, and the public.

New to This Edition

- Chapters begin with Enduring Understandings and Essential Questions to guide readers and help them organize material.

- Chapters have been reorganized and updated.

- Emphasis on early second-language literacy throughout the book includes rich strategies for developing early language literacy.

- Additional descriptions of the characteristics of young learners from the perspective of child development specialists and early language teachers will help teachers plan developmentally appropriate instruction.

- New and additional examples directly from classroom practice, in the words of classroom teachers, have been included throughout the chapters to help readers apply the principles presented in the book.

- Sample webs and thematic units have been cited.

- New activities have been added to the Games and Activities chapter.

Student Population

The primary concern of this book is with the acquisition of a new language by majority-language speakers who are not living in an environment in which their new language is commonly spoken. Students in bilingual and English for Speakers of Other Languages

(ESOL) programs, by contrast, are minority-language speakers in the process of learning the majority language, and they have complex needs in their adjustment to a different society—needs that we have not attempted to address. We believe, however, that the principles and strategies for language teaching offered in this book are also applicable or adaptable for teachers working with English language learners (ELLs) and with teachers of heritage language speakers.

Focus on Beginning-Level Classes

Many of the specific teaching suggestions presented here will be of special value to teachers who work in the first years of elementary and middle school programs that provide foreign-language instruction for less than half of the school day. Numerous programs across the country are new and are staffed with teachers who are relatively inexperienced at these levels. Many of these teachers find it especially difficult to develop activities for meaningful communication in the early stages of second-language acquisition. Therefore, we believe that this emphasis will be the most helpful to the majority of readers. All of the activities can be extended and adapted to higher levels of language complexity and development and to other program models, and most of the ideas can be adapted to almost any level of instruction. In this sense, the ideas can be adapted to programs for heritage language speakers who have language skills that range across an extremely broad continuum. Unfortunately, the focus of this book is not geared to the special needs of heritage language learners; we strongly suggest, however, that these learners have programs that are specially established to meet those needs.

Standards for Foreign Language Learning in the 21st Century

The appearance of the Standards in 1996, and the expanded 1999 edition with supporting Standards for nine languages, refocused the vision and the conversation about language teaching and learning. This book makes frequent references to the Standards document, but does not attempt to teach readers about the Standards themselves. We recommend that readers use this book side by side with the *Standards for Foreign Language Learning in the 21st Century,* available in many libraries. If they are not yet a part of your own professional library, we encourage you to order them from the website for ACTFL (American Council on the Teaching of Foreign Languages), www.actfl.org (on-line store). For quick reference, a brief summary of the goals and Standards is found on page xxiii.

The content of the Standards and the teaching philosophy they represent will be useful in any context, even for those who do not teach in a U.S. school setting.

Terminology

FLES (Foreign Language in the Elementary School) is a term that has often been used to label programs for languages other than English at the elementary school level. Many references in the literature continue to use the term *FLES.* In an attempt to firmly place these programs as part of a K–12 sequence, the profession is moving away from the term in favor of more general terms such as *early start programs, early language learning programs,* and *programs for young learners,* and we have adopted this practice for this textbook. Note that current best practice for these programs calls for 30 to 40 minutes a day, three to five days a week.

No alternative is without its problems or potential for confusion. The term *foreign language,* although still widely used in both the United States and around the world, has negative connotations for some parts of the community. *Second language* is used in some discussions to mean acquisition of the majority language by minority-language speakers. The term *second language* is often inappropriate in any case, because a number of students in these programs may actually be acquiring a third or even a fourth language. The term *language,* when used alone, is easily confused with English language arts.

A number of states have chosen to use the term *world languages,* and still others are using the term *Languages Other than English (LOTE),* a term used in Australia. The National Board of Professional Teaching Standards chose w*orld languages other than English,* abbreviated to *world languages.* In this book we have used primarily the terms *world language* and *foreign language,* occasionally *second language,* and frequently the terms *early language* and *target language.* We make no distinction among the terms—since we don't feel there is a consensus around any one term, we decided to use them all!

We hope that this fourth edition of *Languages and Children—Making the Match* will serve as a useful resource for teachers, supervisors, and planners, and that it will make a contribution to the number and quality of language programs for young learners.

acknowledgments

This book is a testimonial to friendship—first of all, to the friendship between the authors that has grown ever stronger through four editions of this book and numerous other projects. It is also an expression of the personal and professional friendships that have supported our work and enriched our understanding. We are deeply grateful, and we hope the book is worthy of you. We thank:

- Our husbands, Tony Curtain and Duane Dahlberg, who have supported us in countless ways.
- The many early language teachers who have contributed ideas and activities to this book.
- Diana D'Amore and Rose Koremenos whose friendship and support were instrumental in the completion of this fourth edition.
- Kristin Ruud for her work with the citations and additions to the activities chapter (Chapter 13) and Brandee Mau for her work on the technology chapter (Chapter 14).
- Janet Glass, Cindy Kendall, Myriam Met, Cherice Montgomery, and Nancy Rhodes for their willingness to review portions of the manuscript and give advice.
- Shannon Graber, Corey Maslowski, and Marcy Zachmeier-Ruh for their inspiring additions to the immersion chapter (Chapter 11).
- Peggy Boyles, Greg Duncan, David Jahner, and Thomas Sauer for their help in updating teacher and program evaluation checklists.
- The wonderful teachers to whom we referred again and again:

  Vicki Alvis, Fulton County Schools

  Jo Ellen Hague, Douglas County, Georgia

  Patty Ryerson Hans, The Wellington School, Columbus, Ohio

  Jessica Haxhi, Maloney Magnet School, Waterbury, Connecticut

  Hildegard Merkle, Bethesda, Maryland

  Alisha Dawn Samples, Lexington One School District, Columbia, South Carolina

  Kathleen Siddons, Goodwin School, Storrs, Connecticut (Retired)

- The reviewers of this fourth edition for their suggestions and comments: Emilio Garza, California State University, Bakersfield; Nancy Lawrence, Albuquerque Public Schools; Carla Paciotto, Western Illinois University; Marcie J. Pyper, Calvin College; Judith L. Shrum, Virginia Tech; and Juan del Valle, University of Evansville.

This book has been written in the spirit of sharing, which is such a marked characteristic of teachers of young learners whenever they get together. Many of the teaching ideas presented here have been shared with us in classes and workshops, and we continue to learn daily from our colleagues and from our students.

Finally, we celebrate especially the network of early language teachers whose dedication, professionalism, and sharing bring the precious gift of new languages to young learners.

introduction

Languages and Children—Making the Match is about the many ways in which learning a new language with skilled teachers can enrich the world of the learner. There are keys, old and new, to unlock the magic that second languages hold for children.

With this book we offer keys that we have found as we imagine what second languages for children might mean, and the potential it can have for all learners in our schools. These keys may be used by teachers already working with children, by those preparing to teach, and by administrators, parents, and others engaged in the planning that brings successful language programs to life and keeps them vital.

Some keys are found in the experiences of the 1960s, when elementary school language programs were popular and numerous. There were serious mistakes made during that boom time for languages, such as inadequate planning, poor preparation of teachers, and unrealistic goals. By acknowledging and analyzing these mistakes, we can avoid their repetition. The 1960s left us with success stories, as well, and from those experiences came examples that guide our planning for the future.

Research in second-language acquisition and in related fields, much of it undertaken since 1970, offers other keys. Not all can be translated directly into classroom practice, but the insights provided by research can help us evaluate programs, materials, and methodology more effectively and consistently. Perhaps the most significant key to the early language learning experience is a dramatic shift in emphasis from grammar to communication in the language teaching profession. The emphasis on communication as the governing idea in curriculum and classroom practice is reinforced both by research and by the experiences of successful language teachers.

The *Standards for Foreign Language Learning in the 21st Century* (1999) have established a new K–12 vision for language education and supported it with challenging goals and standards for curriculum content. ACTFL Performance Guidelines for K–12 Learners (Swender and Duncan, 1998) translate those standards into student performances that can guide both curriculum development and student assessment. These key documents are shared by the entire profession and will help us communicate effectively with one another and with our students, parents, and community.

Communication is the essential element, the fundamental principle of this book. It unifies the guidelines offered and the methods and materials described. Communication has long been a stated goal of the language teaching profession, but it has traditionally been cast in a secondary role to grammar as an organizing principle. The experienced teacher and the beginner alike face the challenge of adapting the methods of the past to a standards-based, communicative emphasis and of developing new strategies to encourage comprehension and communication. This book suggests guidelines and examples to assist the teacher in creating a standards-based classroom in which communication has the highest priority.

The principles on which this book is based are summarized in the Key Concepts for Success: Elementary and Middle School Foreign Languages, found on page xxi and on the Standards for Foreign Language Learning, summarized on page xxiii. The Key Concepts have been shaped by the collective experience of many classroom teachers and they offer a classroom application of what many researchers have learned about languages and children. These are the keys, some new and many familiar. The door of opportunity—the magic of language acquisition—awaits their use.

Although the focus of this book is on grades preK–8, the principles that underlie it apply to language learning at almost any age.

Key Concepts for Success
Elementary and Middle School Foreign Languages

Children learn new languages best when:

1. Learners are active constructors of meaning and users of language, rather than passive receivers of vocabulary and information.

2. Teachers consistently conduct instruction in the target language with minimal use of the native language and translation. Teachers keep the target language and the native language distinctly separate.

3. Units and lessons focus on a thematic center aligned with content and performance standards. There is a balance among the basic goals of culture, subject content, and language in use.

4. Teachers plan for classroom management as carefully as all other aspects of instruction.

5. Teachers scaffold instruction so that learners become increasingly independent in their use of the spoken and written language.

6. Learning takes place in communicative contexts that carry significance for the student.
   - These contexts include meaningful social and cultural situations and subject content instruction, as well storytelling, music, games, rituals, drama, and celebrations.
   - Students learn grammar in context, through usage and not through analysis. Grammar for its own sake is not the object of instruction.
   - There are meaningful opportunities to use the new language beyond the classroom.

7. Learners internalize culture through experiences with cultural materials and practices in the target language.

8. The language program draws from and reinforces the goals of the general curriculum.

9. Learners experience activities that
   - are intrinsically interesting, cognitively engaging, and culturally connected.
   - take into account the distinctive characteristics found at each level of cognitive, social, psychomotor, and educational development.
   - provide frequent opportunities for student language use in interpretive, interpersonal, and presentational modes.
   - include concrete experiences: visuals, props, realia, and hands-on experiences.

- incorporate frequent opportunities for physical activity.
- appeal to a variety of learning styles.
- move students toward increasing independence and self-direction.

10. Activities, lessons, and units are affectively engaging and made meaningful and memorable through the use of story form. containing a clear beginning, middle, and end.

11. Learners use reading and writing as communicative tools appropriate to their age and interests, even in early stages of language development.

12. Teachers and students assess learning frequently and systematically in order to gather information on progress and language development.

Standards for Foreign Language Learning

Communication

Communities — Cultures

Comparisons — Connections

Communication

Communicate in Languages Other Than English

- **Standard 1.1:** Students engage in conversations, provide and obtain information, express feelings and emotions, and exchange opinions.
- **Standard 1.2:** Students understand and interpret written and spoken language on a variety of topics.
- **Standard 1.3:** Students present information, concepts, and ideas to an audience of listeners or readers on a variety of topics.

Cultures

Gain Knowledge and Understanding of Other Cultures

- **Standard 2.1:** Students demonstrate an understanding of the relationship between the practices and perspectives of the culture studied.
- **Standard 2.2:** Students demonstrate an understanding of the relationship between the products and perspectives of the culture studied.

Connections

Connect with Other Disciplines and Acquire Information

- **Standard 3.1:** Students reinforce and further their knowledge of other disciplines through the foreign language.

- **Standard 3.2:** Students acquire information and recognize the distinctive viewpoints that are only available through the foreign language and its cultures.

Comparisons

Develop Insight into the Nature of Language and Culture

- **Standard 4.1:** Students demonstrate understanding of the nature of language through comparisons of the language studied and their own.
- **Standard 4.2:** Students demonstrate understanding of the concept of culture through comparisons of the cultures studied and their own.

Communities

Participate in Multilingual Communities at Home & Around the World

- **Standard 5.1:** Students use the language both within and beyond the school setting.
- **Standard 5.2:** Students show evidence of becoming life-long learners by using the language for personal enjoyment and enrichment.

Source: From Standards for Foreign Language Learning. Reprinted by permission of ACTFL.

Languages and Children—
Making the Match

Learners
Communication
Teachers
Planning
Programs
Languages
&
Children
Resources
Cultures
Content

Chapter 1

Characteristics of Young Learners

Enduring Understanding

- Successful teachers take into account student differences in developmental levels and individual characteristics.

Essential Question

- What do I need to know about the students I teach?

Children have a reputation for being natural language learners, for very good reason. Almost without exception, they have learned their native language with apparent ease, and by the time they are 6 years old they have brought it to a level of fluency that is the envy of non-native speakers. Parents who bring their children into a second-language setting and immerse them in a new situation—for example, an elementary school taught in the foreign language—often experience a kind of miracle. After around 6 months, their child begins to function successfully in the new setting and at a linguistic level to which the parents cannot hope to aspire, even when they have been studying the language seriously for a similar period of time.

These examples of children's natural language learning ability might seem to suggest that the best thing to do to help a child learn a language is simply to place the child in the target language setting and then stay out of the way to let the miracle happen. Unfortunately, this is not an approach that will make it possible to bring languages to every child. There is, however, both linguistic and psychological theory to help explain children's seemingly effortless second-language acquisition and to provide insights that can make the classroom a better place for such language acquisition to take place. Understanding this theory, showing consideration of learner differences, and understanding the principles of child development and the characteristics of children at different stages of development will help prepare the teacher to create curriculum and activities that bring languages and children together effectively.

● Second-Language Acquisition

Second-language acquisition theory may help explain the puzzling situation of children who acquire languages more quickly and apparently with much less effort than do their parents when placed in a second-language environment. The children are in a setting in which they are surrounded by language that is made meaningful because of the context and because of the way teachers speak to them. They are given time to sort out the language that they hear and understand, until they are ready to begin to use it for their own expressive purposes. Their parents, on the other hand, are usually busy learning vocabulary and grammar rules, and they attempt to apply them later to a setting in which they have something to say. For Stephen Krashen, a linguist who has synthesized much of recent second-language acquisition research in his writing, the children would be *acquiring* language, while the parents would be *learning* it.

Krashen has popularized the idea of comprehensible input, the amount or level of language that the student can fully understand, plus just a little more: $i + 1$. According to Krashen's input hypothesis, the most important factor in the amount of language acquired by a learner is the amount of comprehensible input to which that learner is exposed.

The input hypothesis provides a powerful reason for the exclusive use of the target language for all classroom purposes. However, simply deciding to use the target language is not enough. It must be used in such a way that the message is understood by the student at all times, even though every word of the message may not be familiar. This is accomplished through the use of gestures, examples, illustrations, experiences, and caretaker speech, as described next. When teachers complain that students do not understand them when they use the target language, it may well be because they are using the target language at a level that is too far beyond the child's current ability to understand—actually $i + 10$ or perhaps $i + 50$. Learners who are presented with language too far beyond their current level may well conclude that they are not good language learners and/or that this language is simply too hard to be learned. An important part of the teacher's planning time for a classroom based on the principles of second-language acquisition will be devoted to strategies for making the target language comprehensible to the students.

Paying attention to input focuses on the importance of listening skills and on the potential benefits that can come from increased listening opportunities for all students, especially those at the beginning level. An extended listening period gives learners the opportunity to gather meanings and associate them with language. They can give their full attention to understanding the messages that are being communicated, without the pressure to imitate or respond immediately.

Use of Language—Caretaker Speech

In a classroom designed to encourage second-language acquisition, there is an emphasis on communication. The teacher provides students with an environment in which they are surrounded by messages in the target language that communicate interesting, relevant information in language they are able to understand—language that is comprehensible to them. The teacher uses natural language, not contrived language intended to incorporate all the most recently learned grammar points. It differs from the language used with peers. Part of creating comprehensible input for language acquirers consists of using strategies for making the message understood, variously known as "motherese," "caretaker speech," "teacherese," or "foreigner talk." Some of the characteristics of this speech, as it occurs naturally, will be observed when a grandparent is talking with a young grandchild—or when a skilled teacher is introducing a new language. Here are some features of this kind of speech:

1. A somewhat slower rate of speech (still with the normal rate of speech for that speaker, but at the lower end of the range).

2. More distinct pronunciation (not a distorted pronunciation, however, which actually changes the sounds of the language). For example, most American speakers of English pronounce the "tt" in the word *letter* as if it were spelled "dd." When asked to pronounce clearly, they often change their pronunciation of the sound to "tt," thus distorting the language through an attempt to pronounce it "accurately." Such distortions are not in the long-range best interests of the learner.

3. Shorter, less complex sentences.

4. More rephrasing and repetition.

5. More frequent meaning checks with the listener to make sure that he or she understands.

6. Use of gesture and visual reinforcement.

7. Greater use of concrete referents.

8. Scaffolding. The teacher surrounds the learner with language, allowing the student to be a participant in dialogue. In early language acquisition, the teacher actually provides both verbal parts of a conversation. Later, the teacher might embellish one- and two-word responses by the learner into complete utterances in a natural, conversational manner, at the same time modeling extended discourse and providing meaningful listening experiences. Students will become capable of taking over increasing responsibility as participants in the conversation.

Conditions Necessary for Second-Language Acquisition in the Classroom

According to Krashen and colleagues (1982), as well as other researchers, language acquisition takes place most effectively when the input is meaningful and interesting to the learner, when it is comprehensible ($i + 1$), and when it is not grammatically sequenced.

These ideas contrast sharply with some practices that have been common in language teaching. Language acquisition theory suggests that the language to which learners are exposed should be as natural as possible—that the past tense, for example, should not be postponed until students are able to analyze the past tense themselves. The key factor in the usefulness of input is whether or not it is comprehended.

In general, the grammatical details of a message do not have as much impact on comprehensibility as does the context surrounding the verbal message and the vocabulary with which the message is communicated, especially in the early stages of language acquisition. Meaningfulness and interest for the learner may well be the most significant factors of all.

Michael Long (1983) and others suggest that acquisition takes place best in a setting in which meaning is negotiated through interaction, so that the student has influence on the message being communicated. Of course, the greater the language skills of the listener, the more effectively the interaction can influence the message. This suggests to the teacher that early attention must focus on providing students with the ability to communicate messages such as, "I don't understand," "Could you please repeat that?," "Did you mean . . . ?," "Could you please speak more slowly?," and so forth.

Comprehensible Output

Merrill Swain (1985) has taken Krashen's idea one step further with her suggestion that students acquire language most meaningfully when they also have the opportunity for comprehensible "output," or "pushed output." That is, they need to have a setting in which their attempts at communication are valued and shaped to make them acceptable and understandable, through communicative rather than grammatical means of correction. When learners are pushed to express themselves in the new language, they begin to listen to the grammar of the language, and not just to the vocabulary. Output also allows learners to test hypotheses about the target language grammar (Ellis, 2008).

Mounting evidence suggests that direct error correction has little or no influence on the accuracy of messages (Dulay, Burt, and Krashen, 1982). Correction that responds to the meaning of a message, however, has a much greater likelihood of making a difference for the speaker. Frequently correcting grammatical errors and interrupting to prod for accuracy tends to shift students' attention away from the message being communicated and toward inhibiting their willingness to speak.

Essential Concepts of Second Language Acquisition for Teachers

Awareness of how languages are learned is a part of the essential background of any language teacher, and this is especially the case at the K–8 level. A group of K–6 foreign language teachers and teacher trainers developed the following list of essential concepts of second-language (L2) acquisition for early language teachers. They were part of a Teacher Partnership Institute at the National K–12 Foreign Language Resource Center at Iowa State University. The following list grew out of their experiences and discussion:

- Second-language acquisition proceeds according to predictable stages.
- The degree of acquisition is correlated with the time available for instruction.
- Children acquire language best in a low-anxiety environment.
- Culture is closely related to language and is an essential component of instruction.
- Meaning can be communicated in L2 without the use of English (or L1).
- Children acquire language through a focus on meaning rather than on grammar.
- Children involve many senses in the acquisition process.
- Meaning in L2 is established, in a school setting, through thematic, integrative approaches incorporating the content of the general curriculum.
- Meaning is established through visual cues.
- Children acquire language through extended listening experiences and negotiation of meaning.
- A relevant, meaningful context is necessary for effective language acquisition.
- The teacher can use a variety of techniques to make the language understandable to children (comprehensible input).
- Children acquire language through the tasks appropriate to their developmental level:
  a. More manipulation is necessary for younger students.
  b. Language analysis begins later (philosophic layer/late adolescence).
  c. Older students often demand more translations.
- The rate and the degree of L2 acquisition are affected by differing student learning styles.
- Learner-centered instruction facilitates second-language acquisition.

This is a concise summary of our current understanding of effective foreign language pedagogy for young learners.

Factors Affecting Second-Language Acquisition

Many factors are at work in the early language classroom. There is variation among the characteristics of the input to which students are or have been exposed, as well as factors relating to individual students.

Some of the most important of these issues are summarized in Figure 1.1. The input factors in this diagram work together to create an environment and a learning career for the student that can lead to eventual fluency in the target language.

How long has the child been learning the language? The amount of language to which the student has already been exposed is a critical element in his or her current and future levels of language acquisition. Time is the great ally in development of language proficiency.

● **FIGURE 1.1** Input and Attributes in L2 Acquisition

Source: Adapted from Brown (1991).

Does the program offer language every day for at least 30 to 40 minutes, for optimal learning in a program for young learners, or is there less time available? Met and Rhodes (1990) identified time spent in language instruction and the intensity of that instruction as the two most critical factors in rate and amount of language acquisition. The American Council on the Teaching of Foreign Languages (ACTFL) Young Learner Task Force (Swender and Duncan, 1998) established 30 to 40 minutes per day, three to five days per week, as a minimum time allocation for achievement of the performance goals outlined for K–12 learners (p. 482).

Within the amount of time that is allocated to language in the school day, how much of that time is actually spent on language instruction? How often is the class canceled because of school programs or field trips? How much time is spent moving the students to the language classroom, or taking out and putting away materials, or handling discipline problems? All of these factors cut into allocated time; time on task is the real measure of the input available during a class period.

In addition to how much time is spent, we also have to look at the quality of that time. What kind of instruction is taking place? Is there use of the target language **95** percent of the time in cognitively engaging, developmentally appropriate activities?

On the other side of the chart are the attributes that the student brings to the language learning process. These are the factors within the student and the student's social setting.

First, how old is the learner? Age is strongly related to learning another language. Children are more likely to develop native-like proficiency before age 10, and they are also at a maximum of openness to other cultures. Second, how literate are the learners in their first language? These skills will influence the ability of the learner to benefit from written forms of input.

In the model (Figure 1.1) there is interaction between the two sides. The best input can also fail a student if it does not take into account the attributes of the individual learner. Every learner brings significant cognitive abilities to the classroom. These are related to the student's capacity for analogy and intellectualization. Each learner has a unique array of abilities and capacities, of intelligences, and of learning styles and strategies. All of these dimensions affect the types of experiences that will best facilitate language acquisition for a specific learner, no matter what the learner's age.

What factors in a student's personality will affect her or his ability to profit from target language input? Is the student a risk taker or an extrovert? Is the learner inhibited? What other personality factors might support or hinder language learning?

How strong is the student's motivation to learn the language? Highly motivated students seek out input and benefit from every opportunity to experience the new language.

What is the child's social environment? Is language learning valued at home and among peers? What is the learner's attitude about speakers of the new language?

Once the input and attributes have been taken into account, the next step is interaction. The learner must have the opportunity to use the language, to engage with the language, and to construct meaning with the language in order to learn it! With enough opportunities for communicative interaction, the final stage is, of course, proficiency in the new language.

● Cognitive Characteristics of the Learner

Just as second-language acquisition research has helped us better understand the language development of the students in our classrooms, cognitive psychologists have given us information about learning in general. Information about the brain can lead us to better ways to reach our students, and to make our time with them more effective. Multiple intelligences and learning styles models have been developed by psychologists and educators in order to assist the teacher in planning for a whole classroom of learners whose learning preferences and strengths may be different from those of the teacher—and they are certainly not identical with those of each other!

Information from Brain Research

The study of the brain and intensive work in cognitive psychology have resulted in a significant shift in orientation away from the behaviorist principles that once dominated educational thought and practice. Rote learning, habit formation, and observable outcomes are being replaced by an emphasis on meaningfulness, metacognition, and process.

For the behavioral psychologist, the student is considered to be a relatively passive subject, to be manipulated through reinforcement techniques and drill. The cognitive psychologist, by contrast, sees students as active participants in the learning situation, controlling and shaping their own learning processes. In the behaviorist classroom, the students respond to stimuli and reinforcement, whereas in the classroom based on cognitive psychology, the students' own internal motivation drives the learning process. One of the most important principles of cognitive psychology for the early language teacher is that information is best learned and retained if it is made meaningful to students.

Teresa Kennedy (2006, p. 479) identifies several implications of brain research for the language teacher, highlighting the importance of engaging many senses and an enriched environment. She also notes:

- We use our *emotions* to tell us what is important to learn and what to remember.
- The brain stores information based on *functionality* and *meaningfulness*.
- Emotions drive *attention*.
- Attention drives *learning* and *memory*.
- *Repetition* is necessary but it requires *novelty* with regard to instructional design (which should incorporate all five language processes—observation, listening, speaking, reading, and writing—and utilize a variety of methods and approaches).

Renate Caine and Geoffrey Caine (1997), in their Brain/Mind Learning Principles (pp. 104–108) point out that the search for meaning is innate. Meaningful and meaningless information are stored separately. Meaningless, or relatively unrelated, information requires far more conscious effort to learn. Meaningful information is stored in a "spatial/autobiographical" memory that does not require rehearsal and can be recalled as a complete experience.

Rod Ellis (2008) also emphasizes the significance of meaning, listing it as the second of his 10 principles of instructed second-language acquisition: "Instruction needs to ensure that learners focus predominantly on meaning." He notes that activities focused on creating meaning are intrinsically motivating for learners; they help develop both communication skills and the vocabulary and grammar needed to use the language effectively (pp. 1–2).

Patterning   One of the most important points about the brain and learning is the fact that the brain's search for meaning occurs through patterning. The brain looks for patterns as it organizes information according to schematic maps and categories. As young learners in language classes search for meaning in the experiences we provide for them, we must be sure to create complex, meaningful experiences from which they construct their own patterns of understanding.

What we now know about the brain suggests that it resists having meaninglessness imposed on it; facts and skills that are presented in isolation need more practice and rehearsal to be stored. For example, if we were to ask students to memorize a random series of letters such as *f z g i h r c t u w d h,* students would be able to do this task, but it would require great effort since the series of letters is presented in isolation and is meaningless.

If we were to ask students to memorize a series of letters that are put together into words such as *yet, paper, snow, drive, boat, when, through,* the task would be somewhat easier, since the brain can attach some meaning to the words even though the words themselves are not connected in any way.

If, on the other hand, the teacher uses a meaningful sentence such as *The boy is going to Disneyland when school is over for the summer,* the brain has much more of an opportunity to attach meaning and make connections. This last series of letters combined together into a sentence expresses a complete thought.

A child presented with this sentence may think of his or her favorite Disney character or some of the pictures she or he has seen of the exciting events at Disneyland. This sentence has a much better chance of being remembered because it connects to an experience that is already in the child's brain and it activates the child's prior knowledge. If the sentence is actually the climax of an engaging and emotion-filled story, it is likely that the whole experience will be stored in memory quite easily.

Although it may seem to teachers that they are making things easier for learners by reducing learning to isolated "simple" words and sounds, such as letters of the alphabet or the names of various vocabulary items, it requires more work for the brain to remember these things, since it has no meaningful experience to which to attach the learning. In the example of asking the student to learn a series of isolated letters or words, the task is actually made more difficult because the student has to rely on rote memory rather than on the context and the connections that make the learning meaningful.

The brain processes parts and wholes simultaneously. While it is sometimes necessary to focus on individual pieces or discrete skills, these individual pieces or discrete skills should be presented within a rich context. Any focus on discrete items, such as individual vocabulary or writing details, for example, must be made for a clear purpose, so that the parts become building blocks for holistic learning.

Emotions   Many researchers have described the importance of emotion in the learning process and in the construction of meaning. Emotions and thoughts cannot be separated, and thus emotions have a great effect on all learning. One of Caine and Caine's (1997) guiding principles states that emotions are critical to the brain's patterning (p. 105). If an event is related to positive emotions, there is a greater chance for successful patterning to take place. Jensen (2005) puts it even more forcefully: "Emotions drive attention, create meaning, and have their own memory pathways."

The role of emotions applies both to the types of experiences we provide for the students and to the classroom atmosphere we create. Many of our student activities have positive emotions associated with them, such as games, songs, rhymes, and lessons involving movement and physical activity. Creating a warm emotional climate in which children feel self-confident, free, and highly motivated is equally as important as providing activities that have emotional connections. Periodic celebrations of learning, of target culture festivals, or of individual achievements can contribute to the positive classroom atmosphere we hope to create. Mascots for the classroom can enhance the positive environment as well, such as a frog puppet "class member" or a "target language only" bear that goes home with the children on a rotating basis.

Story is another vehicle for integrating emotion in instruction. Pink (2006) describes story as "context enriched by emotion" (p. 103). As humans, we are natural story makers, storing and retrieving our experiences as stories. Shared stories bind us to our culture and help us understand our world.

Eric Jensen (2000) points out that for many content areas a moderate level of stress optimizes learning. However, for subjects with high complexity and novelty, such as language and mathematics, students learn better with the lower stress environment just described (p. 78).

Stephen Krashen (1981), in his discussion of the "affective filter," highlights the importance of emotions in the language learning process and the fact that children are known to resist learning when learning is unpleasant, painful, or being attempted in a punitive environment. Students' ability to learn more readily those things they want to learn is well recognized. Krashen relates these experiences to language acquisition by describing a filter that the brain erects to block out second-language input, no matter how carefully designed that input may be. The filter goes up in the presence of anxiety or low self-confidence, or in the absence of motivation. The filter goes down, and the language input can come through, when motivation is high, when a student is self-confident, and when the learning takes place in a relatively anxiety-free environment.

Social Dimension   Construction of meaning also has a social dimension, especially in a world language classroom. As Frank Smith (1994) put it, "Language is not a genetic gift. It is a social gift." Meaning can be constructed much more readily if social interaction is an important part of the learning. One of Ellis's principles (2008) affirms that "the opportunity to interact in the second language is central to developing second language proficiency" (p. 2). Games, role-plays, and partner and small-group activities motivate learners at the same time as they enhance learning.

The social dimension of games and classroom rituals provides another way in which the brain can attach meaning. Once the students have learned a concept, they can practice it in partners and small groups. The social relationships of partner and small group activities add to the richness of meaning-based experiences for the brain. Following are some examples of simple social activities that can be done in the classroom.

- At the beginning of class, the whole class can greet the teacher in the target language, but then the students can also greet several of their classmates in a very short, motivating, social partner activity.

- Students can practice classroom dialogues with partners, or "read" to each other a memorized story that they have written either individually or as a class activity.

- Students can do a partner weather report. After a class member has looked out the window and reported on the weather, the other students can tell their partners about the weather outside.

- Students can turn to their partners to practice or process a new phrase or a new concept. Chapter 4, on partner and group work, will provide many other examples.

Learning Styles

The individual learners in foreign language classes differ in many ways, at every level of instruction. Writers and researchers on learning styles have provided a plethora of ways to analyze and describe learner differences, and all are useful. Learners can be characterized as visual, auditory, and kinesthetic learners; they can also be classified as holistic or linear learners. Some researchers place learners on a continuum from concrete to abstract or from sequential to random. Perhaps the most important insight from this information is the realization that almost all students are different from their teachers, and from each other, in a large variety of ways. This section describes a few of them.

Some learners thrive in a highly social and interactive environment; others feel more comfortable and may do better when they can think and learn alone. Some learners are motivated and empowered by carefully structured, linear tasks and unvarying routines; they may find it annoying and distracting when bulletin boards or visuals are not carefully aligned and the classroom isn't neat and orderly. Other students feel suffocated by so much structure and long for the freedom to solve problems and be creative. These same students enjoy classes in which the teacher keeps them guessing and sometimes makes random leaps from one topic to another. These students don't usually mind a little clutter—it makes them feel at home!

Many students need a supportive emotional climate in which to learn, and regular assurance that they are valued as people, regardless of their performance. A few students, on the other hand, just want to be left alone to learn—on their own!

Some students need to touch, or move, in order to learn. (That's probably true of almost every primary school child.) Some students benefit most from visuals and teachers' gestures when they are learning or reviewing language; others won't feel confident of the information until they see it written out; still others, with poor vision or a brain that processes visual input poorly, don't benefit from either.

Some children learn very well just from listening attentively to what is taking place—they may remember well without ever writing things down. Still others need to take notes and rework the information several times before it is firmly anchored.

These examples just begin to describe the ways in which students differ from one another—and from their teacher!

There are many other differences, too. Does a student learn best in a busy environment, perhaps with a music background, or in a quiet setting? Some students learn best when they can volunteer and try things out; others need to feel very secure before trying anything new.

Nancy Foss (1994) points out that when students are asked to learn in a way that makes them uncomfortable, they experience stress. In a classroom where a student's learning style is never included, that student is constantly operating under stress, and learning is likely to be seriously affected. Foss recommends that teachers should be aware of when an activity or an assignment will cause stress for one or more groups of students, and try to find ways to make the activity more comfortable. For example, some students who prefer very linear, clearly defined tasks will be under stress when assigned to create a skit with a group. Providing clear written directions and a template for the skit, as well as a written component as part of the skit preparation, will help to make these students more comfortable and help them to learn more effectively.

Multiple Intelligences

As we look at our classes closely we can make an important discovery. Each class is brimming with intelligence—but as with learning styles, each student's profile is different. The work of Howard Gardner (1983, 1993, 1999) and applications by Thomas Armstrong (1993, 1994) make us aware of eight distinct forms of intelligence that exist in our students, identified in Table 1.1. Each of the forms of intelligence is valuable and necessary in society, although most schools have tended to support and nurture only the first two: linguistic and logical-mathematical intelligence. This practice has tended to leave other forms of intelligence with far less recognition in the school setting. Armstrong (1996) points out that despite the emphasis on the first two intelligences, U.S. students are not excelling in these areas, and he questions whether it might not be the case that children learn best when "their entire range of capability is addressed and when multiple connections are encouraged in a balanced way" (p. 2).

As language teachers in a system that has long valued linguistic and logical-mathematical intelligence above all, we are in a good position to support other kinds of intelligence, too. Some teachers, as they plan their units and lessons, lay out all the intelligences on a grid and systematically include some activity for each type of intelligence. Such an approach respects the value of all the intelligences and encourages students to do their best work at all times.

In a 30-minute class period, touching on every intelligence might be quite a challenge, but we certainly can try to keep a balance among all of them over a week, or throughout a unit. Many of the activities and examples in this book show how we can touch on a number of different intelligences in our classes.

One of the important lessons that teachers can take from the research on learning styles and multiple intelligences is this: What interests and appeals to us as learners and as teachers is an important consideration as we plan. However, it is a very unreliable guide to meeting the needs and interests of all the students in our classes. In every class we teach, there are bound to be more students who are unlike us than there are those who are like us. It is our job to build bridges to all learning styles, helping students to learn, as much of the time as possible, in a way that is natural and comfortable to them. Our goal as language teachers is to support the learning of every student, appealing to a variety of learning styles, and to nurture all of the forms of intelligence represented in each of our classes. Our goal is for every learner to experience success—on his or her own terms as well as on ours.

TABLE 1.1 Multiple Intelligences and Their Applications to the Language Classroom

Intelligence	Excels at	Language Application
Linguistic	Reading, writing, telling stories, playing word games, etc.	Almost everything we do in class!
Logical-Mathematical	Experimenting, questioning, figuring out logical puzzles, calculating, etc.	Surveys, making charts and graphs
Spatial	Designing, drawing, visualizing, doodling, etc.	Illustrating a Gouin series; creating a picture of an object by writing the word for the object over and over
Bodily-Kinesthetic	Dancing, running, jumping, activities adding motions to songs and chants	Total Physical Response (TPR), building, touching, gesturing, etc.
Musical	Singing, whistling, humming, creating melodies for favorite rhymes	Using songs and rhythmic chants, tapping feet and hands, listening, etc.
Interpersonal	Leading, organizing, relating, manipulating, mediating, partying, etc.	Small group and partner work
Intrapersonal	Setting goals, meditating, dreaming, planning, being quiet	Journaling, portfolio building
Naturalist	Understanding, categorizing, explaining things in the world of nature	Photography, field trips, classifying

Sources: Adapted from Gardner (1983, 1993, 1999) and Armstrong (1993, 1994).

A second lesson, every bit as important as the first, has to do with the use of the information on learning styles and multiple intelligences. Each student in the classroom is an individual of remarkable complexity. No single category or set of categories is adequate to describe or explain that individual student, although at times the categories can be useful in finding a way to reach an individual student. If teachers begin to think in terms of "that concrete sequential in the second row" or "that naturalist right in front of me," however, we have missed the point and also missed the precious individuality of each student in our classes. The categories are useful in helping us plan our classes and diversify our teaching, but they should never be used to sort our students into "boxes" that limit our understanding of the whole person. Howard Gardner (1999) identified this danger very clearly: "People so labeled may then be seen as capable of working or learning only in certain ways, a characterization that is almost never true. Even if it has a certain rough-and-ready validity, such labeling can impede efforts to provide the best educational interventions for success with a wide range of children" (p. 91).

Thematic Teaching and Construction of Meaning

Thematic instruction is an integral part of early language learning and provides an ideal environment for constructing meaning. In thematic teaching, the curriculum is organized around a thematic center, which can originate in the classroom, the school, the environment, or the target culture. Language concepts and concepts from the regular curriculum and the target culture are interrelated and presented as a whole, within a thematic framework. Language is tailored to the developmental level of the students; activities address a variety of learning styles and call forth a range of multiple intelligences. Students have many opportunities for identifying patterns and connections, experiencing engaging activities with emotional content, and interacting with their peers. It is the goal of the thematic instruction described in this book to reach every child with meaningful language and culture experiences.

● Developmental Characteristics of the Learner

The most important factor in teaching and learning in any setting is the learner. Learners of any age differ from one another in significant ways: Individuals may learn best through listening or reading, they may learn more easily alone or within a small group, they may require heavy visual reinforcement or learn better through verbal explanations, or they may respond better to a sequential or to a random organization of materials or experiences. Each learner's experiences differ from those of class peers in a variety of ways. Children and young adolescents, however, differ from older learners in certain patterned and predictable ways as they progress through stages of development. An understanding of these general developmental characteristics is essential for the elementary and middle school language teacher.

Piaget and Stages of Cognitive Development

The teaching of children has been profoundly affected by the work of Jean Piaget, who identified four stages of cognitive and affective development in childhood and adolescence. The child develops cognitively through active involvement with the environment, and each new step in development builds on and becomes integrated with previous steps. Because two of the four shifts in developmental stage normally occur during the elementary school years, it is important for language teachers working with children to keep the characteristics of each cognitive stage in mind (Piaget, 1963). They are as follows:

   1. *The stage of sensory-motor intelligence (age 0 to 2 years).* During this stage, behavior is primarily motor. The child does not yet internally represent events and "think" conceptually, although "cognitive" development is seen as schemata are constructed.

   2. *The stage of preoperational thought (age 2 to 7 years).* This stage is characterized by the development of language and other forms of representation and rapid conceptual development. Reasoning during this stage is pre-logical or semi-logical, and children tend to be very egocentric. Children often focus on a single feature of a situation at a time—for example, they may be able to sort by size or by color but not by both characteristics at once.

   3. *The stage of concrete operations (age 7 to 11 years).* During these years, the child develops the ability to apply logical thought to concrete problems. Hands-on, concrete experiences help children understand new concepts and ideas. Using language to exchange information becomes much more important than in earlier stages, as children become more social and less egocentric.

   4. *The stage of formal operations (age 11 to 15 years or older).* During this stage, the child's cognitive structures reach their highest level of development. The child becomes able to apply logical reasoning to all classes of problems, including abstract problems either not coming from the child's direct experience or having no concrete referents.

   The thinking skills of most children in elementary school are at the concrete operations stage, and experience plays a major role in all learning. Piaget points out that children are not simply miniature adults who have less experience and thus less knowledge to work with as they approach problems and new situations. They do not think like adults because their minds are not like adult minds. It is the privilege of the elementary school teacher to share their world and learn to work within it. Characteristics of children as learners at different ages and implications for language teaching are described next.

Egan and Layers of Educational Development

The work of the Canadian educator Kieran Egan (1979, 1986, 1992) provides insights about educational development that are especially applicable to the elementary and middle school language program. Egan describes development in terms of the characteristics that determine how the learner makes sense of the world. He thinks of educational development as a process of accumulating and exercising layers of ability to engage with the world. As individuals develop, they add new layers of sophistication without leaving behind the qualities characteristic of earlier layers. As he puts it, "Each stage contributes something vital and necessary to the mature adult's ability to make sense of the world and human experience" (1979, p. 86). The final stage, the ironic layer, is made up of essential contributions from all the earlier stages, governed by the ironic orientation to the world. The characteristics of each of Egan's four layers are as follows:

The Mythic Layer: Ages 4 to 5 through 9 to 10 Years

- For these early elementary-school learners, emotions have primary importance. The students always want to know how to feel about what they are learning. They make sense of things through emotional and moral categories (e.g., good versus bad, happy versus sad, etc.).
- Young children are drawn into a topic or an idea through simple polar opposites. For example, they find it hard to resist the appeal of very tiny versus really huge, freezing cold versus burning hot, a wicked witch versus the perfect princess, and so on. Once presented in this way, concepts can be developed by filling in between the poles.
- The world of the imagination is vivid and real to these children, so they move easily in and out of a world where animals talk or activities take place on a magical trip to another world.
- Learners in the Mythic Layer often believe that the world thinks and feels as they do.
- These learners interpret the world in terms of absolutes, in the same way that a fairy tale world operates. The wicked witch is all bad; the daring prince is all good.
- Using story form is the ideal approach for teaching Mythic Layer learners. Like a fairy tale, instruction should have a clear and strong beginning, middle, and end; it should introduce things using strong opposites; it should address absolute meanings; and it should have strong emotional and moral appeal. Although it does not have to be a story, instruction should incorporate these strong story elements.

The Romantic Layer: Ages 8 to 9 through 14 to 15 Years

- Upper elementary and middle school learners begin to separate the world around them from their internal world—they no longer assume that the world thinks and feels as they do. They are developing a sense of their own identity within this wider world.
- Romantic Layer learners tend to see this outside world as both fascinating and frightening. As they seek out the limits of this world, they are drawn to extremes (e.g., the highest mountain, the longest word, etc.). They are also attracted to realistic detail—the more different from their own experience, the better.
- These learners are great collectors of everything from baseball cards to amazing facts about a country on another continent. They often enjoy research on topics of their own choosing, and they are good at memorizing.
- Because the outside world can seem threatening, elementary-age students learn best when new information incorporates and emphasizes qualities that can over-

come the threat—"transcendent" qualities such as courage, nobility, genius, ambition, energy, and creativity.

● Story form continues to be important for the Romantic Layer learner, with emphasis on realistic detail and real-life heroes and heroines.

● Although it may not seem evident, Romantic Layer learners are searching for and developing a sense of romance, wonder, and awe.

The Philosophic Layer: Ages 14 to 15 through 19 to 20 Years

● These learners have integrated their inner world with the outer world. They now understand the world to be a unit, of which they are a part.

● Learners in the Philosophic Layer try to organize the facts and details they collected in the Romantic Layer, creating their own systems for making sense of the world.

● Once they have developed a system of organization, these learners tend to believe that they have found *the* system, and they become (over)confident that they know the meaning of everything!

The Ironic Layer: Ages 19 to 20 through Adulthood

● The learner recognizes that no one system is adequate to organize all knowledge, but that systems are necessary to make sense of information. If one system does not work well, it can be discarded in favor of another one.

● This is the mature, adult learner.

Classroom Considerations for Elementary and Middle School Learners

Several experienced pre-K to middle school teachers have added their observations about students in different grade levels, primarily from the point of view of the language teacher. They are:

Vicki Alvis, Fulton County Public Schools, Georgia

Myriam Chapman, Bank Street School, New York City, New York

Hal Groce, Anoka-Hennepin Public Schools, Minnesota

Alan Hans, NBCT Early Adolescent Science, Hilliard Tharp School, Hilliard, Ohio

Patty Ryerson Hans, The Wellington School, Columbus, Ohio

Jessica Haxhi, Maloney Magnet School, Waterbury, Connecticut

Ana Lomba, Ana Lomba Early Languages LLC, Princeton Junction, New Jersey

Hildegard Merkle, Bethesda, Maryland

Kate Naughter, Amman, Jordan

Joel Swanson, Mounds Park Academy, St. Paul, Minnesota

Preschool Students (Ages 2 to 4)

Preschool children are in a sensitive period for language development. They absorb languages effortlessly and are adept imitators of speech sounds. Because they are very self-centered, they do not work well in groups, and they respond best to activities and learning situations relating to their own interests and experiences. Although they have a short attention span, they have great patience for repetition of the same activity or game. Preschoolers respond well to concrete experiences and to large-motor involvement in language learning.

> *Ana:* Young children are very active and have short attention spans. It is important to plan your curriculum with that in mind. For a one-hour class I may have somewhere in the order of 10 to 15 different activities, but many of them are repeated from previous classes. Also, these activities are varied in nature to appeal to the diverse personalities of the students. It is a good idea to always carry an extra "life saving" activity. No matter how wonderful your activities for the day are and how great your expertise is, some days will be rough. In days like this I would take out a bag of play-dough or another tactile activity and postpone my wonderful plans to the next day. That's how it is.
>
> Developing phonological awareness in preschool is a critical skill in alphabetic languages. These phonological skills transfer from one language to another. Therefore, by including activities that develop phonological awareness in—say—Spanish, you are also helping young children move forward in their path to building reading skills in English. Now, that's something all early language educators should know! By using rhymes, poems, stories, tongue twisters, and many other language-rich activities in your instruction you are not only helping young children acquire better communicational skills in the new language, but also taking them a huge step further in their path to becoming proficient readers in their first languages.

Primary Students (Ages 5 to 7): Kindergarten and Grades 1 and 2

Most primary-grade children are still preoperational, and they learn best with concrete experiences and immediate goals. New concepts and vocabulary are more meaningful when presented as pairs of binary opposites. Children like to name objects, define words, and learn about things in their own world; they also have vivid imaginations and respond well to stories of fantasy. They need to know how to feel about something in order to learn it well. Primary-age children learn through oral language; they are capable of developing good oral skills, pronunciation, and intonation when they have a good model. They learn well, especially beginning in first grade, through dramatic play, role-play, and use of story form with a strong beginning, middle, and end. Because of their short attention spans, they need to have a great variety of activities, but the teacher must keep in mind that children of this age tire easily. They require large-muscle activity, and they are still rather unskilled with small-muscle tasks. Teachers of primary students must give very structured and specific directions and build regular routines and patterns into the daily lesson plans.

Kindergarten

Patty: Prekindergarten and kindergarten students need to know that there will be daily opportunities for moving, wiggling, manipulating objects, and using songs and/or rhythm. They love to share their favorites (favorite color, animal, fruit, etc.). They love to use every available sense and to experience "magic" (using colored water, magic boxes, [and noticing] the appearance of unusual things in the classroom). It is crucial for them to "have a turn." When playing games, they are most comfortable when they can see the system for assuring that everyone will have a turn (cards or Popsicle sticks with each child's name).

Hildegard: I often "forgot" that my kindergarten students were not German, they followed my commands and instructions with such ease. They need to feel accepted, liked, part of the group, and to be noticed and smiled at by the teacher. Feeling uncomfortable in class makes them physically sick (tummy ache). They like to move constantly, manipulate three-dimensional things, put things together and take apart, be enchanted by stories.

Jessica: Kindergartners are capable of much higher levels of conversation and content than we ordinarily assume. They enjoy short dialogues (name, likes, etc.) performed with puppets—especially talking about themselves! They are engaged when making predictions and experimenting, such as with "sink and float" lessons. They also like being able to comment at every stage of the class, using expressions such as "I'm done!" "Look at this!" and "I did it!"

Joel: These kids are a lot of fun. They will tell you what they are thinking and will not hold back. If you've gone too long someone will ask when the class is over. If they need to move, they will. When I am planning for kindergarten, I shoot for 9 to 10 activities in 35 minutes. Of course the "new" activity might just be a slight variation. You can throw in a twist on your song, or start making mistakes in a poem, but you have to plan ahead to keep them where you want them.

Grade 1

Patty: First-graders still crave structure and routine, but also like more surprises within that routine. Using chairs to help define each child's space is more helpful by this age. A system for turn taking is also still important. My first-grade students enjoy creating and playing games that reinforce whatever language elements we are working on. Games that involve closing eyes and hiding objects are especially successful. I generally have one bulletin board dedicated to whatever the first-grade students are learning about and they love seeing mysterious changes on the board and trying to figure out what caused them (i.e., What animal broke the branch off our apple tree?). They enjoy songs with big motions and the opportunity to add a silly twist to a song or game. Pretending is still very well received as well.

Hildegard: They need to feel successful. They like to take things home, tell endlessly about themselves, move, make things (crafts), draw, and label. They are interested in almost everything—holiday celebrations, fairy tales, themselves. Play, play, play! It is a good age to introduce and practice partner work and cooperative learning. Have a take-home folder for the parents to see.

Jessica: Our first-graders have enjoyed cultural activities that they can participate in physically, such as a summer festival dance, tea ceremony, or pretend "flower viewing" picnic. As fifth-graders, they often remember these early cultural experiences. They also respond well to carrying out classroom tasks, such as handing out and collecting scissors, crayons, pencils, and glue while using the target language.

Joel: They are learning to read and write and love it when they can do those things in the target language. I take advantage of that every time that I can. They love to be read to and are amazed that they can read some things in the target language. Don't forget the short attention span. You will still need to plan a lot of activities for a 30- to 35-minute class.

Grade 2

Jessica: The energy of second-graders must be cherished! They are most willing to participate in story-form pretending, physical acting out of adventures [TPR], and even repetitive dialogues. As with each grade, though, units must be meaningful and have a driving purpose. Since second-graders get so excited, it is helpful to have a "cool-down" song or chant that leaves them quiet at the end of class.

Joel: Every day they remind me that they may be bigger than the kindergartners, but developmentally they have a lot in common. They can do a lot in the target language, but watch out for expecting too much. They still aren't to the point where they can deal in abstracts. They also have difficulties with too many instructions at once. Don't forget to break complicated instructions down into easy chunks.

Patty: Second-graders enjoy silly, surprise endings and having the opportunity to pretend that they are in a variety of situations. They also like to get specific when learning about various animals and enjoy a scientific twist to a lesson whenever possible.

Intermediate Students (Ages 8 to 10): Grades 3, 4, and 5

Intermediate-grade students are at a maximum of openness to people and situations different from their own experience. For these children, a global emphasis is extremely important, because it gives them an opportunity to work with information about countries in all parts of the world. As intermediates develop the cognitive characteristics of the concrete operations level, they begin to understand cause and effect. Students in intermediate grades can work well in groups. They can begin a more systematic approach to language learning, but they continue to need firsthand, concrete experiences as a starting point and to benefit from learning that is embedded in context. The phenomenon of "boy germs" and "girl germs" begins to develop during these years, and children may resist partner situations with children of the opposite sex. They continue to benefit from experiences with imagination and fantasy, emphasis on binary opposites, and strong emotional connection to what is learned, as well as story form with distinctive beginning, middle, and end. In addition, they will benefit from themes based on real-life heroes and heroines who display transcendent qualities in overcoming the challenges of life.

Jessica points out that learners in these grades are bringing together much of the vocabulary and functional chunks learned in earlier years and can apply them in more complex situations. In assessment, they should be given meaningful contexts in which to use the language they already know and to create new language, such as when designing commercials or skits, responding to picture prompts, or writing letters to pen pals. Students can work readily with rubrics and they usually enjoy peer editing and scoring activities. Teachers can balance their picture of students' language progress through keeping a record of mini-assessments that check for understanding during a unit, along with larger, rubric-scored assessments at the end of the unit.

Grade 3

Patty: My third-grade students enjoy legends, geographic facts and details, drama, and dressing up. By this age they appreciate the addition of gross details from time to time (as with the hole in the skull of St. Aubert in the legend of Mont St. Michel). They still need structured dialogues and writing tasks (like postcards) but crave an increased amount of choice within that structure. Math tasks incorporated into our lessons are also well received at this age. For example, during our study of the Loire Valley the students prepare floor plans on graph paper of a dream château. We then spend some time finding and comparing the area and perimeter of each student's château and the various rooms.

Joel: Most of the kids can read and write in their first language. Working on the same skills in the target language (TL) is a lot easier at this point as well. They love fairy tales and I have yet to meet the third-grader who doesn't enjoy trying to make up their own in the TL. They are also at a point where they can help with younger kids because they have such strong language skills. I like to combine classes and have the third-graders read to the kindergartners.

Jessica: Our third-graders always seem more settled down and academic than the previous year. They enjoy more complicated story-based themes but still love pretending. They can also handle more independent activities, such as making charts and illustrative pictures for presentations, surveying others, and working in pairs or groups.

Hildegard: They like to collect (the water museum, where students collected all kinds of water and labeled it, was very successful), create with language, write their own texts with the help of word banks, work with a partner (help each other, "proofread" and correct for each other, create together). Competitive games! They love humor, riddles, jokes. They are interested in everything about the country [of] the language they are learning—geography, foods, and climate.

Grade 4

Joel: You have a new kind of learner in fourth grade. They are getting into a new developmental level. Abstract thought is coming into play. So are hormones and a new kind of peer pressure. In many schools there is pressure to start "dating." Try to push yourself to see what the kids are really capable of. They will surprise you.

Hildegard: They need to feel like little scientists, discover, cook, make models, write creatively, perform and memorize plays. I used a "Let's Eat!" and "Let's Be Healthy!" unit with great success. We cooked and baked with each different food group, put on three different plays for the younger students and the parents, planned a healthy meal that everybody liked, cooked it, and served it to the community. After the meal we danced to traditional (live!) German music. The music, physical education, and art teachers were involved, as well as the classroom teacher.

Patty: My fourth-graders enjoy a bit more friendly competition within games than my younger students do. They are fascinated with history, facts, and legends. They are more eager to do written tasks and actually appreciate the responsibility of a little homework as long as it is a clear part of the routine. (I give homework every Wednesday that is due every Friday. The parents and homeroom teachers are aware of this from the beginning of the year.) Students this age seem to enjoy putting themselves in other people's shoes, so we create imaginary families as we visit French-speaking countries across the world. In this way they choose a new name and must share their likes and dislikes based on research they have done about the country in which they now "live." We do more activities in the computer lab at this stage. We don't do free Internet searches (not allowed in most elementary schools), but with book-marked sites the students can do guided research as we explore various topics.

Jessica: Students in this grade seem to be more metacognitive about their language learning. They ask questions about "why" the language is used in certain ways and they see patterns and differences. I begin doing some direct strategy instruction in this grade to help them see how to extend their conversations and really respond to other speakers, as well as how to find meaning in context (while both reading and listening).

Grade 5

Jessica: Fifth-grade is a challenge! The "newness" of learning another language has worn off long ago, and the language students can use is becoming more difficult. Some students may have decided that they don't like learning the language. The key is to provide experiences that reignite students' interest in the language and culture while building on their language ability. They enjoy Internet-based activities, dialogues that they can manipulate to be funny and interesting, assignments with multiple intelligences-based choices (a song, a drawing, a written piece, etc.), and learning about teens in the target culture. Some recent student interviews in our schools showed that they are most interested in being able to choose their own groups and partners at this age and throughout middle school.

Hildegard: They like to sit in their chairs (surprise!), memorize lists and poems and plays, write extensively, create books and projects, and perform. They like to work seriously and be seen as "adults." They used the Internet to research about Germany. They are interested in German peers and their social life; they like to display posters with writing and art. Successful strategies: Give clear expectations at [the] beginning of [a] unit; make students responsible for their own learning. Allow time before or after school (or by email) for extra help and questions. Give directions in written form, in the target language, of course. Students had German pen pals, and many kept them until graduation.

Vicki: Fifth-graders are often the oldest students in an elementary building. They are eager to serve as school and classroom leaders so it makes sense to involve them in leadership roles where they can show off their skills in the target language. My fifth-graders enjoy using fun props to report the weather and give the lunch menu in Spanish for the school's daily newscast. Teachers and administrators appreciated fifth-grade students using their language skills to promote special emphases during the school year. For D.E.A.R. Day (Drop Everything And Read) my students read books from the school media center in Spanish or about Spanish language cultures, and then wrote and shared mini-book reviews for broadcast on the TV news. A good way to wrap up the school year is to have fifth-graders write letters to tell incoming students what to expect in Spanish class. The next year's crop of new students loved receiving the letters, and writing them gave my fifth-graders a chance to reflect on their journey as language students. Provide fifth-grade students a chance to shine beyond the school day by performing songs or skits for PTA meetings or International Night and entering foreign language association spoken language and poster contests. Making your oldest elementary-age students and their language skills visible will result in leadership opportunities for students as well as a valuable advocacy tool for your program.

In the classroom set routines and procedures that will allow students to assert their growing sense of independence constructively. For example, early on in the school year have students practice moving into groups quickly and efficiently by saying something as simple as "You have one minute to form groups of _____ (two, three, five, etc.)." Keep in mind that older students may have extended seat time in their other classes, so build in opportunities for students to move in every lesson. Fifth-grade students are school-savvy enough to consciously begin to develop a sense of how they learn. Create self-assessment checklists and offer students choices between various products for assessments. Children at this age are developing literacy skills in the target language as they fine-tune the skills in their first language, and they are quite empathetic and social. Consequently, it is a good time to introduce pen pals/e-pals or just exchange hand written and personally illustrated postcards between "secret classmates" in the same building. Be sure to recycle vocabulary and structures from prior grades, but not activities, unless the activities can be made more challenging, meaningful, engaging and developmentally appropriate for this age. Above all, keep in mind that fifth-graders may be the "seniors" in the building, but they want to have fun as they learn.

Early Adolescent Students (Ages 11 to 14): Grades 6, 7, and 8

During the middle school and junior high school years, students are undergoing more dramatic developmental changes than experienced at any other time in life, and on widely differing timetables. The early adolescent must learn to deal with a variety of experiences: emerging sexuality in a changing and often unpredictable body; reaching a cognitive plateau for a time, and then finding new, adult intellectual tools; multiplying and rapidly shifting interests; a fluid and flexible self-concept; a need to rework interpersonal relationships with adults; turbulent emotions; extreme idealism; a need to assert independence; and a powerful peer group. A major goal of all schooling for children of this age is the encouragement of positive relationships and positive self-image. Middle school learners need the opportunity for broad exploration, as well as an introduction to the demands of academic disciplines.

Because exploring the limits of the real world is very important at this age, students will respond well to opportunities to learn in exhaustive detail about subjects that interest them. Heroic figures with qualities that transcend threats are especially good choices for emphasis, and middle school–aged children need learning experiences with a strong affective component. Students show high interest in the unusual and the extremes in the real world.

Myriam describes middle school students in loving terms: "They have not yet become disaffected with school; they wear their hearts on their sleeves as long as it doesn't show too much; and they can be 'won over' if what you want from them doesn't interfere with their friendships or humiliate them in any way. They want to succeed in school, they enjoy mastery ('Hey, we really learned a lot today'), and they'll do just about anything so long as the expectations are clear and within the range of their abilities. I love their complexity and their struggles. I dislike their pettiness (squabbles over what seem to adults to be silly issues), their defensiveness ("She started it!"), and their occasional thoughtless cruelty to each other (especially among seventh-grade girls). I find that the hardest thing to keep in mind is that they are children. As their teacher, I can become so identified with them that I forget that they are still at the beginning of their lives as learners and developing human beings."

Myriam also notes: "Content-based units with a definite culminating product work very well with all these groups. In every case, students must have something to show at the end of their unit of study: a book, a skit, a video presentation, a poster, a mural."

Grade 6

Alan: What motivates a sixth-grader? Extremes—things that are really outrageous or gross. Hearing stories about real life and real problems. Personal tales of challenge and triumph, especially from the teacher's own life. The safety of working and presenting with others. Integrating elements from television, pop culture, and general teen *angst* (remember what it was like to be 11?) into the curriculum in some way. Don't assume they are adults when giving directions and tasks, but remember they love to be treated as if they are grown up. They need and want someone to lead, to look up to, even if they don't act that way at times. They love challenges, to beat a certain score, time, or amount of something—make this attainable and you'll get more out of them. Pets, music, and team sports are good topics from which to draw activity ideas, especially helpful when trying to connect with students who are frequently disengaged.

Give them opportunities to assess their own learning. Have them grade their own rubric before finishing a project or task, then verify. This will yield valuable information on the students' perceptions of themselves and the clarity with which you communicated expectations.

Provide sixth-graders with structure—they need it. Partner tasks work well. We often assume they can do more than they are able to, and we tend to get frustrated when they don't understand things in which we should provide them more guidance. Yet within this structure, they have the freedom to create, to share their funny, creative, outrageous, and unpredictable side. They'll typically share experiences of a painful injury, a "disgusting" thing they did, or sometimes will show a part of themselves which reveals wisdom and reflection beyond their years. These unpredictable behaviors, their ups and downs of everyday living and their outward expression of these feelings makes teaching young people of this age eternally fresh and interesting.

Hal: Sixth-graders want to know the "weirdities" in their own culture, as well as in others. They love to compare and contrast. Venn diagrams work extremely well, and prove to be beneficial at proving similarities. They love to research other cultures and find the "strange" points of interest. They also like to determine what would be "strange" to others about American cultures.

   Activities must change about every 10 to 15 minutes. Transition is very important. It's hard to keep kids on task when they can't use what they've just learned in the next activity. They like partner work, but still want to work with same-sex groups. They don't seem to mind when partners switch every 2 to 3 minutes, such as with interviews, however. Activities are always timed. When I give them less time than I think they will need to complete an activity, it becomes more of a challenge for them and it keeps them on task. If they're working and on task, I extend their time. I've found with all language students, including English Language Learners, accountability is imperative. They must have something produced, and quality is important.

   The teacher is a "monitor." The students must be given information to use. Once they have enough, they need the opportunity to be creative with it and explore their world. They don't want "peer" teachers—teachers who act like they do. They do want teachers who can relate to them and understand their vocabulary and interests. The adult role is extremely important.

   Learners at this age level love to create new things and show them off. They especially like making menus and doing projects that can be displayed. They love supplemental language that doesn't appear in books and that "only they" know.

Vicki: Sixth-graders are willing to take chances and try out new language and cultural experiences, but at the same time they need the security of regular classroom routines and well-established procedures. They can be very empathetic toward others, which makes them willing to accept and appreciate cultural differences. They are very social, so I provide frequent and meaningful partner and small group activities. They like games, not so much for the competition as for the opportunity to try out the language while they play. Sixth-graders are eager to participate when tasks are based on real-life situations, such as expressing and supporting their personal opinions in creating a "Best and Worst of" brochure to introduce visitors to business in their community.

Grade 7

Hildegard: [Seventh-graders] like to go outside the classroom to conduct interviews, and help with and teach the younger grades. They learn (and even
study hard!) when it is for a reason.

They like to read authentic texts and discuss them. Nobody liked our
textbook. The best-liked unit was "Besuch im Zoo," where groups of students
created posters and prepared presentations for the rest of the school and the
public, and then talked about their animal at the German Day at the Zoo. It
was a good opportunity to use correct spelling and grammar and to work on
precision.

Hal: This age is more concerned with getting their point across than correctness
of language, although accuracy is starting to develop. They are interested in
what kids their own ages are doing in the target culture, and the vocabulary
they use in everyday speech. They're more willing to work in mixed partner
activities, depending on the time of year. The teacher is more "instructor."
Information is still given for immediate use. Students are more intimidated to
use it creatively, though.

Seventh-graders are beginning to prefer age-appropriate activities, such
as telephone conversations, or shopping, or TV prompts. [They are] a bit
more self-absorbed than sixth-grade students. As with sixth-graders, however,
all language learning must have a purpose. These students aren't concerned
with register, the grammar, or whether or not the language is totally correct.
Their concern is using the language and having others use it with them in
return.

Myriam: The common assumption is that seventh-graders are ready to look at
language as a system, but this is the case for only a very few. I try to teach the
language before I get students to analyze it, and I make grammar fun with all
sorts of approaches, balls thrown in the air, magical sentences, etc. But in the
end, I have concluded—teach grammar if you must, but don't expect it to stick!

Kate: Seventh-graders are both playful and intellectual. They need to be motivated by doing something that has meaning for them. They appreciate routine
and clear guidelines (e.g., . . . homework is [assigned] every day). They need to
have the teacher say things over and over again. When you have 20+ kids,
they're not all hearing you at the same time. I like how they surprise themselves. They really do like to learn, even though they put on this persona that
maybe it's not cool, or pretend they're not smart.

Grade 8

Hal: The "real" world starts rearing its head in the eighth grade. Students are
interested in technology and how to communicate with others. As with
seventh-graders, these students like to use the language in realistic situations,

such as giving and taking direction, asking and denying information, and so on. This age group still likes to explore, but a little more outside their "safe" world. This is where technology makes teaching profitable. They're curious about what they don't understand, but are hesitant (at times) to pursue it without guidance. An abundance of vocabulary, especially slang, is a must. Most cultures are interested in music, and modern music plays a vital role at this age level.

Students in eighth grade want more direct answers. They also want to learn things and share with their peers in an "informal" setting. Since seventh- and eighth-grade culture focuses so much on school and peers, much time should be devoted to this study in the target culture as well. The emphasis should be on similarities rather than on differences. Partner work is much easier at this age level (in comparison to sixth grade). Activities must change about every 20 minutes, depending on interest level. Students begin writing notes and postcards to others at this level as well.

Eighth grade is a good time to "reintroduce" fairy tales and other things kids learned while growing up. They like to be teachers for others (younger students or brothers and/or sisters). They especially love to compare and contrast fairy tales of their own culture with those of the target cultures, as well as rewriting fairy tales as much as their language level permits.

Hildegard: They need to feel grown up and almost equal to the teacher, respected—their opinion has to count. They like to do their own things their own way. They become self-motivated (some). They are interested in justice, global awareness, world peace, religion(s), and they are out to better the world. The teacher needs to tell students what needs to be done, give them strategies to accomplish the task, and then give them time to do it independently. Give clear descriptors of expectations and grading procedures; rubrics worked best for me. Unfortunately, many students come to our classes with loads of problems, so be gentle with their feelings.

Myriam: My eighth-graders keep journals. They must write 12 sentences in French every week. I respond to their entries, commenting and keeping a conversation going. I also point out simple errors and I may include information that is not in the curriculum but which can be useful to the writer. I do not correct all grammatical errors since this journal writing is about self-expression and experimenting with language and not about being grammatically correct. Some students like to share their journals with friends or with the whole class, and some want to write continuing stories. These are collected and become class books that everyone can read.

Kate: Eighth-graders are more receptive and more socially aware. They are finding out about themselves; they can be reflective and see their own growth. When even one or two have political or social savvy, they can lead the class into a great place—sharing opinions, asking questions. Like seventh-graders, they are very curious and very vulnerable, despite the façade.

Summary

- Second-language acquisition theory, learning styles, multiple intelligences, brain research, cognitive psychology, and information about cognitive and educational development all contribute to a greater understanding of languages and learners.

- Information in these areas is always evolving and is subject to new questions and interpretations as our understanding of human development and the mind continues to change and grow.

- Thematic teaching is an approach to curriculum development and classroom planning that can help the teacher capitalize on the information we have about learners and their wonderful diversity.

For Study and Discussion

1. Choose a topic or a lesson (such as animals, foods, geography) that could be of interest to children at several age levels and explain how you would approach it differently at each of three different levels:
   a. kindergarten
   b. grade 3
   c. grade 6 or grade 7

2. Examine a lesson you have designed, taught, or found in a book of lesson plans. What learning styles and intelligences are supported in this plan? Are any left out? How could you adjust the lesson to be more inclusive?

3. Choose the grade level with which you are the most familiar, and reread all the descriptions of students at this grade level found in the chapter. How well do they reflect your own experiences? What descriptors would you add or change?

4. Read additional information about learning styles and multiple intelligences, using references at the end of this chapter or others. Then create a profile of yourself as a learner, in terms of both learning styles and multiple intelligences. Which students in your classroom will you need to pay particular attention to because of differences in style and intelligences? What types of activities will you need to include in the class if you are going to meet their needs?

For Further Reading

The following sources are recommended for additional information about material covered in this chapter. Chapter citations are documented in Works Cited at the end of this book.

Armstrong, Thomas. *Multiple Intelligences in the Classroom.* Alexandria, VA: Association for Supervision and Curriculum Development, 1994.

Armstrong, Thomas. "Utopian Schools." *Mothering* (Winter 1996). Available on-line: www.thomasarmstrong.com/articles/utopian_schools.htm.

Bredekamp, Sue, and Carol Copple (Eds.). *Developmentally Appropriate Practice in Early Childhood Programs Serving Children from Birth through Age 8* (rev. ed.). Washington, DC: National Association for the Education of Young Children, 2000. Some portions available online: www.naeyc.org.

Caine, Renate Nummela, and Geoffrey Caine. *Education on the Edge of Possibility.* Alexandria, VA: Association for Supervision and Curriculum Development, 1997.

Ellis, Rod. "Principles of Instructed Second Language Acquisition." *CAL Digest.* Center for Applied Linguistics (December 2008). Available online: www.cal.org/resources/digest/instructed2ndlang .html.

Gardner, Howard. *Intelligence Reframed: Multiple Intelligences for the 21st Century.* New York: Basic Books, 2000.

Gurian, Michael, Kathy Stevens, and Kelley King. *Strategies for Teaching Boys & Girls: Elementary Level.* San Francisco: Jossey-Bass, 2008.

Jensen, Eric. "Brain-Based Learning: A Reality Check." *Educational Leadership* 57:5 (April 2000): 76–79.

Jensen, Eric. *Teaching with the Brain in Mind* (2nd ed.). Alexandria, VA: Association for Supervision and Curriculum Development, 2005.

Kennedy, Teresa J. "Language Learning and Its Impact on the Brain: Connecting Language Learning with the Mind Through Content-Based Instruction." *Foreign Language Annals* 39:3 (Fall 2006): 471–486.

Kennedy, Teresa, and Susan Reese. "A Look at Research on Foreign Language Learning and the Brain." *The Language Educator* 2:6 (November 2007): 32–35.

Websites of Interest

Center for Teaching and Learning (Learning Styles): www1.indstate.edu/cirt1/facdev/pedagogies/ styles/ls1.html.

Foreign Language Study and the Brain: http://ivc .vidaho.edu/flbrain/.

Lazear, David G. New Dimensions of Learning site: Exploring Multiple Intelligences: http:// newdimensionspress.com/whatismiq.htm.

Learning Styles Resource Page: www.oswego.edu/ ~shindler/lstyle.htm.

Enhance Learning with Technology: Learning Styles: http://members.shaw.ca/priscillatheroux/styles .html.

Chapter 2

Creating an Environment for Communication

Enduring Understanding

- Students are active constructors of meaning in meaningful, communicative contexts.

Essential Question

- How can I create meaningful contexts for everything I teach?

There is a compelling thrust in language teaching toward a new organizing principle for language instruction: meaningful communication in the context of a holistic approach to learning. The first goal of the *Standards for Foreign Language Learning in the 21st Century* (1999) is communication: Communicate in languages other than English. The other four goals—cultures, connections, comparisons, and communities—all flow from and are dependent on the ability to communicate. As the introduction to the *Standards* points out, "to relate in a meaningful way to another human being, one must be able to communicate" (p. 11).

The new focus on communication has developed, in part, from the insights of second-language acquisition research, from the communicative competence movement, from brain research, from experience with immersion programs, from cognitive psychology, and—of course—from the *Standards for Foreign Language Learning in the 21st Century*. The principle of meaningful communication replaces the grammatical focus that has been so common in secondary and postsecondary language programs, as well as the emphasis on memorization and recitation that has frequently characterized language instruction for young learners. Grammar has taken on a secondary role—that of supporting communication. The orientation toward communication places language learning in a living laboratory, in which process is the primary focus of planning and instruction.

As communication takes on a central position, it is important to understand what it is and how it can be encouraged. Rivers (1986) explains that "students . . . achieve facility in using a language when their attention is focused on conveying and receiving authentic messages—messages that contain information of interest to speaker and listener in a situation of importance to both—that is, through interaction . . . between people who have something to share" (p. 2). Krashen and Terrell (1995) refer to the "Great Paradox of Language Teaching: Language is best taught when it is being used to transmit messages, not when it is explicitly taught for conscious learning" (p. 55). Savignon (1997) reports that "the development of the learners' communicative abilities is seen to depend not so much on the time they spend rehearsing grammatical patterns as on the opportunities they are given to interpret, to express, and to negotiate meaning in real-life situations" (p. xi). The *Standards for Foreign Language Learning in the 21st Century* (1999) define successful communication as "knowing how, when, and why, to say what to whom " (p. 11).

Canale and Swain (1979) contribute the idea that communicative competence is actually the combination of competence in four areas: (1) grammatical competence, the ability to apply the rules of grammar to produce or interpret a message correctly; (2) discourse competence, the ability to connect several ideas together appropriately and to maintain an extended exchange of messages; (3) sociolinguistic competence, the ability to choose language usage according to the social situation; and (4) strategic competence, the ability to understand a basic meaning or to be understood, even when adequate vocabulary and structures are lacking.

● Meaningfulness as a Priority for Classroom Activity

The key element in all of these communicative developments and approaches is meaning—that is, a primary focus on meaning rather than a focus on form. The brain research that has contributed so much to our understanding of the classroom highlights the crucial role of meaning in learning and teaching. This research offers several insights to guide us in this direction. The brain is always searching for meaning and for patterns in the information and experiences that we encounter. Both attention and memory are focused on what is meaningful (Wolfe, 2001; Sprenger, 1999; Sylwester, 1995; Caine and Caine, 1997). The overriding factor in both attention to and retention of new information is emotion—the conscious or unconscious decision that some element of an experience or of new information is emotionally significant and worth remembering (Goleman, 1995; Sylwester, 1995). We can facilitate the development of communication skills as we provide students with classroom experiences that have both a meaningful context and emotional content.

Meaningfulness—and real communication—always occurs within a context. Genesee (2000) points out that "instruction for beginning language learners, in particular, should take into account their need for context-rich, meaningful environments." Clear, meaningful, and interesting contexts provide settings in which new language is understandable, and familiar language becomes more memorable and useful. In fact, context creates an environment that allows the brain to do what it does best:

- Identify patterns and make connections.
- Link new information to existing knowledge for effective storage and recall.

● When Is "Communicative" Not Communicative?

A common danger for every innovation is that it will be trivialized into a slogan and robbed of its power for genuine change. Not every text, drill, or activity bearing the label "communicative" is an example of communication; not every textbook or unit labeled "standards based" is actually designed to reflect the philosophy of the *Standards for Foreign Language Learning in the 21st Century.* Many attempts to "personalize" activities in a language classroom are actually thinly disguised drills that provide no opportunities for genuine sharing of information. For example, the question, "What is your name?" has no communicative value when the name of every student in the class is already known to every other student. The question, "Are you a boy or a girl?" would be considered both ridiculous and insulting to a student of any age if it were asked in the native language instead of the target language. If, on the other hand, one student is blindfolded and trying to guess the identity of another student in a game setting, both the questions "Are you a boy or a girl?" and "What is your name?" could be genuine requests for information; the questions and the answers would have a communicative purpose.

The gap described by the Center for Applied Linguistics (Campbell et al., 1985) between the results of immersion and those of early language programs may have been aggravated by the noncommunicative ways in which instruction has frequently been organized in these more limited programs. Programs for young learners have historically had many of the following characteristics:

1. An emphasis on recitation:
   - lists
   - labels
   - language mainly used at the one-word level
   - memorized patterns and dialogues, usually cued by a teacher question
   - songs, many of which are not integrated into the rest of the language curriculum
   - games, used as a change of pace or for grammar practice
   - rhymes and poems chosen at random
   - reading for recitation; reading aloud
2. Pervasive use of English during the class:
   - for discipline
   - for giving directions
   - for clarifying the target language

- for checking comprehension
- for teaching culture

In content-based classroom settings, such as immersion and bilingual education, the context within which communication takes place is well established. The context is the regular day and the regular curriculum of the school with all of its givens. The language becomes a tool of instruction and information exchange is assured. In most classrooms for young learners, however, in order to avoid the emphasis on recitation and one-word labels, a context for communication must be created, and the teacher must be the one to create it.

A parallel can be drawn between early language programs and music programs with regard to creating a communicative setting. In a music program, the goal of every music teacher is to provide students with the skills necessary to perform music written for aesthetic purposes, both for the sake of their own enjoyment and to communicate a musical experience to others. This process takes a long time and many years of practice, even for very talented students. However, students in a successful music program are not limited to practicing skills, drills, and scales for all those years without any actual musical experiences. In the absence of music originally written at a level that enables novices to perform it, sensitive teachers have prepared music at the ability level of the students—music that students can perform with enjoyment and with an authentic musical message for the listeners. These selections are planned and chosen carefully, taking into account the skills of the musician and the limitations of the school setting. Young people in programs like these gain both pleasure and confidence from their experiences with performance and with the communication of musical ideas.

There is a marked analogy between the music setting just described and the foreign-language classroom. The young learner in the early language program has neither the skills nor the opportunity to use the target language in a natural communicative setting, but the teacher can create settings within the classroom that will satisfy the learner because there is a genuine exchange of information taking place. These experiences also prepare the learner for the day when the opportunity for natural communication will be available. The language teacher who thinks only in terms of memorizing lists of basic vocabulary, drilling and mastering a body of grammatical forms, and practicing a series of pronunciation tasks, is not giving students the opportunity to exchange authentic messages nor providing inherently motivating tasks.

● Developing Contexts for Tasks and Activities

Revision of Traditional Activities

Even though the shift to communication as an organizing principle has been in place for quite some time, materials available from commercial sources or through exchanges among school districts frequently provide little help in developing communicative tasks for young learners. Teachers may have to do extensive adaptation of materials in order to provide opportunities for communication, as in the following example.

> A suggested game from the teacher handbook for a textbook series calls for identification and guessing. As one student leaves the room, the others choose a classmate then draw a rough figure of the child on the board. The child who is "it" returns to the room, looks at the picture, and asks, "Is it the teacher?" "Is it Mary? John? Is it Miss Jones?" until the child has guessed the identity of the outlined figure. The child then goes on to ask questions such as, "Is it a teacher or a student? Is it a boy or a girl? Does the person have red hair or green hair?" and so on.

In its present form, about half of the game is noncommunicative, because once the name of the person is known, the other information is clearly known to all participants as well. If the questioning had started by identifying first the role, then the sex, and then other information such as hair color, color of clothing, and so forth, the entire task might have been communicative.

Of course, there is a place in a communication-based classroom for practice and drill; the difference is in the motivation and the context for the practice and drill. In a communication-based classroom, the practice and drill take place not for their own sake, but in order for a student to participate in a specific communicative setting: to talk about classroom material, to discuss information related to specific interests, or to contribute in some other way to an information exchange that is meaningful to all the participants.

As another example, the teacher may wish to have students practice the phrase "My name is" (for example, in German, *Ich heisse*). This phrase will enable them to introduce themselves, perhaps to a visitor in the class, to members of a partner school on a videotape, or in some other natural communication setting. The students in most cases already know each other's names, so to go around the class and have each student say, *"Ich heisse Fritz," "Ich heisse Maria,"* carries no communication value. The teacher must create a context within which *"Ich heisse Maria"* is used in a more meaningful way. One possibility would be for the teacher to put on the nametag of one of the students in the class and claim to be that student. The teacher persists until the student responds with her or his own name. This can be done, as a kind of game, until everyone in the class has had a chance to practice. Another possibility, after the phrase is well established but still needs practice, would be to blindfold the students one at a time and create a game in which they must identify speakers by voice who claim to be the teacher, a favorite fairy tale character, or a famous person.

Surrounding Experiences with Language

An important strategy for creating context falls into the general category of surrounding concrete experiences with language. Many content-related activities lend themselves to this technique. The teacher plans a group lesson in which students are involved with a concrete, hands-on activity. For example, in a French classroom the lesson might be centered on the French food crepes. Together the teacher and the students work through the steps in making crepes, if possible by actually preparing the crepes in small groups, or through pantomime as the teacher gives a demonstration in front of the class. The teacher surrounds the activity of the crepes preparation with descriptions and explanations in the target language, using far more language and repetition than would normally be called for with the same activity in the native language. Some part of this language use might involve invitations for students to imitate phrases, respond to questions, or even initiate comments in the language as they participate in the activity.

> Now let's make the batter.
>
> I take a bowl. Look how big the bowl is. It's a big, shiny bowl.
>
> I set the bowl down.
>
> I take an egg. Let's see . . . shall I take a white egg or a brown egg?
>
> (Students respond.)
>
> The egg is white and round. (And so forth.)

Later, in recall of the entire experience, the language is reentered and reactivated. Language used to recall the experience provides the basis for discussions, for demonstrations, for a videotape or a PowerPoint presentation, for scrapbook activities, for class group storybooks, and for a variety of other possibilities. Within the context of this experience, the teacher can embed functions or purposes that are transferable to future settings. The link between language and action enhances the impact of the language itself and encourages its retention in long-term memory.

Games

Games are a familiar method by which elementary and middle school teachers create a setting for second-language acquisition. In addition to context, games also provide an emotional connection and a sense of play that brain research and teacher experience indicate can enhance both learning and memory. Teachers choose or invent games for introducing and practicing language that students can later use in natural contexts for communicative purposes. Egan (1986) points out that games share with stories the characteristic of a strong beginning, middle, and end, an important factor in making learning meaningful for elementary and middle school students. These games should be communicative themselves, whenever possible, rather than heavily drill oriented. Often, just a simple twist, as in the examples described earlier, can change a mechanical practice or drill enough to provide a game-like character that makes it consistent with communicative goals for the classroom.

Games can also provide a structured setting for the practice of common social and conversation-starting formulas for which there is not sufficient authentic opportunity in the everyday classroom. A good example of this is one of the games in Fluegelman's *The New Games Book* (1976), which is easily adaptable to any target language:

> Children stand in a circle, facing the center with hands joined. A child who is IT walks around the outside of the circle, touches another child on the shoulder, and begins to

run in the same direction around the circle. The child who has been tapped runs in the opposite direction around the circle. At whatever point the children meet, the two must shake hands, greet one another in the target language, perhaps even adding "How are you? I'm fine" and then race to see who can be the first back at the empty place left in the circle.

There are a number of "new games" that build on everyday social language and can easily be adapted to the foreign-language setting. These can be very useful as a way of providing context for the practice of language that will later be used in a genuine communicative situation. More examples of games, songs, and rhymes are provided in Chapter 13.

Songs, Rhymes, and Finger Plays

Other powerful vehicles for linking language with action include songs, rhymes, and finger plays that involve large- and small-motor physical actions. Many songs and rhymes for young children are designed to incorporate actions, and the finger play is a rhyme built entirely around the use of the hand and the fingers to enter into the performance of a rhyme. The power of these language resources is clear when one considers how many adults can respond without thinking to the following:

> Here's the church,
> Here's the steeple.
> Open the doors and
> See all the people.
>
> Where is thumbkin?
> Where is thumbkin?
> Here I am.
> Here I am. . . .
>
> Teddy bear, teddy bear
> Turn around.
> Teddy bear, teddy bear
> Touch the ground.
> Teddy bear, teddy bear
> Show your shoes.
> Teddy bear, teddy bear
> Read the news.

These rhymes are just a few examples of the shared childhood language experiences that unite many adult speakers in the United States. Songs, rhymes, and finger plays from the target culture can be located to bring concepts and common expressions to life for children and to add a cultural dimension to the lesson. In some cases, songs and rhymes may also be adapted from their English counterparts. In an early language classroom, action-oriented songs and rhymes, especially those with humorous actions, become favorites of the children, who want to recite or sing them again and again.

What distinguishes the use of songs and rhymes in a standards-based, communicative approach is their careful integration with the thematic context of instruction. Further ideas for using games, rhymes, and finger plays are found in Chapter 13.

Props, Materials, and Hands-On Experiences

Another important factor in creating context for communication is the use of props and concrete materials. Learners throughout the elementary and middle school years continue to learn best from concrete situations; the more frequently the manipulation of actual objects can accompany language use, especially objects representing the cultures being taught, the greater the impact of the language itself. Hands-on activities with these props and materials can range from manipulating puppets to performing science experiments, and they are engaging for students at every grade level. Other possibilities include experiences with art, crafts, and sports activities. Examples of props and materials are found in Chapter 12, together with suggestions for their use.

Stories

Telling and reading stories is one of the most beloved contexts for young children, and students of all ages can become engrossed in a good story. The familiar structure of a story helps to make the meaning comprehensible, especially when it is richly supported with visuals, gestures, and student participation. Many teachers have also found that stories make a good unit focus.

Dialogues

Another set of strategies for creating context to motivate communication is the development of simulations, dialogues, and role-plays. Dialogues, the hallmark of the audiolingual method, have value for young learners because they provide a structure for a series of expressions that combine to develop a situation, an idea, or an experience. When they are carefully constructed and chosen, dialogues can provide an outlet for children's natural love of dramatization and role-play. A dialogue can prepare students for conversations and situations that will later be part of a story or a fairy tale in the curriculum. The dialogue can also develop as a means of recreating a story that the learners loved when the teacher read it or when they saw it in a video or a movie.

Patty Ryerson, pre-K–4 French teacher, uses dialogues that include options for student creativity, beginning in second grade. Here is an example of one of her dialogues. The italicized portions are decided on by the students, using vocabulary they have been learning in class. Patty notes that the students love to make the dialogues silly!

A: Hi!
B: Hi!

A: Where are you going?

B: I'm going into the desert.

A: How?

B: By bicycle.

A: Me too.

B: Great! Let's go!

A: Look! A *snake!*

B: Oh! It's *slithering.*

A: Look! *A kangaroo rat.*

B: Oh! It's *jumping.*

A: Look! A *butterfly.*

B: It's attacking! Let's get out of here!

The following guidelines will assist teachers in the choice or creation of a dialogue:

1. It should be short, including short utterances for the students to say.

2. It should feature natural use of language that is not restricted by artificially imposed grammatical limitations.

3. It should be open to many variations so that it can be recast to serve as the basis for future dialogues in other settings.

4. It should be flexible so that the students can shape it according to their own creativity and sense of humor.

5. It should incorporate a large proportion of previously learned vocabulary and functions so that the learners are not overwhelmed by the quantity of new language to be learned.

Role-Play

Role-play moves a step beyond the dialogue and places students in a situation in which they are called on to cope with the unexpected or with a new setting, using the material they have memorized through dialogues and other classroom activities. For example, after working with a dialogue drawn from a shopping situation, students of Spanish might be called on to develop a role-play in which they go into a Peruvian market to buy an item that represents new vocabulary or a new challenge. Perhaps they look for their favorite American brand of breakfast cereal at the food store, or the clerk has only sizes that are too large or too small in the clothing store. They then work together in a group to develop an unscripted conversation around the new situation.

In most cases, role-play is beyond the resources of the beginning language learner, who can mainly be expected to provide short, memorized utterances in new situations. It can, however, be a very valuable strategy beyond the beginning level.

Partner and Small-Group Work

Another very powerful context for communication in the classroom involves the use of small-group and partner activities within the framework of cooperative learning. Pair and small-group work incorporates the benefits of cooperative learning, an excellent vehicle to help students communicate in the new language. When students work cooperatively in pairs or small groups, their opportunities for language use are multiplied many times over. Often, while learners are engaged in pair work, meaningful communication stems from "information gap" activities in which one partner or member of the group has information that the other partner does not have. Language has to be used to "bridge the gap" and solve the problem or otherwise achieve some goal.

Cooperative learning (see Johnson and Johnson, 1987; Kagan and Kagan, 2008) offers an approach to small-group work and student–student interaction that has natural applications for a foreign-language program in which communication plays a key role. Goals of social development can be reinforced through cooperative group work in the foreign-language class, as students are placed in a position where they have need and motivation to communicate with one another.

Nancy Foss, who has researched the connection between language proficiency and learning styles, notes that pair work seems to be comfortable for all learning styles. Learners who prefer to work alone can tolerate working with a partner; learners who like to work in groups will be happy when working with another person (personal communication, 2002).

Specific guidelines for conducting partner and small-group work are provided in Chapter 4, together with a variety of sample activities.

Content-Related Instruction

The content of the curriculum is a natural context for foreign languages in the school setting. The integration of the language program with the rest of the school day brings interest and relevance to language instruction. Content-related instruction is further developed in Chapter 10.

● Teaching in the Target Language: Context for Communication

One of the most valuable elements of the context for communication is the target language itself. We know from research in second-language acquisition that learners need to be surrounded with comprehensible language—or input—in order to facilitate the acquisition of the new language. This input should be both meaningful and of interest to the learner. Otherwise the brain is not likely to engage with either the language or the information it carries.

Teachers must provide this input consistently, from the very first day and throughout every class period. Many successful early language teachers make it a point to speak exclusively in the target language; others recommend use of the new language 95 to 100 percent of the time. It is especially important that the teacher use the new language for regular classroom tasks, such as giving directions, organizing activities, and managing behavior. It is these regular classroom tasks that demonstrate that the new language "works"—that it can be used for all the important business of the classroom (and by natural extension—of life).

Language is the key or the "ticket" to the culture. We give our students this "ticket" as we give them the language with which they can enter the culture and participate in it. Even though not all teachers are native speakers, all teachers are the culture bearers, the representatives of the culture in the classroom. When students have the feeling of being surrounded by the language, they also have the feeling of what it might be like to actually be in a place where this language is spoken on an everyday basis. We are preparing them for the time when they will actually be in the culture of the new language. In the meantime, the time they spend in our classrooms is the only time they have to experience the new language. If we spend much of this time in English, we are actually denying them access to the language and the culture.

Of course, as we use the new language, we must make sure that our students understand what we are saying and that we use techniques that will make what we say concrete and comprehensible.

We also need to give our students both opportunities and tools so they can use the new language themselves, for meaningful purposes. Young learners, such as young children in their first language, will learn most quickly the language that "makes things happen." Asking for permission, telling others what to do, claiming a toy or a place to sit—these situations and many more can motivate meaningful language use when the language has been modeled and made available to the learner.

How Do We Keep the Classroom in the Target Language?

Use the Target Language Consistently   Show that the target language is important to the students because it will get them what they need and want: attention, a pencil, help, approval, and permission to leave the classroom.

Surround Students with the New Language

- Talk to them as if they understand, and use visuals and gestures to make sure they do.
- Use a "think-aloud" approach to your own activity in the classroom. As you move to the front of the room, for example, you might say (in the target language), "I'm going to my desk now to get the paper and pencils we will need for the next activity. Where did I leave those pencils? Oh, here they are—under my grade book," and so on.

- Increase student understanding with the help of predictable activities and verbal routines that you use over and over.
- Use caretaker speech, the kind of speech that parents use with their children. (Caretaker speech was discussed in detail in Chapter 1.)

Monitor and Assess Target Language Use

Make sure that the students understand that using the new language is important to you! One way of doing this is to keep track of their language use and to build it into student assessment. This may involve circulating around the classroom during partner or group work to gather information and to remind students that they are expected to use the target language. Jessica Haxhi, a Japanese teacher in Waterbury, Connecticut, circulates with her clipboard while wearing her Japanese "police hat," on which "Speak Japanese" is written in bold Japanese characters.

Another strategy is to reward student target language use with some visible token— perhaps a reward strip in a pocket chart or a piece of imitation currency from the target culture. This kind of token reward is effective only on a short-term basis, since it cannot replace intrinsic motivation for language use. Language use must become a part of the management of the classroom and an integral part of the classroom culture.

Separate the Native Language from the Target Language—Avoid Translation

Evidence from bilingual education shows that students in classes in which the languages are kept separate end up with much greater language proficiency than those in classes that do not maintain such careful separation. Mixing languages, and translating from one language to the other, can cause confusion and tends to be counterproductive for early language learners.

There are two main reasons why language mixing and translation are inefficient. First, if the students know that the teacher is going to use both languages, they will not engage with the target language and will patiently wait for the English "version" to appear. Second, the teacher who knows she or he will be clarifying or repeating in English will not expend as much effort to make the target language comprehensible. It takes considerable effort and many visuals and other materials to maintain a target-language environment. The English "shortcut" robs students of the opportunity to construct meanings and experience the situations that will make the new language meaningful and move it into long-term memory. Our goal is for students to experience concepts through the new language, and not through English!

Sometimes students who have understood directions or new vocabulary may call out the English, either as a way to help their classmates or to show the teacher that they have understood. A teacher may appreciate the enthusiasm these students show, but it is important not to encourage or reinforce this practice. When it becomes a habit, the language lesson can turn into a translation guessing game or puzzle, and the communication goal of language learning fades into the background.

Using a sign to indicate which language is being spoken has proven to be a very helpful tool for teachers, because it is a tangible reminder for them and for the students that they should stay in the target language. Some teachers make a ritual out of the transition into the target language at the beginning of class and back to English at the end. Rita Gullickson, for example, beats a tambourine as she and the students turn slowly around and count to three, in English at the beginning of class and in Spanish at the end. After a few days of leading the routine, Rita lets the students take turns as the leader. The tambourine, as an instrument used in both Spain and Latin America, adds a nice cultural touch to the activity.

Beginning students cannot always conduct themselves entirely in the new language, of course. When they ask a question or give a response in English instead of in the target language, we can respond to them in the target language by rephrasing what they said and then responding to their question or their comment. This strategy will often provide interested students with new vocabulary or phrases that meet a need or an interest.

Evidence from bilingual education shows that students in classes in which the languages are kept separate end up with much greater language proficiency than those in classes that do not maintain such careful separation. Mixing languages, and translating from one language to the other, can cause confusion and tends to be counterproductive for early language learners.

Role of English   There certainly are times when it may be necessary and even advisable to use English. There may be an emergency in which the welfare of the students is at stake. Under some circumstances, especially in times of emotional upsets, individual students may need a private conversation in English. There may be extremely important concepts in a teachable moment that absolutely won't be communicated in the target language.

If English is used, it should be intentional, and it should be for a purpose. The use of English should be a conscious decision, not just something the teacher slides into without thinking. The following process can be helpful in making a decision to use English instead of the target language.

The teacher should first ask the following questions:

- Can I find a way to communicate the idea in the target language?
- Can I simplify the concept or the information?
- Can I add concrete materials, visuals, or experiences to enrich the context and to make the concept or the information comprehensible in the new language?

If the answer to these questions is "no," there is another series of questions to consider:

- Can I substitute a different concept?
- Can I delay this topic until the students are ready to do it in the target language?
- Can I ask the classroom or content teacher to follow up in English?

- Could this be part of the lessons I leave for an English-speaking substitute teacher on the days I am absent?
- Could this be a homework assignment using English language resources?

If the answer is "no" to all of these questions, there is one more question to consider:

- Is this really important enough to sacrifice valuable time in the target language in order to speak English?

Of course, if after all these deliberations, the teacher finally makes the decision to use English for a specified purpose, it will still be important to stay within the guidelines of target language use 95 to 100 percent of the time.

Some teachers think that they need to discipline in English, just to make sure that the students understand. Yet the very reason we need to discipline in the target language is that it is too important to do in English! When the target language is used for all the important business of a classroom, the message to students is clear: This language is important to me, and worth learning.

Make the Language Comprehensible   The most important technique for keeping the classroom in the target language is, of course, to make the language as comprehensible as possible. We may attempt to use the target language consistently and constantly, but it will not result in student learning if we fail to use a variety of means to make the language understandable for the students.

There are four key teaching tools that help to make the new language comprehensible.

1. The teacher presents the information in simple, direct language (i.e., caretaker speech) and chooses vocabulary and structures that incorporate considerable material that is familiar to the learners.
2. Break down directions and new information into small, incremental steps. The younger the learner, the smaller these steps need to be.
3. Make lavish use of concrete materials, visuals, gestures, facial expressions, and bodily movement.
4. Model every step of the process or the directions being presented. This modeling often takes place with exaggerated gestures or materials. After presentation, the teacher might go through the directions again and have the students pantomime the actions required.

Maintain a Physical Classroom and School Environment to Support the Target Language   Make the classroom and the school an environment where it is obvious that the target language is spoken. For example, the teacher might label the classroom, classroom objects, and the school in the target language. It is very effective to post the class schedule, class objectives, helper charts, and rules for classroom management in the target language. Hallway displays and bulletin boards in the school corridors are effective reminders of the fact that the target language is important in this environment. These displays are especially effective when they incorporate student work in the target language.

In addition to making the language comprehensible and maintaining a language-rich environment, we must make sure that through all of this we are checking that the students are understanding.

Monitor Comprehension How can we check for comprehension? Shall we ask the students to tell us in English what we have just said in the target language? Never! We want the students to experience the language through the language, not to learn it in reference to English. We need to find other ways to have the students show us what they know.

We can ask the students to use signals to indicate their response to a comprehension check. They can hold their thumbs up for "yes," hold their thumbs down for "no," and wiggle their thumbs for "I'm not sure."

If the answer to a question is a number, students can hold up the correct number of fingers for the teacher to see, write the number on a piece of paper, or hold up the correct numerals from an envelope full of numbers that they keep at their desks or in their language folders.

Students can also draw pictures to signal their comprehension or they can write on small whiteboards or chalkboards. They can act out the behavior or imitate the performance that the teacher has demonstrated.

Teachers—or students—can ask yes–no, either–or, or who, what, where, when, why questions. Students can complete open-ended sentences or supply missing information. They can supply the next step in a set of directions or the retelling of a story. Students can correct the teacher's (intentional) errors, or contribute to the cognitive mapping of a concept.

When students are working together or alone on the completion of a task, the teacher can circulate and observe student performance, as a measure of understanding.

Teach Functional Chunks of Language (Prefabricated Language) Our last strategy for keeping the classroom in the target language is teaching students functional chunks of language. Young children first learn to interact with others in their native language by using these functional chunks, absorbed from what they hear over and over. "Sit down," "bye-bye," and "thank you" all start out as imitated chunks and are repeated because they can make something happen. In the classroom, these unanalyzed chunks of functional language make it possible for learners to make their needs known, to contribute to the conversation, and to understand more of what their teacher and others say to them. Phrases such as, "Please, may I have . . ." or "I don't understand" and "I really like . . ." can give students a head start on language acquisition and communicative competence. More information on functional chunks will be provided in Chapter 3.

Summary

- The central task for the elementary or middle school language teacher is to create a communicative climate focused on meaning, within which language acquisition can take place naturally.

- Meaningful, age-appropriate contexts for language use provide the best support for language development. Examples are games, songs, rhymes, hands-on activities, dialogues, role-plays, arts, crafts, sports, stories, content-related instruction, and partner or small-group work.

- One of the keys to teaching for communication is keeping the classroom in the target language.

- When learners are surrounded with their new language 95 to 100 percent of the class time, and when teachers use the language for all classroom purposes, language use has a purpose and there is motivation to learn.

- Mixing languages, and translating from one language to the other, can cause confusion and is counterproductive for young learners.

- Teachers use many strategies to support the target-language environment:

  1. Using language to accompany every activity in the classroom and making a clear separation between the use of English and use of the target language

  2. Using caretaker speech to ensure that students understand them

  3. Using visuals, concrete objects, gestures, and physical actions

  4. Creating a target-language presence in the classroom and the school; monitoring for comprehension and language use; and teaching functional chunks of language

For Study and Discussion

1. Why is it often so difficult for teachers to make the change from a grammatical to a communicative orientation to language teaching? What kinds of assistance can help them make the transition?

2. Choose a drill-oriented activity that you have observed or used in a K–8 language classroom or have located in a language teacher's manual. Redesign it so that the same goal is being met in a communicative way.

3. Another teacher tells you that she has tried teaching in the target language but gave it up. The students, she reports, just got too confused, especially those in kindergarten and first grade. She might be willing to try again, if someone could tell her how to go about it. What could you suggest to her for her next effort?

For Further Reading

The following sources are recommended for additional information about material covered in this chapter. Chapter citations are documented in Works Cited at the end of this book.

Asher, James J. *Learning Another Language through Actions: The Complete Teacher's Guidebook.* (6th ed.). Los Gatos, CA: Sky Oaks Publications, 2008.

Krashen, Stephen D., and Tracy Terrell. *The Natural Approach: Language Acquisition in the Classroom* (rev. ed.). Englewood Cliffs, NJ: Prentice-Hall, 1995.

Richards, Jack C. *Communicative Language Teaching Today.* Cambridge: Cambridge University Press, 2006.

Sprenger, Marilee. *Learning and Memory: The Brain in Action.* Alexandria, VA: Association for Supervision and Curriculum Development, 1999.

Terrell, Tracy. "The Natural Approach to Language Teaching: An Update." *Canadian Modern Language Review* 41:3 (1985): 461–479.

Terrell, Tracy. "The Role of Grammar Instruction in a Communicative Approach." *The Modern Language Journal* 75:i (1991): 52–63.

Chapter 3

Building toward Communication in All Three Modes

The image in the top right contains the following text arranged around an octagon: Learners, Teachers, Communication, Programs, Languages, & Children, Planning, Resources, Cultures, Content

Enduring Understanding

- Effective two-way communication skills develop over time as a result of careful scaffolding with a variety of activities that include opportunities for negotiation of meaning.

- Strategies for developing one-way communication skills require particular attention to context and audience without opportunity for negotiation of meaning.

Essential Question

- What contexts and activities will help to develop interpersonal, interpretive, and presentational communication skills?

The *Standards for Foreign Language Learning in the 21st Century* have helped us think more clearly about how we use language, and they provide us with new vocabulary for discussing communication. The communication standard incorporates three dimensions, or modes: interpersonal communication (1.1), interpretive communication (1.2), and presentational communication (1.3). In the balanced approach to communication described in the *Standards for Foreign Language Learning in the 21st Century,* students take on many roles in the language classroom. They are conversation partners in oral and written language, they are audience, and they are presenters. The teacher needs to plan a variety of activities to help students develop the competencies necessary for each of these roles.

> ### *Communication*
>
> **Communicate in Languages Other Than English**
>
> Standard 1.1:
> Students engage in conversations, provide and obtain information, express feelings and emotions, and exchange opinions.
>
> Standard 1.2:
> Students understand and interpret written and spoken language on a variety of topics.
>
> Standard 1.3:
> Students present information, concepts, and ideas to an audience of listeners or readers on a variety of topics.

● Three Modes of Communication: Interpersonal, Interpretive, and Presentational

The first communication standard (1.1) addresses the interpersonal mode: two-way communication, both oral and written, in which participants engage in an exchange of ideas, information, or opinion. Communication can be negotiated—that is, either partner can ask for clarification or explanation of the message. Contexts and building blocks for interpersonal communication are addressed in this chapter and in Chapter 4.

The other two communication standards focus on non-negotiated, one-way communication. In Standard 1.2, the interpretive mode, the listener, reader, or viewer is separated from the creator of the message by distance, time, or the logistics of the situation. Thus, the message cannot be altered or influenced by the learner, who cannot request clarification, repetition, or rephrasing. The listener or reader is essentially an audience and has little or no interaction with the source of the message.

In Standard 1.3, the presentational mode, written or oral presentations must be so clear that our listeners or readers can understand them without asking for repetition or clarification. The writer or speaker cannot check for understanding and alter the message accordingly. Inadequacies in the areas of language competence or cultural awareness will hamper the flow of communication for either the interpreter or the presenter of the message.

This textbook is a good example of these two types of communication. For the reader, this is interpretive communication—1.2. For the authors, as writers, this is presentational communication—1.3. As readers, you need to understand the vocabulary of pedagogy for early language learning and something about the culture of the classroom and the profession. As writers, we need to make sure that we choose our language and our examples carefully, to help you understand our message clearly. We must always be aware of our audience.

It is important to emphasize here that communication is a holistic concept. The three modes do not occur in isolation during instruction; rather, they flow from one to the other. The interpersonal mode is often used to introduce, reinforce, and connect work with the other modes of communication in the classroom, in addition to being an instructional focus in its own right.

● Communication in the Interpersonal Mode (Standard 1.1)

Standard 1.1 is the most challenging of all the communication standards. Although the definition of interpersonal communication involves spontaneous interaction and negotiation of meaning, novice learners require extensive preparation before real interpersonal communication can take place. The stepping stones provide tools and strategies for helping beginning language learners develop the resources necessary for true interpersonal communication. These strategies and stepping stones can lay the foundation for full participation in spontaneous interaction and negotiation of meaning. They include an early focus on vocabulary building: methods of introducing, elaborating, and practicing vocabulary and functional chunks of language.

We know from research in second-language acquisition that extended listening is a crucial first step in developing skills in a new language, and at early stages this listening is highly interactive, even though students do not have much language at their disposal. Students respond to directions, imitate teacher movements, or otherwise indicate that they have—or have not—understood the message. Yet, even during these early stages, students want—and often try—to respond with language; they want to communicate, and vocabulary is the key.

Functional chunks, introduced and reinforced through a variety of different activities, provide a bridge from single words to complete utterances, and they are essential building blocks for communication and for later work with grammar.

Approaches that combine language with actions and story, such as the Natural Approach, Total Physical Response, Stories with Gestures, and the Gouin Series, move students from interacting primarily through physical responses to using language in a more nearly interpersonal way.

All of these approaches involve meaningful language use and continuous invitations for learners to interact, using both oral and written language. From the earliest stages of language learning, these stepping stones help students develop the ability to engage in conversations, provide and obtain information, express feelings and emotions, and exchange opinions (Standard 1.1).

Stepping Stone: Vocabulary Development

Vocabulary is the essential foundation for communication in the second language. The primary task of the novice learner is the development of a strong and useful vocabulary. Early language learners understand what they hear and read largely in terms of the vocabulary they recognize, and their ability to express meaning is limited by the vocabulary they have internalized. One of the first tasks of the teacher, then, is to help students develop a useful working vocabulary.

Most of us, when we hear the word *vocabulary,* think about individual words, often in categories. Sometimes when we talk about what our students have learned, we list things like colors, numbers, family members, farm animals, and so on.

Single words are certainly one element of vocabulary development. They are the first clues to meaning for the beginning learner, and the first building blocks for expressing meaning. With each new thematic unit we can present essential vocabulary in a variety of ways and in rich contexts.

Storytelling and story reading provide especially valuable contexts for new vocabulary. Teachers can highlight important or interesting vocabulary and perhaps comment on how it makes them feel, all in the target language, or they may involve students in a physical or emotional reaction to the word. For example, in a spooky story about a haunted house, the teacher might pause at the word *ghost,* shiver and repeat "ghost," and make a comment such as, "A ghost is scary—ooo! A ghost! A gho-o-o-st!" The teacher might encourage students to repeat the word and pantomime the scary ghost. As part of the process, she or he might also write the word on the chalkboard, perhaps creating a ghost-like outline around the word. A sequence like this engages both the kinesthetic and the emotional paths to memory.

Graphic or cognitive organizers can show how new words relate to one another and to a theme. The Venn diagram in Figure 3.1, for example, shows relationships among vocabulary used to describe a dog and a wolf.

There are many other ways to encourage vocabulary development with individual words, and most teachers have a repertoire already—listing all the foods you would buy if you were shopping for dinner instead of your mother, naming all the animals you can

● **FIGURE 3.1** Venn Diagram. Renate Grant and her students developed a Venn diagram comparing dogs and wolves.

Soure: Reprinted by permission of Renate Grant.

think of that begin with a certain letter, building a word chain in which the first letter of each word is the same as the last letter of the word before it, playing the "Suitcase Game," in which students list all the items packed in the suitcase by the players ahead of them and then add their own. In addition to being valuable and enjoyable activities on their own, these vocabulary builders can serve as effective "sponge" activities: quick activities for the end of class when there are only a few minutes remaining, or for any other class time that might otherwise go to waste.

As students work with new vocabulary in a variety of ways, that vocabulary becomes more securely connected in long-term memory and more available for future use. Students might sort foods according to whether they like or dislike them; the teacher might organize activities in which students provide opposites for new vocabulary, or rhyming words; students might rank-order activities from most to least favorite, and so on. The greater the personal connection to the vocabulary, the more likely it is to be moved into long-term memory.

What all of these strategies have in common is the fact that they take place in a context, and any vocabulary listing is done for a purpose. They do not incorporate translation to or from English. Whatever variety of approaches we use, it is helpful to keep in mind the guidance offered by Genesee (2000), based on cognitive research: "Students' vocabulary acquisition can be enhanced when it is embedded in real-world complex contexts that are familiar to them" (p. 1). With this advice in mind, teaching vocabulary as lists or in translation would miss the mark. Instead, complex, language-rich environments and contexts provide the most fertile ground for vocabulary growth. Each child learner will acquire the vocabulary that has meaning and purpose to her or him.

Stepping Stone: Functional Chunks (Prefabricated Language)

The students' working vocabulary consists not only of single words and their meanings, but also—perhaps even more importantly—of "functional chunks," which are memorized and unanalyzed phrases of high frequency. The most useful of these are flexible, in the sense that they can be used in several different contexts with the substitution of a word or two. There are many terms for these chunks, including lexical phrases, formulaic expressions, and prefabricated language. The phrase "How're you doing?" is one example of such a chunk in English. Other examples include "I don't _____ (understand, sing, swim)," "Let's ___ (go, run, play)!," and "Please may I have ___?" Most of the polite formulas in any language are learned first as functional chunks—they are learned as a unit long before the individual words are understood in themselves. Functional chunks can be any length, and for the novice learner, all learned language is a chunk.

Much of the early language that toddlers amaze us with is really made up of functional chunks, used because they can always get a reaction. Phrases such as "That's not the point!" and "I've told you a thousand times!" reflect what parents or caregivers have repeated many times, and young children often use them in inappropriate—though logical—contexts.

These functional chunks are an especially important part of language development for two reasons. First, they allow students to participate more fully in interpersonal communication even at very early stages. Functional chunks can communicate complete ideas in an efficient and clearly understood way. Functional chunks can "make things happen" in a way that single words never can manage—but they are stored in the brain just as if they were a single word. Functional chunks are a very important part of the young learner's working vocabulary.

Second, functional chunks are a first step toward later grammar acquisition. As vocabulary expands and students become more sophisticated language users, the functional chunks they have stored become the basis for discovery—and for grammar. In fact, these memorized chunks of language are among the best building blocks of grammar.

A memorized chunk becomes more meaningful when students have an opportunity to use it to express something about themselves. In a unit on professions, for example, they can use the phrase "I would like to be . . ." to express real intentions. The memorized chunk "Please may I have . . ." can become part of regular classroom routines and exchanges. Students become fluent users of the phrase "I'd like to _____" if they have many opportunities in class to express preferences, or choose among options. Once a chunk has been introduced, the teacher should provide many contexts within which the students can use the expression for genuinely communicative purposes.

Passwords and Language Ladders   These selected phrases give students the language they need to deal with recurring situations in the classroom. Their use has often been demonstrated in workshops by Dr. Constance Knop of the University of Wisconsin–Madison. The phrases usually embed patterns that can later be used for a variety of purposes, but initially they are learned as memorized chunks.

Passwords are phrases, such as "Please, may I sharpen my pencil?" that are taught directly and then posted on the wall with some identifying visual to assist students in recalling the meaning connection. Passwords are frequently taught one each day or each week, and students are then required to produce the password before leaving the class for some desired activity such as lunch, recess, passing to another class, or going home for the day. When a learner struggles to express an idea contained in a password that has already been learned, the teacher can simply refer the student to the password posted on the wall and thus assist the student in recalling the information that has already been learned. These are examples of sample passwords:

May I go to the bathroom (office, drinking fountain, etc.)?

How do you say that?

Can you help me?

I can't find my eraser (paper, book, homework, lunch ticket, etc.).

Please give me the _____.

It's my turn.

Please leave me alone.

I have a stomach ache (headache, sore throat, etc.).

I am almost finished.

May I get my coat (book, pencil, band instrument, etc.)?

I need paper.

I'll help you.

This is very nice of you.

Hello. How are you?

Close the door (window, desk, locker), please.

Please pull down the shade.

May I borrow that?

That's mine. (That belongs to me.)

I'll share that with you.

My bus was late.

Sit down next to me.

He was sitting in my place.

What are we having to eat?

I was absent yesterday.

_____ is absent today.

I don't know how to say that.

I can't say that.

What time is it?

Please may I have a tissue?

One good strategy for choosing passwords to teach is to listen to student conversations and note which expressions they use frequently, but always in English. Passwords will be most effective if they are learned because of a real need to communicate the information involved.

Language ladders are similar to passwords in that they are also phrases taught one per day or per week. They usually represent a series of different ways in which to express a similar idea or a similar need, often in different registers, degrees of politeness, or social context. For example, a language ladder might include levels of reaction to a homework assignment, or different ways of giving a compliment or encouragement to fellow group members in a cooperative learning situation. Language ladders, like those seen here and the one shown in Figure 3.2, are posted on the wall in the classroom with accompanying visual cues, and they are usually sequenced or clustered to show their relationship and to assist the student in remembering their meaning.

Praise	Conversational Management	Excuses for Not Having Homework
Spitze!	J'ai une question.	Estaba ocupado(a).
Erstklassig	Pouvez-vous m'expliquer?	Estaba cansado(a).

Wunderbar	A quelle page sommes-nous?	Estaba enfermo(a).
Prima	Je crois que???	Tenía sueño.
Grossartig	Pardon je n'ai pas compris.	Salí con mis padres.
Klasse	Répétez s'il vous plait.	No pude hacerlo.
Phantastisch	Parlez plus fort.	No entendí.
Farewells	Est'ce que . . .	Se me olvidó.
Arrivederci	Excusez moi.	No sabía cómo hacerlo.
Buona Sera	Pourquoi	No tenía el libro.
Ci vediamo domani	Parce que	Dejé mi libro en la escuela/cass.
	Un instant	
Ciao	Pour quelle saison . . .	Tuve práctica de . . . fútbol, piano, coro, ballet, gymnasia . . .
Addio		

Games Games are an ideal setting for practicing functional chunks and making them habitual. The challenge for the teacher is to devise games that elicit chunks of language, rather than just one-word responses. In the "Hot–Cold Game," for example, one student goes out of the room and the class decides where to hide an object "in plain sight." When

● **FIGURE 3.2** Language Ladder. Language ladders help students recall language they can use in managing their lives in the target language. Here is a series of praising statements in Arabic.

the student returns, the class chants the name of the object, louder or softer depending on whether the student is moving nearer to the object or farther away. The same game could practice a whole chunk of language if the class were to chant "I'm missing my ___," or another appropriate phrase, rather than the name alone.

"Twenty Questions," or other question games, give students the chance to practice phrases, or functional chunks. Many of the activities and games listed in Chapter 13 provide excellent opportunities to practice these chunks of language and to move into genuine interpersonal communication.

Rhymes, Chants, and Songs   Nothing makes a phrase "stick" like a catchy rhyme or a rhythmic chant. Nursery rhymes or finger plays from the target culture make the link with children in other countries; jump-rope rhymes and counting-out rhymes can move from the classroom to the playground. All can be chosen for their potential to give learners practice with the functional chunks that form the bridge to later fluency.

Any phrase the teacher wants to imprint on children's memory can become a chant with which to play. Brigitte Jonen, a German early language specialist, uses a magic wand to create a chorus of chanters who repeat a rhythmic phrase over and over. The teacher directs them as if they are an orchestra, calling for the chant to become louder, softer, faster, slower, and finally ending with a grand climax. Other techniques for practicing the same (or another) phrase include:

- Marching single file around the room while chanting
- Repeating the phrase as if each student were a baby, a big elephant, a tiny mouse, or a hissing snake
- Repeating the phrase with varied emotions—as if the students are sad, angry, happy, afraid, or proud
- Turning to a partner and repeating the phrase as fast as possible, then as slowly as possible
- Taking turns with a partner saying the phrase as directed by the teacher (e.g., one partner might be angry, another might be sad)

Many of these activities appeal to several different learning styles, and they also connect the phrase and the experiences to emotions, a powerful motivator and memory aid.

Songs add the dimension of melody to the power of rhymes and rhythms. Songs with refrains or motions in particular make the learning and repetition of vocabulary and functional chunks effective and meaningful.

Presenting and Teaching Functional Chunks

The Natural Approach   The Natural Approach (Krashen and Terrell, 1983, 1996) is an effort to apply the insights of second-language acquisition, and especially Krashen's five hypotheses, in the beginning language classroom. Curriculum and activities are designed to be compatible with the stages of language acquisition as outlined here:

Oral Language Development in the Natural Approach (Krashen and Terrell, 1996)

Student Stage 1: Comprehension (pre-production)

    a. Total Physical Response (TPR)

    b. Descriptions of pictures and persons

        Information is associated with class members

        Students respond with names

Student Stage 2: Early speech production

    a. Yes–no questions

    b. Either–or questions

    c. Single/two-word answers

    d. Open-ended sentences

    e. Open dialogues

    f. Interviews

Student Stage 3: Speech emerges

    a. Games and recreational activities

    b. Content activities

    c. Humanistic-affective activities

    d. Information-problem-solving activities

In this approach, the teacher seeks to help students "bind" new language by providing experiences and associations with vocabulary in a meaningful context, thus making the language both more meaningful and more memorable. Extended listening experiences are provided during stage 1 of language acquisition, drawing on TPR, use of vivid pictures to illustrate concepts, and active involvement of the students through physical contact with the pictures and objects being discussed.

In stage 2, students are drawn into oral participation by means of yes–no questions, choice making, and open-ended statements. The Natural Approach outlines a useful sequencing of teacher questions to help move students from a listening mode to a speaking mode:

Step 1: *Students respond with a name or respond by pointing to the object.*

    Who has the cheese?   Point to the cheese.

    Who forgot his pencil?   Point to the pencil.

Step 2: *Yes–no question*

    Does Helena have the cheese?

    Did Duane forget his pencil?

Step 3:   *Either–or question, using nouns, verbs, adjectives, adverbs*

(The student answer is contained in the question)

Does Helena have the cheese or the bread?

Is it Swiss cheese or cheddar cheese?

Is the cheese on the bread or on the floor?

Did Duane forget his ruler or his pencil?

Step 4:   *What, when, where, who questions*

(Students answer with a single word, moving toward a phrase answer)

What does Helena have?

What kind of cheese is this?

Where is the cheese?

What did Duane forget?

Step 5:   *Students answer with the entire sentence or action*

What did Duane do this time? Or Tell us about the cheese.

Many teachers plan their questioning of students according to this Natural Approach sequence, from easiest to more difficult: If students are unable to respond to questions at one level, the teacher can move back to an easier level, still giving students a chance to succeed. There are a number of teachers who have posted this sequence, in the target language, at the back of their classroom, as a reminder of the levels of difficulty of the questions they are using with their students.

Through the use of context and personalization, the listening and speaking practice of Natural Approach stage one and stage two are made meaningful rather than mechanical. Only at stage three does communication really begin to take place, after language and meanings have been acquired and nurtured over some time.

Direct Teaching of Speaking   Although most aspects of the audiolingual methodology of the 1960s are a poor fit in today's communicative climate, audiolingualism did lead to the development of several useful strategies to assist with the direct teaching of oral skills. Most student speaking should occur naturally, in communicative settings, but teachers may choose direct teaching to introduce activities such as passwords or phrases in a song or a dialogue. The following suggestions will help them to do so in an effective manner.

1. *Teacher Repetition.*   During activities that call for a group or whole-class response, the teacher should never repeat a response with the students. It is very tempting to try to model a quick, clear, vigorous response by playing the role of cheerleader, but students quickly become dependent on the teacher's leadership. Moreover, teachers who speak with the students are not in a position to evaluate the quality of the student response and the degree to which students may actually have mastered the material.

2. *Modeling.*   Teachers should always model the language with natural speed and intonation, especially in practice settings when they might otherwise tend to emphasize the components of the message that they expect to cause the students problems. When students seem to be having difficulty with a sentence, it is a better strategy to repeat the message several more times, using natural speed and intonation, than to distort the language by slowing it down or giving difficult segments inappropriate emphasis.

3. *Backward Buildup.* Most language in songs, passwords, rhymes, and dialogues should be simple and direct enough for learners to understand and learn it in complete utterances. When an utterance is longer than about seven syllables, however, it is often necessary to teach the utterance part by part instead of in a single stream. Under these circumstances, it can be helpful to segment the utterance into meaning units so that, for example, prepositions and their objects are not separated into different practice segments. It is also useful to begin teaching the utterance with the segment closest to the end. In the sentence, "I wasn't able to get my homework done yesterday," the teacher might proceed as follows:

> yesterday.
>
> done yesterday.
>
> my homework done yesterday.
>
> to get my homework done yesterday.
>
> able to get my homework done yesterday.
>
> I wasn't able to get my homework done yesterday.

Backward buildup should be used only in very specific situations, with language that is understood by the learners and highly motivating, such as a very important password, a song that is integral to the rest of the lesson, or the language necessary for a game or for expressing a message of considerable importance to the children.

4. *Answer Precedes Question.* When dealing with question–answer exchanges, it is useful to teach the answer first, followed by the question. For example, one might teach, "It's three o'clock," "Today is Wednesday," "My name is Mary," or "I feel terrible." All of these are statements that can stand alone and that clearly communicate information that might have value to the hearer. Once the answer has been learned, the statement can be cued with the question, and the question becomes a form of input: "What time is it?" "It is three o'clock." As a final step, the question is learned, and the question and the answer can then be used together in natural settings. This is a much more natural approach than teaching the question first, since questions really cannot stand alone without an answer. When the answer is taught first the question is always practiced in combination with an answer, thus creating much more meaningful, realistic practice settings. These experiences lead naturally to awareness of typical adjacency pairs in the target language—in other words, typical questions and answers that always occur together.

Teaching Pronunciation Although direct teaching of spoken language may have its place, and there are useful techniques for accomplishing it, there is probably far less justification for the direct teaching of pronunciation, at least in early stages of language acquisition. As Berty Segal (n.d.) has pointed out, focusing instruction and correction on pronunciation increases the potential for creating problems and for communicating some inappropriate messages. Segal describes three problems that may arise when pronunciation is taught and drilled directly:

1. Students often do not know which sounds to say. They sometimes cannot separate the teacher's command from the word or phrase to be repeated. They frequently cannot determine which part of the phrase is causing difficulty, so they do not know where to focus their attention.

2. If a sound does not exist in the native language, over 40 hearings are required before the students even recognize the sound they are trying to imitate. Drilling with a single student who is not able to hear the sound in question is frustrating for both teacher and student.

3. The frustration inherent in premature individual drill work in pronunciation leads to student anxiety and a loss of self-confidence in all areas of the language acquisition process.

In addition to these issues, and perhaps most important of all, the direct teaching of pronunciation at early stages of language acquisition encourages students to focus attention on the surface features of language rather than on the meaning. It is a way of inviting learners to listen for speaking rather than to listen for meaning, of encouraging them to parrot language rather than truly developing language competence.

Avoiding a focus on pronunciation does not mean that pronunciation should be ignored. Teachers need to be sure that they provide an effective language model, both in terms of pronunciation and language structure. An accurate teacher model is a key to accurate student pronunciation. Teachers should also anticipate potential pronunciation problems and plan strategies to give students additional exposure to these sounds. Teachers can playfully emphasize a specific problem sound in a song, a game, or a chant, for example, and students will imitate enthusiastically. As is the case with other errors, early pronunciation problems can effectively be dealt with when teachers restate student messages correctly as a form of reflective listening, rather than in a correction mode. Most learners tend to be good imitators, so there is no serious danger of reinforcing poor pronunciation habits.

When students have gained confidence and comfort with the new language, and the emphasis on communication has been established, attention to pronunciation becomes more appropriate. Teachers can assist experienced students in communicating more effectively and more precisely by guiding improvement in pronunciation as well as in grammar, structure, and vocabulary usage. When correction takes place in the interest of improved communication of meanings and ideas, it is more compatible with how the brain works and thus more effective.

Invitations for Students to Speak   One of the challenges that early language teachers face is moving students from the comfortable role of listener to the "riskier" role of language user. The strategies described so far in this chapter, and others developed within the same philosophy, function as invitations to the student to be a participant in the action and the interaction of the language classroom. Students will learn to communicate by talking about familiar topics of interest to them, using the vocabulary that their teachers have systematically helped them to acquire. One of the best forms of "invitation" is to give students the opportunity to be the teacher.

Students draw extensively on their repertoire of functional chunks when they are given the opportunity to take the role of the teacher. After considerable experience with the opening class routines, for example, students can become the leaders. In the Total Physical Response activities in the next section, one of the goals is to have the learners begin to issue the commands. Some teachers begin every class period with a question–answer session, and learners enjoy taking over this responsibility as well. All of these possibilities, and many more, move learners toward being full participants in classroom communication.

Stepping Stone: Linking Language with Actions and Story

When teachers link language with actions, they provide additional context, and they also appeal to additional learning styles and intelligences. Gestures help students remember key vocabulary in passwords, rhymes, and songs. The youngest learners respond immediately to finger plays and songs like "Itsy-Bitsy Spider."

The addition of a story line to the actions adds an emotional component, and it draws on the ability of the brain to organize, store, and recall information by means of story. Teachers can use the following strategies to introduce and develop the vocabulary and functional chunks that form the critical basis for language use in the interpersonal and presentational modes.

Total Physical Response (TPR) The TPR strategy uses movement to help establish meaning and set a purpose for language use. This systematized approach to the use of commands was developed by the psychologist James Asher in the late 1960s (see Asher, 2000). Total Physical Response has become a common and effective means of introducing learners to a new language through listening and physical involvement, especially in early stages of instruction. Many teachers find it to be an especially engaging and effective way of introducing new vocabulary and making it meaningful. This strategy may be at its most effective when it is used playfully, and both teacher and students are having fun.

In TPR, teachers interact with students by delivering commands, and students demonstrate comprehension through physical response. The following sequencing is recommended by Berty Segal (n.d.); examples have been added by the authors.

1. Commands involving the entire body, large-motor skills
   - Point to your ear.
   - Put your left hand on your head and turn around three times.
   - Walk backwards to the front of the class and shake the teacher's hand.
   - Clap your hands for Mary. She did a good job.
2. Commands involving interaction with concrete materials and manipulatives, beginning with classroom objects
   - Take the red circle and place it in the wastebasket.
   - Pick up your green crayon and lay it under your chair.

● Walk to the chalkboard, take a piece of yellow chalk, and draw a picture of the sun.

3. Commands relating to pictures, maps, numbers, and other indirect materials
   ● Go to the map and trace the outline of Paraguay.
   ● Go to the picture of the bathroom and (pretend to) brush your teeth.
   ● Go to the wall chart and point to a food from the fruits and vegetables group.

When giving a command for the first time, the teacher models the desired behavior, removing the model after several repetitions of the same command. After students respond confidently to a number of single commands, the teacher begins to combine commands in original and unexpected ways, so that students discover that they can understand and respond to language that is expressed in ways that they have never heard before.

Students are not expected to respond orally until they feel ready. Early oral responses involve role reversal (a student takes on the role of the teacher and gives commands to others in the class) and some yes–no and one-word replies to the teacher questions. This strategy involves little or no pressure to speak in the early stages.

Some very important aspects of the strategy include the creation of novel commands, which encourages careful and creative listening, and the combination of commands so that students perform several actions in sequence. The sequence of commands must never become predictable, and students must be confident that the teacher will never embarrass them. It should also be a clear ground rule that students who take the role of teacher in later stages will show the same consideration of their classmates.

In its simplest terms, TPR seeks to teach new concepts through the body, as shown in Table 3.1. Students discover that they can make the connection themselves between new language and its meaning, without translation into English or explanation by the teacher.

TABLE 3.1 Useful Vocabulary for Beginning TPR

Verbs		Adjectives/Adverbs		Nouns
stand up	turn around	fast	low	body parts
sit down	clap	slow	backwards	classroom objects
lift/raise (hand, etc.)	open	___ times	forwards	parts of the room
lower	shut	(to the)	sideways	colors
point to	wave	left	above/over	numbers
lay/place	draw	right	below/under	
take	write	front	in	
jump		back	on	
		high	next to	

Steps	*Examples*
1. Give a command while modeling the action.	
a. Start with actions using the body.	**a.** "Raise your hand." "Put your hand on your foot (knee/head/elbow)." "Turn around." "Put your hand on the floor."
b. Give commands involving objects.	**b.** "Pick up your pencil and lay it on the floor."
c. Use commands relating to pictures, maps, charts, etc.	**c.** "Go to the whiteboard and draw a dress." "Go to the (picture of the) bedroom and comb your hair."
2. After several repetitions of the command while modeling, the teacher removes the model. If students can respond without the model, give the command a few more times. Mix up single commands and give them in a different order.	"Put your hand on your elbow." "Raise your knee." "Turn around." "Jump backwards three times."
3. After students can respond successfully and confidently to a number of single commands, combine them in original and *unexpected* ways. Surprise and humor help to keep TPR fresh and engaging.	"Put your elbow on your knee and *turn around*." (new combination)
4. Call on volunteers to respond to commands of increasing length and complexity (often silly), *using familiar language in new combinations.*	Who can do this: Raise your hand. Walk backwards to the map, put your left hand on your head and put your right elbow on South America. All right, Maria."
5. String commands together to tell a story or create a sequence that has a beginning, middle, and end.	"Angie, hold the (stuffed animal) monkey with your right hand. Mario, put your right elbow on the monkey's head. Kim, put your elbow on the monkey's nose (and so on, using body parts of class and the monkey and finally creating a kind of silly picture). Class, take out your (imaginary) cameras and take a picture of the monkey and his friends. Smile!" *continued*

Steps	*Examples*
6. Invite student volunteers to "play teacher" and give commands to the rest of the class (role reversal). It is important that students volunteer for this step and not be called on randomly.	"Who would like to be the teacher today?"
7. (optional) After step 6, TPR can be extended into experiences with reading/writing."	What was the hardest command Mary gave you today? Let's write it down on the board." "Who can do the command I just wrote on the board?"

Total Physical Response is especially engaging when the commands can be strung together in unexpected ways to actually develop a story line with a beginning, middle, and end. (See Step 5.) Sometimes the playful quality of TPR can be intensified when the teacher delivers an outrageous command, such as "Put your elbow on the ceiling," and students have learned to respond with "That's impossible." Here are some examples of what this might look like.

Stories with Gestures

Total Physical Response Storytelling (TPRS) is an approach to combining language with actions and story. It was introduced by California teacher Blaine Ray in 1990, as a way to motivate his high school Spanish students and help them succeed. Based on TPR and the Natural Approach, TPRS embeds new vocabulary and structures as functional chunks in a story line and provides extensive listening practice before students are expected to speak. Since its introduction TPRS has undergone many variations, as teachers have adapted it to their own philosophies and practice. Most recently, it has morphed into new terminology and a somewhat different approach: Teaching Proficiency through Reading and Storytelling.

Among the many variations, the authors find the approach of Janet Glass to be especially appealing. For clarity, we will call this variation "Stories with Gestures." Glass notes that her stories are always embedded in a thematic unit with a cultural focus, and she never finds it necessary to use translation.

One of her favorites is from her unit "The Llama's Secret," based on the book *El secreto de la llama* by Argentina Palacios, a Peruvian flood story (now out of print). In this story, a llama, our hero, can suddenly speak. He warns the people and animals that there will be a big flood. He saves them by leading them to the highest peak in the Andes Mountains. After five days, the flood waters subside, and the llama never speaks again. Figure 3.3 shows the sequence of pictures that Janet Glass uses to tell the story. Like Janet Glass, teachers can devise their own stories and illustrations based on the following model and examples from the Internet.

● **FIGURE 3.3**   Visuals for the Story, *El secreto de la llama*

Source: Reprinted by permission of Janet Glass.

Storytelling Step 1   Step 1 in the process is to identify the key vocabulary in the story, draw or find pictures, and assign a motion for each item. For a folktale or fairy tale, it is best to break the story into short segments and present them one at a time. Each of the segments should function as a mini-story, with a clear beginning, middle, and end, in order to sustain interest. Then teach a few items from the first segment using variations of TPR. For example, the key vocabulary for the first segment of Janet's story might be as follows:

niño	(boy)
agua	(water)
sube	(rises)
miedo	(afraid)
ve	(see)
pico	(mountain peak)
corre	(run)

At first, students just listen as a new word is presented. Then they practice the motions with the teacher. Next, they respond as the teacher combines the vocabulary words in a variety of ways, creating a variety of sentences or questions, such as, "The water rises and rises. When it rains, does water go up or down? Birds go up and down. In this classroom, do you go up or down? What else goes up and down? The boy is afraid. Are the fish afraid? Is the boy's father afraid? Are you afraid? Who else is afraid?" And so on. One of the means of checking understanding is to have students do the motions with their eyes closed.

Storytelling Step 2   In the second step, the students work in pairs to say or read the vocabulary words to each other and see whether or not they can do the actions. Then the process can be reversed, and the students do the actions for each other to prompt the vocabulary words.

Steps 1 and 2 can be repeated until all the key vocabulary has been introduced with actions and with many opportunities to practice various combinations of words.

Storytelling Step 3   Step 3 is to use the vocabulary in a story. The teacher can use pictures, puppets, or student actors to tell a mini-story using the key vocabulary words. A mini-story for this set of vocabulary follows:

Hay un niño.	There is a boy.
Hay agua.	There is water.
El agua sube y sube.	The water rises and rises.
El niño tiene miedo.	The boy is afraid.
Ve un pico.	He sees a mountain peak.
El niño corre.	The boy runs.

The teacher retells the story several times while students do the gestures, embellishing it in different ways each time, but the basic story stays the same. Each telling should provide an opportunity for students to participate and for the teacher to check for understanding: The students provide gestures; the teacher leaves pauses for students to fill in words; the teacher makes mistakes and the students correct them; the teacher uses yes–no and either–or questions as the story progresses (e.g., "Is the boy running or swimming?").

Storytelling Step 4   Step 4, after many retellings by the teacher, is for students to practice retelling the story to each other in partner practice. At this point, the teacher may want to elicit student volunteers to tell the story, or a variation of it, to the class. Other students may act out the story in front of the class as their peers narrate it. In some classes, the teacher may wish to have students write out the story, perhaps first as a copying exercise.

Storytelling Step 5   The mini-story is revised in Step 5. The teacher may want to cover up the last frame of the story and ask the students to come up with their own new ending, or have students retell the story, adding new characters and/or new vocabulary. Other possibilities are for the teacher to present a revised story as a model, or for teacher and students together to experiment with revisions. The waters can rise and the boy sees a boat instead of a mountain peak, or he's not afraid and he swims instead. Anything is possible. The teacher might also help students to revise the story so that it is told in the first person: "I am walking." "I see the water rising." And so on. Students then work in pairs to create their own revisions, which are then presented to the class or written and illustrated for a portfolio or a class book.

For the story of *El secreto de la llama,* additional segments would be taught as separate stories, creating a kind of soap opera effect. As a culminating activity, the entire legend could be presented and dramatized, an example of presentational communication.

Using stories with gestures clearly moves students from the interpersonal mode of communication into a limited experience with presentational communication, both oral and written. Students build both vocabulary and structure resources that are readily available for future use. Janet Glass is enthusiastic about this approach: "One thing I know from experience—the students remember it long term. I think it's the simultaneous combination of seeing the pictures, hearing the words, doing the gestures, having the repetition, and enjoying the story. They really like making one up with slight variations and sharing them. This gives them a lot of chances to hear and speak the language."

For a complete monarch butterfly unit incorporating storytelling with gestures, go to http://senoraglass.com/wlo/monarch/page6.php.

Gouin Series (Action Series)

The Gouin Series, or Action Series, is a great activity for moving students from listening to speaking, and it also provides a good context for embedding functional chunks of language. In a Gouin Series the teacher prepares a series of six to eight short statements describing a logical sequence of actions that takes place in a specific context, such as getting up in the morning, cooking a meal, using the library, or making a phone call. A Gouin Series can be used to introduce vocabulary in context, basic structures in the language, and verbs that follow the same grammatical pattern. Unlike a dialogue, where exchange of information takes place, the Gouin Series focuses on narrating a step-by-step sequence of actions. It is a narration, not a dialogue. Only one person is involved and talking.

The Gouin Series dates back to the 1890s to François Gouin, who invented what was called the "Series Method." This method is very similar to TPR and to TPR Storytelling in that it involves a series of actions. In TPR, the actions tend to be random, but in a story, the actions take the form of a narrative with a beginning, middle, and end. The Gouin (Action) Series is also a narrative. It can be used to teach culture, to reinforce class or school procedures, or to reinforce various subject content areas. It can also be used to review and retell a story. All statements in a Gouin Series should include action verbs and use the same tense and the same person throughout. The teacher presents the statements to the class orally, accompanying them with pantomime of the actions involved. The class responds first through pantomime and later by imitating the statements while doing the actions. In preparing a Gouin Series, it is useful to have simple props and visuals for at least some of the activities.

Here are several samples of Gouin series written by classroom teachers:

Going to Class

I look for my materials.

I go to the class.

I take off my hat.

I take out my gum.

I greet the teacher.

I sit down.

I hear the bell.

I take out my homework.

We Make Our Bed (Japanese)

We are tired.

We open the closet doors.

We take out the futon.

We put the futon on the floor.

We cover the futon with the sheets.

We lay the pillow and the quilt on top of the futon.

We sleep and dream.

Making a Sandwich the German Way: I'm really hungry!

I lay my hands on the table.

I take the fork in my left hand.

I take the knife in my right hand.

I stick my fork into the cheese sandwich.

I cut (a piece of) the cheese sandwich.

I eat the cheese sandwich.

I say, "That tastes good!"

Constance K. Knop from the University of Wisconsin–Madison has identified the following values of the Gouin series in language instruction:

1. It links language to action and visuals, leading to improved comprehension.
2. It teaches appropriate verbal and physical behavior, making it especially useful for teaching cultural behaviors and shaping classroom behavior.
3. It is easy to recall because it has multiple meaning reinforcers:
   - Physical actions
   - Visuals and props
   - Logical sequence
   - Appeal to the senses
   - Beginning, middle, end (story form)

The Gouin Series has the following components:

1. Its introduction sets the scene and motivates the action.
2. It includes six to eight statements (can also use commands).
3. There is a seven-syllable limit for most statements.
4. It has a logical sequence of actions.
5. It has a single, specific, clear context.

6. It includes action verbs.

7. Only one tense is used (not necessarily present).

8. Only one person is involved (not necessarily first-person singular).

9. Simple props or visuals are used to dramatize the action.

Sequence for Teaching Gouin Series

1. The teacher presents the series orally, accompanying words with pantomime and props.

2. The teacher repeats the series orally and the class joins in with pantomime, *not with words.*

3. The class pantomimes the series as the teacher repeats orally but does not model actions. When moving to this step, the teacher first repeats the phrase and hesitates to see if the students perform the pantomime on their own. If they cannot, the teacher models the action again. Continue this once or twice, until the students can perform the pantomime confidently.

4. The teacher makes a "mistake" in the sequence, perhaps leaving something out, to see if the students catch it and correct the teacher.

5. Individual *volunteers* pantomime the series as the teacher repeats orally, without modeling. This step is done until everyone has had a chance to "solo." With very confident students, the teacher can "make mistakes" to test for listening comprehension.

6. The class imitates the series orally as well as physically, first together and then as individual volunteers leading the class. At this point, student volunteers can also lead the series, sometimes with interesting variations.

Literacy Transition (Optional)

7. The teacher distributes cards with the steps of the series written on them, holding each card up and having the students repeat the phrase as they "read" the card.

8. The class and the teacher repeat the series, and students hold up the correct card as their phrase is recited and then stand in front of the room in the order of the series.

9. The whole class "reads" the series from the cards in the front of the room.

10. The teacher distributes sheets of paper on which the steps of the series are written in the correct order, with a picture frame above each step. Students illustrate the "story" and read it aloud to one another, or take it home to read there.

The cultural potential of a Gouin Series and the extension of the series to a reading and writing activity is illustrated by Figure 3.4, a Gouin Series about Columbus.

● **FIGURE 3.4**   Example of How a Gouin Series Can Be Extended into Reading and Writing

Source: Created by a student of Rita Gullickson.

A Note about Written Language in the Interpersonal Mode

Most of the discussion thus far has been focused on the development of oral language. Students also need experiences that prepare them for writing in the target language, so that they can begin to use the written word as well as oral language for interpersonal communication. This kind of writing involves students in focusing on expressing and exchanging personal messages, not engaging in mechanical drill exercises. For example, they might write notes to each other and put them in the classroom mail or message box. They can write messages (perhaps on self-stick notes) to be placed on a message board. In a game-like setting, they might exchange written TPR commands with one another, or develop components of a reading action chain (see Chapter 13). Pen pals or "key pals" provide other rich opportunities for communication in the interpersonal mode.

Dialogue Journals   A dialogue journal is a written conversation in which a student and teacher communicate regularly (Peyton, 1993). Students write about topics of their choice, and the teacher writes back with responses, advice, comments, and observations, acting as a participant in an ongoing written conversation, rather than as an evaluator who simply corrects or comments on the writing. Because dialogue journal writing involves exchanging genuine messages for real purposes to a known and interested audience, it provides a valuable context for language and writing development. Dialogue journals can be used with students from beginning to advanced stages of learning a new language. At the very beginning stages, students can write or copy the few words they have learned and combine them with pictures. At more advanced stages, they can engage in discussions of cultural issues or other course content, as well as express more personal feelings and opinions.

Borich (2001) reports the value of using dialogue journals as an assessment of a second-grade thematic unit on the Yucatan. She concludes, "The data suggest that student dialogue journals provide documentation of student learning from a cultural unit taught in Spanish" (p. 16).

The success of dialogue journal writing depends in part on the prompt return of the journals by the teacher. With large numbers of students to deal with, teachers can find a dialogue project to be a practical impossibility. Another appealing possibility for effective use of this strategy is journaling with advanced high school or college students, especially students in methods for early language programs. With older learners, journaling might be facilitated by the use of email.

● Communication in the Interpretive Mode (Standard 1.2)

Listening and Reading

Listening is considered by many teachers and researchers to be the cornerstone of language development. In beginning classrooms, listening is the main channel by which the student makes initial contact with the target language and its culture. The challenge with listening in the interpretive mode is to provide students with opportunities for extended, purposeful listening and viewing in addition to the listening that takes place as a part of conversation.

One simple activity that helps learners move in this direction is the game "I See Something That You Don't See." The teacher describes a student or an object in the classroom at some length, and the students try to guess who or what is being described. Later, a student volunteer may do the describing, after student speaking skills have developed and as the students become familiar with the language of description.

Storytelling and Story Reading   Few listening experiences can compare with a good story, told or read by the teacher. In early stages of language development, the story may be heavily supported with visuals or actions. Using visuals and actions to support the listening experience helps learners draw on all the resources they have available to understand the message—background knowledge, tone of voice and gestures, pictures or visuals, and motions. This experience helps prepare learners for more independent listening activities in the future.

Many values come together in the story: Egan (1986, 1997) identifies the story form as one of the most effective tools for communicating new information to young learners, and Bruner (1990) makes the even stronger claim that our perception of the world is shaped by the stories to which we are exposed and that we have internalized. Certainly the myths, folktales, fairy tales, and legends of a culture constitute a direct and pleasurable means of communicating cultural ideas and values, and in the language classroom these stories can give learners a cultural experience in common with those living in the target culture.

Storytelling   Storytelling has special pedagogical values for the foreign language classroom. Wajnryb (1986, pp. 17–18) identifies the following reasons for telling stories in the early language classroom:

1. The purpose of telling a story is genuinely communicative.
2. Storytelling is linguistically honest. (It is oral language, meant to be heard.)
3. Storytelling is real! (People do it all the time.)
4. Storytelling is sensual.
5. Storytelling appeals to the affective domain.
6. Storytelling caters to the individual while forging a community in the classroom.
7. Storytelling provides listening experiences with reduced anxiety.
8. Storytelling is pedagogically sound.

Wajnryb suggests several steps in the storytelling process that will help beginners prepare successfully. After choosing a suitable story, the teller can "skeletalize" it—write out the major features and characters of the story in the order of the action, but in words and phrases. As an alternative, the teacher might devise a story map (described later in this chapter). This information serves as a reminder of the story line, yet allows the teller to narrate in a natural oral style, adapting to the responses and the understanding of the learners. At this point, the teacher can also plan for specific vocabulary or linguistic features to be emphasized through repetition, in order to intensify the opportunities for acquisition of useful language.

The next step is to develop some form of advance organizer, perhaps presenting or recalling key vocabulary using visuals, physical actions, or other devices, and then setting the stage for the action to follow. Then the storyteller begins the tale, using visuals and dramatic expression, and involving learners through actions and prediction whenever possible. Once the story has been told, many follow-up activities are possible, depending on the story itself and the aspects to which students have responded most enthusiastically.

Storytelling can provide experience with the interpretive mode for learners, even at very early stages of language acquisition, when the stories meet the following criteria:

1. The story is highly predictable, or familiar to the learners from their native culture, with a large proportion of previously learned vocabulary. In early stages, it is especially helpful to choose stories that include vocabulary representing the home and school environments of the children.

2. The story is repetitive, making use of formulas and patterns that occur regularly and predictably. In the best story choices, these repeated elements provide language that learners can later use for their own expressive purposes. Pattern stories like *Brown Bear, Brown Bear* (1983) by Bill Martin Jr., or cumulative stories like "The House that Jack Built," are good examples of this type of story. Stories written for children in the target culture, if they have a story structure like those detailed by Wajnryb, can be successfully presented in the target language from very early stages of language development.

3. The story line lends itself to dramatization and pantomime.

4. The story lends itself to heavy use of visuals and realia to illustrate its content and progress.

Stories that meet these criteria can be presented without the use of English, relying entirely on visuals, pantomime, and the children's existing knowledge of the story or the situation to make meaning clear. "The Three Bears" is an example of a story containing all of these features. The teacher may check comprehension during or after the telling by using physical responses (point to the big bear, hold up the little bowl), yes–no questions, and other levels of the Natural Approach sequence described earlier.

After the story has been told several times, learners may pantomime the story as the teacher tells it again. This "physical storytelling" can be carried even further, as the teacher recombines previously learned TPR commands with familiar story material to create a new story that the students act out as the teacher tells it.

Many teachers pull stuffed animals, puppets, or other concrete objects representing story vocabulary from a magic box, a mystery bag, or another special hiding place. As the teacher introduces or reviews the vocabulary for the items, one item at a time, he or she distributes the objects among class members. These objects can be the focus of a game before the storytelling begins, used to reinforce the vocabulary. Also, students can hold up the objects as they occur in the story, perhaps using them to help dramatize the action.

One of the special benefits of storytelling in the early language classroom is that the teacher can tailor the story to the interests and background knowledge of the class. Joe Pennington, a Spanish teacher in Douglas County, Georgia, created a magical listening experience for his second-graders to explain the exaggerated limp that he appeared to have from the time the class began. He told his wide-eyed students about his encounter with a dinosaur in the local discount store, at the end of which he saved a little girl from the dinosaur's jaws. Joe's body language, familiar context, and choice of vocabulary empowered his students to gain meaning from context, an essential element of the interpretive mode.

Story Reading   Reading stories aloud has the additional benefit of connecting narrative with the printed page. The teacher can successfully read very familiar stories aloud at an early stage of language acquisition, especially if the book is heavily illustrated. While reading aloud, it is helpful to point to the words or lines as they are read, to emphasize the connection of oral language to print, even before learners are actually reading. Most primary school teachers follow a pattern of introducing the book by title and identifying the author and the illustrator, and then reading dedications aloud, so that children think of books as communication created by real authors and artists, often with a specific audience in mind. During the reading, the teacher may pause frequently to comment on the illustrations or the action, to involve students in reactions or predictions, or to clarify some aspect of the story.

Story Mapping   Story mapping is a strategy used to identify and visually organize the central structure and main components of simple stories. Story maps help students understand what they are reading. They can be used before, during, and/or after reading. Since story mapping simplifies and graphically organizes the story, it helps the foreign language student to sort out the more important information from the less important information in the story, and thus to comprehend the story better. It is also a helpful tool for teachers to use in their planning as they prepare stories to tell or read to their students. Story maps can take many shapes and forms; several sample story map formats are shown in Figures 3.5 and 3.6. The teacher reads the story and constructs the story map based on the components of the story and the language ability of the students. The teacher may simplify the story or the number of events in the story according to the needs of the students.

The teacher decides how and at what point in the lesson to use the story-mapping strategy. The map framework can be the basis for asking appropriate comprehension questions. It can also be used at the beginning of the story as a prereading organizer to help the students understand what they are going to read or hear, or it can be filled in by teachers and students together as the story is being read. Students can use the story map to write a summary of the story, or to rewrite the story by changing one or more elements; for example, they can change the setting or invent a new hero. Students, individually or in groups, can develop a story map and then use it to write an original story.

Typical questions to ask when putting together a story map include the following:

What is the setting?

Who is the main character?

What did the main character want (goals)?

What was the problem?

What did the main character do to solve the problem?

What happened next?

How was the goal met and the problem solved in the end? Or not solved?

How did the main character feel in the end?

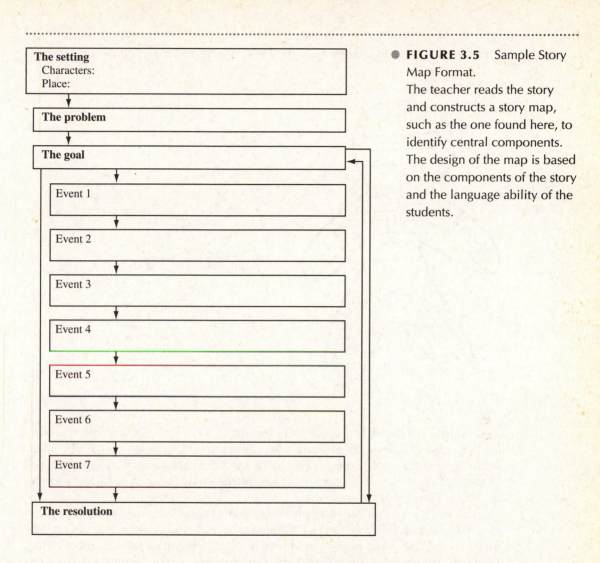

The setting
Characters:
Place:

The problem

The goal

Event 1

Event 2

Event 3

Event 4

Event 5

Event 6

Event 7

The resolution

● **FIGURE 3.5** Sample Story
Map Format.
The teacher reads the story
and constructs a story map,
such as the one found here, to
identify central components.
The design of the map is based
on the components of the story
and the language ability of the
students.

Listening and Reading for a Purpose   Listening, reading, and viewing can all be
enhanced when they take place for a purpose. Of course, the purpose in the "I See Something" game mentioned earlier is solving the puzzle. The purpose of story reading and
telling may simply be the pleasure of following an interesting narrative.

Sometimes a purpose for listening can be established through use of a worksheet,
such as the format shown in Figure 3.7, used for filling in the information from a recorded
weather forecast in the target language. The purpose of this kind of activity could be made
more meaningful if the learners had to decide which clothes to wear for an imaginary outing, based on the weather forecast, or if they needed to tell a family member how to pack
for their coming trip to the city or country in question.

● **FIGURE 3.6**   Sample Story Maps for *The Gingerbread Man* and *Where the Wild Things Are*

As with any formal listening activity, the teacher would prepare students by activating their existing knowledge of weather vocabulary and expressions, perhaps by brainstorming what they could expect to hear in the weather forecast and creating a word bank or a web of vocabulary. Thus prepared, the students would be much more likely to succeed in the listening experience.

Students need to be carefully prepared for any formal listening or viewing experience. For example, before viewing a DVD about the celebration of Karneval in Germany, students could talk about celebrations they enjoy in this country—in German, of course. The teacher might lead them to share ideas about costume parties, costumes, parades, festive foods, and music—while the teacher or a student writes these ideas on the board. Their purpose in viewing the DVD might be to identify characteristics of this celebration that are the same or different from those they are familiar with at home.

There are many ideas for activities that will give students practice with listening and viewing in the interpretive mode:

● Students might view television advertising in the target language, or listen to radio commercials, in order to choose among several options for the same product on the basis of preestablished criteria. Using the same materials, they might compare the most important criteria (adjectives) listed in the target language

● **FIGURE 3.7** A Worksheet to Guide Listening or Viewing Experience with a Weather Report

High Temperature ____ ° C	Low Temperature ____ ° C	Precipitation	Wind Conditions	Sky Conditions	Humidity
High temperature feels: ● warm ● hot ● very hot	Low temperature feels: ● freezing ● cold ● cool	● light rain ● heavy rain ● snow ● sleet ● hail ● mist ● thunderstorm	● windy ● light breeze ● still	● sunny ● cloudy ● partly sunny ● partly cloudy	

with those that would be stressed in an American commercial for a similar product and develop a Venn diagram, creating a good opportunity for addressing the comparisons standard.

● Directions for a task or a project can be an opportunity for extended listening practice. A CD or DVD might be set up at a learning center, for example, with directions for completing a puzzle, coloring a picture or chart, or doing a paper-folding activity.

● Some teachers have recorded a story or a set of directions—perhaps for a homework assignment—on a telephone answering machine. Students call the number and listen to the message in order to complete a task or solve a problem. This is a natural type of listening activity for the telephone-addicted middle school student!

● Sometimes background information about a new unit or project can be presented in modified "lecture" format—another opportunity for practice with interpretive communication.

Many activities that begin as an opportunity for extended listening flow naturally into reading, speaking, or writing—in fact, these competencies are closely interconnected. The Gouin Series is a good example of this flow. It begins as a listening activity, heavily supported with actions and sometimes visuals. The series can become a reading activity, as students place written statements from the series in order; or it can develop into a speaking activity, in which students recite the series and perhaps make variations on it.

Reading

Reading is another dimension of one-way, interpretive communication, Standard 1.2. As with listening, reading activities are most successful when they take place for a purpose. Many reading activities will parallel those designed for listening—only the medium for the message has changed. As with listening, the challenge of reading in the interpretive mode is to provide students with opportunities to use reading as a tool, for a purpose, within a familiar and meaningful context.

Reading activities that are primarily interpretive will build on and use the literacy skills discussed in Chapter 5. The interpretive standard is primarily concerned with reading to learn, rather than with learning to read. The goal of these activities will usually not be simple one-word or one-sentence-at-a-time reading. Instead, students will work with longer, connected texts, including authentic materials.

The process of understanding written language involves drawing on experiences and information already stored in memory. Frank Smith (2006) explains, "Reading depends more on what is behind the eyes—on nonvisual information—than on the visual information in front of them" (p. 34). Preparing students for new reading experiences involves activating this nonvisual information. If students do not already have a conceptual framework for what they are about to read, it will be impossible for them to have a successful reading experience. These structures for organization of meaning are called *schemata*. Reading can be understood, then, as a complex process of meaning construction by the learner, who takes information from the printed page and constructs meanings based on schemata already held in memory. The following activities all draw on existing visual and nonvisual information that learners already possess.

Sample Reading Activities for Developing the Interpretive Mode   Students can use selected target language ads or websites, for example, to gain information about products that they might want to buy on an imaginary trip to the country in which the language is spoken. There are numerous websites available for children who speak the target language, and many of these contain games or information appropriate for American target language learners. They all involve reading the target language for a purpose.

For example, fifth-grade German students might read letters from German children describing their household pets, in preparation for writing a description of their own pets. These letters are available on the Blinde Kuh website for German children (www .blindekuh.de). The students might later write their own letters to be submitted for inclusion on the same website.

Middle school students might read brochures or Internet sites from a variety of cities in the target culture, scanning for several predetermined characteristics, and then make recommendations as to which city the class should choose for an imaginary trip to the country.

Clearly, there is a very close connection between reading and writing. Some of the best reading materials for early language learners are those written by themselves or by their classmates. Some very meaningful writing experiences flow from what students have read. Because both the language and the context are familiar, students can read one another's written work for interest and enjoyment.

The Language Experience Approach, described in detail in Chapter 5, is an excellent starting point for this type of reading. The teacher and the class together write a brief story about some shared experience, such as a cooking activity, a field trip, or a story they have enjoyed. Students then read the new story aloud, copy it, perhaps illustrate it, and then take it home to read to others.

The little "puzzles" shown in Figure 3.8, written by students, provide reading experiences for their classmates—with the purpose of solving the puzzle. The puzzle frame in Figure 3.9 provides opportunity first for student writing at the single-word level, filling in the blanks of a self-description. The self-descriptions can then be posted on a "puzzle board," and students will experience reading for a purpose as they try to guess who is being described.

● **FIGURE 3.8**   Puzzles by Students. Students fold down the flap on these puzzles to see if they have the correct answers.

Source: Reprinted by permission of Patty Hans.

....

● **FIGURE 3.9**   Puzzle Frames. These self-descriptions can be posted for reading
practice.

Wer bin ich?	Who am I?
Meine Augen sind _____.	My eyes are ____ (color). _____
Meine Haare sind _____.	My hair is ___ (color). _____
Meine Lieblingsfarbe ist _____.	My favorite color is ___ (color). _____
Ich habe im _____ Geburtstag.	My birthday is in ___ (month). _____

Many of the examples of student writing presented later in this chapter can be used
to provide reading opportunities for other members of the class. Poetry of various types,
silly descriptions, new versions of familiar stories, and theme and picture books can all
serve as effective reading materials in the early language classroom.

Reading aloud to others is an interesting mix of interpretive and presentational
communication. Students can read class-developed books to family—or even to students
in other classes.

One of the important elements of the interpretive mode is the ability to recognize
and interpret the cultural information embedded in a written, oral, or visual text or product. In order to help students progress toward meeting this standard, we need to provide
them with many authentic listening, viewing, and reading experiences. Unfortunately,
much of the reading material designed for native speakers of the same age as our students
is far too sophisticated linguistically to be appropriate for novice readers.

Materials designed specifically for language learners can serve as a bridge to later
independent reading of authentic texts. We need to be careful, as we choose these texts,
that the reading material is interesting, communicates needed and important information,
and is at the appropriate linguistic level for our students. Teachers have created their own
texts, based on the interests of their students and on the themes presented in their teaching units. Some teachers have even made such materials available on their websites, for
their own students as well as for other teachers and their students. One good example is
Lori Langer's website, www.miscositas.com, on which she provides beautifully illustrated
retellings of authentic stories from Spanish-language and French-language cultures.

Before early language learners attempt to read longer passages or stories independently, it is essential that considerable preteaching and preparation take place. Phillips
(1984) suggests the following:

Preteaching

1. Brainstorming to generate ideas (and maybe vocabulary) that are likely to occur in
   the text. These might be written on the chalkboard and later used as a word bank.

2. Looking at visuals, headlines, titles, charts, or other clues that are provided with the text.
3. Predicting or hypothesizing on the basis of the title, first line, or other clues what might happen in the text.

Of course, there are many different elements of reading that our students need to develop, some of which are natural components of the elementary and middle school curriculum. They can read a weather forecast to determine what clothes to pack for an imaginary trip to Hamburg; they can read clues to help them decide where to find a hidden treasure. Reading for specific information can become part of any unit or theme. We need to give our students practice with the skills that will help them to become effective readers.

Among other things, Phillips (1984) suggests these activities:

1. Getting the gist of short readings, paragraphs
2. Identifying topic sentences and main ideas
3. Selecting the best paraphrase from multiple-choice options of the main idea of a text or of the conclusion
4. Matching subtitles with paragraphs
5. Filling in charts or forms with key concepts
6. Creating titles or headlines for passages
7. Reacting in some global fashion to a reading passage

Students can learn to skim a passage to determine in general what it is all about. Then they can scan the passage to locate a few of the main ideas related to its general meaning. Finally, the students can read more carefully in order to achieve their intended purpose. These activities, like the activities in Phillips's list, need to take place within a meaningful context, in which reading is done to accomplish purposes that are important to the student and not just to the teacher.

The goal of all these activities is to move students toward ever-greater independence as readers, whether their purpose is reading for information or for personal enjoyment. This is an important step in moving their learning beyond the classroom into the community (Standard 5.1) and into their personal world (Standard 5.2).

● Communication in the Presentational Mode (Standard 1.3)

This standard involves oral or written presentation of information, concepts, and ideas to an audience with which there is little or no interaction. In most cases it involves one-way communication in which the audience cannot modify the message or interact with the writer or speaker for purposes of clarification.

In presentational communication, oral or written language is used to accomplish a meaningful purpose. Because there is an important audience, or an important purpose, the learner is more likely to recognize the value of clarity and accuracy in communication. Grammatical accuracy and cultural appropriateness take on greater importance, and careful editing and practice become shared goals for the students and the teacher.

The presentational mode builds on and may go beyond the single words, memorized chunks, and shorter utterances that are characteristic of interpersonal communication for novice learners. In early language classrooms, presentational communication will rely heavily on memorized language, of course, and will need to be heavily scaffolded—that is, it will require a considerable amount of instructional support.

Speaking

One of the best ways to encourage the development of speaking competencies in the presentational mode is through the performance of skits and dramatic songs. Children love to act out stories, songs, and skits for each other and for other classes. Of course, these presentations also serve as interpretive listening experiences for their audience.

Many of the songs presented to students in primary school involve physical actions, accompany dances, or tell a story. All of these types of songs can be presented dramatically to an audience of parents, other students, or community members.

Presentations and performances are popular culminating activities for a unit, and they are great for sharing with a wider audience. Some types of performances include:

- Plays in which every student takes a role
- Performances of authentic songs, accompanied by culturally appropriate instruments, such as recorders or rhythm instruments
- Small group presentations of scenes from an authentic story that accompanies a thematic unit.
- Student-created skits that tie together the language and information from a thematic unit
- Puppet plays, written by the students and presented before an audience
- PowerPoint or other types of media presentations to share the information gained through research into a topic drawn from the thematic unit
- Short speeches advertising the attractions of a city or a famous landmark in one of the countries in which the language is spoken
- Videos or podcasts of commercials for real or imaginary products that are useful or practical in the target culture
- Video production of "how-to" shows, such as how to prepare a recipe or the steps in a craft project—taken from the target culture, of course
- Production of a video essay or podcast about the students' school and school life to send to a class or school in a country where the target language is spoken

Presentations can be excellent culminating activities for a unit or a series of lessons. In stories with gestures, for example, one of the goals is to bring students to the point where they can write and act out their own variations of the stories originally presented by the teacher. Many other classroom activities lend themselves to polishing up and presenting for an audience. Opportunities for making presentations abound. Parent–teacher organization meetings are always looking for willing program participants. Students can perform for other classes, as part of school assemblies, and for special "classroom programs" to which family members are invited. Some teachers record student performances and students can borrow copies to take home to show their families.

The important element in all of these activities is the audience. Preparing for an audience motivates concern for accuracy and effectiveness. In the case of presentations for an audience of native speakers, attention to cultural expectations also becomes important.

It is evident from many of the examples we have identified that there is a close relationship between oral and written communication for presentation. Students usually write their skits and edit them before presenting them orally. Written revisions of a story can be read aloud to an audience.

Writing

The writing dimension of presentational communication has much in common with speaking. The emphasis here is on developing a product for an audience and for a purpose. Unlike worksheets, or comprehension questions at the end of another language exercise, writing in the presentational mode has a purpose that goes beyond fulfilling an assignment just to satisfy the teacher. In planning activities that help students work toward this standard, teachers might ask themselves, "When and why would they do this activity in the real world?"

Carolyn Andrade and Julie Benthouse Banner (1993) clearly summarized the potential and the focus of writing in a Central States Conference presentation. Most of their summary is especially applicable to the presentational mode:

Writing

- expresses meaning
- allows for practice (this would be an exercise, or a building block—see Chapter 5)
- provides opportunities to combine learned elements
- results in a product that is a measure of proficiency, and is viewed as an accomplishment by both the author and the teacher
- lends itself to sharing of a social event in the school with classmates or across grade levels, at home, or in other settings
- lends itself to collection
- reflects the creativity and individuality of the author
- involves complex operations that are different from those required for speech

Successful writing activities provide the following:

● A framework of linguistic structure

● Outlets that allow for self-expression and creativity, so that the student's writing can extend beyond the model

● Realistic, reliable, appropriate, and understandable products

Written Products Using Individual Words   Students can use single words to make a creative representation of a vocabulary item or a concept. Sometimes classified as *concrete poetry* or *shape poetry,* these products are enjoyable for both the creator and the audience. One strategy is to use the repetition of a single word to develop a picture that represents the meaning of that word. More frequently, several words are used, each outlining a different part of the picture. Figure 3.10 shows several pictures developed in this way using German and Spanish vocabulary words.

● **FIGURE 3.10**   Repeated Words Shaped to Form a Picture. This strategy requires accuracy and creativity.

Sources: (top left) Students of Melanie Engel Unger, *(top right and bottom left)* Milwaukee Spanish Immersion School, *(bottom right)* Helena Curtain.

There are many possibilities for using the repeated-word strategy for creating written products for an audience. Teachers must be careful, however, that whatever the student is writing so many times is being written correctly, since practice tends to lead to permanence.

Another single-word strategy is presenting a single word, often a new vocabulary word, in such a manner that the way in which the word is written or drawn portrays the meaning of the word. Figure 3.11 shows four examples, one from Chinese and the others from Spanish.

A more sophisticated use of shape or concrete poetry at the one-word level would be to have the students draw a shape such as a heart, but instead of using the word *heart* over and over, they might use the word *love*.

Scaffolds. Writing in the presentational mode needs to be heavily scaffolded at early stages of language learning. That is, the writing is based on a clear and well-established pattern, and students succeed by contributing their own content to the preexisting pattern.

● **FIGURE 3.11**   Word Pictures That Reflect the Meaning of the Words Themselves

Sources: (top) Helena Curtain, *(bottom)* Created by students of Rita Gullickson, Whitnall (WI) Middle School.

The following poem frame, found in a second-grade classroom, would be an excellent starting point for creative writing with beginning language students. The frame, of course, would be provided in the target language, not in English.

Snow

Snow is as _____

    as _____

Snow is as _____

    as _____

Snow is as _____

    as _____

Snow is as _____

    as _____

by _____

A similar activity, conducted in the target language, would begin with brainstorming of some of the words associated with snow, listed on the board as a word bank. Then the class would brainstorm some things that are similar to snow in some way, listing these words in a separate word bank. The class might then create a group poem as a model, and then each student would create her or his own poem. The poems might be posted in the classroom, or gathered into a class book.

Here is another example of a poem built on a similar type of frame—an ode to the color white—in Spanish!

Blanco	**White**
Blanco es el color de la nieve.	White is the color of the snow.
Blanco es el color de las nubes.	White is the color of the clouds.
Blanco es el color del invierno.	White is the color of winter.
Blanco es el color al opuesto de negro.	White is the color opposite of black.
Blanco es el color de un oso blanco.	White is the color of a white bear.
Blanco es el color de mi papel.	White is the color of my paper.
Blanco es el color de un cisne.	White is the color of a swan.
Blanco es el color mío cuando estoy miedoso.	White is my color when I am afraid.

The fantastic pictures in Figure 3.12 were the product of another type of writing template or frame. Each middle school student created her or his own fantasy animal by combining the characteristics of three different animals. They then named the animal

● **FIGURE 3.12** Fantasy Animals Created by Writers in Middle School

Mi animal es un ofanteafa. Tiene la cabeza como el elefante y las piernas como la jirafa. el es lento, grande, feroz y pesado.

Caridad Falkowski

Mi animal es un jirafpingüpaj. Tiene la cabeza como la jirafa. Tiene el estómago como el pingüino y las piernas como el pájaro. El es tímido y lento. También es alto y grande.

Linda Zoltak

Source: Created by students of Rita Gullickson, Whitmal (WI) Middle School.

and described it, using a grammatical framework provided by their teacher, Rita Gullickson. Here is the writing frame:

My animal is a _____.

It has the _____ of a _____.

It has the _____ of a _____.

And the _____ of a _____.

It is _____ and _____ (characteristics).

(It is also) _____ and _____.

One of the beauties of this type of writing activity is that the products can be used in so many different ways. Each student's writing serves as interesting reading material for other students in the class—and it is almost guaranteed to be at an appropriate reading level.

The fantasy animal descriptions could be separated from the pictures and placed on notecards. Each student could be given a different notecard to see whether he or she can match the description with one of the animals posted around the room (interpretive communication).

The teacher or a student could read a description aloud and class members could try to draw a picture of the fantasy animal. They could then compare their animals with the originals (interpretive communication).

Finally, the pictures and their descriptions could be used in partner activities, in which one partner reads a description and the other partner tries to draw the animal. The partner doing the drawing can request clarification along the way. After the activity, they can check to see how close their pictures came to those of the original artists (interpersonal communication).

Teacher Janet Glass follows up a similar activity with a reading experience at an "art gallery":

> We have come across about 25 or 30 animals in the stories, songs, and games we've done so far this year. I elicited the words and wrote them on the board. I asked them to draw a new animal (a composite) from three different ones and write on the back what they were. As an example, I drew an *oveja-elefante-pajaro* on the board. I told them not to copy from anyone and to keep it a surprise.
>
> The next day I had prepared an Art Gallery with all their pictures hanging around the room. Each one had a number. I gave out a sheet that listed them but not in order. The students had to walk around the room and find which one matched, for example, *vaca-mariposa-gallina.* They then wrote down the number of what they thought matched. Of course they talked about it (all in Spanish) while they were doing it and they read it. They all used their imaginations, too, which made it great fun.

A favorite idea among drawings and descriptions of this type is the monster activity in Figure 3.13. A careful look at the description reveals the supportive framework in place that helps to ensure student success! This would be a natural follow-up to an experience with the book *Go Away, Big Green Monster!* by Ed Emberley (1992). This student used many different adjectives, some of which might not have been in the shared vocabulary of the class. An early step in preparing any work for an audience is considering what the audience will be able to understand, as it relates to language structure, vocabulary, and cultural context.

Pattern Poems.   The pattern poem has many possibilities for harnessing the creativity of young learners and focusing it through writing. One example is the *acrostic poem,* in which a word is spelled vertically, and words or sentences are arranged around the central word to describe it or express its meaning in some way. This kind of poem can also be used as a self-description, or to elaborate any key word related to the theme. The example in Figure 3.14 is by a middle school student in Spanish 2. He also enhanced his poem, "Gracias" ("Thanks"), with computer images that are not shown here.

● **FIGURE 3.13**　Fantasy Animal. Creating and describing a monster is an engaging activity for learners.

Me llamo Norte.
Soy una persona.
Tengo dos narices y dos cabezas.
Tengo cuatro manos y cuatro orejas.
Tengo tres bocas y tres pies.
Tengo viente dientes y quince dedos en los pies.
Mi pelo **es** corto.

Vivo en el océano ártico.
Soy agresivo y áspero.
Soy liviano y timido.
Soy rayado y chulo.

My name is Norte.
I am a person.
I have two noses and two heads.
I have four hands and four ears.
I have three mouths and three feet.
I have twenty teeth and fifteen toes on my feet.
My hair is short.

I live in the Arctic Ocean.
I am aggressive and rough.
I am lightweight and timid.
I am striped and _____?

Source: Created by students of Rita Gullickson.

● **FIGURE 3.14**　An Acrostic Poem Using "Gracias"

Gracias por	Thank you for
Ropa que es comfortable	Comfortable clothes
Una c**A**sa que es bonita	A beautiful house
Comida deliciosa	Delicious food
M**I**s amigos	My friends
Cuando h**A**ce buen tiempo en octobre y noviembre	Nice weather in October and November
Dia de acción de gracia**S**	Thanksgiving

Early creative writing experiences might include simple forms of poetry like concrete poetry, diamante, cinquain, or haiku.

A *diamante poem* might first be constructed by students and teacher in a whole-class setting, and then individual students or pairs working together might construct their own. It's called a diamante because the shape of the poem, when it is finished, is like that of a diamond. The directions for a diamante and an example in English follow:

one word: noun	Cats
two words: adjective describing noun	soft, warm
three words: participles (or verbs)	play, leap, purr
four words: nouns related to subject	tails, tongues, paws, whiskers
three words: participles (or verbs)	bite, lick, tease
two words: adjectives	elegant, rough
one word: synonym for first word	Siamese

Some teachers also use a shorter version of this pattern, with three words in the center of the poem instead of four. The *cinquain* is similar to the diamante, and follows this pattern.

1. Choose a subject; identify it in one word.   winter
2. Describe the subject in 2 words   white snow
   (noun + adjective, adjective + adjective).   skiing, skating, sliding
3. Describe an action associated with subject   excitement, joy
   3 words (often 3 verbs).   wonderland
4. Express an emotion associated with the word,
   using 2 words.
5. One word to sum up, express the essence.

These formats have the advantage of requiring only single words, a natural task for the novice learner, but when they are placed together in a poem they are both interesting and expressive. The format also helps students to recognize words according to their grammatical category—subtly, of course!

Haiku is a more complex format in that it involves whole sentences rather than just single words. It is a type of Japanese poetry that paints a picture of nature with words in a very controlled pattern of three lines containing 17 syllables, as shown here.

Line 1: Five syllables	Summer sun is hot
Line 2: Seven syllables	Making grass and gardens brown.
Line 3: Five syllables	Hurry, bring water!

The most important quality of this format, as with others already presented, is that it provides interesting reading for other learners because it is personally expressive.

Other Writing Activities   Writing is one of the best ways to reinforce learning and bring it into focus. Of course, it is most effective when it has a clear purpose for the writer—and a ready audience.

The examples in Figure 3.15 from Patty Hans's third-grade French classroom at the Wellington School in Columbus, Ohio, are from the culmination of a unit on the French *voyageur* in Canada. Each of the students describes herself or himself in comparison with a typical *voyageur*. The products can be posted as reading material for others, or they can be compiled into a class book and shared in many ways.

The culminating activity for an imaginary trip to France is a postcard home, giving important information about the trip. With this type of activity, students can learn to work with the cultural conventions for writing in the target language. Postcards provide a good context for early experiences with writing in the presentational mode, because the message is short and highly structured, but the context and the purpose are very realistic.

There are many possibilities for meaningful and purposeful products for early language writers. The outcome of a research project on a country or a city, for example, might be a brochure encouraging visits from class members. A successful project of this type will require clear guidelines, models of what a quality brochure might look like, and careful development of the language and structures necessary to communicate the ideas.

Advertising brochures work for other types of units, too. As a culminating activity to a solar system unit, fifth-grade French students developed advertising brochures for their favorite planets. How about a visit to Saturn, with its 23 moons? Or if you love the heat, maybe a visit to Mercury is for you!

....

● **FIGURE 3.15**   Writing as Culmination to a Unit. Third-grade students in Ohio compare themselves to a *voyageur*.

Source: Reprinted by permission of Patty Hans.

After reading a heavily patterned book like *Brown Bear, Brown Bear* (1983) by Bill Martin Jr., or *The Very Hungry Caterpillar* (1983) by Eric Carle, students might work in pairs or individually to create their own version of the book, written, illustrated, and made available for other students to read and enjoy.

Diane Harris described this writing project on the Ñandu listserv for K–8 foreign language teachers in June 2002:

> A book project that I completed with fourth grade classes (in their third year of Spanish) was to have students produce a class book about the year, "El libro del año," which incorporated vocabulary for months, seasons, activities, and expressions for weather and preferences ("me gusta/no me gusta").
>
> In pairs, students produced several pages about their specific month. This included writing short sentences (in several short paragraphs) with illustrations and graphics as they chose. I then added a title page (ideas for same provided by class), compiled and spiral bound the book for display.
>
> The students enjoyed this project very much and were very proud (and quite surprised) with the finished product and their ability to "write" in Spanish!

For students who have studied the same language for many years, more extensive writing is an appropriate option. The inspiration for a short story or another writing project can come from anywhere. A piece of art or a cartoon could inspire a story—what happened before, what will happen next? A headline from a newspaper in the target language could be used to create the story behind it, perhaps for inclusion in a class newspaper. The slogan and the picture from a magazine advertisement for a culturally significant product, such as a small car from Germany, could lead to a whole advertising campaign for the product, using different methods of presentation.

More advanced learners can create wonderful reading and listening experiences for younger learners. Middle school students can create picture books for primary school learners and then read them to the children, touching on both writing and speaking in the presentational mode. Of course, this also addresses Standard 5.1. Depending on the program, older elementary students would be able to create reading materials for younger students, as well.

As projects become somewhat more complex, students will benefit from the "quality control" that is an important component of process writing. That is, because of the importance of the message and of the audience, there is a concern for clarity, accuracy, and cultural appropriateness that goes beyond the need to please the teacher. When students work together to help each other write as well as they are able, the products—and the students' language—are bound to get better and better.

The process approach to writing incorporates the following steps:

1. Prewriting—often in large group, directed by the teacher
2. Drafting—alone or with a partner

3. Sharing and responding to writing—done with partners or in small groups

4. Revision—alone or with a partner

5. Editing—with partners or in small groups

6. Publishing—final draft!

This process can be introduced and developed from the earliest stages of writing in the presentational mode.

As students become more and more proficient in their language ability, teachers will be guiding the students' second-language writing and looking to improve it based on the same characteristics that they would use to improve their first-language writing. They will make sure that their writing is appropriate according to these primary, or six, traits of writing:

Primary Traits of Writing/Six Traits of Writing

1. Main ideas and content

2. Organization
   - chronological
   - spatial
   - logical
   - order of importance
   - compare/contrast
   - clarification

3. Voice

4. Word choice and usage

5. Sentence sense and variety

6. Correct spelling, punctuation, capitalization

As we have seen, students can use even very limited language to write information, ideas, and personal expression for an audience. Although this chapter has emphasized activities for early stages of language development, the principles of writing in the presentational mode remain the same at every level. As learners become more sophisticated language users, they can take over an increasing proportion of the responsibility for structuring and monitoring their own work. To paraphrase a famous observation by Vygotsky (1962/1986), what learners can do with the assistance of the teacher today, or with the assistance of peers, they will be able to do by themselves tomorrow.

In all the communication modes—interpersonal, interpretive, and presentational—the key element is purpose. As learners discover that they can use their new language to achieve purposes that they feel are personally important, their motivation and their language competencies will continue to grow.

Summary

- The interpersonal mode is the most challenging of the communication standards, but many strategies and stepping stones can lay the foundation for full participation in spontaneous interaction and negotiation of meaning.

- Before students can participate fully in the interactions of the classroom (interpersonal mode), and in the interpretive and presentational modes of communication, they must build a meaningful and usable vocabulary consisting of both individual words and functional chunks of language.

- Early student responses are primarily nonverbal, such as in beginning TPR sessions.

- As students gain experience, vocabulary, and confidence, they take part in interaction with the teacher and with one another and begin to function verbally in the interpersonal mode.

- These experiences build toward the greater independence demanded by the interpretive and the presentational modes.

- The one-way communication called for in Standards 1.2 (Interpretive) and 1.3 (Presentational) draws on the same vocabulary, functional chunks, and contexts as those described for Standard 1.1, but with greater attention to context and audience. The greater independence demanded by these standards will require careful preparation and additional scaffolding in order to ensure student success.

- The listening, reading, and viewing activities suggested in this chapter are intended as idea starters, not as an exhaustive list. Many of them are drawn from resources available through the target culture, because cultural awareness is a key factor in the interpretive mode. Stories, videos, magazines, and other texts with cultural relevance will help students become more sensitive to the cultural messages embedded within the text.

- Similarly, the ideas for the presentational mode in this chapter are just the beginning. As teachers provide students with a wide range of opportunities for presenting oral, written, or visual information to an important audience, students will become increasingly aware of the relevance of linguistic accuracy and cultural sensitivity.

For Study and Discussion

1. Novice learners in a communication- and standards-based classroom have a greater need of experiences with vocabulary and functional chunks than they have for systematic grammar instruction. Yet, grammar is the element that allows learners to create with language, and then create their own communication. What is an appropriate role for grammar in the early language classroom?

2. Choose a phrase that students will need in order to function in the target language in your classroom. Design a sequence of several activities to teach that phrase, and try them out on your students, colleagues, or classmates. Were you able to address several learning styles? Were you able to play with the language?

3. Choose a topic that has value either for helping learners deal with their classroom environment in the target language or for teaching appropri-

ate cultural behavior. Use it as the basis for a Gouin Series of six to eight sentences; try it in your classroom and demonstrate it to your colleagues.

4. Under what circumstances is the direct teaching of speaking skills necessary or desirable?

5. Create a list of potential writing activities in the interpersonal mode. Identify the level of language development for which each would be appropriate.

6. Communication is a holistic concept, and the three modes of communication are closely interrelated in "real life." What value is there for the teacher in the early language classroom to consider and plan for them separately?

7. How do listening, reading, and viewing in the interpretive mode differ from listening and reading in the interpersonal mode?

8. How does the factor of audience influence the speaking or writing task in the presentational mode?

9. Choose a story that meets the criteria for successful storytelling as detailed in this chapter. Develop a story map and plan an advance organizer for use in telling the story; plan the visuals and activities you will use to accompany the story, and tell the story to a group of peers or of children.

10. Teacher guides for language arts and other sources can be used to develop a collection of simple forms of poetry for early stages of foreign language instruction. Create sample poems in your language, based on models from this chapter or from other sources, and plan a lesson in which you guide students in the development of their own poem.

11. Add at least three possible writing activities to the list in this chapter. What characteristics do they have that qualify them as activities in the presentational mode? For what grade level and language proficiency level would they be appropriate?

For Further Reading

The following sources are recommended for additional information about material covered in this chapter. Chapter citations are documented in Works Cited at the end of this book.

Asher, James J. *Learning Another Language through Actions: The Complete Teacher's Guidebook* (6th ed.). Los Gatos, CA: Sky Oaks Publications, 2000. Available through www.tpr-world.com.

Caine, Renate Nummela, and Geoffrey Caine. *Education on the Edge of Possibility.* Alexandria, VA: Association for Supervision and Curriculum Development, 1997.

Ellis, Rod. *Principles of Instructed Second Language Acquisition.* www.cal.org/resources/digest/instructed2ndlang.html.

Krashen, Stephen D., and Tracy Terrell. *The Natural Approach. Language Acquisition in the Classroom* (rev. ed.). Englewood Cliffs, NJ: Prentice-Hall, 1996.

Peyton, Joy Kreeft. "Dialogue Journals: Interactive Writing to Develop Language and Literacy." *ERIC Digest* (April 1993). Available on-line at www.cal.org/resources/Digest/peyton01.html.

Porto, Melina. "Lexical Phrases and Language Teaching." *Forum* 36:3 (July–September 1998): 22–25.

Redmond, Mary Lynn (Ed.). *Teacher to Teacher. Model Lessons for K–8 Foreign Language Educators.* Lincolnwood, IL: National Textbook Company, 1999.

Terrell, Tracy. "The Natural Approach to Language Teaching: An Update." *Canadian Modern Language Review* 41:3 (1985): 461–479.

Chapter 4

Focusing on Interpersonal Communication

Partners and Small Groups

Enduring Understanding

- Well-designed partner and small-group activities are powerful tools for building interpersonal communication skills.

Essential Question

- How can I design effective and meaningful partner and small-group activities?

● Cooperative Structures: Cooperative Learning and Interactive Language Tasks

Interaction is the key to the interpersonal mode and to language development for second-language learners, and interactive language tasks are among the most important means by which this communication can be accomplished. Part of the challenge for the early language teacher is giving students sufficient opportunity for interaction and for building interpersonal communication within the limits of a short class period.

The traditional large-group, teacher-led classroom structure has severe limitations. Communication flows primarily in one direction, from teacher to students, and learners have few opportunities to test their own use of the language for personal communication. Yet both cognitive learning theory and second-language acquisition theory state that in order to acquire language, learners must express themselves orally. Expressing concepts, putting them in our own words, explaining them to others and speculating about them aloud, making applications of concepts to new situations, and finding creative and personalized ways to remember new concepts or language materials all contribute to genuine, successful learning.

Cooperative learning in the form of partner activities and small-group work holds much promise for the early language classroom. When students learn to work cooperatively in small groups or in pairs, their opportunities for language use are multiplied many times over, as are their opportunities for active participation in concrete and meaningful experiences. Small-group and partner activities, as contrasted with large-group, teacher-fronted activities alone, have numerous advantages for the language learner:

- Many opportunities for language use
- A chance for natural language practice
- More student talk
- A higher percentage of student talk in real communicative activities
- A "safe" environment for communication, more like one-on-one conversation
- Two-way communication—a chance both to ask and to answer questions

In addition to the language benefits, partner activities specifically provide other benefits (Nerenz and Knop, 1982):

- Variety in class routines and activities
- Opportunity for students to practice social skills
- Students are "center stage" rather than the teacher
- More on-task behavior

According to Nancy Foss (2002), who has researched the interaction between learning styles and foreign language proficiency, partner activities in the foreign language classroom may be the only type of speaking activity that is comfortable for every learning style. For the learning style that likes groups, pairs were determined to be almost as good, and for other styles, pairs were preferred to groups.

It is important to emphasize here that partner and small-group activities are not a strategy for *teaching* language. They are a very effective strategy for *practicing* language that has already been learned through a variety of other activities, and for *using* that language to achieve important goals. When partner and small-group activities are introduced prematurely, before the needed language is readily available, students will be frustrated and they are likely to revert to English in order to accomplish the task. One teacher observed that the more engaging the activity is, the more likely the students are to complete it in English, especially if they are not comfortable with the language needed for the task.

Developing Cooperative Skills

Learners need just as much guidance in developing cooperative skills as they do in developing communication competencies. The early language classroom is a natural setting for this growth.

Small groups and pairs, in order to function successfully, require that certain elements of cooperative learning be in place (Johnson and Johnson, 2005):

1. Positive interdependence means that everyone depends on one another and that no one feels exploited, unnecessary, or left out.

2. Face-to-face interaction is possible only when learners are in a physical setting in which they can talk with one another and work together easily, without raising their voices.

3. Individual accountability is in effect when each learner knows that she or he may bear full responsibility for the information or the skills being learned by the group. There are no hitchhikers—only full participants.

4. Social skills training is an integral component of all the work in the cooperative classroom (see Figure 4.1). The teacher helps learners to understand the skills

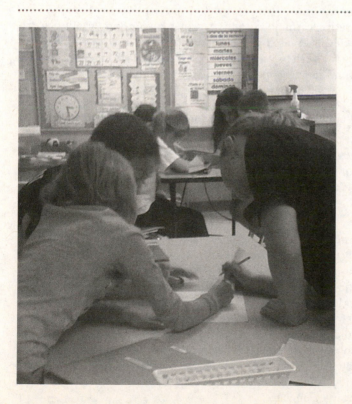

● **FIGURE 4.1** Human Relations Skills. Children develop both language and human relations skills when they work in cooperative groups.

they will need to work successfully together and helps them to practice and monitor them. As is the case with language skills, a few specific cooperative skills will be highlighted at the beginning, such as making sure everyone has a turn to speak, giving encouragement, and listening when other group members are talking. Additional skills can be added after the first skills have become habitual. Only with the development of the skills of working and living cooperatively can communication become possible, in either the target language or the native language.

5. Group processing of the cooperative skills is just as important to the classroom routine as are quizzes and other strategies for determining progress in the subject content. The teacher helps learners analyze what is working well in their group and what can be improved, offers suggestions when individual groups are having specific problems, and focuses the attention of the entire class on a limited, manageable number of skills at a time. Much of the group processing can take place in the target language, providing an additional area for meaningful communication within the classroom. At the end of an activity the teacher might ask, for example, "How did your group do today about making sure everyone had a chance to speak? Hold up three fingers if you feel you did great, two fingers if you need some improvement, and one finger if you need to really work at this." As an alternative, the responses could be written, or decided on by the group and then reported.

Proponents of cooperative learning indicate that roles have an important place in the development of social skills. They also have an important place in the development of language functions, since the roles can be used to help develop language functions that are an integral part of the second-language curriculum. Some of the roles that could be assigned include:

Encourager/Praiser: Reinforces group members for performing well or staying on task.

Manager/Timekeeper/Supervisor/Checker: Organizes the group, keeps the group on task, and makes sure everyone contributes.

Recorder/Secretary: Records group answers.

Spokesperson/Speaker/Reporter: Reports back to the whole class.

When roles are explained, the teacher might teach and practice the language needed for each of the roles, possibly posting the information on the wall as a reminder. For example, the encourager might say, "That's a good idea," "Good job, Mary!," "We're doing a great job of getting this done." The manager might need to say, "Do you have any ideas, Dave?," "We just have three minutes left," "What shall we do first?" The recorder would need to be able to ask for clarification and repetition. The spokesperson and reporter would need to check for clarity. Roles should shift with each task, so all group members have the opportunity to perform all the roles. Before each task begins, the teacher might ask, "When I come around to listen to you work, what will I hear the encourager say that will show me that she or he is doing a good job?," "What will I hear the manager say?," and so forth. This should all take place in the target language.

Olsen, Winn-Bell, and Kagan (1992) present a useful list of group and task roles that are valuable in themselves, but in addition carry with them an important language component. Learning how to interact in a group will have both short-term benefits in the students' own cultures and long-range benefits, should they have the opportunity to travel to the target culture. This kind of experience will enable them to be more open and receptive to speakers of the target language. Some of the group-related social skills for which the teacher will provide language and support include the following:

Asking for help

Complimenting

Sharing courtesy

Following directions

Listening

Talking in turn

Using first names

Acknowledging others' contributions

Praising others

Recognizing others

Verifying consensus

Keeping the group on task

Mediating disagreements or discrepancies

Some of the task-related social skills are:

Asking for clarification

Asking for explanations

Checking for understanding

Elaborating the ideas of others

Explaining ideas or concepts

Giving information or explanations

Paraphrasing and summarizing

Maintaining eye contact (a culturally based behavior)

● Classroom Management with Small-Group and Partner Activities

Teachers who have not had a lot of experience with small-group and pair work may have concerns about placing students in a situation in which they have more independence than in traditional large-group instruction. These teachers may also have anxiety about classroom noise and the potential for off-task behavior and disruption. But if partner and small-group activities are carefully planned, the benefits to student learning will far out-weigh these challenges.

Classroom management changes dramatically in the implementation of cooperative learning activities. Traditionally, class activities are relatively simple, and students do lit-tle talking and interacting. In fact, the goal is often to keep students from talking at all. Cooperative learning activities are more complicated and do not offer the simple, quiet classroom found in other types of classroom management. Cooperative activities can be noisy, the classroom furniture will need to be arranged differently, and the teacher may have to function as a resolver of conflicts, especially among students who are resistant to working with others. Most of all, the teacher has the role of a facilitator rather than that of a manager.

Grouping Students for Interactive Activities

Small Groups   Students in a classroom might be divided into long-term groups by "family," with each family seated around its own table. This allows learners who are given target language names to have a last name as well as a first name. Within the small group each member might be assigned a role: mother, father, sister, brother, grandparent, and so on. The teacher can use the family groupings to assign tasks within the group—for exam-ple, today the mother will be the leader, the father will be the recorder, and so forth. The small group could form the basis for a simulation in which one family encounters another family on an outing and introductions are made all around. This type of simulation allows for meaningful use of language in an imaginary setting.

Organizing small groups for short-term activities can be done in a number of ways. Rita Gullickson keeps a basket of plastic-colored clothespins near her classroom door. As students enter the room, they take one of the pins and clip it to their clothing. For exam-ple, all those wearing purple clothespins work in one group and all those with yellow pins work in another. Colored pieces of paper, colored toothpicks, colored teddy bear coun-ters—manipulatives used for helping primary school students with mathematics con-cepts—colored tokens, or any other manipulatives could function in much the same way. Deborah Roberts (2002) takes this strategy one step further by having the students choose a group name based on the color—for example, yellow might be the sun group.

Roberts offers a number of other interesting ways to form groups. She suggests that students can be given a simple arithmetic problem on a notecard, and they form a group with others whose arithmetic problem has the same solution: 12×5, $30 + 30$, 15×4, and so on. Students can be grouped in categories, and items belonging to those categories are written on index cards. For instance, one student has food and others have hamburger, bread, and grapes. In a similar strategy, the teacher might use countries and cities: Deutschland, Berlin, Frankfurt, and München. Another variation of this strategy would be for students to receive index cards, some of which have single letters. Other students have combinations of letters that, when combined with the single letter, form a word— for example, c/offee/ and g/old.

Groups can also be formed by counting off. The teacher first decides how many students will be needed in each group for the planned activity. Then the teacher divides the number of students in the class by the number of students planned for each group, and students count off by that number. For groups of five in a class of 35 students, for example, the students would count off by seven—students count from one to seven and then begin again with one, counting until everyone has received a number between one and seven. With young learners especially, it is helpful to have the children hold up their fingers for their number until all the counting is completed—so they don't forget their number. After the number count-off is finished, all the number six students form a group, as do all the twos, and so on.

Another way to organize groups is to put together the pieces of a cut-up shape or a puzzle to make a whole, or simply to draw names of other class members. Groups could be formed by historical figures. For example, the kings and queens of France could be one group, and others could be French musicians, French artists, French sports figures, and French scientists. Food in various parts of the food pyramid could constitute another method of grouping, as could animals in different habitats.

Some ways to organize students into groups require little preparation and can be language activities in themselves. For example, students can form groups according to the make of their family car. If there are unbalanced numbers, the teacher can intervene and quickly make two or three groups out of a very large one, or send a few students to another group. Other ways to organize include:

Number of hours they slept last night, or time they went to bed

Number of siblings/family members

Number of syllables in their name

Shoe size or color

Partners/Pairs   In most cases, it is desirable for students to work with a variety of partners over a period of time, and not choose their own partners. Classes can be organized for pair activities in a variety of ways. Partners can be organized informally, simply by saying, "Turn to the person next to you," "Turn to the person in front of you," "Go to another person in the room who is wearing the same color you are," and so on. One middle school teacher gives students 10 seconds to make eye contact with a partner and get together with that person—silently. Counting-off works for partners, too—in a class of 20 students, students could count from one to ten twice, or use letters A to J twice, for example.

Inside-Outside Circles   Figure 4.2 shows another effective way of organizing the class so that students have a chance to work with several partners in succession. The teacher divides the class into two groups, perhaps by having them count off by twos. Ones form a circle and face to the outside of the circle. Twos form another circle around the first circle and face to the inside. Each student should be facing a partner. In this situation the students can practice a conversational exchange, such as giving a simple greeting, asking

● **FIGURE 4.2**   Inside-Out Circles

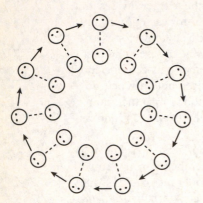

someone's age, discussing favorites, or whatever interaction needs practice at the time. It is most effective if the students are actually learning something of interest about their partners. As soon as the exchange has been completed, on a signal from the teacher, students in the outside circle move one partner to the left around the circle. Only one circle moves, in the direction indicated by the teacher. The conversation is repeated with a new partner, and on signal the outside circle moves again. The circle keeps moving until it returns to the place it started.

"Line-Ups"   Using two lines of students facing each other, which is especially useful when there isn't room to create circles. One of the lines rotates, with the person at the head of the line moving to the end of the line each time (Figure 4.3). Sometimes students in both lines can move, with the students on each end moving to the other line after each exchange (Figure 4.4). This gives students a greater variety of partners to work with. This use of rotating lines is especially useful if partners are practicing two lines of a dialogue, because it feels more like real communication when students work with different partners.

● **FIGURE 4.3**   Two Lines of Students. One line rotates, the other stays in place.

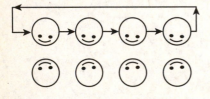

Matching Pairs   Partners can be organized more formally. The teacher can prepare sets of cards with identical matching pairs and distribute them to the class; the students circulate until they find the person who has the matching picture card (numbers, shapes, animals, foods, etc.). For example, a student who has the number three must find a partner who also has the number three, or a student who has a picture of an animal must find the person who has the same picture. Alternatively, the teacher might prepare card pairs in which one card has a picture or a numeral and the other card has the word written out.

The teacher can prepare and distribute sets of cards with pairs that are matched by relationship; students find their partner by locating the person who has the related card. In this way, the matching of partners becomes a learning experience in itself. For example, one partner has the name of a country and the other has the name of the capital, or one partner has one-half of a proverb from the target culture and must find the

● **FIGURE 4.4**   Two Lines of Students. Both lines move, and new partners face each other.

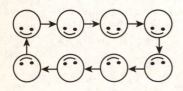

partner with the other half. Matches can be organized using many different categories, such as:

- First names and last names of artists or historical figures
- Various forms of a verb
- Antonyms or synonyms
- Puzzle pieces of pictures or words (art pictures, proverbs, and common sayings also add a cultural dimension)
- Common expressions, such as "Happy/Birthday" and "Good/Morning"
- Two-line conversational exchanges or dialogues
- Associations, such as hammer/nail, hospital/nurse, red/apple

"Partners around the CLock"   Another way to organize partners is to use a procedure in which partners are assigned for a period of time. One such procedure is called "Partners around the Clock." Each student has a piece of paper with a blank clock face large enough to write names next to each hour on the clock (see Figure 4.5). The teacher might draw a line on which students can sign their names. The teacher gives directions for the activity and sets a time limit. Students arrange to meet a different classmate for each hour on the clock, so that there is a different name written next to each number. They cannot arrange more than one meeting per hour. Students arrange their meetings by moving around the classroom and asking each other questions such as, "Are you free at one o'clock or three o'clock?," "Are you busy at noon?," "Can we meet at five o'clock?" After the designated time period is over, the teacher makes sure that each student has a partner for each hour by quickly asking who still needs a partner for each hour in turn. Those who are missing certain hours can then make appointments with each other. This is especially helpful for those students who are shy or who may not be the first ones asked by other students.

> ● **FIGURE 4.5** "Partners around the Clock." A large clock can be used to organize communication among partners.

If at the end there are still some students without partners, those students can "double book" and make some groups of three. It is important that each student be represented in the activity, even absent ones. Students can make appointments with the clock on the absent students' desks, for example.

Once all the times have been filled in, the teacher can then use the clock as the basis for organizing interviews or for any other language tasks—for example, "For the next activity you are going to be working with your three o'clock partner" or "Discuss with your ten o'clock partner the solution to the puzzle on the chalkboard." The students can keep their clocks for use over several days or weeks, or for the duration of a unit. The teacher could collect the clocks and distribute them the next time they are needed. If students keep the clocks, it is a good idea for students to make an extra set of the clocks for the teacher, in case one or more students lose them.

This activity can take on a greater cultural dimension by using a map of the target language country or city with lines for signatures drawn in various places. For example, students with a map of Japan can ask another student, "Can I meet you in Tokyo?," "Can we see each other in Kobe?," or "Do you have free time in Kyoto?" Using a variety of devices such as this for organizing partners over a specified period of time frees the teacher from always having to find a different way to get the students to work together. Geography connections could be emphasized by using a world map and arranging meetings on every continent.

"Snowball"   Deborah Roberts (2002) uses an engaging activity called "Snowball" to bring partners together. The teacher prepares pairs of antonyms (or synonyms) on separate pieces of paper, preferably recycled, and gives every person in the class a piece of paper. The class then forms a circle, crumples the paper into a "snowball," and tosses the snowballs up into the air toward the center of the circle. Each student then picks up a snowball, opens it up, and looks for a person in the group who has the antonym (or synonym) of the word on the paper. Together they make a sentence including both words.

Questions for the Teacher When Planning Small-Group and Partner Activities

In order to plan for cooperative learning activities and to effectively manage student behavior, several factors must be taken into account. The following guidelines are helpful in developing successful activities and in choosing appropriate activities from a variety of sources. Not all of these criteria will be applicable to every activity, but each of these items should be considered as the activity is developed.

1. What is the source of the message(s) to be exchanged? What motivates the communication?
   - Is there an information gap or opinion gap?
   - Is there a reason for the students to want to know the information?
2. What language will be required to complete the activity? How much of it will need to be practiced or reviewed?
3. What will be the product that results from the activity? Can this product be shared or evaluated?
4. How is the language to be used guided, controlled, or scaffolded?
   - Is there a natural limitation because of the task itself?
   - Is most of the language provided in written form?
5. How will partners or group members take turns?
   - Is there a built-in indicator for taking turns, such as an asterisk in front of the item for the partner who is to ask the question, or have roles been assigned to group members?

- ● Does each partner or group member have an opportunity to participate approximately equally?

- ● Is there a means to prevent either partner or any group member from dominating the conversation?

6. Can the partners or group members find out immediately whether they have been successful?

   - ● Is the activity self-correcting?

   - ● Is there a way for the partners to monitor their own accuracy or success?

7. How can the teacher follow up on the activity in a communicative way?

   - ● What kind of communicative follow-up questions can the teacher ask about the activity? For example, can she or he ask, "What did you find out about your partner or other group member that you didn't know before?" or "Which of the problems did you have the most trouble with?" "Which response or idea surprised you the most?"

   - ● Will the follow-up to the activity be interesting to the students as well as holding them accountable?

   - ● What potential exists for oral or written follow-up or homework?

8. If partners or groups finish their task early, how can the activity be extended so that they will be engaged while the rest of the class is finishing?

9. What is the plan for dealing with a student who does not have a partner?

   - ● Will the teacher take the role of the extra partner? (Although tempting, this role removes the teacher from the important role of monitor, and makes it hard to determine how the task is progressing and what kind of intervention might be needed.)

   - ● Will the teacher prepare one set of materials for three students instead of two, so that the extra student will be accommodated smoothly?

Step-by-Step Guidelines for Small-Group and Partner Activities

Although one of the advantages of small-group work is that it takes the spotlight off the teacher for a period of time, it can be effective only if it is carefully organized and consistently monitored. Especially for the first few times, preparing and conducting such activities may actually require more teacher effort than the traditional teacher-centered classroom style. But the many benefits make partner and group work more than worth the extra effort. The following guidelines, adapted from workshop presentations by Knop (1985), Johnson and Johnson (2005), and Kagan and Kagan (2008), will help the teacher plan effectively for pair or small-group activity in the classroom.

1. Keep the group size small; start with pair activities. It is easiest to start with pairs for the first experience with group activities. Cooperative groups are usually most effective

when they are comprised of no more than five people, and they should never be larger than seven.

2. Set the stage; motivate the activity. When the teacher sets the context for the activity dramatically, using actions and visuals, it enhances motivation. It is also helpful to give each activity a name, making it easier for students to request it again and to recall the rules the next time the activity is introduced.

3. Set clear goals; describe the outcomes clearly for the students. Students should understand how the language task relates to the context provided by the teacher and recognize the outcome as satisfying some purpose or interest. Included in the goals should be clear expectations about the use of the target language during the activity.

4. Make sure the students have the target language they need to accomplish the activity, that they know how to say what they will need to say. Review and practice the language needed by each partner in order to complete the activity successfully. For many activities the actual language to be used can be printed on the task sheet, so that students can focus on communication and practice accurately at the same time.

5. Give exact directions for every step of the task. Carefully prepare and sequence the instructions for the activity so that they are as simple as possible and can be presented in the target language. To appeal to different learning styles, directions should be both oral and written, perhaps provided on the activity itself, or written on the overhead projector or chalkboard.

- Model the sequence of the activity in precise steps, so students know exactly what is expected of them at every step of the way. You may model both parts yourself, or begin by working with the whole class so that the teacher plays the part of Partner A and the rest of the class plays the part of Partner B. An individual student might play Partner A while you play the role of Partner B, or you might bring up two students and have the class watch them go through the steps of the entire activity.

- Get student feedback on all the steps to be sure students know how the activity will proceed and will not waste time during the activity itself:

  Who begins the activity?

  What does Partner A start with?

  What does Partner B do?

  What else does Partner B do?

  What if Partner B doesn't agree?

  What does Partner A do next?

6. Set a time limit to help students feel accountable and to make the best possible use of the time available to them. It is effective to use a kitchen timer with a loud bell or buzzer to provide a neutral timekeeper and a clear signal for the end of the activity. Adjust the time limit if necessary during the activity, to allow for less time if students are finishing early or more time if the activity takes longer than expected.

7. Circulate among the students throughout the activity. Circulating allows you to monitor use of the target language, language problems the students are having, and the success or failure in the use of cooperative skills. You can also show interest in the students' conversations and give suggestions when they need help. Moving among the students, especially if you have a clipboard in hand, is also a form of control for on-task behavior. Provide positive feedback and give attention and special recognition to the teams that are most on task.

8. Establish a system for getting the attention of the students back to you and for getting the noise level down when it is necessary. Many teachers use a hand signal such as a raised right hand to get the students to give their full attention to the teacher and to keep their hands and bodies still. The teacher initiates the signal by raising the right arm in the air. The students respond by stopping their activity, becoming quiet, and showing the signal back to the teacher and to the other students with whom they are working. (This helps give some of the responsibility for control back to the students.)

9. Elicit communicative feedback and process group effectiveness at the end of the activity. Not every pair or every student needs to be reached after every activity, but call for responses at random so students always feel accountable. Rather than simply checking only for the correct solutions for the task, use communicative feedback techniques that extend the language used in the task. This can be interesting to the whole group. For example, in an activity related to foods, the teacher might ask, "Is the dinner your partner planned one you would eat?" or "What did you like about the tamales?" Also, regularly use the feedback period to assist students in evaluating the effectiveness of their groups.

● Sample Cooperative Group Activities for Beginning Language Learners

Students can work together in a small group to solve a problem or develop a response to a situation the teacher designs. There are many types of interactive language tasks. A pair or small group might design a series of commands to give to another small group or to the teacher, orally at first and perhaps later in writing. The members of the small group might rehearse with one another to make sure that everyone in the group is able to ask to go to the bathroom or to sharpen a pencil, to request having something repeated, to agree or disagree. The shared teaching task creates a kind of validity for the communication in and of itself, because it is being directed toward a goal and being managed and monitored by the students themselves.

"Jigsaw"

A pair or a small group of three to four students might work with a "Jigsaw." Each individual has a certain amount of information that, when combined with the information from the rest of the groups, will lead to the completion of an assignment. For example, each student might be given a part of the information necessary to find a location on a map, to choose an appropriate gift for a parent, to identify another member of the class, and so on. As they share the information orally, the students solve the problem and also practice the language involved.

In the "Jigsaw" activity in Figure 4.6, a group of four is given an envelope with four strips of paper, one for each student. Each student in a group of four has a piece of information about an animal from the unit just completed. Each student reads the information on the sheet that he or she has been given. Student A reads number one ("It's an African mammal") then student B reads number one ("It has stripes"). Next, Student C

● **FIGURE 4.6**   "Jigsaw" Activity for Groups of Four Students

Student A	Student B	Student C	Student D
1. It's an African mammal.	1. It has stripes.	1. It lives in small groups	1. It ends in *a*.
2. It's a type of ape.	2. It ends in *n*.	2. It has long arms.	2. It lives in trees.
3. It has black spots.	3. It lives in forests.	3. It's found in Africa and Asia.	3. It belongs to the cat family.
4. It lives in the savanna.	4. It travels in small groups.	4. It's up to 5.5 meters tall.	4. It eats from trees.
5. It can be under water for 15 to 20 minutes.	5. Its babies are white.	5. From 1 to 6 inches of fat keep it warm.	5. It has flippers.
6. It has powerful back legs.	6. It hops.	6. It's found in Australia.	6. It carries its baby in a pouch.
7. It begins with *L*.	7. It's found in South America.	7. It belongs to the camel family.	7. It can work at high altitudes.
8. It's the largest living land mammal.	8. It's an endangered animal.	8. It's very intelligent.	8. It lives in Africa and Asia.

reads number one ("It lives in small groups") and finally Student D reads number one ("It ends in *a*"). After all the students have read their clues, the group must decide the name of the animal and write it down on a sheet of paper. The group then works on number two and proceeds in the same way until the group of students has identified all the animals on the sheet.

If the group needs more scaffolding, the teacher might insert in the envelope, along with the four strips of paper, the pictures of the animals in the activity so that the group can check with the pictures if they are not sure of one or more of the animals. Another option would be for the teacher to provide the answers in a separate location so that the group could self-correct and make sure that it has found the correct answers. There are many options for follow-up to this activity and many ways to adapt it to various levels of language learning. Albert Martino from the Guilderland School District in Albany, New York, has provided the following options:*

1. Once the students have completed the speaking component of the Animal Jigsaw this can now be converted into a writing activity. Students will continue to work in their groups for this activity. They will also continue to need to use the four lettered jigsaw strips with the sentences from the jigsaw activity.

   Students receive a worksheet entitled My Favorite Animal _____ (which should be in the target language). Students are to use the list of animals from the previous jigsaw speaking activity in choosing their favorite animal. They complete the sentence with the name of their animal and then they are to draw a picture of that animal in the space provided.

   The students will now write a description of their favorite animal using the sentence strips as follows: Each student will take one of the jigsaw sentence strips and find the line that describes his or her animal and then copy that in the first line below the drawing. The students then pass their strip to the next person in their group and find the same line and copy that statement on the second line and so on until they have written four lines that describe their animal.

   While sitting in their groups they can take turns reading aloud their mini-compositions about their animals. Students might be encouraged to read aloud their compositions using the kind of voice they would imagine this animal might have if it could speak!!!

2. The next two activities require the students (or the teacher) to fold the worksheets in half so that the picture of the animal is folded back and what the students will see is just the mini-composition. A paper clip can be used to keep it folded back.

   These can now be exchanged with other groups. Students can now read aloud the compositions from another group and guess the name of the animal. Or, these can be read by individuals aloud while others listen and guess the name of the animal.

---

*Source: Reprinted by permission of Albert Martino.

3. Another writing exercise again uses the sentence strips from above. Students will not need a special worksheet but rather just a plain piece of paper to write on. They will silently choose an animal as they did above and begin to copy down the descriptions from the jigsaw strips. However, as they do so they are asked to include *one* sentence from one of the strips that *does not* match or describe their animal.

   These "crazy descriptions" can be shared in writing in the group and students can guess which line does not belong! These may also be read aloud by one student in the group while the others listen to determine which line does not belong.

4. A further extension activity is a listening activity that the teacher does with the large group. The teacher chooses to describe one of these animals and tells the class. The teacher then reads aloud one of the sentences and the class calls out *true* or *false* in the target language.

5. The teacher will need to have large cutout pictures of the animals for this activity. Also, the teacher will need to have each of the sentences from the jigsaw strips printed on a strip of paper (laminated if possible).

   The teacher will post these pictures around the room. Under each one the teacher will place a series of four sentences to describe that animal. Some may be correct and others may not be. Students working in groups/pairs are assigned an animal. They read the strips together and determine which ones are true and which ones are false. They take their false ones and go to the appropriate animal and ask the students if they need their strip (which they can read aloud to them). If so, they place that strip under the animal and move on until all animals have the correct statements. This requires some student negotiation using language like: "Do you have? Do you need? Do you want?"

6. This activity is very similar to number 5 except that it is done in groups of four. Each group has two small clear plastic bags: one with the pictures of the animals and one with the sentences typed up and cut out. They take out the pictures and the sentences and try to match up the sentences with the appropriate pictures.

   Once they have done this they can make a crazy animal by using any four random sentences to describe a new animal. They will then draw their new crazy animal on a separate sheet of paper and write the description below the animal!

"Let's Have a Dinner Party"

This cooperative learning activity, appropriate for early language learners, is called "Let's Have a Dinner Party!" (Figure 4.7). In this activity, students are assigned various roles and tasks and work in a cooperative group to plan a meal. Students are given food options (in their target language) and are helped with the language they may need in order to accomplish the activity. Each group member is responsible for making sure that one food group is represented. The menu must include a variety of colors, shapes, and textures, and every member must agree to the entire dinner and enjoy eating it! This activity adds a kinesthetic dimension since the students must draw (using crayons or markers) the dinner

● **FIGURE 4.7**   Task Sheet for Cooperative Activity "Let's Have a Dinner Party!"

Tasks:

Create a dinner menu with your group of four.

1. The menu must include a variety of colors, textures, and shapes.

2. Every member must agree to the entire menu and enjoy eating it!

3. If necessary, you may use foods not listed on this sheet.

Roles:

Each group member is responsible for making sure one of the food groups in the food pyramid is represented. (The fats/oils/sweets group can be left out.)

Task master: The task master assigns group members to the food groups they represent.

Recorder: The recorder draws the menu on a paper plate and writes the items on the back of the plate.

Spokesperson: The spokesperson presents the menu to the rest of the class.

Encourager: The encourager gives encouragement as the group makes decisions and draws the menu.

Examples of Language to Be Used

Let's serve …

I really like …

I don't like …

We need a different (shape, texture, color).

FATS/OILS/ SWEETS	BREAD/ CEREAL	MEAT/PROTEIN		
butter	French bread	beef steak	baked chicken breast	sliced tomatoes
vegetable oil	rice	pork chop	roast turkey	cucumbers
olive oil	pancakes	sausage	fried chicken	tossed green salad
DAIRY	tortillas	hamburger	eggs	French fries
milk	whole grain bread	beef roast	**VEGETABLE**	cole slaw
Swiss cheese	blueberry muffins	ham slice	broccoli	**FRUIT**
cottage cheese		veal	spinach	peaches
custard		meatballs	green beans	fresh grapes
ice cream	sourdough rolls	lamb	cauliflower	fruit cups
yogurt	cornbread	frankfurter	mashed potatoes	sliced apples
chocolate pudding	popovers	shrimp	carrot sticks	
cheddar cheese	white bread	walleye fillet	acorn squash	
		salmon steak		

they have planned on a paper plate. As a follow-up, the class can vote on its favorite dinner of those presented. Students can write about the dinner their group has planned or write about a dinner that they would like to plan for themselves. As a variation to this activity, students can plan a trip, listing the clothes they will take and creating the itinerary they will follow. In order to integrate mathematics, they can be given a certain budget to work with.

● Sample Partner Activities for Beginning Language Learners

Because of the power of partner activities in the development of communication competencies, especially the interpersonal mode, there are a growing number of resources commercially available for older learners. Many high school and college textbooks incorporate partner activities, for example, and some books of activities focus on one-on-one interaction. Partner activities can be fully as effective and useful with young learners, as the following examples will show.

Partner activities can range from "drill in disguise" to a meaningful exchange of information, depending on the degree to which the participants have real motivation to complete the task, the degree of investment in the outcome, and the level of autonomy in setting up the task. When the students see a clear purpose for the activity and it results in a product or a solution that has individual meaning, it is more likely that real interpersonal communication is taking place. For example, in the "Let's Have a Dinner Party!" group activity, the decision about a meal that every member would eat reflected a real-world challenge and called for genuine communication to negotiate a result—the "real" answer was not predetermined by the teacher. The resulting menu was shared with others as a culmination of the task.

The "Jigsaw" task relating to animals in Africa was predetermined by the teacher, but the puzzle context was more motivating than a simple drill. In the examples that will follow, there is a range of activities from "drill in disguise" to more communicative tasks. All types of partner activities have value. Those on the drill end of the spectrum give needed practice in a sheltered setting. More communicative, personally motivated activities help students develop their interpersonal language competencies. As teachers we can work toward increasing the level of communication in our partner and group tasks and regularly raise for ourselves the nagging question from Kieran Egan: "Why should it matter to children?"

Informal Pairs: Students Working Together to Complete a Task

In an informal pair, partners work together to get a task finished or to share information that is available to both of them. Informal pairs can be as simple as "Turn to your partner and say 'good morning,'" "Turn to your partner and tell her or him your favorite color," or "Tell your partner the first step in this activity." This use of pairs is a kind of sheltered practice that helps create a climate of cooperation and move the focus from the teacher back to the students.

Partners can show each other their answers to a problem or a question in order to check it. They can turn to each other with greetings at the beginning of the class and say good-bye at the end of the class. In Tara Kraft-Mahnke's Spanish class, the students greet three fellow students each morning and exchange one polite comment, such as "How are you?" Informal pairs might take turns reading from a text or reading to each other the stories they have written. They might work together on a task assigned by the teacher.

Patty Ryerson Hans does partner work even with her prekindergarten and kindergarten students, but she notes that the teacher is nearly always the leader in the activity, guiding the children in the process of sharing, cooperating, and taking turns (e.g., "Partner A, hold up the bag," "Partner B, take the red block out of the bag," and so on).

For early stages of language development, a back-to-back TPR partner activity can be both fun and useful. After learning a number of colors, for example, students might stand back to back with crayons in their hands for all the colors they have learned. Partner A might call out, in the target language, "Show me red!" and at the same time pull out the red crayon and hold it out. Partner B also finds the red crayon and holds it out. Together they count to three in the target language, and then they turn to see if they have chosen the same color. Then the partners go back to back again and Partner B gives the command. The same type of activity could be used with body parts, emotions, or any vocabulary to which a gesture has been attached. It might be especially useful with stories with gestures. This activity is self-correcting in that the person giving the command is unlikely to choose something about which he or she is not certain, and it could be used as a sponge activity when there are only a couple of minutes left in a class.

Information Exchange Tasks

In contrast to informal pairs activities, information exchange tasks require students to interact in order to exchange information to accomplish a task. These exchange-of-information tasks are sometimes referred to as *information gap* or *opinion gap* activities. One partner has information or an opinion that the other partner needs or wants to find out. After the task is completed, each partner will have obtained new information from the other and will have completed some type of informational objective. These types of activities give students the opportunity to develop skills of negotiation of meaning, which are essential for interpersonal communication.

Several common variations of information exchange tasks are:

- Interviewing or surveying
- Finding and giving information
- Following and giving directions
- Finding differences and/or similarities
- Solving problems

Interviewing or Surveying

In interviewing or surveying activities, each partner interviews the other, or interviews other members of the class one at a time in order to gain information. Here are some examples, all of which could serve as a model for others on different themes, and with different structural emphases.

"Find Someone"   The "Find Someone" interview activity can be used again and again. It is often used as an icebreaker activity but it can be used in many other ways. In Figure 4.8, Marianne Soldavini, an English as a second language teacher in the Milwaukee Public Schools, uses it as part of a nutrition unit.

"What's Your Pastime?"   For this interview activity, students are given a list of pastimes, all of which have been studied recently in class. Their task is to find a student in their classroom who does each of the activities on the list. The interview sheet would look like the one in Figure 4.9 (written in the target language, simplified as necessary).

The activities here would be chosen from among those the teacher knows the students enjoy, based on activities earlier in the learning sequence. After the students have finished the interviews, the teacher will follow up by asking:

Who plays tennis? (Someone will give the name of a person whose name he or she has written down.)

••

● **FIGURE 4.8**   Worksheet for "Find Someone" Activity

Find Someone: Nutrition Unit

Find someone who likes to go to McDonald's.   Name _____

Find someone who ate breakfast this morning.   Name _____

Find someone who can name a protein.   _____   Name _____
                                                                                 Name of protein

Find someone who can cook something.   _____   Name _____
                                                                              What he or she can cook

Find someone who can tell you one
of the food groups.   _____   Name _____
                                                                                    A food group

Find someone who hates to eat broccoli.   Name _____

Source: Marianne Soldavini, Milwaukee Public Schools.

● **FIGURE 4.9**   Surveying Activity Related to Pastimes

Preparations for the Visitors

The principal has just announced that several students from Switzerland will be visiting our school for two weeks. Their teacher provided us with a list of interests and hobbies for these students, in the hope that there would be students in our class with whom they would have something in common. Interview the other members of the class until you find at least one person interested in each activity—no more than one activity per person, please. Conduct the interview using the following format:

Hi, Mary.

Hi, Johnny.

Do you (like to) play _____?

Yes, I do.

Good. Write your name on the line: _____

When you have all the blanks filled, see if you can find additional people for some of the activities. You will have ten minutes to complete this survey.

Do you play tennis? _____

Do you play the piano? _____

Do you play chess? _____

Do you play soccer? _____

Do you play jazz music? _____

Do you play classical music? _____

Do you play cards? _____

Do you play the violin? _____

Do you like to read? _____

Do you like to swim? _____

Who else plays tennis? (Other names will be read.)

Does anyone else play tennis? Raise your hand. (Possible hands are raised.)

Who plays the piano? (One student says, "Mary plays the piano.")

Who can tell me something else about Mary? (Some students may have Mary's name listed for another activity, so the teacher gets a description of Mary's interests.)

Mary, do you play anything else? (Mary may add something.)

The follow-up can continue in this manner until the teacher is satisfied that the students have achieved the purpose of the task and their curiosity has been satisfied.

● **FIGURE 4.10**　"How Was Your Weekend?" Activity

On the Weekend... A			
This weekend did you...	Ludovic	You	Your Partner
Eat an apple			
a pizza	−		
a sandwich	−		
rice			
pâté	+		
gruyère cheese			
Drink water	+		
Coca Cola			
milk			
café au lait	+		
wine	+		
Go to a soccer match			
Spend 5 hours eating with your family	+		

On the Weekend... B			
This weekend did you...	Ludovic	You	Your Partner
Eat an apple	+		
a pizza			
a sandwich			
rice	+		
pâté			
gruyère cheese	+		
Drink water			
Coca Cola	−		
milk	−		
café au lait			
wine			
Go to a soccer match	−		
Spend 5 hours eating with your family			

Source: Designed by Nancy Foss.

"How Was Your Weekend?"　This activity (Figure 4.10), designed by Nancy Foss, is a "missing information pair activity" that combines a personal interview with a kind of jigsaw, in which each partner has different information. The first step is for each partner to answer the questions for himself or herself, using a + sign for yes and a − sign for no. Then the partners ask each other what they ate/drank/did on the weekend. The third step is to ask about Ludovic, a young boy from France with whom the teacher has contact. Each of the partners has different information about Ludovic, so they have to ask yes–no questions to determine how his weekend went. The partners, and later the class, can then compare their weekends with that of Ludovic. The addition of a real French boy adds a valuable cultural connection to this activity. Of course, when used in the classroom, the interview sheets would be written entirely in the target language. This template can be used with any topic, and the column for Ludovic could be replaced with the teacher, the music teacher, or a real contact from the target culture.

"ESP!"　This activity is adapted from Dr. Constance K. Knop, who has presented many helpful workshops about partner activities. The activity is called "ESP" because it gives students a chance to test their extrasensory perception. The key factor in this activity is the

● **FIGURE 4.11**   "ESP" Activity for a Unit on Pastimes

???????

¡¡ESP!!

Do you know your partner? Can you read your partner's mind?

1. Predict your own level of ESP on a scale of 1–5 and write it down in the last blank.

2. Decide how you will answer each of the questions. You must choose one answer.

3. Look at your partner. What will your partner answer?

4. Write down what you think your partner will answer for each question.

5. Partner A asks the questions first. Score one point for each correct prediction.

6. Partner B asks the questions second. Score one point for each correct prediction.

Who has the most ESP?

If you have time, work with your partner to predict how the principal would answer.

		Partner	Principal
Do you prefer soccer or football?		_____	_____
Do you prefer popular, jazz, or rock music?		_____	_____
Do you prefer movies or concerts?		_____	_____
Do you prefer cards or board games?		_____	_____
Do you prefer to watch tennis or golf?		_____	_____
How much ESP do you have?	ESP Score:	_____	
How much ESP did you predict you have?		_____	

fact that students predict their partner's answers, thus intensifying their own involvement in the activity and making them more interested in the answers to their questions.

Each student receives the same list of forced-choice questions about her or his preferences, based on theme vocabulary from recent class work. Each partner makes a personal choice for each item, and then looks intently at his or her partner in order to see if she or he can sense what the partner has decided for each item. Then each partner writes down a prediction for each item for the other person. The partners take turns asking the printed questions in order to determine whether their predictions were accurate. The number predicted correctly is the "ESP score." If students finish early, they can predict the teacher's answers, or the teacher might give the list to the principal or another familiar school figure ahead of time and then ask students to predict that person's responses. The answer sheet might look like Figure 4.11. As a variation on the "ESP" activity, the teacher might email a teacher in a classroom in the target culture and use a student from that classroom as the third person to predict.

The "ESP" activity is especially versatile because it may be redesigned to use the concepts in nearly every unit. The process would continue to be engaging, as the information would be new each time, and probably the partner would be different as well.

Interviews like these are usually intrinsically interesting because students want to know what other students think, or what other students have to say about a topic. Some topics that could be developed into effective interviews include:

- Favorite TV shows
- Favorite/least favorite foods
- Favorite animal
- Names of pets
- Tasks that are liked/hated
- Profession in the student's future

Finding Differences and Similarities

A typical pair activity for young learners is based on the idea that each partner has different information and the partners must find the differences in order for the pair to reach a common goal. The information can be text or pictures or a combination of both. This activity can be done with each partner having just one picture or with each partner having a series of pictures. In Figure 4.12, each partner has been given a sheet of paper with several series of pictures. This activity comes from a unit on animals and their habitats.

Finding Differences: More Than One Picture   Partner A begins the activity because Partner A has an asterisk next to number one on the first set of pictures. Partner A names the pictures in number one in order, and Partner B compares what Partner A reads with what is found on her or his sheet of paper. Partner A says "I have . . . in my pictures." Partner B says "I have . . . in my pictures." If they match, Partner B says, "They are the same." If they don't match, Partner B says, "They are different." When the partners decide they have a match, they place a plus sign on the line following the item. If they decide they don't have a match, they place a zero or a minus sign on the line. Then Partner B names the animals in order as they are found in item number two on her or his sheet because Partner B has an asterisk beside that item. The activity continues until the students have made decisions on all the groups of pictures on their page. Only then do the partners compare sheets to see if all their decisions are correct.

This activity can be a two-level activity (an idea adapted from Mari Haas). After students have decided whether each of their rows is the same or different, they can take another step. Do all of the animals in number 1A and number 1B actually live in the same habitat? This activity could become more of a puzzle and less of a drill if part of the task was to find the misplaced animals—that is, animals in the wrong habitat—and determine to which habitat they all belong. Then the directions might be something like this:

"After we made these lovely groups of matching animals for you, some animals wandered into rows where they don't belong. Tell your partner the names of the animals in each row that has an asterisk, and see if it is the same or different from your partner's row. If it is different, decide which animal doesn't belong in the habitat and write down that animal's name (or draw a circle around that animal). When you have finished comparing your rows, decide what habitat all those wandering animals belong to and draw a picture of it."

● **FIGURE 4.12**   Finding Differences: More than One Picture

Partner A

Match My Animals

Partner B

Match My Animals

This type of matching activity can have endless variations, depending on the language skills of the students and on the goals of the activity. Students working on reading skills might match a picture with a word, or a more complex picture with a written description.

● **FIGURE 4.13**   Finding Differences: One Picture

Finding Differences: One Picture   In another "Finding Differences" activity (see Figure 4.13), students compare single pictures that have relatively small but noticeable differences. Each student has a different version of the same picture, and students have to find the differences between them without looking at each other's pictures. This activity is considerably more difficult than the preceding activity because partners must use descriptive language and questions as they try to determine how their pictures differ. To avoid frustration, it is helpful to tell the students how many differences there are to find. Another variation might be to set a time limit and challenge students to see how many differences they can find. This version of finding differences, in which each partner has a single picture, is a template for practice of any language, culture, or curriculum concept. All that is needed is a black-and-white picture of the items to be practiced and a bottle of white cover-up liquid or white cover-up tape so that the picture can be slightly changed.

In another variation of finding differences, one partner has a single picture and the other has two or more similar pictures. The first partner describes the picture and the other partner tries to determine, from the description and by questioning, which of the pictures is the same as the one being described.

Following and Giving Directions

Pair Activities with Manipulatives   In this pair activity, one partner gives instructions and the other partner carries them out. For example, in such an activity using blocks, Partner A has a picture showing an arrangement of colored blocks. Partner B has actual colored blocks, which she or he must arrange to match the picture, based on instructions given by Partner A. If the instructions are not clear, Partner B can ask questions to clarify the task. After the task is successfully completed, the partners switch roles and build an arrangement based on a new picture. Variations of this activity include giving directions for placing furniture in a room, moving a token on a map, or arranging a variety of shapes to form a picture.

As a cultural variation for this activity, the teacher could download a series of pictures by one or more artists from the target culture from the Internet and duplicate small copies so that each student has an envelope with eight or more pictures. The task is for one partner to arrange a display of pictures, using some but not all of the pictures, as if it were to be a school hall display. They imagine that the partner is in the hall, getting ready to mount the display, and the first partner has to use an imaginary cell phone to describe how the display is to be put together. After the second partner arranges the pictures, they compare to see if the communication was effective.

Not all pair activities have to involve reading or paper-and-pencil tasks. The children from Yinghua Academy in St. Paul, Minnesota (see Figure 4.14), are working with mathematics manipulatives.

"Mystery Dots"　This activity involves a "dot-to-dot" picture in which the numbers have been scrambled. One partner has the picture, and the other partner has a card with the correct sequence of numbers that must be followed in order to connect the dots properly. The student with the card tells the partner how to connect the dots, number by number, to complete the picture. (When the teacher puts the activity together, it is helpful to add "distractor" numbers and dots so that the picture being drawn is not immediately apparent.) One way of increasing student motivation is to ask students to write down or circle the dot number at which they first thought they knew what the picture was going to be. Then in the feedback phase the teacher can find out when pairs of students figured the puzzle out, or ask whether the first guess was right or wrong, and so forth.

"Dress the Bear"　Each partner has a picture or figure of a bear and a variety of pieces of clothing to place on the bear (see Figure 4.15). Partner A dresses the bear and then tells Partner B how to dress her or his bear. Partner B can ask questions for clarification. After the directions are completed, the partners compare bears to see if they are identical.

This activity could also be extended into a "Finding Differences" activity. After partners each dress their own bears, they interview each other to find out how the bears are the same and how they are different.

● **FIGURE 4.14**　Pair Activities with Manipulatives. Not all pair activities have to involve reading or paper-and-pencil tasks. These children from Yinghua Academy in St. Paul, Minnesota, are working with mathematics manipulatives.

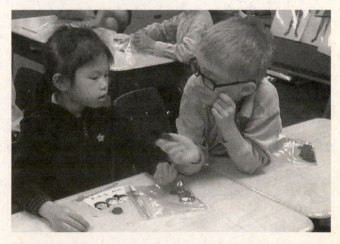

● **FIGURE 4.15** "Dress the Bear" Activity

Finding and Giving Information

"Let's Make a Sandwich"   Visuals are cut out and each partner receives an envelope that contains small food pictures, including two pieces of bread. Each partner has the same visuals (see Figure 4.16).

First, each partner individually "makes a sandwich" (using the paper bread and food cutout pictures) with a specified number of items in it. The partners should not be able to see each other's sandwiches. After each has made a sandwich, they each predict how many things they think will be the same in their two sandwiches, writing down the number secretly. They then interview each other to find out how many things are the same and how many things are different in their sandwiches.

Communicative feedback involves asking questions such as, "Did your partner have anything in the sandwich that you would never eat?" "Did your partner make a sandwich that surprised you?" "What was in it?" "How many of you would eat that sandwich?" And so on.

As a variation of this activity, students can make "sandwiches" with culturally appropriate bread products and fillings. Some teachers have given students half sheets of paper, folded, and had them write or draw the fillings for their sandwich. Curriculum connections can be made by adding prices, calories, or food groups, and asking students to make sandwiches within a certain budget, within a certain calorie content, or representing certain food groups. This task has great appeal because it has a kinesthetic dimension. Students can manipulate the pictures in the envelope in different ways. And, of course, many different kinds of pictures with language, culture, and curriculum connections can be put into the envelope.

"What's in My Backpack?" Each student draws a picture of a backpack or bookbag on a half sheet of paper or construction paper, folded over (see Figure 4.17). Students draw and label a specified number of items in the backpack, consulting a list of possible items posted on the bulletin board or on the chalkboard. The students then consult with their partners to determine what things are in each other's backpacks, keeping a list of what each partner has and doesn't have. At the end of the activity, students can give an oral report to the class about their partner. For example, "Maria has a ruler; she doesn't have a pencil," and so on.

As a variation, students could walk slowly among their classmates, looking for students who have chosen the same items to put in their backpack. At the end of the time period, the teacher could determine which student located the most identical backpacks. As another option, students might chart the number of duplicates they find for each of the items in their own backpacks.

Using the same idea, students might pack a suitcase for an imaginary trip, pack a picnic basket, or collect any other logical combination of items to compare.

"What's on Your Shopping List?" Similar partner activities can be done with written language. Students learn to write by writing, and this occurs first at the word level. In this activity, students choose from a posted list of possible items to create a five-item shopping list for their trip to the beach. They then compare their list with that of a partner, or they could interview other classmates to find someone who has the same list. Better yet,

● **FIGURE 4.16** "Let's Make a Sandwich" Activity. Food in Row 1: hamburger, eggs, jelly. Row 2: peanut butter, ham, lettuce. Row 3: chicken, cheese, tomatoes.

Source: Reprinted by permission from Myriam Met.

● **FIGURE 4.17**   "What's in My Backpack?" Activity

each student might seek someone with a completely different list, so that he or she could share products at the beach!

"Where's the Teddy Bear?"   Each partner has a large picture of a house with various rooms, similar to the house in Figure 4.18. Each partner has some small object or party favor—for example, a teddy bear counter (a small plastic manipulative in the shape of a teddy bear used for mathematics in primary school)—that he or she can "hide" in the house.

Partner A places the teddy bear counter or other small object in a room of the house and Partner B must ask questions to find out where the object is hidden. The object can be hidden in the middle of the room in order to make the questioning and vocabulary easier, or it can be hidden *in, on, under,* or *next to* a certain object in the house, thus increasing the amount of vocabulary being practiced. When Partner B has found the object, then Partner A must look for the missing object that Partner B will hide. The house visual can be used as the basis for other class activities— for example, a next step would be to guess or describe what the teddy bear is doing in the house.

The beauty of this activity is that the teddy bear or other object could be hidden anywhere. There is an endless variety of language, curriculum, and cultural connections that

● FIGURE 4.18 "Where's the Teddy Bear?" Activity

can be made as the teddy bear is "hidden" on a picture of a monument, a map, a painting, or in one of the layers of the rain forest. Patty Hans, PK–4 French teacher at the Wellington School in Columbus, Ohio, has her first-graders draw a picture of (my garden), adding to the yard or garden gradually as they develop language about animals, fruit, fruit trees, and the prepositions for *on* and *under.* Then they use the yard scene as a game board and one student "hides" a token representing an animal or "under" one of the trees in the *mon jardin (my garden),* adding to the yard or garden gradually as they develop language about animals, fruit, fruit trees, and the prepositions for *on* and *under.* Then they use the yard scene as a game board and one student hides a token representing an animal *on* or *under* one of the trees in the drawing. The second person guesses where the animal is.

"Hear–Say"   This activity calls for careful listening and speaking. Each partner has a grid arranged in two columns, one with an ear or other symbol or words to indicate "I hear" at the top. The other column has a mouth at the top, or another symbol or words to indicate "I say." Partner A begins by saying the word in the "I say" column that has an asterisk beside it. Partner B finds that word in the "I hear" column and says the word next to it, in the "I say" column. Partner A looks for that word in the "I hear" column and says the word next to it, and so on, until the process works its way back to the language item with the asterisk. See the example in Figure 4.19. This activity can be repeated with any lan-

● **FIGURE 4.19**   "Hear-Say" Activity: Plants

Partner A

👂	👄
Plants make our world beautiful.	* A seed is a plant.
Animals carry seeds.	People plant seeds.
Seeds need sunlight.	The roots come first.
Then the fruit grows.	A plant can be a bush.
Wind blows seeds.	Water carries seeds.
A plant can be a tree.	Plants are food for us.
The leaves grow next.	Flowers come.
Seeds need good dirt.	Seeds need water.

Partner B

👂	👄
Plants are food for us.	Plants make our world beautiful.
Flowers come.	Then the fruit grows.
People plant seeds.	Seeds need good dirt.
Seeds need water.	Seeds need sunlight.
A seed is a plant.	Wind blows seeds.
The roots come first.	The leaves grow next.
A plant can be a bush.	A plant can be a tree.
Water carries seeds.	Animals carry seeds.

Source: Created by Marianne Soldavini, Milwaukee Public Schools, 2000.

guage items, including pictures, and can be used at any language level. Students might listen to whole sentences, or even descriptions, or put stories in sequence. Once students have done an activity like this several times, they might work as partners to create a "Hear–Say" activity for their classmates, using familiar vocabulary or concepts.

"Corners"　　This activity, adapted from Kagan and Kagan (2008), provides a valuable and flexible format for early language communication tasks. The teacher posts visuals in each corner of the room (or other appropriate places) and asks the students to think about why they might want to go to that corner, or what kinds of things they might want to do there. The activity is most effective if it takes place within a context. For example, the teacher might explain (in the target language):

> "Imagine that we have just received approval for a class vacation trip later this year. We have four options: the seashore, the mountains, the woods, or the lake. Think about which one of these you would most like to visit on a class trip, and what you would like to do at this location."

> "In a moment you are going to walk to the vacation spot you would choose. When you get there, find one partner and raise your hand silently. Now walk to the picture of the vacation spot you would choose."

> "Now that you have a partner, tell your partner one thing that you would like to do at that vacation spot. Raise your hand when you have both had a chance to speak."

> "Now find another partner and tell your new partner what you would like to do. Raise your hand when you are finished."

> "Now find a third partner and tell that partner what your first two partners want to do."

> "Who can tell me what Mary wants to do at the beach?"

> "What does Richard want to do in the mountains?" (and so on)

The visuals in the corner could represent any number of topics, such as seasons, food, months, days of the week, clothing, cities, countries, continents, occupations, places in the city, types of houses, types of museums, and activities.

The language for this activity can be carefully controlled and teachers can plan for the grammatical structures they would like to highlight. Here is the procedure summarized:

- The teacher announces the corners. It is helpful to have visuals—either pictures or words posted in each corner.
- Students are given time to think about which corner they would like to go to and why. (Some teachers ask students to write the name of the corner to which they are going on a piece of self-stick notepaper. This ensures that students will think for themselves and not go to the corner to which their class friends may be going.)

- Students go to their chosen corners and find a partner with whom to share the language task. For example, the teacher may post pictures of the four seasons, and the students may be asked to tell the partner their favorite activity during that season, such as "I like swimming."
- Students then find a second partner with whom they share the same information.
- Students then find a third partner and tell that third partner what the first two students they have spoken with have said.
- There is then a feedback period and the results are shared with the class.

Other ideas for the "Corners" activity are posting pictures of different types of shoes or clothing in each corner and asking students where they like to go wearing that shoe or that article of clothing. Scenes or art prints from the target culture could be posted and students could go to the corner of their favorite one and tell their partners why it is their favorite.

This activity can have a greater narrative structure if students are also asked to make a prediction. For example, at the beginning of the class trip activity the students might be asked to think about which vacation spot their teacher would choose, based on what they know about the teacher or the enthusiasm with which the teacher described each of the corners. At the end of the activity, the students could be asked to predict which of the spots the teacher would choose by pointing to that corner. The teacher could end the activity by going to that corner and telling what she or he would do there.

Although there are increasing numbers of commercial sources for partner activities, some of them with copying rights for the teacher, many teachers will find these sources to be useful primarily as models for their own creations. Partner and group activities will be the most successful when they are designed specifically for the interests and the curriculum of a specific group of learners.

Summary

- Partner and small-group activities are effective and motivating tools for encouraging interpersonal communication. They have the advantage of giving students language practice in a sheltered, interpersonal setting.

- Partner and small group activities can be used only to practice language that has already been learned, not to introduce new language.

- Although these activities take the teacher off of "center stage," they require, if anything, even more careful planning than traditional teacher-fronted instruction.

- The teacher must plan for developing the social skills, as well as the language skills, that are necessary for effective interaction and use of time in partner and small-group activities.

- Organizing the class into groups and partners should be part of the learning experience, and can take place in a variety of ways.

For Study and Discussion

1. What different concerns would you anticipate in planning partner activities for students in middle school, as compared with students in first grade?

2. How would you explain the purpose of partner or small-group activities to a parent or a principal who walked into your classroom in the middle of an activity? Assume that the person is somewhat taken aback by the fact that students are not sitting in rows.

3. Design two different types of partner activities for a thematic unit you have designed, or one that you find in other resources.

4. Create a "Hear-Say" activity that summarizes the most important guidelines for conducting small-group or partner activities.

For Further Reading

The following sources are recommended for additional information about material covered in this chapter. Chapter citations are documented in Works Cited at the end of the book.

Dreke, Michael, and Sofia Salgueiro. *Wechelspiel Junior. Bilder & Mehr.* Munich: Langenscheidt, 2000.

Johnson, David W., Roger T. Johnson, and Edythe Johnson Holubec. *Cooperation in the Classroom* (6th ed.). Edina, MN: Interaction Book Company.

Kagan, Spencer, and Miguel Kagan. *Kagan Cooperative Learning*. San Clemente, CA: Kagan Publishing, 2008.

Klippel, Friederike. *Keep Talking. Communicative Fluency Activities for Language Teaching*. New York: Cambridge University Press, 1985.

McConnell, Mary. *Español en Pareja*. Munich: Langenscheidt, 1991.

McDonnel, Wendy. "Language and Cognitive Development through Cooperative Group Work," in Carolyn Kessler (Ed.), *Cooperative Learning: A Teacher's Resource Book*. Englewood Cliffs, NJ: Regents-Prentice-Hall, 1992.

McGroarty, Mary. "The Benefits of Cooperative Learning Arrangements in Second Language Instruction." *NABE Journal* 13:2 (Winter 1989): 127–183.

Putnam, JoAnne. *Cooperative Learning in Diverse Classrooms*. Upper Saddle River, NJ: Prentice-Hall, 1997.

Sánchez, Juana, and Carlos Sanz. *Jugando en español*. Munich: Langenscheidt, 1993.

Chapter 5

Literacy in the Early Language Classroom

Languages & Children

Enduring Understanding

- Literacy development and activities are essential components of language learning beginning in the earliest stages.

Essential Question

- Why and how can I incorporate the reading and writing in planning and instruction?

This chapter will explore the building blocks of literacy in a second language and answer some basic questions about second-language literacy. In order for students to be able to function in both the interpretive and presentational modes, they must develop the tools to communicate effectively using reading and writing skills in the new language.

● Connection between Oral and Written Language

From both first- and second-language acquisition theory, we know that oral language is acquired in real-life, natural settings through interactions with others. Oral language provides the basis for both first- and second-language reading. Meaningful reading experiences in both first- and second-language classrooms are dependent on the students' oral language comprehension and on their existing background knowledge and experiences. As students develop their listening comprehension, they begin to make connections between oral language and the print that represents this oral language. Some students make this connection much faster than others, and some students find great security and support in having written language available. This is more likely to be the case in grades 2, 3, and higher.

When Should Reading Begin?

In the classrooms and in the methods texts of the 1960s, reading and writing were considered a potential obstacle to the development of speaking because of interference from native language sound–symbol association. Some methods texts of the time recommended that children in early language programs should not be exposed to the written form of the language for up to three years. We have come to realize that this view was counterproductive, since it does not allow students access to visual stimulus, an important means of conveying meaning.

If reading experiences are related to what they have been exposed to during other classroom activities, students can experience success with reading in the new language even at very early stages. Delaying reading in the new language may be very frustrating to students whose learning styles are more visually oriented. Reading delay may also cause some students to develop their own covert writing system.

Here is an example from a fourth-grader in a summer school French class. On her nametag on her desk she had written the following: *un du twa kat sank sees set weet nerf dees* (for *un, deux, trois, quatre, cinq, six, sept, huit, neuf, dix,* or one to ten). This student needed to see the written word and its visual reinforcement. She was trying to remember the numbers in French, and since she did not have access to the written version, she made up her own way to write them.

The best answer to the question of when reading should begin is: As soon as possible! This does not mean that we hand out texts to first-graders, or that we focus on reading as the primary way to deliver instruction in the new language. It means that we do not leave literacy out, even in the early grades, and that in the later grades we refer to and reinforce the reading skills that the students have already acquired. We focus on literacy as a tool for communication.

Transfer of Skills from the Native Language to the New Language

Second-language reading differs from first-language reading in that most of the students (except for those in immersion programs) have already made the connection between meaning and written symbols in their first language. They transfer the skills they have acquired in one language to their new language. Cloud, Genesee, and Hamayan (2000) have described and organized important reading skills.

Decoding Skills: Figuring Out Words

- Sounding out the word
- Recognizing a sight word
- Using context

Text Processing

- Directionality of text (not always left to right, as in English)
- Capitalizing a word at the beginning of a sentence
- Skimming, scanning, and using other previewing techniques
- Using the title and illustrations to understand a passage

Reading Comprehension

- Identifying the main idea and important details
- Predicting outcomes/anticipating events
- Identifying story sequence
- Summarizing and paraphrasing

Critical Reading Skills

- Discriminating between fact and opinion
- Recognizing cause and effect

Literature Study

- Recognizing important feelings and motivations of characters
- Identifying the conflict

These skills, depending on the language level and developmental level of the students, can be called on in second-language classes and reinforced through reading in the new language.

Communicating with Mainstream Classroom Teachers

As we address the issues of literacy in a new language, we must work with the concerns of classroom teachers. Mainstream classroom teachers of students in the early grades, especially kindergarten and first grade, are often concerned about confusion if students see print in two languages. Their concerns are understandable, especially if they have had no previous experience with how children learn new languages. However, in some schools the reading specialist is one of the most enthusiastic supporters of a foreign language program in which reading and writing are introduced early.

In the early grades, foreign language instruction does not focus on new reading skills; rather, we work on building the oral language base that provides the foundation for literacy in the second language. The print environment that we provide supports the oral language the students already have. We can reassure classroom teachers that we will not spend our time focusing on reading skills, but instead we will take advantage of the skills students have already acquired in their first language. We use literacy as a tool for interpersonal or interpretive communication in the new language, rather than focusing on teaching reading skills and subskills.

Schema

One of the most important aspects of literacy is background knowledge. The process of understanding written language involves drawing on experiences and information already stored in memory. For example, if a person does not have a schema for the term *carburetor*, he or she would need a lot of scaffolding in order to understand a text about carburetors. Considerable visual support and other explanations would help that person understand the meaning of the text. In the same way, learners who are approaching a text in any language need to have enough background knowledge so that they can make sense out of it. This is especially true in second-language literacy. There must be intensive work before, during, and after reading the text to ensure that the students will comprehend what they read, because in second-language literacy there are two elements to deal with: the concept itself and the label for the concept in the new language.

Reading and Writing as Tools for Communication

In the language classroom, we want to use reading and writing primarily as tools for communication in the interpersonal, the interpretive, and the presentational modes, and not as ends in themselves. Isolated fill-in-the-blank exercises do not provide meaningful reading and writing experiences. A focus on reading subskills and isolated exercises puts students who are already having difficulty in the first language at a special disadvantage, and reduces their chances for success. In a standards-based early language program, these students can have an opportunity to begin anew with success-building reading and writing experiences in their new language.

In an integrated standards-based approach to language learning, listening, reading, speaking, and writing activities do not take place in isolation, but are interrelated and flow out of the communication task that the learners are performing. The amount of time devoted to reading and writing experiences will vary according to the grade level of the students and the amount of time available for instruction.

● Building Blocks of Second-Language Literacy

In this section, we will examine what meaningful reading and writing experiences might look like in a standards-based classroom. As with native-language classrooms, working on literacy in a foreign-language classroom has at times been limited to drill and practice, with a focus on spelling and grammatical accuracy. Within a meaning- and standards-based curriculum, however, reading and writing can be much more. Copying isolated letters and words has no purpose except for drill and practice. We can find ways to put even necessary drill and practice into a communicative context that makes literacy activities more meaningful for the learners.

In preschool and primary school classrooms, beginning reading experiences can focus on teacher storytelling and story reading, with incidental exposure to the written language. This means that the classroom and school can be labeled and that students will see, posted around the room, the written version of the vocabulary and structures that they are learning. A simple way for the teacher to include literacy in the early foreign-language program is by modeling the processes of reading and writing during the class. For example, the teacher might write a message to the students to be read at the beginning of class. As literacy skills are established in the first language, we can use and reinforce them in the new language. With students in second grade and above who are beginners, we may be able to proceed more quickly with written language than with beginners in earlier grades.

Key Words and Word Banks

The key vocabulary words and word bank strategy was initiated by Sylvia Ashton-Warner in her seminal work titled *Teacher* (1963). *Key words* are sets of words requested by students, which are of personal interest for them. These students keep a word bank—the words they have requested are written on cards that can be saved and referred to when needed.

Students can store their word banks in a notebook or in a small file box for index cards. Key words of interest to the entire class can be posted around the room. Word banks can also be developed by a whole class and posted in the classroom in preparation for a specific written or oral activity.

These strategies are used in first-language classrooms to help students make a transition to literacy through their own experiences. In the early language classroom, they help students acquire and use the language that will be most valuable to them in dealing with their own needs and interests.

Environmental and Functional Print

Many children in their native language become readers naturally as they begin to make sense of environmental and functional print—the words on the milk carton or their favorite brands of cereal or candy; names of buildings, stores, and products of interest; traffic and information signs; and many other items. Foreign-language programs usually do not exist in an environment that is rich with public written information in the target language; however, filling the classroom with opportunities for reading can create some of the same opportunities. Environmental print, for this purpose, includes all the second-language print that exists in the classroom, such as:

Charts	Lunch menus
Bulletin boards	Signs
Displays	Calendars
Passwords	Lesson plans on the board
Language ladders	Class rules
Posted Gouin series	(and many more)

Environmental and functional print also includes the type of written information found in authentic materials from the target culture, writing that communicates needed information that is of immediate value to the reader. Such print might include labels and directions on packages, ads, CD covers, and TV and radio guides. Teachers can use environmental and functional print to add a dimension of written language to learning activities, even if they are not necessarily literacy-focused activities.

The Language Experience Approach to Reading

A third building block for meaningful literacy experiences in early language classrooms is the Language Experience Approach to reading. This approach incorporates all the communication skills—speaking, listening, writing, and reading—and moves from the interpersonal mode to the interpretive mode and possibly to the presentational mode.

The Language Experience Approach to reading is based on the idea that children will be able to read printed words if these words are part of their everyday language and experience. Familiar experiences are translated into oral expression, then recorded and read. When a visual symbol is connected to the spoken word and the word is part of the learner's experience, the meaning is readily understood and has immediate relevance. The students are not asked to read material for which they have no background knowledge.

Initially, the teacher elicits language from the students through group discussion of an experience. Such an experience might be one in which the teacher, students, and parents in a language class go to a restaurant specializing in that culture's cuisine. In order to write a language experience story about this activity, the teacher might proceed as follows: After the restaurant activity is over, the teacher and the class talk together about what they have experienced. The teacher speaks only in the target language, but the students may volunteer some information in their native language. As the activity progresses, the teacher writes down the students' words and ideas, usually on a large chart or on the chalkboard.

The final story for a Japanese class's visit to a Japanese restaurant might be something like this:

We went to the Tokyo Sushi Restaurant.

We took off our shoes.

We sat down on the floor.

We looked at the menu.

We ordered sushi.

We ate with chopsticks.

Our parents ate with chopsticks, too.

We like sushi.

The story might be shorter or longer, or more or less complex, depending on the age and language level of the students, but it is written in the target language.

After the story has been written, the teacher and the students read the story aloud together. Then the story can be copied and illustrated by the students and read and reread at school and at home. In later stages of elementary school language programs, where there is considerable contact time, students might write their own stories and share them at a class story table or in the library.

This approach to beginning reading makes the task easier and less frustrating because reading materials match oral language patterns and draw on personal experiences. We are not asking the learners to try to decipher the unfamiliar or confusing language of texts that are not yet meaningful. In spite of the students' marginal control of the oral language, the introduction to print by way of the Language Experience Approach ensures that learners will understand what they are reading and will find it meaningful.

The Language Experience Approach can be used successfully with both first- and second-language learners. There are some differences in how it is conducted in the two settings, however. Although the steps in the process are similar for both groups, the language teacher spends much more time structuring the experience and guiding the dictation process. In first-language classes, the teacher writes down anything and everything the learners say, with little editing. In second-language classes, the teacher usually has to prompt language and supply vocabulary. The actual language dictated by the learners is usually modified (rephrased correctly, where necessary) and sometimes translated by the teacher at this step.

The Language Experience Approach must be adapted somewhat for second-language classrooms to allow for firmer direction from the teacher, but the central concept remains the same—using the students' own background of experiences and their own words, as much as possible, to create the reading text.

Shared Reading

A last building block for literacy experiences in the early language classroom is shared reading: Teachers read books aloud to language learners, thus giving them oral language input and a bridge to literacy in the new language. *Big books* have become a popular way for teachers to engage students in story reading. A big book is an enlarged piece of commercial or student-made literature, intended to re-create the intimacy and good feelings of one-on-one "read-aloud" sessions with an entire class. These are sometimes referred to as *extended lap* experiences. They are labeled *big books* because they are large enough so that the entire class can see and share in the experience. Most big books have a predictable story line with strong rhythm, rhyme, repeated patterns, logical sequence, and supportive illustrations.

Students follow each word in the big book as it is read, thus reinforcing the reading skill of directionality. Students in native language literacy development programs begin to "read" by reciting and memorizing, recognizing sight words, and decoding the text. Students in early language programs can use shared reading experiences to begin matching oral language with the written word. Being able to see the text easily along with the teacher and the other learners helps students make the connection between the oral language and the print. Reading to students in the new language is a very valuable experience, even if the students do not have access to the text, as in shared reading, because it provides them with the valuable input they need in order to begin to construct meaning in the new language. Figure 5.1 shows an example of how a shared reading experience using Eric Carle's *The Very Hungry Caterpillar* might be developed and adapted for second-language learners.

● Building Literacy in the Early Language Classroom

In this section, we will examine a selection of literacy-building activities that can be done at various levels of language and literacy. We'll start with the most basic: visual discrimination and directionality.

Visual Discrimination and Directionality

Visual discrimination and directionality are some of the most basic literacy experiences. Students need to be able to discriminate shapes and also need to know in which direction the eyes move in order to follow the print within the text. Does the print move horizontally from left to right, or from right to left? Does it move vertically? Books in Arabic open from what we would call the "back," for example. Teachers in Arabic programs who are adapting materials often have to reformat books so that they open in the proper direction. When students are reading in Arabic, Hebrew, and other non-European languages, they must learn that directionality is relative.

Figure 5.2 (page 142) shows the cover and a page from a Japanese class book written by Lynn Sessler and her kindergarten students from Menasha, Wisconsin. The book is titled *Keroppi What Do You See?*, patterned on Bill Martin' Jr.'s *Brown Bear, Brown Bear, What Do You See?* Each student contributed to the book by making an origami fish, pasting it on the page, and then embellishing the page with artwork. Lynn added the word for *fish (sakana)*, along with each child's name, to every page. Lynn uses this book to help her students with visual discrimination. She has created an activity that assists them in matching the word for *fish* with its occurrence on their page. The book has a string attached to it with a paper fish on the other end, on which is written the Japanese word for *fish*. Students take the fish and match what is written on the paper fish with the same word on each page of the book. The other word on each page of this class book

● **FIGURE 5.1**   Sample Shared Reading Experience with *The Very Hungry Caterpillar* by Eric Carle

These procedures are spread out over time with some of the activities being performed each day.

Items Needed

- Three books, one to read and two (paperback) to cut up. (You need two books to cut up so that you can use the pictures on each side of the page.) For reading, you can use the "big book"version or a version with large print for the whole class to see.

- Vocabulary pictures posted around the room (large enough for all to see): apple, pear, orange, strawberry, plum, sun, moon, leaf. Other possibilities are egg, and foods that the caterpillar ate on Saturday.

- Pictures of each of the events in the story. (Use cut-up book pages and mount on heavy paper.)

- Text to go along with the pictures of about 10 major events in the story. (Done on the computer, large 36 pt.) Mount on heavy paper.

- *Hungry Caterpillar* puppet, plastic caterpillar, or picture of real caterpillar.

- Bag or box in which to hide the caterpillar puppet or plastic replica.

- Optional: A set of small pictures exactly the same as the larger ones. Put them in an envelope for each person. Ask the class to get out of the envelope and hold up, for you to see, the picture of the events you describe—for example, "Hold up the picture of the apple," and "Hold up the picture of the foods that gave the caterpillar a stomach ache." This is another way to check comprehension of the story. This would be done immediately after the story is read.

Procedures

Before the Story

- Have students point to various pictures on the walls, or have students touch or pick up actual food replicas.

- Give each student a manipulative (paper or a plastic replica) of the things from the story. Ask all children to hold up the manipulatives as you call them out. Or ask them to stand up if they are holding the manipulative you are calling out. Later on, as you read the story, ask the students to hold up their manipulative as it is mentioned in the story.

- Put a plastic caterpillar or caterpillar toy in a bag or box and have students guess what is inside. Begin reading the story after someone guesses correctly. If it takes too long, you can take the item out of the bag.

The Story

- Read the story, acting out and embellishing various parts to increase understanding.

● **FIGURE 5.1**   (Continued)

After the Story

- Make a graph of food items the caterpillar ate on each day. Put days of the week across the bottom of the graph and then make a bar graph with the pictures of what was eaten on that day. Repeat text from the story as the students are putting the items on the graph for the correct day.

- Read the story again.

- Show pictures (out of sequence) of the events in the story. As you show each picture, motion for someone to come to get that picture and take it back to his or her place.

- After all the pictures have been passed out, ask which picture represents the first thing that happened in the story; show number one with a finger gesture. Have the person holding that first picture go to the front of the room and hold up the picture for everyone to see.

- Do the same with the second picture, and so on, until all the students with pictures are standing in the correct order of the story in the front of the room.

- Next, show the text posters (out of sequence) for the students to read silently. As you show each poster, ask if anyone can match it with the text. Ask those who volunteer to do this to stand behind the person holding the picture and hold the text above their heads. (If it is a small group, ask the "class" to identify which picture goes with the text and then give the text to the person holding the picture. Ask that person to hold up both the text and the picture at the same time.)

- Review with the class each picture and text.

Follow-Up

- Continue to read the story several times. Retell the story using manipulatives or pictures only. Have students begin to tell the story.

- Give the students the story text on strips of paper and have them put the text in the correct order, working with partners, in groups, or individually. (This can also be done with story pictures.)

- Have the students illustrate and write their own *Hungry Caterpillar* story to take home and share with their parents. Ask parents and others to sign an interactive homework form indicating that they have heard the student reading the story.

- Choose possible follow-up activities such as writing another *Hungry Caterpillar* story using the same language patterns, but having the caterpillar eat different foods, or writing a story replacing the caterpillar with another animal eating different foods (possibly culture specific). Have students illustrate the story and write short captions using sentences you have generated. Other follow-up activities include true–false, fill-in-the-blank, cloze, songs, and poems.

● **FIGURE 5.2** Japanese Class Book. Students match the Japanese word for *fish* in their class book.

is the name of the student who created the page. Lynn also has students match up their names with a card. She is helping her students make the connection between oral language and print in Japanese.

As we have seen, students in Japanese programs and programs in other less commonly taught languages often have to start at the very beginning with visual discrimination, since they are learning a totally new writing system or systems. Of course, students are also working on visual discrimination and figuring out sight words when they put together a word bank, or participate in a language experience or shared reading activity.

Literacy Building Activities at the Word Level

Most young language learners are familiar with the process of reading and writing and have probably already had the experience with both in their first language. At very early stages, many activities will be in the form of reading, copying, and labeling, especially at the word and sentence levels. It is possible that at the word and sentence levels the students are able to communicate meaning.

Labeling   There are many ways to begin second-language literacy activities with labeling. Students can label real objects, either with a label they write themselves or with a label prepared by the teacher. They can hold up labels in response to questions asked by the teacher. They can label diagrams and graphic organizers. They can also label the classroom, including not only the objects and furniture but also expanding the effort into such areas as labeling the walls with the cardinal directions—north, south, east, and west. Students in early language programs are often engaged in labeling activities in which the basic objective is to connect printed language with the oral language they have learned.

Other Word-Level Literacy Building Activities

Here are some other examples of word-level activities:

- Match the written word with a picture on the whiteboard or magnet board, or in a game such as "Concentration" or "Dominoes."

- Respond to true–false questions about familiar stories.

- Given a list of items sold in a store, make a list of things to buy for a parent, for friends, for a party, and so on.

- Create collages with visual representations of specific vocabulary.

- Choose a movie from the movie page in a target language publication and write down information to share with a friend.

- Complete graphs, charts, and maps to give personal information or show preferences.

- Write the names of people in a family picture.

- Make as long a "word snake" as possible—write strings of words in which the last letter of one word is the same as the first letter of the next.

- Label the items in a picture.

- Write a menu for a restaurant, choosing items from a list.

- Write a restaurant take-out order, choosing from items listed on the menu.

- "Shop" from a target language catalog and make a list of items to buy and fill out an order form (simplified for beginning students).

- Given a chart on which foods are listed by food groups, write a menu for a balanced meal.

- Make a list of items in a picture and sort them according to category.

Sorting and Classifying as a Word-Level Activity   Sorting and classifying is an inherently meaningful activity because it is cognitively engaging. When students sort and classify words, they must attend to them carefully so they can put them in the correct categories. Each time a word is repeated in a different categorizing exercise, the students must attend to it again. Each repetition forces the brain to deal with that word again, and after enough repetitions, sooner or later the word will "stick." Here is an example of how this might work: Given a set of vocabulary words related to food, you can ask the students to sort them in various ways. For instance, Which foods grow above the ground? Which grow below the ground? For which foods do we eat the stem, the root, and the leaf? Which foods do we eat cooked or raw? There are many more possibilities: foods I like or don't like, hot or cold foods, processed or unprocessed foods, salty or sweet foods, and so on.

Sentence-Level Activities

Here are some suggestions for sentence-level activities:

- Read and write songs, rhymes, and poems that have been learned orally.
- Write weather reports and include pictures.
- Compare the weather in two countries.
- Write action (TPR) commands for students to give to each other or to the teacher.
- Rewrite a story.
- Write mathematics problems.
- Fill in balloons in a comic strip with very simple captions.
- Supply simple dialogue for pictures or picture books.
- Write simple captions for pictures in a class or personal album.
- Have students keep their own journals or notebooks of classroom requests and classroom-centered survival vocabulary.
- Write recipes.
- Write and deliver a note in a classroom mailbox or on a classroom message board.
- Write questions for interviews about favorite television shows, pets, travel, favorite foods, teachers, subjects, and so on.
- Write invitations.
- Write birth announcements.
- Write a reading action chain (see Chapter 13) or a "Hear-Say" (see Chapter 4) activity.
- Write learning logs using memorized chunks of language.
- Write questions to a historical figure about his or her place in history.
- Fill in the end to a sentence that begins with a prompt such as "I feel happy when . . ." or "I feel sad when . . . ."

Paragraph-Level Activities

The following activities are recommended for increasing students' skills in developing paragraphs:

- Create pattern stories according to a model that students have heard and seen.
- Draw a picture and write about how you are dressed now, then draw a picture and write about what you will be dressed like when you are grown up.
- Describe the house you live in now, then describe the house you will live in when you grow up.

- Write class experience stories.
- Write introductions (to people, places, books, etc.).
- Write daily journals.

Hildegard Merkle uses a literacy-building activity from Germany in a game-like context. She gives these directions for a *Laufdiktat,* or walking dictation:

Goal/Purpose: To read and write from memory.

Materials Needed: (Teacher) Different cards/strips with the target vocabulary. (Students) Paper and pencil.

Procedure: After reading a picture book, telling a story, cooking following a recipe or any language activity, write the target vocabulary or sentences on cards and place the cards face down in different locations in the room. To ensure high success, review the target vocabulary by helping the learners to imagine the items with closed eyes and then drawing them in the air, on a partner's back, on their own arms, or something similar. Using TPR commands, instruct the students to take paper and pencil and draw the target vocabulary items.

Then model (don't just describe it!) the walking dictation carefully:

1. Put down paper and pencil. Pick up your imaginary camera.
2. Go around the room, looking for a card. Turn one card over.
3. Take your imaginary camera and take a picture of the writing on the card ("exposure time" can vary as needed by the student).
4. With the picture in your mind, go back to your place, pick up your pencil, and write the word(s) you see in your mind to label the picture you have drawn.
5. Look carefully at what you have written, put down the paper and pencil, go back to the card, and compare the writing with your mental picture.
6. If it is incorrect, go back and correct your writing. If it is correct, go to the next card and repeat.

Set a time limit and instruct learners to begin.

Closure: Read the story again and allow learners to compare their work with the original.

Suggestions for Intermediate and Advanced Students: Instead of single words, write a story or a poem in several sentences on the cards. Follow the same procedure as above. The students first write all the sentences in random order and then sequence them. Closure would be the reading of the story or poem. It is more interesting if there are several possibilities with surprise endings!

Phonics and Grammar

Using phonics methods alone is not sufficient for young language learners. Younger students who are not yet at the stage of abstract thinking are not able to focus on grammatical rules and reading and writing activities based solely on grammar. These students need reading and writing experiences that are connected to their lives in a natural way. They also need to have real-life experiences or experiences with exciting books in order to develop a base of interesting things about which to write. It is very difficult to make the connection between reading and writing if the only experiences students have with writing are connected to isolated drills and practice exercises in workbooks.

What about Accuracy?

Young language learners may not yet be accurate spellers in their native language since accurate spelling is something that does not develop until the late elementary grades. It is important to have flexibility, so that in some early writing experiences the focus is on communicating important and meaningful messages and not necessarily on accuracy for everything that is written. Accuracy will increase as the students progress toward accuracy in their native language and as they develop skills over time in the second language.

Students who are dyslexic in their native language will experience similar difficulties in a second language. A reasonable accommodation can be found by not holding them to a higher standard in the second language than they can show in their first language.

Round Robin Reading

One practice that is not beneficial to early language learners is commonly called "Round Robin" reading (students reading from a selection one after the other in a predictable order). Reading should be approached as a process for deriving meaning from the printed word and not for using the printed word as a stimulus for speaking, or a kind of recitation. Round Robin reading, often seen in elementary school language classrooms, is not an appropriate strategy for developing reading skill in a second language.

Round Robin reading tends to encourage students to respond to the surface features of the language and not to the message. Many students master the "trick" of sound–symbol association without developing skill in comprehension or communication. Because reading aloud is a practice with such a long tradition, it gives many teachers a sense of security to use it as a strategy; however, current understanding of the reading process does not support its continued use.

Reading aloud can be very useful when it is done for meaningful communicative purpose, such as:

- Sharing part of a story that students especially liked
- Reading part of a story that students have written or something that they want to share

- Reading parts of a play as practice for a performance
- Reading to a child in a younger grade
- Reading to a partner in order to practice for reading the same book at home to their parents
- Practicing reading to a partner in order to prepare for reading in another setting

Summary

- There is sometimes controversy about when reading and writing in a foreign language should begin, but experience has shown that language learners can be exposed to written forms of the language from the beginning of the language learning experience.

- Students transfer the literacy skills they have learned in their first language to their new language, although this process is more complex when writing systems in the new language are very different from those the students have already learned. As we communicate with classroom teachers and reading teachers, we can reassure them that we will be building on language and literacy skills that are already in place, and that literacy skills in the first language will not be threatened by the process.

- The first steps in reading and writing in a new language include using key words and word banks, enriching the classroom environment with environmental print in the target language, employing the Language Experience Approach to reading and writing, and enjoying regular shared reading experiences. Helping students to build literacy skills in their new language requires many meaningful opportunities to read and write, at the word, sentence, and even the paragraph levels.

- A few strategies found in some first-language classrooms are not useful in the foreign-language setting. A phonics focus is not as effective as reading and writing experiences that are directly connected to students' lives and interests. An emphasis on accuracy in spelling and grammar is not appropriate in early stages of learning a new language.

For Study and Discussion

1. Imagine that you are a K–1 foreign-language teacher in a new program. It is your job to explain to the classroom teachers how the new language program will work. You know that concerns are bound to arise about possible interference between the writing system of the new language and the emerging literacy skills in the native language. Prepare yourself for one of these conversations by outlining the message you plan to deliver.

2. Choose one of the first steps in reading and writing and build a lesson plan around use of this step.

3. Round Robin reading does not seem to be a very useful strategy in an early language classroom. Describe some possible alternatives that would involve meaningful experiences in reading aloud.

4. Choose a storybook and develop a walking dictation activity to use as a follow-up to reading the story aloud several times.

For Further Reading

The following sources are recommended for additional information about material covered in this chapter. Chapter citations are documented in Works Cited at the end of the book.

Cloud, Nancy, Fred Genesee, and Else Hamayan. *Dual Language Instruction: A Handbook for Enriched Education.* Boston: Heinle and Heinle, 2000.

Cloud, Nancy, Fred Genesee, and Else Hamayan. *Literacy Instruction for English Language Learners: A Teacher's Guide to Research-Based Practices.* Portsmouth, NH: Heinemann, 2009.

Guillaume, Andrea M., Ruth Helen Yopp, and Hallie Kay Yopp. *Fifty Strategies for Active Teaching Engaging K–12 Learners in the Classroom.* Upper Saddle River, NJ: Merrill/Prentice-Hall, 2007.

Herrell, Adrienne L., and Michael Jordan. *Fifty Strategies for Teaching English Language Learners* (3rd ed.). Upper Saddle River, NJ: Pearson Merrill/Prentice Hall, 2008.

Peregoy, Suzanne, and Owen F. Boyle. *Reading, Writing and Learning in ESL: A Resource Book for K–12 Teachers* (4th ed.). Boston: Pearson Allyn and Bacon, 2008.

Tompkins, Gail. *Fifty Literacy Strategies Step by Step* (2nd ed.). Upper Saddle River, NJ: Pearson Merrill/Prentice Hall, 2004.

Yopp, Ruth Helen, and Kallie Kay Yopp. *Literature-Based Reading Activities* (5th ed.). Boston: Allyn and Bacon, 2010.

Chapter 6

Designing Instruction

Integrated Thematic Planning for Curriculum, Unit, and Lesson Design

Enduring Understanding

- Careful planning is at the heart of all effective instruction.

Essential Question

- How can I design effective and meaningful curricula, units, and lessons?

● Why Thematic Instruction for the Early Language Curriculum?

Thematic planning and instruction are among the most important elements of an effective early language program. Our standards orientation calls for integrated learning, with connections to other content areas and to new information through the use of the new language. Our growing insight about brain-compatible learning supports thematic instruction, as well. As we teach new languages to children, our focus is making meaning, rather than making accurate new sounds or grammatically correct sentences (important though these may be). Eric Jensen (2005) suggests that for meaning-making to take place, we should evoke three important ingredients in our general practice: emotion, relevance, and context and patterns (p. 96). A carefully designed theme can incorporate *emotion,* one of the most powerful channels for learning; *relevance,* a critical motivator for language learning; and *rich context,* an element that brings language learning to life and activates the pattern-making functions of the brain.

Much of elementary school curriculum in all content areas is built around themes, often as a means of integrating several subjects during the school day. Middle school curriculum is also growing ever more theme-based, as schools respond to the intellectual, social, and developmental needs of the early adolescent learner. As the language teacher connects language instruction to existing themes or creates language-specific themes, the language class is clearly an integrated part of the school day, and languages are perceived to be meaningful components of student learning.

Here is a listing of some of the advantages of thematic planning:

1. *Thematic planning makes instruction more comprehensible because the theme creates a meaningful context.*

In a thematic unit, students can interpret new language and new information on the basis of their background knowledge. They are not just learning vocabulary in isolation; they are using words to identify which animals are endangered in South America, or which foods came from Europe in the Columbian exchange (the goods and foods that were exchanged as a result of Columbus's encounter with the Americas).

Thematic instruction makes the learning more relevant to the learner. When themes are well chosen, students will be more engaged with the learning because they can see its purpose and find it interesting—and fun.

2. *Thematic planning changes the instructional focus from the language itself to the use of language to achieve meaningful goals.*

In thematic instruction, we focus on using the language to communicate something related to a theme, rather than repeating words in isolation with no connection to the classroom or the student. Instead of focusing on how to say or write something, thematic instruction shifts the focus to communicating a message for a reason.

As we shift the focus to what language means and can do, students become motivated to acquire language and to be accurate because they want to communicate about information that is of interest to them.

3. *Thematic instruction provides a rich context for standards-based instruction.*

One of the important features of the National Standards for Foreign Language Learning is their emphasis on working toward a goal, and focusing on the "big picture"— or the "big idea." A German teacher who helped pilot the Standards commented that with the Standards orientation, she began planning in bigger "chunks"—essentially, developing themes that worked toward an important goal, over a longer period of time. Many of the scenarios found in the Standards document are also examples of integrated thematic units.

4. *Thematic instruction offers a natural setting for narrative structure and task-based organization of content.*

Wiggins and McTighe (2005) suggest that the story structure is an ideal curricular design, in which meanings unfold as a unit works its way from beginning to middle to end. Stories make learning easier because the brain is naturally structured to use narrative to organize memory. Task-based learning also has a narrative structure, as students work through the challenges of the unit in order to complete an important final task. Both of these powerful strategies for structuring learning are natural components of a thematic unit.

5. *Thematic instruction involves the students in real language use in a variety of situations, modes, and text types.*

Thematic instruction, especially when it is organized in a story structure, gives students the opportunity to use language in a variety of situations, including simulations of cultural experiences. A theme lends itself to all three of the communication modes: interpersonal, interpretive, and presentational. Text types within a thematic unit can range from preparing and reading poetry, to reading headlines, to creating or listening to a description, to participating in a conversation, to listening to a play. The list goes on and on.

A thematic unit is organized in terms of meaningful experiences with language, focused on a theme and on theme-related tasks. These experiences prepare students to use the language for a variety of purposes—their own purposes—beyond the classroom.

6. *Thematic instruction involves activities or tasks that engage the learner in complex thinking and more sophisticated use of language.*

Even though learners may have very little language at their disposal, they are still capable of using that language in a complex and sophisticated way, if they have the opportunity and the interest. An engaging theme built around endangered animals, for example, led one student to use simple vocabulary to make a very sophisticated statement. On a picture of a leopard, the student wrote the caption *No soy un abrigo (I am not a coat).* This is a far more sophisticated and meaningful use of the verb *to be* than the obvious statement *I am a boy* or *I am a girl.*

7. *Thematic instruction avoids the use of isolated exercises with grammatical structures, practiced out of context, that tend to fragment language at the word or sentence level and to neglect the discourse level.*

The thematic unit provides many opportunities for students to hear and use language in a variety of meaningful contexts. We have learned from brain research that manipulation of vocabulary and grammar in a drill setting is less efficient than the meaningful use of language in rich contexts. Students need contexts for extended listening, for conversations in which real information is exchanged, and for oral and written presentations of information and ideas. Fragmented language is not as memorable as language learned in context—and it certainly isn't as usable.

8. *Thematic instruction connects content, language, and culture goals to a "big idea."*

What is really worth understanding? Is it the past tense of the irregular verbs? Is it the names of six modes of transportation? Wiggins and McTighe (2005) advocate the organization of curriculum around "big ideas": ideas, topics, or processes that reside at the heart of the discipline and have enduring value beyond the classroom. These are ideas, topics, or processes that are not obvious, about which students may even have misconceptions, so that learning can become a process of discovery or "uncovering." Topics like these are likely to be of great interest to students, especially when they are approached as questions, issues, or problems (pp. 10–11).

Glastonbury Public Schools has developed a curriculum based on the principles of Understanding by Design, the curriculum design principle developed by Wiggins and McTighe (1998). The Spanish curriculum is organized around key "big ideas" at each grade level, and these are developed through the use of guiding questions that focus each unit. For example, the first-grade curriculum is focused on the question "How do we name things in a different language?" The "big idea" question in third grade is "Why is my day the way it is, and is it different from other countries?" The guiding questions include "What is school for?" and "How is my family different from others?" In fourth grade, the central question is "Why do we explore and what do we find?" Some of the guiding questions are "What is an explorer?," "What influences have the explorers left on the types of homes we have today?," and "What types of transportation do explorers use?"

Thematic instruction helps students go beyond knowledge and skills in their language use and bring them to the point of actually using these skills to gain access to important ideas that are worth understanding. These important "big ideas" have enduring value, beyond the classroom and beyond the context in which they were learned.

For example, learning the terms for a variety of foods is typical content for the early language classroom. By itself, this food vocabulary is static knowledge, easily forgotten. When it is encountered in the context of a unit about the Columbian exchange, however, the same vocabulary takes on relevance and importance as a tool for learning about something of lasting value—and thus the vocabulary becomes more memorable. This thematic unit begins to uncover the "big ideas" of what happens when cultures interact with one another, and how things change over time.

Another common early language topic is animals, and sometimes this topic can also result in limited, static knowledge. Jackie Dove's fourth-grade students in a beginning French class, however, used the animal vocabulary they had learned to uncover and share information about endangered animals. This experience gave her students a connection with the "big idea" of the interaction of all living things with their environment.

Curriculum and lesson planning are the most important components of an early language program. Each day's lesson fits into a larger framework of planning, which makes it a part of long-range goals and unified, sequenced objectives. A planning process organized around Standards, communicative principles, and the framework introduced later in this chapter will develop experiences for students that enable them to function effectively in a variety of situations and modes of communication. This planning process will first attempt to give children control over their immediate environment and then move outward, enabling them to discuss interests, needs, and concerns in the school beyond their classroom, in their families, and in their community. At the same time, students will acquire and use the new language in contexts that are planned to be rich with cultural meanings and associations.

● Thematic Planning for K–8 Classrooms

In order to achieve and maintain high student interest and motivation in the early language classroom, planners must organize the curriculum and the everyday activities of the classroom around the needs and interests of students. In the elementary and middle schools, this is an individual challenge from school to school and from class to class. Faced with a perpetual lack of published materials, the elementary school language teacher will no doubt always have to develop a great many materials personally, as the existing materials usually require adaptation to meet the needs of a specific school or class. Middle school language teachers often find that published materials are not appropriate to the language level or the developmental levels of their students. A commitment to thematic planning can free the language teacher from the limitations of existing materials and lead to more interesting lessons and greater learning on the part of their students. Whether at the elementary or the middle school level, planning for foreign language instruction should be standards-based, thematic, and multidisciplinary, addressing the needs and the development of the whole child. Close cooperation with teachers of other subject areas can lead to an effective integration of languages with the emphases and the goals of other content areas. Several tools to assist the teacher are described in the following sections of the chapter.

Framework for Curriculum Development

The Framework for Curriculum Development for FLES Programs (Pesola, 1995) was developed to help teachers make sense of the competing demands for time and attention in curriculum planning. It is a visual representation of priorities and relationships among elements of curriculum design (see Figure 6.1). The thematic units developed according to this framework will fit within a curriculum design that accounts for the entire sequence of instruction. In other words, as the unit is being developed, the teacher must take into consideration what part of the entire language sequence is being addressed. The unit is part of an overall K–12 curriculum plan. (See Figure 6.10 on page 182.)

This framework is designed to guide decisions encountered in the process of curriculum development and to inform the process of curriculum and program evaluation. It is an effort to capture a dynamic relationship among elements that are in constant and continuously changing interaction with one another. Each of these elements is addressed next.

Learner and Teacher Characteristics   The characteristics of the learner guide and constrain all curriculum decisions. All elements of curriculum planning and evaluation must take into account the developmental level of the learners, and the presence among learners of a variety of learning styles. Previous language learning and the experiential background of the learners will also have significant influence in curriculum planning. The urban child who encounters public transportation, museums, and street vendors on a daily basis will likely be motivated by somewhat different themes and activities from those that are successful with rural students, whose world is very different.

● **FIGURE 6.1**   A Curriculum Development Framework for Language Learning

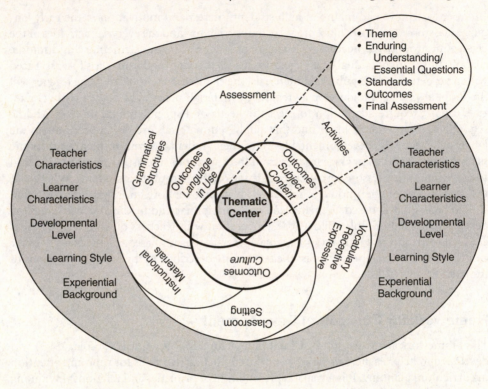

Teacher characteristics are also significant factors in curriculum planning. The teacher's language skills and experiences with the target culture will influence all aspects of instruction. The classroom should be a comfortable place for the teacher as well as for the student. Teachers will be most effective if they teach their strengths and their interests. The teacher who has spent several years in Quebec, for example, and who loves French-Canadian music and history, will probably—and appropriately—design the curriculum that reflects those interests. The teacher who loves to sing will infuse the curriculum with music.

Thematic Center   This framework establishes the thematic center as the focal point for curriculum development. The thematic center includes the theme, the targeted standards, broad unit outcomes, enduring understandings/essential questions, and culminating performance assessments. Choice of a thematic center is based on interests of the pupils and the teacher, relationship to the goals of the curriculum for the grade level or age of the class, potential for integration with the culture of the language being taught, and potential for the application and development of appropriate and useful language functions and communication modes. The focus of a thematic center might be a topic from the general school curriculum or it could be drawn from the literature or culture of the target language. The enduring understandings and essential questions of the thematic center focus all the activities of the unit and shape the decision-making process.

The curriculum for a school year consists of several thematic centers, each related to the others by systematic reinforcement of the unit just completed, and by careful preparation for and transition to the units that follow. Language functions and basic vocabulary are encountered and reinforced from unit to unit, due to the spiral character of the general elementary school curriculum. The units fit within the K–12 language framework.

Targeted Standards.   An important element of the thematic center is the standards that will be targeted during the unit of study. National, state, and local standards will play a role here. Not all standards will be addressed in every unit, but each unit should take into consideration the range of possibilities that the standards suggest.

Outcomes.   Three major groups of outcomes give substance to the thematic unit:

1. *Outcomes for language in use, or functional language outcomes.* This is the language necessary for dealing appropriately with the theme. These outcomes are not grammatical categories or vocabulary lists, but rather the functional uses of language: asking permission, explaining, giving directions, describing, and so on (see Figure 6.2). These outcomes reflect the communication goal in the Standards for Foreign Language Learning in the 21st Century.

2. *Subject content outcomes.* This is the reinforcement and extension of concepts and goals from the general elementary and middle school curriculum, reflecting the connections goal in the Standards.

3. *Culture outcomes.* These reflect experiences with patterns of thinking and behavior that are distinctively representative of communities in which the target language is used—the products, practices, and perspectives of the cultures goal in the Standards.

Making choices in these three areas and maintaining a balance among them is the fundamental work of curriculum development. Like a three-legged stool, each goal should carry equal weight in order to provide a solid foundation.

Each of these three categories for decision making overlaps with the others in significant and sometimes problematic ways. For example, at the intersection of functional language and culture, the close relationship between language and culture is evident. This relationship is so deeply and tightly established that it is sometimes difficult to separate language and culture in instruction. Such a close relationship can lead to the inappropriate assumption that whenever the language is being used, the culture is inevitably being taught. At times, this assumption has resulted in a failure to identify specific cultural outcomes and content for language curriculum. This framework represents visually the idea that even though there may be significant overlap between two of these areas, each of them also plays a distinctive and valuable role in instruction that must be planned for separately and carefully.

· ·

● **FIGURE 6.2** Communicative Functions

Functions: Ways language is used for communicative purposes (involving both initiating and reacting)

Socializing	**Getting Things Done**
Using different modes of address	Requesting
Inquiring about health	Suggesting
Greeting	Making arrangements
Introducing	Reacting to offers, requests, suggestions,
Thanking	invitations
	Inviting
Exchanging Information	Instructing
Identifying	**Expressing Attitudes**
Asking for/giving information	Admiration
Describing	Approval/disapproval
Narrating personal experiences	Interest/disinterest
Inquiring about or expressing knowledge	Friendship
Inquiring about or expressing opinions	Regret
Asking for/giving permission	Apology
Stating necessity and need	Need
Inquiring about or expressing	**Organizing and Maintaining Communication**
likes/dislikes/preferences	Attracting attention
Inquiring about or expressing wishes	Expressing lack of comprehension
	Asking for repetition or rephrasing
	Asking how to say something in the target
	language
	Asking how to spell something mentioned
	Asking someone to explain what they just
	said

Source: Adapted from *Australian Language Levels Guidelines, Book: Syllabus Development and Programming.* Woden, A.C.T.: Curriculum Development Centre, 1988, p. 69.

Both culture and subject content serve as opportunities for meaningful use of language. *Subject content* is the integrative component that melds language learning with the immediate, relevant world of the learner. *Culture* is the distinctive contribution of the language classroom to the general education of the learner. As balance is sought among these three essential components of the curriculum, it is important to avoid choosing trivial or superficial cultural and subject content elements simply to provide a token representation in the plan.

Performance Assessment   The final element of the thematic center is a culminating performance assessment. In a standards-based curriculum, the final assessment (or cluster of assessments) is the opportunity for students to show that they are able to use the language and concepts from the unit in a setting that reflects real-world language use. The American Council on the Teaching of Foreign Languages (ACTFL) recommends that the culminating assessment include the interpersonal, interpretive, and presentational modes. This culminating performance task pulls together the goals of the unit and guides all the other planning choices that have to be made.

Additional Decisions   Once all the elements of the thematic center have been established, the teacher begins to plan the unit that will lead to the outcomes and the assessment, and thus address the standards that have been selected. These decisions relate to the specific language functions that will be needed to accomplish the communication tasks and vocabulary, both receptive and expressive, necessary for interacting with the content of the unit and for successful completion of the final performance; the grammatical structures necessary for dealing appropriately with the unit; the materials and activities that will be used to advance the development of the unit; the classroom setting in which the teaching and learning will take place; and the assessment strategies that will be used during the course of the unit to measure student progress toward the final performance. The teaching of grammatical structures is understood to take place through usage and practice, rather than through analysis and drill.

Each of the decisions in this framework interacts with all earlier decisions and with one another to create a dynamic planning process that can be responsive to the particular environment of each individual setting. The framework is also intended to reflect a flexible planning process. The planner can begin with any of the elements in the process, and make decisions in any order, but all those decisions are held together with the focus of the thematic center and with the ultimate performance task(s) in mind.

The Framework and the Standards   The Framework for Curriculum Development is fully compatible with the *Standards for Foreign Language Learning in the 21st Century*. Each of the outcomes circles ties directly to one of the goals in the Standards. "Language in Use" could also be named "Communication"; "Culture" and "Cultures" are fully compatible; and "Subject Content" could easily be renamed "Connections." The remaining Standards, Comparisons, and Communities interact with the framework outcomes at several points, as illustrated in the diagrams in Figure 6.3. Standard 4.1 deals with comparing languages, and Standard 4.2 addresses comparison of cultures. The community's goal brings the learning of language, culture, and curriculum content beyond the classroom, and engages the learner with the language and the culture for lifelong learning.

• **FIGURE 6.3**   Interactions of a Curriculum Development Framework for Language Learning with Standards for Foreign Language Learning

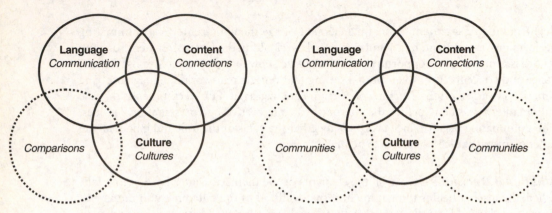

Narrative as a Design Principle/Story Form

Narrative structure has emerged as one of the most valuable of all teaching tools. Cognitive researchers such as Bruner (1990, 1996) and Sylwester (1995) have identified narrative, or story form, as one of the most significant cognitive tools available to us. The brain is wired for narrative, and as humans we use narrative as a means of organizing our own experience. The emotional component of narrative permeates experiences of all kinds and makes them more memorable. Wiggins and McTighe, in their first edition of *Understanding by Design* (2005), go so far as to suggest that planners use the logic of narrative as a principle of curricular design (p. 139).

In his seminal book, *Teaching as Story Telling* (1986), Egan lays out an entire approach to curriculum based on the power of story, suggesting that lessons or units should be approached as good stories to be told rather than sets of skills or objectives to be mastered. Egan does not mean that we must create stories around every concept we plan to teach, although incorporating stories is always effective. Instead, we should give every unit, lesson, and activity the qualities of a good story, with special attention to a clear-cut beginning, middle, and end. His emphasis on placing *meaning* at center stage, through the use of story form, makes this design principle especially appropriate for the language classroom.

Story form, or narrative structure, goes well beyond the use of stories as part of a unit or a lesson. The principles of a good story are found in a count-out rhyme, in an experiment in which students predict whether a vegetable or fruit will sink or float, and in a game, a puzzle, or a problem to solve. Task-based, project-based, and problem-based learning are other examples of story form in a curriculum.

Several strategies can help teachers design or redesign activities in story form. One way to think about it is to structure every unit and lesson toward some kind of culminating activity—and every activity toward a sense of completion and accomplishment. Like the gymnast "sticking" a landing, the learner can experience a sense of accomplishment and the "aha!" of understanding.

> **Story Form Structure**
> **Beginning**
> • Motivation
> • Engagement of the Learner
> **Middle**
> • Activity toward a Goal
> • Participation by the Learner
> **End**
> • Outcome • Product • Solution • Resolution
> • Achievement of Goal by the Learner

Prediction can be one of the most powerful tools for engaging student attention, and it is often overlooked. If students predict an outcome before they begin an activity, they are likely to have greater motivation to carry the activity through to the end. In doing a count-out rhyme with the whole class, for example, the teacher might stop when five children are left standing and ask the class to predict who will be the winner. In a popular science-related language activity, learners predict which fruits (or other items) will sink or float, and then summarize the results of their hands-on experience. These kinds of activities intensify the story form structure, and at the same time they lead to greater and more meaningful language use.

Sometimes a unit—or an activity—can lead up to a performance. Music teachers have a big advantage here—every rehearsal can be working toward a performance. But so can classroom work—it could be a play, a skit, or a conversation with a native speaker. Performance of a song, a dance, or a rhyme is a powerful motivator for accuracy and attention.

A unit that works toward a product, such as a storybook, an art display, or some other tangible and sharable product, is almost guaranteed to be in story form—and to motivate learners! Sometimes the product might be a publication, like a class newsletter or an announcement on local cable TV.

The story form strategy might be a puzzle or a problem to solve. Computer games—for instance, "Where in the World Is Carmen Sandiego?"—are a great example of this strategy. Some teachers have built entire units on a search for a "stolen" or disappeared item. The search takes them from one country to another where the target language is spoken, or from one place to another in a city in the target culture. The simple, popular activity "I See Something That You Don't See" is a much simpler example of the puzzle strategy. In this game, the teacher (or later a student) describes something or someone in plain sight and students try to identify it. Another example is the "Jigsaw" activity in cooperative learning, in which each student holds a different piece of information and the group must communicate in order to solve a problem or complete a task. The story form strategy might be like many children's picture books—establishing a repetitive pattern and then culminating with a surprising break in the pattern.

What all of these strategies have in common, and those the reader might be able to add, as well, is the fact that they give purpose to the unit, the lesson, and the activity. They have a clear-cut beginning, middle, and end. The story form, and the anticipation of the outcome, add an emotional component to learning that increases the probability that it will find a place in long-term memory.

Strategies for Developing or Intensifying Story Form:

Prediction	Puzzle
Performance	Problem to solve
Product	Pattern ⇨ surprise
Publication	Provide a frame
Pose a challenge	Play a game

Purpose

Kieran Egan Frameworks   One effective tool for organizing both the thematic unit and the daily lesson is Kieran Egan's Story Form Framework for the Mythic Layer (1986, p. 41). His suggestions for organizing instruction take into account the educational characteristics of learners at different developmental stages (see Chapter 1).

The first step in this story form framework (Identifying Importance) includes three key questions that are relevant to any grade level and to every unit, lesson, or activity we might teach:

What is most important about this topic?

Why should it matter to children?

What is affectively engaging about it?

In Egan's Planning Framework for the Romantic Layer (Middle School Years) (1992, p. 94) he suggests additional questions specifically relevant to the older learners. He advises a focus on heroes and "transcendent human qualities" such as loyalty and courage, as well as emphasis on extremes and the "limits of reality." Among his provocative questions for this group of students are the following:

What transcendent human qualities can be seen as central to the topic?

How can the content be shown in terms of human hopes, fears, intentions, or other emotions?

Does the content expose some extreme or limit of reality within the topic?

What content best allows students to pursue some aspect of the content in exhaustive detail?

These questions can help define the thematic center of the Framework for Curriculum Development, and they address the basic purpose of everything we do.

Egan's planning considerations are intended for teachers in all subject areas, and they do not specifically address the teaching of another language. In planning a daily lesson or a unit based on a thematic center, the language teacher might also ask these questions:

What language will students need to communicate about the concepts in this unit?

What kind of activities will help the students communicate?

What can I do as a teacher to motivate the students?

What kind of materials will help clarify the new information and make the experiences come alive for the learners?

What language will the learners need to practice in order to experience success in communicating throughout the unit?

What will the payoff be? What performance tasks will bring resolution to the story of the unit and show the teacher and the students themselves that the goals of the unit have been met?

Both a unit plan and a daily plan must include a variety of possible activities for meeting each goal.

Backward Design

In their landmark book *Understanding by Design,* Wiggins and McTighe (2005) describe an approach to curriculum development that builds on and enriches the educational focus on standards and performance assessment. They describe the design process in three stages.

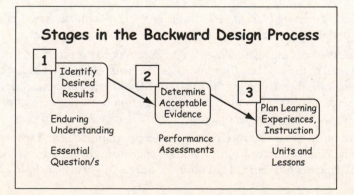

Stages in the Backward Design Process

1 Identify Desired Results

Enduring Understanding

Essential Question/s

2 Determine Acceptable Evidence

Performance Assessments

3 Plan Learning Experiences, Instruction

Units and Lessons

Stage 1 is the identification of desired results. The questions they ask bear remarkable similarity to those listed by Kieran Egan: "What should students know, understand, and be able to do? What is worthy of understanding? What enduring understandings are desired?" (p. 17).

In stage 2, the planner determines acceptable evidence that students have achieved the desired results and met the standards. The assessment possibilities range from informal checks for understanding to a performance task or project. The unit will be anchored by performance tasks or projects (pp. 22–23).

During stage 3, the teacher plans learning experiences and instructional activities. At this stage, the planner needs to (1) identify enabling knowledge and skills that students will need, (2) identify activities that will equip students with this knowledge and these skills, (3) determine what needs to be taught and how it should best be taught, (4) decide on materials and resources, and (5) determine whether the design is coherent and effective.

As with the Framework for Curriculum Development, the details of planning follow the identification of the instructional focus, or desired results, and decisions about final performance assessment.

Planning Integrated Thematic Units

Thematic teaching, as described in the Framework for Curriculum Development, provides context for concepts and activities through their relationship to a thematic center. One significant function of the theme is to focus on meaningful and interesting information and experiences as reasons for learning and using language. It also helps to connect ideas and information to make them more understandable and easier to remember. Possible themes might be selected or rejected on the basis of their potential for appropriate language in use, for salient and child-appropriate culture experiences, or for reinforcement of important concepts or skills from the general curriculum.

Resources for Thematic Planning   The first step in thematic planning is to assemble the resources and guidelines available for the planning process. At a minimum, this should include the following:

1. *Standards for Foreign Language Learning in the 21st Century,* as well as state and local foreign language standards.

2. An inventory of language-in-use (language functions) appropriate for the language level of the students. In some cases, this will be provided in a scope and sequence already existing for the program. State curriculum guidelines or a textbook series may offer inventories of language functions, or the teacher might draw from a list such as the one provided in Figure 6.2.

3. A set of outcomes for culture, drawn from a program scope and sequence or from the Framework for Cultural Competence from the American Association of Teachers of French. The culture resources might also include a locally

developed collection of cultural symbols, products, and practices, as described in Chapter 9.

4. Outcomes and standards for the content areas of the general curriculum, including mathematics, science, language arts, social studies, health, music, art, and physical education. In general, related content for thematic units can successfully be drawn from concepts and skills at grade level or from earlier grade levels. Although many curriculum concepts and skills in preschool and primary grades can be communicated successfully in the target language at grade level, language skills of students in programs may not be equal to the more sophisticated content of some curriculum areas in the middle and upper grades.

5. ACTFL Performance Guidelines for K–12 Learners (see Appendix).

Choice of Theme   Choice of a thematic center should take into consideration:

- The interests of the learners and the teacher
- Relationship to the goals of the curriculum for the grade level or age of the class
- Potential for integration with the culture of the language being taught
- Potential for story form—that is, an interesting, unfolding story line and a clear beginning, middle, and end
- A meaningful response to the question posed by Egan: "Why should it matter to children?"
- Potential for the application and development of appropriate and useful language functions and communication modes
- Potential for a meaningful culminating performance assessment with links to real-world language use

Other factors influencing the choice and development of a theme might include schoolwide or across-the-curriculum emphases, holidays or special school or community events, available materials and resources, or the presence of individuals in the school or the community with special background they can bring to the language classroom.

The focal point for a thematic center may be a topic from the general school curriculum or it may be drawn from the literature or culture of the target language. Broadly based thematic units may be designed to last for weeks—explorations, for example, or change. Other units may have more focused themes, based on a single story, a holiday, or a special occasion like a birthday celebration.

From Topic to Theme   There are many possible starting points for this process. You might start with an idea or a topic based on a curriculum concept, a poem, a story, a book, a school or grade focus, a piece of art or an artist, or a piece of music or a composer.

Deciding on a topic is really only the first step. The next step is to move from a topic to a theme. A theme is a richer basis for a unit, one that has greater potential for meaning and purpose. A topic usually involves just a loose collection of ideas, but a theme suggests a "big idea" and more focus for the unit. It provides a goal, or a destination for the learning, resulting in a planned culminating activity. We often express this goal or destination by means of a focus question that guides the activities of the unit, as we saw in the examples from the Glastonbury curriculum. We might think of the theme as a way of "putting clothes on" the topic, to make it more appealing and colorful, and to give it more personality—and a much stronger affective impact.

The topic of "house," for example, has very little potential for the richness of a theme that will really matter to learners and to their teacher. Here are some possibilities for themes developed from the topic "house," each of which suggests a possible story line and many connections:

My house of the future	The haunted house
The enchanted castle	A house of hedgehogs

The topic of "animals," as another example, may address concepts from the regular curriculum but has no focus to tie it together. Where is such a unit going? Is there enough focus for the learning to be memorable? How can we ensure that such a broad topic will provide the learners with meaningful experiences that lead to lasting learning? There is danger that such a loosely based unit will have only superficial learning results. A unit entitled "Where Do Animals Live?," on the other hand, clearly has a focus and suggests rich opportunities for learning. (See Figure 6.9 on page 171.)

Brainstorming a Web of Ideas   Once a theme has been established, the next step is to begin a brainstorming process that yields a web-like organization of ideas related through meaning to one another and to the central theme. A web is a cognitive organizer, a visual representation of concepts and their relationships that allows the curriculum planner to see how the ideas and activities relate to each other in a nonlinear fashion. Using a web allows the planner to extend the theme in many directions and to flesh out the topic with meaningful categories and subcategories (Pappas, Kiefer, and Levstik, 1990, p. 51). Although not every element from the brainstorming web may find its way into the unit, ideas and activities gathered in this way form the basis for further planning.

There are various ways to build a web, such as by subject content areas, by multiple intelligences, or in a free-form fashion.

1. *Subject Content Web.* Webbing by subject content areas (see Figure 6.4) enables you to think of activities that might otherwise be overlooked and provides a rich source of ideas for the unit. Of course, webbing around subject content topics also provides valuable links to the regular curriculum and supports content-related instruction.

2. *Multiple Intelligences Web.* Planners may also use a web based on multiple intelligences, such as that found in Figure 6.5. Using multiple intelligences as the basis for the web ensures a variety of activities to meet the needs of diverse learners.

● **FIGURE 6.4**   Webbing by Subject Content Disciplines

● **FIGURE 6.5**   Webbing by Multiple Intelligences

● **FIGURE 6.6**   Free-Form Webbing

3. *Free Form Web.* Free-form webs (see Figure 6.6) do not have any predetermined format but flow out of the brainstorming process in no particular order. When using a free form process, it is best that the planner carefully screen the web to be sure that there is a variety of activities and that all the elements (language, subject content and culture) are included.

Organizing the Planning Information   The next step is to choose targeted standards, broad unit outcomes, and culminating assessments for the theme. The assessments should include interpersonal, interpretive, and presentational tasks. Together these components constitute the thematic center for the unit. These elements and those that follow can be organized in a Unit Plan Inventory (see Figure 6.7). The Unit Plan Inventory serves as a chart for organizing information from the web. The final step in the preliminary organization may be to reexamine and refine the student outcomes for the unit. A detailed explanation on how to fill in the Unit Plan Inventory follows.

Unit Plan Inventory	Unit Title: Author(s):	Language/Level: School:

Scenario/Unit Overview:

Stage 1:   What students should know and be able to do

Enduring Understanding(s)   (Big Idea) (Students will understand that . . .)

Essential Question(s):

Targeted Question(s):

Targeted Standards: (Local, State, National)

Outcomes/Objectives/Progress Indicators: (Students will be able to . . .)

Stage 2:   How students will demonstrate what they know and can do: Performance-based Assessment

Interpersonal Task and Rubric	Interpretive Task and Rubric	Presentational Task and Rubric

Stage 3:   Preparing students to demonstrate what they know and can do

Language/Communication		Culture(s)	Subject Content (Connections)	Essential Materials	Learning Activities, Performances
Language Functions	Grammatical Structures				*(Use separate page for this section)* **Beginning** **Middle** **End**
	Vocabulary				

Comparisons:

Communities:

Explanation of Unit Plan Inventory (UPI)

Scenario

This is a short description in a few sentences summarizing the unit, including the beginning and end.

Stage 1: What Students Should Know and Be Able to Do

Enduring Understanding(s): The enduring understanding is the "Big Idea" of the unit.

Essential Question(s): The essential question gives the unit focus.

Targeted Standards: These can be the national/foreign language standards and/or local standards.

Outcomes/Objectives: Here you will list what the students will be able to do at the end of the unit (not what you are going to teach). There do not necessarily have to be three objectives; the number will depend on your unit. Remember that the outcomes must be measurable and observable and must specify what the students will be able to do. Use action verbs such as *identify, describe, demonstrate, explain,* and *classify* to help you in this process.

Stage 2: How Students Will Demonstrate What They Know and Can Do

Performance Assessments   At various points in the unit (not all at the end), you will provide assessments for the students that show that they have mastered the objectives. Be sure to assess language objectives as well as content objectives. Please provide an assessment for each of the three communication modes: interpersonal, interpretive, and presentational. Include the rubric for each of the assessments attached to the unit.

Stage 3: Preparing Students to Demonstrate What They Know and Can Do

This section of the UPI contains the inventory of functions, structures, vocabulary, materials/resources, and major learning activities/performances. As you work on your UPI, look at your web and begin to narrow down the ideas that you will actually use in this unit. Some of the ideas that you brainstormed for the web might be useful in another unit. As you refine your outcomes and assessments, you will begin to see what parts of the web you can use most successfully and what parts might not work so well, or might take too long, or might not work for other reasons.

Functions: (See Figure 6.2 earlier in this chapter.) List the language functions that you will have the students perform in the unit. Two or three functions are sufficient. Write in which context the functions will be used. For example, instead of just saying "Identify," you would say, "Identify geographical areas of Peru" or "Describe foods available at the market."

Structures: List the grammar the students will be using in the performances for this unit.

Vocabulary: List the vocabulary for the unit. You do not have to list every word, but be specific about the vocabulary so that the scope is clear. For example, say "Adjectives such as *tall, short, cold, hot*" rather than simply "Adjectives." This column helps you identify the scope of the vocabulary for the unit.

Essential Materials/Resources: What materials will you need to complete the unit? List books by name and author, name songs, and give Web addresses. Be as specific as possible. Remember others will be using your unit.

Learning Activities/Performances: This is not a complete list of all the activities but a general framework for the unit. This shows the "story form" and the flow of the unit. In the *"Beginning"* section, list some ideas for how you will motivate your students at the beginning of the unit. In the *"Middle"* section, list the skill-building activities that you will do in the middle of the unit. In the *"End"* section, include how you will end the unit and what the culminating activity will be.

Comparisons and Communities   List how the unit will relate to the Comparisons and Communities goals of the 5C's.

It is important to emphasize that all these categories relate to the thematic center; in other words, the categories flow from the choice of themes, standards, outcomes, and culminating assessment. Essentially, these are all the planning elements listed on the Planning Framework, except for classroom setting, which would likely be indicated under activities.

Laying things out on the Unit Plan Inventory helps you see the balance among the choices and assures that you are emphasizing the elements that you have decided are most important. (See Figure 6.8 and Figure 6.9 for a sample completed web and Unit Plan Inventory.)

The process we have described here is not a linear process—it is more of a spiral. At every step along the way, we need to monitor and adjust our work, so that it reflects the characteristics and content of good unit design. Throughout the planning process, it is important to monitor at each step for:

- Unit focus
- Culture elements related to outcomes
- Subject content elements related to outcomes
- Functional language related to outcomes
- Vocabulary and grammar to support functional language
- Standards-related content and activities

- Opportunities for general student growth
- Accommodation for diverse learners (styles, intelligences, thinking skills, differentiation)
- Feasibility

     Classroom setting

     Materials

     Time

- Strong beginning, middle, end

     For unit

     For activities within unit (story form)

- Engaging culminating task/activity/performance

The next step in the planning process is to organize the activities and assessments in a logical sequence, to ensure that there is a careful progression and a well-developed beginning, middle, and end. At this point, it is time to begin planning the daily lessons.

● **FIGURE 6.8** Sample Completed Web

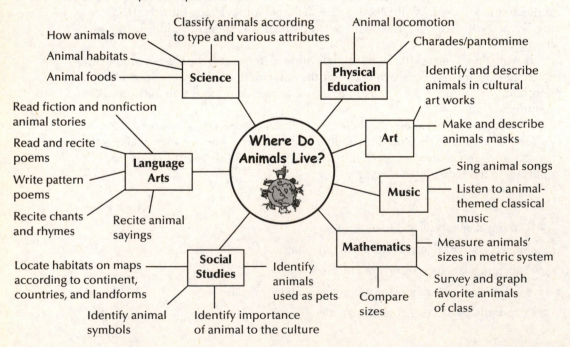

● FIGURE 6.9   Sample Completed Unit Plan Inventory

Unit Plan Inventory	Unit Title: Where do Animals Live?	Language Level: Novice Grade Level:

Unit Overview: After learning about animals and their various homes, students at the end of the unit show that they have integrated their learning by creating an imaginary animal and describing it from various aspects.

Stage 1:   What students should know and be able to do

Enduring Understanding(s):   Students will understand that all living things need a place to live.

Essential Questions(s):   Where do animals live?

Standards: (Local and/or National) 1.1, 1.2, 1.3, 2.1, 3.1 (*Local standards are not filled in here because the sources will vary.*)

Outcomes/Objectives/Progress Indicators: Students will be able to compare and contrast selected animals based on specific criteria such as habitat, size, movement, color and cultural connections

Stage 2:   How students will demonstrate what they know and can do: Performance Assessment

Interpersonal Task and Rubric	Interpretive Task and Rubric	Presentational Task and Rubric
Each student will take on the role of one of the animals and interview another student.	Students will listen to (or read) a story about an animal looking for its habitat and draw a series of pictures that retell the story.	Create an original product relating to animals and present it to the class or another audience. For example: Create an imaginary animal and describe its appearance and habitat

Stage 3:   Preparing students to demonstrate what they know and can do

Language Functions	Grammatical Structures	Key Vocabulary	Culture(s)	Subject Content	Essential Materials	Major Learning Activities/ Performances
Describe animal appearance and characteristics Identify animals by name and habitat Express likes and dislikes Ask questions concerning animal characteristics	Comparisons 1st- 2nd- 3rd-person singular of verbs: like live eat be see Verb to be is, are	Adjectives to describe: color speed size texture personality Nouns for animals habitats geographic regions continents Verbs for animal movement	Animal sounds Symbolic animals Cultural importance of animals Animal sayings Animal stories Animal songs Artists and animals	• Science habitats, animal food locomotion • Mathematics measuring, animal sizes, comparing sizes, graphing favorite animals of class • Geography locations of habitats • Fine Arts animal paintings make masks • Language Arts animal stories fiction and non-fiction pattern poems	Maps Animal pictures Art prints Art supplies Pattern poem examples	BEGINNING • Fantasy (virtual) trip to various habitats MIDDLE • Identify animals using art prints • Match animal with habitat • Locate world habitats on a map • Ask questions about animal hidden in bag • Do animals jigsaw activity • Do Finding Differences partner activities • Use rhymes, songs related to animals • Survey animal likes and dislikes in class • Graph animals according to attributes, habitats • Compare & contrast pets in various countries • Identify animal symbols in various countries • Classify animals in various categories, e.g. number of legs, color, locomotion, etc. • Take on animal identity and participate in interviews • Move like an animal • Make and describe animal masks • Write animal poem (cinquain/diamante) END • Create a story about favorite animal OR • Create fantasy animal and describe it and its habitat

Comparisons: Compare and contrast pets in various countries.
Communities: Share presentations with audience outside school.

171

Some Challenges of Planning Thematically

When putting together a thematic unit, there are sometimes so many possible connections that it can be hard to know when to stop! It is likely that not all of the activities developed during the brainstorming process will be used in the current unit, and that is how it should be. These good ideas are not wasted, since many of them can be used in future units.

It is possible to push thematic teaching to the extent that it could seem artificial. One of the authors heard about a primary school teacher who decided on a "bears" focus in her class. Her students did math with teddy bear counters, solved bear word problems, read story after story about bears, ate bear cookies, put up a bears bulletin board, and so on and on and on. Although each of these activities was engaging in itself, the bear focus went on for so long that one of the students asked, "Do we have to talk about bears again?" The lesson here is that we need to be aware of how far to take a topic and also to gauge our students' interest in a topic. This example illustrates a topically based and not thematically based web, but it still brings across the idea that we must not overdo any material. Common sense must rule when we are planning thematically!

When planning thematic units that are content-related, we do *not* expect young learners to master all aspects of the content area we are drawing from, in contrast to immersion and bilingual programs where students must master the grade-level curriculum. In content-related instruction we are using various subject areas to make connections with the regular school curriculum and to give the students rich, cognitively engaging materials for language use. The focus in content-related instruction is on language learning; the content is used as a vehicle to make that learning more engaging.

● Planning the Daily Lesson

The importance of a written plan cannot be overemphasized. There is a remarkable correlation between the presence of a detailed written plan and the ability of a teacher to be creative and flexible in the actual class setting. Many early language programs have a very limited amount of class time in which to give children experiences with the target language. Only careful planning can prevent the loss and misuse of time, which is already in very short supply.

Objectives/Outcomes

The careful formulation of written objectives (sometimes called *outcomes*) will help the teacher plan relevant activities and coherent lessons. Effective objectives always describe what students will be able to do at the end of the lesson. The statements include action verbs that represent a student activity that is observable. Verbs such as *teach, learn,* and *understand* are not useful because they describe process rather than outcome, and because they are essentially unobservable. It is often helpful to think of each objective as beginning with the phrase "The students will be able to . . . ."

Here are some examples of objectives for a beginning elementary school foreign-language class.

Students will be able to do the following:

Communication

- Exchange appropriate greetings with the teacher or a classmate.
- Point to a day of the week on the calendar when it is named.
- Identify numerals 0 to 5 when they are not in sequence.
- Respond correctly to the following commands, individually and in a group:

stand up	sit down
point to . . .	touch . . . (color, number, body part)
walk	turn around

- Respond with name when asked "What is your name?" (Some children will also say "My name is . . . .")

Cultures

- Identify items or pictures relating to celebrations, traditions, holidays, or events of the target culture.
- Imitate classroom gestures and courtesy expressions commonly used in target culture.
- Name important customs, holidays, or events.
- Sing songs, play games, and celebrate events from target culture.

Connections

- Use numbers to count and tell the date; describe the weather and seasons.
- Sort objects according to attributes (e.g., color, shape, length, and size); identify units of time (e.g., days of the week and months).
- Name and demonstrate the relative position of objects (e.g., over, under, inside, and outside).
- Identify simple land forms; identify common animals in students' own culture as well as the target cultures.
- Categorize foods into groups (e.g., fruits, vegetables, grains, and meat).
- Count to 100; identify elements (e.g., shape and color) in their own and others' art works.
- Identify and use appropriate terms of measurement, currency, and time (e.g., measure clothing in centimeters, count target culture money, and tell time).
- Locate target language country/countries on the globe or world map, using a visual or an oral cue.
- Retell a story by charting or graphing important elements, with teacher assistance.

Elements of the Daily Plan

The daily lesson plan should provide the teacher with easy reference to the key elements of the day's instruction. One format that works well is the following:

Sample Lesson Plan Format

Theme:
Lesson Title or Topic:
Standards Addressed:

Outcomes or Objectives:
    Language
    Culture
    Content

Assessment:

Materials:

Lesson Outline:
    Warm-Up
    Introduction
    Lesson Activities or Procedures
    Closure

Follow-Up/Homework:
Reflection:
Special Considerations:

Theme   Begin by listing the theme. This helps you to keep in mind where you have been and where you are going with the theme on which you are working. It's also helpful to list a lesson title or topic. This title, of course, refers to the theme.

Standards   Here, you list the foreign language standards that you are targeting in this lesson, and possibly other standards that support the goals of the lesson. It isn't realistic to try to include all eleven Standards in a single lesson, but communication Standards should always be represented.

Outcomes or Objectives   Next, identify observable student outcomes for the lesson. Outcomes or objectives also describe student behavior at the end of the lesson. The components of Language, Culture, and Content are listed as a reminder to keep them in balance over the course of the unit. Some teachers note which of the components are represented in each objective. Individual objectives might include more than one of these key components.

Assessment   The assessment category describes any procedures for determining student performance during this lesson. If you are doing a formal assessment, provide the needed rubrics or checklists on separate pages at the end of the lesson. This would also be a place to indicate names of students for whom you intend to do an informal assessment.

Materials   It is valuable to indicate on the lesson plan which materials you need for the lesson, so you can see at a glance what you have to bring with you to class or to prepare in advance. This is especially important if you are a traveling teacher.

Lesson Outline   Here, you provide a step-by-step description of activities and procedures, with a time designation for each one. As you plan for the class flow, it is important to keep in mind what you have learned from cognitive theorists. The first five minutes and the last five minutes of a class period are prime learning time. You must use this precious learning time very carefully, and make sure that it isn't wasted in routine or unchallenging, undirected activity.

Within this step-by-step lesson outline, you should plan for:

- Warm-Up: to help students make the transition from their previous activity to the language class. Often the warm-up consists of an opening routine.

- Introduction: introducing the lesson for the day, and informing the students so they know the objectives of the lesson.

- Lesson Activities or Procedures: a step-by-step guide on how you will present the main part of the lesson and how students will practice the lesson components. Be sure that there is sufficient variety in the activities you have planned. Early language learners need variety and are unable to stay on task if an activity is too long. Eric Jensen (2005) suggests a maximum of 5 to 7 minutes of focused attention time for grades K through 2, 8 to 12 minutes for grades 3 through 7, and 12 to15 minutes for grades 8 through 12.

- Closure: how you will bring the lesson to a close. This could be the culminating activity of the lesson, or an opportunity for students to demonstrate their new learning.

Follow-Up/Homework   How will you follow up on this lesson? If you assign homework, list it here and indicate whether handouts will be needed.

Reflection   How did the lesson go? Here, you make notes on items to remember for the next time that you teach the lesson, or the next time you meet with this class. Observations about individual students might also be listed.

Other Considerations   It is important to plan in advance for strategies within the lesson to help you meet the needs of the diverse student populations in your classes. This includes attention to differentiation, as described later in this chapter, and modifications for students who have special needs.

Alternate Lesson Plan Format

Greg Duncan, national consultant for languages education, has devised a lesson plan format based on *backward planning*. This format very simply and effectively plans for the basic element of the questions posed by Wiggins and McTighe in the three stages of planning.

Sample Lesson Plan Format Based on Understanding by Design

Unit: _____   Lesson Number: _____

Grade Level: _____   Time of Year to Be Taught: _____

Stage One: What will students know and be able to do at the end of this lesson?

Do

Know

Stage Two: How will you know that students can do that?

Stage Three: What instructional activities will be used?

Opening Activity

Activity 2

Activity 3

Activity 4

Activity 5

(and so on)

Closing Activity

Materials needed for this lesson:

Source: Reprinted by permission of Greg Duncan.

Sharing the Lesson Plan with Students

Writing a lesson plan or a lesson outline on the board actually helps students to anticipate the variety of activities they will experience and to feel a sense of progress through the lesson or through the material. The plan itself can become the object of meaningful communication and language practice, as the teacher asks learners to remind her or him of the next activity, or invites them to choose an activity from those remaining. Teachers in some advanced classes write the day's schedule in sentences on the chalkboard, and it becomes a class activity at the end of the lesson or the day to rewrite the sentences in the past tense to show that the activity has been completed. Rather than talking about changing the tense of the verb, the teacher might say, "This sentence isn't true anymore; how can we change it to make it right?" In some classes, especially immersion classes, the revised daily schedule could be written in a class diary, illustrated, and used to maintain a class history.

● Differentiation

We know that all students are unique and bring to the classroom their own strengths and needs. Based on this fact, differentiated instruction attempts to provide students with multiple options for taking in information and making sense of ideas. Differentiated instruction asks that teachers be flexible in their approach to teaching and that they adjust the curriculum and presentation of information to learners rather than expecting all the learners to be able to accomplish the demands of the curriculum in the same way. The intent of differentiating instruction is to maximize each student's growth and individual success by meeting each student where he or she is, and assisting in the learning process. In differentiated instruction, every student is learning the same thing but may be learning it in a different way. The key to a differentiation is that students are offered choices and are matched with tasks compatible with their individual learner profiles.

Differentiated instruction is based on the following beliefs (Tomlinson, 2001):

- Students differ in their learning profiles.
- Classrooms in which students are active learners, decision makers, and problem solvers are more natural and effective than those in which students are served a "one-size-fits-all" curriculum and treated as passive recipients of information.
- Making meaning out of important ideas is the focus rather than "covering information."

Tomlinson (2001) states that curriculum should be differentiated in three areas:

Content. Multiple options for taking in information
Process. Multiple options for making sense of the ideas
Product. Multiple options for expressing what they know

Suzanne Irujo (2008) offers some valuable general principles regarding differentiation:

1. Differentiated instruction is not the same as individualized instruction. Every student is not learning something different; they are all learning the same thing, but in different ways. And every student does not need to be taught individually; differentiating instruction is a matter of presenting the same task in different ways and at different levels, so that all students can approach it in their own ways.

2. The basis for differentiation must be your knowledge of the standards that your students must achieve and of where each of them is with respect to those

standards. In order to know this, you must have a workable record-keeping system based on observation of students' performance during learning activities.

3. If you have classroom management problems, you need to solve those before you can begin to differentiate instruction. Many teachers "aim down the middle" because it's the only way they can keep control of the class.

4. Change only works when it is done one small step at a time. Many teachers make the mistake of trying to change too much at one time. Then nothing works because they can't focus on a large number of new things at the same time, so they give up on trying to change.

5. Reading about examples of differentiated instruction and talking with other teachers who are doing it can be very helpful. Remember, however, that what works in one context may not work in yours.

Factors to Consider When Planning the Lesson

Warm-Up   Each early language class period, regardless of its length, should begin with a brief warm-up. This is a time for communicative use of completely familiar language. The warm-up has several purposes:

1. It provides a review and a basis for new material to be introduced.

2. It provides a transition from the instructional time the students have just experienced in their native language to an intensive experience of learning and thinking in the target language.

3. Because of the relatively easy level at which the warm-up is conducted, it helps students build or regain confidence in their ability to work with the target language. At some point in the warm-up, every child should have the opportunity to say something in the target language, either individually, in a small group, or in the larger group.

4. It provides a time during which teachers and students alike can share dimensions of their personalities and their interests—as they talk about likes and dislikes, families, weather (and how they deal with it)—and they can personalize applications of material they have learned earlier in a more structured setting.

The warm-up does not "just happen." It must be carefully planned to include different material and strategies each day.

Balance of Old and New Material   Learners need a great deal of practice with new material before they are able to appropriate it for their own functional, communicative purposes. Every class period should contain some new and some familiar material; the exact balance will vary from day to day. One of the teacher's tasks is to make the old material seem new and the new material seem familiar. The teacher must plan for many different contexts within which to practice, in order to prevent boredom with the practice and to provide the children with a sense of progress—the old always seems new because the message to be communicated has a new context and the need to communicate that message is also new. For example, when children are first introduced to numbers, they might count objects, participate in a count-out rhyme, guess which number the teacher has hidden in her or his hand, participate in a concentration game with numbers, play the game "Go Fish" with number cards, roll giant dice and call out the numbers, sing a song based on numbers, provide the number preceding or following a number given by the teacher, and so forth. For cultural emphasis, the teacher can show the students how to count with fingers in the target culture since this may be different from the way we count on fingers in the United States. Each activity presents a new context and a new challenge, but in the process the learners have practiced the numbers vocabulary enough for it to become automatic.

Introducing New Material   When introducing new material, the teacher tries to build on what students have already learned so that they have maximum security and self-confidence. For example, on the first day of class, the teacher might point out, if appropriate, some relationships and cognates between the native language and the target language, and show how many of the target-language words the student may already be familiar with without realizing it. When the class hears a new song, poem, story, or another message for the first time, the teacher may invite the students to identify familiar words and phrases. In order to facilitate this task of making the new seem familiar, the teacher will consciously "seed" or plant material in the lesson for Monday that will appear in a larger context on Wednesday or Thursday, so that the later, longer message will not seem entirely new—familiar material is already present.

For example, a German teacher has decided to introduce a birthday song because one of the students has a birthday on Thursday:

Zum Geburtstag viel Glück! (Good luck/happiness on your birthday!)

Zum Geburtstag viel Glück! (Good luck/happiness on your birthday!)

Langes Leben und Gesundheit! (Long life and good health!)

Zum Geburtstag viel Glück! (Good luck/happiness on your birthday!)

On Monday, the teacher introduces the exclamation *viel Glück! (Good luck!)* in the course of a game, demonstrating the contrast between the American gesture of crossed fingers and the German gesture of pressing thumbs to symbolize a good-luck wish. The exclamation is reentered at every opportunity during the course of the week. On Tuesday, the lesson includes the opposites *kurz* and *lang (short* and *long),* applied during a TPR exercise at the chalkboard in which learners draw monsters with long and short hair, long and short arms and legs, and long and short ears and noses. On Wednesday, the teacher pretends to have a cold, sneezing frequently, and the students are taught to wish the teacher and one another *Gesundheit,* which is already somewhat familiar to them. By Thursday, the only new words in the birthday song are the word for *birthday* itself, *Geburtstag,* which the teacher explains by means of showing a birthday cake and presents, and the word for *life, Leben,* which the teacher may explain by contrasting a long life of someone who is 96 years old with a short life of someone who is 2 years old. After listening to the song one or two times (and with a minimum of repetition) the students are ready to sing the birthday song.

Planning from day to day should incorporate these linkages. The teacher should constantly be helping students recognize these links, so that the students discover language learning as a cumulative process, in contrast to what seems so often to be the case in other classes, where learning for the test (and later forgetting) seems somehow to be acceptable and inevitable.

Routines   Every class period, especially in the primary grades, should include a certain number of regular, predictable classroom routines that make heavy use of language repetition and patterned teacher–student interaction. "Show-and-Tell" and the calendar activities that begin the day in many primary classrooms are examples of such routines. These routines provide learners with a sense of security, and they also give "meaning clues" to the content discussed in the course of the activity. Special routines are common for line-ups to leave for another classroom, or for changing activities within the classroom. Passing out or turning in papers becomes an opportunity for routine use of language for many teachers.

A caveat regarding the calendar routine: Calendar activities are especially useful at the beginning stages, but as students progress in the language, the calendar should take up less and less time, in order to leave more time for what the students are currently learning. In some classes, the calendar routines never change, year after year, even though students no longer need practice with the language and the concepts involved. When this occurs, valuable time is lost for new and more engaging material, and student progress and motivation are affected.

Variety   Each class period should also include a number and variety of activities. In general, the younger the students in a class, the greater the number of different activities planned for each class period. The attention span increases with the age of the child, but even in the middle school/junior high, activities should rarely last longer than 10 minutes, and they should usually be planned to last from 5 to 8 minutes.

Activities should be developed with attention to high- and low-energy requirements on the part of both the teacher and the students. The teacher might think in terms of planning for peaks and valleys of excitement, of movement, or of physical and verbal involvement. The early language teacher should plan activities at the end of the class period that leave the children ready to go on to work in other classes. Closing a class period with a game that leaves the children excited, unmanageable, or noisy will not earn the appreciation or the future cooperation of their next teacher.

Each lesson should include a balance of active and quiet activities, of large-group and small-group or partner activities, and of one-way and two-way communication. It is very important for learners to have the opportunity to ask questions as well as to answer them and, especially in the TPR-oriented classroom, to give directions as well as to respond to them. It is also wise to plan for a change of pace and activities that involve movement outside of the desk or the learning circle. Songs, games, and rhymes with actions can change the tempo and the emphasis of a class period, while continuing to further communicative goals.

Interactive Homework   Some teachers find it very useful to use homework as a means of connecting the language classroom with the home. When they give students tasks to complete at home and ask for parent signatures on the work, parents become more aware of what is happening in the classroom, and this can translate into greater support for learning. Students can read a book or a story that they have written or copied, name all the foods at a meal, teach their family a series of TPR commands, perform a TPR Storytelling variation, label the objects in their bedroom—the list is virtually endless. Teachers in Pinellas County, Florida, use a system of interactive homework as an assessment tool (see Chapter 7) (Gilzow and Branaman, 2000). In programs that have very limited class time, interactive homework can be a means of extending the students' amount of exposure to their new language.

● Planning for an Entire Sequence of Instruction

The focus of this chapter is to create thematic units that will be used within a framework of K–12 instruction. The same principles and processes can also guide planning for a year or for a whole program. Figure 6.10 gives an example of how a thematic unit might fit into an entire sequence of instruction.

● Planning for Immersion, Bilingual, and Content-Based Instruction

Planning in an immersion or bilingual content-based classroom will focus on and take its direction from the goals of the subject content area. One major difference between the classroom in which a second language is the medium of instruction and the native-language classroom is that planning focuses on language development and on subject content goals at the same time in the second-language classroom. While the organizing principle for instruction will be the subject-matter content, the language skills necessary to progress in communication about subject matter content must also be intentionally developed through the planning process. This suggests that it will sometimes be necessary to do language development activities in preparation for or as a component of a lesson directed toward subject content goals. The teacher of subject content in a second language must always be aware of the language skills demanded by the concepts and the activities involved in the subject content goals. The teacher must also plan carefully for the concrete experiences and the visual reinforcement that will make the academic language

● **FIGURE 6.10** From Standards to the Classroom

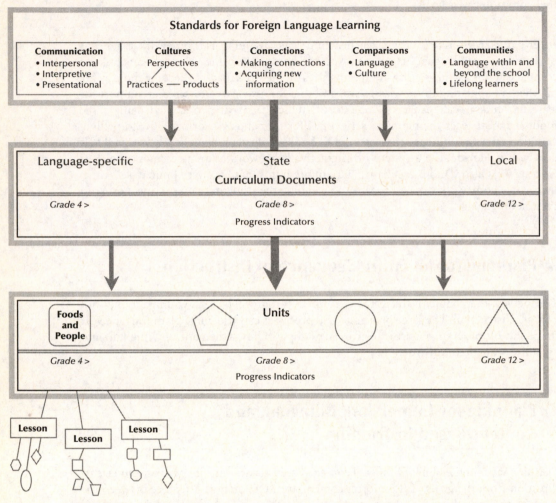

of instruction comprehensible to the students and help them develop the linguistic skills necessary for dealing with the subject content material.

A further difference found in the immersion or content-based language classroom is the added priority of providing cultural insight, information, and experiences as an important part of the curriculum. The time and effort required to deliver significant components of the general curriculum in a second language can sometimes result in a short-changing of culture goals in a content-based curriculum. Like language development, culture must be systematically incorporated into each unit and lesson in order to provide students with the best possible learning experience.

Summary

- Careful planning can help the language teacher make the most of the limited time available for instruction in the target language.

- One meaningful approach to planning curriculum is the development of integrated thematic units that incorporate the key elements of language-in-use, subject content, and culture.

- Effective planning takes into account the educational development of the students and draws on such approaches as story form, backward design, and differentiation to make learning more meaningful and more memorable.

- The careful preparation of student-oriented objectives and a written plan can free the teacher to be flexible and creative during the class period, responding to the needs and interests of the learners as they develop without losing the direction and focus of the lesson.

- Each plan should be organized around the needs and development of the learner and take into account the learner's need for both variety and routine.

For Study and Discussion

1. How can the preparation of student-oriented objectives and a carefully written plan free the teacher to be creative and flexible during the class period?

2. Choose a potential theme for a unit in your language and develop a web of possible concepts and content for the unit. Share the web with a colleague and check for the presence of language-in-use, culture, and subject content. Select the content from the web and lay it out on the unit plan inventory.

3. Write a lesson plan for teaching a content-related topic.

4. Write a lesson plan for teaching a culture-related topic.

5. Choose a song or a game you would like to teach to your class because it reinforces or anticipates basic concepts that are a part of the curriculum. Analyze it for unfamiliar vocabulary, and build a plan for "seeding" that new vocabulary over a period of several days.

6. Write a set of objectives, phrased in student terms, for teaching the song or game in question 5.

For Further Reading

The following sources are recommended for additional information about material covered in this chapter. Chapter citations are documented in Works Cited at the end of the book.

Egan, Kieran. *Imagination in Teaching and Learning: The Middle School Years.* Chicago: University of Chicago Press, 1992.

Egan, Kieran. *Primary Understanding.* New York: Routledge, 1988.

Egan, Kieran. *Teaching as Story Telling.* Chicago: University of Chicago Press, 1986.

Gilzow, Douglas F., and Lucinda E. Branaman. *Lessons Learned: Model Early Foreign Language Programs.* McHenry, IL: Center for Applied Linguistics and Delta Systems Co., 2000.

Gregory, Gayle. *Differentiated Instructional Strategies in Practice.* Thousand Oaks, CA: Corwin Press, 2003.

Gregory, Gayle, and Carolyn Chapman. *Differentiated Instructional Strategies: One Size Doesn't Fit All.* Thousand Oaks, CA: Corwin Press, 2002.

Irujo, Suzanne. "Differentiated Instruction: We Can No Longer Just Aim Down the Middle." *ELL Outlook™*. Retrieved June 18, 2008, from http://www.coursecrafters.com/ELLOutlook/2004/sept_oct/ELLOutlookITIArticle2.htm.

Jensen, Janis, and Paul Sandrock with John Franklin. *The Essentials of World Languages Grades K–12 Effective Curriculum, Instruction, and Assessment.* Alexandria, VA: Association for Supervision and Curriculum Development, 2007.

Patrick, Paula. *The Keys to the Classroom: A Basic Manual to Help New Classroom Teachers Find Their Way.* Alexandria, VA: American Council on the Teaching of Foreign Languages, 2008.

Sandrock, Paul. *Planning Curriculum for Learning World Languages.* Madison, WI: Wisconsin Department of Public Instruction, 2002.

Theisen, Toni. Differentiated Instruction in the Foreign Language Classroom: Meeting the Diverse Needs of All Learners. *Communique.* Austin, TX: Languages Other Than English Center for Educator Development, Southwest Educational Development Laboratory. Retrieved 2006 from http://www.sedl.org/loteced/communique/n06.pdf.

Tomlinson, Carol Ann. *How to Differentiate Instruction in Mixed Ability Classrooms* (2nd ed.). Alexandria, VA: Association for Supervision and Curriculum Development, 2001.

Tomlinson, Carol Ann, and Jay McTighe. *Integrating Differentiated Instruction and Understanding by Design: Connecting Content and Kids.* Alexandria, VA: Association for Supervision and Curriculum Development, 2006.

Wiggins, Grant, and Jay McTighe. *Understanding by Design* (2nd ed.). Alexandria, VA: Association for Supervision and Curriculum Development, 2005.

Chapter 7

Using Assessment to Help Students and Programs Grow

Enduring Understanding

- Assessment is an essential element of planning and instruction.

Essential Question

- What kinds of assessment will help me and my students reach our language learning goals?

● Student Assessment

When elementary or middle school language teachers gather at conferences and in-service meetings, or when they communicate on listservs, there is a constant flow of good ideas. They exchange games and activities, suggestions for songs, patterns for visuals, recipes for in-class food activities, and so on. They rarely exchange ideas for assessment, record keeping, reporting, or grading.

The tendency to focus on ideas and innovations for presenting material and developing activities is not found exclusively at the elementary and middle school levels, or exclusively among classroom teachers. Assessment of student performance has received far less time and attention in many methods classes and methods books, in conference programs, and in teacher in-service sessions than techniques for motivating students, planning curriculum, and managing the classroom. Methods for measuring student achievement within the communication-oriented classroom have not kept pace with methods for presenting materials and for giving students the opportunity to use language in communicative ways.

Assessment of student learning has acquired new relevance, however, in a world language community focused on standards, proficiency, and communication. Instead of being the last priority for consideration in planning curriculum and instruction, standards and assessment have become the starting point for "backward design," a process of working from final student products and performances back to content and activities.

The reorganization of the curriculum around standards and communicative goals requires a similar radical reorganization of assessment philosophy and practices. The results of communicative, standards-based programs can no longer be assessed with the same philosophy and using the same methods that have been used for decades. The popular and familiar discrete-point test, which measures grammar and vocabulary items in isolation, unrelated to meaningful context, is clearly an inappropriate measure for the achievement of communicative goals. It may have been somewhat more appropriate for assessing student performance in programs with a grammar-translation emphasis or based on the behaviorist principles of the audiolingual method. Yet, because these methods of assessment have both the security of familiarity and the illusion of objectivity, they continue to play a dominant role in many classrooms.

The discrepancy between *what is taught* and *what is tested* threatens both the credibility of communicative goals as they are stated and their chance of being realized. When students and parents perceive a discrepancy between the stated goals of a course and the contents of achievement tests, they invariably—and appropriately—believe the message of the testing. Sandra Savignon (1997) summarizes the problem very effectively:

> The most important implication of the concept of communicative competence is undoubtedly the need for tests that measure an ability to use language effectively to attain communicative goals. Discrete-point tests of linguistic structures of the kind developed in the 1960s have not only failed to sufficiently take into account the complexity and dynamic quality of the communicative setting, in some cases, they have also served, in their emphasis on grammatical accuracy, to discourage the strategies needed for communicative competence and thus to hinder the development of more communicative curricula. A language course that sets out to "cover" all the points of grammar presented in a basic textbook, and then tests learners on their "mastery" of these points, has little time left for communication. (p. 223)

Discrete-point tests are particularly inappropriate as a means of measuring the richness and diversity of the language acquired by the young learner in a communicative, standards-oriented classroom. As we grow more sophisticated in our ability to capitalize on the meaning-making ability of the learner, as we allow students to draw from a rich target-language environment in individually meaningful ways, and as we encourage learners to build their own structures of meanings and expression in the target language, we lose control of the bits and pieces that are easily measurable by traditional means. At the same time, the obligation to assess, the need to describe learning in a meaningful way, takes on even greater importance. Both the pressure toward accountability to standards and the requirements of effective articulation from one program level to another demand meaningful assessment practices and clear means of communicating student achievement within the profession, the school, and the community.

This kind of pressure can lead us to embrace familiar assessment measures, and perhaps even to compromise our goals for early language programs in order to make them more easily measurable by available means. The performance of a learner who is participating in a meaning-filled, communicatively oriented, developmentally appropriate early language program must be assessed and reported by meaning-filled, communicative, developmentally appropriate means. Otherwise, the entire basis on which new programs are developed is threatened. As Egan (1988) notes, "We must be wary of the temptation to make learning cruder, so that we can measure it more securely" (p. 240).

Importance of Assessing Student Performance

In many early language programs the problem is not so much inappropriate assessment as it is an absence of formal assessment measures altogether. Because of the nature of program goals and the large number of students each teacher sees in a day or in a week, assessment of student achievement may receive little priority in these programs. Some teachers are concerned that testing or assessment of any kind will raise anxiety levels and lower motivation in their classes, especially among students who have been unsuccessful in much of the traditional school curriculum. Yet, learners and their parents often take seriously only those subjects for which there is regular assessment and reporting; any tendency to regard the language class as an "extra," or as a subject area of less than equal status with the rest of the curriculum, is reinforced by the absence of regular, careful student assessment and reporting.

In fact, assessment is just as essential to planning and instruction as are the choice of theme, identification of targeted standards, and selection of language, content, and culture goals. The culminating performance assessment is a critical component of the thematic center, and the assessment circle is the largest in the third layer of the Framework for Curriculum Development (see Figure 6.1 on page 154), suggesting that it is the first of these six categories to be considered, the doorway to all other planning considerations. In fact, every step in the decision-making process is linked to assessment, from theme selection to decisions about standards and content to be addressed. Well-written outcomes contain or imply an assessment strategy. The first step in structuring any lesson is to ask the twin questions, "What do I expect students to be able to do as a result of this instruction?" and "How will I know if they have met this goal?" The answers to these questions are of interest and importance to students as well as to the teacher, to parents, and to all other stakeholders in the educational setting.

One reason for the uneasiness often felt by early language teachers about the topic of assessment may be common perceptions of testing and reporting that most of us have encountered in our own educational journeys. Often, testing is experienced as something teachers—the empowered—do to students for purposes of rendering (often negative) value judgments about the students' work. It is not surprising that teachers who place a high value on motivating students and helping them to feel competent and successful are uncomfortable with the idea of testing; they might even put it off and try to avoid it altogether.

Some of this uneasiness can perhaps be overcome if all parties in the assessment process change the emphasis in assessment from making judgments to gathering information. This information can be used to recognize and celebrate progress, identify areas for more intense effort, and describe levels of proficiency for the benefit of planning and articulation, among many other possibilities.

It is important to keep in mind, then, that assessment is more than simply giving and grading quizzes and tests and then marking report cards. Effective assessment is a complex and ongoing process.

Assessment Process

Discussion of the assessment process brings to mind a cartoon in which a little boy comes up to the teacher after class and asks, "What did I learn today, Miss Jones? My mother will want to know."

That cartoon is a good reminder that determining what has been learned in the classroom is important—for the teacher, of course, but also for the parent. And probably most important of all, our students also need help in recognizing their own progress in language learning. Before we begin the assessment process, we must identify what information we need in order to determine whether our goals have been met. This question comes at the beginning of the planning process, when we set the goals for our unit or our lesson. Asking this question during initial planning helps us to decide on the performance tasks—the products and performances—that will focus the unit, and to determine the evidence we will need to find out what the students have learned.

Our focus in the assessment process itself, then, is finding out and reporting what has been learned. This process has three major components: assessment, evaluation, and grading.

Assessment   *Assessment,* the first component of the process, is the gathering of data or information. Our question here is: What information do I need to gather in order to find out if the goals for this segment of learning have been met? And how will that evidence best be gathered?

Evaluation   The second component, *evaluation,* is interpreting the data or information that has been gathered. The critical issue is to determine what criteria I will use to judge the quality of the student work. There are many questions at this step, including the following:

What are the most important aspects of the performance on which I will be providing students with feedback?

Have I prepared my students to be evaluated on these criteria (have they had sufficient practice and preparation to hold them accountable on these criteria)?

Are the evaluation criteria focused on the quality of the performance or merely on the completion of the task?

How does the information compare with other information I may already have?

How important is it, in relationship to other information?

What other information do I need?

Grading   The last element of the process is *grading,* the process of transforming assessment data or information into a symbol that communicates the results of an evaluation.

● Performance Assessment

Much of education in the twenty-first century is moving toward standards-based education and alternative forms of assessment, in an effort to match the goals of curriculum more effectively with the assessment evidence we gather. In addition, the effort is to link the assessment tasks with student activity in their world, and to measure achievement of these goals in terms of application of knowledge rather than rote learning. The focus on performance assessment is particularly appropriate for world languages, since proficiency in the use of the language—performance—is the true measure of what students know and are able to do.

This emphasis on performance is a very good fit with both the goals and the practices of standards- and communication-based, integrative curriculum in the elementary and middle school language program. Wiggins (1992) offers several suggestions for the design of tasks for performance assessment (pp. 27–28):

1. Contextualize the task. Provide rich contextual detail.

2. Aim to design "meaningful" tasks—not the same as "immediately relevant or practical" tasks. A context, a problem, or a task can be invented as well as be of actual, direct relevance to a learner's surroundings. Helping to identify an alien's home planet through a series of questions and answers could be a meaningful and interesting way to see if students recognize descriptions, although it is not immediately relevant or practical.

3. Design performances, not drills. A test of many items (a drill) is not a test of knowledge in use. Performance is not about desired bits of knowledge, but about "putting it all together" with good judgment.

4. Refine the tasks you design by building them backwards from the models and scoring criteria. Students should know the target and the standard in advance.

As with language acquisition itself, the most authentic and potentially the richest source of meaningful context for the young learner is the language classroom. Several possibilities for gathering meaningful information about student performance within the classroom setting are suggested next.

What Did I Learn Today?

It is a challenge for teachers—and students—to gather information about what has been learned during a class, a unit, or a marking period, especially when classes are short and the teacher sees many students in a day. The early language teacher needs many different strategies for gathering this kind of information, and the most meaningful and reliable of these strategies are performance tasks, a form of performance assessment.

Performance Tasks

Performance tasks differ significantly from traditional paper-and-pencil approaches to assessment. Like the Standards themselves, they focus on what students can do with language, rather than what they know about language or their ability to manipulate bits of knowledge about language. A *performance task* is a product or a performance that calls for the student to use the competencies and the vocabulary from a unit of instruction in a meaningful context, preferably a context that replicates the challenges of the "real world."

The following performance task was developed for middle school students at the novice-high or early intermediate level, after several years of language study. It was designed to be the culmination of a unit on weather, and it assumes earlier units on clothing and seasons. Notice that there is a careful description of the task and considerable student support for each of the steps along the way. There are elements of all three modes of communication in the task: interpersonal, interpretive, and presentational. This task also incorporates story form: There is a clear-cut beginning, middle, and end for the activities. The directions for the task would probably be written in English, but it could also be written in Spanish if the student language skills were sufficiently sophisticated and if the task were introduced with sufficient modeling and careful explanation.

Performance Task Example Deciding on a Destination   The teacher would begin this performance task by setting the scene.

> An anonymous donor has offered to fund a trip for our class to the capital of any country we choose in the Spanish-speaking world, at exactly this time next year. Our job is to decide which city we would like to visit.
>
> Each member of the class will research the climate of one of the cities that we might like to visit, as well as some of the attractions. Your job is to find the information that will help us decide which city we will choose. This project includes two tasks:
>
> 1. Visit a Spanish-language website for your city on four different days during next week, keeping track of the weather conditions on the chart I will hand out (Figure 7.1, written entirely in the target language). Websites will be

● **FIGURE 7.1**   Worksheet for Student Weather Research

Weather Chart for _____   Date _____

Date				Averages
High Temperature:	____ °C	____ °C	____ °C	____ °C
High Temperature Feels: • freezing • cold • cool • warm • hot • very hot				
Low Temperature:	____ °C	____ °C	____ °C	____ °C
Low Temperature Feels: • freezing • cold • cool • warm • hot • very hot				
Precipitation: • light/heavy rain • snow • sleet • hail • mist • thunderstorm				
Wind Conditions: • windy • light breeze • still				
Sky Conditions: • sunny • cloudy • partly sunny • partly cloudy				
Humidity:				

distributed in class. We will assume that this is typical weather for the city for this time of year. Prepare a weather report for the class, in which you:

- Give the average high and low temperatures over the time period you researched. (*Reminder:* Divide the total of all the temperatures by the number of days in the report.)
- Explain the sky conditions, wind conditions, and precipitation, if any.
- Describe what the weather would feel like and suggest what clothes we would need. (Information about the humidity would be helpful.)
- Prepare a visual that would help us understand your weather report.
- Tell something else interesting about the weather and the city.

Use the weather vocabulary we have studied during this unit, and present your information in complete sentences. It will be more effective if you do not read from a script, but you may use a script if you prefer to do so. Be prepared to answer questions from your classmates.

2. Using the same website, or other links to Spanish-language sites about your chosen city, identify at least five special characteristics or attractions of the city that you think your classmates would find interesting and worth visiting. Then prepare a two-minute "commercial," using PowerPoint or another multimedia format, giving the reasons why this city should be our choice for the trip. If you prefer, you could develop a brochure about the city, either with the computer or by hand.

Evaluating Performance Tasks: Checklists

Sometimes teachers shy away from using performance assessments because they require teachers to make judgments based on criteria rather than on an answer key, and the teachers are concerned about treating students fairly. A checklist or a rubric can help us be consistent and relevant with our observations, so that we are not distracted in a skit, for example, by the clever props the student may have designed, and overlook some major problems with the actual language used.

A checklist for a performance task is simply a listing of the qualities expected or required in a quality product or performance. For example, a checklist for the student oral weather report in the performance task just described is shown in Figure 7.2. When students have a checklist like this in advance, they know what is expected and can compare their own level of performance with that expectation. This checklist has the first four items listed as non-negotiables (Sandrock, 2002). These must be completed before the performance can be evaluated, based on the remaining criteria. It is helpful for students to understand that meeting the non-negotiable criteria is the ticket to presenting work for evaluation.

Some teachers use checklists in a slightly different way. They give students a list of the outcomes for each unit when the unit begins, so that students can keep track of their own progress. This becomes a checklist for the use of both students and teacher. Figure 7.3 is such a list used by Hildegard Merkle with her German students.

● **FIGURE 7.2**   Checklist for Student Oral Weather Report

In my weather report I will remember to:

*___ include information about temperature and humidity

*___ include information about sky conditions and precipitation, if any

*___ suggest appropriate clothing for the weather in the city

*___ use visuals that clarify weather terms or other information

___ pronounce the important vocabulary words correctly

___ use sentences to describe the weather

___ add interesting and relevant information

___ look at my audience and be enthusiastic

___ answer questions carefully and clearly

*Non-negotiable. Performance will not be evaluated until these requirements for the task are completed.

● **FIGURE 7.3**   Unit Checklist: It's My Birthday!

Please check off (✓) what you can do in German.

Now I can:

☐ ☐ State my own age in German.

☐ ☐ Tell the ages of my family members.

☐ ☐ Say all the months and seasons.

☐ ☐ Tell time and the days of the week.

☐ ☐ Tell and measure my height.

☐ ☐ Write a shopping list with the things I want for my party.

☐ ☐ Count money in German.

☐ ☐ Name the stores I have to go to for doing my shopping.

☐ ☐ Write an invitation to one of my friends.

☐ ☐ Sing at least one birthday song and congratulations in German.

☐ ☐ Have fun the German way! (tell favorite activity from unit).

☐ ☐ Bake a cake following a recipe (done at home).

Note: Both the students and the teacher use this checklist.
Source: Reprinted by permission of Hildegard Merkle.

....

● **FIGURE 7.4**   Checklist for Third-Grade Japanese Students

Name _____   December 3rd grade

Things I Can Do in Japanese

Think about what you can do in Japanese. Make a checkmark under the appropriate column for each sentence. After our testing, Jessica-sensei will write a red "O" in the correct column according to how you do on the test.

	Yes!	With help	Not yet
Communication Skills			
I can say whether I have something using "_ ga aru."	O	✓	
I can ask for things using "kudasai."	⊘		
I can say "here you are" and "thank you."	⊘		
I can count to 100 by tens.		O	✓ O
I can count to 1,000 by hundreds.	✓		O
I can read all the hiragana we learned so far (35).	All ✓	Many O	Few
Culture Skills			
I can recognize three kinds of Japanese writing: Kanji, hiragana, and katakana.	✓	O	
I can recognize different Japanese coins.	⊘		
I can play rock-paper-scissors in Japanese.	⊘		
Connections to Other Subject Areas			
I can find Japan and the U.S. on a globe and a map. (geography)	⊘		
If you give me a price, I can "draw" the correct amount of money I need using 1, 5, 10, 50, 100, and 500 yen coins. (math)		⊘	
Comparisons (of language and culture)			
I know the difference between Japanese and American money and I can tell you about how much each Japanese coin is worth in American dollars.	⊘		

Communities (Japanese Beyond the School)

I have done at least two homeworks for Japanese so far this year.   Yes! O ✓   No _____

I have told someone outside of school about the things I learned in Japanese class.   Yes! O ✓   No _____

Source: Reprinted by permission of Jessica Haxhi.

One way that Hildegard uses this checklist is to have students demonstrate mastery of each item on the list as they complete it—probably with the exception of the last two items on the list. The student goes first to a partner, who monitors the performance and checks it off if it is acceptable. After successful performance with a partner, the student goes to the teacher for a final check.

Jessica Haxhi uses the format in Figure 7.4 as a summative checklist at the end of a grading period. Students assess their own progress and then the teacher checks their performance using student interviews.

Checklists should represent clearly the goals and objectives for a unit or a performance task. They need to be written in language and vocabulary that is clear and understandable to students and free of educational jargon, as is the case with the examples just provided. Often the goals of the unit or a task become clearer to the teacher when they are translated into a checklist designed for students.

Checklists can be used at the end of a project or a unit so that students can assess their own work. Usually checklists are most valuable when they are given to students at the beginning of a unit or a performance task, so the students have guidance with regard to the teacher's expectations and with regard to what constitutes quality work.

Evaluating Performance Tasks: Rubrics

The rubric is another very valuable tool for evaluating student products and performances. The rubric and the checklist are similar in that they both describe the characteristics of quality performance. A rubric is somewhat more complex, however, in that it also describes levels of performance. Two of the main types of rubrics are analytic and holistic.

Analytic Rubrics An analytic rubric scores several different components of a performance or a product. Typically, the teacher chooses the three or four most important elements of a quality performance to evaluate. It is important not to overload one rubric with components, or the evaluation task becomes cumbersome. These elements are listed in the first column down the left side of the rubric.

Across the top there are usually three or four scoring categories. On a three-point scale, there would be descriptions for performance that is somewhat below standard, for good performance that meets all the criteria, and for outstanding or exemplary performance that even exceeds some of the criteria. Four categories might be termed "Not Yet Successful," "Successful," "Highly Successful," and "Outstanding." These categories could also be given number values, but these numbers are not easily translatable into letter grades by percentages alone. It's fun to give these categories theme-related titles, such as those shown in Figure 7.5 for the weather report task. A student who receives all 3s in the rubric in Figure 7.5, for example, is at the "Successful" level, and yet the point total of 12 is only 75 percent of the possible 16. On a strict percentage basis, this would be a barely passing score.

• **FIGURE 7.5**   Analytic Rubric for Weather Report

Criteria	Getting Ready to Try Out (1)	Intern at the Local Channel (2)	Weekend Weather Reporter (3)	Ready for the Weather Channel (4)
Appropriate Information	Weather information is present. Added information inappropriate.	Required weather information is present but not clear. Added information is sketchy or not relevant.	Includes all required weather information. Added information is present, not relevant or interesting.	Includes all required weather information. Added information is interesting, relevant.
Appropriate Clothing Suggestions	Suggestions are very unclear or inappropriate.	Suggestions are unclear or not entirely appropriate. Relationship is made to weather conditions.	Suggestions are clearly related to weather. Clothing vocabulary is limited.	Suggestions are interesting, use familiar vocabulary, clearly related to weather conditions.
Use of Visuals	Visual is made but not clear.	Visuals are sloppy or missing, or not clearly related to the presentation.	Visuals are present, but not entirely clear, or not effectively used.	Visuals are highly effective, help to make the information clear.
Presentation	Some single words, mixed with English. Language is hard to understand.	Very dependent on notes. Little eye contact. Makes some pronunciation errors, but still understandable. Enthusiasm is lacking.	Able to look away from notes at times. Some eye contact made. Pronunciation correct with a few errors. Shows enthusiasm part of the time.	Presents with little or no reference to notes. Maintains good eye contact with audience. Consistently correct pronunciation. Enthusiasm is obvious.

A checklist can take on some of the qualities of an analytic rubric if there is a rating scale for each item on the checklist. A three-point scale might indicate these characteristics:

1. Somewhat below the standard of quality
2. Meets the standard
3. Exceeds the standard

When non-negotiables are present on the checklist, they should be indicated simply with a yes or no rather than a scale.

Jessica Haxhi does oral testing twice a year with her first- and second-grade Japanese students at Maloney Magnet School in Waterbury, Connecticut. She records their performance using the checklist shown in Figure 7.6, which combines a simple checklist format with quality categories. The checklist/rubric in that example is used for oral testing at the end of December.

Obviously, the description of the points on the scale can vary, according to the preferences of the teacher. The same rubric or checklist can be used to guide self-assessment and peer assessment of student skits or other student presentations performed in front of the class. When the rubric/checklist is used this way, some teachers add at the bottom a line like this:

I want to present/show to the class the following item(s) without help: _____.

This acts as a check on honesty, because the student now knows that he or she must be ready to prove that the task can be done without any help (and may erase the check in the first column and move it to the second column) (Sandrock, 2002).

Once teachers and students have had regular experience with rubrics, it can be valuable to construct the rubric together for a major product or performance. As the teacher and the class consider together what constitutes good work, the students are likely to have a much greater investment in the quality of their own work.

● **FIGURE 7.6**   Checklist with Elements of a Rubric

Name_____   **Second Grade/December**

Student is able to:

	Yes!	With help	Not yet
Say the class rules according to pictures	_____	_____	_____
Express needs such as, "Can I get a tissue?"	_____	_____	_____
Identify the classroom objects	_____	_____	_____
Name various Japanese and American foods	_____	_____	_____
Tell the difference between *hiragana* and *katakana*	_____	_____	_____
Talk about school lunch in Japan in English	_____	_____	_____
Identify the characters in *Momotaro*	_____	_____	_____
Act out the verbs *give/take, go/return, eat, meet*	_____	_____	_____

Source: Reprinted by permission of Jessica Haxhi.

Holistic Rubrics   Holistic rubrics are most appropriate for summative evaluation; that is, they summarize the overall success of a product or a performance, based on the categories and guidelines provided in advance. Unlike the analytic rubric, they do not break the evaluation down into specific feedback on important points; thus, they provide less detailed feedback and are less effective in helping students to improve.

The Articulation and Achievement Project in New England (Jackson, 1999) developed a useful rubric for holistic scoring, shown in Figure 7.7. This rubric uses three

● **FIGURE 7.7**   Holistic Rubric for Communication

3   **Exceeds Expectations**

- Message very effectively communicated
- Rich variety of vocabulary
- Highly accurate, showing no significant patterns of error
- Content supports interest level
- Self-correction increases comprehensibility

2   **Meets Expectations**

- Message generally comprehensible
- Vocabulary is appropriate, with some groping
- Accuracy appropriate to the stage, although some patterns of error may interfere with comprehensibility
- Content is predictable, but adequate
- Occasional self-correction may be successful

1   **Does Not Meet Expectations**

- Message communicated with difficulty and is unclear
- Vocabulary is often inappropriate, leading to miscommunication
- Significant patterns of error
- Content repetitious
- Self-correction is rare and usually unsuccessful

0   **Unratable Sample**

- No consistent use of target language, only isolated words in target language
- Off task

Note: Evaluators applying these rubrics must refer to the Language Learning Continuum for verification of expectations at each stage. Because this is a criterion-referenced scoring, student work samples should be held accountable to the specific criteria rather than to each other.

Source: A Challenge to Change: The Language Learning Continuum. Copyright © 1999, the College Board, www.collegeboard.com. Reproduced with permission.

categories that serve as a very useful backbone for rubrics and checklist rubrics of all kinds:

1. Does not meet expectations
2. Meets expectations
3. Exceeds expectations

When students have checklists to provide guidance in the development of a project or a performance, the holistic rubric is both more meaningful to the students and more usable by the teacher. The checklist, in that case, serves as a *developmental tool,* and the rubric is a *summative evaluation.* A sample holistic rubric for the weather report task is found in Figure 7.8.

A checklist can be combined with the categories of a three-point rubric to form another convenient means of evaluating a student product. When the three-point scale is always understood to mean the same thing, it can be used effectively for many different products and performances and save the teacher time. The weather report checklist in Figure 7.2, when converted to a checklist/rubric, would look like that shown in Figure 7.9 on page 201.

The teacher can provide for student self-assessment by having students complete their own copy of the checklist/rubric, or they could fill in their own rating in the blank on the left of the checklist.

Rubric Development   Development of either an analytic or a holistic rubric will follow approximately the same steps:

1. Decide on the key elements that will be taken into account. In the case of the analytic rubric, these elements will be listed on the left side of the rubric, and will usually number either three or four. In the case of a holistic rubric, these characteristics will be described at each level of performance, in a parallel manner.
2. Decide on the levels of performance—usually three to four, but sometimes more. In the case of an analytic rubric, these might be labeled in a way that reflects the theme. For the analytic rubric, these will probably be listed across the top of the rubric chart.
3. Describe the performance at the highest, exemplary level. For the analytic rubric, this will involve descriptions for each of the elements being evaluated. For the holistic rubric, this will involve a single description that takes into account all of the important elements of the product or the performance. This description should be achievable but challenging. Be sure that your descriptions include only observable behaviors, so that students can easily understand the rubric.
4. Describe unacceptable performance, the lowest end of the scale. Students who do not complete the task will receive no credit, but unacceptable, or the lowest level of performance, implies that the task has at least been completed.

● **FIGURE 7.8**   Holistic Rubric for Weather Report

3   Exceeds Expectations

- All required information is presented and organized in an interesting way.
- Spanish is used consistently, with complete sentences and varied sentence patterns.
- Visual strongly supports the message; relationship to the content is clear and helpful.
- Information is mostly presented without reference to the text, using good expression and accurate pronunciation.
- Student makes eye contact with the audience and adjusts the presentation according to their response.

2   Meets Expectations

- Presentation includes all required information and is organized in a satisfactory way.
- Spanish is used consistently, mostly with complete sentences.
- Visual generally supports the message; relationship to the content is generally clear and helpful.
- Information is mostly read from the page, with good expression and pronunciation.
- Student makes some eye contact with the audience.

1   Needs Work

- Presentation includes all information but is poorly organized.
- Spanish is used, but mostly single words and short phrases.
- Visual is not clear, or not closely related to content.
- Information is read from the page with many stops and inaccuracies.
- No eye contact with the audience.

0   Unratable Sample

- No consistent use of Spanish, only isolated words in Spanish.
- Off task.

---

5. Describe the level(s) of performance that are acceptable but not exemplary. As you do this, go back to the "exceeds" and "unacceptable" descriptions and adjust to make sure you are comfortable with the quality of the "meets expectations."

6. Assign a value to each of the levels of performance in the rubric. Be sure that the line between unacceptable and acceptable is clear. Also be certain that the differences between one level and the next are fair and equal. For example, the differ-

● **FIGURE 7.9**   Checklist/Rubric Giving Information about Quality of Performance

The student is expected to:

___ include information about temperature and humidity	y = yes		n = no		
___ include information about sky conditions and precipitation, if any	y = yes		n = no		
___ suggest appropriate clothing for the weather in the city	y = yes		n = no		
___ use visuals that clarify weather terms or other information	1		2		3
___ pronounce the important vocabulary words correctly	1		2		3
___ use sentences to describe the weather	1		2		3
___ add one piece of interesting and relevant information	1		2		3
___ look at the audience and show enthusiasm	1		2		3
___ answer questions carefully and clearly	1		2		3

1 = needs improvement; 2 = meets expectations; 3 = exceeds expectations

ence between a rating of a 2 and a 3 should not be greater or less than the distance between a 3 and a 4. Be sure that there is an expectation of quality in the acceptable level(s).

7. Check the rubric to make sure that it really addresses the most important characteristics of the product or the performance, and that it reflects the priorities of instruction.

8. Check the analytic rubric to see if all the characteristics are equally important. If you are recording accumulated points from the rubric, you may wish to give greater value to characteristics that are more important. In the case of the weather report (Figure 7.5), for example, "Appropriate Information" or "Presentation" might be more important than "Use of Visuals," so the teacher might give two points for each level of quality for the more important categories and only one point for "Use of Visuals."

Rubric for Gouin Series Activity   Vicki Welch Alvis (2002, p. 3) describes a helpful assessment sequence for a hands-on class activity based on a Gouin Series:

1. The students act out a Gouin Series to make and describe skeleton sweets using Brach's Dem Bones candy (sold in grocery stores in October).
   - I put a napkin on my desk.
   - I put a cracker on top of the napkin.
   - I spread frosting on the cracker with a Popsicle stick.
   - I open the package of candy.

- I place the candy on top of the frosting.
- I describe my skeleton.
- At last, I eat it all up!

2. The teacher assesses comprehension with a silent assessment: Students close their eyes and listen to and act out each step of the Gouin Series.

3. After completing (and eating!) the activity, the teacher assesses student recall of the steps of the Gouin Series by having them create a storyboard. They draw pictures and write sentences to reproduce the Gouin Series on paper. The teacher uses the rubric shown in Figure 7.10 to communicate progress.

Providing Examples of Quality Student Work   Rubrics and checklists are most useful for students when they are accompanied by examples of quality student work. When students can see several examples of successful products, as in the case of a menu or a travel brochure, and perhaps one or two less successful examples, they have a clearer idea of what they are working toward. When these examples are shown *before* the development of a rubric, they can help to guide student thinking as they plan rubric categories and descriptions. When examples are shown *after* a rubric is already in place, they can be used for practice in evaluating the product examples. Effective student performance can be shared by means of videotape and used in the same way.

When providing samples of finished products and performances, it is important for the teacher to include a variety of successful examples, preferably very different from one another. If a single good example is shown, students may feel compelled to follow that

....

● **FIGURE 7.10**   A Rubric Giving Students Feedback about Their Progress with the Gouin Series

Criteria	Necesitas más esfuerzo	Bien hecho	¡Fenomenal!
Meaning	Drawings do not match steps.	5 of 7 drawings match steps.	Drawings accurately match written steps.
Accuracy	Many misused words or phrases; steps not written in order.	Some misused words or phrases.	Steps are written correctly and in order.
Completion of task	Less than 5 of the steps are written and illustrated.	Illustrations and written sentences for 5 of 7 steps.	Illustrations and written sentences for all 7 steps.

example as closely as possible. When a range of successful possibilities is shown, students are more likely to express their own ideas and to exhibit creativity. Usually it is best when examples are not identified with student names—especially less successful examples.

● Structuring Observation for Effective Assessment

Much of the assessment for many teachers, especially at early language learning levels, is done through observation, either of performance in class or of a performance task. In order to gather information successfully and reliably using this strategy, teachers need to consider two major factors: (1) a rubric or checklist to help them focus on the most important elements of what they observe and (2) a method for recording the information they gather through observation.

Observation is one of the most natural and appropriate ways to gather information about what early language learners know and can do. For some aspects of learning, it may be enough for a teacher just to gather information about whether a student can perform a task or not.

Can the student point to at least three colors when asked to do so?

Can the student describe a partner's clothing?

Can the student choose and name a piece of clothing?

These are all tasks for beginning students, where observation is a very common assessment strategy.

Strategies for Recording Observed Performances

Well-designed activities that reflect the outcomes of an integrated thematic unit or lesson are inherently also tools of assessment. Many teachers record observations of individual students after each class session, using a format that lists unit outcomes and names of class members.

Of course, it isn't possible to record observations about every student every day. Most observation takes place over time; thus, it is imperative that the teacher have a careful recording procedure to keep track of who has performed and who has not. It is practical, even for the teacher who sees many classes in a day, to record daily observations of three to five selected students, including any students whose performance was especially outstanding or notable, with some observation recorded for each student at least once a week. Not only does this procedure serve as a record of actual student performance but it also is a reminder to the teacher of students who need more attention or who might otherwise be overlooked.

"Clipboard Observations"   Some teachers keep a grading sheet on a clipboard, one sheet for each class, and take notes on student performance as it occurs each day. Jennifer

....

● **FIGURE 7.11**   Weekly Form to Record a Variety of Information about Student Performance

Class _____   **Week of** ___10/2 - 10/6___

Theme/Objective_____

Name	P	C	D	W
John Smith				
Jane Doe				
Alice James				
Hannah Adam				
Josh Cook				
Kim Burns				
Britney Top				
Sandra McVeigh				

P = Participation

C = Content

D = Discipline

W = Assigned Work

S = Satisfactory

N = Needs Improvement (Not yet)

U = Unsatisfactory

General Observation

lundi *Alice ↑ participation* *Sandra ✓ talk*	mardi *John - not following* *Sandra ✓ removed* *from group, own seat*	mercredi *Assembly 9 a.m.* *Sandra ✓ excessive* *talk (phone call)*
jeudi *Class very loud,* *talkative*	vendredi *Jane very verbal*	other *Britney moved* *10-2*

Source: Reprinted by permission of Jennifer Roth, Coweta County, Georgia.

Roth, a K–5 French teacher in Chapel Hill, North Carolina, uses a sheet like the one shown in Figure 7.11 for each class every week. Every student's name is listed. She can summarize performance in each category weekly, and make note of any special information each day in the boxes at the bottom.

Other teachers use a pad of sticky notes together with a clipboard. A planned assessment is written on top of a sheet of paper, one for each class. When a student successfully performs an assessment, the teacher writes his or her name on the sticky note and puts it on the class sheet. At the end of the day the teacher can transfer the information from each class sheet to the grade book, or to folders that are kept for each student.

The "Boxes" Strategy   Alisha Dawn Samples developed a useful assessment and recording strategy when she was teaching French in a K–5 program in Dahlonega, Georgia. She begins with two recipe boxes of different colors—for example, one blue and one green. She has colored index cards in the blue box, one color for each class, with an individual card for each student. In her lesson plans she writes what the goal of the assessment with the boxes will be for each day. At the end of a class period Alisha regularly plays the game of "Boxes" with the students, and students are eager to participate.

At the beginning of each unit all students' names are in the blue box. Alisha draws a name from the blue box and asks a question or asks the student to perform an action that was taught in that day's lesson. Students know that if they were good listeners they will have a chance to show it by completing a task relevant to the day's lesson. If the student is successful, the teacher moves the card to the green box and places it on end. If the student is not successful, she puts the card back in the blue box and places it on end. At the end of the day she records the successful performance of the students whose cards were transferred to the green box and the unsuccessful attempts made by the students whose cards were put back into the blue box. The students understand that they will have another opportunity to get the task completed successfully if their card goes back into the blue box. They do not perceive this as a failure but rather as a first attempt.

Students also understand that once their card is in the green box it will stay there until everyone else's card joins them. At that time, Alisha returns all the cards to the blue box to begin again. Some units have multiple assessments of all the students using "boxes" and some have only one. When all the cards have been moved from one box to the other, the assessment for that unit or task is completed. The students celebrate their success and eagerly move on to another round. It is important to note that this activity only takes about five minutes total of class time. All students are not assessed on exactly the same task or on the same day. Sometimes only five to seven students are assessed on a given day. At the end of each day the teacher records their responses in her grade book and replaces the cards in the box they were moved to during that day's assessment.

If students still have their names in the blue box at the end of a unit and have not been able to move to the green box, the task level of difficulty can be adjusted (and noted) so that the remaining students can respond and feel successful. At the end of a unit Alisha is able to look back over her students' overall performance of physical and/or oral language responses to gauge their progress. This is only one of several means of assessment that Alisha uses in her classroom.

Some teachers have altered the boxes strategy slightly by using tongue depressors or ice-cream sticks and small plastic boxes or cans. The sticks have names of the students written on them with a permanent marker, and they are color-coded by class with a color on only one end of the sticks. Successful performance is indicated by moving the stick from one box to the other and placing it upside down until it has been recorded. Unsuccessful performance is indicated by placing the stick upside down in the original box until it has been recorded. One teacher has three plastic boxes attached together so the sticks can be placed in the appropriate box to indicate shaky, satisfactory, and outstanding performances. Of course, if a learner is unable to perform at all, the stick would go back into the pile so the student can try again.

Recording and Grading with the "Boxes" Strategy   Alisha Dawn Samples uses both her lesson plan book and her grade book in order to accumulate and evaluate the assessments in her classroom. In her lesson plan, under "Assessment," she writes what the assessment task of the day will be (as a reflection of what the lesson was on). For example:

> Boxes—R task (receptive). Students will be able to identify the colors of the described item by pointing or jumping from item to item. Or
>
> Boxes—P task (productive). Students will be able to describe the shape of the house in each picture (using big, small, medium, triangle, square, circle, or rectangle). Or
>
> Students will complete the activity by placing the correct number called out next to the correct item on the handout (8/8).

In her record or grade book Alisha uses the following key for recording data:

+: Answered correctly	MC: Multiple choice
-: Answered incorrectly	HO: Handout
P: Productive response	D!: Discipline/behavior issue
R: Receptive response	Abs: Absent
NP: Would not participate when called on	T: Test

In her record book Alisha Dawn Samples records the date and a one- or two-word description of the assessment. She can go back to the plan book to see in greater detail what the assessment was and to review progress later. She records the student responses according to the key above. She can later tabulate the progress of each student using his or her marks in receptive versus productive language and their "written" or other verbal responses. She can also note the effects of their behavior and/or absenteeism on their progress. Going from left to right she can determine over time which students are both responsive and verbal, which ones are able to understand but not yet speak very much, and which ones are not able to perform due to absences, lack of participation, or poor behavior. Alisha is not able to evaluate every objective with each student, but she can see their language ability as a whole. She also includes anecdotal notes in her record book, as well as samples of student work. A sample from Alisha's record book is shown in Figure 7.12.

One of the issues that every teacher deals with in using observation as an assessment tool is assessing participation. Vicki Alvis uses the rubric in Figure 7.13 (page 208) to keep track of her students' participation.

Participation

The frequency and accuracy of the students' class participation is an important gauge of student understanding and progress. To encourage and keep track of participation, as well as to reward it, a number of teachers have used a system in which they award students a slip of paper for each contribution to class or for individual performance of a teacher-

● **FIGURE 7.12**   Sample from Alisha Dawn Samples's Record Book

	11/4 color id (R)	11/6 color id (R)	11/7 color id (P)	11/10 color id (P)	11/11 review colors (P)	11/13 color id HO 6/6	11/15 shape id (R)	11/16 house/shapes (R)	11/17 shapes game (R)	11/18 shapes game (P)	11/19 shapes story (P)	11/21 shapes/house HO 8/8	11/22 shapes song (P)
Erica	+R		+P	+P		6/6	+R	+R	+R	+P	+P	6/8	+P
Michael		+R	-P		-P	2/6	+R		+R	-P	-P	4/8	+P
Ashley	+R			+P		5/6	+R	-R	+R		-P	6/8	+P
Nick	-R	D!	-P		-P	0/6	D!		Abs		-P	2/8	+P
Stephanie	Abs	.	Abs		-P	Abs	NP		+R	Abs		Abs	-P

4 = excellent; 3 = good; 2 = satisfactory; 1 = needs improvement

Source: Reprinted by permission of Alisha Dawn Samples.

directed activity, as in TPR. The student places all of the slips of paper earned in a class period in their designated place on a bulletin board or in a notebook. At regular intervals the teacher records the accumulated points for each student. As a variation of this procedure, the students might use similar means to keep track of their success with specific outcomes—for example, using the target language to request permission from the teacher to go to the bathroom.

Comprehension Checks

Comprehension checks are quick ways to see what students understand, before a more formal assessment is used to see how well students are doing. We need to see if students truly understand before we assign practice activities! Here are several examples of quick comprehension checks.

● **FIGURE 7.13**   Rubric for Assessing Participation

Participation		Grade_____
Score	Criteria	Comments
4	✓ Takes initiative to see that group completes project	
	✓ Works enthusiastically	
	✓ Begins and ends tasks promptly	
	✓ Completes own share of the assignment	
3	✓ Takes initiative to complete own share of assignment	
2	✓ Completes own share of assignment with encouragement from teacher or partner	
1	✓ Completes some of assignment with insistence from teacher or partner	
4(A) = excellent; 3(B) = good; 2(C) = satisfactory; 1(D) = needs improvement		

Source: Reprinted by permission of Vicki Welch Alvis.

1. Learners demonstrate understanding, or lack of understanding, by physical responses such as:
   ● Hold up your hand for one answer, your elbow for the other answer.
   ● Touch your ear for yes, your nose for no.
   ● Nod your head for yes, shake it for no.
   Any number of familiar TPR commands could be used for this purpose.

2. Learners demonstrate understanding, or lack of understanding, using objects:
   ● Hold up yes–no cards in the target language.
   ● Hold up objects, such as a pencil, a pen, a ruler, or a crayon.
   ● Hold up tongue depressors that have one end painted one color and the other another color (using felt-tip markers).

3. Learners demonstrate understanding by writing or drawing an answer on a small chalk slate or a dry-erase board. Figure 7.14 shows students using slates in a

● **FIGURE 7.14**   Students Using Slates to Demonstrate Comprehension

second grade classroom at the Yinghua Academy Chinese Immersion Charter School in St. Paul, Minnesota.

● Peer Assessment

Peer assessment can be valuable both to the student being assessed and to the students completing the assessments. It is a very beneficial step toward recognition of quality and honest self-assessment. Clear guidelines, usually in the form of a rubric, are the essential element in peer assessment.

Vicki Welch Alvis (2002, p. 3) uses the simple, student-friendly oral assessment rubric shown in Figure 7.15 for a variety of oral topics and presentation.

Hildegard Merkle uses peer assessment with middle school students to keep them alert and on task during presentations. The assessment in Figure 7.16 (page 211) was used to evaluate the final product of a unit on famous Germans. Each student chose a famous German person from a list, did research, and prepared a class presentation accompanied by a poster. The rubric/checklist shown in the figure was given to the students in German.

● **FIGURE 7.15**   Easy-to-Use Format for Giving Students Feedback on a Presentation

4 ☺ ☺	We understand you easily.
3 ☺	We understand you when the teacher or other students help a little.
2 ··	We understand you a little when the teacher or other students help a lot.
1 ˵	You try a little but we don't understand you.

4 = excellent; 3 = good; 2 = satisfactory; 1 = needs improvement

Source: Reprinted by permission of Vicki Welch Alvis.

● Involving Parents in Assessment

Spanish teachers in Pinellas County, Florida, have developed an assessment system that makes parents and classroom teachers partners in assessment. The language teachers send parents each a sheet of performance activity cards, attached to an explanatory letter. Activities are at 10 different language levels, with 10 performance activities for each level. When a child can accomplish one of the activities, the parent signs the card and sends it back to school with the child. The child files the card in a pocket chart in the classroom, where the classroom teacher reviews the cards with the learners who have completed them. The Spanish teacher may check a few students at the beginning of the class period, as well.

Students are proud to see the cards accumulate, and the cards form a permanent record of their language development. Students can complete the cards in each set in any order, depending on their interest and their individual learning styles. New students can use the cards to catch up on what they have missed. This system helps to develop excellent ties between home and school, as well as between the language teacher and the classroom teacher. The cards are carefully developed to incorporate all the important objectives and competencies of the program in the performance tasks (Gilzow and Branaman, 2000). The Jefferson County Public Schools in Louisville, Kentucky, have created "Can Do" cards modeled on the Pinellas County idea. Some sample cards from Jefferson County are shown in Figure 7.17 on page 212.

● Portfolios

Development of a portfolio by each student has become one of the most popular and widespread of the nontraditional means of assessment. One of the special advantages of this approach is the collaboration between the teacher and the students in assembling and reflecting on the information in the portfolio.

Portfolios are more than just scrapbooks to be stored away with other childhood memorabilia. They should contain examples, selected by the students, that illustrate

● **FIGURE 7.16**   Rubric for Assessment of a Final Oral Project

Directions: Take a new evaluation form for each presenter. Fill in the top portion. At the end of the presentation, circle the points given. At the end, after all questions have been answered, fill in the last two lines, give a comment, and hand in the evaluation sheet.

My name: _____

Name of presenter: _____

Famous person presented about: _____

	1 point	2 points	3 points
Language	Hard to understand. Sentences not complete. Used some English sentences. Past tense missing/incorrect.	I understood almost everything. Sentences complete. Used some English words. Grammar mostly correct. Past tense used mostly correctly.	I understood everything. Sentences complete and flowing. Used no English. Past tense used correctly.
	1 point	**2 points**	**3 points**
Information	There were not many facts and they were not well organized. Only one or two pieces of information were given.	The facts were clear. Three or four pieces of information were given.	I have a picture of the person's life in my head. Six or more pieces of information were given.
	1 point	**2 points**	**3 points**
Answering of Questions	Unable to answer many questions.	Answered briefly.	Answered all questions in detail. Able to tell stories about the person.
	1 point	**2 points**	**3 points**
Presentation	Hard to stay awake. Read most facts. Not loud or clear enough.	Quite interesting. Spoke freely with some reference to notes. Loud, clear voice.	Simply fascinating! Spoke enthusiastically with no reference to notes. Loud, clear voice.
	1 point	**2 points**	**3 points**

Length of presentation: _____   Points given: _____

Comments:

● **FIGURE 7.17**   Examples of "Can Do" Cards

Source: Jefferson County Public Schools, Louisville, Kentucky. Reprinted with permission.

growth in language learning. The students and the teacher can also select items to place in the portfolio together. Sometimes the teacher might suggest to the whole class, for example, "This project would be an excellent item for you all to place in your portfolios, because you are really using some new skills and information here." On other occasions, a teacher might suggest, "Choose one of the writing projects that you completed in this unit to keep in your portfolio at school. The others you may take home to share with your parents."

With each item placed in the portfolio, the student should write a short statement to accompany it, in English or in the target language. This statement should include the student's reason for choosing the item for the portfolio, perhaps what the student is proud of, and what the item shows about the student's learning. It might also include a statement about what the student still needs to work on. Especially with early portfolio experiences, the teacher will need to provide a form for the students to use in supplying this information.

It would be important to include evidence from all three of the communication modes from the communication standard: interpersonal, interpretive, and presentational. A good selection of information in a portfolio might include the following:

- Drawings or photographs that the student can explain or describe
- Written products such as individual versions of a class Language Experience story
- Poetry or other expressive writing
- Letters, invitations, greeting cards, or other "writing for publication"
- Photographs or slides of skits, puppet plays, simulations, or other activities in which the student participated, together with an audiotape of the student contribution, if possible
- Journal entries relating to class or other experiences
- Audio or video documenting oral participation in a meaningful group or individual activity
- Visual products (or photos of them) developed through class activities: maps, charts, displays, bulletin boards, and so on

Written Presentations

Expressive (diaries, journals, writing logs)

Transactional (letters, surveys, reports)

Poetic (poems, stories, plays)

Performances

Role-playing, drama

Dance/movement

Reader's Theater

Mime

Choral readings

Music—instrumental and choral

Maps

Graphs

Dioramas

Models

Mock-ups

Displays

Bulletin boards

Charts /replicas

Visual and Graphic Arts

Storyboards

Drawings

Posters

Cartoons

Mobiles

Media Presentations

Videotapes

Audiotapes

Slides

Photo essays

Print media

Computer programs

Presentations

Debates

Discussions

Interviews

Speeches

Storytelling

Oral histories

Poetry readings

Broadcasts

Evaluating Portfolios

One strategy for using portfolios is to have students select the best example of what they have learned for separate assessment (or comment, or showing off to parents and others). Short (1991) recommends the following criteria for evaluating portfolios. She emphasizes the importance of establishing and announcing these criteria in advance, and suggests the possibility that students and teacher might decide the criteria together. Some possible criteria include:

- Variety—selected pieces display the range of tasks students can accomplish and skills they have learned.
- Growth—student work represents the students' growth in content knowledge and language proficiency.
- Completeness—student work reflects finished products.
- Organization—students organized the contents systematically.
- Fluency—selected pieces are meaningful to the students and communicate information to the teacher.
- Accuracy—student work demonstrates skill in the mechanics of the language.
- Goal-oriented—the contents reflect progress and accomplishment of curricular objectives.
- Following directions—students follow the teacher's directions for selecting pieces for the portfolio (i.e., if a teacher requests eight items, student provides eight, not six).
- Neatness—student work is neatly written, typed, or illustrated.
- Justification or significance—students include reasonable justifications for the work selected or explain why selected items are significant. (pp. 54–55)

The portfolio's ultimate value is that it shows that students have engaged in self-reflection, and that this has resulted in greater learning. At the end of the year, the portfolio should highlight what the student has learned, and where the student is on the continuum of proficiency. In this way portfolios can serve as a valuable means of informing teachers at the next level of language instruction about the skills and progress of the students with whom they are about to work.

Portfolios should be housed in the school and distributed and collected for student use, so that this valuable information doesn't disappear on the trip to or from school, or serve as a nibbling exercise for the family puppy! Portfolios housed electronically would solve this problem.

LinguaFolio

LinguaFolio is a portfolio assessment instrument intended to help individual students set their language learning goals and to track their progress toward achieving them. Suitable for use as either a physical or an electronic portfolio, it includes these three components:

- *Passport:* a place for students to document their formal assessments and their self-assessments (checklists)

- *Biography:* where students record information about their language background and their activities with other cultures
- *Dossier:* where samples of a student's work over time are archived

LinguaFolio was developed from the model of the European Language Portfolio in an effort to provide American students and teachers with the tools to encourage and support a seamless record of progress for lifelong language learning. All parts of the LinguaFolio and information about its use are available for free download from the website of the National Council of State Supervisors for Languages (NCSSFL): www.ncssfl .org/links/index.php?linguafolio. There are also links to the European Language Portfolio and other related resources.

For younger learners, LinguaFolio, Jr. involves the same three components, but with language and format designed for elementary school learners. These quotes from the website convey very well the flavor and the intent of LinguaFolio, Jr.: www.doe.virginia.gov/ linguafolio/junior.html, accessed February 15, 2009:

> LinguaFolio, Jr. is a tool to help me organize information about language learning during my early years. I can use it to describe my language background, show others what I know and can do in other languages, and keep samples of my work.
>
> I can update my Language Passport, Language Biography, and Language Dossier at any time. I can share my LinguaFolio, Jr. with my present and future teachers, my parents, and perhaps others, but it is especially for me!

● Grading

After all the assessment data have been accumulated and evaluated, the final step in the assessment process is grading—transforming the assessment data into a number or a symbol to report the results of evaluation. Grading policies differ from school to school, and from program to program. Some programs have decided to avoid the issue altogether and simply not give grades to students. They cite the rationale that grading can serve to discourage some students, and they prefer to have students just enjoy the program. This approach may well be problematic, for at least two reasons.

First, as we have shown, students want to know what they have learned and how good their progress is—and so do their parents. Second, when students are receiving grades for other subjects in school, but not for languages, there is a strong tendency to believe that languages are not as "serious" or important as the other content areas. This definitely leaves the language program vulnerable when budgets and programs are being cut.

Grading is a far less difficult and uncomfortable task when the teacher has sufficient information—that is, assessment data—with which to work. Number values can be assigned to rubrics and checklists. Results of observations, systematic student checks, and achievement testing can be tallied. Results of all these measures can be weighted and averaged in a variety of different ways.

There are a number of questions a teacher can ask at the point of arriving at a grade. Should completion of homework count toward the final unit, semester, or quarter grade? What weight will class participation carry? How heavily does the final performance assessment count toward a final grade?

These are questions that only the individual teacher can answer, based on the priorities for that unit, that class, and that specific school setting. These decisions should be made at the beginning of planning, however, and not as the teacher sits with the grade book the night before grades are due.

How the grade itself is expressed is largely a matter of school or district policy. It might be a scale of A to F, or a percentage, or Satisfactory/Unsatisfactory. The most important consideration is the amount of information available to parents. Some school systems use an anecdotal report card in the elementary grades. The anecdotal report can be a good opportunity to communicate program information along with the individual student report.

Jessica Haxhi's semester report to parents includes, on one side of the form, a list of the content covered in the class over the semester. The third grade, for example, covered the following:

Communication

- Saying the numbers from 1 to 100
- Building and community helpers
- Describing a scene using "there is/are" (___ga aru), and "there is/are not" (___ga nai)
- Naming Japanese foods and their ingredients
- Reading the 48 hiragana characters

Culture

- New Year's Day in Japan
- All about Tokyo and the flight to Japan
- Mt. Fuji
- Sumo wrestling

Connections to Other Subject Areas

- Using calculators to convert measurements
- Solving addition and multiplication problems in Japanese

Comparisons

- Knowing basic differences between Tokyo and Waterbury (Connecicut), and Tokyo and other American cities and towns

On the other side of the form is the individual student report. One student, whom we will call Mary Jones, received this report:

Effort/Attitude

Excellent

Communication

Uses learned vocabulary to communicate with occasional hints.

Culture

Develops age-appropriate knowledge of cultural practices and products.

Connections

Performs tasks from other subjects in Japanese with accuracy.

Comparisons

Demonstrates ability to compare Japanese language and culture to her own.

Comments Regarding Mary

Mary is a solid student in Japanese classes and her language skills are developing steadily. Nice work!

Even in situations where the language program is not a part of the regular reporting system, the teacher can initiate a method of sharing student progress similar to this one, in order to help both parents and students feel that progress in the language class is noticed and valued.

● ACTFL Performance Guidelines for K–12 Learners

One of the most important tools for the language teacher in designing realistic goals and assessments for the classroom is the ACTFL Performance Guidelines for K–12 Learners (Swender and Duncan, 1998). These guidelines provide the performance levels for students working in a standards-based program beginning in kindergarten and continuing through grade 12. (See Appendix.)

Performance indicators are given in six areas:

Comprehension: How well do they understand?

Comprehensibility: How well are they understood?

Cultural Awareness: How is their cultural understanding reflected in their communication?

Communication Strategies: How do they maintain communication?

Vocabulary Use: How extensive and applicable is their vocabulary?

Language Control: How accurate is their language?

Performance indicators are organized according to three levels:

Novice Learner Range: grades K–4, 5–8, or 9–10

Intermediate Learner Range: grades K–8, 7–12

Pre-advanced Learner Range: grades K–12

Within each level, performances are listed according to the communication modes—interpersonal, interpretive, and presentational. These guidelines will help us all to set realistic goals for our students and choose appropriate performance assessments to measure our students' success. Thus, for example, the teacher in a third-grade early language program might consult the "Vocabulary Use" category. If the students have been learning the new language since kindergarten, they will be nearing the benchmarks identified in the novice learner range (K–4). The teacher can read the descriptions to see what her or his students are working toward in the areas of interpersonal, interpretive, and presentational communication, as shown in Figure 7.18.

After examining these guidelines, the teacher realizes that performance tasks will be most useful and realistic if they prompt students to use memorized vocabulary and phrases in familiar contexts. The teacher also realizes that extended writing or speaking in sentences will not be a realistic expectation. It will be important that activities and tasks directed toward vocabulary in the interpretive mode should use familiar contexts and be accompanied by gestures, pantomime, props, visuals (oral) or illustrations (written), and other contextual clues. Examination of performance indicators in the other five areas should give the teacher a basis for realistic and appropriate lessons and tasks for these third-grade students.

Teachers working with beginning language students in grade 3 would have to recognize that students in their classrooms are at very early stages of development toward meeting these performance levels, but the performance goals are still the same. Teachers working with eighth-grade students in a grades 5–8 program would also find their students in the novice learner range, but their topics and familiar contexts would likely be different from those of the third- or fourth-grade child.

Taken together, the performance indicators in the six domains provide a snapshot of learner performance at each of three points along the K–12 continuum: novice, intermediate, and pre-advanced. Teachers can use the performance guidelines to help focus their planning and assessment, no matter how many years of previous language experience their students may have had.

● ACTFL Integrated Performance Assessment (IPA)

The final step in the standards initiative of the American Council on the Teaching of Foreign Languages (ACTFL) is the development of an assessment document to assist teachers in designing effective measures of student performance. The ACTFL Integrated Performance Assessment (American Council on the Teaching of Foreign Languages, 2002)

● **FIGURE 7.18**   Novice Learner Range Grades K–4 or Grades 5–8 or Grades 9–10

Interpersonal:

- Comprehend and produce vocabulary that is related to everyday objects and actions on a limited number of familiar topics.
- Use words and phrases primarily as lexical items without awareness of grammatical structure.
- Recognize and use vocabulary from a variety of topics including those related to other curricular areas.
- May often rely on words and phrases from their native language when attempting to communicate beyond the word and/or gesture level.

Interpretive:

- Recognize a variety of vocabulary words and expressions related to familiar topics embedded within relevant curricular areas.
- Demonstrate increased comprehension of vocabulary in spoken passages when these are enhanced by pantomime, props, and/or visuals.
- Demonstrate increased comprehension of written passages when accompanied by illustrations and other contextual clues.

Presentational:

- Use a limited number of words and phrases for common objects and actions in familiar categories.
- Supplement their basic vocabulary with expressions acquired from sources such as the teacher or picture dictionaries.
- Rely on native language and phrases when expressing personal meaning in less familiar categories.

is intended to serve as "a prototype to assess students' progress toward the K–12 standards as well as students' language proficiency within the framework of the ACTFL Performance Guidelines for K–12 Learners" (p. 9). The ACTFL Integrated Performance Assessment (IPA) is considered a "cluster assessment" that incorporates three linguistic tasks, each featuring one of the three modes of communication described in the Standards: interpersonal, interpretive, and presentational. The designers of the IPA envision a seamless connection between the performance assessment and standards-based curriculum and instruction.

The tasks of the IPA take place within a single, meaningful context and are designed to build on one another. They are intended to reflect real-world uses for the language that students have learned during the course of a given unit of study. Students are motivated because the tasks are interesting and relevant to their world and their interests. Teachers prepare students for the assessments with ongoing feedback on performance during classroom instruction, as well as by providing rubrics and models of excellent performances for the IPA itself.

Together with the *Standards for Foreign Language Learning in the 21st Century* and the K–12 Student Performance Guidelines, the ACTFL Integrated Performance Assessment provides teachers and curriculum developers with a clear path toward meaningful, communicative foreign language instruction for learners of all ages. Teachers now have access to all the critical resources necessary to make the significant shift to standards-based, performance-guided, communicative language teaching. The website of the Foreign Language Educators of New Jersey (FLENJ) has examples of tasks modeled on the ACTFL IPAs, developed as a part of their Consortium for Assessing Performance Standards, a New Jersey FLAP Grant Project. The assessments are organized around 11 content/theme areas and designed for novice, intermediate, and pre-advanced levels. Rubrics and many student samples, both written and auditory, are also available at the same site: http://flenj.org/CAPS/?page=parent.

● Program Assessment

Program assessment is a concern both separate from and related to the development of classroom testing measures. Elementary and middle school language programs, especially when they are new to the curriculum or are experiencing extensive revision, need to provide evidence that program goals are being met. Classroom achievement testing may provide one component of this evidence. There may also be a need or a desire to demonstrate the impact of the program on student performance in other content areas, on self-concept, on attitudes, or on cognitive or social development. This type of assessment requires careful advance planning and the cooperation of administrators, classroom teachers, and assessment personnel, where available. In the case of programs established with funding provided by a government agency or by a private foundation, external evaluators may be involved in developing an assessment plan. The Pinellas County, Florida, program assessment (Taylor, Feyten, Meros, and Nutta, 2008), referred to in Chapter 15, can serve as a model for other programs as educators design their own assessments.

Assessment of Student Performance as Part of Program Assessment

One of the problems encountered in the process of program assessment is the difficulty in measuring student performance appropriately and reliably. In an educational climate that measures program success in terms of standardized test scores, it is essential to have appropriate instruments for measuring the progress of elementary and middle school students.

Two useful measures of student language attainment have been developed by the Center for Applied Linguistics, with a specific focus on young learners. The Student Oral

Proficiency Assessment (SOPA) is designed for students in grades 3 through 5 who have had at least four years of language instruction. Originally developed for immersion students in 1991, it was adapted for other types of programs in 1996. Validity and reliability testing were completed for both versions in 1999. The ELLOPA, the Early Language Listening and Oral Proficiency Assessment, was developed for children ages 4 to 8 who are learning a foreign or second language in a school setting. Other instruments, the NOELLA and the STAMP (see below) were developed by the Center for Applied Second Language Studies (CASLS) at the University of Oregon.

Student Oral Proficiency Assessment (SOPA)   The SOPA interview is 15 to 20 minutes in length, depending on students' proficiency levels. Students participate in the interview in pairs, to reduce anxiety and to create a more natural assessment situation. There are two assessors, one to conduct the interview and another to serve as a rater. Sometimes the interview is audio- or video-recorded.

After an initial warm-up period, the students perform several tasks that focus on their listening skills, using a bag of colorful and appealing manipulatives, such as plastic fruits or animals. Once the students have been successful in the listening phase, the interviewer moves on to ask simple questions about numbers, colors, and favorites. These tasks are followed by additional tasks, some of them calling for students to interact with one another. Depending on their ability, the students are given the opportunity to give directions, describe, retell a story, or persuade. After the assessment tasks are completed, students participate in a wind-down activity that leaves students feeling successful. The entire interview is designed to assess student ability in oral fluency, grammar, vocabulary, and listening comprehension.

Early Language Listening and Oral Proficiency Assessment (ELLOPA)   "Cow Talk," as the ELLOPA is sometimes called, consists of a series of game-like activities that are appropriate for children in pre-kindergarten through grade 2. Two or three children at a time participate in a series of five language games in which they interact with a Spanish-speaking cow puppet, Señora Vaca, who speaks only Spanish. Of course, for other languages, the cow would go by another target language name. This assessment focuses primarily on listening skills and only secondarily on speaking skills. Topics covered include family members, colors, numbers, size, food, songs, animals, and weather. Student performance is rated holistically, on a scale that measures listening comprehension, fluency, vocabulary, language control (grammar), communication strategies, and cultural awareness.

The SOPA and the ELLOPA make it possible for schools and school districts to assess their students' performance holistically, using the criteria based on the ACTFL Proficiency Guidelines for Speaking (revised in 1999) and the Performance Guidelines for K–12 Learners. The rating scale typically consists of nine levels, from "junior novice—low" to "junior advanced—high." Training for SOPA and ELLOPA is available through the Center for Applied Linguistics, both offered at several language conferences and it is also available to individual school districts, on request, and on-line.

National Online Early Language Learning Assessment (NOELLA)   The NOELLA is an assessment designed specifically for the younger learner, grades 3 through 6. Developed at the Center for Applied Second Language Studies (CASLS) at the University of

Oregon, the NOELLA is intended to measure proficiency in reading, writing, speaking, and listening. It is Web-based and linked to the ACTFL Proficiency Guidelines. The tests are currently available in Chinese, French, Japanese, Korean, and Spanish. When these tests are used in a language program, they will provide validated data for use in effective program assessment, as well as for placement and instructional planning.

Standards-Based Measurement of Proficiency (STAMP)   This assessment tool is similar to the NOELLA in that it is also Web-based and linked to the ACTFL Performance Guidelines. Like the NOELLA, it was developed and continues to be improved by CASLS. Appropriate for grades 7 through 16, it is available in Spanish, French, German, Japanese, Italian, and Chinese (Simplified and Traditional). The STAMP measures from Novice–Low to Intermediate–Mid in reading, writing, and speaking. Reports provide individual results for students and teachers, class-level reports, and building-, district-, and state-level reports for administrators. Teachers can play back all student oral responses and review the writing responses. Further information and a brochure are available from www.avantassessment.com/products/about_stamp.html.

Resources for Program Assessment

Although a full description of program assessment is beyond the scope of this chapter and this text, it must be taken seriously by every elementary and middle school language teacher. Schinke-Llano (1985), Heining-Boynton (1991), and Rosenbusch (1991) offer suggestions and formats for program assessment to assist teachers and program coordinators in developing an effective assessment process. Additional information is found at the end of Chapter 17, and especially in Figure 17.5.

● Student Achievement Testing

Of course, there is still a place for quizzes and tests, even within the performance-based mindset that we have developed as a profession. Written tests and quizzes can demonstrate mastery of specific skills at a specific point in time. They are probably most useful as guideposts along the way, like the comprehension checks described earlier in this chapter. They help the teacher and the students themselves know what building blocks to pay closer attention to before the language can be successfully used in meaningful performance tasks.

Tests and quizzes can be made much more meaningful if they are contextualized, or made to resemble some real-life situation. For example, a multiple-choice test could tell the story of a teddy bear's trip to the rain forest, and students could choose appropriate vocabulary or responses to make the story "make sense."

The following guidelines are offered for the use of teachers who wish to develop a program of student achievement testing, in addition to the performance-oriented assessments we've discussed, that is congruent with both their own goals and with the needs of the learners in their classes.

Guideline One: Use the Achievement Test as an Opportunity for Learners to Discover How Much They Know, Not How Much They Still Have to Learn

Many teachers, like their students, recall testing experiences in which it seemed clear that the test was designed to trick and confuse them, and to demonstrate that they didn't know as much as they might have thought. No matter what grade may eventually have been awarded on the test, the feeling of frustration and inadequacy lingered long after the test items had been forgotten.

In an early language classroom that has focused on providing students with successful experiences in communication, the testing situation can be an extension of the same principle. Just as the teacher attempts to reduce students' anxiety and to enhance their motivation and self-confidence for language activities in the classroom, so can the teacher reduce anxiety and enhance motivation to help students to achieve success in demonstrating what they have learned. For example, teachers can schedule short testing sessions on a regular basis to prevent students from becoming anxious and to avoid placing unwarranted importance on the role of testing in the class.

Guideline Two: Test What Has Been Taught in the Way It Has Been Taught

There should be no surprises on a test designed to help students discover what they know. All the skills that have been used in activities during class should be included in the test in some way. Skills and specific materials should be tested using the same type of communicative activity by which they were practiced. For example, if a teacher wishes to use a paper-and-pencil test to determine whether students understand commands that have been practiced in the classroom, that teacher can prepare the students to feel comfortable with the test item by introducing a game-like partner activity. In one game, students choose a picture that matches a command given by the teacher or by one of their classmates; in another game, they draw stick figures to represent a command and compare their results with one another. If listening has been emphasized in the class, it should be emphasized in the testing situation. If speaking has been practiced during class, it should be a part of the assessment in approximately the same proportion as it was in the class, and using similar speaking situations.

The teacher who plans each lesson on the basis of carefully worded, student-oriented objectives has already laid the groundwork for the activities that will be a part of the assessment. Each objective that appears on the test should bear approximately the same weight of importance that it carried in the development of class activities.

Although performance assessment in its great variety may have the most to offer the foreign language setting at the elementary and middle school level, there continue to be times when more traditional paper-and-pencil measures will also be helpful. These approaches are familiar to students and parents, as well as teachers, and thus can provide valuable corroboration of information gathered by other means. Hadley (2001) suggests strategies for developing "hybrid classroom tests," in which traditional classroom tests are revised to give them a more communicative orientation. One of the key components in this revision is the idea of providing a context for all test items. For example, a series of 10 questions would all refer to the same familiar story and actually develop an idea or a narrative sequence. This allows the learner to use all the information available, both on the page and in her or his own memory, to complete the task.

● Suggestions for Testing

Interpretive Mode: Listening

The best source of ideas for assessment are the activities and contexts used in daily class sessions, since these are the settings within which meanings and understanding have been developed. Additional suggestions are provided next, most of them especially appropriate for early levels of language acquisition, when assessment seems to be the most difficult.

1. *True–False Tests.* In advance, prepare answer sheets numbered from 1 to 10 (or 1 to 15, or 1 to 20, depending on length desired), with the words *true* and *false* given for each number. With no additional preparation the answer sheet shown here may be used for any of the test items described below.

1.	True	False		1.	Oui	Non		1.
2.	True	False		2.	Oui	Non		2.
3.	True	False		3.	Oui	Non		3.
4.	True	False		4.	Oui	Non		4.
5.	True	False	OR	5.	Oui	Non	OR	5.
6.	True	False		6.	Oui	Non		6.
7.	True	False		7.	Oui	Non		7.
8.	True	False		8.	Oui	Non		8.
9.	True	False		9.	Oui	Non		9.
10.	True	False		10.	Oui	Non		10.

   a. Show the class a picture that includes more than one item of information (for example, different types of weather and their effects, a scene with individuals performing a variety of actions, and so forth). Then read statements about the picture, and have the students respond with true or false.

   b. Read a short paragraph or dialogue to the class. Then make several statements about the content of the selection or probable outcomes of the situation. The students respond true or false on the basis of the correctness of each statement.

c. Read a command and perform the action commanded, or show a picture of the action being commanded or described (see Figure 7.19). Have the students indicate true if the command or statement and the action agree; have the students indicate false if they do not agree. Link the actions in a meaningful, story-like sequence to provide maximum context.

d. Base some true-and-false statements on reasonableness or logic. For example, if you read, "The turtle says bow-wow," the students would mark false.

(CAUTION! Never include a negative in a statement used for a true-false item.)

● **FIGURE 7.19**   Sample True–False Item

He is going to lift the box.   T   F

2. *Listening/Picture Stimuli Tests.* In advance, prepare answer sheets with 1 to 10 questions (or more) and the choices of (a), (b), (c), (d), or (e) for each question. This type of answer sheet lends itself to a variety of question techniques, which are described here.

1. (a)___	(b)___	(c)___	(d)___	(e)___
2. (a)___	(b)___	(c)___	(d)___	(e)___
3. (a)___	(b)___	(c)___	(d)___	(e)___
4. (a)___	(b)___	(c)___	(d)___	(e)___
5. (a)___	(b)___	(c)___	(d)___	(e)___
6. (a)___	(b)___	(c)___	(d)___	(e)___
7. (a)___	(b)___	(c)___	(d)___	(e)___
8. (a)___	(b)___	(c)___	(d)___	(e)___
9. (a)___	(b)___	(c)___	(d)___	(e)___
10. (a)___	(b)___	(c)___	(d)___	(e)___

a. Show students several pictures, each of them numbered. When the students hear a statement, have them place the number of the appropriate picture next to the letter for that statement. For best results, the pictures should be related to one another in a meaningful way, perhaps placed in a sequence showing development of a sequence or a story line.

b. Give the students a picture showing several activities. Read sentences describing each of the activities, and have the students place the number of the sentence on the part of the picture that depicts the activity described. As an alternative, show a picture that has numbers on it, and have the students place the number of the activity next to the letter of the sentence read. Make the picture as rich with connections—and even humorous—as possible. For example, an item for a German class combining culture and activities might be as follows:

> "The Heinzelmännchen have stolen into the home of a sick family to help out. Each of the workers has found something to do, but some of them have chosen very strange tools for the job. Mark the number that shows the activity being described. Number 1 is washing the dishes."

c. Present classroom objects or other learned vocabulary in individual pictures, either on the students' papers or on cards in the front of the class. Read statements containing the individual vocabulary items, and have the students number the items to correspond to the sentences (or place the number of the object beside the letter of the sentence that you read). The sentences should be in a connected, meaningful narrative. This type of item tests (and encourages) the students' ability to perceive known language embedded in unfamiliar language (see Figure 7.20).

d. Give a "labeling" exercise: Have students place numbers corresponding to the correct identification of a part of a picture (body parts, table setting, countries, and so forth) when they hear you read the identification, or when they hear you read a statement containing the label. This could be developed as a description of a fantasy creature, which will help to find the creature hiding in the closet.

e. For more advanced students, prepare a short connected story using sentences that the students have learned, but in a different context. Place a collection of large pictures on the chalkboard tray, flannel board, or pocket chart; or display pictures on the overhead projector. Have the students look at the pictures while listening a second (or third) time to the narrative. Then ask the learners to write on their papers the letters of any pictures that represent a part of the story, or perhaps to list the letters in order to show the sequence of the story.

3. *Carrying Out Commands.* For a classroom in which TPR is an important tool, carrying out commands is one of the most natural of all types of assessment techniques. Berty Segal (n.d.) suggests establishing a list of commands that incorporate the key learning elements for each unit of instruction. While other students are working at their seats, working at learning stations, or developing group projects, Segal tests students in groups of three by giving the commands and having the students carry them out. She uses the same list of commands for all student groups, varying the order in which they are given. The teacher uses a grid to check students who do not perform the command accurately. Other options include the following:

a. Make a picture test containing balloons, either in numbered squares or in a picture format on which each balloon itself is numbered. Ask students to color the balloons according to instructions. You can construct other tests in which you ask students to identify some elements of a picture with numbers or colors, or in which students draw a picture or construct figures on command (for example, the monster drawings).

b. Have individual students carry out your commands, either orally or by writing on slips or cards. You can devise these commands to show comprehension of other vocabulary in addition to the verbs involved.

Interpersonal Mode: Speaking

If all instruction in speaking has been in context and communicative, the assessment function should also be contextual and communicative. The scheme of assessment should reflect the ongoing goals of the program rather than focusing on detail and grammar (which often seem easier to evaluate). In many cases, interpersonal contexts are genuine, naturally occurring opportunities for performance assessment. Interpersonal activities that could form the basis for assessment include the following:

1. *Personal Question–Answer:* Have students discuss a familiar topic, something often discussed in class in the same manner, with you or with one another.

2. *Dialogue:* Two (or several) students may perform a dialogue they have created, memorized, or adapted.

3. *Rejoinder:* Make a statement to which students respond appropriately. For example, if you say, "I feel terrible today," the student says, "That's too bad."

4. *Picture Reaction:* Give students a picture; have them respond either by telling about it, or perhaps by giving the command suggested by the picture (at an earlier stage). See the example in Figure 7.21.

5. *Narrative or Dialogue Completion:* Give the students part of a familiar narrative or dialogue, and ask them to complete it, either by choosing the completion learned in class or by providing a new one created for the occasion.

6. *Role Reversal:* You may use role reversal as a means of evaluating the individual student's development of speaking skills, but neither you nor the student should view it primarily as an assessment tool. When role reversal has become a standard and comfortable part of class procedure, you may begin to incorporate some elements from this activity into the assessment format.

7. *Oral Identification and/or Description of Familiar Objects:* Have students draw familiar objects from a sack or from a "magic box" and identify or describe them aloud. (This may also be a good opportunity to work with requests, politeness vocabulary, and other components of the rituals that have been established in class.) This strategy could be structured as a game, in which students describe items to the class and the class tries to guess which familiar object has been drawn.

8. *Puppet Show:* Have students work in pairs or in small groups to develop puppet shows that may serve as a demonstration of what they have learned.

Interpretive Mode: Reading

Creating means of assessing reading as a communicative function can be challenging, but such means are possible. Asking students to perform written commands is a natural first step, and these commands can take on greater complexity as students progress.

● **FIGURE 7.21** Sample Picture Item. Teacher says: "Tell me something about this picture," or "Give a command that would fit the action."

1. Adapt items suggested in the listening section to evaluate reading by changing the stimulus from the spoken to the written word. (Many of the listening items are readily adaptable.)

2. Ask students to perform commands delivered in writing, either individually or as paper-and-pencil responses done by the entire class at one time.

3. Have students read parts of stories written by the group and react to them in some way—true–false items, multiple-choice items, and so forth. They may fill in blanks with words chosen from a list at the end of or on the side of the reading passage (cloze procedure).

4. Have students match labels with pictures or parts of pictures.

Writing: Interpersonal and Presentational Modes

Much writing will be copying in the early years of an early language program, but some assessment of writing, in addition to listening, speaking, and reading, will leave students with a sense of achievement in all four skills.

1. *Labeling.* Have students label pictures or parts of pictures with the appropriate target language term (see Figure 7.22).

2. *Cloze or Completion.* Have students fill in blanks in a familiar passage, or complete an anecdote without an immediate model. In this kind of an assessment the context is very important, so students will be filling in the blanks to make the meaning clear.

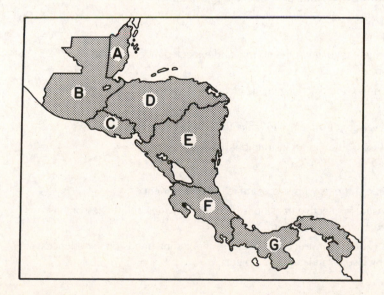

● **FIGURE 7.22** Sample Labeling. Teacher says: "Label the countries on this map from which we have had guests in class."

3. *Commands.* Have students write commands to be performed by the teacher or by a classmate.

● Teacher Evaluation

The teacher is the most important part of any classroom, in any subject area. Teachers who are committed to personal and professional growth and to providing the finest possible learning environment for their students can be the best evaluators of the teaching and learning that take place in their own classrooms. The assistance of supportive peers and administrators can also help teachers achieve new goals and develop new dimensions of their teaching skills. Teachers can work together to give one another feedback and support as they experiment with new approaches and techniques. The reorientation of language teaching toward communication and performance is a major step away from the traditions within which most language teachers have themselves learned languages and have been trained to teach them. Ongoing support and encouragement from peers will play an essential role in making this significant reorientation.

The checklist of teaching behaviors that follows is oriented toward communicative language teaching in the elementary and middle school. It is intended to assist teachers who wish to evaluate their own teaching and to be helpful observers of one another. It will also assist administrators in giving support and feedback to language teachers working in their schools. The observation guide can be used most successfully over an extended period of time, for a series of observations.

The Effective Elementary and Middle School Language Teacher

Use of the Target Language

___ 1. Teacher uses target language as the normal and expected means of classroom communication.

___ 2. Teacher keeps use of the native language clearly separated from use of the target language.

___ 3. Teacher uses a variety of strategies to make the language comprehensible.

___ 4. Teacher avoids translation as an instructional strategy.

Instruction

___ 5. Activities provide students with successful learning experiences.

___ 6. Teacher demonstrates effective transitions between activities and the lesson has momentum and a sense of direction.

___ 7. Teacher uses a variety of instructional strategies, including hands-on experiences, accompanied by visuals and concrete objects.

___ 8. Reading and writing are integrated with listening and speaking experiences.

___ 9. Students ask as well as answer questions.

___10. Grammatical structures and vocabulary are introduced and practiced in meaningful contexts.

___11. Teacher gives clear directions and uses modeling to provide examples for the students.

___12. Teacher allows ample wait-time after questions.

___13. Students are active throughout the class period, and there are varied groupings of students and varied interaction patterns (teacher–student, student–teacher, student–student)

___14. Teacher practices sensitive error correction with primary focus on errors of meaning rather than on errors of form.

Planning

___15. Lesson/unit is standards-based and shows relationship to a guiding thematic idea (thematic center).

___16. Lesson/unit shows a balance of language, culture, and subject content goals.

___17. Language components of lesson/unit include three modes of communication.

___18. Lessons avoid and attempt to counter cultural and other stereotypes.

___19. Lessons incorporate both new and familiar material, and the teacher provides scaffolding to help students comprehend the new material.

___20. Lesson content and activities are appropriate to age and developmental level of the class.

___21. Plans incorporate activities from a variety of cognitive levels, cognitive styles, and intelligences.

Classroom Climate

___22. Teacher appears enthusiastic and motivated.

___23. Teacher shows patience with student attempts to communicate.

___24. Teacher uses varied and appropriate feedback.

___25. Environment is attractive and reflects the target culture.

___26. Discipline is positive, prompt, and nondisruptive.

Assessment

___27. Teacher constantly monitors student comprehension.

___28. Teacher assesses language development in meaningful contexts.

___29. Teacher uses a variety of formal and informal performance assessment tools.

___30. Teacher provides opportunities for self- and peer assessment.

Summary

- A careful and systematic assessment process is an essential component of the early language program.

- The most powerful assessment tools are performance tasks that allow students to use the language they have learned in a meaningful and purposeful way.

- The culminating performance assessment focuses the unit and guides the planning of all unit components and activities.

- Checklists and rubrics can help teachers evaluate performance on these tasks and help develop student skills in self-assessment.

- Students can also benefit from achievement testing that gives them the opportunity to demonstrate what they have learned in a supportive, positive atmosphere designed to help them succeed.

- The most effective assessment tools test what has been taught in the way it has been taught.

Only when the means of testing appropriately reflect the goals of the curriculum can those goals most effectively be achieved.

- Student performance assessment can be an important component of program assessment. The SOPA and the ELLOPA have been developed by the Center for Applied Linguistics to assist schools and programs in evaluating student progress. The NOELLA, developed by the Center for Applied Second Language Studies, is a Web-based assessment for learners in grades 3 through 6. The STAMP, also Web-based, is designed for novice–low through intermediate–mid learners, grades 7 through 16.

- Evaluation of teacher performance is another important component of the effective elementary and middle school program. It is most valuable when the teacher is a critical self-evaluator who receives support and encouragement from colleagues and administrators.

For Study and Discussion

1. In your department meeting, a discussion has developed about the current policy of giving students in the elementary school language program a grade of "Satisfactory/Unsatisfactory" and basing the assessment on observation of the degree of each child's participation and enthusiasm. You have been in the department only a few weeks, but you have some insight to add. What suggestions would you make to the department, and why?

2. You and your fellow teacher have decided to develop some of your tests together in order to be able to write more effective assessments. However, now she is complaining about the tests you write. She claims that if you give the learners only material that you are sure they can succeed with, and test them in the same way you taught them, then the results of your tests aren't worth anything. How do you respond to her?

3. Choose a series of lessons from materials that you know, from observations you have made, or from lessons found on the Internet. Design a short test for one or two of the objectives covered in the lessons, no more than five questions, keeping in mind the testing principles identified in this chapter. What activities in the lessons have prepared the learners to be tested in this way? Or what activities would you have to incorporate in the lessons in order to use the testing items you have written?

4. Examine carefully the K–12 Performance Guidelines for the novice level, including all six of the categories described (see Appendix). Design a performance task that would allow students to show their ability to use the language at this level in interpersonal, interpretive, and presentational modes of communication, and indicate which of the guidelines are being addressed. Create a checklist and a rubric to assist you in evaluating this assessment.

5. Use the teacher checklist in this chapter to evaluate your own teaching performance in the class setting with which you are most familiar. Write a goals statement in which you set objectives for your continued growth as a teacher. Use that personal goals statement to list four things you would like to have your favorite colleague watch for and give you feedback about on her or his next visit to your class (make them very specific).

For Further Reading

The following sources are recommended for additional information about material covered in this chapter. Chapter citations are documented in Works Cited at the end of this book.

Blaz, Deborah. *A Collection of Performance Tasks and Rubrics: Foreign Languages.* Larchmont, NY: Eye on Education, 2001.

Boyles, Peggy. "Scoring Rubrics: Changing the Way We Grade." *Learning Languages* 4:1 (1998): 29–32.

Fisher, Douglas, and Nancy Frey. *Checking for Understanding: Formative Assessment Techniques for Your Classroom.* Alexandria, VA: Association for Supervision and Curriculum Development, 2007.

Gilzow, Douglas F., and Lucinda E. Branaman. *Lessons Learned: Model Early Foreign Language Programs.* McHenry, IL: Center for Applied Linguistics and Delta Systems, 2000.

Goodman, Kenneth S., Lois Bridges Bird, and Yetta M. Goodman (Eds.). *The Whole Language Catalog: Supplement on Authentic Assessment.* Santa Rosa, CA: American School Publishers, 1992.

Heining-Boynton, Audrey. "The FLES Program Evaluation Inventory (FPEI)." *Foreign Language Annals* 24:3 (1991): 193–201.

National Capital Language Resource Center. Portfolio Assessment in the Foreign Language Classroom. Interactive module available on-line at: www.cal .org/nclrc/portfolio/modules.html.

O'Malley, J. Michael, and Lorraine Valdez Pierce. *Authentic Assessment for English Language Learners: Practical Approaches for Teachers.* Reading, MA; Addison-Wesley, 1996.

Sandrock, Paul. *Planning Curriculum for Learning World Languages.* Madison, WI: Wisconsin Department of Public Instruction, 2002.

Taylor, Gregory, Carine Feyten, John Meros, and Joyce Nutta. "The Effects of FLES on Reading Comprehension and Vocabulary Achievement: A Multi-method Longitudinal Study." *Learning Languages* 13:2 (Spring 2008): 30–37.

Websites of Interest

CAL Testing and Assessment: www.cal.org/topics/ta/.

Linguafolio: www.ncssfl.org/links/index .php?linguafolio.

Linguafolio Jr.: www.doe.virginia.gov/linguafolio/ junior.html.

NADSFL Characteristics of Effective Foreign Language Programs: www.nadsfl.org/ characteristics.htm.

New Jersey CAPS Assessment project: http:// flenj.org/CAPS/?page=parent.

NOELLA: casls.uoregon.edu/noella.php.

STAMP: www.avantassessment.com/products/ about_stamp.html.

Planning and Evaluating Highly Successful Foreign Language Programs: PearsonSchool.com/ EndInMind

Chapter 8

Managing the Successful Early Language Classroom

Enduring Understanding

- Goals and plans for student behavior are an integral part of effective classroom instruction.

Essential Question

- What are the elements that contribute to an effectively functioning classroom?

Every teacher steps into a classroom with the intention of being effective, although we may not always have a clear idea of how to achieve that goal. Based on their research, Good and Brophy (2007) identified three characteristics of effective teachers: They have classroom management skills, they teach for lesson mastery, and they practice positive expectations.

These characteristics are clearly closely related, and much of this book supports effectiveness in all three areas. This chapter focuses on the first of these characteristics: managing an early language classroom. Classroom management involves all of those procedures and routines that make our time with our students as productive as possible. Without effective management skills, a teacher's repertoire of units and activities is useless.

Just as we plan the content of the lesson and unit, we must also plan for the management of the class: rules and consequences, procedures and routines. Just as we have objectives and outcomes in our lesson and unit plans, we have goals and plans for student behavior in our management plan.

● Factors beyond the Teacher's Control

A number of factors are involved in classroom management over which the teacher has virtually no control. We have to develop our management strategy by taking these factors into consideration—factors that differ from school to school and even from class to class. This section describes some of these factors.

Time of Day

In the morning, classes are usually full of energy; many elementary school teachers regard morning as prime learning time. On the other hand, an early morning class in middle school might be difficult to wake up. During the last hour of the day, students tend to be tired—or sometimes all wound up such as on a Friday or just before a holiday.

Lunch presents another issue. Before lunch, students may be hungry and preoccupied, or restless and watching the clock, especially in middle school. After lunch, some students may be sleepy, and others may be especially excitable if they had a high-sugar meal.

We need to take into account where students were immediately before the language class. They may have come from outdoor play, or from physical education, and they will need activities and encouragement to help them cool down so they can make the most of class time. They may have come from a relatively quiet activity, or from a long stretch of sitting or concentrating. Then they may need the teacher to energize them and refocus them on the language tasks.

Where the Language Class Is Held

It's possible that elementary school language teachers work in their own classrooms. It is even more likely, however, that they will be teaching from carts and traveling from one classroom to the next. Those teachers have to work within the management styles of the classroom teachers in whose rooms they are guests, and they may need to negotiate some of their own management system with other teachers. Here, the key to success is establishing good relationships with fellow teachers.

Moving from class to class means adjusting to the mood of each new classroom, and sometimes having to wait until the classroom teacher is ready to turn the class over to the language teacher. Once in a while a classroom teacher returns to the class late, causing the language teacher to be late and perhaps breathless for the start of the next class.

Sometimes language classes are held in choir rooms, on stages in the gymnasium, or in a corner of the library. Each of these nontypical class settings has its own challenges and requires specific management planning.

Social and Emotional Factors: Nature of Children

The last and most important of the factors beyond our control is the nature of the students with whom we are dealing. They are just kids! And they carry all the developmental characteristics of students their age.

Teachers need to be knowledgeable about how children develop and about what constitutes typical and predictable behavior for each of the ages we teach. The language teacher who is determined to have kindergartners sit still for 15 minutes at a time will misinterpret the 5-year-olds' need to move around as misbehavior and treat the children accordingly. The teacher who uses regular and frequent partner activities because she or he recognizes the need for middle school students to interact with their friends has learned to turn a developmental characteristic into an advantage for language learning.

These kids we teach tend to be fun-loving and enthusiastic, and they show their enthusiasm and their sense of fun in different ways at different ages. They can be amazingly perceptive and unbearably wise. They can be stubborn and frightened. They can be easily hurt, and sometimes those who seem to have the toughest shell are the most fragile inside.

We may have troubled students who need every bit of our skill to help them manage themselves in our classrooms. We may have students with physical and emotional needs beyond our expertise, but our class needs to be a special place for all of them.

Frank Smith (1988, 2006) has described language learning as a social gift, not a genetic gift. Learning another language is becoming a member of the club, the community of people who speak that language. We can invite all students in.

● Factors within the Teacher's Control: Classroom Management Basics

Advice to new teachers almost always centers around classroom management issues: "Be organized." "Be prepared." "Be firm." "Be consistent." "Be fair." The number of books addressing classroom management could fill one whole wing of a library. The best place to start in developing a plan for classroom management, however, is within the school itself. To plan an effective program of classroom management for a specific school setting, the teacher should:

- Be informed about all school procedures and follow them carefully.

- Find out which classroom teachers have the best reputation for well-managed classrooms—then visit with them and visit their classes. They will have the best understanding of the students in this school and at these grade levels. The observation suggestions in Figure 8.1 will help to make the most of such a visit.

- In the elementary school setting, visit all the classes you will be working with before beginning language instruction, if possible, in order to understand the way each of the classrooms functions and to get a feeling for how students behave generally in their regular classes. This is especially important for teachers who are new to the level they will be teaching.

- Talk with other language teachers in the school or in another school in the same community, if there are other language programs.

● **FIGURE 8.1**   Observation Suggestions for Elementary/Middle School World Language Classrooms

Take notes on the sheet below and use them as a basis for discussion after class.

Grade level observed _____ Date _____ Time _____ to _____

What did the teacher do to gain attention?

What strategies did the teacher use for beginning and ending activities, and for making transitions from one activity or topic to another?

What did the teacher do to motivate pupil interest and engagement?

What kinds of activities did you observe in the class (teacher presentation, partner or small-group work, individual seatwork, problem solving, etc.)? How often did activities change?

What topics and activities seemed to be especially motivating to these pupils?

Did there seem to be any class routines that were followed, or patterns pupils knew to follow? What rules or expectations do pupils seem to understand in this classroom? Explain.

What types of nonverbal communication did the teacher use (eye contact, hands, proximity, etc.)?

How do these pupils behave when they are bored? Excited? Under stress?

What behaviors (individual or group) surprised you? Bothered you? Impressed you? Were there any behaviors that bothered you but didn't seem to bother the teacher? Or that she or he seemed to ignore?

What did you learn about pupils of this age during this visit to their classroom?

● Read books on successful management, such as those suggested at the end of this chapter.

The following major guidelines for classroom management will help teachers organize and evaluate the advice they receive and to build their own management plan that will be effective specifically for the early language classroom.

1. Maintain a positive environment.
2. Establish clear procedures.
3. Plan for every single moment—and beyond!
4. Be proactive: involve parents and the school community.

Guideline 1: Maintain a Positive Environment

The Teacher—Who Am I?   The essential element in a successful classroom is the teacher. Every study of methodology or student performance eventually concludes that the single-most important factor in student success is the teacher. Teachers need to ask themselves: "Who am I? What are my strengths? What are my weaknesses? Am I aware of them so that I can build on my strengths and compensate for my weaknesses? What are my reasons for being a teacher?" If we have a realistic picture of ourselves and feel confident that we have the skills we need to be successful early language teachers, we can also be successful in creating positive feelings in our classrooms.

Haim Ginott (1972) makes an eloquent statement about the significance of the teacher in the classroom environment:

> I've come to a frightening conclusion. I am the decisive element in the classroom. It's my personal approach that creates the climate. It's my daily mood that makes the weather. As a teacher, I possess a tremendous power to make a child's life miserable or joyous. I can be a tool of torture or an instrument of inspiration. I can humiliate or humor, hurt or heal. In all situations, it is my response that decides whether a crisis will be escalated or de-escalated, and a child humanized or de-humanized. (pp. 15–16)

Mission   Another way teachers build a positive focus is by remembering our powerful and important mission. We are giving our students the beautiful gift of another language, in a country in which that opportunity has not always been available. We are opening the door to new ways of thinking, a door that links us to the rest of the world. Many of us have come to believe that this is an important step toward peace.

Sense of Humor   We need to activate our sense of humor, because it is such a help in maintaining a positive atmosphere. If we remember to keep it with us at all times, we may be amazed at how far it will take us. Approaching a situation with humor and patience can defuse many tense moments.

A classroom filled with laughter is likely to be a healthy classroom. It is important to remember, however, that laughter should never be at the expense of the dignity of any student, and laughing at another student should be promptly confronted and stopped.

Keeping Our Cool   Anger has no place in the classroom. Allowing oneself to lose control and to shout is simply inappropriate. And tempting though it may be at times, striking back at a student with a put-down or sarcasm damages everyone in the classroom—including the teacher. These are the same behaviors that we are trying to discourage our students from using. Even though we might be seething inside, maintaining a calm and supportive manner is an essential part of keeping a positive atmosphere.

Motivating Students   Another key to maintaining a positive environment is to motivate our students. Motivation is important both for the content of our lessons and units and to help students understand the value of learning another language. We need to explain the reasons for an early start and a long sequence and why the language they are learning is important. In this way we can empower our students to participate more fully.

Availability and Visibility to Students   We can also nurture a positive atmosphere by being available to students before and after school, for help, and, on occasion, just to talk. We can share a bit of ourselves during our classes, so that they recognize us as people with interests and with interesting experiences. We can greet students by name when we meet them in the classroom and when we see them in the halls or in the world beyond the classroom.

One of the most meaningful ways to be visible and supportive to students is to attend their activities and chaperone their field trips and parties. When we can tell a student, "I really enjoyed your play last night" or "The band concert was very enjoyable," we are affirming them and supporting them in important ways. The additional benefit for the teacher is the discovery of talents and aspects of personality that are not always revealed in the language classroom.

Guideline 2: Establish Clear Procedures

Our second classroom management basic is to establish clear procedures. This means that we have clear and concrete expectations for academic performance and for how the classroom functions, and that we present these expectations to the students in a clear, step-by-step fashion. Many students do not transfer behavioral expectations from the English language setting, where there is relative silence much of the time. The language class is sometimes a real contrast, and students need clear guidance as to what is expected.

Establish Rules   Establishing and communicating a set of classroom rules is an extremely important element in helping the class to function smoothly. We can help maintain a positive environment when we state classroom rules positively and reinforce positive behaviors.

When establishing rules in the elementary school setting, we must also consult with the classroom teachers and set up ground rules for how we will operate together. For example, the language teacher will need to make clear who will do the disciplining during the language class and how well the language class rules will mesh with those of the classroom teacher. Of course, all rules will be consistent with school policies.

The first step in developing a set of rules is to decide which behaviors are important to you in the classroom. Next, you put those behaviors into short and simple statements or commands in the target language, so that the students will be able to understand them. These statements should be positive; for example, instead of "Don't run," state, "Walk." Instead of "Don't touch your neighbor," say, "Keep hands and feet to yourself." Effective rules should be:

1. Observable
2. Enforceable
3. Nonjudgmental
4. An expression of behavior that is important to the teacher in order to teach effectively
5. Stated in the target language

Audray Weber's rules for her K–5 Spanish classes are *¡Paren, Miren, Escuchen! (Stop, Look, Listen!).* When she wants attention, she sings those three words in a familiar pattern and the students respond immediately.

Jo Ellen Hague's rules for her French classes are *Look, Listen, Participate* (by raising your hand), *and Speak French!—Regardez, Ecoutez, Participez, Parlez français!* She writes each of these rules on a paddle, and when students need to be reminded of one of the rules, she holds up that paddle. Jo Ellen also reviews the rules daily by holding up the paddles.

Jessica Haxhi has four rules for her Japanese students: Listen, Raise your hand, Keep hands to yourself, Speak Japanese! She also has an important silence signal: When she wants students to stop whatever they are doing and be quiet, she places both hands on top of her head with her elbows raised. When students see this they put their hands on their heads, too, stop talking, and pay attention to the teacher.

After you have decided on the rules, the next step is to plan how to teach the rules using the target language. The most effective way to go about this is to do a lot of modeling and then to involve student participation. When teachers incorporate a motion with each rule, the students remember it more easily, and the teacher can later use TPR as a form of practice for the rules. In the case of Jessica Haxhi's four rules for Japanese, for example, she has the students cup their hands behind their ears for "Listen." They raise their hand dramatically for "Raise your hand." They cross their arms and hold their hands above the elbow for "Keep hands to yourself," and for "Speak Japanese," they make speaking motions with their hands and repeat a Japanese greeting. Many teachers post their rules in the target language after they have taught them, usually with a picture or other symbol to help students connect the words with meanings.

Jessica Haxhi is able to communicate to the students exactly what they may and may not do in the class when she demonstrates what it looks like to break the rule and then points to the rule or shows the gesture for the rule. Some teachers have a puppet misbehave and ask the students to point to the rule, or show the motion for the rule, or call out the rule, once they have learned the language for doing so.

One of the most important things to remember about establishing and implementing rules in a classroom in which only the target language is spoken is modeling. In fact, some educators say that this is the key to all good teaching. We need to show students in a step-by-step fashion exactly what it is they are supposed to do. Management problems are much reduced when all students are on task and understand how they are expected to behave.

Establish the Connection between Behavior and Consequences—Positive and Negative
Hand in hand with establishing the rules is determining the consequences for breaking the rules. We need to make sure that students understand the connection between a behavior and the consequence attached to that behavior. Consequences will be determined to a certain extent by school policies, but the teacher needs to have a plan for the steps to take when students break the rules.

Some teachers link their consequences with rewards. For example, Jessica Haxhi and her colleague Kazumi Yamashita use a Japanese toy to implement consequences. There are four layers stacked together to make up this toy. When someone disobeys a rule, the teacher removes the lowest layer. For each disruption another layer is removed. At the end of the class, the number of remaining layers is entered on a chart as the class score for the day. There is competition among the classes for the most points over a specified period of time, and when points reach a certain predetermined number, the class qualifies for a party or some kind of special day.

Laura Igarteburu described a similar management strategy on the Ñandu listserv. She gives each class a sticker if the whole class follows her three rules: "Listen. Raise your hand. Speak Spanish." At the beginning of the class period she writes a word in Spanish on the board, and whenever any student breaks a rule she erases a letter from the word. If there are no letters remaining in the word at the end of the class, there is no sticker for the day. As the year progresses, Laura uses shorter words each month, until, by the last month, the "game" is played with a one-letter word! Penny Fields uses a similar strategy with numbers. At the beginning of each class period she writes the number 10 on the board, and after the first breaking of a rule she erases the 10 and replaces it with a 9, usually without comment, so that peer pressure can work its magic. This process continues throughout the class. The number on the board at the end of the class is recorded, and whenever the class total reaches 100 points, the students may have a special day in which they select favorite games or other activities.

Sometimes individual behaviors persist and do not respond to group consequences, especially with students who have recurring behavior problems. In that case, additional measures are called for. For many teachers, the first step is to give "the look." Every teacher needs the skill of looking directly at a student, without smiling, and silently communicating the message "I see what you are doing and we both know you need to stop." For some students and some situations, this is all the student may need to resume the expected behavior.

Teachers often follow this step by "moving in on" the offending student, without interrupting the lesson or calling attention to the student. When the teacher moves close enough, this may stop the behavior altogether. Proximity can also be used to prevent behavior problems from starting, when the teacher senses a potential problem in some part of the room.

Sometimes just calling the student's name will serve as a good reminder, although this strategy must be used carefully. Calling the name as a reprimand also calls attention to the student and that may be just what the misbehavior is intended to accomplish. It is best to use the student's name as a kind of invitation: "Fabian, did you get a good look at this?" or "Claire, I want you to notice this picture especially." Using the student's name in an example can also be a good way to pull a student back in: "Let's imagine that Roberta is walking down the street in Germany looking for a good place to buy a loaf of bread." Calling on the student next to the offending student can sometimes achieve the same purpose. Calling on an inattentive student to answer a question, primarily for the purpose of "catching the student out," communicates the message that questioning is more of a punishment than it is an invitation.

Many teachers find that a disruptive or inattentive student can be best handled by temporarily moving him or her out of the group or to another part of the room until the student is ready to participate more fully. With a very young child, this time-out should be short. When we place a student outside the group, we must be certain to monitor her or his behavior closely and to remember to call the student back to the group as soon as she or he seems ready. We are responsible for every student in our class, all the time.

With repeated misbehaviors, it is time to start keeping a written log of behaviors and the steps we have taken to deal with those behaviors. If misbehaviors persist, a call home is often a helpful step, and we need to be prepared to give a detailed history of the behavior when we consult with the parents. Persistent or troubling misbehavior should also be discussed with the principal in early stages, so that there can be a team approach to helping the student resolve the problems. For any of these steps, a carefully dated log with simple descriptions of behavior can be invaluable.

Here are some helpful tips put together by K–5 teachers in Georgia:

- Know the process that works in your school and grade level.
- Do not plan for a consequence you will not be willing to apply.
- Make sure students know the consequences.
- Make sure parents know the consequences.
- Be consistent, impartial, and fair.
- Follow through with consequences.
- Don't make threats—use your system.
- Remember that the child makes the choice to break the rule and therefore receive the consequence.

Rewards   As with poor behavior, there are also consequences for good behavior—of course, we usually call these rewards. There has been a great deal of professional discussion about the benefits and the risks of rewarding performance or behavior, and about intrinsic and extrinsic motivation. Although we focus on intrinsic motivation for positive behavior and for learning in the long run, in the short run many teachers find it useful to use extrinsic systems for motivating positive behavior and performance.

Many teachers give stickers for good performance or for especially good behavior; these stickers seem to be valued by students in the whole K–8 spectrum. That depends on the sticker, of course; no eighth-grader would feel rewarded by a Barney sticker, for example. Some teachers also use small pieces of candy as occasional rewards. Stickers can be awarded to individuals or to a whole class, as in the Igarteburu strategy described earlier. Similar rewards can be given for target language use or for other forms of excellent performance.

Some teachers use a visual challenge to motivate behavior—for example, learners in a Spanish class move one step higher on an Aztec pyramid whenever they have earned the step through good behavior or good performance. Other teachers keep track of points on a chart, or placing marbles or coins in a jar. When the goal is achieved, there is a celebration—a party, a prized activity, or some other special event. For Penny Fields and Laura

Igarteburu, the special event is a day on which students are allowed to select favorite games or activities, in the target language. (It is not a vacation from the language, nor is it reason for the teacher to pay for an expensive party.)

It is important to keep in mind, however, that extrinsic rewards are a temporary measure, a bridge to positive performance that we want to encourage for its own sake. We should plan to wean our students from these extrinsic rewards once the behavior has been well established.

There are intangible rewards that may be even more powerful than stickers and candy. Sometimes classes or individuals feel rewarded just by the fact that the teacher is pleased, or happy, or even excited by a certain performance. Students can feel rewarded when they are given the opportunity to lead a class. Some teachers lead group applause whenever a student has done a good job on an individual performance.

Students also feel rewarded when they are given a special responsibility for the class or the classroom. Most children love to help, and the teacher needs only to identify specific tasks. Tasks are also a good way to help some students develop a sense of responsibility. Some possibilities for "rewarding" tasks include erasing chalkboards or whiteboards, acting as line leader, passing out materials, leading some familiar group activity, or acting as messenger for items that need to be delivered to the office or to another classroom.

Our ultimate goal is for students to feel rewarded and motivated by their own success. Our role is to praise, support, and encourage along the way.

Establish Procedures for All Classroom Routines   We need procedures for making sure that students understand what we want them to do and how we want them to do it. We need procedures for beginning the class, for ending the class, and for maintaining and refocusing the attention of the class as the lesson is in progress. Procedures are also needed for other aspects of classroom routine, such as asking to sharpen a pencil or to get out of one's seat. With such procedures in place, students know what to expect, and they feel safe and comfortable within the routines we have established.

Beginning Class   Many teachers begin their classes with a song or a chant or a routine greeting—or sometimes all three. Students need a signal for when it is time to begin the language class and give the teacher their full attention. In many cases when the traveling teacher pushes the cart through the door the class starts with a greeting and a song, giving the teacher a chance to take out materials and set the stage for the lesson about to begin. When students come to the language classroom, there have to be procedures for quickly taking assigned places, followed by a teacher-led greeting or another opening routine.

After the opening song, teachers often continue with a calendar routine or song. Naming the day and date, with the use of a large calendar in the target language, gives practice with numbers as well as the names for the days of the week. Another common component of the calendar time is to check the weather and record it. Students enjoy leading this portion of the class and can often do so quite early in the year. Once the students get to a certain point in their language development, calendar time can change so as to incorporate different types of language. If teachers still use a daily calendar routine in a third-grade class, for example, it should look very different from the routine used in a kindergarten or in a fifth-grade class.

Researchers tell us that the first 5 minutes and the last 5 minutes of any class period are prime learning time. We need to be careful not to let opening routines and calendar activities drag on too long or else we fail to take advantage of this prime learning time for important work with the main objectives of our lesson.

Ending Class Routines   The responsibility for ending the class period belongs to the teacher, not to the students. This is of special concern in schools with bell schedules. We need to teach students that the teacher is the one who dismisses the class, not the bell or the second hand on the clock.

As we approach the end of the class period, it is important to be conscious of how we leave the students for the next teacher. If we have engaged the class in some very lively activities, we will make sure that that we have a cool-down activity before we close. When students leave our class, they have to be ready for the next teacher to continue with their learning.

When students leave our language classrooms, they need a routine for lining up at the door and leaving the room quietly and in an orderly fashion. Teachers often dismiss students by table, choosing the most cooperative table first, or the table that was ready the fastest. Sometimes a teacher dismisses by clothing colors, hair color, or some other characteristic, so that this portion of class is a continuation of language learning time.

Many ending routines are similar to opening routines in that they include a good-bye song or a chant and, of course, saying good-bye to the teacher. Japanese teachers usually incorporate a traditional bow at the beginning and end of class. Traveling teachers sometimes include a "heads-down" component at the very end of the class. That is, the last thing students do as part of the language class is to put their heads down on their desks or tables, until the next teacher arrives to "wake them up."

Routines for Maintaining and Refocusing Attention   Elementary and middle school language teachers use various routines for maintaining the focus of the class or getting back attention if it is wavering. These routines are especially necessary with younger students. The younger the students are, the more easily they will be distracted.

Various options are available for focusing student attention, including hand signals, rhythmic clapping, songs, and other activities. It is important to be consistent with these signals and not to introduce too many at one time.

One common quiet or attention signal is sometimes called the *zero noise signal,* or the *universal cooperative learning signal.* The teacher raises her or his hand, and students raise their hands as soon as they see the teacher's hand raised. When they raise their hands, students must also stop the activity, stop talking, and show the hand signal to their teacher and to their classmates. This routine puts some of the responsibility for quieting down the classroom on the students themselves. Students need practice in responding to these signals, too, until they become habitual—otherwise, the signals won't have any effect on their behavior!

Some teachers use a system of counting down or counting up to indicate that the class may be exceeding the bounds of the rules, usually with a raised hand and counting from one to five or five to one in the target language. By the time the teacher has reached the end of the sequence, or the lowest number when counting down, the students must be ready to continue the activity or to begin a new activity. Some teachers use rhythmic clapping to help refocus the students. When Audray Weber needs to regain attention, she might interrupt an activity by singing her three class rules until students are silent and ready to begin again.

Some teachers use special routines when beginning or ending an activity. Audray Weber calls the names of the students who are ready to begin an activity, putting others on notice that they need to get ready themselves. Tara Kraft-Mahnke indicates the start of an activity by calling out *"Luces! Camera! Acción!" (Lights! Camera! Action!),* accompanied by dramatic gestures reflecting the excitement of movie making.

Teachers can also help students by signaling the end of an activity. When students are engaged in group work, hearing or seeing that they have 3 minutes left can help them focus and finish the task. When everyone is engaged with a successful game, the teacher can end the game more easily by indicating (in the target language), "Two more turns," or "We'll play one more time," and then sticking to that format. Jessica Haxhi often wears a thematically appropriate hat when she monitors a class activity such as partner work, interviews, or a simulation. She signals the end of the activity by removing her hat.

Procedures for Performing Other Class Activities   As the teacher creates a management plan, the more carefully procedures are developed for the recurring activities in the classroom, the more successful the plan is likely to be. The teacher should design a procedure and a plan to teach students how to do each of the following:

- *Ask permission* to leave their seats (to sharpen pencils, get materials, go the bathroom, etc.). Passwords can be helpful tools for these procedures.
- *Pass out and collect materials.* Teachers must show students the procedures for picking up and returning materials when they are working in groups, or when materials such as papers, craft materials, or books need to be distributed during class. A few minutes spent practicing these procedures will ultimately save hours of class time over the course of a year.

    Many teachers build the collecting of the materials into the class activity itself so that by the time the activity is over, the teacher has the materials back. Total Physical Response is a useful strategy for this purpose, such as, "Put all the red animals into the basket. Put all the green animals into the basket." And so on.

    Instead of doing everything themselves, some teachers choose student assistants to serve as materials helpers. Students usually feel rewarded by the opportunity to help in this way, and their assistance is especially valuable because of short class times and a need to move quickly from one class to another in an elementary school program.

- *Transitions from one activity to another.* When activities change, when students need to move from one place to another, when the focus moves from the large group to individual or partner work, the teacher needs to plan for an efficient transition. For example, transitions involving movement can be facilitated by means of a chant or a familiar song that relates to the next activity or the one just completed. Teachers can describe exactly what behavior is expected during the change from one group configuration to another, perhaps making a game of finding a partner within 10 seconds or being in the assigned seat and ready to work before the class has completed the singing of a favorite song. The teacher should examine each lesson plan to discover where transitional activities will be needed and then plan for them.

Procedures for Calling on Students Efficiently   Deciding which student to call on can be a difficult process for the teacher, and sometimes it contributes to wasted class time. So many hands are waving in the air! How can we remember who last had a turn? Or whose turn is next? We also know that our field of vision sometimes causes us to favor one side of the group over the other. One strategy is to move the students (or ourselves) so that the same students are not always to our left or to our right during class activities. Another simple strategy for making sure that all students have been included is to begin an activity with all students standing, and then have each student sit down after participating.

A further technique involves writing student names on individual notecards or craft sticks. The teacher draws a card or a stick from the pack and calls on the student whose name is written there. This ensures that students will be called on at random, and it also makes calling on students much more efficient, since no time is lost in deciding who will be called on among the sea of hands that might be raised. The teacher continues going through the pack until each student has had a turn. This technique can also be used for assessment purposes as we go through the pack over the course of several days.

A second way to use the cards or sticks is to put the student's name back with the others, once the student has had a turn. In this way, the students who have already been called on will remain alert since they do not know if or when their name will be called again. Used in this way, however, there is no assurance that every student will have a chance to participate. Another strategy for retaining attention would be to occasionally draw a name from among the students who have already recited, so that no student feels they can afford to let their attention drift.

Another factor to consider when calling on students is wait-time. Research tells us that students need 3 to 5 seconds of thinking time in their native language in order to give a good answer to a question. They are likely to require more time to think of a response in a new language, except for quick memorized responses. Allowing students enough time to think will generate more responses and higher-quality responses.

Guideline 3: Plan for Every Single Moment—And Beyond!

Our third basic for classroom management involves planning, planning, and more planning. You must have a detailed plan for each lesson. There can be no downtime because if there is an unplanned moment, or if you have to stop and think about what to do next, the students will begin to make plans of their own! It is better to have too many activities planned rather than too few.

Teachers must adjust the classroom activities to fit their students' attention span. For kindergarten students, activities must be changed every few minutes, whereas sixth-through eighth-grade students can stay on one topic for longer periods of time. Some researchers suggest that most children can focus for a number of minutes equal to their age plus two. Thus, a 7-year-old can focus for no more than 9 minutes under the best conditions.

The teacher's plan must provide activities in which each student can experience a measure of success and satisfaction, consistent with his or her ability. This principle requires attention to diverse learning styles and to each of the multiple intelligences identified by Howard Gardner (1983, 1999), as well as to the differing academic abilities among the students, and the presence of physical and emotional obstacles that some students have to overcome. Our goal should be that each student is able to succeed with at least one thing in every class period.

Effective planning will involve the students in directing their own activities. Students should have a chance to lead the group, make decisions, and assist the teacher in meaningful ways. The class is usually far more attentive when a student leads a familiar activity like the calendar or a song than they would be if the teacher were the only leader. Older students can check for the completion of homework, monitor attendance, or take responsibility for other important tasks.

Lesson planning must also provide for a balance between movement and sitting-at-desks tasks. It is important to remember that K–1 students have a physical need to move. It is more stressful for them to sit quietly for a long period of time than it would be for them to run around the track for the same amount of time. The same can also be said for middle school students.

Some teachers provide for this variety by moving their students from one side of the classroom to the other when they change activities. This helps keep the class interested and focused. Sometimes a quick TPR sequence can serve as a transition from one activity to another and provide a needed energy lift. A song or a chant, accompanied by movement, can also provide a needed change of pace.

Procedures for Using Every Bit of Class Time

There is so little time in a language class, especially in the elementary school, that every minute is precious. Teachers work hard to take advantage of every moment. A teacher might sing while a student is taking a long time to make a decision. Sometimes students themselves can sing to mark time or while materials are being distributed or collected.

Effective teachers simply don't waste a single minute. For example, when students are engaged in a group activity, the teacher is busy monitoring the group and intervening whenever there is a need for assistance, or for correction of behavior. Sometimes a teacher will also use part of the group time to organize materials for the next activity.

Sponge activities are important resources to have available to make the most of class time. These sponges are used to soak up any extra class minutes with productive student activity. A well-planned teacher has a repertoire of these activities ready whenever they are needed—such as at the end of a class when there's not enough time to start a longer activity but there is a minute or two before the students leave. Sponge activities can also serve as options for students when they have finished their individual or group work.

The following activities are examples of useful sponges for different language levels:

- Playing the game "I Spy," or "I See Something You Don't See" (followed by a description), or "I'm Thinking of a Person Who Is Wearing" (followed by a description).

- Asking, "How many questions can you think of to ask a person from Germany who might come to visit the class?"

- A simple back-to-back partner TPR activity, in which partners take turns giving commands and then face each other to see if their actions match. For example, "Touch your nose, 1–2–3."

- Posing the challenge, "In two minutes, write down as many jungle animals (farm, savanna, ocean) as you can think of with your partner. Did anyone write down anything that no one else thought of?"

- Stating, "I'll say a word and see if you can give me the opposite (or as many synonyms as you can think of," etc.).

- Saying, "I'm thinking of an animal that starts with the letter _____."

Guideline 4: Be Proactive and Involve Parents and the School Community

An early and very important step in management planning is to develop a close relationship with the school principal, or with the administrator who is responsible for student discipline. You might want to share your management plan with this person and invite suggestions. If you make the administrator aware of problems that arise before they become crises, the two of you can work together as a team.

Teachers also need to enlist parent support. Parents need to be informed about class policies and activities, so that there will be no surprises if we have to contact them about a problem situation. A letter home at the beginning of the year is a good starting point in building this relationship. Then we can send notes and make phone calls regularly, with more "good-news" messages than negative ones. Newsletters are another important vehicle for keeping parents informed about classes, expectations, and the philosophy of the program. A note sent out at the beginning of each new unit, or on a regular basis every two to four weeks, can prevent misunderstanding and build parent support for the program.

Students should know that we will follow up on problems that arise in school. When we call a parent, we need to make sure that we talk with parents in person. It is usually best not to leave a phone message that could be intercepted, or that might be misinterpreted before it can be clarified. The phone call itself should be in the spirit of enlisting parent cooperation and inviting their insights about the student who matters to both of us. We should try to follow up negative messages with positive ones as soon as possible. We also need to be aware of family circumstances before sending out negative reports—in some cases, a bad school report could have serious unintended family consequences.

Interactive homework is another powerful tool for connecting home and the classroom. Students take home examples of their work in class, with the expectation that they will share it with some adult in their lives who will sign it, comment on it, and return it to school. This practice gives parents a much better gauge of what their students are learning than if they periodically ask, "What did you learn in Japanese today?" or "How do you say _____ in French?"

The best method of all for building parent understanding of the language class is to invite the parents into the classroom itself. Then they can see for themselves how the class functions and how their children behave and perform. They may even become interested enough to volunteer assistance for special projects and activities.

● Special Issues Affecting the Traveling Teacher— à la Cart

Many teachers in programs for young learners live a mobile life and travel from classroom to classroom using a cart. Although most early language teachers would prefer to have their own room that they could decorate thematically and set up to match their teaching style, there are also some benefits in the traveling situation. In a discussion of the traveling teacher on the Ñandu listserv, several advantages were mentioned.

Mary Sosnowski points out that traveling to the children's space makes it possible to incorporate the posters, bulletin boards, and current student work in the daily lesson. Communication with the classroom teacher is regular and natural. When the language teacher comes to the classroom, there is less disruption of the students' day and the language feels like a more integrated part of their learning.

Susan Fomento teaches in her own classroom in one school and travels in another. She notes that students have their basic tools close at hand when she comes to them, so she doesn't lose time by having to distribute scissors, markers, rulers, or other things that students normally have in their desks. Maintaining a room of her own requires considerable time and effort, and she also notices that she sees far less of her colleagues when she teaches in her own room. All things considered, Susan prefers to have her own room.

Usually teachers don't have a choice as to whether they will teach in their own room or from a cart. When it is necessary for the teacher to travel, there are a number of ways to make the most of the situation, beginning with the cart itself. Figure 8.2 gives a list of ways in which a cart could be adapted, and shows a photo of a commercially available cart. The cart has to serve as a storage place for all the materials needed for the day's classes and as a staging area for most of the classroom activities. Because the cart is so important, design of the cart and planning for its use are crucial decisions for the traveling teacher to make.

● **FIGURE 8.2**   Suggestions for Design and Use of a Traveling Cart

Keep the cart carefully organized. You will need:
- Baskets
- Plastic storage boxes and cases
- Plastic bags

Attach posters to the edges of the cart:
- Place hook and loop tape on the edge of the cart and posters.
- Use jumbo bag clips to attach posters and other items to the cart.

Use sides of the cart for:
- Poster storage and display
- Whiteboard
- Cork board/Bulletin board
- Felt board

Place a small easel on top of the cart for display.

Be sure the cart is enclosed so materials don't drop off when you go over a bump in the floor.

Use hook(s) on the side of the cart to attach posters (use hole punch and reinforcement rings on posters before laminating).

Design a drop-leaf table from one side of the cart for use in simulations.

Design/add fold-out arms from the top of cart to allow for up to three posters side by side.

Designate a space on the cart for each grade level you teach.

Use desk letter-stacker for collecting and organizing student work (by teacher).

Color code classes and class work.

Have a special place for the CD player (easy access and use).

Use hook-and-loop material on inside of the cart door to attach needed materials and to keep them handy.

Have a space reserved for a clipboard and a pen, or other record-keeping materials.

Have a covered space/place to keep items that are meant to be "surprises" for the class.

Keep stickers and other rewards and prizes very accessible.

Have laminated games easily available, as well as other materials for sponge activities.

Create routines to have students assist in repacking the cart at the end of class (or at the end of activities).

Prepare the cart for the next day before you go home each afternoon.

Whenever possible, get to class early in order to get set up before instruction begins.

The wheels of the cart are important. If they roll well, the teacher's back is less likely to be strained. It is helpful if they can be locked. Keep them oiled so you don't squeak in quiet halls.

When you leave the cart parked, place the open end toward the wall (or leave in the room for your next class).

Ask the classroom teacher for a drawer or other storage space in each classroom you visit.

Know the rules and consequences of each classroom you visit; adapt to them as necessary.

Note: The cart pictured is commercially available and could be adapted. See Photo Credits for information.

Working with Many Different Classroom Teachers

A second challenge for traveling teachers is the fact that they must work closely with a number of different classroom teachers, moving from room to room and from one environment to another. Sometimes they have very little time between classes to make the transition. A close relationship with the teachers whose classrooms they share can make this challenging situation much more manageable. Here are some ideas for working closely with classroom teachers and enlisting their help.

How the Language Teacher Can Support the Classroom Teacher Planning together with classroom teachers is extremely important because cooperation improves the quality of instruction. Joint planning inspires shared goals and motivates integration of the language into the classroom. If the program should come under threat, the language teachers are regarded as part of the team, and other teachers become advocates for the program.

There are many ways for the language teacher to make links with the rest of the curriculum. For example, the language arts series may contain stories set in Spanish-speaking countries, and the Spanish teacher might focus a unit on one of the same countries, or teach similar stories in Spanish. The social studies curriculum is often a source of ideas for integrating the language with the rest of the students' day. The classroom teacher will be happy to recognize that the language program can connect with and enrich the existing curriculum.

As language teachers, we need to be prompt in arrival for class and in ending the class. We leave the students ready for the classroom teacher at the end of our lesson, just as we expect them to be ready for us to begin class when we arrive.

We need to leave the classroom the way we found it. We should try to rearrange the classroom as little as possible, but if we change things around, we need to put furniture and equipment back in its place.

It is beneficial to provide classroom teachers with a written lesson plan, or with written vocabulary for their use, as well as written copies of songs, chants, and rhymes. Most teachers are geared to an adult's more visual or reading style of learning and no longer have the child's quick ability to learn languages orally.

We can supply classroom labels in the target language for use with calendars, bulletin boards, and items in the classroom. Along that same theme, if the language teacher and students wear target language name tags during the language class, the classroom teacher should have a target language name tag to wear, as well.

If we need the classroom teachers to provide any special materials for the language lesson on a given day, such as scissors, crayons, or paper, we can notify the teachers at least a week in advance, if possible, and put another short reminder in their mailboxes the day before. We must also be sure to collect those materials at the end of class so the teacher doesn't have any extra work.

Classroom teachers come to rely on the language class at a certain point in their day, and when we are absent they sometimes feel imposed on. We need be sensitive to this issue and to provide lesson plans and materials for days on which we know we must miss school. Some teachers also create simple learning stations for each classroom, for students to use during their free time or for use when the language teacher is gone. Parents are sometimes willing to help create games or other self-correcting activities that will allow students to work with the new language on their own.

How the Classroom Teacher Can Support the Language Teacher   One of the most important ways the classroom teacher can support the language teacher is by being positive about the role of language in the curriculum. The message the classroom teacher sends to the students can make a world of difference! A comment such as, "You are so lucky to be able to study a foreign language at a young age" or "Knowing a foreign language will certainly help you in the future" is a powerful motivator. If a classroom teacher is enthusiastic about the study of a foreign language, it will make a positive impression on the students that is, of course, very helpful to the language teacher when that teacher enters the classroom.

Language teachers can encourage their classroom colleagues to have the students ready for class when the language teacher arrives. This means having other work completed and put away, having desks arranged for the language class, and perhaps having name tags on the desks or around the students' necks. These simple steps will save valuable minutes for language learning.

Sometimes classroom teachers are supportive of the program and want to help in any way they can. One of the first ways to help is by avoiding the temptation to translate what the language teacher says for the students. Experiencing the language through the language itself and not through English will increase students' language skills. Classroom teachers who are familiar with our philosophy of language learning will be in a much better position to support the program in positive ways. For example, the classroom teacher could coordinate the distribution of a language-related book bag that children sign out to take home. Inside the book bag could be books with tapes, maps, language activities for students to complete with parents, and a comments sheet for parents to fill out.

Teachers who feel comfortable with using the new language could work with the students in the following small ways:

- Have the students write the day and date in the target language.
- Give page numbers in the target language.
- Do part of the morning calendar routine in the new language.
- Use numbers and give math answers in the target language.
- Label the bulletin board in both languages.
- Encourage students to give responses or otherwise use the target language they know.

When the Classroom Teacher Is Not Interested or Not Supportive   One language teacher wrote the following to the Ñandu listserv: "I teach 2nd and 3rd grades, and out of the 16 classes that I go to, about 6 do not reinforce what I teach. As a result the students of those teachers do not pick up as much as those where the classroom teacher reinforces what is being taught. I see this a lot especially at the time of evaluations. I feel bad for those students because I know they would do better if the classroom teacher showed some interest herself."

Sometimes, despite our best efforts at cooperation and collaboration, we must work with teachers who are not supportive of what we do. These teachers may require special attention and even some education about program goals and outcomes. The following suggestions, many from teachers on the Ñandu listserv, may help improve the situation.

We can assure teachers that we will not be adding to their workload, and that we will support and reinforce what they are doing in class. Once they see our program in action, they may become as excited about the program as we are. We might do a short demonstration for them in the target language, in which we incorporate information or content that the students already learn in their regular classes. For example, we could do something as simple as counting by 10s, or teaching cardinal directions, or locating several countries where the target language is spoken by using latitude and longitude. At the end of our presentation, we can assure the teachers that we will be using the new language as a tool to reinforce and review skills and concepts from regular classroom, in addition to our focus on language and culture.

One way to help classroom teachers feel ownership in the program is to enlist their opinions and their expertise. This can be done either formally or informally. We might use the following survey with the teachers in order to obtain information:

- What are some ways that you would be willing to be more involved in the language program?
- What are some special topics, projects, or teaching methods you would like to see us incorporate into the program?
- How can we improve communication and planning with you?
- What are some of your general ideas and recommendations on how the program could be improved?

Finally, in our efforts to win over a reluctant classroom teacher, we need to be flexible, but not so flexible that we lose our sense of purpose and our own curricular goals.

Summary

- Managing a successful early language classroom is a complex process in which planning is the essential element.

- Teacher plans always have to adjust for factors beyond the teacher's control, such as the time and place their classes meet and the developmental and individual characteristics of the child in those classes.

- The management plan should include strategies for establishing and maintaining a positive classroom environment, establishing rules, consequences, and routines for the management of all classroom procedures.

- Part of management is making a detailed plan for every class period that uses every available minute of class time and takes into account the students' need for variety, movement, and clear directions for every activity.

- The effective manager is proactive, building bridges to administrators and parents that will create a climate of cooperation when it is necessary to confront a problem.

- Teachers who must travel from room to room with a cart face special issues in classroom management.

For Study and Discussion

1. Plan five rules for your class, worded positively, that are:
   a. observable
   b. enforceable
   c. nonjudgmental
   d. expression of behavior that is important to you in order to teach effectively
   e. in the language you teach

   Word these rules carefully so that they are clear to students.

2. Design a poster for your rules that you can place in your language classroom (or on your cart!). Be sure there is a visual that helps convey the meaning of the rule.

3. List consequences for your rules, both negative and positive. Your consequences should be:

   a. logical
   b. reasonable
   c. designed so they do not require you to stop the lesson

4. Identify and describe at least three procedures that you will use to make your class run smoothly. Design a plan for teaching one of these procedures to your class.

5. Develop a lesson plan for your first day of class, in which you:
   a. introduce your rules and procedures
   b. establish a positive classroom environment
   c. give students some "chunks of language" to take home with them the first day

For Further Reading

The following sources are recommended for additional information about material covered in this chapter. Chapter citations are documented in Works Cited at the end of this book.

Brookhart, Susan M. *How to Give Effective Feedback to Your Students.* Alexandria, VA: Association for Supervision and Curriculum Development, 2006.

Curwin, Richard L., Alan N. Mendler, and Brian D. Mendler. *Discipline with Dignity: New Challenges New Solutions* (3rd ed.). Alexandria VA: Association for Supervision and Curriculum Development, 2008.

Fay, Jim, and David Funk. *Teaching with Love & Logic: Taking Control of the Classroom.* Golden, CO: The Love and Logic Press, 1995.

Ginott, Haim G. *Teacher and Child: A Book for Parents and Teachers.* New York: Macmillan, 1972.

Kohn, Alfie. "The Risks of Rewards." ERIC Digest EDO PS 94 14. ERIC Clearinghouse on Elementary and Early Childhood Education, December 1994.

Levin, James, and James F. Nolan. *Principles of Classroom Management: A Professional Decision Making Model.* (4th ed.). Boston: Pearson Allyn & Bacon, 2006.

Patrick, Paula. *The Keys to the Classroom: A Basic Manual to Help New Language Teachers Find Their Way.* Alexandria, VA: The American Council on the Teaching of Foreign Languages, 2007.

Rothstein-Fisch, Carrie, and Elise Trumbull. *Managing Diverse Classrooms: How to Build on Students' Cultural Strengths.* Alexandria, VA: Association for Supervision and Curriculum Development, 2008.

Wong, Harry K., and Rosemary T. Wong. *The First Days of School: How to be an Effective Teacher* (4th ed.). Mountain View, CA: Harry K. Wong Publications, 2009.

Languages
& Children

Learners
Teachers
Communication
Programs
Planning
Resources
Cultures
Content

Experiencing Culture in the Classroom

Language, Culture, and Curriculum Interact

Enduring Understanding

- Elements of products, practices, and perspectives of the target culture are essential components of planning and teaching.

Essential Question

- How can I create classroom experiences to help students build cultural understanding?

● Experiencing Culture in the Classroom

Even 60 years ago, when language classes were usually taught using a grammar-translation method and students didn't learn interactive or communicative language skills, culture was a part of the standard curriculum for language classes. At that time, the culture goals tended to be primarily what some have called "big C" culture—historical figures, geography, literature, music, and fine arts. Since then, the curriculum for culture has expanded to include patterns of everyday life of the people who use the target language, as well as folklore, contemporary media, and countless other facets of the life and thought of the people who speak the target language.

As our world has grown smaller and our society more diverse, language programs have become an important curricular area for teaching our young people to be empathetic toward people from other cultures. The language courses also help learners to develop a global awareness necessary for a world that is both smaller and more complicated than it was even 10 years ago.

● Culture and the Standards

The *Standards for Foreign Language Learning in the 21st Century* (1999) have redefined the relationship of culture to all aspects of language learning, raising it to new prominence and importance in the curriculum. Not only does culture have its own separate Standards (2.1 and 2.2) but it also serves as a unifying thread throughout the other four areas of the Standards document.

> *Standard 2.1:*   Students demonstrate an understanding of the relationship between the practices and perspectives of the cultures studied.
>
> *Standard 2.2:*   Students demonstrate an understanding of the relationship between the products and perspectives of the cultures studied.

Effective communication is defined by cultural appropriateness and sensitivity (Standards 1.1, 1.2, and 1.3); cultural connections enrich the links made to the general curriculum (Standard 3.1); and the new language gives access to information, ideas, and opinions that are embedded in another culture (Standard 3.2). Comparisons of languages (Standard 4.1) uncover a host of culturally defined patterns of expression and ways to view the world, and comparisons of cultures (Standard 4.2) bring students to greater understanding of both the target culture and their own. Standard 5, Communities, encourages direct and ongoing application of language and culture competencies in the world beyond the classroom.

The Standards have reminded us of what we instinctively knew: Culture is the most important context for language learning. As Lange points out (1999), "The new standards put culture at the core of foreign language learning as a major content." The Standards themselves put it clearly: "In reality, then, the true content of the foreign language course is not the grammar and the vocabulary of the language, but the cultures expressed through that language" (1999, pp. 47–48).

Cultural topics to be included in an integrated and communication-based elementary and middle school foreign language program are often chosen at least in part on the basis of their potential for enabling students to communicate through the target language and for their inherent ability to motivate students to use the target language. Interest in the culture in which the target language is spoken can motivate language acquisition and practice. In addition, the cultural dimension of the language class can assist the learners in better understanding their own culture, as they make comparisons and begin to understand a point of view that is based in the target culture and expressed in the target language.

Even more important than the potential for communication, the interests and developmental levels of the students in the class must guide the choice of cultural information selected for instruction. There may well be parallels between the acquisition of a second language and the acquisition of a second culture. Many similar criteria could be said to apply. Students will not understand or be open to cultural information and practices that are so divorced from their own experiences as to seem funny or even bizarre, any more than they will learn language that is not directed to their interests and built on their own experiences. They are also unlikely to "acquire" cultural information that primarily affects adults in the target culture, since they have yet to penetrate the adult culture of their own world and often find it confusing. Perhaps most significantly, just as children do not acquire a language primarily by being told about it, but rather through meaningful, communicative experiences with the language, so also do children penetrate a new culture through meaningful experiences with cultural practices and cultural phenomena that are appropriate to their age level, their interests, and the classroom setting.

The Culture Triangle

With the cultures goal, the Standards have given us an additional, more challenging set of lenses to use when planning to integrate culture with our language classes: Gain knowledge and understanding of other cultures. Although the goal itself seems quite general, the two standards associated with it turn our thinking sharply in a new direction.

The Standards define *culture* to include the philosophical perspectives, the behavioral practices, and the tangible and intangible products of a society. The diagram shown in Figure 9.1 represents the close relationship among these three elements.

● **FIGURE 9.1** The Culture Triangle

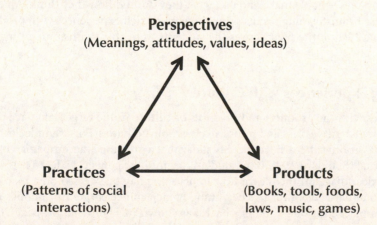

Source: Standards for Foreign Language Learning in the 21st Century. Yonkers, NY: National Standards in Foreign Language Education Project, 1999, p. 47. Reprinted by permission of ACTFL.

An example may help to illustrate the relationship among the three elements of culture. The drum is a product and a familiar artifact of Native American culture, sometimes a tourist item bought as a plaything for children. The drum is also a practice, a group of drummers sitting around a large drum and playing or chanting for a powwow. The product and the practice reflect the perspective, or the value and importance, of community gathered around the drum to share traditional ritual, rhythm, and dance. To present only the drum product without the context and the values in which it holds an important place is to miss the meaning of the drum entirely.

Another example comes from a German setting. American visitors to a large German city are likely to be struck by the fact that many of the cars are very small, in comparison to most vehicles driven in America, and that cars are parked on the sidewalks all over the city. The Smart Car, a very small car, is particularly adept at parking in these tiny spaces. Here, the product is the Smart Car, and the practice is parking on the sidewalk. The perspective emerges when we realize that many German inner cities have been retained or restored to the way they were centuries ago, so valuing of the past might be one of the perspectives represented here.

The relationship among products, practices, and perspectives might not always be so easy to trace, especially with young learners, but this goal and these Standards challenge us as teachers to be aware of the perspectives represented in the cultural products and practices we incorporate into our classes, and to build our plans around these perspectives. In early language classrooms we are laying the groundwork for perspective through experiences with the products and practices that infuse every aspect of our language program.

Jessica Haxhi and her fifth-grade students developed a summary of some of the things they had learned about Japanese culture, based on the culture triangle (see Figure 9.2). Although normally the Japanese class is conducted entirely in Japanese, this discussion took place in English.

Notice that Haxhi renamed the points in the triangle to be more child-friendly: what the Japanese people make and use, what they do, and how they think. An examination of these brainstorming results shows how many rich experiences with products and practices have led to the perspectives the students were able (with some prompting) to identify.

Creating Experiences with Culture

Experiences with the products and practices of culture in the target language can begin with the first language class and infuse all classroom activities. For example, learners in a German classroom can learn from the first day that a greeting is accompanied by a hand-shaking ritual (Standard 2.1). Young students beginning Spanish can learn first the colors of the Mexican flag and then learn how to place the flag on Mexico on a map of North America (Standard 2.2). Learners beginning French can celebrate April Fool's Day with fish shapes placed on one another's backs, as shown in Figure 9.3 on page 262 (Standard 2.1). A teacher of Japanese might greet students with a bow and expect them to greet one another in the same way (Standard 2.1). Children learning any European language can

● **FIGURE 9.2**   Brainstorming the Culture Triangle

Source: From Maloney Magnet School, Waterbury, CT. Reprinted by permission of Jessica Haxhi, Japanese teacher.

learn to count on their fingers starting with the thumb representing the number 1 (Standard 2.1). Students in a German class can learn very early to press their thumbs for good luck, or to knock on their desks instead of applauding to show approval (Standard 2.1). None of these experiences requires an elaborate explanation, but each is a step toward identification with another way of thinking and another way of behaving in everyday situations.

Many cultural practices blend easily with regular classroom routines. Choice of the next person to recite or to participate in a game can be made using a culturally based counting-out rhyme. A tie in a Japanese class could be broken with the traditional "Rock-Paper-Scissors" game. Learners in the French classroom might learn to raise two fingers rather than waving a whole hand when they want to be called on.

Simple crafts and food activities can provide experiences with products of the target culture that extend over a longer period of time, and some of them address both Standards 2.1 and 2.2. An activity such as building and later breaking a class piñata, or perhaps individual piñatas made with paper bags, can be both an opportunity to apply language to a new activity and an experience in preparation for a celebration common to the target culture. Mask making can be a prelude to the celebration of an in-class version of a

● **FIGURE 9.3**   "Fish" Game.
Playing the "Fish" game on
April 1 gives students who are
learning French an
experience with French
culture.

festival specific to the target culture, such as the pre-Lenten carnivals observed in several German-, French-, and Spanish-speaking cultures. A Japanese class could learn to follow directions in an origami paper-folding activity and then decorate the classroom with their creations. A food activity—such as preparing an open-faced sandwich in a German class, and then eating it with a knife (in the right hand) and a fork (in the left hand)—provides an opportunity for experiencing several cultural contrasts in food presentation and eating behavior. A food activity for a Chinese class could include cooking noodles and then using chopsticks to eat them.

These crafts and food activities can later become the focal point for language experience stories and for writing or copying activities. They can serve as the central feature of simulations or the starting point for student-prepared skits or presentations to parents. Preparations for a festival, including making such crafts as piñatas, paper flowers, or masks, might culminate in a festive celebration, either within the class or as a joint experience with other classes or invited guests.

The use of a variety of visuals representing the target culture can help to relate interests of the learners to the wider world in which the target language plays a role. Posters and bulletin boards can create an awareness of the cultural settings in which the target language is spoken. Magazines and comic books from the target culture can be used to illustrate vocabulary items or to communicate a bulletin board message. Coins from the culture used as counters for math activities or as playing pieces in a board game bring a reality to these everyday cultural objects. Board games, puzzles, and picture books, when made available to learners in a learning center or in a special foreign language corner of the classroom or the library, open doors to the daily life of the child in the target culture and invite the learner to experience a small portion of that culture.

When Jo Ellen Hague visited Paris, she developed a wonderful cultural resource for her classroom. She took along the class mascot, Gustave the Frog, and took pictures of him in many different situations—for example, receiving his boarding pass, Gustave with Sacre Coeur in the background, and so on (see Figure 9.4). Reiko Aya, a Japanese immersion teacher from Portland, Oregon, had a similar idea when she took her class mascot, Barney, to Japan, and photographed him in Japanese settings. Seeing the familiar mascot in the target culture brings a special kind of credibility and reality to the pictures of these unfamiliar places.

● Comparing Cultures (Standard 4.2)

As teachers and students work with the practices, products, and perspectives of the target cultures, it is natural that students should begin to compare these new cultures with their own. The teacher can encourage and invite these comparisons and help students move toward the understanding that cultural behavior is systematic and governed by the perspectives of a culture. With enough experience and guidance, the students can begin to hypothesize about cultures in general and to reflect on their own culture as one among many.

One simple example of this kind of comparison can be accomplished by the use of contrasting maps of the world. A map printed for a U.S. audience almost always has North America at the center. A map printed in Europe for a European audience almost always has Europe at the center, and a map printed in Asia has Asia at the center. Drawing

● **FIGURE 9.4** The Adventures of Gustave the Frog

students' attention to these contrasts can lead to questions about why each orientation is appropriate for its audience.

Jessica Haxhi uses a popular Japanese children's movie, *Totoro,* to draw out a number of cultural comparisons. The movie is about a furry creature that is only visible to children, and the creature's adventures with two little girls. One of the class activities is to compare some interesting cultural contrasts between suffixes on names in Japanese. Later, the class makes a comparison chart with the "Girls' Home from *Totoro*" on one side and "My Home" on the other. Students draw pictures of beds, baths, tables, eating utensils, and so on, for each side, taking from what they saw in the movie. This is a good way to compare without making broad generalizations about "Japanese homes" and "American homes."

Jeanette Borich (2001) developed a unit rich with opportunities for cultural comparisons, although her primary goals were cultures and connections. As second-grade students participated in an imaginary trip from their home in Iowa to the Yucatan Peninsula, they had the opportunity to compare many cultural elements: concepts of spring and other seasons because of contrasting climates, celebration of birthdays, typical foods, housing in villages and cities, and other elements. Through a journaling activity, the children were encouraged to reflect on these cultural experiences: "Mérida is a large city and Tinum is a small town in Yucatán. What did you notice about the houses in those places? Tell how María celebrated her birthday in Yucatán" (p. 19). The entire experience helped the children become observers of differences and similarities and discouraged making quick judgments based on first impressions.

The guided and thoughtful reflection about cultural experiences and observations, conducted in the target language as described in the preceding examples, gives students the opportunity to construct meaning. Genuine, personal understanding of culture cannot be "transmitted" through a lecture or a multimedia presentation by someone who already has that understanding. It comes through personal experiences with products and practices, recognition of differing perspectives, and thoughtful comparisons of all three dimensions of culture. It may be that this comparisons Standard holds the key to real culture learning.

● Identifying Resources for Integrating Culture

Many teachers find the integration of culture and cultural experiences to be among their most challenging tasks, because they lack the firsthand experiences that would give them a rich background on which to draw. Even for teachers who have spent considerable time in a foreign country, or who were raised in a foreign setting, it is often difficult to know where to begin with cultural instruction. The following are intended as starting points for integrative culture planning.

Identifying Cultural Information for a Thematic Unit

When considering what culture one might draw into a thematic unit, it can be useful to think in terms of cultural products and cultural practices. Some examples from Pesola (1991, p. 339) follow:

Cultural Products

- Flags or insignia related to learners' interests
- Significant national or geographic monuments
- Symbols associated with holidays
- Good luck and bad luck symbols
- Symbolic meaning of animals
- Heroes from history or myth
- Significant examples of the visual arts (and artists)
- Significant examples of the musical arts (and composers)
- Important characters, events, and themes from folk literature
- Traditional children's songs, rhymes, games
- Traditional stories and legends
- Examples of folk arts
- Currency and coins, stamps, and other realia
- Traditional and holiday foods

Cultural Practices

- Forms of greeting
- Celebration of holidays
- Use of gestures
- Meals and eating practices
- Shopping
- Favorite playtime and recreational activities
- Home and school life
- Patterns of politeness
- Types of pets and attitudes towards pets
- How children and families move from place to place

Any of these items might serve as the starting point of a thematic unit or as a component of instruction.

Children's literature—folktales and fairy tales, contemporary children's books, songs, rhymes, and finger plays—provide an especially valuable resource for cultural information. Use of literature designed for children in the target culture allows learners of the target language to share cultural experiences and attitudes in a very direct way, thus offering an experience very similar to that of a child growing up in that culture. Location and use of culturally authentic stories may be among the most valuable and successful of all cultural activities.

Story and Culture

Story, or narrative, is a powerful vehicle for experiencing culture. Values and concepts of the culture that are embedded in myths and folktales can be shared through storytelling, story reading, and dramatization. In this way they become part of the childhood experience that is a foundation for later understanding on a deeper level. In addition, stories, as we have seen in Chapter 6, have special effectiveness in giving learners access to ideas and feelings. Stories about historical figures or legendary heroes are infused with the personal qualities and behaviors valued in the culture. In fact, stories may be one of the best ways of bridging the relationships among products, practices, and perspectives—they are, quite simply, an expression of the perspectives of the culture. As is the case with the native language and culture, experiences with these stories in childhood lay the groundwork for cultural insights and culturally sensitive behaviors.

One of the ways to give greater meaning to objects, or realia, from the culture is to weave them into a story, often linking them to a practice. For example, Jo Ellen Hague builds a story around the king's cake tradition in France that her kindergarten students will never forget. Instead of just telling the students about the cake and the tradition that are part of the Celebration of the Three Kings, the students "bake" an imaginary king's cake. Students take turns placing imaginary ingredients in a two-dimensional bowl, pushing down the "beaters" and "whirring" as the ingredients mix. Every child is involved, as each one passes each ingredient around the class before it is added to the batter while singing a song about a cake. The last ingredient to be added is the all-important bean. Jo Ellen pours the imaginary batter into a two-dimensional cake pan and places it in a cardboard oven with a hinged door.

The cake "bakes" while the learners sing another song, and anticipation builds. When the cake comes out of the oven, it has magically baked—thanks to a bit of sleight-of-hand on the part of the teacher, who has placed a tagboard cake shape in the pan while manipulating the oven door. There are four large pieces of the cake, which is now placed on a tagboard picture of a table with four people sitting around the cake: the father, the mother, the sister, and the brother. The family member who finds the bean in her or his piece of cake will be king or queen for the day.

The teacher asks learners to predict which piece of cake is hiding the bean, calling for a show of hands with each piece of cake and writing down the number of votes. Then they look under each piece of cake in turn to see where the bean is hidden. When the bean is found, a crown is placed on the head of that family member, and everyone applauds.

Art and Artists

The visual arts can draw students into the culture in a number of ways, and art can play a role in almost every kind of language activity. For example, we could use reproductions of famous paintings to illustrate vocabulary or concepts, or as props in a corners activity (see Chapter 4). The stories of famous artists often draw students in and can encourage them to learn more about the artist's work, life, and environment. Some teachers have focused on the work of a single artist and had their students copy the artist's style in their own creations. This focus could serve as a thematic center for an entire unit that integrates study of colors, descriptions, shapes, and artistic techniques.

As a first step in an artist unit, the teacher would introduce the artist, perhaps by telling a story that captures something of her or his spirit, and then show a number of the artist's creations. This would lead to many opportunities for student language use: description of what they see, identification of specific objects or elements of the work, and so forth. In the case of a realist painter, the students might describe or identify those things that contribute to a sense of reality in the work. In other cases, the students might explain what clues they used to identify what is represented in the picture. During this phase students become acquainted with the vocabulary needed to discuss basic elements of artistic design.

After they have seen and discussed many examples of works by Franz Marc, for example, the students are ready to create their own artworks in the same style. The culminating activity for this kind of unit might be a gallery showing. Each picture should be given a title by the student artist, and then each student might give a brief oral description of the painting and its most important characteristics, as if it were part of a gallery tour.

Some artists seem particularly appropriate for this kind of an activity. Franz Marc produced a large number of pictures of animals, many of them in bright colors. Joan Miró uses a style of drawing that would be easy for students to imitate. Matisse has many images that could be imitated creatively as an art project. The teacher does not need to be an art expert in order to develop activities like these. Many art books for young readers provide engaging and useful information that can guide the development of such a unit.

Never has locating artwork for use in classrooms been easier. Museum stores often have books of art for children; calendars often feature the work of a specific artist—and they are best bought on sale in January or February. And of course the Internet can provide pictures by almost any artist with whom a teacher would like to work.

● Fantasy Experiences/Virtual Trips

It is possible to create more extended experiences with culture in the classroom, even for students who have very limited language background. By combining fantasy, culture, story form, and elements of Total Physical Response, the teacher can create a vivid, living connection between the learners in the classroom and the target culture. Like simulations, fantasy experiences can place students in a setting that replicates important elements of the target culture and offers the opportunity to experience new feelings, new combinations of circumstances, and new solutions to familiar problems. The fantasy experiences described next are highly structured and teacher controlled, designed for use in early stages of language instruction, when it is often considered very difficult to deal with culture in the target language. Variations and adaptations of this technique can be used at every level of language instruction.

Fantasy Activity for the First Day of Class

Experience with fantasy can begin as early as the first day of class. With Baroque-style string music playing softly in the background, the teacher explains to students that they are to imagine themselves as learners in the target culture and to choose a name by which they will be called during the course of the class. They close their eyes and listen as the teacher reads a list of names expressively, then a second time in an angry voice, so students know how a name might sound in case the teacher should ever become angry during class. Finally, the students open their eyes and listen as the teacher reads the names a third time, raising their hands when they hear a name they would like to use. When two or more students choose the same name, the teacher goes on, continuing through the list until only one child chooses each name. In the case of very popular names, which several students want, the teacher might either give more than one child the same name, or simply remove the name so that students make other choices.

This activity establishes the connection between background music and use of the imagination. It also gives children an opportunity to take the first step toward identification with a new culture, a new way of thinking, even a new way of being addressed.

Fantasy Activity for Early Stages of Language Acquisition

Here is a plan for a simple fantasy experience that can be used in early stages of instruction. With music in the background, the teacher talks about being very tired and directs the learners to stretch, to yawn, to lay their heads on their arms, to close their eyes, and to sleep (perhaps even to snore). The teacher counts off the hours of the night, reminding the children to sleep, perhaps to snore (or not to snore). At seven o'clock, the teacher plays a recording of church bells (reflecting German culture) or sets off an alarm clock, and then directs the learners to wake up, to stretch (again), to wash their faces, brush their teeth, dress, make their beds, and sit down for breakfast. The culminating portion of this fantasy might be a small continental breakfast, if the class can include food experiences, or the pantomiming of leaving home to go on to other activities.

Airplane Fantasy

A longer fantasy experience might involve taking the students on a trip. Children are issued passports and airline tickets and prepare for a "trip" to Germany, China, Colombia, Senegal, or any other destination appropriate to the language being taught. In addition to the Baroque music in the background, the teacher prepares an "aircraft" with a masking tape outline on the floor. This takes up much of the room, especially in a large class, with chairs placed side by side, in twos or in fours depending on the size of the class, and labeled with letters and numbers, as in a real aircraft. In the airplane fantasy experience carried out by one of the authors there were actual airline ticket folders, luggage tags, and air-sickness bags, as well as some in-flight magazines and other realia typically found in an airplane. As the fantasy experience proceeds, children are directed to show their tickets and their passports to the flight attendant, to find their seats, to buckle their imaginary seat belts, and, of course, told to refrain from smoking and to participate in all the other activities associated with the beginning of any flight. During the course of the flight, children look out their imaginary windows at drawings of clouds and of other aircraft. When they experience turbulence, they jiggle up and down and back and forth in their seats. When the teacher comments on the unease in the stomach that they all feel, many children discover an imaginary use for their real air-sickness bags.

In an extended fantasy, the teacher might distribute in-flight meals, consisting of half a sandwich, a pickle, fruit, and a mint or a cookie assembled on small trays from a meat department and wrapped in plastic food wrap. The children are directed to close their eyes and sleep, as the teacher counts off the hours and notes the change of time through the time zones. The children finally arrive at their destination and exclaim over large pictures of the city in which they have landed, as they are directed to look at and point to special landmarks they should note. Classes that have shared this experience often remember a feeling of actually having traveled in an airplane to a distant place. As a follow-up to the airplane trip, classes might write a language experience story together or draw pictures of the trip on postcard-sized tagboard and write messages from their destination to send home (see Figure 9.5).

When Jo Ellen Hague wanted to transport her kindergarten students to a Paris environment, she had the class mascot, Gustave, do the flying. In fact, one of the children took on the role of the airplane as Gustave, fastened to the child's clothing, rode around the room from Georgia to Paris!

Steamer Trip Fantasy

Another example of a fantasy, this one taking place in Germany, is a trip on a Rhine steamer, again to the accompaniment of Baroque music, using inexpensive sunglasses and a simple paper camera as props, and with the outline of a Rhine steamer taped to the floor. Learners are directed to exchange coins for tickets, to give their tickets to a ship attendant, and to board the steamer. As the steamer progresses down the Rhine, the children are directed to go to the left and the right on the deck, to look at and point to castles and other landmarks as they go by, and to pass the camera back and forth to "take pictures" of the special features along the Rhine. If a snack is desired, it might be some kind of finger food, an ice cream bar, or some juice. A day or two after the Rhine trip, the students might view slides of an actual Rhine trip, once again point out the special landmarks they have seen, and perhaps even pick out themselves and their classmates in pictures of Rhine passengers. (Although of course they are not actually present in the pictures, learners usually have no problem in "finding" themselves in a large group of people from an actual Rhine photo.)

Other Fantasies

Other examples of potential fantasy settings might include a bus trip or a walking trip around Paris, Cairo, Madrid, Tokyo, or Berlin, with important tourist attractions along the way to look at and point to. It could be a canoe trip down a river in Canada, during which

● **FIGURE 9.5**   Fantasy Experience. Just a few props can create a fantasy environment with great potential for culture and language acquisition.

animals from the woods appear and disappear on either side of the masking-tape river "flowing" through the center of the classroom. The boat trip could be on the Loire, or a tourist boat in Paris, a raft on the Amazon River, a pirogue on the Niger River, a junk in Hong Kong, and so on. Fantasy subway rides can also be fun and instructive, especially if accompanied by actual tape-recorded subway sounds.

In some fantasies, all learners can take part at the same time, as in the airplane trip and the simple morning fantasy. In other fantasies, a few students may take part and the rest of the class serves as observers. There can be several episodes of the same fantasy, involving different members of the class. In each repetition the script might change so that children never know exactly what to expect and thus remain attentive through several repetitions. In a fantasy that takes place in Berlin, for example, several students stand in line, press the call button outside the elevator, choose the correct floor, and press the button to reach the observation tower. Many variations are possible in this fantasy: The door might fail to open or become stuck partway, one student might be left behind, a child (or the teacher) might get a hand or a piece of clothing caught in the door; thus learners will be directed to perform different activities in each variation of a similar situation. For the elevator fantasy, only a masking tape elevator, the up-down buttons on the outside, and the floor buttons on the inside of the elevator are required as props. (The elevator door "opens" when the masking tape door is temporarily lifted from the floor.) Passengers in the elevator might discover their stomachs growing queasy, as the elevator goes very high very fast (see Figure 9.6).

Planning a Fantasy Experience

Some of the key components to be considered by a teacher wishing to plan a fantasy experience include the following:

1. Precede major culture-bearing fantasies with shorter experiences.
2. Choose background music that is regular and unobtrusive. (Baroque string music works very well.)
3. Set the scene in a physical way, using masking tape, chair arrangement, or other physical means.
4. Choose cultural features that have dramatic potential.
5. Select topics that include possibilities for movement, props, and sounds as a part of the dramatic sequence.
6. Plan the sequence to include a beginning, a middle, and an end.
7. Build in elements of humor and surprise.
8. Choose a few appropriate props; do not use too many.

● **FIGURE 9.6** Elevator Fantasy Experience. Even a school classroom can include an elevator—at least for the purposes of fantasy.

9. Use familiar commands with new content or introduce new commands carefully in advance.

10. Plan for natural communicative follow-up during succeeding class periods.

Fantasy activities can provide very vivid, memorable experiences with the target culture. Since fantasy requires the suspension of disbelief, it is important that major or extended fantasies not be overused, or they will lose their special quality.

● Classroom Exchanges

A classroom exchange project is a particularly effective means of combining linguistic and cultural goals, as it offers learners the opportunity to experience aspects of the target culture in a very direct and personal way. This idea can be used as the core of the foreign language curriculum for a period of time or as an effective supplement to any program model.

The elementary or middle school language teacher establishes a relationship with a teacher, preferably an English teacher, at a comparable grade level in a school in the target culture. Together, they set goals for a variety of activities involved in an exchange of class projects. Setting up individual pen-pal or key-pal relationships is not part of the early stages of this program, since the emphasis is on group work within each class. The program takes place in two phases; in the first phase the students in each school plan and prepare the projects they will send to their partner school, and in the second phase they interpret and respond to the project they have received from their partner school.

A fourth-grade class in a parochial school in Northfield, Minnesota, developed a classroom exchange with a fifth-grade group in Hamburg, West Germany, in a project designed by Dahlberg. As a first step, the two groups exchanged group photographs of class members, class lists, and school schedules. Then the Northfield group discussed the best way to show their partner group what it meant to be a fourth-grade child, in their school, in Northfield, in Minnesota, and in the United States. At the same time, they began to generate questions about the life of the German children. The project resulted in the following activities:

1. A questionnaire based on students' questions about life in Hamburg was developed. The questions reflected interest in family and pets, modes of transportation, size of families, hobbies, and favorite film, TV, and pop music stars. The children also took the questionnaire themselves and analyzed the results to gain insight into their own lives. Because these students were beginners, the questionnaire was developed in English and translated by the teacher before it was sent to Germany. With more advanced learners the same activity might be conducted in the target language.

2. Materials containing information about the community and aspects of the children's daily lives were collected. This involved visits to the local chamber of com-

merce, letters to the state tourist agency, and visits to many local businesses and service organizations. The final collection of materials included these items:

- TV and movie schedules
- Mail-order catalogs
- Telephone book
- Weekly food ads and coupon pages
- Comic books
- Brochures about the city and the state
- Colorful information about community businesses
- Seed catalogs and packets for favorite garden products
- Circus flyers
- School student handbooks
- Copies of the school paper and the local paper

3. Photographs of selected aspects of the children's daily lives were taken. Different children's homes were selected for each room of the house; other children had pets or hobbies photographed. The final slide collection included pictures of the following:

- All possible rooms in a home
- A school bus
- The school, the classroom, the gymnasium
- Stores and businesses familiar to the children
- Pets and children engaged in hobbies
- The cafeteria
- School athletic, music, and drama events the children liked to attend
- Individual pictures of the children with a favorite pet or toy

4. Music and other information that held meaning for class members were recorded. The recorded information included the following:

- Favorite songs from German class and music classes
- School song and cheers
- Favorite pop or rock music (determined by class vote)
- Self-introductions by each child in German

(The German partner class also made recordings of the material the American children were learning in their German classes, but there was no interest in having American children return the favor, because at the time an American accent was not considered acceptable in the partner school.)

5. To see how the climates compared, the weather was charted day by day over a period of several months, and later compared with information sent from Hamburg.

The period of preparation for the exchange lasted about six weeks and was an experience with inquiry and interdisciplinary involvement that resulted in better knowledge of the children's own class and environment and heightened interest in life in German-speaking countries. The activity would have been valuable even if nothing had ever been received from Hamburg. When the Hamburg projects actually arrived, there was considerable excitement throughout the school.

Many of the Hamburg contributions had been prepared by individual children, who enclosed drawings, favorite rhymes and games, family pictures, postcards, maps, and short descriptions of favorite activities. The responses to the questionnaire provided material for investigation and discussion for the rest of the school year: Why would so many American film stars appear in the list of favorites? Where were the Saturday-morning cartoons on television? The contact with authentic materials and the awareness of the lives of real children of about their own age provided a context for the study of language and a springboard for a continuing interest in culture.

Finding a Partner for an Exchange

Teachers wishing to develop a classroom exchange project may find a potential partner teacher in several ways. Several of the professional associations and journals have teacher pen-pal opportunities with fellow teachers abroad, and these contacts can be developed into classroom exchanges. Many colleges and universities have programs of study abroad, and students in these programs are often willing to serve as liaisons in setting up such a program. The best route for developing a program is a personal contact with a teacher or a school during a trip to a country of the target culture. The goals of the project should be fully discussed and agreed on before the project begins, and the project should begin in the fall, to allow enough time for materials to be developed, to reach their destination, and to receive a response before the end of the school year.

Many variations on the classroom exchange are possible. Technology would now permit exchange of digital photos, presentations, and movies, as well as email questionnaires, electronic bulletin boards, and Internet-based telephone calls. Developing exchange relationships with several different countries in which the target language is spoken, and focusing on a different country each year, would help students to appreciate the variety of approaches to daily life that can be discovered through the use of a single language. Exchanges between students learning the same language in different parts of the United States or different parts of the world can be motivating and revealing, as learners discover that lifestyles and customs are not identical even where others speak their own native language.

Classroom exchanges can go even further, of course. Sometimes a communication exchange will precede an actual exchange of visits between groups of students. Several teachers have pointed out the advantages of bringing preadolescent youngsters on trips abroad. Although in some cases they may be more likely to experience homesickness than older students, they might be more likely to welcome the family experience and be less resistant to the necessary rules and restrictions that a trip abroad entails. Teachers report success in exchanging visits with children as early as the end of fifth grade, provided that there is a close working relationship between the teachers involved, as well as close cooperation with parents. Exchange programs involve a great deal of preparation and supervision, but they provide powerful opportunities for language use and cultural contact that cannot be obtained any other way.

Placing students in contact with students of their own age in the target culture makes it possible to address several of the national standards in a meaningful way. Much of the information exchanged invites comparisons, especially cultural comparisons (Standard 4.2). Students become more aware of their own culture as they explain it to others and see similarities and contrasts with their partner school. They have ready access to information and opinions in the partner class (Standard 3.2), and they are clearly moving their language learning beyond the classroom walls (Standard 5.1).

Flat Stanley—Where Have You Been?

Flat Stanley, a book for young readers by Jeff Brown, has sparked the imagination of teachers and children all over the country and even spawned several websites. It tells the story of a little boy who is flattened by a falling bulletin board so that he is a mere half-inch thick. Being flat has some advantages, as Stanley discovers when he travels through the U.S. mail in a very large brown envelope to visit a friend across the continent.

In the Flat Stanley project, students make a paper or electronic Flat Stanley to exchange with other classrooms. Sometimes they use a copy of the "Stanley" from the book, and sometimes they use their own faces on the flat paper figure. The recipients treat the visiting Stanley as a guest and record events from Stanley's visit in a journal and through photographs, postcards, and so forth. These are then returned to the original group of students. Some classes mail Stanleys to relatives and friends all over this country. A few language classes have used Flat Stanley as a way of exchanging with young learners in other cultures and other countries. The potential for geographic and cultural learning through a project like this one is almost endless. The website for the Flat Stanley project has extensive information, photos, and stories about successful projects: www .flatstanley.net.

● Education for Global and Multicultural Awareness

The early language classroom provides an especially favorable setting for introducing the learner to the whole world of cultural diversity. When the language teacher limits the attention of the class to a single country, or even to one region of a country in which the target language is spoken, an important opportunity is being missed. Almost all of the languages most commonly taught in elementary school in the United States are used in a number of countries with customs and lifestyles that vary greatly from one to another. The classroom experience will be much richer if this variety is brought into the classroom through activities, visual representation, and specific songs, games, crafts, foods, and other experiences reflecting a variety of cultures.

Global awareness can be further enhanced when teachers use every opportunity to show relationships between countries where the target language is used and other nations around the world. The presence of many Germans in South America, the trade of a local business with Japan, and the role of French explorers in the United States and in other parts of the world can all become a part of the information exchanged in an early language classroom. The teacher can invite speakers of the target language who have had experiences in any part of the world to show the class slides and to discuss the countries they have visited—in the target language. In more advanced classes, the teacher and students together can discuss implications of events in any part of the world, both for countries in which the target language is spoken and for the students themselves.

Broadening culture study to include ideas and practices from a more global perspective can also help students see the contrasts they experience between their home environment and the target cultures in a wider context. Instead of perceiving a conflict or a set of either–or choices, learners can begin to see the options in their own and another culture as simply two of many alternatives within a rich variety of possibilities.

Language teachers, like teachers in all other areas of the curriculum, have a responsibility to plan lessons with sensitivity to the racial and ethnic diversity present in their classrooms and in the world in which their students live. The early language classroom that incorporates the goals of global and multicultural education into carefully developed culture instruction can help students take on a new and broader perspective. By learning to appreciate the point of view of someone living in the target culture, they can also learn to value the points of view of many others whose life experiences are different from their own.

Rosenbusch (1992b) describes a process for developing thematic units for young learners that are based on global education concepts and that incorporate insights and information from the target culture. She maintains that foreign language teachers can be leaders in helping students develop a global perspective and in preparing them for responsible world citizenship. This may be just what H. Douglas Brown had in mind when he wrote, "Language is a tool for overcoming powerlessness. Our professional commitment intrinsically drives us to help the inhabitants of this planet to communicate with each other and to negotiate the meaning of peace, of goodwill, and of survival on this tender, fragile globe" (1991, p. 257).

● Additional Activities

Early language teachers who are committed to providing cultural experiences for their classes will be constantly in search of authentic games, music, crafts, foods, and customs to share with them. In addition, many of the following activities (Standards numbers shown in parentheses) will contribute to developing the standards described in this chapter.

1. Invite foreign visitors or target language speakers to visit the class and share their experiences, using visuals, slides, and as many concrete materials as possible (2.1, 2.2, 5.1).

2. Learn and perform folk dances and singing games from the target culture (2.1).

3. Celebrate holidays and festivals of the target culture in the class, especially those that do not have an American counterpart (2.1, 2.2).

4. Where possible, make field trips to a neighborhood, restaurant, museum, or store that reflects some aspects of the target culture (2.2).

5. Invite learners to bring to class any items from the target culture or samples of the target language that they may come across in their homes. Many students become very good at finding the target language on directions, store labels, and advertisements. These items can become the stimulus for a great deal of language when the child or the teacher shares them with the class (2.2).

6. Identify local or regional place names that may be derived from the target language and investigate the reason for the choice of name. Some communities may have namesakes in the target culture, or sister cities in another country, and these relationships can be the source of many activities (2.2).

7. Ask students to skim target language newspapers or magazines to find illustrations for concepts they are learning in the foreign language class or in subject content classes (2.2).

8. Tell or read fables, folktales, and legends that come from the target culture or from other cultures around the world (all in the target language) (2.2, 3.1).

9. Read to students from picture books written for children in the target culture and reflecting that culture (2.2).

10. Students can view videos made for children in the target culture.

11. Visit a supermarket or a gourmet shop and list foods that are imported from countries where the target language is spoken (2.2).

12. Encourage students to read fiction and nonfiction books about children in the target culture. The school media center director is often willing to help develop a list or a collection of these books for each grade level (2.2, 5.2).

13. Use collections of games from around the world to locate suitable games played in the target culture, and incorporate these into units and lessons (2.1).

14. Establish contacts through email or professional channels with language teachers and their classrooms in the target culture. Use these contacts to answer teacher and student questions about life in the target culture, and to exchange cultural products, children's literature, and up-to-date cultural information (2.1, 2.2, 3.2).

15. Subscribe to magazines written in the target language and produced in the target culture, both those intended for young people of the same age as the language learners and those intended for parents and caregivers. These can provide students with direct contacts with authentic cultural materials and can give teachers insight about life and concerns affecting young people in the target culture (2.2, 3.2, 4.2).

16. Incorporate animal sounds in the target language into any unit dealing with animals. These sounds are fun to use and reinforce the differences among languages (4.1, 4.2).

Summary

- Cultural goals can best be met by giving learners experiences with the culture rather than by talking about cultural facts and artifacts. Many of these experiences can be part of daily classroom activity, integrated with the use of language in an authentic, communicative setting.

- Teachers may identify cultural information to integrate with language and subject content by considering the categories of cultural products and practices and considering the perspectives they represent.

- In all cases culture requires careful and systematic planning, to provide developmentally appropriate information and experiences at each developmental level and a well-designed sequence of instruction.

- As teachers plan lessons that incorporate cultural products and practices, they are also building a foundation for awareness of the perspectives of the culture. Although perspectives may not always be overtly taught, the teacher needs to be aware of the perspectives underlying the cultural experiences of the classroom.

Guiding students in the comparison of cultures helps them develop a deeper and more personalized understanding of both the target culture and their own culture.

- There are two types of extended cultural experiences—the fantasy or virtual trip and the classroom exchange. The fantasy makes use of a few props and the child's imagination to bring the child together with the culture in a fantasy setting. In the classroom exchange, two cultures actually meet, as a language class exchanges projects and information with a partner class in the target culture.

- Global awareness and multicultural education are additional goals that have special importance in the elementary school foreign language classroom. The target language can be used as a point of departure for making connections with the entire world, and gaining access to the perspective of the target culture can help learners appreciate other perspectives in their community and their world.

For Study and Discussion

1. Explain to a colleague why you have chosen to spend a considerable amount of time seeking out authentic songs, games, rhymes, and stories for use in your primary school classes, rather than simply retelling or translating the things learners are already familiar with in English.

2. You have invited a native speaker to speak to your class of sixth-graders who are in their second year of learning the language you teach. Based on what you know about language and culture, what instructions and help will you give your speaker in advance to ensure that the experience will be valuable for the children in your class?

3. Together with a classmate or a native speaker of the language you teach, develop an inventory of cultural products and cultural practices that you can draw from as you develop integrated thematic instruction. Can you identify the perspectives reflected in the items you have written down?

4. Choose a feature of the target culture that you feel would be suitable for the development of a classroom fantasy or virtual trip experience.

Follow the guidelines in the chapter and plan a virtual trip for the grade and language level with which you are the most familiar.

5. You have made contact with a teacher of English in an elementary school in the target culture, and the teacher is eager to take part in a classroom exchange but has no idea how to begin.

Write a message in which you describe the mechanics and the potential of the idea.

6. List seven ideas for meaningfully linking the target language that you teach with worldwide cultures, beyond the limits of the countries in which the target language is spoken natively.

For Further Reading

The following sources are recommended for additional information about material covered in this chapter. Chapter citations are documented in Works Cited at the end of this book.

Bosma, Betty. *Fairy Tales, Fables, Legends, and Myths: Using Folk Literature in Your Classroom* (2nd ed.). New York: Teachers College Press, 1992.

Brown, Jeff. *Flat Stanley.* Steve Björkman, Illus. New York: Harper Trophy, 1996. Flat Stanley project website: www.flatstanleyproject.com.

Lange, Dale L. "Planning for and Using the New National Culture Standards." In June K. Phillips (Ed.), *Foreign Language Standards: Linking Research, Theories, and Practices.* The ACTFL Foreign Language Education Series. (Lincolnwood, IL: National Textbook Company, 1999), pp. 57–135.

Lange, Dale L., Carol Klee, Richard M. Paige, and Yelena Yershova (Eds.). *Culture as the Core: Interdisciplinary Perspectives on Culture Teaching and Learning in the Language Curriculum.* CARLA Working Paper Series #11, November 1998. Minneapolis, MN: University of Minnesota, The Center for Advanced Research on Language Acquisition.

Lange, Dale L., Carol Klee, Richard M. Page, and Yelena Yershova (Eds.). *Culture as the Core: Integrating Culture into the Language Curriculum.* CARLA Working Paper Series #15, November 1999. Minneapolis, MN: University of Minnesota, The Center for Advanced Research on Language Acquisition.

Pesola, Carol Ann. "Culture in the Elementary School Foreign Language Classroom." *Foreign Language Annals* 24:4 (September 1991): 331–346.

Rosenbusch, Marcia. "Is Knowledge of Cultural Diversity Enough? Global Education in the Elementary School Foreign Language Program." *Foreign Language Annals* 25:2 (April 1992):129–136.

Websites of Interest

http://anacleta.homstead.com
Spanish and world language and cultural links and resources.

http://miscas.tas.com
Contains many culture resources, including visuals for virtual trips.

Chapter 10

Connecting Content with Language and Culture

The Connections Standards and Content-Related Instruction

Enduring Understanding

- Language instruction draws from and reinforces the goals of the general curriculum.

Essential Question

- How can I use the content of the general curriculum to enrich and extend language instruction?

Regarding language as a medium of learning naturally leads to a cross-curriculum perspective. We have seen that reading specialists contrast learning to read with reading to learn. Writing specialists contrast learning to write with writing to learn. Similarly, language education specialists should distinguish between language learning and using language to learn. Outside the isolated foreign language classroom students learn language and content at the same time. Helping students use language to learn requires us to look beyond the language domain to all subject areas, and to look beyond language learning to education in general. Therefore we need a broad perspective that integrates language and content learning.—Mohan, 1986, p. 18

● Making Connections between Language and Content

The connections goal of the *Standards for Foreign Language Learning in the 21st Century* emphasizes the role that languages can play in extending and enriching student learning in all content areas. Languages give students access to information, opinions, and ideas that would be otherwise inaccessible. The Standards-based language classroom gives students the skills and the practice needed to acquire information in their new language, and it connects the foreign language curriculum with other parts of students' academic lives.

Content-related instruction ties directly to the connections goal in the Standards document: *Connect with other disciplines and acquire information.* There are two standards under the connections goal:

Standard 3.1: Students reinforce and further their knowledge of other disciplines through the foreign language.

Standard 3.2: Students acquire information and recognize the distinctive viewpoints that are only available through the foreign language and its cultures.

Standard 3.1 recognizes that foreign languages can be used to acquire new knowledge by making connections between other subject areas and the foreign language. An important benefit of this connection is that the new language is used as a tool for thinking and learning.

In Standard 3.2, students use the new language to gain access to information and points of view that are not available to some other students who do not know the language. This standard reminds us that a second or third language broadens our students' horizons and resources for all aspects of learning.

Some of the main purposes of content-related instruction are:

- To provide cognitively engaging contexts for language practice
- To integrate language development with content learning
- To provide a vehicle for reinforcing the academic skills and processes and the cognitive skills required by the regular curriculum
- To enrich concepts learned in other content areas with the unique experiences and insights available through language study

● Programs That Relate Language and Content

The goals of foreign language teachers and content area teachers have not always been congruent. Too often the foreign language curriculum was conceived and taught independently from, and to the exclusion of, the content area curriculum. This situation accounts in part for the resistance classroom teachers sometimes exhibit to the addition of a language program to an already crowded school day.

The integration of subject content and academic skills with language and culture is a positive step toward meeting the goals of both language teaching and content teaching, and toward identifying a place for languages in every student's program. In fact, integration of language and subject content is already being successfully accomplished in many language programs.

Immersion and bilingual programs have demonstrated for more than four decades that students can learn subject content and language simultaneously and successfully. Sheltered English programs, when used as a component of bilingual education, have also proved to be very effective in providing successful content-based instruction for second language learners. Sheltered English programs are designed to teach English and subject content to English language learners using specially adapted (but not watered-down) curricula and materials. Students in these classes learn the subject content in the target language, but they are not required to compete with native speakers or to work with the same linguistic tools that are used by native speakers. In the sheltered English class, as in the immersion class, language is a tool through which subject content is learned and not primarily the object of instruction.

Content-Related Programs in Elementary Schools

Immersion, bilingual, and sheltered English programs are designed to teach grade-level content. Content-related programs use the regular curriculum as a vehicle for making language activities more cognitively engaging. Although such programs may teach some grade-level topics, they do not commit to teaching a specific portion of the general school curriculum at a specific grade level. A standards-based language program at the elementary or middle school level will always be content related because it incorporates the connections goal into the curriculum. Integration of curriculum content is an important factor, but it does not overbalance the other goals.

Use of curriculum content in this way provides a rationale for fitting the foreign language program into an already crowded school day. Content-related programs reinforce the curriculum and may or may not use content directly associated with the grade level of the students. More and more school districts are recognizing curriculum integration as a powerful vehicle for convincing parents, school board members, and regular classroom teachers of the value and viability of second-language instruction.

● Reasons for Content-Related Instruction

The reasons for having content-related instruction are twofold. First of all, the movements toward communicative competence, proficiency, and standards all support the use of meaningful content in the language classroom. In order for communication to take place, some knowledge or information must be shared. Incorporating subject content instruction into the elementary school world language classroom provides a meaningful context for language use, and encourages language use for interesting and engaging purposes.

The second area of support for content-related instruction comes from what we know about second-language acquisition and what we know about the brain. Subject content instruction fills the need for "comprehensible input." When providing subject content instruction, the teacher surrounds the students with language to which they can relate by means of a concrete experience, or on the basis of their previous experiences with the information.

Lessons on mapping and graphing, estimating, measuring, endangered animals, the solar system, or the rain forest provide rich opportunities for making language input comprehensible through meaningful visual and tactile experiences. The language used is comprehensible to the students because teachers make sure that ideas and concepts are being communicated clearly and concretely in language the students understand. The language is supported by contextual clues, often in the form of visuals or concrete objects.

Content-related instruction supports what we know about how the brain makes connections and how learning takes place. Students are actively engaged in constructing meaning and making sense of the interesting world presented to them through the vehicle of the target language.

Another source of support for content-related instruction relates to the notion of how time is allocated in the elementary school day. The perennial question asked by administrators and classroom teachers is: "What will we have to take out of the curriculum in order to include language instruction? There is currently not enough time in the curriculum for us to accomplish our existing goals." A language curriculum that introduces or reinforces some mathematics, social studies, or science concepts, and that also makes activities cognitively engaging by focusing on academic skills and processes, provides a powerful rationale for justifying a stable place in the curriculum for elementary language instruction.

● Curricular Areas with Potential for Content-Related Instruction (Standard 3.1)

There are many subject content curriculum standards or benchmarks that are suitable for making connections with languages. Curricular areas such as physical education, family and consumer education, health, art, and music have potential for content-related instruction. Because they deal with highly experiential, often very visual learning, the use of a second language in communicating the concepts could be a natural and successful alternative for instruction. Several of the areas with special potential are the social studies, mathematics, and science.

Social Studies

The social studies curriculum for the elementary school deals with many of the same concepts traditionally taught in language programs in a less systematic way. Such topics as home, family, community, social patterns, and comparative cultures are natural choices for the foreign-language curriculum. Geography and map skills are also easily incorporated into content-related instruction, and there is a natural culture connection. It is also true that U.S. students lag far behind those in other countries in the area of geography. Learning geographical concepts in another language can reinforce a weak curricular area and perhaps heighten student interest.

Many of the techniques and resources used for the teaching of social studies are also appropriate for presenting the same concepts in another language. For example, the use of media; the inquiry method; the use of photos, pictures, and study prints; the use of historical artifacts; and reference to colorful periodicals all provide rich stimuli for meaning-based language instruction.

Although the social studies, especially geography, offer a wealth of language and materials for content-related instruction, there are both advantages and disadvantages to using social studies as a basis for early language learning programs. On the one hand, there is the potential for a great deal of meaningful language and vocabulary use in topic areas that are closely related to the language and cultures curriculum. On the other hand, there may be more vocabulary and language proficiency required for the content and processes of social studies than novice-level language students can adequately develop. This problem becomes evident beginning as early as grade 3 in a K–5 curriculum. Many important geography concepts, however, such as identification of places, use of maps, and map directions, work well with novice learners even though they may be cognitively complex.

Mathematics

Conceptual mathematics explanations and abstract concepts at higher levels of mathematics instruction may pose difficulties, but computation and concrete problem-solving situations can be very useful in content-related instruction. Concepts of size and shape are easily communicated in the target language, and elementary school language teachers have long used simple computation as a means of practicing number concepts. We have included here some of the components of the elementary school mathematics curriculum in order to illustrate in just one subject area a sampling of a few possible curriculum connections that could be made in the language program.

Measurement

- Learn to measure—in inches/feet/centimeters/meters.
- Estimate measurements with reasonable accuracy, using appropriate unit (length, mass, area, volume, time, temperature).
- Identify standard measures and intrasystem equivalencies.

Statistics

- Read, interpret, and construct graphs.
- Given a set of data, determine the mean or average of those data.
- Classify numbers as prime or composite.
- Tell, read, and write time to the nearest minute.

Arithmetic

- Make simple calculations, using the foreign language to review and reinforce math "facts" and measurement.
- Read, write, and say whole numbers from 0 to 100 billion.
- Round numbers to nearest 10, 100, 1,000, 10,000 or 100,000.
- List multiples of a given number.
- Find products and quotients of whole numbers.
- Multiply mentally by 10, 100, or 1,000.

Graphing Activities   Graphing is an excellent mathematics-related activity that can be used with many different themes in a language classroom, even when children have relatively limited expressive language ability. Graphing is also an essential concept in science and social studies. In a Japanese program, students created a graph of their favorite foods (see Figure 10.1A). Figure 10.1B shows an example of using weather to create a graph in a Spanish program.

A first experience with graphing might be entirely teacher directed and involve only physical responses on the part of the children. (Students have already learned to understand colors and various items of clothing when the teacher describes them.)

● **FIGURE 10.1A**   Students in a Beginning Japanese Program Indicate Their Favorite Foods

Teacher: Everyone who has brown shoes on, stand up.

Lift up your left foot so we can see your brown shoe.

(Walks around class to check for shoes and to comment.)

Mary has brown shoes—they look new, Mary!

Tom has brown shoes.

Let's see how many people have brown shoes (counts).

1–2–3–4 . . . (or children may count along).

(Goes to prepared chart on overhead projector, chart paper, or chalkboard.)

Seven children have brown shoes.

(Colors in graph—seven squares, perhaps with brown marker, or places colored shoes on the graph.)

Everyone who has brown shoes, sit down.

Everyone with black shoes, raise your hand.

Wave your hand back and forth!

Lift up your feet so we can see your black shoes.

(Continues in this way, changing things slightly with each color.)

● **FIGURE 10.1B**   A Chart of the Daily Weather Can Also Give Students Experience with a Bar Graph

At the end of this activity there will be a completed graph that the children can talk about. If the activity is used with more than one class during the day, the graphs for the different classes can be compared and contrasted, and concepts such as *more* and *less* can be practiced.

With very young children, a graph is more meaningful if it is created with real objects. In the shoe graph activity, a first step with kindergarten children might be to have each child place her or his own shoe in the appropriate space on a graph outlined on the floor. As a next step, the child might trade the shoe for a piece of paper in the color of his or her shoe, thus making the connection between the number of papers and the number of shoes.

Measuring and graphing heights of class members using centimeters has a cultural "shock value" for students of all ages—even college students find this experience to be engaging. The heights of the class can then be graphed, following a procedure similar to that of the shoe graph.

Another type of graphing activity involves food (or other item) preferences. Pictures of different foods might be placed on each of the walls of the room, and learners "vote" for their favorite first by pointing to it and then by walking to that section of the room. (In a class in which learners are already doing a lot of speaking, they might express their preferences orally.) The teacher counts the number of students at each of the options and colors in the results on the graph. As an alternative, the students themselves might place a square representing their choice on the chart, perhaps with their name printed on it, to help build a graph. Once the graphing activity has been completed, it can be the basis of discussion and used for comparisons, for recalling favorite foods of individual classmates, for games, and for a variety of other communicative activities.

At more advanced speaking stages, learners might take surveys among their classmates about topics that interest them and graph the results, using their graphs to help explain their discoveries to their classmates. Some sample topics would be number of sisters and brothers, number or kind of pet(s), and favorites (e.g., colors, day of the week, season of the year, vegetable, and so on).

Science

Science is especially well suited to content-related foreign language instruction. Hands-on science activities involve many opportunities for interaction and meaningful exchange of language. Activities such as formulating hypotheses and reformulating them when the outcomes vary are important opportunities for the exchange of real information with learners beyond the novice level. Science instruction incorporates the use of many graphics and charts that contribute to understanding.

One of the most powerful strategies in science instruction is the use of prediction. Students encounter a puzzling situation or develop an experiment and predict the results they expect, thus investing personally in both the project and the solution. This strategy can be implemented even when students still have very limited expressive language skills, if the teacher surrounds the experience with language and uses carefully designed questioning techniques. The following example illustrates how the student involvement might be guided:

> *Teacher:* Who believes that the pear will float? Raise your hand.
>
> Who believes that the pear will not float? Raise your hand.
>
> Let's see (counting) . . . 16 believe that the pear will float, and 12 believe that the pear will not float.
>
> (The teacher or student records responses on the chalkboard or on a graph.)
>
> I wonder who is right. Does anyone want to change his or her mind? Raise your hand if you want to change your mind.

> *Teacher:* Rose, do you believe that the pear will float? Yes or no.
>
> *Rose:* Yes.
>
> *Teacher:* Rose says yes. Let's mark X for yes.
>
> (The teacher asks one child after another, and records the response on a graph, or has a student recording responses.)

> *Teacher:* Luc, do you believe that the pear will sink or float?
>
> *Luc:* Sink.
>
> *Teacher:* Luc believes that the pear will sink. Let's put one mark by "sink."
>
> (The teacher asks one child after another, and records the response on a graph.)

● Using the Language to Acquire Information and Insight That Is Only Available through the Target Language (Standard 3.2)

The focus of Connections Standard 3.1 is integration with the school curriculum. Standard 3.2 pushes the student beyond the classroom and beyond the general curriculum in search of information and opinions that have personal importance to the learner: "Students acquire information and recognize the distinctive viewpoints that are only available through the foreign language and its cultures" (*Standards for Foreign Language Learning in the 21st Century,* 1999, p. 56).

Young language learners have many experiences inside a world language classroom that they could not have anywhere else. They hear and read folktales, stories, poems, and music written for native speakers, or sometimes adapted to their language level. Sometimes virtual trips or fantasy experiences such as those described in Chapter 9 can help them to better understand a point of view or a piece of information that would otherwise seem inexplicable.

When teachers work with world maps from the target culture, learners discover that other cultures place their own country or continent in the center of the world—not North America, as U.S. students are accustomed to seeing in the central position. Country names are different in another language, and many familiar cities go unrecognized in the language of the country where they are located.

All of these experiences lay the groundwork for greater independence in seeking out new information from the target culture and in the target language. Jessica Haxhi in Waterbury, Connecticut, builds a unit around the Japanese movie *My Neighbor Totoro*. Learners identify many characteristic cultural features in the movie and contrast them with their own homes and lives. These activities are closely related to the cultures and the comparisons goals, but they also build a foundation of experiences and understandings that would be inaccessible to them any other way. Because the movie was designed for peers in the target culture, it is an especially valuable experience for these learners of Japanese.

Learners who use the target language to sing songs and play games from the target culture are also gaining insights that would be unavailable to them outside the language classroom. These games and songs—like the picture books and stories that enrich early classrooms, or the Japanese movie mentioned earlier—give students a foundation that only young children can receive, because childhood is a natural time for such experiences. The ability to express understanding of information and distinctive viewpoints available through these experiences will come with time.

If teachers in classrooms for young learners have established a partner relationship with a classroom in the target culture, they are in a good position to guide student inquiry about the target culture and the lives of their peers. The class might develop a questionnaire or a survey for their peers in response to an international event, or perhaps the students will check information in a storybook they have read or in a textbook. They might request information about birthdays, holidays, or other celebrations in the target culture, and then share their own customs. What the teacher carefully structures and guides in early stages can blossom into interesting and meaningful independent or group projects.

Older learners who have had more experience with the language and the culture will be more independent in accessing information and opinions. Students in middle school will be able to use such sources as Key Pals, websites, and magazines written for young adolescents in the target culture to prepare reports on topics of personal interest. They may even become motivated to research such topics as popular music, movies, and teen pastimes on their own.

This independent research is truly the goal of Communication Standard 3.2—motivating students to seek out information that goes beyond the limits of the curriculum and often beyond the teacher's own expertise. The role of the teacher in the language classroom is to give students the skills and the language foundation that will allow them to do so. Standard 3.2 links closely with the Communities Standards (5.1—students use the language both within and beyond the school setting; 5.2—students show evidence of becoming lifelong learners by using the language for personal enjoyment and enrichment). It can also provide the opportunity for students to develop the perspectives called for in the cultures standards, often in areas that are well beyond the teacher's own expertise (see Chapter 9). The new perspectives may also be compared with the students' own worldview, thus addressing the Comparison Standard 4.2: "Students demonstrate understanding of the concept of culture through comparisons of the cultures studied and their own." As Connections Standard 3.2 moves students beyond the classroom, teachers and students can become co-learners within the classroom.

All of the activities in this Connections Standard have the goal of giving students a "new window on the world," and helping them to achieve ever greater independence in the use of their new language for personally meaningful purposes.

● Context-Embedded and Context-Reduced Language Tasks

The work of Cummins (1981) continues to be very helpful in explaining some of the strategies that are useful for subject content instruction. Cummins states that first- or second-language proficiency can be looked at in terms of the degree of contextual support available for expressing or comprehending through a language. He describes "context-embedded" language, which is supported by a wide range of clues, and "context-reduced" language, which has very little extra support, so that everything depends on the words themselves. Cummins also says that language proficiency can be viewed in terms of cognitive involvement, or the amount of information a person must process simultaneously or in close succession in order to accomplish a task.

According to Cummins's model, tasks involving language use can be classified into four categories, as seen in the four quadrants in the chart in Figure 10.2. These categories are as follows:

A. Cognitively undemanding and context embedded (embedded in context that helps to make the meaning clear)

B. Cognitively undemanding and context reduced (little context provided)

C. Cognitively demanding and context embedded

D. Cognitively demanding and context reduced

Figure 10.2 helps illustrate the level of contextual support and academic complexity found in various areas of the curriculum. They range from quadrant A, in which the activities are context embedded and relatively simple, to quadrant D, where the activities are more language dependent, context reduced, and relatively difficult.

● **FIGURE 10.2**   Range of Contextual Support and Degree of Cognitive Involvement in Communicative Activities

Source: Based on James Cummins, "The Role of Primary Language Development in Promoting Educational Success for Language Minority Students," in *Schooling and Language Minority Students: A Theoretical Framework* (Los Angeles: California State University), 1981.

As concepts characteristic of quadrant B and quadrant D emerge in the course of instruction, the teacher can make them more accessible to students through the incorporation of extensive visual and concrete referents and through the careful establishment of a context.

The teacher can make the math story problem from quadrant D intelligible through visual or graphic representation. Conceptual explanations can be made more vivid with the addition of appropriate graphs, charts, illustrations, and hands-on experiences. With the addition of context, materials that would otherwise be unintelligible in the target language can contribute to student learning.

The Cummins grid has clear implications for teaching in early language programs, as described here:

Make New Concepts Less Language Dependent

1. Make increased use of visuals and realia.
2. Provide for hands-on involvement of learners.
3. Increase the number and vividness of examples and analogies.
4. Establish a clear, meaningful context.
5. Draw on learners' past experiences and previous learning from the curriculum.
6. Make generous use of rephrasing and repetition.

Make Language Tasks More Cognitively Engaging

1. Relate foreign language curriculum to the concepts in the general school curriculum.
2. Make use of academic skills and processes to engage learners at higher cognitive levels, even when the language itself may be quite simple: classifying, categorizing, graphing, estimating, predicting, comparing, sequencing, identifying patterns.
3. Create opportunities for learners to practice new language in communicative and problem-solving situations, including games, rather than relying on imitation and drill.

● Application of General Academic Skills

As world language teachers begin to incorporate content teaching into the class period, their planning will take on a three-dimensional character. They will design lessons to develop the students' skills in the content area, their understanding of and experience with the culture, and the language necessary for them to achieve both of the preceding goals. Cutting across all three dimensions are intellectual or general academic skills.

One of the useful contributions of cognitive psychology to teaching and learning is a new attention to learners' thought processes. Like language, thinking skills are best developed in context, in the process of grappling with an important idea or decision. At the same time, purposeful implementation of a variety of academic skills and processes can also add to the meaning-making potential of their new language. Teaching these skills enables learners to manipulate information in order to plan, make judgments, decide, and solve problems. Learners need to be able to use academic skills and processes so that they can raise questions as well as support possible answers. Children also need to become aware of their own mental processes and to assess what they know so that they can determine what they still need to learn.

Inventories of thinking skills can be useful to language teachers as a reminder of the need to make activities more cognitively engaging by increasing the sophistication of the thinking required. Bloom's Taxonomy of Thinking Processes (Bloom, 1956) is a helpful tool that is familiar to many educators.

Bloom's Revised Taxonomy of Thinking Processes

Bloom (1956) outlined six levels of skills, including knowledge, comprehension, application, analysis, synthesis, and evaluation. Anderson and Krathwohl (2001) revised the original taxonomy to include remembering and understanding, applying, analyzing, creating, and evaluating. They juxtaposed the last two levels because they indicated that creating is cognitively more advanced than evaluating. The circle diagram (Clark, 2002) in Figure 10.3 contains the taxonomy levels in the inner circle. The first two levels, Remembering

● **FIGURE 10.3**   Bloom's Taxonomy of Thinking Processes: Examples of Activities and Assignments (Products) That Demonstrate Bloom's Levels of Cognitive Skills

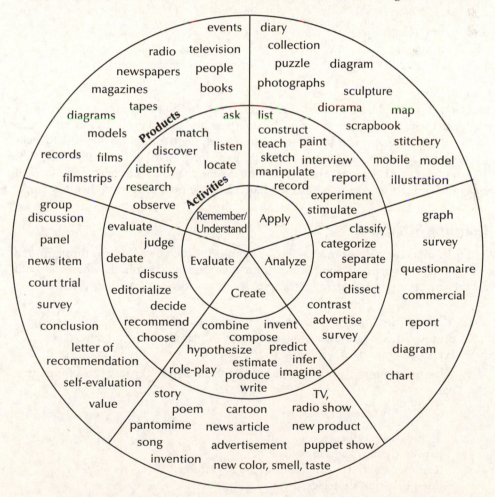

Source: Based on B. Clark (2002). *Growing up Gifted: Developing the Potential of Children at Home and at School* (Upper Saddle River, NJ: Merrill Prentice-Hall, 2002). From www.apa.org/ed/new_blooms.html.

TABLE 10.1   Process Skills across the Curriculum

Science	Reading	Mathematics	Social Science
Classifying	Comparing & contrasting characteristics	Sorting, sequencing	Comparing ideas
Collecting data	Taking notes	Collecting data	Collecting data
Interpreting data	Organizing facts, recognizing cause & effect	Analyzing	Interpreting data
Communicating results	Logically arranging information	Graphing, constructing tables	Making maps
Predicting	Predicting	Predicting	Predicting

Source: From *INSTRUCTOR*, March 1991, Copyright © 1991 by Scholastic Inc. Reprinted by permission.

and Understanding, are contained in one section. The middle ring contains verbs associated with each level, and the outer ring contains possible student products for that domain of cognitive processing. This taxonomy should be helpful to teachers as they seek to incorporate academic skills and processes into their teaching. Another chart, shown in Table 10.1, outlines the skills that are needed in various subject areas. Both charts provide teachers with helpful information needed for addressing cognitive process in their teaching.

Learning Strategies

Young learners can become more skilled at monitoring their own learning through attention to learning strategies. Some students use these strategies naturally, whereas for others they must be taught. Learning strategies are usually divided into three groups:

1. *Metacognitive Strategies.* Strategies for planning and reflecting on the learning process, such as previewing the main ideas, or planning what is going to be expressed orally or in writing.

2. *Cognitive Strategies.* Strategies learners apply directly to the task itself, for example:
   Outlining
   Summarizing
   Using context clues
   Grouping and clustering
   Compensation strategies, such as use of gestures
   Memorization strategies
   Study skills

3. *Affective and Social Strategies.* Learners use these strategies to reward and encourage themselves, to lower anxiety and frustration, or to ask for help. Some examples are:

> Questioning for clarification
> Self-talk
> Asking for help
> Working with other students

● Strategies for Helping Students Access Content

Marzano, Pickering, and Pollock (2001) have suggested several important strategies that help students access content, which can be especially helpful when that content is presented in a new language. Two of the research-proven strategies they suggest are identifying similarities and differences and using nonlinguistic representations.

Identifying Similarities and Differences

Presenting students with explicit guidance in identifying similarities and differences, or asking students to identify similarities and differences independently, enhances students' understanding of and ability to use knowledge. Strategies for identifying similarities and differences include comparing, classifying, using metaphors, and using analogies. These strategies can be extended into the language curriculum as well, of course. For example, students might compare a birthday celebration in the target culture with their own, or they might classify clothing vocabulary according to whether the item is worn in the winter or the summer or both. Students might create writing projects based on a metaphor: "Winter Is a Polar Bear," for example. More advanced students might create more sophisticated products. Creating analogies based on combinations of old and new vocabulary could be an interesting way to intensify the understanding and the memorability of the words. Even at the single-word language level, students could play word games with analogies, such as "Dark is to light as night is to . . . ."

Nonlinguistic Representations

Nonlinguistic representations represent a second system of storage for knowledge—an imagery form, which is different from linguistic forms of representation. When students use both systems, they are better able to think about and to recall knowledge. Marzano, Pickering, and Pollock (2001) identify the following nonlinguistic representations as ways to aid student learning:

- Making physical models, such as using math manipulatives to solve a story problem, can make otherwise abstract concepts more concrete and more meaningful.

- Generating mental pictures can create a story-like or emotional connection to vocabulary or information. A teacher who describes the setting in detail before telling a story to the class is helping them generate a mental picture that will aid comprehension.

- Drawing pictures and pictographs could be a means of anchoring vocabulary in the new language. Students might create an individualized picture dictionary, for example.

- Engaging in kinesthetic activity is a popular means of helping students to understand and remember language. TPR, TPR Storytelling, the Gouin Series, and songs and rhymes with actions all capitalize on the value of connecting language and ideas with motion.

- Creating graphic representations can help to clarify relationships among ideas and concepts.

In the next section we will focus on using graphic representations to help students access content knowledge through the new language.

Using Graphic Representations as Cognitive Organizers

A graphic or cognitive organizer is a visual that displays words or concepts in categories to show how they relate to one another. This organizes the information in such a way that it can be easily understood, remembered, and applied. Cognitive organizers connect linguistic and visual information, thus facilitating both learning and retrieval of what has been learned.

For the novice language learner, who finds listing and naming to be the most natural ways to use a new language, graphic organizers provide an ideal and cognitively engaging context for using and practicing vocabulary. The teacher who uses a variety of cognitive organizers is moving language instruction from area A in the Cummins grid (Figure 10.2), cognitively undemanding and context embedded, to area C, cognitively (more) demanding and context embedded. At the same time, the student is experiencing vocabulary in a variety of meaningful contexts and will be much more likely to store that vocabulary in his or her long-term memory.

Charts, graphs, time lines, flowcharts, tables, maps, Venn diagrams, and many other types of organizers are used to help students place vocabulary and information in a comprehensible and engaging context. Cognitive organizers can be used to list concepts in various ways. One of the ways to classify the many different types of organizers is in terms of how they structure information, such as:

- Simple listing/mapping/webbing/clustering
- Time sequence/chronology

- Compare and contrast
- Process/cause and effect

We will examine examples of each of these four types in turn.

Simple Listing/Mapping/Webbing/Clustering   This type of organizer presents information or clarifies and categorizes information in a structured way. These organizers can be linear or nonlinear depending on the relationships being described. They are used to describe and list attributes or patterns or to organize information about specific events, settings, or people. They can organize information into general statements with supporting examples, or they can clarify concepts relating to a word or phrase that represents entire classes of people, places, things, and events.

Mapping/webbing/clustering organizers might be used to list everything the students can think of related to a central concept, such as a geography concept, an animal, or a specific person. The concept word can be placed in the center of the map, with the other ideas listed as spokes coming out from the central concept. A picture map of Africa, for example, will help students visualize the range of various animals that are native to the continent. Other organizers, such as the brace map, the tree map, and the topic category organizer, show how ideas and concepts are related to one another in a hierarchical fashion. A family tree is a simple example of this kind of organizer. Figure 10.4 shows some of ways that these organizers can be depicted.

● **FIGURE 10.4**   Forms of Simple Listing Organizers

Time Sequence/Chronology This type of cognitive organizer categorizes information according to some kind of sequence or chronology, as in a time line or a flowchart. Flowcharts can be linear or cyclical. A cycle flowchart shows how a series of events can produce the same results again and again, as with the water cycle or the life cycle of a butterfly or a frog (see Figure 10.5A).

Sequence/chronology organizers could also show a chain of events, the stages of an event, the steps in a procedure, or the actions of a character. A story map fits into this category of organizers. (See the section on story maps in Chapter 5.) Another way to graphically organize a sequence or chronology is with a continuum that shows the beginning and ending points of a process, or the range of some quality, such as student heights within a class, between extremes. Figure 10.5B is a chronology in the form of a foods time line that could become an interesting part of a nutrition unit.

● **FIGURE 10.5A** Cycle Flowchart

● **FIGURE 10.5B** Foods Time Line

4000 B.C.	Oranges and watermelons
3600 B.C.	Popcorn
2000 B.C.	Marshmallows
490 B.C.	Pasta and macaroni
1395	Gingerbread and Lebkuchen
1484	Hot dogs
1553	Potatoes in Europe
1762	Sandwiches
1819	Spaghetti
1830	Soft drinks in America
1894	Hershey bars
1941	M & M's and Cheerios
1947	Betty Crocker cake mix
1954	TV dinners
1955	McDonald's restaurants
1965	Gatorade
1998	Grape tomatoes

Source: Adapted from "The Food Timeline" (www.gti.net/mocolib1/kid/food/html).

Compare and Contrast

A third way the graphic organizers can classify information is by showing comparisons and contrasts. These types of organizers help students to distinguish between similarities and differences. The chart comparing the Mayas of Mexico and Central America and the Incas of Peru shows the similarities and differences on a simple chart (Figure 10.6). The first column lists the elements to be compared while the second and third columns specify how each group manifests this element.

The Venn diagram is frequently used for comparison and contrast. A Venn diagram consists of two or more intersecting circles that graphically depict logical relationships between or among concepts. The Venn diagrams displayed in Figure 10.7 show two overlapping circles, each circle representing one of the concepts to be compared. One circle lists the characteristics of the first item, while a second circle lists the characteristics of the other item. The segment where the two circles overlap in the middle shows the similarities between the two items, whereas the characteristics outside of the center show the differences. This activity serves as an exercise in logical thinking, and it can also be the basis of a meaningful writing exercise with each area of the diagram serving as the starting point for a separate paragraph.

Venn diagrams can also be used for simple sorting activities conducted entirely orally. Two large hula hoops or two jump ropes laid out in adjoining circles could form the diagrams. Learners could be asked to sort a group of objects into things that are blue in one circle, for example, and things that are round in the other. The teacher would include some items that are both round and blue. When students realize that these items should go in both circles, they are faced with a problem. They can usually solve the problem by moving the circles so that they intersect, leaving a space in the middle for items that have both characteristics. If students do not arrive at this solution within a reasonable time, the teacher can help with hints, or actually make the circles intersect.

● **FIGURE 10.6**   Comparison/Contrast Worksheets Can Reveal Similarities and Differences

	Incas	Mayas
Food Supply		
Shelter		
Location		

● **FIGURE 10.7**   Comparison and Contrast. Venn Diagrams show similarities and differences.

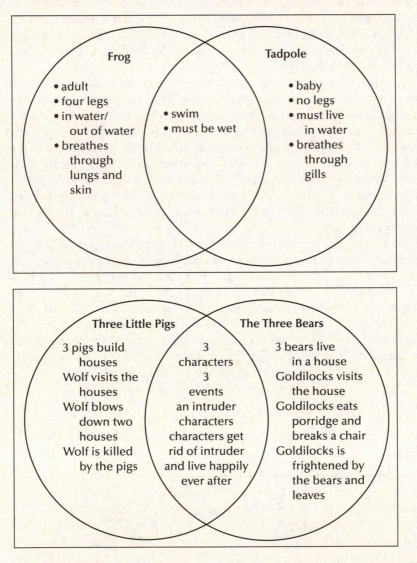

Process/Cause and Effect   This last type of organizer shows the logical relationships between causes and effects. These organizers can be used to show relationships among events within a story, for example, or steps in a process. The causes and effects must be specifically labeled "Cause" and "Effect" in order to make the relationship clear (see Figure 10.8).

● **FIGURE 10.8** Cause and Effect Organizers

● Factors to Consider in Planning for Content-Related Instruction

Numerous factors must be considered when planning connections with the content curriculum for an integrated thematic curriculum, unit, or lesson. Most of the same considerations apply for the teacher in an immersion, bilingual, or content-based program:

- The content-area skills and concepts that can interrelate most effectively with the language goals
- The language competencies needed in order to work with the content selected
- The cognitive skills necessary in order to perform the tasks in the lesson
- The potential for integration with cultural concepts and goals

It is important to emphasize the point that when teachers incorporate general curriculum content into a thematic unit, they should not ignore the balance among language, content, and culture goals. There may be some lessons in a unit that emphasize subject content, but elements of the Cultures Standard and the Communications Standard should also be present.

Balance of Language, Culture, and Content Goals

Both authors of this book have had the experience of working with school districts where content-related instruction is the primary emphasis in programs for young learners at the expense of other goals. In these situations, other dimensions of the curriculum appear to suffer. Students are still learning, of course, but the full potential of an early language program is not being realized. When this happens, it is often because school administrators seized on the idea of reinforcing the regular curriculum to the virtual exclusion of the other important elements of language teaching. In our enthusiasm for content-related instruction, we must remember that our vision is shaped by the interrelatedness of language, content, and culture, and by all five of the national Standards, not by the Connections Standard alone.

Curriculum Resources

The best resources for the teacher who is interested in content-related instruction are the curriculum documents for the elementary and middle school level of the school district in which the second-language program takes place. If such materials are not current or are not available, the state department of education will have available standards for instruction at various grade levels. National Standards for each subject can also provide guidance. Language teachers may find, when they examine school curriculum documents, that they are already addressing some of the concepts but in an unsystematic way. For example, the teacher who regularly teaches the location of French-speaking countries in a fifth-grade class may choose to expand these lessons to include locating capital cities on simple maps using elementary grids, thus reinforcing additional map-reading skills taught at this grade level.

Teachability through the Target Language

The language teacher looks for concepts that lend themselves especially well to the kind of concrete, hands-on, activity-oriented teaching that is necessary in the early language classroom. Thus, the teacher must ask: Can these concepts be taught using the simple language that novice-level learners are able to understand and use? Or do they require more abstract, complex, and sophisticated language?

For the fourth-grade science curriculum of a partial immersion program, for example, the staff chose a unit on rocks and charts as a likely candidate for Spanish instruction. They selected this topic because so many of the activities involved handling and observing characteristics of rocks and then classifying the rocks according to visual criteria.

This staff, however, decided that a unit on magnetism would require an inappropriately sophisticated command of the target language because of the expectation that conclusions would be evaluated and discussed in great detail. Figure 10.9 shows an example

● **FIGURE 10.9** Rain Forest Pattern Story

1. Here is the rain forest in South America. It is hot, humid, and it rains a lot.

2. This is a hummingbird. He is purple, blue, green, and yellow. He is a little bird that drinks nectar. He is sleeping and rain drops are falling on his head.

3. 3a. The hummingbird awakens and flies up a Kapok tree to see from where the rain drops are coming.

   3b. The hummingbird starts to fly upwards and sees a tapir. He asks the tapir, "Who are you?" The tapir replies, "I am the tapir. I am a black mammal. I eat insects. I live on the forest floor." "No, you are not the rain. Thank you. I am going to continue."

4. The hummingbird flies higher and sees a leaf cutter ant. "Who are you?"

   "I am the ant. I am a small, black insect. I eat leaves. I live on the forest floor and in the understory."

   "No, you are not the rain. Thank you. I am going to continue."

5. The hummingbird flies higher and sees a boa. "Who are you?"

   "I am the boa. I am a brown reptile. I eat small mammals. I live in the understory."

   "No, you are not the rain. Thank you. I am going to continue."

6. The hummingbird flies higher and sees a jaguar. "Who are you?"

   "I am the jaguar. I am a white, yellow, and brown mammal. I eat small mammals. I live in the understory."

   "No, you are not the rain. Thank you. I am going to continue."

7. The hummingbird flies higher and sees a toucan. "Who are you?"

   "I am the toucan. I am a black, yellow, red, green, and white bird. I eat fruits. I live in the canopy."

"No, you are not the rain. Thank you. I am going to continue."

8. The hummingbird flies higher and sees a sloth. "Who are you?"

   "I am the sloth. I am a brown mammal. I eat plants. I live in the canopy."

   "No, you are not the rain. Thank you. I am going to continue."

9. The hummingbird flies higher and sees the sky. It is sunny and it is warm. He sees a macaw. "Who are you?"

   "I am the macaw. I am a red, blue, green, and yellow bird. I eat fruits. I live in the canopy and the emergent layer. Why do you ask?"

   "I live in the understory. It rains a lot there. Where does the rain come from?"

   "It rains up here too. The rain comes from the clouds above. Look! You can see it raining over there."

   "Thank you. I now understand." The hummingbird returns to the understory. He drinks some nectar and it starts to rain again.

   "I now know where the rain comes from."

Source: Jackie Dove and Stephanie Metrusias. Reprinted with permission.

of how two teachers of young learners scaffolded their introduction to a rain forest unit so that it would be understandable to their fourth-graders. Jackie Dove and Stephanie Metrusias wrote a pattern story to illustrate the layers of the rain forest.

Content-Compatible and Content-Obligatory Language

When planning for the language aspects of the lesson, it is important to include both content vocabulary for the particular subject area and the other new language the students will need to know in order to understand the lesson. The teacher must decide how much subject content language can reasonably be taught in the second language.

Content-obligatory language is the language that must be taught in order to teach or reinforce the curriculum concept, drawn from content curriculum. *Content-compatible language,* drawn from the language curriculum, is that language for which the curriculum concept or information provides a convenient context. For example, although the teacher knows that the basic language functions that will be needed for a rain forest unit are probably identifying and describing, the teacher recognizes this as an opportunity to work on other language functions such as asking for and giving information, and expressing admiration. Students could conduct role-play tours of the rain forest and ask about the animals in various levels, or express admiration for the beautiful colors of animals and flowers.

The teacher could decide to develop a fantasy theme in which the animals take on personalities. Then content-compatible language could even extend to socializing. Perhaps the teacher could have the animals greet each other like this:

Student A: Hello, I'm Mrs. Jaguar, I live in the understory, and I am pleased to meet you.

Student B: Hello Mrs. Jaguar, I'm Ms. Hummingbird. I live in the understory. I'm pleased to meet you.

Availability of Relevant Materials

Early in the planning process it is important to identify the instructional materials you will use. Are sufficient materials available in the target language or will most materials have to be translated? If materials are available in the target language, how much adaptation is necessary?

It may be necessary to simplify the instructional materials if the print involved is too difficult, or amplify them if they do not provide enough comprehensible input for foreign-language students. Also, make sure that the materials needed to teach the lessons you have chosen are readily available (and that they are easily portable if you are a traveling teacher and do not have your own classroom).

Adapting Materials

Echevarria and Graves (2007, p. 131) have developed a useful list of techniques for adapting materials. Although some of these are primarily directed at the content-based or immersion setting, many of the ideas can be used by teachers in other programs as well.

1. Using graphic depiction
2. Outlining the text
3. Rewriting the text
4. Using audiotapes
5. Providing live demonstrations
6. Using alternate books

Active, Hands-On Teaching Strategies for Helping Students to Understand the Concepts

These strategies should not demand heavy verbal involvement of the students but should focus on receptive language. Surround the activity with language, and use visuals, demonstrations, and vocabulary the students already know to explain the new content vocabulary. Make sure the components of the lesson are observable and manipulable. Total Physical Response and Natural Approach activities can help provide the meaningful context necessary in content-based classes (see explanations in Chapter 2). Close communication with classroom teachers will be helpful in evaluating these teaching strategies and rethinking those that may need improvement.

● Challenges in Integrating Language and Content

A great challenge inherent in the integration of language and content instruction, especially for immersion and other content-based programs, is that not enough attention will be paid to the other crucial elements involved in elementary school language teaching—namely, language and culture. Incorporating content alone does not ensure that effective language learning will take place. Content-related instruction incorporates concepts and activities from the general curriculum to enhance the language class, because they provide meaningful, motivating, and intrinsically interesting experiences on which to build language learning. Foreign language teachers who are attempting content-based or content-related instruction for the first time often lack a strong professional preparation in specific content areas. As a result, they need to focus most of their attention on the content aspects of planning and, given the limited planning time available, they may not plan as carefully for the language and culture components.

Another danger, especially for immersion and other content-based programs, is the possibility that some of the problematic practices from first-language teaching will be carried over into second-language instruction. A traditional content class might consist of a series of teacher questions about what students have read, or to elicit students' background knowledge. The teacher often asks rapid-fire questions that require a specific answer, perhaps only a one-word or very short answer. The follow-up to the teacher questions during class might be a worksheet with more questions that students answer individually. In this example, there is a lot of teacher talk and little opportunity for students to process what has been learned or to engage in extended discourse. If these practices are used in the world language class, it is likely that there will be no opportunity for students to use their new language in a meaningful way. When they do use the second language, under these circumstances, their teacher may focus only on errors of content and never address—or even notice—errors in syntax, grammar, or pronunciation.

Solutions to these challenges could include designing a systematic plan for language development; providing purposeful, theme-based activities that give the student opportunities to present a product to an "important audience"; and providing opportunities for students to engage frequently in extended discourse thorough cooperative learning and interactive tasks. Ideas and activities presented in this book can be directly useful in addressing many of these challenges. The solutions lie in a meaning-based, thematic curriculum that purposefully and continually integrates the teaching of language, content, and culture.

Summary

- Content-related instruction, properly implemented, gives us a valuable source of cognitively engaging and intrinsically interesting activities with which we can enrich our programs. It connects the foreign-language curriculum with other parts of students' academic lives, and it extends their access to meaningful information through the target language.

- Including content from the general curriculum and paying attention to general academic skills, while also teaching students to communicate in another language and culture, can increase the intensity of the language learning experience, thus enhancing motivation, accelerating language development, and contributing to the overall academic achievement of the learner.

- Especially in programs for young learners, the incorporation of content-related instruction can give increased impetus to language study at that level, not only because of the more effective language learning it will bring but also because it offers a solution to the perennial problem of how to find time for elementary school foreign-language instruction.

- When subject content is integrated with elementary school foreign language curriculum, the classroom teacher who struggles to schedule a multitude of curricular areas into a limited amount of time may see the elementary school foreign-language teacher as an ally in this effort, rather than as a competitor in a zero-sum game for control of instructional time in the school day. Integrating subject content with foreign language and culture instruction can be a powerful way to build a stable place in the curriculum for foreign-language programs.

For Study and Discussion

1. Examine an elementary or middle school foreign-language curriculum to identify concepts from other subject content areas that are already present there. What role do they play? How could the teacher increase their importance within the existing curriculum?

2. Locate a curriculum guide for social studies, science, language arts, mathematics, health, or physical education at the elementary level with which you are most familiar. What concepts do you find that are already touched on in foreign-language classes? Which concepts lend themselves to instruction in a second language? What criteria did you apply for choosing these concepts? List five of the concepts that you feel have the best potential, and give reasons for your choice.

3. Using the curriculum guide in item 2 (above), choose two concepts that are located in quadrant D of Cummins's chart shown in Figure 10.2 (context-reduced, cognitively demanding) and explain how you would develop lessons and materials to move them to quadrant C (context-embedded, cognitively demanding) in order to include them in a foreign-language curriculum.

4. Which of the advantages of integrating subject content with language and culture instruction do you think would be most important in the elementary school language situation you know best? What obstacles will need to be confronted in order to implement it?

5. Design an activity in which you use a cognitive organizer to help students understand and remember vocabulary for a thematic unit. What other cognitive organizers could you use with the same vocabulary?

6. Plan two activities addressing the Connections Standard 3.2, one for a middle school classroom in which students have already had six years of language study, and one for a class of second-grade students who have begun instruction in first grade.

For Further Reading

The following sources are recommended for additional information about material covered in this chapter. Chapter citations are documented in Works Cited at the end of this book.

Caine, Renate N., and Geoffrey Caine. *Education on the Edge of Possibility.* Alexandria, VA: Association for Supervision and Curriculum Development, 1997.

Chamot, Anna Uhl, and J. Michael O'Malley. *A Cognitive Academic Language Learning Approach: An ESL Content-Based Curriculum.* Rosslyn, VA: National Clearinghouse for Bilingual Education, 1986.

Echevarria, Jana, and Anne Graves. *Sheltered Content Instruction: Teaching English Language Learners with Diverse Abilities* (3rd ed.). Boston: Pearson Allyn and Bacon, 2007.

Echevarria, Jana, Mary Ellen Vogt, and Deborah Short. *Making Content Comprehensible for English Language Learners: The SIOP Model* (3rd ed.). Boston: Pearson Allyn and Bacon, 2008.

Gibbons, Pauline. *Scaffolding Language, Scaffolding Learning: Teaching Second Language Learners in the Mainstream Classroom.* Portsmouth, NH: Heinemann, 2002.

Hill, Jane D., and Kathleen M. Flynn. *Classroom Instruction That Works with English Language Learners.* Alexandria, VA: Association for Supervision and Curriculum Development, 2006.

Hyerle, David. *Visual Tools for Constructing Knowledge.* Alexandria, VA: Association for Supervision and Curriculum Development, 1996.

Marzano, Robert J., Debra Pickering, and Jane Pollock. *Classroom Instruction That Works.* Alexandria, VA: Association for Supervision and Curriculum Development, 2001.

Marzano, Robert J., Jennifer S. Norford, Diane E. Paynter, Debra J. Pickering, and Barbara B. Gaddy. *A Handbook for Classroom Instruction That Works.* Alexandria, VA: Association for Supervision and Curriculum Development, 2001.

Met, Myriam. "Learning Language through Content: Learning Content through Language." *Foreign Language Annals* 24:4 (1991): 281–295.

Met, Myriam. "Making Connections." In June K. Phillips (Ed.), *The ACTFL Foreign Language Education Series.* Lincolnwood, IL: National Textbook Company, 1999, pp. 137–164.

Met, Myriam. *Content-Based Defining Terms, Making Decisions.* Washington DC: National Foreign Language Center, 1999. Retrieved February 2008. www.carla.umn.edu/cobaltt/modules/principles/decisions.html.

Rhodes, Nancy, Helena Curtain, and Mari Haas. "Child Development and Academic Skills in the Elementary School Foreign Language Classroom." In Sally S. Magnan (Ed.), *Shifting the Instructional Focus to the Learner.* Middlebury, VT: Northeast Conference on the Teaching of Foreign Languages, 1990, pp. 57–92.

Vogt, Mary Ellen, and Jana Echevarría. *99 Ideas and Activities for Teaching English Language Learners with the SIOP Model.* Boston: Pearson Allyn and Bacon, 2008.

Websites of Interest

Although the following websites are focused on English language learners, they include a variety of valuable resources on the topic of teaching language through content.

Center for Applied Linguistics: www.cal.org. The Integrated Language and Content page of the Center for Applied Linguistics' (CAL) website includes a complete listing of CAL projects and products: www.cal.org/topics/ilc.html.

National Clearinghouse for English Language Acquisition and Language Instruction Educational Programs (NCELA): www.ncela.gwu.edu/. NCELA (formerly the National Clearinghouse for Bilingual Education) offers many resources for teaching language through content, such as the "In the Classroom Toolkit," with sample activities for teaching grade-level content in K–12 educational settings: www.ncbe.gwu.edu/library/curriculum/index.htm.

Chapter 11

Immersion Programs

Reaching toward Bilingualism

Enduring Understanding

- Experiences with immersion programs provide models of exemplary instructional practices for all language programs

Essential Question

- What can immersion programs tell me that will help me to provide more effective instruction in my own classroom?

● Immersion: What Is It? What Makes It Work? What Are the Results?

Since immersion programs have the greatest amount of time dedicated to language learning, this is the program model that has the greatest success in terms of language outcomes. Immersion programs are part of a subgroup of programs that, according to Fortune and Tedick (2008), fall into the category of dual-language education. Students in immersion programs become functionally proficient in the second language at a level appropriate to their age and grade in school. Immersion students not only become bilingual but also master the subject content of the regular elementary school curriculum that is taught through the second language. As an approach to early language learning, immersion is easily able to provide a holistic language learning experience for students of a new language, since the teachers and students are able to communicate throughout the entire school day on topics spanning the full range of the curriculum.

● Types of Programs

Immersion programs vary in the amount of time devoted to instruction in the second language (total or partial immersion), in the level of entry (early, middle, or late immersion), and in the population of students who enter the program (two-way and indigenous language immersion). The following definitions clarify terms and concepts associated with immersion in the United States and Canada.

- *Total or Full Immersion* The second language is used for the entire school day during the first two or three years. In early total immersion programs, reading is taught through the second language. In some programs, instruction by means of English is introduced gradually, often in second grade, and the amount of English is increased until the fifth or sixth grade (the last grade in elementary school), where up to half the day is spent in English and half in the second language. In other programs, once English is introduced (usually at grade 2 or 3) the percentage of time spent in English remains constant throughout the program, at approximately 20 percent. In some other programs, the entire day is conducted in the second language for a much greater period of time and English is not introduced until grades 4 or 5.

- *Partial Immersion* All instruction is in the second language for part (at least half) of the school day. The amount of instruction in the immersion language usually remains constant throughout the elementary school program. In early partial immersion programs, students frequently learn to read in both languages at the same time; in some programs, notably Arabic, Chinese, and Japanese partial immersion, literacy skills are taught first in the native language. Partial immersion has also become the most popular type of immersion model in the United States. Most partial immersion programs maintain a ratio of target language use to English use of approximately 50/50 throughout the elementary grades.

- *Early Immersion* Students begin learning through the second language early in the elementary school sequence, usually in kindergarten or first grade. In some programs, such as some in Milwaukee, immersion programs begin in 4-year-old kindergarten.

- *Late Immersion* Students begin learning through the second language later in their schooling, either at the end of elementary school, at the beginning of middle school/junior high school, or in high school. Many students entering late immersion programs have had previous instruction (30 to 60 minutes per day) in the second language. Late immersion programs may involve 90 to 100 percent of the instruction in the second language for the first year and 50 to 80 percent for one or two years after that, or 50 to 60 percent throughout. This model is more common in Canada than in the United States.

● *Continuing Immersion* Continuing immersion programs are found at the middle school/junior high school or high school level. These programs are designed to maintain the language skills already developed in total or partial immersion programs and to further develop them to as high a degree as possible.

● *One-Way Immersion* The term *one-way immersion* refers to the fact that in total and partial immersion programs in the USA, the students are generally monolingual English speakers who are learning the immersion language. The focus of the program is "one-way" in that all the students are learning the same new language.

● *Two-Way Immersion* Two-way immersion programs, also known as *two-way bilingual,* or *developmental bilingual education programs,* are similar to one-way immersion programs except that the student group includes native speakers of the target language as well as native speakers of English. Thus, all students learn subject matter through their native language as well as through the second language, and both language groups have the benefit of interaction with peers who are native speakers of the language they are learning. The ideal student population of such programs is a 50/50 combination of majority and minority speakers. In most programs, native English speakers make up anywhere from one-half to two-thirds of the population. The ideal goals of two-way immersion, in addition to subject content mastery, are that the English-speaking students become functionally proficient in the second language and that the second-language speakers become functionally proficient in English. At the same time, all students continue to develop skills and proficiency in their native language. These programs have been successfully implemented at both elementary and secondary school levels. Two-way language development programs promote bilingual education as an enrichment program for all students rather than as a compensatory education mode for English language learners. These programs most often involve Spanish and English, but they also exist in other languages.

● *Indigenous Immersion* Indigenous immersion programs are designed as language and culture revitalization programs in Native and Aboriginal communities. Depending on the student population in the programs, they can be either one- or two-way immersion programs. Indigenous programs differ in that they have a very strong cultural emphasis. Much of the education program is organized through the central focus of the perspectives, practices, and products of the Native culture.

One of the strongest indigenous immersion programs is Hawaiian. Hawai'i is the only state in the United States that has a designated native language, Hawaiian, as one of its two official state languages. In 1987, the Department of Education established the Hawaiian Language Immersion Program, Ka Papahana Kaiapuni Hawai'i. The goal of the Hawaiian immersion program is to provide a quality education based on knowledge of the Hawaiian language and culture as the foundation on which individuals become responsible, sensitive, and productive adults who contribute significantly to all levels of Hawai'i's community. The students understand that they will be responsible for the perpetuation of the native Hawaiian language and be the stewards of the cultural heritage of the indigenous people of Hawai'i. The program has grown from 2 sites in 1987 to 19 sites with a student population of about 1,500 in grades K–12 on five islands. (See www.k12.hi.us/~kaiapuni/.)

Immersion Goals   Immersion program goals may be summarized as follows:

1. Functional proficiency in the second language
2. Maintenance and development of English language arts skills comparable to or surpassing the achievement of students in English-only programs
3. Mastery of subject content material of the school district curriculum
4. Cross-cultural understanding

How Did Immersion Start?

The idea of immersing second-language learners in an environment in which they must use the language is certainly not a new one. Immersion programs have appeared throughout history and can be found in many private schools throughout the world. The first North American public school immersion program in recent times began in 1965 with a kindergarten in St. Lambert, Quebec. It was prompted by a group of English-speaking parents who were concerned that traditional French programs were not sufficient to meet their children's needs for greater comprehension of and fluency in French, at a time when bilingualism in French and English had become a necessity in Canada.

As research information from Canadian immersion programs began to be disseminated, and as immersion programs were spreading rapidly in Canada, similar programs began to be established in the United States, where a different set of realities regarding second-language learning existed. Whereas Canadian immersion programs were developed because of a demonstrated need for bilingualism, immersion programs in the United States were established for a variety of reasons, most of which centered on a search for alternative approaches to successful second-language teaching for young children.

The first immersion program in the United States was started in 1971 in Culver City, California. The number of immersion programs in the United States grew slowly. In 1974, three programs were added, and by 1977, the number had grown to five. In 1977, the Milwaukee Public Schools began the German component of its immersion programs, and San Diego Schools began a program in Spanish. One of the authors was involved with the founding of the Milwaukee program and has seen it grow to French, German, and Spanish elementary schools and a middle school/high school. The elementary schools have celebrated more than 30 years since their founding and have "grown their own" teachers, since there are now teachers at each of the schools who were originally immersion students!

In 1987, a total of 50 school districts offered immersion, and by 1999, these numbers had grown to 72 districts and 10 languages in 29 states plus the District of Columbia. In 2006, the numbers increased again to 83 districts in 23 states and Washington DC. Since the 2006 survey, the numbers continue to grow, especially in the area of Chinese immersion. Table 11.1 summarizes the locations of immersion programs in the United States according to a 2006 survey by the Center for Applied Linguistics. Table 11.2 (page 315) shows the various immersion languages being studied in immersion programs.

Two-Way Immersion

A distinctive U.S. contribution to the inventory of immersion program models, two-way immersion programs have been developed in a number of U.S. cities as an alternative to transitional bilingual programs. These programs contrast sharply with transitional bilingual programs that feature homogeneous native-language classes. Minority language students begin their studies in their native language until they have learned enough English to be transferred to a mainstream classroom. In these transitional classes, students study English as a second language (ESL) but do not benefit from language reinforcement through interaction with native-English-speaking peers in the classroom. In contrast, a two-way program targets both language minority and language majority students. In each half of the day, one of the groups is receiving instruction in its native language and one of the groups is learning in its new language. This format provides English language learners (ELLs) with the opportunity to learn English without lagging behind academically, and it gives native-English-speaking students the chance both to learn a second language and to develop an understanding of another culture.

Two-way programs share with one-way immersion programs the basic assumption that a new language is best learned not as the object of instruction, but rather as the medium of instruction, through a content-based curriculum. Immersion programs have traditionally been designed as language enrichment programs for language-majority students. Two-way programs in the United States, on the other hand, are designed to serve the needs of both language-majority English speakers and ELL populations. In a two-way program, native English speakers are not separated from ELL students during instruction; the two groups are in the same class. Such a model takes advantage of the fact that children learn new languages most naturally and effectively when they have peers—classmates and playmates—as language models.

Program designs vary from district to district, but three typical designs are described in detail by Christian and colleagues (1997). (See Tables 11.3 and 11.4 on page 316.) This Center for Applied Linguistics publication profiles River Glen Elementary School in San Jose, California, and Inter-American Magnet School in Chicago. Two of the variables among these programs are percentage of instruction in Spanish and English, and initial reading instruction. The tables show two of the differences among the three programs studied.

TABLE 11.1 Summary of U.S. Immersion Programs, by State: 2006

State	Number of Schools and Districts by State						
	Schools	Districts	Private	Pre-school	Elementary	Middle	High
Alaska	9	2	0	0	5	2	2
Arizona	4	2	2	3	4	1	0
California	13	7	5	7	11	7	3
Colorado	1	1	0	1	1	0	0
Connecticut	1	0	1	1	1	0	0
Wash. DC	4	1	2	3	4	2	0
Florida	5	4	0	0	4	2	0
Georgia	1	0	1	1	1	0	0
Hawaii	26	1	3	4	15	10	9
Iowa	1	1	1	0	1	0	0
Illinois	5	1	4	4	5	0	0
Indiana	7	2	1	1	3	3	3
Kentucky	2	1	0	1	2	1	1
Louisiana	30	10	2	5	23	8	0
Massachusetts	14	4	0	0	9	5	2
Maryland	16	3	0	0	9	9	1
Michigan	4	2	2	2	3	2	0
Minnesota	24	11	1	1	15	7	5
Missouri	3	1	0	0	3	2	0
Montana	1	0	1	1	1	1	0
North Carolina	4	2	0	0	3	1	1
New York	1	0	1	1	1	0	0
Ohio	3	1	0	0	3	3	0
Oklahoma	2	1	1	0	1	1	0
Oregon	25	5	6	6	13	7	6
Pennsylvania	6	4	0	0	4	2	1
South Carolina	4	2	0	2	4	0	0
Tennessee	1	1	0	1	1	0	0
Texas	8	5	1	2	7	1	0
Utah	5	1	0	0	4	1	0
Virginia	24	4	1	1	14	9	1
Washington	4	1	1	1	2	1	1
Wisconsin	5	2	1	4	4	1	1
Total 33	**263**	**83**	**38**	**53**	**181**	**89**	**37**

Source: Center for Applied Linguistics. (2006). Directory of Foreign Language Immersion Programs in U.S. Schools. Retrieved February 10, 2009, from http://www.cal.org/resources/immersion/. Reprinted by permission.

TABLE 11.2   Summary U.S. Immersion Programs: 2006 (by Language of Instruction)

Languages of Instruction in Total and Partial Immersion Programs		
Language of Instruction	**Number of Programs**	**Percentage of Total**
Spanish	132	42.6%
French	90	29.0%
Hawaiian	26	8.4%
Japanese	22	7.1%
Mandarin	12	3.9%
German	10	3.2%
Ojibwe	3	1.0%
Arabic	2	0.6%
Italian	2	0.6%
Russian	2	0.6%
Yup'ik	2	0.6%
Cantonese	1	0.3%
Chinook	1	0.3%
Danish	1	0.3%
Diné	1	0.3%
Greek	1	0.3%
Norwegian	1	0.3%
Swedish	1	0.3%
Total 18	**310**	**100.00%**

Source: Center for Applied Linguistics. (2006). Directory of Foreign Language Immersion Programs in U.S. Schools. Retrieved February 10, 2009, from http://www.cal.org/resources/immersion/. Reprinted by permission.

The distinctive goals of two-way language development programs are as follows:

● Language-minority students will become literate in their native language as well as in English.

● Language-majority students will develop high levels of proficiency in a second language while making normal progress in first-language development.

● Both language groups will perform academically at their grade level, develop positive attitudes toward the two languages being learned and toward the communities they represent, and develop a positive self-image.

Two-way immersion programs are most appropriate for communities that have a large and fairly stable population of native speakers of the target language. Ideally, approximately equal numbers of the students should be native speakers of each language. When

TABLE 11.3   Program Design by Grade Level and School Site: Percentage of Instruction in Spanish and English

Grade Level	Key	River Glen	IAMS
Kindergarten–First	50–50	90–10	80–20
Second	50–50	85–15	80–20
Third	50–50	80–20	80–20
Fourth–Fifth	50–50	60–40	60–40
Sixth	50–50	50–50	60–40

Source: Christian et al. 1997. *Profiles in Two-Way Immersion Education.* Washington, DC: Center for Applied Linguistics and Delta Systems, Inc., 97–98. Reprinted by permission.

TABLE 11.4   Initial Reading Instruction by Grade Level and School Site

Grade Level	Key	River Glen	IAMS
Kindergarten–First	ALL: English and Spanish	ALL: Spanish	English Proficient: English Spanish Proficient: Spanish
Second			ALL: Add L2 (approx.)
Third		ALL: Add English	

Source: Christian et al. 1997. *Profiles in Two-Way Immersion Education.* Washington, DC: Center for Applied Linguistics and Delta Systems, Inc., 97–98. Reprinted by permission.

language-majority students outnumber language-minority students, there tends to be greater in-school use of English, the language that is already reinforced outside of school.

Both the National Clearinghouse for English Language Acquisition and Language Instruction Educational Programs (NCELA) and the Center for Applied Linguistics (CAL) serve as rich sources of information regarding two-way language development programs.

The *Guiding Principles for Dual Language Education*

The *Guiding Principles for Dual Language Education* is a tool to help dual-language programs (two-way immersion, heritage language, foreign language immersion, or developmental bilingual programs) with planning and ongoing implementation. The publication is based on the New Mexico *Dual Language Program Standards* and is grounded in research on effective schools. It was developed by the Center for Applied Linguistics in 2005 with an expert panel of researchers and practitioners from across the United States, and revised in 2007. It is available online at www.cal.org/twi/guidingprinciples.htm. Since the Guiding Principles give such a detailed and excellent picture of the elements that quality programs should have, Figure 11.1 contains an overview of the guiding principles of this document. We encourage readers to access the entire document, since it provides much needed guidance regarding the basic characteristics needed to make a quality program. Most aspects of these guiding principles relate to all types of immersion programs.

How Does Immersion Work?

In early total immersion programs, students begin their study of the new language in kindergarten or first grade. When the children arrive at school in the morning, they hear the teacher speak only the new language, and all classroom conversation and instructions are in the target language. In this way the children acquire the new language in play and work situations that are related to meaningful communication. Even though the teacher is constantly using the target language, the students may use English among themselves and also when speaking to the teacher. This reduces anxiety and frustration and allows the children a period of time in which they can build up comprehension skills in the second language. Within one to two years in the program, the children move rather automatically into speech production.

The children tend to show little anxiety or frustration about learning in another language because the things they learn are within their experience and because every effort is made to put messages into a meaningful context. For example, they learn to speak and write about things they understand: in kindergarten a lesson on objects that sink and float, in first grade a trip to the fire station, in second grade a lesson on magnets, in fifth grade a lesson on geography, and so forth. In the beginning stages of the program, the students learn to say things like "I have a hot lunch today," "Can we go out for recess?," "I want to be first," and "Give me the ball."

Children in total immersion programs learn to read through the second language rather than through the first. They read about things they have been exposed to through various experiences and can already speak about. This approach is markedly different from that used in most bilingual education programs, in which reading is always introduced in the first language. Parents of kindergarten and first grade students in immersion programs are advised that they should feel free to encourage any natural interest in reading expressed by their child, but that they should not try to formally teach English reading at home.

After two or three years in a total immersion program, formal English language arts is introduced for about 30 to 60 minutes each day—in the second or third grade, depending on the school district. A few districts wait until fourth or fifth grade to introduce instruction in English. Children continue to study the remainder of their subjects through the new language. Once children begin to read in English, the many skills that transfer from the second language enable most of them to "catch up" in English reading within one or two years. In some immersion programs, as the students progress through the middle

● **FIGURE 11.1**   Overview of *Guiding Principles for Dual Language Education*. Full document is available at www.cal.org/twi/guidingprinciples.htm.

Strand 1	Assessment and Accountability
Principle 1	The program creates and maintains an infrastructure that supports an accountability process.
Principle 2	Student assessment is aligned with state content and language standards, as well as with program goals, and is used for evaluation of the program and instruction.
Principle 3	The program collects a variety of data, using multiple measures, that are used for program accountability and evaluation.
Principle 4	Data are analyzed and interpreted in methodologically appropriate ways for program accountability and improvement.
Principle 5	Student progress toward program goals and NCLB achievement objectives is systematically measured and reported.
Principle 6	The program communicates with appropriate stakeholders about program outcomes.

Strand 2	Curriculum
Principle 1	The curriculum is standards-based and promotes the development of bilingual, biliterate, and multicultural competencies for all students.
Principle 2	The program has a process for developing and revising a high-quality curriculum.
Principle 3	The curriculum is fully articulated for all students.

Strand 3	Instruction
Principle 1	Instructional methods are derived from research-based principles of dual language education and from research on the development of bilingualism and biliteracy in children.
Principle 2	Instructional strategies enhance the development of bilingualism, biliteracy, and academic achievement.
Principle 3	Instruction is student-centered.
Principle 4	Teachers create a multilingual and multicultural learning environment.

Strand 4	Staff Quality and Professional Development
Principle 1	The program recruits and retains high-quality dual language staff.
Principle 2	The program has a quality professional development plan.

● **FIGURE 11.1** *(Continued)*

Principle 3	The program provides adequate resource support for professional development.
Principle 4	The program collaborates with other groups and institutions to ensure staff quality.

Strand 5	**Program Structure**
Principle 1	All aspects of the program work together to achieve the goals of additive bilingualism, biliteracy and cross-cultural competence while meeting grade-level academic expectations.
Principle 2	The program ensures equity for all groups.
Principle 3	The program has strong, effective, and knowledgeable leadership.
Principle 4	The program has used a well-defined, inclusive, and defensible process to select and refine a model design.
Principle 5	An effective process exists for continual program planning, implementation, and evaluation.

Strand 6	**Family and Community**
Principle 1	The program has a responsive infrastructure for positive, active, and ongoing relations with students' families and the community.
Principle 2	The program has parent education and support services that are reflective of the bilingual and multicultural goals of the program.
Principle 3	The program views and involves parents and community members as strategic partners.

Strand 7	**Support and Resources**
Principle 1	The program is supported by all program and school staff.
Principle 2	The program is supported by families and the community.
Principle 3	The program is adequately funded.
Principle 4	The program advocates for support.
Principle 5	Resources are distributed equitably within the program, school, and district.

Source: Elizabeth R. Howard, Julie Sugarman, Donna Christian, Kathryn J. Lindholm-Leary, & David Rogers. *Guiding Principles for Dual Language Education* (2nd ed.). Washington DC: Center for Applied Linguistics. Reprinted by permission.

grades, the amount of English is gradually increased until by fifth or sixth grade, there is a balance of instruction in the target language and in English. In other immersion programs, after students have been exposed to English for one hour per day, the amount of English continues at one hour per day for the duration of the program. The result is that 80 percent of a student's day is spent in the second language and 20 percent of the day is spent in English through the sixth grade. Variations in program design reflect the needs, desires, and resources of the individual school district.

Students in one-way immersion programs are generally monolingual English speakers who are learning another language for enrichment purposes. Students in two-way programs are a combination of native English speakers and native speakers of the immersion language. Immersion teachers are elementary-certified teachers who are native or near-native speakers of the second language.

What Are Immersion Results?

Initially, parents and school administrators might express fear that immersion students will not achieve well in the basics and will fall behind their peers in monolingual English classes. The original St. Lambert study documented the positive effects of the immersion approach (Lambert and Tucker, 1972). Since then, for more than 30 years there have been abundant research reports on immersion programs (e.g., Genesee, 1987, and Johnson and Swain, 1997).

Immersion students acquire remarkable proficiency in the second language compared with students in other second-language programs. But it must be noted that this proficiency is not native-like in every aspect. Immersion students are able to communicate on any topic appropriate to their level of intellectual development, but they do make grammatical errors, and they have to use circumlocutions and other strategies to express themselves when they are lacking the appropriate vocabulary.

One reason that immersion students do not have native-like speech in every respect is that they do not usually have the opportunity to interact with native-speaking peers. Often, the only native-speaker model that the immersion students have available to them is their classroom teacher. The other models that they hear constantly are their non-native-speaking classmates. Immersion students who have moved into a native-speaking environment, however, have been able to adjust their speech successfully. This issue is far less frequent in two-way immersion classrooms, since there are native speakers among the learner's peers in addition to the teacher.

● *English Skills* Research results show that students in early immersion programs perform as well as or better than their English-educated peers on tests of achievement in English. Immersion students are initially behind in their English skills but catch up within a year after the English component is introduced into the curriculum. In any case, by fifth grade, immersion students have caught up with all aspects of English and there are no differences in English test performance between immersion students and monolingual comparison groups who have been taught through English.

- *Subject Content Mastery* Immersion students perform as well as or better than their monolingual English-speaking peers on tests of subject content mastery in mathematics, science, and social studies. The academic achievement of immersion students is equivalent to that of monolingual students who are studying the same subjects in their native language.

- *Cross-Cultural Understanding* Results from research show that Canadian immersion students "develop more friendly and open attitudes toward French-Canadians" (Lambert, 1984).

- *Second-Language Skills* With respect to second-language skills, according to Canadian research on French immersion, immersion students demonstrate a high level of functional proficiency in the immersion language. Compared to native speakers, the receptive skills of students are much better developed than their expressive skills. By the end of grade 6, children are close to the level of native speakers in reading and understanding French, but they are very different from native speakers in terms of spoken and written French. This difference is especially noticeable in terms of their mastery of grammar (Harley et al., 1991).

● Integrating Language and Content

In immersion, the focus of instruction is on the curriculum (social studies, science, mathematics, language arts, health, art, music), and the second language is used as a tool to teach the curriculum. It has been said that immersion teachers are elementary teachers 100 percent of the time and are also language teachers 100 percent of the time. They plan lessons that focus on language development and on subject content goals at the same time. Immersion teachers must take the time to develop the language skills necessary for communication about subject matter content. This suggests that it is frequently necessary to do language development activities in preparation for or as a component of a lesson directed toward subject content goals. The immersion teacher also must also plan carefully for the concrete experiences and the visual reinforcement that will make the academic language of instruction comprehensible to the students and help them develop the linguistic skills necessary for dealing with the subject content material.

Since the syllabus is oriented toward the regular curriculum of the school district, and since the students need their new language to communicate on a daily basis, immersion programs are usually able to avoid the pitfalls of many second-language programs that are grammar driven. They are truly able to base language learning on real communication needs.

It has sometimes been pointed out that immersion students, although fluent, lack proper grammar and are not accurate speakers. Immersion researchers have often found that immersion students are not given enough opportunity to actually use the language in class. James Cummins (1981) states that many French immersion teacher classrooms have tended to be highly "transmission oriented," in that they have focused on presenting the curriculum in such a way that students have minimal opportunities to use oral or written language for creative or problem-solving activities.

Cummins encourages immersion educators to be conscious of the potential for enhancing student's awareness of language by having them carry out individual and group projects focusing on structural or sociolinguistic aspects of language. He advocates that language and discourse become a part of the immersion curriculum.

Roy Lyster's work (2007) has been extremely helpful in looking at the kinds of interactions that happen in immersion classrooms and in pointing out the need to work on language concepts as well as content concepts. Lyster states that "initial conceptualizations of immersion and content-based instruction underestimated the extent to which the target language needs to be attended to" (p. 3). Lyster cites studies that show varied language outcomes depending on the kinds of activities that were being done in class. Classrooms in which students demonstrated better second-language achievement included the following instructional options:

- More teacher–student interaction
- More opportunities for meaningful interaction among peers
- Less reliance on nonverbal cues for meaning
- More explicit than implicit correction

Lyster (2007) advocates more focus on language form and suggests that implicit feedback is not always as effective as explicit feedback. In other words, errors need to be systematically attended to and students must have an active part in rectifying their language output. (See also Lyster, 1999, 2005.)

Sheltered Instruction

In programs for English language learners, *sheltered instruction* is the name given to making grade-level content more accessible to language learners while at the same time providing help with language development. Sheltered instruction is exactly what happens in the immersion classroom on a daily basis. Several books dealing with all aspects of sheltered instruction are highly recommended: Echevarria and Graves (2007), *Sheltered Content Instruction*; Echevarria, Vogt, and Short (2010), *Making Content Comprehensible for Elementary English Learners: The SIOP Model*; and Echevarria, Vogt, and Short (2010), *Making Content Comprehensible for Secondary English Learners: The SIOP Model*.

Strategies for Developing Access to Language and Content

A number of strategies mentioned in the sheltered instruction literature are the same as those used in immersion classrooms for integrating language and content. Among these strategies are:

- Ensuring background knowledge
- Making language comprehensible and contextualizing

- Checking for understanding
- Developing language and allowing for student interaction
- Adapting academic content to the language proficiency of the students

Ensuring Background Knowledge   The process of understanding language and new concepts involves drawing on experiences and information already stored in memory. Since background experience plays such an important role in learning, it is crucial that teachers pay attention to providing or activating the background knowledge that language learners need to understand texts and instruction.

Making Language Comprehensible and Contextualizing   This is the most basic way the teacher can help learners understand the language of the classroom and the curriculum. He or she helps the students understand the language through use of gestures, visuals, and concrete examples, and through the routines and rituals of the lesson and the school day. Especially in the early stages of immersion, it is important that teachers use their acting abilities, as well as concrete objects, to illustrate meaning. Following are some ideas for making language comprehensible and providing context.

- Gather materials such as visuals, models, manipulatives, videos, and other tangible referents to contextualize the lesson.
- Avoid doing all the talking for extended periods of time.
- Pace the class and provide opportunities to interact and move about.
- Set up a cooperative learning environment.
- Develop thematic units that make information more accessible to students, since it is put in a meaningful context and is not presented in isolation.
- Personalize the language or the information.
- Support verbal explanations with nonverbal cues:
  Gestures/facial expressions
  Props, realia, manipulatives, concrete materials
  Visuals, graphs, pictures, maps
  Demonstrating, or "acting out," the meanings of words
- Make language modifications such as the following:
  Defining words in a meaningful context
  Paraphrasing in simple terms when using more complex expressions
- Teach vocabulary by using the following strategies:
  Using realia or visuals with words
  Giving antonyms or providing synonyms
  Placing new words on a continuum (e.g., show how "warm" and "cool" would fit on a continuum with "hot" at one end and "cold" at the other end)

Using words in context

Suggesting logical relationships

● Maintain a physical classroom environment to support immersion language learners.

Checking for Understanding   Although it is very important to make language comprehensible and to provide context for lessons, this is not sufficient. Checking for comprehension must be a part of every lesson. Teachers can assess understanding in various ways:

● Check comprehension with nonverbal responses (nodding of heads, raising hands, signaling, actions, drawing, etc.).

● Personalize questions.

● Repeat and, if necessary, review main ideas and key vocabulary.

● Provide many ways for students to practice what they are learning: orally, in writing, using pictures, and using actions.

● Use a variety of question types.

● Ask students to apply the concept being taught.

Developing Language and Allowing for Student Interaction   Please see Chapters 2, 3, and 4 for many ideas on accomplishing this goal.

Adapting Academic Content to the Language Proficiency of the Students   Modifying instruction and adapting texts is an important part of working with language learners in an immersion setting. It is also extremely challenging and time consuming. Experts in this area recommend that teachers adapt only those portions of texts that are the most central to the learning of the desired concept.

● Life in Immersion Programs: From the Teachers' Perspective

Several experienced immersion teachers have added their observations about life in immersion programs. Although these comments are very insightful, they cannot possibly cover all of the aspects of teaching in an immersion program. In the For Further Reading section at the end of this chapter are excellent resources for more detailed information. The immersion teachers who have shared their thoughts here are:

Corey Maslowski, St. Louis Park Public Schools, Minnesota

Shannon Graber, former French immersion teacher, Edina Public Schools, Minnesota

Marcy Zachmeier-Ruh, Twin Cities German Immersion School, St. Paul, Minnesota

Why Immersion Works

Shannon: In your heart, you believe that immersion will work, but to see the truth unfold is a fabulous experience. However, [immersion] only "works" because of very articulate planning, organization, varied instructional strategies, solid teaching skills, and *humor*.

Effect on Students: Student Anecdotes

The students are coloring independently and a kindergartner begins to cry. When asked why, he responded, "I don't know how to color in Spanish!"

Another student walked through the door on the first day of school and shook the teacher's hand. He said, "I'm Johnny; I'm the one that speaks English."

"My teacher speaks only in French . . . but she laughs in English!"

After the first day in immersion, the mother asked, "Did you understand everything the teacher said?" The child responded, "No, but I did everything she told me to do."

Corey: What I have learned over the years is that at the beginning stages most students did not even realize that other kids go to school and learn in English. Because their reality was that they spoke Spanish at school, they did not know any different.

Balance between Content and Language

Corey: In immersion, there is a delicate balance between teaching the content and the language. Ultimately, we are responsible for delivering content as determined by local districts and state standards. However, if we did not also assess student language and focus on error correction, we would be doing a disservice to the students.

At the beginning, I was trying to figure out how to use the materials that were available to me and to make them easily accessible to the students at their language level. This is not always easy! Knowing what I know now, I would have been much more intentional with *error correction* and doing minilessons as the need arose to teach language structures. When creating lesson plans, strong language objectives need to be embedded in the content. Simultaneously, I would be working with other teachers to create a *defined language scope and sequence* for student language acquisition.

Use of the Immersion Language

Corey: NO ENGLISH should be used in the classroom. Because appropriate materials do not always exist in the target language, it is important to "think outside of the box" and ask how we can achieve the same learner outcomes without using materials in English. What language will students need to be able to accomplish their tasks without breaking into English?

It is important for immersion practitioners to craft a *vision* for the type of school that they want to be in. What will it look like in the hallways? How will teachers interact with one another? Will they use formal register? As the students get older, will it be appropriate for them to speak English at recess? Can they in the cafeteria? At what point in kindergarten or first grade will it be important for them to only speak the target language? Some schools have a big celebration on day 100 of first grade. . . . They are then expected to use only the target language in the classroom.

Shannon: If the staff is united with their commitment to 100 percent second-language use in the classroom, they will be united to find creative methods to preserve the target language use. For example, a kindergarten teacher needs to talk about safety issues: fire drills, health issues, bus issues, and so forth. With the early grades, these issues can be dealt with by inviting a guest speaker into the classroom. The nurse explains health issues in English, the principal or social worker explains fire drills, and so on.

Attention to Immersion Language Development

Marcy: The main pitfall that I have seen is to use the district curriculum and expect that the kids will gain the language more or less by osmosis. This actually works fairly well at the lower grades at the early stages, but when the kids get older and there is no attention paid to a method by which to acquire new vocabulary and grammatical structures, their linguistic ability suffers greatly from lack of accuracy, no matter that their fluency level is very high.

Teachers need to remember that kids, no matter how fluent they have become, are still second-language learners. Since we are using German text-books, there is much vocabulary which needs to be pre-introduced, and cultural concepts which need to be explained because children are not bringing with them the same background knowledge as the native speakers for whom the texts were intended.

Immersion Teaching Settings versus Monolingual Teaching Settings

Corey: We must remember that we need to scaffold lessons more than we would if we were teaching in the students' native language. Repetition becomes commonplace. Routines become even more essential.

Shannon: In an immersion school, there is only one kind of teacher: a quality teacher. The reason this is true is that immersion teachers, in order to help students make sense of their learning world, *must* incorporate a variety of teaching strategies and techniques; they *must* use visuals, media, literature, music, and so on; they *must* involve the five senses; they *must* welcome movement, dance, art in their classrooms. The list could go on and on. Regular teaching settings may have these components. Immersion settings must have these components.

Marcy: One of our biggest issues was not at all apparent the first year, as we were all caught up in the overwhelming whirlwind of founding a new school. What has started to come up now is the disconnect between being an effective classroom teacher and an effective language teacher. If a good teacher conducts all instruction in German, the kids will learn at a phenomenal rate, as we have experienced. What we are struggling with now is that, given our documented success, some of our teachers (those without prior training as language teachers) are feeling that additional training in language teaching methods is not necessary, especially after the kids are already speaking in German. Because they are not language teachers, they don't realize how much better/faster the kids could learn. (They don't know what they don't know.) We must set the expectation that it is an *ongoing* process to become just as skilled as a language teacher as it is to be a classroom teacher.

Background Needed for Immersion Teachers

Marcy: If the immersion teachers are coming from a language teacher background and moving into an elementary setting, I would emphasize presenting content in ongoing, thematic settings, as younger students need this to be able to meet the high cognitive demands being placed on them as they learn language and content at the same time.

If the staff is primarily bilingual elementary teachers, I would really emphasize the language teaching methodology and how important it is to ensure that they are becoming *purposefully fluent* (i.e., teachers can control to a very fine degree what and how well kids learn vocabulary, phrases, etc.).

For any type of staff, I would stress the Understanding by Design approach. If the curriculum is not already designed that way … , then teachers need to focus on why they are doing particular activities.

Exhaustion

Corey: The teachers will probably feel exhausted during the first months of the year (for some, the exhaustion never subsides). It can be exhausting to speak a language (that may or may not be their own) to students who most likely do not speak the language at home.

Shannon: I wish that someone would have warned me about the incredible amount of *physical and mental energy* that would be expended those first few weeks of school. It is so important to "pace" oneself so that fatigue doesn't overwhelm you. Scheduling the day with chunks of quiet activities is beneficial for both the teacher and the students. An example for a kindergarten classroom would be to have a simple, quiet art activity with classical music playing.

Building Program Support

Corey: I also think it is really important to have clear communication with any other teachers in the building (or the school system) about the goals of the program. Unfortunately, I have not seen a program yet that has not struggled with political backlash because of the perceived "elitist" immersion program. Why does the program exist? What are the benefits to students? What are the benefits to the larger district? In light of any struggles that may occur, how will the staff deal with them?

Qualities of an Immersion Teacher

Shannon: An immersion teacher:

Provides a well-established routine that gives students a sense of security
Uses many visuals, visual clues, and gestures, to convey meaning
Uses repetition in varied forms, changing rhythm and beat to add flavor to repetition
Creates intrigue and mystery with small and great items
Makes the old material seem new and the new material seem familiar
Is constantly aware of students' comprehension and monitors and adjusts to fit their needs
Seeks to personalize learning to spark the learners' interest
Nurtures an inviting and positive environment where students are not afraid to take risks
Is adept at quickly changing teaching strategies to convey meaning
Reviews student outcomes frequently and assesses students accordingly

● The Anchorage School District (ASD) Immersion Programs: Models of Excellence (Japanese, Russian, and Spanish Partial Immersion and Spanish Two-Way Immersion)

The Anchorage Immersion programs have a reputation of excellence around the country. Janice Gullickson, the World Languages Curriculum Coordinator, has diligently worked to build outstanding programs. Here is a "case study" of some of the qualities that make for excellence as described by Janice.

Immersion Program History

Historically, the language immersion programs in the Anchorage School District [ASD] are the result of the voice of the local community requesting that second language learning begin with children in the elementary school and within the academic program. With school board approval the first language immersion programs began in 1988 and 89 at two schools, for Japanese and Spanish. A two-way bilingual Spanish immersion program was added in 1993 to meet the needs of an increasing Spanish-speaking population. This model is a win-win for both English and Spanish speaking children. Bilingual speakers achieve above average test scores on standardized English tests and SATs. Likewise, those who are studying English as a second language (ESL), and continue to study their native language while learning English excel academically. These programs expanded by one grade level each year until all were K–12. Their popularity, along with an interest from the business community for proficient Russian speakers, paved the way for the first Russian language immersion program in the U.S. In 2004, ASD began a Russian immersion program in kindergarten and first grade with plans to expand each year until the program is K–12.

Immersion Program Model

The Anchorage School District Partial Immersion programs are "school-within-a-school" programs in neighborhood schools, and immersion students achieve the same academically as their monolingual English peers. Students have a "team" of two teachers, one an English speaking teacher and the other a speaker of the target language (Spanish, Japanese, German or Russian). For one-half of each day, students are immersed in the second language while receiving instruction in the local district curriculum. Students learn content, i.e. math, science, social studies, while becoming bilingual and biliterate in a second language.

Immersion Secondary Program Model

Each of the Anchorage School District four elementary immersion programs transitions to designated middle and high schools to ensure students a 13 year language immersion sequence. Students who complete the K–12 program are honored with language immersion completion cords at end of year ceremonies prior to graduation. Students, adorned with the immersion language completion cords, are awarded recognition at high school graduation.

Middle school students continue the immersion program model of learning language through content in social studies and language arts. Coursework is integrated and in Japanese, the curriculum incorporates comparative study of Japanese history and culture. Three of the four immersion programs also provide an immersion experience in the target language country that is connected to the academic program giving students an opportunity to use their language in real life setting.

Immersion students continue in the program at high school in four year upper level courses designed to increase their language skills while learning through content. Spanish courses include *Vistas Juveniles del Mundo Hispano, Perspectivas Literarias, Estudios Latinoamericanos,* and Advanced Placement (Language and Literature.) Students of the Japanese for Fluent Speakers Course are partnered with members of the local Japanese community in an "adopt-a-student" program. High school immersion courses are designed to be rigorous and challenging for students while preparing them for upper division university coursework.

Immersion Program Parent Support

Families are an important component to the parent, student, teacher, [and] team, and are encouraged to support the program by becoming involved in the learning of a second language and culture with their child. A parent orientation is required for those who have children entering an immersion program. Entry is by a lottery process and for English speakers. Children enter the program at kindergarten or by the end of first semester of first grade. Older bilingual students who meet literacy standards may enter on a space available basis through the lottery process. Parent advisory committees support the program with fund-raising, travel exchanges, extracurricular activities, including community celebrations of language and culture that are open to the public.

Teacher Teams and Curriculum

Beginning in kindergarten there are two classrooms and two teachers: the target language teacher and the English partner teacher. Instruction follows the partial immersion model with one half-day in the target language and one half-day in English.

Immersion teacher teams for each grade level comprise an English partner and target language teacher. These teachers collaborate and plan for instruction, taking into consideration the need to separate languages and, to some extent, support one another for each content area. When the target language teacher is responsible for science the English teacher will provide support by having students read science books that have more difficult text. Together teachers design thematic units that integrate content areas and maximize time for instruction. Teachers mirror one another's classroom management rules and strategies and conference with parents as a team. Planning together is one of the key components of program success.

Historically, the curriculum has been divided as follows. However when appropriate, for linguistic purposes, content areas are shared by both teachers.

	English	*Spanish*
Kindergarten	All content areas integrated	
Grades 1–6	Reading and Language Arts	Reading and Language Arts
	Mathematics	Social Studies
	Health	Science

Assessment

Students are assessed for oral language annually by classroom teachers using the FLOSEM (Foreign Language Observation Evaluation Matrix). Immersion teachers are currently working with a consultant for assessment, Robert Marzano, to design new standards-based assessments for oral and written language proficiency that are aligned with the national standards and ACTFL Performance Guidelines for K–12 learners.

External Funding

The language immersion teachers and staff are funded in full by the local school budget. Over the years the district has earned additional funding by way of the competitive FLAP (Foreign Language Assistance Program) for resources to develop curriculum, [obtain] materials and provide professional development with experts from the field of second-language acquisition. The additional funding has also supported travel for staff to observe and learn from other programs around the U.S.

Professional Development

Immersion teachers and administrators receive support by ongoing professional development. This includes an annual summer institute, L2 literacy grade level workshops, and a mandatory new-to-program workshop for immersion teacher teams. Teachers of Japanese, German, Russian and Spanish work frequently throughout the school year to revise and create target language content materials, e.g. L2 science tubs for district science kits. Experienced language immersion program teachers mentor new-to-district teachers in the district's formal mentorship program.

Entrance into the Program

A lottery determines entry into the program at kindergarten and first semester of first grade. Students entering at second semester and in grades 2–12 are evaluated for target language and literacy skills for eligibility.

Teacher Qualifications

All language immersion teachers employed by the District are native or near-native speakers of the target language. Applicants are interviewed and rated for oral and written language proficiencies. All teachers are certified and hold Alaska teacher licenses.

Separation of Languages

One of the "non-negotiables" is separation of languages by teacher, by classroom, and by instruction; for the immersion teacher, delivery of instruction is consistently in the immersion language (NO ENGLISH). Switching homeroom classrooms at each quarter grading period maximizes time in the target language. If students have an English homeroom in the morning for the first quarter they will have an immersion language homeroom in the morning for the second quarter. The number of minutes of the instructional day devoted to the target language is also periodically monitored.

Celebrations of Learning

Language immersion programs are enriched by a variety of celebrations of students' language and culture learning throughout the school year. These range from after-school hands-on classes, summer camps, Latin American dance lessons, Japanese Taiko-drumming teams, and the visual arts. Each program sponsors special school-wide culture celebrations. For example, Russian "Maslenitsa" good-bye winter celebration, Japanese Cherry Blossom Festival, and Spanish Cinco de Mayo. The district language immersion programs are well known in the community and respected as potential language and culture resources. On the night of the terrorist attack, September 11, 2001, the Japanese immersion teachers and their students were summoned by the mayor's office to interpret for the many stranded Japanese passengers of a Korean airline.

Long-Term Commitment

Parents, students and school staff need to commit to a K–12 program.

Summary

- Immersion programs place children in a school environment in which all subject content is taught in a new language, beginning as early as kindergarten or first grade.

- Carefully designed immersion programs in Canada, the United States, and other countries have produced remarkable results, both in terms of the amount and quality of the second language acquired and in terms of the level of achievement in subject content and native-language competencies.

- Children who are given the opportunity to learn in immersion programs can achieve a degree of fluency in the target language that would otherwise be attainable only through an extended period of study in the target culture. In addition, their performance in first-language basic skills and their mastery of subject content is as good as or better than that of their peers who are studying in an English-only curriculum. Research results in Canada have been replicated in immersion programs in the United States.

- While intensive, long-term exposure to a second language is available only in an immersion program, other distinctive components of immersion instruction can be applied in every early language classroom.

- Even though immersion instruction will always be a limited program option, available only to some students in some school systems, insights gathered from the experiences of immersion can contribute to improved language instruction for all students.

For Study and Discussion

1. As the new curriculum coordinator for your district, it is your job to present an information session for parents who are considering enrolling their children in a new immersion program in your language in the district.
   a. Outline the information you will include in your presentation.
   b. What questions do you expect the parents to ask? How will you answer them?

2. Despite the compelling research evidence of success, immersion programs are found in relatively few locations in the United States. Why do you think this is the case? What steps might you recommend for increasing the number of immersion programs?

3. As a consultant to the early language teachers in your district, choose one or two of the characteristics and strategies of immersion that you

think would be important first steps toward teaching within the immersion philosophy, and explain how you would present them to the teachers. Use concrete examples in your explanations.

4. What implications would the implementation of an early immersion program in one elementary school in a mid-sized U.S. city have for the language offerings in other schools and at other levels in the same school system?

5. What benefits can two-way immersion programs provide that are not available through traditional bilingual education or immersion programs? Under what circumstances would you recommend that a school or district consider instituting such a program?

6. What issues could be anticipated when planning an immersion program in a less commonly taught language such as Arabic, Chinese, and Japanese?

For Further Reading

The following sources are recommended for additional information about material covered in this chapter. Chapter citations are documented in Works Cited at the end of this book.

Baker, Colin. *Foundations of Bilingual Education and Bilingualism* (4th ed.) Clevedon, UK: Multilingual Matters. 2006.

Calderon, Margarita Espino, and Liliana Minaya-Rowe. *Designing and Implementing Two-Way Bilingual Programs: A Step-by-Step Guide for Administrators, Teachers and Parents.* Thousand Oaks, CA: Corwin Press, 2003.

Center for Advanced Research on Second Language Acquisition (CARLA). University of Minnesota, Minneapolis. Available on-line at http://carla .acad.umn.edu/.

Center for Applied Linguistics. Total and Partial Immersion Programs. Washington, DC: 2006. Available on-line at www.cal.org/resouces/ immersion.

Cloud, Nancy, Fred Genesee, and Else Hamayan. *Dual Language Instruction: A Handbook for Enriched Education.* Boston: Heinle and Heinle, 2000.

Cummins, James. "Immersion Education for the Millennium: What Have We Learned from 30 Years of Research on Second Language Immersion?," in M. R. Childs and R. M. Bostwick (Eds.), *Learning through Two Languages: Research and Practice. Second Katoh Gakuen International Symposium on Immersion and Bilingual Education* (pp. 34–47). Katoh Gakuen, Japan. 1998. Available online at http://carla.umn.edu/ cobaltt/modules/strategies/immersion2000.html. Accessed February 7, 2009.

Cummins, James, and Merrill Swain. *Bilingualism in Education: Aspects of Theory, Research and Practice.* Burnt Mill, Harlow, UK: Longman Group, 1986.

Day, Elaine M., and Stanley M. Shapson. *Studies in Immersion Education.* Clevedon, UK: Multilingual Matters, 1996.

Directory of Two-Way Bilingual Immersion Programs in the U.S. Washington DC: Center for Applied Linguistics, 2008. Available on-line at www.cal .org/twi/directory/.

Fortune, Tara Williams, and Diane J. Tedick. *Pathways to Multilingualism: Evolving Perspectives on Immersion Education.* Clevedon, UK: Multilingual Matters. 2008.

Freeman, Yvonne S., David E. Freeman, and Sandra P. Mercuri. *Dual Language Essentials for Teachers and Administrators.* Portsmouth, NH: Heinemann, 2005.

Genesee, Fred. *Learning through Two Languages: Studies of Immersion and Bilingual Education.* Cambridge, MA: Newbury House, 1987.

Howard, Elizabeth, Kathryn Lindholm-Leary, Julie Sugarman, Donna Christian, and David Rogers. *Guiding Principles for Dual Language Education* (2nd ed.). Washington DC: Center for Applied Linguistics, 2007. Available on-

line at www.cal.org/twi/Guiding_Principles
.pdf.

Howard, Elizabeth R., and Julie Sugarman. *Realizing
the Vision of Two-Way Immersion: Fostering
Effective Programs and Classrooms.* Washington
DC: Center for Applied Linguistics and Delta
Publishing, 2007.

Lenker, Ashley, and Nancy Rhodes, "Foreign
Language Immersion Programs: Features and
Trends over 35 Years." *The ACIE Newsletter*, 10:2
(2007): 1–8.

Lessow-Hurley, Judith. *Foundations of Dual Language
Instruction* (5th ed.). Boston: Pearson Allyn &
Bacon, 2008.

Lindholm-Leary, Kathryn J. *Dual Language
Education.* Clevedon, UK: Multilingual Matters,
2001.

Lyster, Roy. "Immersion Pedagogy and Implications
for Language Teaching," in Jasone Cenoz and
Fred Genesee (Eds.), *Beyond Bilingualism:
Multilingualism and Multilingual Education* (pp.
64–95). Clevedon, UK: Multilingual Matters,
1999.

Lyster, Roy. *Learning and Teaching Languages through
Content: A Counterbalanced Approach.*
Philadelphia: John Benjamins Publishing, 2008.

Met, Myriam. "Elementary School Immersion in Less
Commonly Taught Languages," in Richard D.
Lambert and Elana Shohamy (Eds.), *Language
Policy and Pedagogy*. Philadephia: John
Benjamins Publishing, 2000.

Potowski, Kim. *Language and Identity in a Dual
Immersion School.* Clevedon, UK: Multilingual
Matters, 2007.

Soltero, Sonia White. *Dual Language Teaching and
Learning in Two Languages.* Boston: Pearson
Allyn & Bacon, 2004.

Swain, Merrill. "French Immersion Research in
Canada: Recent Contributions to SLA and
Applied Linguistics." *Annual Review of Applied
Linguistics* 20 (2000): 199–212.

Swain, Merrill. "Manipulating and Complementing
Content Teaching to Maximize Second Language
Learning." *TESL Canada Journal* 6:1 (1988):
68–83.

Swain, Merrill, and Robert Keith Johnson.
"Immersion Education: A Category within
Bilingual Education," in Robert Keith Johnson
and Merrill Swain (Eds.), *Immersion Education:
International Perspectives* (pp. 1–16). Cambridge,
UK: Cambridge University Press, 1997.

Chapter 12

Stocking the Early Language Classroom with Materials and Resources

Enduring Understanding

- Materials provide a basis for creating the concrete contexts that are especially necessary for young learners.

Essential Question

- What materials and resources will be most effective in creating meaningful contexts for my classroom?

● Useful Supplies, Materials, and Equipment

Materials represent a significant portion of the time and resources invested in an early language program, no matter what program model has been chosen. This chapter describes materials that will provide the means for creating the concrete context that is so necessary for meaningful communication. Because young learners require hands-on learning experiences with concrete objects, the early language classroom must have a wide variety of objects and materials available, as many of them as possible from the target culture. Such materials offer a richness and texture not available even in the most carefully designed textbook. This need for a wide range of materials is one of the most marked differences

335

between teaching elementary or middle school/junior high school children and older students. While high school and university teachers often emphasize the written word and written homework early in the learning experience, the early language teacher works with the development of oral language skills over an extended period of time.

The need for a wealth of materials creates special problems for the traveling teacher, who must devise practical ways of transporting props and realia that are often bulky and unwieldy. Some teachers have devised a traveling cart especially for this purpose, and many other early language teachers have become well known for the large bags and satchels they carry with them. Some types of materials, especially those used for crafts and projects, are already present in the regular classroom, but they must be specially ordered and stored in a classroom that is being equipped for foreign-language instruction.

You can tap many sources in the process of stocking the early language classroom. You can arrange for the short-term loan of some items with preschool and elementary school teachers, or teachers in the ELL or the bilingual program. Some types of visuals and media resources are available through the school media center, especially CDs and DVDs, videos, audiotapes, and equipment. School supply houses are good sources of most basic classroom supplies, and many other materials listed in this section are available from distributors of curriculum materials, supplies, and equipment for early childhood and elementary education. Early language teachers will find it useful to be on mailing lists for as many of these catalogs as possible. Browsing through such catalogs often suggests new activities and new uses for materials already present in the classroom.

Locating authentic materials from the target culture is usually more difficult and more time consuming. A number of companies specialize in importing realia and materials for foreign-language teachers, but these materials are often chosen to appeal to older students. The foreign-language teacher traveling in a country where the target language is spoken can find many teaching materials in toy stores, bookstores, media stores, and novelty and souvenir shops. DVDs or CDs of children's stories, songs and rhymes, and simple picture books for storytelling are especially valuable "finds" for the classroom. Toys, books, and music can sometimes be located on the Internet, when local sources fail and a trip to the country is not an immediate option. Language teachers who are able to travel abroad collect items ranging from empty packaging for candy and soft drinks to menus, coins, and ticket stubs. Those who do not have regular opportunities to travel must find other sources for child-appropriate authentic materials and realia.

One of the best ways to obtain teaching materials from the target culture is to correspond with an elementary school English teacher in one of the countries where the target language is spoken. This type of relationship can make it possible for teachers to exchange pictures, music, and realia spontaneously, either to complement a theme of interest or to serve as a focus for an entire unit of instruction. Technology now makes it possible to exchange materials like these very quickly, once a relationship has been established. This type of cooperative exchange provides the opportunity for both teachers to obtain meaningful materials at a reasonable cost, although there is usually considerable delay in receiving any materials that cannot be transmitted electronically.

You can sometimes obtain posters and travel brochures without cost from embassies, consulates, or tourist agencies representing countries in which the target language is spoken. As a starting point for contacting such agencies, teachers can search the Internet and write letters requesting materials to all possible sources. A letter or e-mail requesting posters and city information from the visitors' bureau in capital cities or other cities in the country where the target language is spoken can also yield valuable resources. Multinational businesses sometimes make materials developed for another country available to teachers; posters and travel brochures can also be obtained from travel agencies and airline companies that are sometimes willing to provide such material to foreign-language teachers.

There are also less formal sources for obtaining materials and resources for classroom use. Garage sales and rummage sales are often good places to find plastic fruit, flowers, and other replicas, as well as toys, costumes, puppets, and other realia. Learners themselves enjoy sharing favorite toys or helping to create a visual or a device that will bring classroom instruction to life. Always on the lookout for a new way to make a concept or a communicative situation more vivid, many early language teachers are regular customers at toy stores, variety stores, and souvenir shops.

The time and the budget devoted to developing the materials and resources available to the early language teacher will have a significant impact on the quality and the success of the elementary school language program. Some of the items that are valuable to the elementary or middle school language teacher are listed next.

Supplies

Butcher/Chart Paper (1,000-foot roll) Because this paper can be cut to varying sizes as needed, it can be used for classroom collages, art projects, tracing body shapes, and making life-sized paper dolls.

Butcher/Chart Paper (precut), Chart Tablets, Flip Charts These are used for language experience stories, developing charts and graphs, demonstrations, and explanations. Chart tablets are excellent for displaying the results of small-group projects or brainstorming.

Construction Paper Construction paper can be used for craft projects, visuals, and games. It should be available in at least 12 colors, and in at least two different sizes, 9″ × 12″ and 12″ × 18.″

red	blue	white
black	green	yellow
brown	gold	purple
pink	orange	gray

Tagboard, Oaktag, Posterboard Available in 9″ × 12″, 12″ × 18″, and larger pieces, these are useful for mounting pictures and for making flash cards, posters, signs (such as passwords), language ladders, and classroom charts.

Self-Adhesive Plastic, in Clear and Assorted Colors/Patterns This is used for preserving visuals, classroom crafts, game boards, and teacher-prepared materials.

Paper Plates These are a basic supply for the early language classroom, and they are usually less expensive than tagboard. They can be used as a background for almost any picture; to display meals using food pictures; as a basis for crafts, visuals, clocks, masks, mood faces, weather pictures, and mobiles; as well as for serving snacks.

Masking Tape This can be used for changing the environment by creating shapes and defining spaces on the floor; it also has many commonplace uses such as attaching labels and attaching posters and visuals to walls by making a circle out of masking tape. (When attaching masking tape to pictures and posters, first place a strip or two of tape on the item itself, at each point where the masking-tape circle will be applied. Then, when the masking-tape circle is removed, the picture or poster will not be damaged.)

"Easy Release" Tape and Notes This is good for labeling anything on a temporary basis. (This tape sticks but not permanently and does not damage surfaces.)

White Glue This is especially suitable for adhesive jobs that are similar to model building and for putting a magnet or pin on the back of an object. It is used mainly for crafts.

Glue Stick This is a handy item for quick jobs or for non-permanent stickups and paper crafts. (For some tasks, a glue stick is easier for children to handle than white glue.)

Paper Fasteners These are for making clock faces and jointed figures and for joining booklets.

Paper Punch This is for making name tags, clock faces, and many crafts.

Colored Chalk Color adds variety to chalkboard activities. Some chalkboards do not tolerate colored chalk well, so be sure to check with a custodian before using this chalk extensively.

Whiteboard Markers and Erasers Where whiteboards are available, the use of color is very engaging.

Colored Tissue Paper Many crafts call for tissue paper, including paper flowers, piñatas, mosaics, papier-mâché figures, mobiles, and many crafts.

Chenille Stems or Pipe Cleaners These can be used for paper flowers and other crafts.

Yarn in Assorted Colors Crafts and game activities often require yarn, as well as name tags, mobiles, mini-books, and other projects.

Notecards Available in 3″ × 5″ and 4″ × 6″, these are useful for making games, and for multiple other uses, including activities with flags (4″ × 6″ cards are the same size as silk flags that are commercially available).

Portfolios or Other Carrying Cases Artist portfolios or other means of carrying posters and large teaching visuals are essential for helping the teacher to stay organized. Using different portfolios for each theme is also helpful.

Zip-Closure Plastic Bags of Various Sizes These bags can keep materials organized and prevent small pieces from becoming lost. They are used for the teacher's materials and also to keep manipulatives for partner and other student activities sorted and organized.

Stickers in a Colorful Variety Many teachers use stickers as a reward for performance, or as a way of brightening student work when it is returned. These kinds of rewards are most effective when they are unpredictable celebrations of student work or effort, and when they relate to the theme of the class.

Craft Sticks, Tongue Depressors, Dowels These items can be used for randomly calling on students or creating groups or teams, as well as for craft activities. They can also serve as the basis for several kinds of puppets.

General Resources

Folk and Fairy Tales (books, videos) These are good for reading aloud, planning units, or student browsing at a reading table or in a learning center.

Songbooks A selection of songbooks from the target culture will make it easier for the teacher to choose songs that reinforce specific topics and vocabulary in the curriculum. Teachers should not overlook target-language songs in the music series currently being used in the school district.

Coloring Books and Dot-to-Dot Books These are a good source for visuals and activities, especially when they come from the target culture.

Paper Dolls These may be used for individual students at a learning station with recorded instructions on how to dress the doll, or in a partner activity in which one student tells the other how to dress the doll. Large dolls can be used for whole-class activities.

Books of Simple Poems, Rhymes, Finger Plays Regularly used with preschool and primary-level students, finger plays are rhymes with corresponding actions. Using poems and rhymes from the target culture rather than translations of ones that exist in English can be a way to provide more cultural experiences in the early language classroom.

Flannel Board Manipulatives Available from various publishers, they are used as props for telling fairy tales and other stories and are also available in sets depicting various vocabulary categories such as the house, family, foods, clothing, weather, opposites, and animals. Magnetic sheets can be used in the same way on a chalkboard or a whiteboard that has a steel core.

Rubber Stamps and Ink Pads These may be used for creating realia (coin, clock, shape stamps), for incentives and rewards, and for creating pair or partner activities.

Peel and Stick Plastic Activity Kits These cutout vinyl shapes adhere to a glossy surface. They are valuable for learning center activities and for TPR activities with individuals and small groups. The teacher can put together a scene, take a picture of it, and record directions for constructing the scene on an audiocassette. The child re-creates the scene, following the directions, and uses the photograph to check for accuracy. If the vinyl pictures are large enough, they can be used for TPR activities with the whole class.

Board Games Some board games from the target culture are useful for small group and learning center work. Certain native-language board games can be adapted to activities conducted entirely in the target language.

Bingo and Lotto Games Many commercial games are available to reinforce vocabulary of all kinds. Games specifically keyed to vocabulary and concepts of an individual lesson can be made by the teacher and laminated, often with student help in a class project.

Picture Books and Easy Readers in the Second Language Picture books with very simple texts, if they are well illustrated to provide the necessary visual reinforcement, can be read aloud to a class or a small group or used for beginning reading experiences. It is difficult to find books with the right text-to-picture ratio. Some schools have taken English books and labeled over them in the second language; however, this results in a loss of cultural exposure for the learners.

Elementary School Second-Language (Picture) Dictionaries These resources help learners develop early skills in dictionary use and provide target language visuals for important concepts.

Rhythm and Orff Instruments Simple instruments are useful for developing accompaniment to songs and rhymes and for creating sound effects for simulations and fantasy experiences/virtual trips.

Realia

Plastic Fillable Eggs in Several Sizes Eggs can be hidden one inside the other for discovery activities. They can also be used to hide various objects and to hold scrambled sentence parts, pictures for sequencing, or objects for guessing games. Graduated sizes in various colors are available at Easter time.

Magnetic Numbers, Letters These are used on the magnet board or chalkboard for manipulating number concepts or creating words.

Foam Numbers, Letters These provide a different texture and an alternative way of dealing with the same vocabulary. Children love to touch soft letters and numbers.

Math Counters or a Large Number of Any Small Objects Such as Mini-Erasers Counters can be used for math activities, of course, and also for games of many kinds.

Empty 35mm Film Cans Useful for storage, for guessing games, and as containers for surprise vocabulary items, these are very handy to have on hand, but they are disappearing as digital cameras replace film cameras.

Magnetic Mirror Use this as a prop on a magnetized chalkboard for pantomime and action chain activities. For example, the teacher might draw a sink on the board and have students go there individually to pretend to comb their hair and wash their faces, looking in the mirror while performing the actions. The simple prop of the mirror makes the activity more meaningful.

Oversized Combs, Toothbrushes, Sunglasses, and Other Props The use of exaggerated sizes for props dealing with any relevant vocabulary adds to the feeling of play and fun and incorporates an element of surprise.

Inflatable Figures (Dolls, Animals, Skeletons, Globes) Inflatable figures can be used in classroom activities or serve as giant-sized manipulatives.

Clocks with Movable Hands This is a necessary prop for activities dealing with time. These clocks are available commercially in both individual student and teacher sizes, or students can make their own as a craft activity.

Large Dice Dice are available with dots, numbers, or blank faces for adding pictures. These are useful for practicing numbers, creating math problems, and developing vocabulary games of many kinds.

Wand, Baton, or Pointer Teacher or students can direct chants or singing with a "magic" wand or baton. These items can also be used for pointing out objects in a game, choosing students, and creating fantasy transformations.

Jump Ropes Jump ropes are useful for TPR activities such as jumping a specified number of times or jumping forward, backward, sideways, fast, slow, high, and low. Jump-rope rhymes from the culture are a good way to move the language beyond the classroom. Two jump ropes laid on the floor in circles side by side can become a Venn diagram.

Hoops (Hula Hoops or Foldable Mathematics Hoops) Use hoops for sorting activities and creating Venn diagrams with actual objects. They can also be used as props in TPR activities designed to illustrate terms such as *into, over, out of* and *next to* (jump over the circle, sit down in the circle, step out of the circle, and so forth).

Balls Sponge balls can be thrown around the classroom with no danger of injury or breakage. They can be thrown to the person who will respond to a question, provide the next question, or be the partner in some kind of exchange. The ball can also be used for various games and activities.

　　Bouncing balls can be used for TPR activities that are similar to the jump rope activities described earlier. The balls can be bounced high and low, fast and slow, or a specified number of times.

Colorful Fabric Backdrops with Thematic Illustrations Available by the yard from fabric stores, a yard or more of these 36″ or 45″ wide fabric pieces can set the tone for a unit and sometimes become part of unit activities. Such prints might have various themes such as the rain forest, foods, oceans, sports, and many other topics.

Puppets, Stuffed Animals, Dolls These items may be used as partners in modeling a conversational exchange. Puppets can be the stimulus for getting information: They can have a secret, speak for a shy child, or be part of an impromptu skit in which the puppets themselves are the characters. Puppets can also be the desired objects in a classroom activity in which students ask to hold or to play with certain things. If they are of the right size and design, a large number of them can be placed in the "magic box" to surprise everyone when all the puppets appear.

Puppets can be of various types: hand puppets, stick puppets, paper bag puppets, folded paper puppets, sock puppets, finger puppets, and others. The children can make many types of puppets themselves.

Plastic Fruit, Vegetables, Flowers, Toys Especially when they are life-sized, plastic models are the next best to the real thing for vocabulary of all kinds.

Suitcase of Clothing Children enjoy dressing up for games or role-plays. Oversized clothing in adult sizes is the easiest to use because students can put it on and take it off quickly and easily. Activities such as relay games and fashion shows are especially effective. The suitcase itself can be a prop in simulations. Smaller suitcases can be used for doll clothes or other small-sized items.

Blindfolds Blindfolds are useful for games, and for changing drill to communicative activities by removing the obvious stimulus from sight.

Brightly Patterned Tablecloth or Scarf, Preferably from the Target Culture The cloth spread out on the floor can define the stage, or set the scene for a story, for classes that sit on the floor. Activities and materials can be laid on the cloth, and the students stay in a relatively well-defined circle around it.

Portable Electronic Keyboard, Rhythm Box The teacher can choose a rhythm as a background for practicing rote material like numbers, lists, or rhymes. Providing a background rhythm changes the character of the activity, making it more fun and adding a right-hemisphere dimension.

Silk Flags These 4″ × 6″ flags are a colorful reminder of the variety of places where the target language is spoken; students will learn to identify flags with geographic locations. Flags are also useful for work with colors. Flags for almost any target-language country are also available on the Internet, or in many software drawing packages.

Dollhouse and Furniture These are useful props for vocabulary dealing with household items and everyday activities.

Sequencing Materials Pictures and manipulatives designed for sequencing activities in early childhood education can be used as the basis for simple storytelling and vocabulary reinforcement as well as for sequencing practice.

Playing Cards There are many kinds of commercially available playing cards, including games such as "Go Fish" and "Old Maid," many of which can be labeled over for the elementary or middle school world language classroom. Target-language card games such as the German "Quartett" or French "Jeu de la Famille" games are valuable for small-group activities because they put students in physical touch with objects from the culture. Regular playing cards can be used for a variety of games that involve reviewing numbers. Cards can also be made with clip art, a copier, card stock, and a paper cutter.

Mathematics and Numbers Flash Cards Flash cards for addition, subtraction, multiplication, and division facts, as well as for numbers and fractions, reinforce the regular mathematics curriculum while providing practice in the target language.

Individual Chalkboards or Whiteboards These can be used for comprehension checks and for listening comprehension and TPR activities. They can also be used for a variety of games. Whiteboards can be made inexpensively by cutting up large sheets of the same material purchased at a builder's supply store. Sometimes the store will even cut up the smaller boards for the teacher. Even more inexpensive are heavy-duty page protectors with a piece of posterboard or cardboard inserted. The surface can be written on using dry erase markers just the same as on a whiteboard.

Beads, Blocks, Rods, Counters These are manipulatives for listening comprehension and communicative language activities. They are also useful for dealing with mathematics concepts such as patterns. Students might organize the blocks or beads according to the teacher's directions, then hold them up to confirm that they understood. They can also be used for partner work in which partners take turns giving directions.

Toy Telephones These make good props for skits and simulations. Toy coin telephones into which plastic coins can actually be inserted are available, making them a good prop for a Gouin Series. (Some telephone companies will lend or donate real telephones for classroom purposes.)

Toy Money This is useful for simulations and for reinforcing mathematics concepts. (It is preferable to use toy money from the target culture.) Teachers can also duplicate replicas of actual money used in the target culture by using actual currency or models available on the Internet.

Toy Cash Register This is for simulations of making change. (It is preferable to use one from the target culture or one that doesn't have a dollar sign.)

Menus from the Target Culture These are useful for pair work, for stating preferences, in simulations, for room decorations, and for reinforcing vocabulary.

Thermometer (Demonstration) The classroom demonstration thermometer should have both Fahrenheit and Celsius scales and a movable temperature indicator. It is used for temperature reports and comparisons with temperatures in foreign countries. (Using thermometers reinforces science concepts and knowledge of the metric system.)

Metric and Balance Scales Both a small food scale and a larger scale for weighing people are useful. Scales are especially valuable for cooking activities reflecting cultures in which ingredients are weighed rather than measured with a cup. Simple balance scales are useful for a number of science activities.

Meter Stick or Measuring Tape   These are for measuring activities and reinforcing the mathematics and science curricula.

Postcards, Letters, and Stamps   These can serve as classroom decoration, as props in simulations and partner work, and for cultural inquiry activities.

Newspapers and Magazines   When written in the target language, these provide browsing and early reading activities, material for art projects, bulletin board backdrops, and props. English language magazines can also be a source of materials for visuals and collages, but they lack the cultural perspective.

Empty Food Packaging   Preferably from the target culture, these are useful for simulations and as props and decorations. Some teachers set up a "store" in part of the classroom as a part of the regular classroom environment.

Table Settings   Flatware, dishes, glasses, cups, napkins, and tablecloths are useful for practice in table setting. Real food, food replicas, or pictures for nutrition lessons and simulations provide the finishing touches.

Coins from the Target Culture   Coins are useful for role-play and simulations and are a good source of cultural information. Coins can also be used to make rubbings, as counters in board games, and for mathematics activities.

Sporting Goods   Sports equipment from the target culture is useful for games and demonstration purposes. For example, boules in a French class or bocce in an Italian class provide an authentic cultural experience for the students. These games are best played outside, since enthusiastic participation might disturb the class next door.

Calendars   When made in the target culture, these show different customs for formatting the date and the month, and they provide attractive pictures reflecting the culture. Other calendars can be useful sources for visuals and student projects. Some software can create calendars in several languages.

Picture Visuals

Pictures provide context and stimuli for a variety of classroom activities. For use with the entire class, they should be mounted and be large and clear enough (at least 8″ × 10″) so that all students can see them. Smaller pictures are appropriate for small-group and pair work. When used to illustrate a concept, pictures must not be cluttered or confusing; only one thing should be represented by each picture.

Pictures are very helpful in keeping the classroom in the target language. They should provide the focus for meaningful, communicative activity, and not just be used to elicit one-word responses and naming. For example, students can sort a series of pictures into the categories of the food pyramid, or arrange them to plan menus. Other pictures might be used to classify types of clothing by appropriate season, color, or degree of formality or informality. In the beginning stages, pictures help the teacher to convey meaning, but later the same or similar pictures can be used as cues for partner activities or group work so that they become aids to communication as well as to vocabulary.

Picture Files It is important to have a variety of materials so that students do not become bored with the same picture used over and over. A variety of visuals for the same concept or vocabulary term can help to ensure that students understand the concept itself, and do not simply have an automatic reaction to a single picture. Picture files can be developed from magazines, postcards, calendars, catalogs, brochures, posters, wall charts, and commercially available flash cards, among many other possibilities. Pictures and clip art available on-line and in software packages can also be useful resources for pictures.

Travel Posters and Brochures Posters and travel brochures provide an especially colorful point of reference for the target culture in the classroom, and they can sometimes be used to set the stage for a fantasy or a culture activity. They should be changed periodically so that they do not lose their appeal for students. Posters, maps, and charts should be laminated before they are displayed if they are to be used for an extended period of time.

Flash Cards Flash cards can be either commercially produced or teacher prepared. They provide picture or symbol stimulus for a wide range of vocabulary and for sequencing activities. Tagboard, oaktag, or posterboard is a good base for making flash cards. It is helpful to make all flash cards in a series the same size for convenience in storage and in dimensions that can be easily held and manipulated by small hands if they are intended for individual or small-group activities, or viewed by an entire class if they were meant for work with large groups. If the flash card is rectangular, it is also helpful to have each flash card oriented the same way vertically or horizontally so that the pictures do not have to be constantly rotated from horizontal to vertical when they are shown in a sequence.

Artworks that Represent Significant Artists or Folk Arts from the Target Culture Fine arts and folk art are important facets of the target culture that can be a part of the learning environment from the first day of class. They can also be the focus or components of thematic units. Prints are available commercially from museums, in calendars and books, and in study prints (see below). There are also numerous websites from which teachers can download both the artworks themselves and information about artists and their times.

Study Prints and Charts Many curriculum libraries and school libraries have files of study prints and charts that can be borrowed for a period of time. These pictures are centered on a theme, such as "Children around the World" or "Community Workers." They are especially useful for content teaching.

Blackline Master Books Available from various publishers, these books are useful as sources for visuals and student activity sheets. Activities developed from these sources must be meaningful and must be an integrated part of the curriculum.

Visuals Available from Computer Clip Art and on the Internet   Visual materials have never been so abundant as they are now, given the availability of clip-art software at reasonable prices. Libraries of clip art are often included with word-processing and other software programs. The Internet offers numerous sites with downloadable free images, and many webpages offer visual materials for teach-ers, as well. Use of a search engine such as www.google.com will often yield web-sites that have visuals available for the exact topic the teacher needs to illustrate a concept or enrich a theme. Teachers often exchange information about these sites on listservs such as Ñandu, or some teachers have built links to useful sites from their own webpages.

Classroom Equipment

Chalkboard/Whiteboard   This is probably the most used classroom aid. Using both colored and white chalk on a chalkboard or markers on a whiteboard makes it more effective, provided that the board surface can handle colored chalk. Walk-ing up to the board is a change of pace for the students. In some schools, the board has a steel core, making it possible to use it like a magnet board.

Pocket Chart   The pocket chart is a standard tool for reading instruction in the primary grades. Charts are made of sturdy cardboard or vinyl and contain pockets that are useful for holding word cards and picture cards. Pocket charts are available from school supply sources, or teachers can develop their own. A long pocket chart with only one pocket can be placed along the chalkboard for use with unscrambling sentences, creating time lines, organizing pictures to retell a story, and so on (see Figure 12.1).

Flannel Board   Flannel boards are commercially available or can be made by stretching a piece of cotton flannel or felt over a backing such as stiff cardboard,

● **FIGURE 12.1**   Pocket Chart

wood, or styrofoam. They should be about 3″ × 2″ in size if they are to be used with the entire class, or they may be smaller if they will be used by small groups or individuals.

Lightweight items with a piece of flannel, felt, or sandpaper on the back will stick to the flannel board so that scenes can be put together and changed easily. Pieces of dress-stiffening fabric or interfacing can also be cut out and colored for use on the flannel board. The flannel board provides an excellent device for storytelling and manipulating objects. The board can be divided into rooms of the house, roads, farms, calendars, and many other spaces with felt strip dividers. Other materials that adhere easily to the flannel board include paper with flocked backing, pipe cleaners, string, yarn, suede, and sponges. Many flannel board manipulative materials are available from school supply stores and catalogs.

Magnet Board Magnet boards are commercially available in sizes similar to those available for flannel boards, and they can be used in much the same way. Magnets can be placed on top of figures to hold them in place, or they can be glued to the back of objects or figures to be used. Magnet strips with adhesive backing are available from school supply stores and stationery stores. Magnetic letters, numbers, pictures, and other magnetized items can also be obtained commercially. Some teachers have bought sets of words designed for "refrigerator poetry" in countries where the target language is spoken, to be used in learning centers or for special projects. Sheets of magnetized paper suitable for use with a computer printer make it possible for the teacher to create words and pictures for use on a magnet board. Teachers can create their own magnet boards using a large cookie sheet or a piece of sheet metal. Many chalkboards and some whiteboards have a steel core and can be used as magnet boards.

Peg Board The peg board consists of a sturdy board perforated with a regular pattern of holes and with a series of fixed or movable pegs or hooks that protrude from it. The pegs or hooks can be used to hang flash cards, numbers, pictures, or letters that have a hole punched in them. The items can be moved from peg to peg. Boards with hooks can be used to display three-dimensional items or to mount shelves for storage and display.

Hook and Loop Boards and Strips Hook and loop material—commercially known as Velcro®—is sometimes used for fasteners in sewing. It consists of two different types of surfaces that attach very tightly to one another. Hook and loop boards can be used for displaying three-dimensional materials because the system creates a very strong bond. Even without a hook and loop board the teacher can attach a strip of the hook and loop material along the side of a chalkboard or bulletin board and use it to mount various items. Some teachers use hook and loop pieces to attach and remove visuals from charts, calendars, and other games or displays.

Chart Stand, Easel These are useful for displaying large visuals and maps and for supporting chart tablets and flip charts. When teachers read "big books," the easel is a very helpful aid.

Globes, World Maps, Maps of Countries Where the Target Language Is Spoken
Frequent reference to globes and world maps will help students put learning into
a global context. Ideally, these resources will be printed in the target language,
although first-language maps and globes can also be useful. Inflatable globes are
available in English and in some target languages. These can be tossed around
the classroom and used in a very personalized way; they are usually less expensive
than traditional classroom globes.

Audiovisual Equipment

Overhead Projector The overhead projector allows the teacher to control the
focus of class attention by turning the projector off and on and by revealing only
one part of the transparency at a time. The overhead projector is especially valuable for the traveling teacher, provided that there is a projector in every classroom the teacher visits, or room on a traveling cart for a portable projector.
Many instructional materials can be prepared ahead of time and projected when
they are needed during the class; this saves class time that would otherwise be
spent in writing on the chalkboard.

Transparencies are especially effective when they include color, which may
be added even to commercially prepared transparencies with transparency pens.
Transparencies for use with color printers make it possible for the teacher to
create excellent color transparencies that are suited precisely to the current
theme. Figures on transparencies can be cut out and moved around on the glass
projector stage to achieve a variety of effects. (A number of additional activities
for the overhead projector are listed in Chapter 13.)

Document Projector/Visualizer The document projector is like an overhead
projector with the added advantage that it projects an image of pictures or three-
dimensional objects that would otherwise be too small to show to an entire class.
This is used in combination with a digital projector.

DVD Player/Videocassette Player DVD and videocassette players make it
possible to view commercially prepared lessons or supplementary materials,
many of which provide an image of the target culture that is nearly impossible to
achieve in any other way. Some classrooms also exchange videotape "letters" or
projects with learners studying or speaking the target language in other parts of
the country or with children living in the target culture. Multistandard
equipment is essential for use with DVDs or videotapes made in some other
countries.

CD Player, Audiocassette Recorder/Player, MP3 Player with Speakers These can
be used for learning stations as well as in the whole-group setting. Students can
read a book and listen to the accompanying audio, or they can listen to a set of
instructions for performing activities such as completing a scrambled dot-to-dot
puzzle or dressing a paper doll. There are many possibilities for individual listening
activities in which there is a product at the end and the opportunity for self-check.

The CD or cassette player is also useful for playing accompaniments to songs, providing background music for a variety of classroom activities, and for recording and playing back special songs or skits done by the class—either for their own enjoyment or for sharing with other classes through a tape exchange. If the teacher is still using audiotapes, and she or he plans to play the same song repeatedly in a class, or in a series of classes, it is helpful to record the song several times on the same tape, so there is no need to rewind and try to find the starting point for each repetition.

The CD player has several advantages for teacher use in the classroom. It is easy to find the beginning of a recorded segment, and the sound quality is often better than with an audiotape. It is practical for the teacher to have a combination CD/audiotape machine in order to have maximum flexibility.

Sound equipment should have a good-quality speaker that does not distort the sound when played at a volume high enough to be heard by the entire class.

Slide Projector Slides can still be useful for imparting cultural information, especially when they have been taken by the teacher in the target culture. The drawback to slide projection is the fact that the projector must be set up in advance and the room has to be darkened for the best viewing of the slides. Some teachers have learners illustrate a play with drawings for each scene, and then scan them (or photograph the drawings on a copy stand) to create a slide sequence telling the story. Children then record a dramatization of the play and present the slide-sound story to parents or other students. A similar process could be used to create a PowerPoint or other multimedia presentation. Slides can be scanned and converted into a digital format so that they can be used with a digital projector.

Digital Projector The digital projector has largely replaced the slide projector—and to a certain extent the overhead projector—as the preferred format for showing visuals. The projector can be used to show videos, PowerPoint presentations, or to project any computer image. For the classroom with an Internet connection, the projector gives access to the endless resources of the World Wide Web.

Interactive Electronic Whiteboard The interactive whiteboard fulfills all the functions of the digital projector but has the added capability of allowing interaction with the whiteboard itself without having to use the computer keyboard. The touch-sensitive board connects to the computer and digital projector to show the computer image. Teacher and students can manipulate images and words with a touch to the board, and they can even browse the Internet in the same way.

Computer, Internet Connection, Scanner, Printer The computer has a lot of potential for providing interactive and communicative practice. There are increasing numbers of interesting and useful programs that allow learners to use the language in a game-like setting, or that provide review and practice. Word processing in the target language offers creative writing opportunities for early language classes. With an Internet connection, the computer provides electronic links for powerful class-to-class and student-to-student exchanges.

If the teacher has a scanner and a color printer available, as well as Internet access, the job of developing materials and activities is much more efficient. Scanners with slide adapters make it possible for teachers to make computer images from selected slides in their collection. Internet resources can simplify teacher preparation by offering downloadable lessons, worksheets, activities, visuals, and authentic materials of all kinds. Clip art and visuals from websites in the target culture make it possible for teachers to provide students with authentic materials and experiences that have previously been accessible only by a visit to the country itself. See Chapter 14 for a more extended discussion of technology.

Visual Reinforcement in the Early Language Classroom

Labels All classroom furniture and classroom features can be labeled in the target language (chalkboard, desk, door, erasers, electric outlets). It is also effective to label other parts of the school with target language names—toilets, offices, specialty classrooms, exits, and so forth (see Figure 12.2). Where there is more than one language taught in the school, labels from all languages may be used side by side.

Name Tags Name tags can be an effective reinforcement of the second-language atmosphere if the students have chosen names in the target language. Name tags may be placed on the desks for the language period every day or they may be hung around the neck or pinned on an article of the students' clothing. Some teachers create classroom rituals around the distribution of name tags every day; others prefer to have the students keep the name tags in their desks and take them out as a sign of the beginning of class. Name tags may not be needed beyond the first several weeks of the year; although, for teachers who see many students in a day or in a week, the name tags may be necessary for a much longer period of time. Name tags permit teachers to call students by name, even when a target-language name has not been assigned, in a situation where it is otherwise very difficult to learn all the names of the students.

Calendar Having a calendar in the target language is an easy way to have the target culture present in the classroom at all times. For some teachers an opening routine for each class involves the calendar and the weather. They use the same calendar format as the base, and then they have month headers and calendar numbers (different ones for each month). Many teachers add the new calendar number each day, attaching it with a hook-and-loop tab or with masking tape.

Weather Cards, Chart, Weather Wheel As part of the calendar opening for class, students identify the weather for the day and post it with the calendar. Some teachers keep a weather chart on which the class records the weather over the course of a week or longer.

Lynn Sessler, Japanese teacher in Menasha, Wisconsin, uses weather pictures for each type of weather likely to be encountered in the local climate.

● **FIGURE 12.2**   Classroom Labeled in the Target Language

She attaches a hook or a link to the bottom of each picture. Each day the students decide on the weather—in Japanese, of course—and add a link to the chain under that weather picture. At the end of the week, or the month, the class has a graph of the weather conditions and can use it to describe the weather over that period of time.

Signal Indicating Language Being Spoken This signal can be a sign or a flag or an apron or some other device that indicates whether English or the target language is being used. The teacher changes the signal when the language of the classroom is changed.

Symbols to Hang from the Ceiling Signs with specific vocabulary items, such as weather, months, or time of day, can be hung from the ceiling in various parts of the room. They can be used as a way of organizing the class or as a part of TPR activities. Passwords or language ladders might also be hung from the ceiling instead of being placed on the wall. This possibility assumes that the language is always taught in the same room.

Mobiles Coat hangers are the easiest base for creating classroom mobiles that reflect some aspect of the thematic unit. Directions for making mobiles can be found in many classroom craft books.

Reference Charts Charts can be student or teacher made, or they can be obtained from commercial sources. They visually represent the concepts taught in class. For example, a food pyramid might be used in conjunction with a food unit.

Helper Chart This is a list of classroom jobs performed by students, with visual cues to make the meaning clear (see Figure 12.3). This is obviously appropriate for a classroom devoted to the target language, but sometimes classroom teachers are willing to use a target-language chart for the helpers each week, instead of an English language chart.

Classroom Rules Chart Classroom rules should be spelled out in the target language with a visual cue to make the meaning clear.

Color and Number Charts In primary and early elementary school language classrooms, these are helpful reference points for early activities with colors and numbers.

Bulletin Boards Bulletin boards captioned in the target language and reflecting the target culture can be a source of cultural stimulation in the classroom, and

● **FIGURE 12.3** Sample Helper Chart in Chinese

they can also serve as valuable teaching tools. They should be changed frequently, often with the help of the students themselves, and they should reflect the concepts and the vocabulary being taught in the classroom. Bulletin boards in hallways and entryways of the school provide an opportunity to gain attention for the language program. Some classroom teachers are willing to devote one portion of the classroom board space for the traveling language teacher.

Teacher-Produced Materials

Teacher-made materials are among the most effective means in communicating a concept, structuring an activity, or motivating a lesson, because they are usually tailored to the special needs and interests of a specific class and situation. Both the teacher and the students value the extra effort that has gone into making these materials and use them with special pleasure. Supplementary materials like most of those represented here should contribute to the goals of the lesson and not become a separate entity in themselves.

Many of these items can also be produced by students or with student assistance. All items prepared for the classroom should be of good quality, carefully prepared, durable, and colorful. Edges should be straight and squared, cut with a paper cutter. Pinking shears should be used to cut any cloth with a tendency to ravel, or to provide a decorative edge to paper or fabric.

Three methods for protecting a visual are binding, mounting, and making surface coverings. Binding (with masking tape or other strong tape) protects the edges and makes for longer wear.

Mounting a visual keeps it flat and makes it easier to handle and file; mounting material must be sturdy so that the pictures are not flimsy and do not become dog-eared. Two effective techniques for mounting involve using the dry-mount heat press and spray adhesive. Visuals should be mounted on backings of similar sizes so that they are easier to store.

The surface of visuals can be protected through lamination or by use of clear self-adhesive plastic. Lamination tends to enhance the colors of the visuals and to give a more professional, long-lasting finish. It is frequently no more expensive than other techniques, but it may sometimes be a source of glare, making it difficult for some students to see the visual under certain lighting conditions. With clear self-adhesive plastic there is often a loss of vividness of color, but no machine is necessary, so projects can be completed at home. Do not use permanent ink pens to mark materials that will be laminated or covered with clear contact paper, as the color may bleed; instead, use water-based pens.

Magic/Mystery Box This resource can conceal or reveal vocabulary items and can be a recurring source of surprises and motivation in the classroom (see Figure 12.4). Specific suggestions for its use are found in Chapter 13. Here are the directions for making a magic box:

1. Cover the bottom and sides of a 42-ounce (large) oatmeal box with two layers of self-stick plastic covering. If patterned covering is not used, decorate the box with symbols cut from contrasting plastic.

● **FIGURE 12.4**   Magic Box

2. Cut away the heel and the foot from a large heavy sock, or use a portion of a leg warmer. Pull the sock over the top of the oatmeal box until the entire sock is stretched around the box.

3. Staple the sock around the top edge to fasten it to the box.

4. Place a strip of the self-stick plastic around the top edge of the box, covering the staples and the top edge of the sock.

5. Pull the sock up from the bottom, inside out, to form a "handle" for the box.

Laminated Circles and Numbers   Make large- and small-colored circles (at least one set of each, 12″ and 6″ in diameter) out of construction paper for every color to be taught. Other laminated shapes are useful for mathematics concepts. Make large numbers out of 9″ × 12″ colored tagboard. Laminate or cover with clear self-stick plastic. These materials are all useful for TPR activities, creative play, and subject content instruction.

Floor Maps and Pattern Games   Use a sheet of heavy-gauge vinyl table covering (preferably without texture) to make a floor map of countries, continents, or cities. (If the vinyl is white on both sides, each side can be used for a different map or activity.) It also works to use a heavy shower curtain. Attach the vinyl to the chalkboard or the wall and project a copy of the map using an opaque projector or an overhead projector. Trace the map onto the vinyl using a permanent felt marker or a laundry marker. For additional interest, add colored markers to indicate bodies of water and other features of importance.

This teaching tool can be used for teaching geography concepts by TPR as learners step, sit, or jump on a country, a city, or a physical feature. (Additional teaching suggestions are found in Chapter 13.)

Use the back of the map or another piece of vinyl to create a game board, a chart, or a geometric grid for use with TPR activities associated with a variety of concepts.

Name Tags Punch holes in the two top corners of a piece of tagboard, pull yarn through the holes and tie it, write the student's target-language name on the tagboard, and hang it around the student's neck. The name tag can be shaped to represent elements of the culture being learned, such as berets, flags, and pretzels. (If name tags are laminated, they will last much longer. They must be laminated if they are made out of construction paper.)

Booklets, Theme Books, Shape Books Use booklets or theme books as initial, developmental, or culminating activities for just about any topic. When you create a booklet that represents concepts just learned in pictures (and perhaps also in words), the students have something tangible to take home with them and share with their parents, and the second-language learning becomes more concrete for them. You can prepare the illustrations for the booklet, or the booklet pages themselves, before class, and have students complete them as a classroom activity. Typical booklet topics include weather, feelings, the alphabet, a group trip, foods, and animals.

For variety, you can prepare the cover and the pages for a theme book or booklet in the shape of the topic of the booklet, and have students assemble the booklet and use it to record information about the topic. For example, an experience with a rabbit might be recorded in a booklet shaped like a rabbit, or a nutrition experience might be described in a book shaped like an apple or an egg. These experiences give students both tactile and verbal reinforcement of the concepts under discussion.

Clothesline A clothesline provides an easy way to display visuals or student work in the classroom. For example, the teacher might hang paper or doll clothing on it, use it as a time line, or hang up weather signs or other symbols.

Wheel of Months, Seasons/Weather This teaching tool provides a way of looking at the months of the year and the seasons as a whole and associating them with distinctive characteristics representative of the target culture. The teacher uses heavyweight tagboard or posterboard to cut two large half circles that will be hinged together to form a complete circle. The circle is divided into 12 equal segments, each representing a month of the year and identified by a picture reflecting special activities or occasions for that month and with the name or initial of the month. The board can be used for teaching months of the year, locating class birthdays, and songs and rhymes dealing with months and seasons.

Clothespin Matchups (Self-Correcting Activity) To create clothespin matchups, use the following materials: a large circle (or other shape if preferred) made of cardboard or tagboard divided into 8 to 12 sections, and wooden clothespins—enough so that there is one pin for each section of the wheel.

There are many varieties of activities with clothespin matchups. The circle can contain pictures of vocabulary words, and the clothespins can have the correct word written on them; the activity can deal with rhyming words, opposites, various tenses, or many other topics; students must match the clothespin with the section of the wheel that has the correct picture. To make the activity self-checking, place a number or symbol on the back of the clothespin and the same number or symbol on the back of the correct section of the wheel (see Figure 12.5).

Dominoes (Number or Picture) You can create domino games using colors, numbers, or pictures representing current vocabulary. Use the dominoes for small groups or whole-class activities on the chalkboard or on the floor. Commercial domino games are also useful for many activities.

● **FIGURE 12.5** Sample of a Clothespin Matchup Activity in Russian

Yarn-Board (Self-Correcting Activity) To make a yarn-board, use these materials: an 8½″ × 11″ piece of tagboard divided in half lengthwise, and into four to six sections horizontally; colored yarn (either enough pieces of one color or a different color for each horizontal section); hole puncher; and reinforcements for three-hole-punched paper.

Arrange various pairs for matching practice so that one member of the pair appears in the left-hand column and the other member of the pair appears in a random position in the right-hand column. Attach one piece of the yarn to each segment on the edge of the left-hand column and punch one hole on the edge of each segment in the right-hand column. The student places the yarn in the hole representing the correct match. Many items can be matched: vocabulary pictures with vocabulary words, opposites, and so forth (see Figure 12.6). This activity can be self-correcting in two ways: *Variation 1:* Cut the yarn various lengths so that each piece can fit into only the hole with the correct answer. *Variation 2:* Use

● **FIGURE 12.6**   Sample Yarn-Board in Japanese

multicolored yarn strands all the same length and color-code the correct answers on the back of the hole by placing a round reinforcement for three-hole-punched paper over the hole. Color-code the reinforcement the same color as the yarn.

Game Boards You can make simple game boards similar to those popular with students and create games to reinforce concepts that you are teaching. Game boards can be of any shape and design.

Felt Beanbags in a Variety of Colors Here are instructions for making beanbags:

1. Cut two pieces of felt in a circle shape with a 5″ diameter.

2. Stitch them together with a ⅜″ seam around the edge, leaving about 1½″ opening for filling the bag.

3. Use light cardboard to make a funnel for beans.

4. Fill bag with a rounded ¼ cup of navy beans.

5. Sew shut.

Beanbags can be used for TPR activities, in games involving a floor map or game board, and in other common children's games.

Scrolls Scrolls can be used as a dramatic way of telling a story or presenting a sequence of events or steps, and they are often student produced. They are made by rolling a long strip of paper from one stick or dowel to another. They can also be used as a way of keeping a class or individual record of language learned or experiences shared.

● Choosing and Using Materials Wisely

The materials and realia described in this chapter constitute a significant investment of time and resources. They are important because they make the classroom come alive and they meet the developmental needs of our students. They are also precious. As we create materials and consider their purchase, we must be sure that our time and funds are wisely spent. Materials should be usable in a variety of ways, not purchased or made for a single activity on one day and then never used again. Busy teachers don't have hours to spend on visuals or on manipulatives that can only be used once, for a single purpose, nor do they have budgets large enough to purchase a costly manipulative that will likely only be used once.

For example, a teacher created a large two-story house from posterboard, using hook-and-loop tabs to place furnishings in the house, and creating fold-out walls and doors so that the rooms could be revealed one at a time. During one class session she introduced the rooms of the house by opening the doors to each room and having the class pantomime the kinds of activities that would take place in that room. On another day she removed the furnishings from the rooms and used TPR commands to have students place the furniture in the appropriate room. On another day she hid family members in different rooms of the house and the class tried to guess where each family member was hiding. There are many more variations that could take place with this one, labor-intensive visual, and with each variation the students' language development grows.

Another way to make the most of valuable materials is to share them within a team of teachers. Especially when there is more than one teacher per grade level, sharing materials and ideas makes everyone's load lighter and enhances learning for all the students.

Criteria for Evaluating Nontextbook Materials and Realia

Whether they have been prepared by hand, commercially produced, or obtained directly from the target culture, materials will be most effective when the following questions can be answered affirmatively:

- Are the materials durable? Can they stand up to repeated, ungentle handling?
- Are the materials culturally authentic? (Some items, such as balls, numbers, shapes, animal replicas, and models of uncooked food, are culture free.)
- Are they free of non-essential detail?
- Are they brightly colored?
- Are they safe for use by children?
- Is their size appropriate to their intended use?
- Are they appealing to the intended age and developmental level?
- Do they have a versatility that lends itself to multiple use?
- Are they free of gender and racial bias?
- Do they collectively incorporate a variety of textures (soft, hard, rough, smooth)?
- Are the materials functional and simple to use?
- Are they easy to keep clean?
- Are they aesthetically pleasing?
- Do they reflect quality workmanship?
- Is the cost within the budget?

● Choosing a Textbook and Other Curriculum Materials

Choosing a textbook is one of the most important tasks for the foreign-language teacher at any level. In the elementary school the process is made much more difficult by the fact that there are few text series from which to choose. A number of programs do not reflect current insights about communication and language acquisition. Other materials have been developed for specific purposes and are not easily transferable to the early foreign-language classroom. Spanish materials from bilingual education, for example, are designed for children who already speak Spanish, at least to some extent, and who function at least some of the time in a Spanish-speaking environment. Thus, the linguistic level of these materials is inappropriate for English-speaking children who live in an all-English setting.

In the absence of satisfactory commercial text series, some school systems have invested the funding and the effort necessary to create successful locally developed materials for an entire elementary school sequence. Current curricula and program descriptions can be located using the CAL Early Language website (www.cal.org/earlylang/), the resources of the National Network for Early Language Learning, or those found at the National K–12 Foreign Language Resource Center (http://nflrc.iastate.edu/).

As the interest in elementary and middle school foreign-language programs continues to grow, publishers are producing curriculum materials to add to the small number of contemporary early language text series already developed for the U.S. market, and some of these materials use videotapes as a core component. Many of these will be welcome resources that can provide a useful core for the language program.

Special Considerations at the Middle School Level

Awareness of the distinctive characteristics and learning needs of early adolescents has led to significant changes in the middle school curriculum and organization. Middle school philosophy permeates curriculum and planning for students in grades 5 through 8, and hands-on integrated learning has begun to replace classic textbook-driven instruction. For language programs beginning in the middle school, it has been common practice to choose foreign-language materials designed for high school students and "slow them down" for the middle school, often covering the materials for the first high school year over a two-year period. This practice is intended to prepare middle school students for a smooth integration into the high school sequence, but it fails to address the special needs and interests of the early adolescent at the romantic layer of educational development (see Chapter 1).

Middle school programs that continue an early language learning program or immersion program require materials that build on earlier learning and extend it in developmentally appropriate ways. Few foreign-language materials have been developed specifically for the middle school level, except for some exploratory programs, and teachers must revise and adapt extensively. The middle school student will be best served with a continued emphasis on integrated thematic units, with reference to textbook materials only when they are appropriate to the goals of the curriculum and the learning needs of the students.

Even when satisfactory curriculum materials are available, they represent only one of the tools for curriculum development. Standards-based, thematic planning is the core of any early language program, and curriculum materials need to support these integrated thematic units. Materials and activities chosen or devised by the teacher respond to the interests and needs of students in each specific school setting, and they constitute the most dynamic part of early language instruction.

The materials described in this chapter and the sample activities discussed in Chapter 13 are intended to serve as useful components of both those programs that draw on the resources of a text series and those that have been developed locally.

Criteria for Evaluating Textbooks and Other Printed Curriculum Material

As teachers of young learners evaluate text series or curriculum materials developed in other districts, the following questions are recommended for the screening process:

Goals

- Are the materials standards-based and oriented toward student performance?

- Are the goals of the program or authors clearly stated? Are these goals compatible with local program goals?

- Is the scope and sequence for the entire series carefully developed and clearly presented?

- Do the materials reflect authentic use of language? Is this the way people in the target culture really express themselves?

- What is the intended grade level for the materials? Are the materials suitable for the interests and maturity level of the proposed audience?

Communication

- Does communication rather than grammar serve as the organizing principle? Does work with grammar concentrate on functional use rather than on analysis? Do the activities focus on meaning rather than on form?

- Is the use of English avoided in student materials and discouraged in the activities described in the teacher's manual?

- Do the materials reflect an understanding of the use of current methodology?

- Is the material oriented to activity and experience rather than to exercise and drill?

- Do the materials provide opportunities for meaningful, purposeful language use in the interpersonal, interpretive, and presentational modes?

- Are the materials designed to develop a solid oral language base on which to build reading and writing skills?

- Do the materials provide for a variety of types of classroom organization (pairs, small groups, individual work)?

Culture

- Is culture integrated into the program materials? Is there emphasis on experiencing culture rather than on learning about culture?

- Is culture presented from a global perspective rather than focusing on a single country, region, or ethnic group?

- Are the situations and language presented culturally authentic and up to date?
- Do the materials promote an appreciation of the value and richness of cultural diversity?
- Are there resources provided or suggested for authentic songs, games, and children's literature?

Subject Content and Thinking Skills (Connections)

- Is there provision for the teaching of grade-appropriate subject content in the target language? Are there suggestions for interdisciplinary content and activities?
- Are the materials conducive to the development of higher-order thinking skills, and not restricted to rote learning?
- Are there opportunities for students to personalize both languages, cultures, and content learning?
- Are there opportunities for students to seek out new information using the target language?

Bias

- Are the illustrations and text free of racial, gender, and cultural bias?

Flexibility

- Are the materials adaptable to different program models and time allocations?
- Do the materials provide options for a variety of student learning styles—visual, auditory, kinesthetic?

Physical Characteristics

- Are the student materials visually oriented and colorful?
- Are there color photographs and other visuals clearly linked to the printed material?
- Is the size of print in student materials the same as that used in subject content textbooks used at the same grade level?
- Are the materials durable? Can they withstand handling by many children over the period of time covered by a textbook adoption?

Support Materials

- Is there a teacher's manual with abundant suggestions for the teacher? Does the teacher receive adequate guidance in the use of the materials?
- Are there relevant and effective charts, transparencies, flash cards, pictures, tapes, and other support materials available in addition to the basic program?
- If taped materials are available, do they feature native-speaker voices speaking naturally in the presentation of songs, rhymes, and stories? Are there tapes available that include program-relevant sound effects and background music?

Budget

- Are the materials affordable?

Summary

- Every aspect of the classroom and all of the materials and realia have potential for contributing to the language experiences from which language acquisition develops.

- An ample inventory of supplies will make it easier for teachers to prepare materials tailored to classroom communication needs.

- A good selection of manipulatives and realia makes it possible to vary the contexts within which students communicate, giving them the practice that they need while maintaining high motivation.

- A variety of picture visuals to supplement the realia helps students to stretch the concepts they have learned to include a variety of occurrences.

- Audiovisual equipment can make it possible for learners to have a direct visual or auditory experience with the target culture and with speakers of the language, and it can also facilitate many types of individual instruction.

- The classroom environment can illustrate that a foreign language is an important part of the curriculum, through bulletin boards, charts, calendars, and other vivid evidence. Even when the early language teacher must travel to several rooms in a day, each classroom should be able to find a place for some evidence of the new language and its culture.

- Teacher-produced materials and visuals add a personal quality and investment to any lesson, and they are often the most effective of all teaching tools.

- Equipment and materials necessary to conduct in-class food activities provide for some of the most motivating and memorable of all classroom activities.

- Textbook series appropriate for U.S. elementary and middle school language programs are more difficult to find than are locally produced curriculum materials. The same standards of quality apply to all materials being considered.

- All materials must be carefully chosen and evaluated, with the goals and philosophy of the local program serving as the main criteria.

For Study and Discussion

1. What special advantages might be expected from the use of teacher-made visuals and realia? What are the drawbacks of their use?

2. Choose an item from one of the materials lists and describe four different ways in which you could use it in the early language classroom. Identify the grade and language level of the learners for whom you plan the activities.

3. Choose a textbook series or a teacher-developed curriculum designed for an early language program and evaluate it in terms of the criteria questions found in this chapter.

4. How do the criteria for choosing and evaluating materials for elementary and middle school language classes differ from criteria used in other content areas?

5. One of the exhibitors at a foreign-language conference has announced the publication of a new textbook in your language for children in kindergarten through grade 6. Write down seven questions you would ask the publisher's representative to help you determine whether or not the series is worth a closer look.

Languages & Children

Bringing Language to Life

Classroom Games and Activities

Enduring Understanding

- Games and game-like activities provide a natural context for communication in the classroom.

Essential Question

- What games and activities can I use to develop meaningful classroom language learning?

Games and game-like activities are among the most natural means available for developing a context for communication with young learners. Play is often described as a child's work, and games form a natural part of the child's most important work setting: the classroom. Middle school students are also very responsive to games—in fact, playing with language is a powerful tool no matter what age the learners may be. Games and game-like activities might be credited with carrying the largest role in the acquisition of language in the early language classroom. Although some educators make a distinction between games and activities, it is often very difficult to draw a clear line, and the differences between them are far less important than is the impact they have on the motivation and the language acquisition of the children in the class. Many teachers of young learners have discovered that students regard any well-designed, successful activity that they enjoy as a "game." This chapter treats activities and games as a single category and makes no distinction between them. The suggestions and guidelines presented are applicable to all classroom activities.

The most successful games are very simple, requiring a minimum of explanation and rules. The simple addition of a competitive factor, or an element of mystery or surprise, can convert an otherwise meaningless but necessary practice activity into a game. Most games should flow naturally within the class period from the topics and vocabulary being worked on, and only rarely will they be set apart as major events in themselves.

● Guidelines for Games and Activities

The most important requirement for a game is that it should be fun for the students to play. Before planning a game activity, the teacher should consider whether the students would enjoy the topic and the game outside the classroom. Here are some guidelines for choosing and using games in the language classroom.

1. Choose games or adjust them so that the students need to understand the language and express themselves in it. Then they will realize that the language is useful and they will be motivated to communicate. It is to be expected that the teacher will produce most of the language during the early stages of language acquisition; this is perfectly natural and acceptable, but the target language must play an important part in every game. Some games, such as dominoes and certain board games, can be played successfully with virtually no use of the target language by the students or the teacher. These games need not be abandoned, however, if the teacher can devise a playing routine that involves use of the target language. If the language is not truly required, however, students will choose to use it only when the teacher is within hearing distance.

2. Provide maximum opportunity for students to participate. All learners should be engaged in the activity all the time. Some activities, such as "Simon Says," are designed so that children who miss are "out," which leaves many learners inactive for most of the game. These games can be redesigned to allow for students who are "out" to contribute to the game in a new way, such as by taking turns at giving commands to other students, or to give them a method for reentry into the competition by paying close attention or by completing a special performance of some kind.

3. Organize and score the game so that most of the playing time can be spent communicating in the target language.

4. Add an appealing element of suspense or competition, but structure the game to avoid intense individual competition that could carry over into bad feelings outside the classroom. The healthiest type of competition takes place when teams or groups are evenly matched and have equal opportunity for success. When a higher level of competition is desired, it often works out to pit the class against

the teacher or against an imaginary villain, like the ghost in some computer games. That way, the entire class works together to "win," and when the class wins, so does the teacher.

5. Choose a game that is easy to play so that it will move quickly. In most cases, short games that can be repeated in several rounds during one class period are preferable to longer games, which may not be completed by the time the language class is over.

6. Stop the game or the activity at a point when the class still wants more, rather than continuing it until interest begins to wane.

7. Do not repeat successful activities, except those designed to be played with several rounds, during the same class or on the following day, even when students request them. Using any specific game sparingly helps keep it fresh and motivating.

8. Structure activities when possible in the spirit of New Games (Fluegelman, 1976, p. 13), in which everybody plays to the level of her or his ability: "Play Hard, Play Fair, Nobody Hurt!"

9. Give games a name, especially if they are likely to be used again in a similar form. Young learners regard the game as something special if it has a name, and a name makes it easier for them to talk about the game outside of class or to request it at a future time.

10. Incorporate games played in the target culture or in other cultures around the world whenever possible. Several sources for games with global roots are listed at the end of this chapter. The physical education teacher may have suggestions for references on international games and may also be willing to include such games in the physical education curriculum at the teacher's suggestion. The Internet and the Ñandu listserv and FLTeach listserv, together with their archives, are rich resources for finding games and activities.

● Classroom Games and Activities

The games and activities that follow have been gleaned from many sources; they represent only a sampling of the kinds of activities that are possible in an early language classroom. Two types of activities receive specific attention within the chapter: the role of puppets and stuffed animals, and the use of songs.

This collection includes many activities with an emphasis on listening, although games and activities in which young learners play an active speaking role are also featured. In games and activities that require only minimal or no speech, it is important for the teacher to surround the activity with meaningful, communicative language. Every game in the early language classroom is a language game; every activity is a setting for language acquisition.

The activities that follow do not include every content for the language classroom. Rather, they are templates that can be used to create a game-like activity to develop concepts or information from any content area or any target culture.

Name Games

Names or Numbers "Concentration"   Sit with the students in a circle, if possible, and set up a rhythm, slowly at first, as follows:

>   slap, slap (knees)
>   clap, clap (hands)
>   snap, snap (left hand)
>   snap, snap (right hand)

On the left-hand snaps, call your own name, and on the right-hand snaps, call the name of one of the students. On the next left-hand snaps, have the student call her or his own name, and on the right-hand snaps, call the name of another student. The chain continues until someone misses a turn or loses the rhythm, at which point the teacher begins the game again. When this game is introduced, it is often helpful if you tell students to practice by always responding with the teacher's name on the right-hand snaps for the first few times, until the rhythm and the name-calling have become coordinated. As students increase their confidence and ability and begin to call on one another, you can speed up the rhythm. You can also play with numbers, letters of the alphabet, or any other vocabulary by placing the visual representing each student on the floor in front of her or him.

Another variant for older children who already know one another is "Hollywood Rhythm." Use categories such as animals, countries, foods, and so forth. Students name an item that hasn't been mentioned yet from within the category, without breaking the rhythm.

"Spin the Plate"   With children sitting in a circle, if possible, set a metal pie plate on its edge in the center of the group. Spin the plate and call the name of one of the students. If the student reaches the plate and catches it before it stops spinning, the student takes your place. If the student does not reach the plate in time, you take another turn spinning the plate. The game continues, with each successful participant taking the role of plate-spinner and calling another student's name, until most or all names have been called at least once. This game can also be played with numbers, colors, or any other set of vocabulary.

"Seven-Up"   Here is a variation of a favorite elementary school game: Call seven students to the front of the room, and tell the rest of the students in the class to place their heads down on their desks with their eyes closed. The seven students move around the room and each touches one class member on the shoulder, after which they return to the front of the room. You can recite (or have the seven students recite in chorus) a routine such as "1, 2, 3, eyes open!" The class members whose shoulders were touched take turns guessing which student touched them. If they guess correctly in a single try, they trade places with the student in the front of the room. Students who are not correctly guessed stay in the front of the room for another round.

Chalkboard or Whiteboard Activities

Total Physical Response with Chalk or Marker   Ask the students to respond to commands such as the following:

- Walk (jump, run, crawl, walk backward) to the board.
- Pick up the _____. (color, chalk, marker)
- Write _____.
- Circle _____.
- Make an x on _____.
- Draw (part of a face, body, and so forth).
- Take the eraser and erase _____.

This is an especially good activity for giving young learners practice in remembering a series of commands.

"Chalkboard Monster"   Have one or two students go to the chalkboard and create a monster by following your directions, preferably using colored chalk. In more advanced situations, the monster might develop from the joint commands of the class. For example, you might say, "Draw a big head; draw an ear," and then ask the class, "Do you want large ears or small ears?" so that students can contribute to the development of the monster in various ways, depending on their language level. If more than one student is at the chalkboard at the same time, it is interesting to compare the efforts of each student in a class discussion, always being careful to avoid comparative judgments.

"What's the Weather?"   Draw a window on the chalkboard. Direct the students to go to the board and draw the weather in the window as you describe it. (As a variation to this activity, use a felt or magnet board and have children choose elements to place in the window.) To activate the language, you might lead a discussion about what time of year this weather represents, whether children like or dislike this kind of weather, and what kinds of activities they enjoy in this weather.

Activities with a Magic Box (Bag, Backpack)

(See directions for making a magic box in Chapter 12.)

1. Remove items from the box, describe them, and have students ask for them.
2. Pull familiar items from the box, revealing a little bit at a time, and have students take turns either guessing each item or describing it.

3. Have students describe and/or guess an item in the box from touch alone.

4. Stuff the box with a number of items; have each student pull out one item and use it as a speech stimulus.

5. Use the box and the items it contains with physical-response activities such as *take, put, give,* and *throw.*

6. Have students pull words or phrases from the box and string them together into a narrative or combine them into a command.

7. Play "I'm Going on a Trip and I'm Taking . . . " with items (or pictures of items) pulled from the box. Each student repeats all previous items before they say their own.

8. Stuff food items—real or artificial—into the box. Have students remove three to five items, construct a menu, and identify the meal.

9. Play "Twenty Questions" about an item or group of items in the box.

10. Place items in the box that suggest a specific person and have students guess who it is as each item is revealed.

11. Place items in the box that represent two different categories, such as water creatures and animal creatures. As students take turns removing the items, they classify them using a Venn diagram.

12. Seat students in a circle. Place a number of familiar items in the magic box and pass it around the circle until a bell rings, the music stops, or some other prearranged signal is given. Have the student holding the box draw out one of the items and identify it. The game proceeds until all the items have been removed. Also try this variation: Place items that were incorrectly identified in the center of the circle. When the box stops, the student holding it has the option of drawing an object from the box or choosing one from the center of the circle. The reward for correct identification is the opportunity to hold the object (and perhaps to play with it) during the course of the game.

Activities with Laminated Circles, Shapes, and Numbers

(See Chapter 12 for directions.)

Total Physical Response Commands

1. For giving commands at the beginning stages of learning, use short specific directions, such as:
   Take red!
   Touch red!
   Give me red!
   Sit down on red!
   Jump over red!
   Jump from red to blue!

Lay red on Mary's head, arm, leg, knee, hand, stomach, and so on.

Lay red under the chair, in front of the chair, beside, behind, left of, right of, and so on.

Take the colors of the German, United States, Puerto Rican (etc.) flag, and lay them on the flag.

Make the numbers 19, 21, and so on (by placing two numerals together).

2. "Clock Face": Lay numbers out in a circle to make a clock face; have students move large, laminated hands to tell time or lie down and make their own arms tell the time.

3. "Number Match": Pass out a set of numbers from zero to nine to each of two teams (or more, as class size suggests). Call (or have another leader call) a number; the first team whose "number" stands up gets a point; if more than one student stands, the team cannot win a point.

4. "Who Has It?" Use this at the end of an activity, when each student has either a number or a color. Tell the students to lay their number or color in front of them on the floor or hold them up so everyone can see. Set rhythm as for "Concentration": slap knees, clap hands, snap left fingers, snap right fingers. Ask a question in rhythm; have students answer in rhythm. If they cannot answer, either repeat the question or give the answer.

Teacher: Who – has – sev - en?

Students: (slap) (clap) Su - san.

Teacher: Loud - er (snap) (snap)

Students: (slap) (clap) Su - san!

This activity also works with using items from the magic box.

Activities with Floor Map (Shower Curtain Map)

(See Chapter 12 for directions for making a shower curtain map.)

1. Using the floor map, direct students to do the following:
   - Step from country to country or area to area or lay various parts of their own body on different countries.
   - Lay flags on the appropriate countries.
   - "Swim" in rivers, lakes, or oceans; "ski" in the mountains, and so forth.
   - Jump over rivers or borders.
   - Locate capitals.
   - Lay maps of political subdivisions on the larger map (as in a jigsaw puzzle).
   - Place mountains, major cities, or other geographical features on the maps. For example, direct students to put various sizes of colored plastic drinking cups and thick blue yarn on the map in order to indicate the mountains and rivers.
   - Place products on the region where they originate.
   - Trace routes from place to place using a toy car, boat, or train.

This kind of activity can make geographical and cultural concepts very concrete (see Figure 13.1).

2. Using a geometric grid or randomly placed numbers, students can be directed to:
   - Step from number to number or shape to shape
   - Toss beanbags or lay objects on various parts of the board
   - Perform on the board in response to commands
   - Lay vocabulary flash cards on various parts of the board
   - Perform other activities similar to those described for the floor map

Carol Meyer, from Bennington College, uses a shower curtain map for a number of geography activities in her Spanish classes. They would be adaptable to any language, with just a few changes. She posted these ideas to the Ñandu listserv in April 2002:

● **FIGURE 13.1**   Floor Map Activity

1. With the map itself you can ask students to go to a certain country, in stocking feet. I find that this is difficult, given the small size of some of the countries, so I prefer activity 2.
2. With the cutouts, I can give the students commands to go, pick up a country, and put it in its place.
3. With the cutouts, ask "What color is Chile?" and so forth.
4. With the cutouts, a student has a country that [he or she] describes, and the other students have to guess the country. As an alternative, the rest of the students can play "Twenty Questions" about the country the student is hiding (depending on the amount of language that the students have).
5. With the cutouts, give each student a country and have them form Central and South America. They can then describe their relationships using [the target words for] *south, north,* and so on.
6. With the cutouts, play "What's missing (from among the cutouts on the map)?"
7. With the cutouts students can compare the sizes of the countries, for example, Country X is twice the size of Country Y. Or you can use language like *bigger than, smaller than.* The teacher can ask, "How many countries can fit into Argentina, and which ones are they?" Any kind of compare and contrast activity

that has the students working with the countries will help to make the content memorable.

8. With the cutouts, have the students sort them into categories such as Central America and South America (North America if you include it), countries that speak Spanish and countries that don't, countries from which we import goods, and so forth, depending on the content studied.

Paper and Pencil Activities

Dot-to-Dot Puzzle   Modify a simple dot-to-dot puzzle by renumbering the dots randomly. Call out the numbers in the prearranged order for students to connect the dots to complete the puzzle. (*Note:* Be sure you have solved a copy of the puzzle for yourself, so you do not forget which numbers to call and in which order!) Success is measured by whether the completed puzzle looks as it is supposed to look! You can make this activity more challenging by adding several numbered dots to the puzzle that are not used in the completion of the picture. As a reading and writing exercise, write out the numbers in the target language—for example, *uno, tres, ocho.* Students can then solve the puzzle as an independent reading activity. A dot-to-dot puzzle can also be done as a partner activity with one partner calling out the numbers and the other partner drawing the lines to connect the dots. If at some point, the partner drawing the lines thinks that they know what the picture will be, they can dictate the sequence to the first partner to see if they are correct or not.

"Monsters"   Give each student a blank piece of paper and have them take out their crayons, pencils, or markers. Direct the students to write their names on one corner of the page and then to draw a head only. Then have the children pass their papers a specified number of times to the left or right (or front or back) and tell them to draw another part of the body (or of the face). Keep adding face and body parts and move the papers around after each new part has been drawn. The result is the product of listening comprehension and a series of works of "group art." As a variation, have the children take turns telling the class which parts of the anatomy to draw.

"List Bingo Game"   Have the students choose 5 or 6 words from a list of 8 to 12 previously learned vocabulary words written on the chalkboard, an overhead projector, or a handout. Have the students list the words they have chosen on a piece of paper. Then call out words from the large list in random order and have students cross off the words on their own lists as they are called. The first student to cross out all the words on her or his list is the winner.

Word Find (without word bank)   This activity incorporates places in a city with prepositions. The teacher creates a word find with the vocabulary, such as *bank, school, airport,* and so on, but doesn't include a word bank. These word finds are passed out to the students and the teacher has a large version taped to the board or has made a transparency to be placed on an overhead projector. The students begin looking for the hidden words.

When one student has found one, he or she "directs" the teacher and fellow students to find the word using appropriate direction verbs and prepositions. After playing as a large group, a new word find can be passed out and partners can work together to find the new places in the city. When one student finds a city word, he or she directs the partner to find it without showing his or her paper.

Activities with Playing Cards or Small Flash Cards

For the activities listed here, if you are using playing cards, remove the jacks, queens, and kings from the deck. Use only the the cards numbered one (Ace) to ten.

"Go Fish"   Have students play in groups of three or four. Each student receives five cards, and the remaining cards are placed in a pile in the middle of the group. The student to the left of the dealer begins by asking for a card from any other player, in the hope of finding a matching card to one in her or his hand. If the player has the card, she or he must give it to the player requesting it, and that player places the pair on the table (or floor) in front of her or him and receives another turn. If not, the player says "Go fish!" (or an equivalent phrase in the target language), and the first player draws a card from the pile. If the first player draws the card for which he or she asked, that player lays down the pair and receives another turn. The winner is the player who completes the most pairs.

Try this variation: The children seek to accumulate groups of four rather than two. German "Quartett" or French "Jeu de la famille" games are cultural examples of these games. The teacher can make sets of cards with groups of four, using whatever vocabulary the class needs to work on—for example, four chairs, tables, and so forth if the unit is the home; four hats, shoes, coats, and so forth if the unit is clothing. See suggestions for making these cards in Chapter 12.

"Ugly Monster"   This game is played like "Old Maid" but with an "Ugly Monster" as the extra card. Any category of vocabulary sets can be used.

Changing the Classroom Environment with Masking Tape

Masking tape can be used to create shapes, games, and imaginary settings on the classroom floor. Children might respond to such commands as, "Jump backward from the triangle to the square!" or "Sit down in the middle of the rectangle!" "Human Tic-Tac-Toe," "Hopscotch," and many other play environments can be created. Masking tape will peel off most floor surfaces, including carpet, without damaging them, provided the tape is removed promptly.

You might lead the class on an imaginary trip with the help of a large airplane (or boat or train) taped in outline to the floor. Other fantasy environments might include the floor plan of a house, an elevator with "up" and "down" and floor buttons, a map with rivers and mountains indicated. (See Chapter 9 for more details.)

"Tic-Tac-Toe"   Use masking tape to create a large "Tc-Tac-Toe" board on the floor. Make large Xs and Os out of laminated tagboard. Many variations are possible. Place different colors or numbers in the squares, and hand out smaller versions to the class. Call a color or number; the student who has it chooses the X or the O to place in the square, or sits on the square holding the symbol.

Variations on "Safe Tag"   In an open area of the classroom or the gymnasium, outline several rectangles on the floor using masking tape. Within each of these possible "safe zones" place a different color. The person who is "it" must begin and return to a designated spot. The game begins when you (or a child, later) call out "Go to (a color)!" As of that moment, the person who is "it" is free to tag anyone not touching the indicated safe zone. The first person tagged becomes the new "it." As soon as every player is touching the correct safe zone or there is a new "it," call a different color, creating a new "safe zone." The beauty of this fast-paced game is that it demands immediate recognition of vocabulary items.

As variations, (1) Tape different geometric shapes instead of just rectangles to the floor. (2) Give more complex commands, such as "Everyone wearing tennis shoes go to the blue!" or "Hop backward to red!" (3) Substitute numbers for colors and indicate the "safe zone" with numbers or with simple equations. (4) Use features of the classroom environment as "safe zones," such as the chalkboard, the door, and so forth.

"Side to Side"   This activity is for expressing preferences. The teacher places tape on the floor in three long vertical lines. She or he has cards with pictures of vocabulary such as food, sports, household chores, and so on. Students stand in a single line on the middle line of tape. They face the teacher, who is standing on a chair so that all students can see the picture well. The teacher asks, "Do you prefer bananas or strawberries?" He or she then holds up cards to the left and right and students move to the "side" they prefer. If students have no preference, don't care for either, or like them equally, they can stay on the center line. The teacher can either count the students on each side, ask further questions to particular students about strong preferences, if they have eaten that food that day or week, or if it is currently in their refrigerator at home. Students move back to the middle line for the next question and next pair of cards. As a variation, students can predict what the teacher's preference will be by choosing a side.

Games Focusing on Body Parts

"Living Statues"   Give commands to one student at a time, such as, "Put your left hand on John's right elbow and kneel on your right knee." Use a number of students (in a small class, the entire group) and build a "Living Statue" of class members connected to one another. As a final, interesting, and dramatic gesture, take a photograph with an instant camera and display it on the bulletin board. (Be careful to avoid "connections" that are potentially embarrassing, and avoid placing students together who have a strong antipathy for one another.)

It can be even more effective to have the rest of the students, who are not in the picture, be the picture takers with imaginary cameras.

"Body Collage"   Cut individual arms, legs, eyes, noses, mouths, and ears from magazines so there are many options for each child. Have students ask for their choice of individual body parts in the target language. They then glue them to construction paper and draw in their own heads, hair, torsos, and clothing. You or the students may label the creations, or give the students captions written on self-stick labels and have them select the appropriate label for each body part. As an alternative version for a comprehension emphasis, direct students to choose different body parts one at a time.

"Balloon Bounce"   Give each student a balloon; for younger children the balloon should be already blown up, but for older children blowing up the balloon could be part of the chain of commands used. Have the children toss the ball into the air on command, then continue to bounce it in the air, using various parts of the body as you direct: "Hit the balloon with the head, with the knee, with the elbow, with the back, with the little finger of the right hand." There is almost no sound from the children, so the listening opportunity is excellent. There is no winner or loser—the challenge of keeping the balloons in the air is sufficient.

"Doctor's Bag"   Students color photocopied instruments found in a doctor's bag: stethoscope, thermometer, Band-Aids, tongue depressor, reflex hammer, auriscope, and so on. The teacher laminates them if possible and puts them in the students' *"trousse de medecin."* Students bring in their favorite stuffed animal and tend to them as their patients. Teacher guides this TPR activity with commands such as: "Take the stethoscope and listen to the heart," "Put the stethoscope on its back and listen to it breathing," "Tell your patient to open its mouth and look at its throat," "Put a Band-Aid on its arm," and so on. Later the teacher can ask students to lead this activity.

"Finger Twister"   Marie Consuelo Lopez shared an interesting game for practicing colors and fingers on the Ñandu listserv:

> I pass out color wheels and tell the students that we will be playing *"Twister de dedos."* The students are immediately interested in this game. I begin by introducing the names of the different fingers in Spanish and then explain that I will tell them which color to put each finger on. The object of the game is to be able to put all fingers on all of the colors and keep them there. I begin by telling them to put their *pulgar* (thumb) on *rojo* (red). The students keep their thumb on the red section while placing other fingers on the sections as they are instructed to do so. We play the game several times and each time I speed the commands up. By the last time I am giving chain commands rather than individual commands. While playing the game I observe that the students' affective filters have gone down and they are focused more on the physical challenge than on the language.

Activities Related to Curriculum Content

Geography   Julie Barros described these activities for fourth-grade students on the Ñandu listserv. They are a good illustration of the idea that any of the games in this chapter can be used to bring any of the subject content areas to life.

> I just finished teaching the countries of Central America. We played, and still play, several games using a colored map of Central American countries (drawn on a shower curtain and colored in) labeling the countries first so that students learn where they are. Then I drew blank maps of Central America on index cards and colored in one country. I asked "*¿Donde vives?*" and the student had to stand on the country that he or she received and say "*Vivo en . . .*" Then we took the labels off to see how many the students could remember. The cards were also color coded with the shower curtain so that we could give hints such as, "*Nicaragua es azul. La Republica Dominicana es amarillo y es parte de una isla.*"
>
> We played a game using a song to the tune "This Is the Way We Wash Our Clothes": *asi asi camino, camino, camino* (This is how I walk), *asi asi camino por america central* (This is how I walk in Central America).
>
> We walk around the map singing this song until I clap. Then they stop and I pick a student and say "(child's name) *camina por Honduras.*" The student then has to walk through Honduras.
>
> We also played "*¿Qué pais tengo?*" We put the shower curtain map on the board and one student picks a country out of the bag. The students have to ask yes-or-no prepositional questions to find out what country it is. Of course I listed the questions on the board and went over them first. I used: *Está encima de, está abajo de, al lado de,* and also the locations east, west, north, and south (in Spanish) (also, *¿Es una isla?*).
>
> We also divided into three teams and had a timed race to see who could label the countries fastest. They loved that one too!

This same game could easily work with Francophone Africa, or the countries of the European Union.

The Compass Rose   Kathy Siddons teaches the Compass Rose in her Spanish classes with a lot of imagination, and she shared this strategy on the Ñandu listserv.

> In our district, "*la rosa naútica*" is taught in third grade in the regular classroom curriculum—not second. Therefore, I find that once the regular classroom teacher has covered the material, the reintroduction is very easy. My goal is to have the children experience the concept of north/south/east/west through a simulation.
>
> To review the directionals, I place four children as markers, holding signs for north/south/east/west in the correct spots according to the real compass—which takes some thinking as I am in eleven different classrooms daily in two schools! I display the Spanish flag and use Almirante Cristóbal Colón and his sailors as the main characters.

Colón marches in with great authority, holding a telescope under his arm and wearing a small Italian flag, and greets his marineros. Then he says, *"Marineros, miran al norte."* The children as sailors turn in that direction and receive commands from him to turn to the other directions. The children learn *"noroeste"* too. The children love it and beg to take a turn being Colón.

I transition from this simulation about directionals, to a similar scenario where the sailors experience different weather and physical conditions on board the carabelas. When it rains a lot, Colón says, *"¡Marineros, llueve mucho! Hay mucha agua en la carabela!"* and they have to bail water. When the weather is good, the sailors raise the sails and say, *"Hace buen tiempo. Almirante, tengo hambre."* When it is hot, they cry, *"¡Hace mucho calor! ¡Almirante, tengo sed!"* When it is foggy, *"¡Hay mucha neblina! ¡Tengo miedo!"* and someone rings a bell. When it is very windy, *"¡Hace mucho viento!",* the sailors hold on to the sides of the boat and pantomime being blown around. The children really ham it up here, of course.

The game character of this activity could be intensified by using cards or dice to change the weather arbitrarily on every turn.

Science and Art Activities

Science and Art Activities　Sara Palacio has used this project in grades 1 through 4 to help teach the science concept that water and oil don't mix. She shared it on the Ñandu listserv.

Marbling and Silhouettes Art Project

a. I buy two different colors of oil-based paint (I've used blue and green). Pour some of each color into a shallow pan covered with about 1–2 inches of water. Swirl the paint with a stick; it should float on top of water. Place a white piece of paper gently on top of water. Pull off. And you should have a cool swirly design. Let dry.

b. Have students cut out 3–4 different animal shapes on black construction paper— ocean animals whose names they have learned.

c. Glue on top of the marbled paper. You now have an ocean scene! This project can stand on its own, be framed by black construction paper, or serve as a cover to an Ocean Portfolio or Ocean Alphabet book!

I usually follow up the art activity with an Oil Spill Activity. I get some used motor oil and put it in some tubs, and I gather a variety of items found around the ocean: egg (hardboiled!), feathers, sand, fur (fake), hair, dirt, leaves, bushes, wood, and so on. Then the students work in small groups and test to see what happens to the items in the oil. It's a great vocabulary builder and motivational as well.

Variation on "Simon Says"

Variation on "Simon Says"　To learn the French mountain chains from smallest to largest, the class plays a variation of "Simon Says." Students have learned the names of the mountain chains and touch a part of the body to represent their altitudes: *Les Alpes* (head), *les Pyrénées* (shoulders), *le Massif Central* (waist), *le Jura* (knees), and *les Vosges* (toes).

When the students hear a phrase such as *"Je fais du ski dans les Alpes"* (I ski in the Alps), they may touch their heads. If they do not hear the key phrase and only the mountain chain, they must not move.

"Greater Than"   This is played like the popular card game "War." However, in this version of the game, the students are comparing the populations of the cities of France, Spanish-speaking countries of South America, neighboring countries of Germany, the length of rivers in China, the altitude of mountains in France, and so forth. Each student has the same deck of cards (10 to 20 cards) prepared by the teacher with the name of a city and population— cards can be easily photocopied on different colored paper then cut and put into envelopes to be passed out to students. Students with different color decks (easier to reassemble when they're mixed) play in pairs each taking one card from their decks, asking each other "Where do you live?," and both stating, "I live in _____." Then each card is placed on the table and populations are compared. The student with the larger city says, "Lyon is larger than Dijon" and takes the two cards. Next round could be with a new partner and the smaller city wins. The teacher provides additional game playing language appropriate for level of students. Later students could work together to put their cards in order smallest to largest.

The teacher can also use these cards by passing one card from the deck to each student or a pair. She or he reads off a population and student/pair with that card says, "It's my city," "I live in Lyon," or "We live there. It's Lyon." The teacher could also ask students from cities with populations greater than (or fewer than) a given number to stand. Students can also line up from smallest to largest by comparing populations on their individual card orally.

Action Games

"Command Chairs"   Give many commands in a row, sending students as a group all over the room touching doors, walls, jumping, and so forth. In the meantime, remove one chair, so there is one less chair than there are students. When the command "Sit down on your chair" comes, the students scramble for a chair and the one left standing is "out." The game goes on until the last person is "out." After the students are "out," they can assist you in giving commands to the rest of the class.

"Fast Corners"   One student stands at the front of the class and orally gives each corner a name such as *cat, dog, horse,* and *cow.* This student then turns and counts to 10, from 20 to 30, or in 10s up to 100. As that student is counting, the other students each choose a corner and moves to it before the count is up. The student counting then says the name of one of the corners and turns around. The students in the chosen corner then return to their seats or assist with naming corners and counting. This continues until only one student is left standing. When the number of students left is small, the corners can then be cut down to two. This will make the game go a bit faster, so that the game can begin again.

A Game for Hands—and Plurals   Silvia Pontaza posted this activity, adapted from the Global Child program, on the Ñandu listserv:

> To practice plurals, have students trace their hands on a piece of paper. Make sure both hands are traced on one side of the paper. Ask them to put their hands on the hands that are traced on the paper. When you say *"La mano"* they hold one hand up. Then you say *"El papel"* and they put the hands back on the papers. Then you say *"Las manos"* and they have to hold both hands up. To go back to the normal position (hands on hands traced), you say something like *"El papel,"* or *"Abajo,"* or whatever works for you. You play this game saying *la mano la mano el papel las manos . . .* They love when you try to trick them, and they listen for the difference when the word is plural (you can add *arriba la mano, arriba las manos, cierra el ojo,* or *cierra los ojos,* and so forth).
>
> Another option is to play "Duck, Duck Goose." Students are in a circle with both hands behind them. The person walking around touches each child's hand and says, *"La mano, la mano . . . "* When he or she touches both hands, saying *"las manos,"* that's when it's time to chase.

"Clothing Race"   Have the students form two (or more) teams. Give each team a pile of clothing, the names of which have been learned in the class. Tell the first person on each team to put on selected items of clothing. The list and order of clothing changes each time. The team members can help by reminding the contestant of items they have forgotten, but only in the target language. The first contestant to put on all the right clothing (and only the right clothing) wins a point for the team. (It is helpful if all the clothing is a little too large for the participants, so it can be easily put on and removed.) Lists of clothing can grow longer with successive rotations, to stretch the listening memory.

"Story in Third Person"   As a variation on a fantasy or virtual trip (see Chapter 9), give each person a role in a narrative, preferably with a prop for each character. As you read the story, the students act out their parts. If there is dialogue, the characters simply repeat their lines. This is most effective if there is considerable action and emotion involved, such as laughing or crying. (This technique can also be used with a familiar story, but it is perhaps most effective when only the teacher knows what will happen next, so everyone has to listen carefully.)

"Color Walk, Number Walk"   This is an adaptation of the old carnival "Cake Walk." Place laminated colored circles or numbers in a circular pattern on the floor and have one student stand on each circle or number. Turn on the cassette player or music keyboard and have the students walk around the circle until the music stops, when they will stop on the circle or number nearest them. Draw a color or a number out of a box and ask the class, "Who is standing on _____?" The student standing by that color or number wins and receives applause. You can set up more than one "Cake Walk" in the room so that the entire class can play at one time. As a variation, pictures or written vocabulary words could be used instead of numbers and colors.

Numbers Game from Austria   The class forms a circle around a student chosen as "it." That student is blindfolded and stands; the other children are seated. Give each student a number, beginning with 1. When the student who is "it" calls out two of the numbers, the children who have these numbers must trade places immediately and silently. Should their movements be detected by the student who is "it," she or he must try to catch one of the students and exchange places. If their movements go undetected and the two reach their new places safely, everyone in the circle claps hands (or calls out a predetermined phrase in the target language), and whoever is "it" tries once again by calling two other numbers. For variety, instead of numbers, use names of animals, colors, foods, or other current vocabulary.

"Going Fishing"   Place numbers, colors, or pictures of vocabulary on small paper fish with paper clips attached to them. Students "catch" their fish with a fishing pole that has a string and a magnet attached to the end. If the student names the number, color, or picture, that student may keep the fish; if not, the fish goes back into the "pond." For variety, attach individual words or familiar commands to the fish. If the student can label the correct object with the word or perform the command, that student may keep the fish. Or, if reading and speaking are well established, the student may repeat the word or give the command to another student in order to keep the fish.

"Follow the Footpath"   Place footprints in a variety of colors and sizes around the room, forming a path that the class can follow. Have the students proceed along the path by placing their own feet on one print at a time, naming the color or whatever might be posted next to the footprint, and then proceeding to the next print. The goal is to follow the path to its destination. Also try these variations: (1) Place pictures or symbols for familiar vocabulary on the footprints and tell the students they must name the vocabulary before proceeding further. (2) Point out prints of various sizes and have the students respond with their guesses as to who might have left such a print: the principal, a bear, a well-known young sibling of someone in the class, and so forth. The teacher might ask, "Do you think this print was made by the principal? By a bear? By Mr. Jacobson or by Tommy? By a lion or by a mouse?"

"Typewriter"   Have students holding letter flash cards arrange themselves to spell words, or have students holding numeral flash cards arrange themselves to form several-digit numbers. Distribute the flash cards to a group of students and then call out the word or the number they are to form. This can also be done with words to form sentences.

"Pierre's Clothes"   Have several students stand in front of the class, each of them holding a picture from a group of related vocabulary items. Begin the game by saying, "Pierre is going to school, but he doesn't have a cap." The student holding the cap responds by saying, "Oh, yes, he has a cap, but he doesn't have any shoes (picture held by another student in the group)." The student holding the shoes continues the game using the same pattern, and the game continues until one student misses after being called on or until a player mentions an item that no one has a picture of. If a student misses, he or she names another student from the class to take her or his place in the group in the front. The class may play this game with any type of vocabulary by changing the situation established in the "frame" sentence.

Another way to play this game is to give all students a card and tell them to stand in a circle with the picture facing outward so that the other students can see the picture. This activity begins and is conducted in the same manner, but the goal is to get through all the cards within a certain time. Students learn how important it is to listen to each other and to be attentive and ready to answer. The first round is to practice. In the next rounds, the students are timed and the goal is to improve their time each round. The importance of listening to each other is strongly reinforced. Hopefully this will carry over to all other activities and in turn, will improve the students' skills.

Calisthenics and Fitness Path   Use commands to lead the class in regular calisthenics movements, using many of the same exercises that they perform in physical education classes, if possible. This makes a good change of pace when students become restless, and as they become more verbal they may wish to lead the exercises themselves.

On the playground, in the gymnasium, or in a nearby park if there is one, prepare exercise stations at various points around a walking path, using illustrations to help students understand what they are to do in each case. For the first several times, lead the class around the course, directing the students to perform the activity for a specified number of times at each station. The stations need not all be typical of an authentic fitness path. Some possible stations might include the following:

- Do 10 jumping jacks.
- Touch your toes six times.
- Do four windmills.
- Join hands and form a circle.
- Take four large steps forward.
- Raise your hands high.
- Take six small steps backward.

Also, students might wish to prepare stations themselves, in small groups, and take responsibility for giving the directions when the class arrives at their stations. With older students, these stations might imitate activities from the Olympic games.

Aerobic Dance   Obtain an aerobic dance record or tape in the target language, preferably one with directions that are clearly pronounced and easy to understand. First teach the students the actions without music, and then spend a few minutes every few days doing the aerobic dance exercises with the music.

"Master Says/Maître dit"   Studying animals or pets with first-graders, I changed the game "Simon Says" into "Master Says." The first-graders loved becoming cute little puppies and did what their "master" said only when hearing *"Maître dit"* before the command. Various commands taught to the students were: fetch the ball, dig a hole, wag your tails, turn around, shake, sleep, pant, jump, chase your tail, come here, sit, stay, and others. Students took turns being the *"Maître"* and were later put into pairs to "train" their dogs and present to the class. Teacher and students respond to their "puppies" with a variety of praise phrases. A variation could be "Mother/Father Says" (chores: make your bed, vacuum, wash the windows, dust, iron, and so on, or bedtime routine: brush your teeth, wash your face, put on your pajamas, lie down, drink some water, pick up your toys, turn off the light, give me a kiss, and so on).

"Stand Up/Sit Down"   This is the only game where I divide the class into boy and girl teams/groups, as this is to work with adjectives. Each group sits on opposite sides of the room. Students listen for the form of the adjective spoken. If the girls hear the feminine form "sportive," they stand up and the boys remain seated. If the boys hear the masculine form "intelligent," they stand and the girls remain seated. If the adjective could be identified aurally as either masculine or feminine, such as *rouge, timide, fatigué,* both groups stand up. After the group has practiced and nearly mastered this activity, two chairs may be placed in the front of the room and one girl and one boy come up to play. Both may win a point at the same time by correctly sitting or standing when hearing the given adjective.

Alternatives include (1) Students must stand or sit by looking at the adjective form written on the card. Plural adjectives could then be implemented into the game. (2) This game can also be played dividing the class into "parent" and "child" groups. When the teacher states "Eat your peas *(Qui le dit?),*" the parents stand up. When the teacher states, "There's a monster under my bed *(Qui le dit?),*" the children stand up. If teacher states, "I love you" or another phrase that could be said by both parent and child, both groups stand! After some practice, two chairs may be placed in the front of the room and one "parent" and one "child" come up to play. Both may win a point at the same time by correctly sitting or standing when hearing the phrase that pertains to them.

"Ducks Fly/Birds Fly"   Have the players stand in aisles or beside their chairs. Have the person who is "it" (you may be "it") stand in front, facing the group, and call out "Ducks fly!" "Birds fly!" "Horses fly!" and so forth. When whoever is "it" names an animal that does fly, the players go through the motions of flying, raising their arms high above their heads and lowering them to their sides. When whoever is "it" names an animal that does not fly, they must not "fly." Anyone who "flies" when a nonflying animal is named, or anyone who does not fly when a flying animal is named, becomes "it" (or gives a forfeit).

"Scrambled Eggs"   In this activity the students exchange conversation with one student at a time. Once the conversation has been exchanged, the student who has initiated the conversation must sit in the second student's seat. The second student then must find a third student, initiate the same conversational exchange, and sit down in the third student's seat once the exchange is finished. The third student then finds another student, and so on. The activity is completed when each student is sitting in someone else's seat.

A variation is three or four students begin initiating conversations at once so that several students are talking at the same time and the activity progresses at a faster pace.

The conversational exchange could be on any topic. Here is an example:

1. *First student*   Hello my name is _____.
   My favorite _____ is _____.
   What's your favorite _____?
2. *Second student*   My favorite _____ is _____.

"Bear Hunt"   Sit in front of the class and narrate the following sequence in the target language, accompanying each statement with an appropriate motion. Have students copy the motions throughout. With each retelling, you might change the order or add new complications, in order to maintain suspense and surprise. Eventually the students will want to repeat the statements, echoing you, and some may even volunteer to lead the bear hunt.

"Let's go on a bear hunt!"

"Everybody ready?" (Class responds "Yes!" or "Yes, ready!")

"Let's go!"

"Look at the big woods!" (Make hand gesture for *big*, point to visual of woods.)

"We can't go around it!" (Make hand gesture for *around*.)

"We can't go over it!" (Make hand gesture for *over*.)

"We have to go through it!" (Make hand gesture for *through*, or *straight ahead*.)

(Slap hands on legs rhythmically to represent walking through the woods.)

"Look at the tall grass!" (Make hand gesture for *tall*; point to visual.)

"We can't go around it!" (Make hand gesture.)

"We can't go over it!" (Make hand gesture.)

"We have to go through it!" (Make hand gesture.)

(Rub hands together rhythmically, fingers pointing forward, to represent walking through the tall grass.)

"Look at the big lake!" (Make hand gesture for *big*, point to visual.)

"We can't go around it!" (Make hand gesture.)

"We can't go over it!" (Make hand gesture.)

"We have to go through it!" (Make hand gesture.)

(Move arms rhythmically in a swimming motion.)

"Look at that tall tree!" (Make hand gesture; point to visual.)

"Let's climb it!" (Pantomime hand-over-hand climbing motion.)

"Look for the bear!"

(Pantomime looking, hand over eyes, and moving head slowly from side to side.)

"Do you see a bear?" (Class responds, "No!" or "No, no bear!")

"Climb down the tree!" (Pantomime.)

"Look at the thick vines/bushes!" (Make hand gesture; point to visual.)

"We can't go around them!" (Make hand gesture.)

"We can't go over them!" (Make hand gesture.)

"We have to go through them!" (Make hand gesture.)

(Do rhythmic motion with arms, pushing vines or bushes aside.)

"Look! I see a cave!" (Make dramatic pointing motion.)

"Let's go inside!" (Pat cheeks with mouth open to get hollow sound.)

"It's cold [hug arms and shiver] and dark." (Pass hands over eyes.)

"Let's feel around with our hands." (Make groping motions with hands in all directions.)

"I feel something!" (Touch tentatively, withdraw hand, touch again.)

"It's furry!" (Stroke as with an animal.)

"And wet!" (Withdraw hand quickly.)

"IT'S A BEAR!" (Pantomime shock and horror.)

(Pantomime each of the actions from above in the reverse order, quickly, as the narration proceeds.)

"Run out of the cave!"

"Run through the vines/bushes!"

"Climb up the tree!"

"Look around!"

"Is that the BEAR?"

"Climb down the tree!"

"Swim the lake—fast!"

"Run through the tall grass!"

"Run through the woods!"

"We're home!" (Relax and slouch in the chair.)

"Lock the door!"

Reading Action Chain   This activity provides silent reading practice in a communicative setting. Give all students a card describing an action they are to perform and the action they will observe that triggers their response. (An example of a series of such cards follows.) Instruct students not to show their card to anyone else, to listen and watch very carefully, and to wait to start their action until at least two seconds after the preceding action has been completed. The object of the game is to proceed through the entire series without making mistakes and without leaving anyone out.

You will need to have a list of the actions in the correct order so that if the chain is broken, you will know what went wrong. If the chain breaks, the entire sequence starts over from the beginning, and the suspense grows.

This activity is easy to create, although it appears complicated; and it can be tailored to the personalities and special characteristics of each individual class and classroom. Write commands on 3″ × 5″ notecards, one command on the bottom half of each card; make enough cards so that there is one card for each member of the class. Place the cards in an interesting sequence, including a beginning, an end, and surprises. Then write the first half of each card in the form of a subordinate clause referring to the card just preceding it (see below). Type out the directions for reference during the game and for future use, mix the cards, and distribute them for the game. You can make the game more complicated and longer if you make two cards for each student in the class. This game is very flexible and can be adapted to any thematic unit.

If students have good writing skills, they often enjoy working in groups to create their own games. Group 1 might write the first five commands for the game and give a copy of its final command to group 2. Group 2 uses that command as the cue for the first command in its series, then gives a copy of their final command to group 3, and so on, until the commands of all the groups are linked into a complete chain.

Here is an example of a master plan for a reading action chain:

- After the teacher says "Begin," stand up and say "Good morning."
- After someone says "Good morning," go to the board and draw a triangle.
- After someone draws a triangle on the board, clap your hands slowly four times.
- After someone claps her or his hands four times, jump to the teacher's desk and back to your seat.
- After someone jumps to the teacher's desk and back to her or his seat, count backward from five to one.
- After someone counts backward from five to one, say "Blast off!" (appropriate target language equivalent) very loudly.
- After someone says, "Blast off!," stand up, turn around two times, and sit down.
- After someone stands up, turns around two times, and sits down, turn off the lights.
- After someone turns off the lights say "It's dark in here."
- After someone says "It's dark in here," turn on the lights.
- After someone turns on the lights, go to the teacher and shake hands.
- After someone shakes hands with the teacher, go to the board and write the numbers one to ten under the triangle.
- After someone writes the numbers one to ten on the board, jump four times beside your desk.
- After someone jumps four times beside her or his desk, go to the pencil sharpener, and sharpen your pencil.
- After someone sharpens her or his pencil, go to the board and erase numbers one to five.

- After someone erases numbers one to five from the board, meow like a cat.
- After someone meows like a cat, say "Stop that!"
- After someone says "Stop that!," erase the triangle and numbers six to ten from the board.
- After someone erases the triangle and numbers six to ten from the board, say "That's all—good job."

Guessing Games

"What's Missing?"   Place any number of objects, animals, colors, and so forth on a tray and make sure that all the students have a chance to see the contents of the tray clearly. Let them study what is there and explain that you will remove something and that they must guess what it is. Remove one item and hide it while the student's eyes are closed. Use a cover cloth for "peekers" (and to add a touch of drama). Repeat with a different item. Adapt the game to desired vocabulary. Overhead projector variations include placing small items with clearly identifiable silhouettes on the overhead projector. Turn off the projector, remove an item, and turn it on again. Have the students guess what is missing. Or make color or black-and-white transparencies of pictures or words. Cut them up and do the same activity by removing one item. With any of these variations, students love to have the chance to move items around on the overhead projector themselves.

"Hot and Cold"   One student leaves the room and something is hidden in the classroom. The student returns and must find the hidden object. The rest of the class gives clues as to the location of the object. When the student is near the object they say "Hot" and when the student is far away from the object they say "Cold" (or anything else you decide.) To play this game another way, have the students count slowly, or repeat the name of the hidden item, or repeat a rhyme or other memorized material as a group. When whoever is "it" comes nearer to the hidden object, the students recite louder; when that person moves away from the object, the students recite more softly.

"I'm Thinking of . . ."   Begin the game by saying, in the target language, "I'm thinking of a student in the third row." The students guess the names of students in that row, saying in the target language, "Is it Juan? Is it Marie? Is it Fritz?" until they guess the correct student. Continue with another student (The game can include more language if you choose from the whole class and describe a student a little at a time until the class guesses who it is. Of course, you will start with details that many students share and withhold the clear identifiers until the end.)

   You may play this game with clock times, numbers, objects in the classroom, cities in the target culture, or other suitable vocabulary. Examples of starter statements are: "I'm thinking of a time to meet my friend. What time is it?" "I'm thinking of a number between seven and thirty. What number is it?" "I'm thinking of a city in South America to visit on my vacation. What city is it?" Another way to enjoy this game is to allow the student who makes the correct guess become the leader for the next round. Also, students in small groups can develop descriptions of class members not in their group.

"How Many Do I Have in My Hand?"   Play this game with beans, buttons, seeds, marbles, candy-covered chocolates, coins from the target culture, or any other object that comes in handfuls. Reach into a container and take a number of the objects into your hand (not the one you write with), asking "How many _____s do I have in my hand?" The students guess the number and you write the guesses on the chalkboard. After the students have guessed 10 to 12 numbers, you and the students count the objects together and determine if anyone guessed the exact number—or who made the closest guess. For variety, play the game with a known number of items in the hand. With each guess the leader tells whether the guess is "more than" or "fewer than" the correct number. This adds the element of logical thinking to the game.

"Hot Seat/La Chaise Chaude"   This game is played as an entire class, but there are teams of 4 or 5 students. The teacher prepares picture or word cards of recently studied vocabulary. The first team sends one of its players to sit in the "hot seat" facing the remaining team members. The teacher stands behind the "hot seat" with picture or word cards. The team has one minute to describe in the target language as many pictures or words held above the hot seat to the seated student. Beginning students may use one or two word descriptions. For example, if the word is *bird,* team members might say, "flies," "little," "wings," or "animal." It's wise to brainstorm all the possible descriptions of one word before playing. When the student in the hot seat correctly identifies that picture/word, the card is given to him or her. At the end of that minute, the student counts the cards and tells the teacher, who tallies the points on the board. In the first few rounds, the students may use gestures along with oral descriptions. Then they must either sit on their hands using only oral descriptions or the hot seat must be turned so that the student may not see his or her teammates. To keep all students engaged, be sure they can all see the picture/word cards and are thinking of descriptions that they might use during their turn. Also tell them that they may use a clue/description from another team for a word that has not yet been identified. It's fun to put the teacher in the hot seat sometimes!

"Word Association"   The idea for this game was found at http://www.lingolex.com/ userpages/Ernie.html. The teacher prepares a bag full of recently studied vocabulary words from a thematic unit. One student starts the game by pulling a card from the bag and reading the written word or naming the picture on the card. He or she then states a word that is associated with that first word. Here is an example of what a beginning class who is studying animals and habitats might say:

Student A (reads the word or states the name of the picture on the card): *Dog*

Student A: Tail

Student B: Feathers

Student C: Duck

Student D: Swim

Student E: Fish

Student F: Lake

Student G: River

Student H: Water

Student I: Milk

Student J: Cow

Student K: Farm

"What Am I?"   The idea for this game was found at http://www.lingolex.com/userpages/Ernie.html. The teacher writes random nouns on Post-it notes and places a Post-it on each student's forehead. The students much circulate amongst themselves asking yes/no questions until they have figured out which word they have on their foreheads. In addition to random nouns, the names of famous people, places, or events can be used. The teacher should model this activity, particularly modeling a variety of questions by placing one of the Post-it notes on his or her forehead and asking the students yes/no questions.

"What's Behind You?" (Memory Game)   The idea for this game was found at http://www.lingolex.com/userpages/Ernie.html. The teacher instructs the students to remain looking forward and asks them to recall what is behind them. The students may answer with the names of classmates, furniture, the decor of the room, items on the walls, counters or tables, and so on. The teacher may ask the students to provide more details for the items they remember. She or he might also ask what they can remember about the street outside the school—for example: *Teacher:* Think about the street outside the school. What can you remember? *Student:* There are some trees . . . *Teacher:* Are there trees on both sides of the street? (and so on). In a variation of this game, a student is asked to close his or her eyes and describe his or her neighbor's appearance.

"ESP Guessing Game"   Penny Fields shared this guessing game on the Ñandu listserv:

> The ESP Game is something I got from someone on either this or another listserv, so I will not take credit for it. It is a good game for reviewing different vocabulary. Since I have small picture flash cards for all the units I teach, I just use those. To play, your class should be in groups of four students. You start with a category of vocabulary—for example, colors. Sight unseen you select one of the flash cards and set it aside. Give the students just a short time to decide what color they think the card is. I usually have six groups so I number 1–6 on the board. In turn, you ask each group to report their choice. It is OK for several groups to have chosen the same thing. I write their choice on the board, under their number. When all groups have reported, I reveal the card and give a point to the group or groups who were correct. If no one guessed correctly, no points are awarded. We usually do several rounds with the same vocabulary and then change topics. At the end of the game you count up points for each group and the group with the most points has the best ESP (extrasensory perception).

"Hide and Seek in the School"   This game is a version of "Clue." Penny Fields described this guessing game on the Ñandu listserv. She also gives several stages of activities that work up to the game itself.

I also teach a unit on places in the school to third-graders. My students love to hide a person in a room and work with a partner to guess where he is. I have prepared a sheet [that lists the various rooms in which] we teach (about 7 or 8) and I have two versions, one with the words and one without. In the early stages, I give them the one with the words and they each put the paper behind their folder and hide the figure of a boy or girl. They take turns guessing—"*¿Está en el gimnasio* (Is he/she in the gym)?" or "*¿Está en la biblioteca* (is he/she in the library)?" To tie in our clothing items I will put one clothing item (a small flash card) in a room (behind one of the rooms on a poster in the front of the room). The kids close their eyes while I hide the item and then they must guess where it is.

But the one that they really like is a version of "Clue." I have prepared a sheet with the pictures of the school people at the top, the pictures of the rooms in the middle, and the articles of clothing at the bottom. . . . Each student has a sheet. I pick a small flash card from each category and put them in envelopes on the chalkboard tray. Then the kids have to give me a sentence, i.e., "*La profesora está en el cuarto de baño con los pantalones.*" ("The teacher is in the bathroom with the trousers.") The kids have piles of chips and they cover the incorrect pictures. This keeps them from repeating items already given. If one of the items is correct, I display it on the chalkboard. We keep going until the "mystery" is solved.

New Games and Activities

"People to People" Follow these simple rules:

1. Establish a rhythm and have the students snap or clap the beat, as you say, four times, "People [snap] to people [snap]" (translate into desired language).
2. Call out "Hand [snap] to hand [snap]" four times.
3. Have each student find a partner and place one hand on the partner's hand, repeating the action four times in the rhythm you set.
4. Return to "People to people" and have the students clap and move around four more times.
5. Call out another body parts combination (elbow to elbow, nose to nose, knee to knee) and have the students match up with a new partner. The game continues until all the body parts have been practiced, in a variety of combinations. Be careful not to suggest combinations that will embarrass the students (see Figure 13.2).

"Quick Lineups" Have the students line up by month of birthday, height, color of shirt, pants, shoes, hair, and so forth.

"Animal Calls" Give the students the name of an animal whose "call" they have learned, with two students for each animal. They find their partners by making their animal sounds, and then complete a language task. This could also be done by having students

● **FIGURE 13.2**   New Games—
People to People

sing a familiar song or say a familiar phrase and form groups with all of those saying or singing the same thing.

Board Games

Teacher-created board games are an enjoyable option for reviewing many aspects of language learning. Any simple children's board game can serve as a model, with circles or squares winding around the board from a starting point to a destination. Players advance with the throw of a die, or according to directions on cards. Some game boards may also be downloaded from the Internet. Here are two descriptions of teacher-created board games that were shared on the Ñandu listserv.

Jean Pacheco uses this board game with very young students:

One of the games that I use with kindergarteners is the game "Waggles." Each student has a game board that has been run off on cardstock and laminated. The game board shows a worm. They work in partners and each group of two has a die. The partners take turns throwing the die and saying the number shown in the target language. Then the partner covers that number on her or his worm with a unifix cube. Some numbers are repeated several times on the worm. If the number on the die is already covered on the worm, the player loses the turn. The first partner to cover up all of the numbers on their worm is the winner. This is a good way to practice the numbers 1 through 6.

Bettina Hoar uses a math and numbers game called *la serpiente de los números* (the number snake) for fourth-grade students (see Figure 13.3). The game proceeds like this:

For listening comprehension, read out preselected numbers and have students put the numbers in the boxes that make up the body of the snake. The objective is to see who gets the final tally answer correct after all the mathematical computations indicated within the body of the snake have been completed. This activity changes each time the teacher dictates a different set of numbers for the students to write into the boxes that make up the snake. At the beginning of the year, Bettina uses the numbers 0 to 20, but later continues with numbers up to the hundreds. She has also changed the plus and minus signs to multiplication and division for a much more complicated version of the activity. Sometimes rather than the teacher dictating the number, the students pick numbers out of a hat and dictate the numbers to the class.

Making a Game Board   Kathy Siddons offered some good advice on the Ñandu listserv:

When I create a new game I start work on a blank sheet of 8½″ × 11″ white paper. I sketch things out first with a light pencil and then I go over the pencil outlines with a

NOMBRE:_____ FECHA:_____

La serpiente de los números::

● **FIGURE 13.3**   La Serpiente de los Números

Source: Reprinted by permission of Bettina Hoar.

narrow black marker, using correction fluid as needed to make things perfect. Sometimes I use graph paper with those light blue lines if I really want things to line up exactly by hand. Then I photocopy the final black and white sheet. Then I color in the outlines well and add colorful clip art wherever needed to jazz things up and make it interesting for young children. (Sometimes I am able to complete everything with Microsoft Word and the "AutoShapes" features with color added.)

I then go to a retail copy store and get several copies made, enlarged to 11″ × 17″. This size fits nicely on a large piece of oaktag (lightweight poster paper). I use rubber cement for "glue," let it dry, and then laminate before the children use them. I make enough boards so that there are small groups of students (best size of the group is three) at each game board. One student sits in front of the game board and the other two are on the right and left sides of the game board so everyone can see clearly. I try to use small manipulatives that complement the game theme for the individual game pieces that the students move around. But the children's real favorites are small plastic fruits and animals, and "plain old beans or buttons."

However, before the game is played by everyone, I devote class time to having a mini-demo with a small, hand-picked group of children surrounded by the rest of the class. And I use www.puzzlemaker.com to make exercises to reinforce the necessary vocabulary and symbols that were introduced beforehand, several days before the actual "game day." ("Puzzlemaker" now allows teachers to "file" their created exercises for access later.)

A Potpourri of Additional Games and Activities

Common Games

Relay racing

"Charades"

Spelling bee

"Hangman"

Mystery guest

"Twenty Questions"

Auction

"Simon Says"

Miscellaneous Activities

Go on a treasure hunt or scavenger hunt.

Draw favorite foods on paper plates.

Draw and cut out items for a pretend store.

Draw a community map and label it.

Participate in a play with stick puppets or props.

Do folk dancing.

Make simulated target country currency.

Make rubbings of coins from the target culture.

Make murals.

Make picture dictionaries.

Plan a menu.

Collect simple recipes for culturally appropriate foods.

Cook specialties from the target culture.

Go on a field trip.

Write a class poem.

Dress dolls in native costumes.

Model animals or other figures with clay.

Make clocks.

Make paper bag puppets, dolls, and/or masks.

Draw faces on paper plates to show feelings.

Make mobiles on many topics: five senses, food groups, pets, family, and so on.

Make a home or school floor plan.

Pantomime feelings and/or illnesses.

Make or wear costumes from other countries to learn about clothing.

Make dioramas in a shoebox.

"Shop" from a target language catalog.

● Using Puppets in the Early Language Classroom

Few teaching aids in the elementary school are as versatile and appealing as puppets and stuffed animals. Puppets can take on the role of personalities otherwise not present in the classroom, such as an adult male if the teacher is female, a person who is much older or younger than members of the class, a foreign visitor, a pet, or a special friend to all. A puppet can serve as an alter ego for the teacher, performing exaggerated or foolish actions that the teacher can react to or build on. Puppets can become the second fluent speaker in a conversational exchange, modeling the kind of interaction that the students can someday hope to achieve. Sometimes a puppet becomes the "difficult student" who can't do anything right, or who repeatedly gets into trouble by forgetting to obey the rules. These personalities make all class members feel proud of what they know and how they behave, and the puppet misbehavior gives the teacher a chance to model the rules in a very effective way—and the consequences of breaking them.

Because puppets can be so colorful and often have such distinctive personalities, they provide the ideal subject for descriptions that go beyond simple clothing, size, and colors to include disposition, family, and imagined background. The puppet can also take on the role of the teacher, modeling the process of role reversal for the class and encouraging the students to try being the teacher. While the puppet is the teacher, the actual teacher can demonstrate actions or behaviors that will later be expected from the class (see Figure 13.4).

A puppet is an ideal foil for many mini-dramas that help to create a meaningful classroom context. One favorite puppet character, a colorful frog with a tongue that can be made to pop out of its opened mouth, helps to teach a class to say "please" in the following situation:

● **FIGURE 13.4** Puppets Are Useful Tools

Teacher: (holds up frog as if talking very seriously to it) "Show us your tongue, Mr. Frog!"

Frog: (shakes its head)

Teacher: (pleadingly) "Please?"

Frog: (shakes head)

Teacher: (more emphatically) "Please?"

Frog: (shakes head vehemently)

Teacher: (even more urgently) "Please? PLEASE?"

Frog: (shakes head almost violently)

Teacher: (conspiratorially to class) "You say 'please.'" (Implying, "Maybe he'll listen to you.")

Class: "Please!"

Frog: (shakes head less emphatically)

Teacher: (to class, in a stage whisper) "Say please—louder."

Class: "Please!"

Frog: (shakes head again)

Teacher: (to class, in a stage whisper) "Say 'please' twice."

Class: "Please, please!"

Frog: (pauses, looks at the class, shows the tongue)

Teacher: (to frog, beaming) "Thank you, Mr. Frog!"

In any such exchange it is always important for the teacher to play the "ham," overacting from beginning to end.

Students, as well as teachers, enjoy working with puppets and bringing their personalities to life. In early stages, the desire to hold a puppet or a stuffed animal can motivate even a very shy student to tell the teacher or a classmate, "Please give me the frog." In one popular activity, the teacher draws puppets, stuffed animals, and other items from a magic box or from a large bag and hands them to students who volunteer to hold them. When it turns out that there are not enough items to go around, the students are invited to request them from one another, using the phrase the teacher has already used dozens of times in class to collect objects after a circle activity: "Please give me the _____." A lively exchange of puppets and animals inevitably results, all triggered by language use.

In certain activities the puppet can "take the place" of the student, just as sometimes a puppet takes the teacher's place. Many students who are hesitant about speaking in class will do so much more easily if they are speaking through the new personality of a puppet, especially if the puppet has an established classroom personality to maintain and if all class members are familiar with the routines in which the puppets take part. Some class periods might begin with the call for volunteers (in the target language, of course): "Who would like to be Mr. Frog today? Who would like to be Schnick-Schnack, the witch?" As students develop more speaking skills and come to know their puppet friends well, they may wish to work together to plan conversations between the puppets, or even short puppet plays.

On the Ñandu listserv, Leigh An Gilson has contributed her ways to work with a puppet at the beginning of the year.

After I introduce some basic vocabulary at the beginning of the year (this is my students' first experience taking a language), I tell the students that I have a friend that only speaks Spanish. I find myself talking to the puppet because I really play up the fact that my puppet doesn't speak English. I work my way through the class and try to have the puppet develop a connection with as many students as possible. [For example, here's how I involve my puppet in classroom routines]:

- My puppet Leo usually has a crush on one of the girls, and one of the students is the "go to" when it comes to dancing or whatever.
- Leo participates in all of the games, songs, and classroom activities.
- The funniest part about my puppet is that I think I sound like Elmo in Spanish when I am playing the part of the puppet.

I have had mostly positive experiences with my students when I use the puppet.

Sources of Puppets

Puppets can be obtained from commercial sources, or they can be teacher made or created by the students in the class. A few puppets that specifically reflect elements of the target culture are especially precious participants in the class, but any puppet with personality is a good choice. It is wise to avoid choosing puppets with high commercial visibility, such as those representing popular cartoon characters, so that students are free from prior associations and can participate fully in the imaginary lives of their friends in the language class.

Treatment of Puppets

When we invest puppets or other props in the class with personality and "feelings," we are creating an illusion that can be very powerful. This illusion can build a magical atmosphere in the classroom and serve as an important support for student learning. In order to sustain the illusion, it is important to treat these "personalities" with respect, even when they are not the focus of attention. At the end of an activity, for example, the puppet or other prop should be placed carefully in a special spot, sometimes referred to as a puppet tote, rather than being dropped carelessly onto the desk or the floor. When we take our creatures and our mini-dramas seriously, they are more likely to be meaningful and memorable to our students.

Using Exaggeration

A very small comb or tiny sunglasses might be hidden in an egg or in a magic box or somewhere else in the room. The exaggeration lends a sense of excitement and enjoyment to a "seek-and-find" activity. In a Gouin Series or a TPR sequence in which a student goes to the mirror to comb her or his hair, using a huge comb adds humor to the activity. A regular comb or an imaginary comb does not have the same appeal. When an activity is repeated with the added factor of exaggeration, it becomes a new activity for the class, and the students will participate with enthusiasm.

● Songs in the Curriculum

Music is one of the most appealing and effective entry points into a new language and culture. When used for background or listening experiences, music from the target culture adds to the authenticity of the language setting. Songs learned in the target language have the double benefit of giving students experience with an important dimension of the target culture and helping them to internalize the sounds, the vocabulary, rhythms, and structures of the new language. Students can often sing with a better accent than they can speak with at first.

Songs can play an important role in every unit and every class period. They are most effective when they are an integrated part of the curriculum, selected for their relationship to all of the activities and vocabulary in a class period and not regarded as an add-on or time-filler.

Choice of Songs

Choose songs with a vocabulary that is limited and compatible with the language being used in the classroom so that the words and concepts in the song reinforce or introduce material used for many other activities in the curriculum. Some children's songs from the target culture have a greater vocabulary load than children in the first several years of an early language program can manage.

Choose songs with a limited musical challenge, especially in the primary grades. A song that is musically very difficult will require considerable time just to learn the music, and the language objectives will be overshadowed. Consult with the music teacher about the skills of a specific class, but in general be aware that a simple song moves stepwise from note to note, rather than including wide melodic leaps, and it should have a limited range of notes from low to high. The rhythm should be straightforward and repetitive. Even when they are very simple, songs should be interesting in both melody and rhythm. Also, the topics for songs should be within the experiences of the students in the class and of real interest to them.

Select songs that have a potential for actions, dramatization, rhythm accompaniment, or performance (such as a round or canon). Children in elementary school grades have great difficulty singing rounds, but they participate enthusiastically in songs accompanied by actions, and the actions help students remember the words and their meanings.

Especially in the early stages of instruction choose songs that are highly repetitive in their text, rhythm, and melody. It is also very helpful to use songs that have a refrain.

As a teaching strategy, you can introduce the refrain first, so that as the verses are learned the singers can always return to something familiar when they reach the refrain.

The best song choices are those that are popular in the cultures of the target language, because they reflect the target culture and provide students with an experience in common with native speakers. Songs translated from English have the advantage of familiarity, but they lack cultural authenticity.

Teaching a Song

Teachers do not have to be solo singers to be effective in presenting a song to their students. If teachers know a song, they can present it to the class. A less-than-perfect voice can be an especially good model for students, because it is easier for them to identify with, and even shy singers may feel that they can safely participate.

Some highly repetitive songs that accompany games or dramatic play can be presented informally, with the teacher singing alone at first. Students, especially at the elementary school level, are motivated to participate in both the activity and the singing, and they often learn the words and melody of the song with little formal teaching.

Middle school learners may seem reluctant to sing, but they can often be enticed by an engaging contemporary song that is popular in the target culture. They often respond well to hearing a recording of the song while reading the text for the song. One good strategy for learners at this level is to give them the text with blank spots for significant vocabulary that they should be able to recognize (a variation on a Cloze procedure). They will listen to the words more carefully as they try to fill in the blanks and will eventually learn the song quite well.

The students will also be drawn into viewing video clips of these songs. The video clips of many contemporary songs as well as traditional songs in the target language can often be found on YouTube or the singers' websites. A website for many contemporary French songs with the French subtitles is http://www.youtube.com/user/clipsenFLE. Creating and filming their own video clips of songs is an extension activity that will demonstrate the students' understanding of the lyrics and motivate those who may not feel comfortable as singers.

In most cases, however, especially with older learners, systematic teaching of the song results in the most efficient learning.

The teaching of a song will proceed more smoothly if a careful sequence is followed:

Step One—Prepare the Students   Prepare the students by telling them what the song is about, preferably in the target language, making heavy use of visuals and gestures. Motivate the students to learn the song by sharing something about the setting of the song, the possibilities for actions or dramatization, or when or how it is sung in another country. Play a recording or sing the entire song so that students know what they are working toward. Note that some recordings made by children's choirs in the target culture are pitched so high that they cannot comfortably be used to provide an accompaniment for classroom singing, even though they may be very successful in motivating the activity.

Step Two—Go through the Words Go through the words to make sure the students understand them, or at least that they understand the key words necessary for singing the song meaningfully and with enjoyment. Have the class listen for vocabulary they already know, and ask them to recall the context in which they have used it before. For example, if there is a vocabulary item they know, they can recall a song, game, or situation in which they used it and perhaps some of the things they know about the item. This helps learners to appreciate the cumulative nature of language acquisition and to listen for known vocabulary and meanings even in new material. Place new vocabulary in context and illustrate with gestures and visuals, using English only as a last resort. There should be very little new vocabulary in any new song, as most of it should have been introduced in other contexts several days before you introduce the song.

Step Three—Speak the Song Line by Line Speak the song line by line and have the students repeat the words. This step may be skipped, depending on the nature of the group, the degree to which the language is already familiar, and the difficulty of the song.

Step Four—Sing a Line at a Time Sing the song a line at a time and have the students sing it back. Practice each line several times, until the students can sing it independently. Then practice it two lines at a time (for a song that has about four lines), and then put the entire song together.

Four lines of a song is a good amount to teach during a single class period. If the song is longer and if it has a refrain, teach the refrain first, so that there is a sense of closure even though the entire song cannot be completed in one day.

Step Five—Add Rhythmic Accompaniment After the students have learned the song and enjoy it, begin to add rhythmic accompaniment such as clapping, finger snapping, foot stamping, or hand shuffling. Use Orff and rhythm instruments to make the background even more sophisticated. Consult the music teacher for additional suggestions.

If the song includes motions, teach them together with the words and the music; learning each part of the song will reinforce learning the others. If the song can be used for a game or dramatic play, the students can use it for its real purpose as soon as they have learned the words and music thoroughly.

If the song is a round, perform it first with the class taking one part and the teacher the other. Then divide the class into two parts, then three or more, as the round dictates. Rounds are especially satisfying when they end on a chord rather than just by having groups drop out at the end. If the first group holds the final note and the second group holds the note at the end of the next-to-last phrase, and so on, then the final sound is sometimes very impressive.

Step Six—Create New Verses for the Song After the song has become familiar, students often enjoy creating their own verses for a song. Lauren Schaffer of Portland, Oregon, uses Matt Maxwell's song "Café Crocodile" in this way. Her students brainstorm other animals not mentioned in the song and create additional lines to fit into the song's rhythm and structure, incorporating old and new vocabulary. This activity is similar to student creation of pattern books based on well-loved stories, and it could be extended into a writing activity in much the same way.

Step Seven—Enjoy Singing!　Enjoy singing a growing repertoire of lively, interesting songs with students in your classes!

Here are some suggestions if you consider yourself to be a nonsinger:

- Ask a friend or an advanced student in your language to record the song for you, line by line, just as you will teach it.
- Use an electronic keyboard; program the melody or have someone do it for you; play the melody line by line in class.
- Use a tape or CD that comes with a songbook and play the song line by line during the teaching phase.
- Play the melody on a recorder or another instrument.

Don't Sing? Won't Sing? Try Chants and Raps

Rhythmic speech has many of the same benefits as song for making language memorable and enjoyable. Almost any content or occasion can find its way into a chant. Here are a few examples.

Lois Ann Folliard uses this chant when her French students do something special:

Fabuleux! (arms cheering in the air)

Fantastique (arms cheering in the air)

Excellent (arms cheering in the air)

Trés bien (clapping the two syllables)

Bravo (clapping the two syllables)

Lynn Sessler uses a Japanese chant to reward her students for good performance:

Yoku dekimashita.

Yoku dekimashita.

Shu goy! Shu goy!

Here is a German chant to celebrate something well done:

Toll! Toll! (Clap, clap)

Prima! (rap on the table)

Toll! Toll! (clap, clap)

Das ist ausgezeichnet! (wave hands in the air)

Rita Gullickson developed the following chant to introduce her unit on the Columbian exchange. It is accompanied by finger snapping and gestures.

1. Cristóbal
   Cristóbal Colón
   pidió permiso
   permiso de navegar.
   La reina Isabela
   dijo que ¡no!
   El rey Fernando
   dijo que ¡no!
   Cristóbal Colón
   dijo ¡ay caramba!

2. Cristóbal
   Cristóbal Colón
   pidió permiso
   permiso de navegar.
   La reina Isabela
   dijo que ¡si!
   El rey Fernando
   dijo que ¡no!
   Cristóbal Colón
   dijo ¡ay caramba!

3. Cristóbal
   Cristóbal Colón
   pidió permiso
   permiso de navegar.
   La reina Isabela
   dijo que ¡si!
   El rey Fernando
   dijo que ¡si!
   Cristóbal Colón
   dijo ¡bravo!

This chant in Italian was developed by Italian teachers in Ohio:

Pasta! Pasta!
Chi mangia la pasta?
Tutti! Tutti!
Alti! Bassi!
Biondi! Bruni!
Tutti mangiano la pasta!

Pizza! Pizza!
Chi mangia la pizza?
Tutti! Tutti!
Italiani! Americani!
Francesi! Cinesi!
Tutti mangiano la pizza!

This French chant is recited to a marching rhythm:

À gauche
à droite
à gauche
à droite
J'ai mal au dos
J'ai mal aux pieds
Zut alors j'ai mal au nez!

À gauche
à droite
à gauche
à droite
J'ai mal au ventre
J'ai mal au genou
Zut alors j'ai mal au cou!

This Spanish chant could be a nice review of clothing vocabulary—with variations, for any other set of related vocabulary items:

Me pongo el sombrero.

¿Qué te pones tú?

Me pongo el suéter.

¿Qué te pones tú?

Me pongo los zapatos.

¿Qué te pones tú?

(Go on to other clothing items.)

Raps and chants are contagious. Many of them start out in an echo form, in which the teacher says a line, usually with body motions and snapping fingers or clapping, and students echo the line. It isn't long before the rhythm carries the chant or the rap and everyone is performing together. When introducing the chant, it is important to keep the rhythm going throughout, rather than stopping at the end of each line. Repetition will help students pick up all the words, and the rhythm will make the experience fun.

Some teachers make chants out of vocabulary words themselves—perhaps representative foods from a certain layer of the food pyramid could become a chant:

> Milk, milk, ice cream, yogurt
>
> Cheese, cheese, (clap) cottage cheese.
>
> Buttermilk, buttermilk, yum, yum, yum.

● Craft Activities

Students enjoy creating crafts that reflect the target culture, as well as participating in other art-related experiences. These activities sometimes challenge the teacher to develop new areas of vocabulary and to perfect the skills of giving directions and modeling. The art activity is an extension of the lesson or unit, not a vacation from it, so planning needs to include both the language that will be used and practiced and the craft activity itself.

A number of challenges await the teacher who plans an art or craft activity for the early language classroom. Because class periods are short, it is difficult to complete an activity of any complexity within a single class period. Children of different ages differ greatly in their ability to handle tasks like gluing, cutting, and assembling projects, and it is wise to check with a classroom teacher about the feasibility of an intended project. We always have to keep in mind that the art or craft project is an occasion for using the target language and not allow the complexity of the project to overshadow the language objectives.

Kathy Siddons, Spanish teacher at Goodwin School in Storrs, Connecticut, manages to do successful projects with her second- through fourth-grade students in 15-minute classes, and she has learned how to accomplish this very efficiently. She shared this advice on the Ñandu listserv:

> The more I teach FLES [Foreign Language in Elementary Schools], the more strongly I feel about giving children hands-on experiences of creating their own projects to reinforce what's taught in the classroom.
>
> 1. Pre-cut as much as possible! Super-large paper cutters are wonderful, since large sheets of paper generally cost less in bulk. Also invest in some really good, sharp scissors and don't be afraid to cut several sheets of construction paper at a time. Just trace the pattern on the top sheet only and cut away at six or more sheets.

Your cutting doesn't have to be perfect, you know. Pre-measure exactly what size you need and order/cut accordingly.

2. Copy designs right onto construction paper instead of plain copy paper. We have a copier that makes wonderful copies onto construction paper, fast and inexpensively. The "art" project will last longer and seem more special than on plain paper. White construction paper works very well here.

3. Always allow some part of the project to be designed [the students'] own way so you won't end up with cookie-cutter projects. Offer different colors of paper or a choice of texture or placement. One project I did called "La Flor Multicolor" was a flower in a pot with different colors of petals. The children had to color the petals according to the word in Spanish that appeared on the petals. But the children added a disc with a paper fastener in the center that they colored the way they wished, and they put designs on their pots that made each flower look completely different. (We did this the first day of spring.)

4. Use commercially made paper trimmers, sheets from designed notepads, paper fasteners, stickers, "Scotch" invisible tape, and staples to eliminate the mess and drying time of gluing. I have successfully used PURPLE glue sticks, however. These allow the children to see exactly where they have placed the glue so they don't use more than they need. Too much glue takes forever to dry, and nothing is worse than having beautifully done projects stuck together in piles! I ask the classroom teachers to share their staplers or tape dispensers for project day. I borrow a cafeteria tray and collect all I can. I fill them with staples/tape and carry my tray [from] class to class. The children love to do their own stapling and taping. (I am even contemplating trying a project with the use of double-sided tape.) Prompt return of staplers and dispensers to the teachers is necessary to keep good relations going. To keep track of my own, I put special toucan stickers or "flags" of colored masking tape on my own supplies.

5. Regarding trimmers, notepads, and stickers, take your time to order and peruse catalogs. Some educational firms offer a wide, wonderful selection of cleverly designed trimmers, notepads, and stickers. Working with themes in your curriculum helps you to eliminate unusable ones and think about how to use ones that go along with your theme creatively. Don't shy away from "office-type" stickers at office supply stores. I use the large dot stickers available in many colors that are ordinarily used for files. Also, take the time to estimate just how much of a particular material you will need; you don't want to be short, and you don't want to spend money if not needed. If the catalog doesn't offer the information you need, such as size and count, call the Customer Service Department.

6. Days before the "art" project, ask the classroom teachers to have the children super-ready on project day—desks cleared, pencils sharpened, crayons, scissors ready, etc. A cute reminder in their mailboxes on the morning of project day is a nice touch, too. Plan to stay a few minutes extra if possible to help in any cleanup. With pre-cutting the cleanup is really minimal, which classroom teachers appreciate.

7. Use pre-cut shapes from a commercial source, or make your own using a die-cut machine, available in many teacher work centers or resource centers.

8. Colored masking tape and crepe paper for your "art" are inexpensive, quick, and easy ways to add color and different textures. Consider also using the more expensive "fadeless" construction paper, which doesn't tear easily and cuts beautifully, for special situations and crafts.

9. Work out the sequencing of construction of the project ahead of time. Make several mock-ups (for display) at adult speed. I even make a super-size one for display. Time it and then double or triple the time, depending on grade level. I find if I can't make up the project in less than five minutes, then it's not suitable for a fifteen-minute class. (Sometimes a simple enlargement of the pieces will speed things along for little hands.) If your schedule allows, let your first class of the day be "guinea pigs." By the last class, you will have techniques down pat. The children are always anxious to take their projects home immediately, so I really avoid things that cannot be finished in less than fifteen minutes. Passing out pieces in large manila envelopes, or clipped together with a large paper clip, saves passing-out time.

10. Last, but not least, I just came across a catalog by way of my school's art teacher that has potential for fifteen-minute FLES "art" projects. If you already have access to an Ellison die-cut machine to cut out letters and numbers for bulletin boards, be aware that dies in other designs are available as well. The dies are expensive but I plan on asking the other members of the district's FLES team to share the cost so we can start building a collection year by year. Just to give you an idea, there are llamas; outline maps of Mexico, North America, Puerto Rico, and South America; sombreros; a woman from Spain; and palm trees. (I haven't even considered what dies would pertain to other languages and themes.) Next year I hope to have one or two in the system to try out. At first glance, they would serve nicely as attractive backgrounds for lyrics of songs just learned or to display poetry. Again, the emphasis is on quickness. *¡Buena suerte!*

The possibilities for art and craft activities in classrooms are endless. A book of elementary school craft activities should get the thought processes going, and those focused on a variety of cultures are especially helpful.

Lavender Sachets   During the study of Provence, the students talk about all the vibrant colors and products found in that region of France. As the beautiful purple lavender fields are found throughout the region, we make sachets. Students begin decorating a white cone coffee filter with a memory of what has been studied from that region such as olives, lavender, sunflowers, and so on, or with a floral design found on Provence tablecloths. It's best to put an index card inside the filter while drawing with markers to make sure the color doesn't bleed through to the other side. The student or teacher can then write *la Provence* or *la lavande* on the front of the sachet. The student then fills the filter with a teaspoon of sachet filler, which can be found in perfumed sachet envelopes at craft stores. To complete the sachet, the two outside corners are folded in at an angle and stapled. The top flap is then folded down in attractive way. A purple ribbon is tied into a bow, placed on the top flap and stapled as well.

Stained Glass Windows of Notre-Dame   We "visit" the Notre-Dame Cathedral on our trip to Paris with the kindergartners and admire the beautiful colors of the stained glass windows. We decide to create our own stained glass creations and place them in our classroom windows! There are many stained glass coloring pages available on the Internet that can be printed and photocopied onto transparency sheets. The students color the transparencies with markers and we tape their stained glass masterpieces in the windows. The students may also create their own stained glass designs on a transparency sheet with a black permanent marker and then fill in with colorful markers.

Cornstarch Play-Dough Gargoyles   The kindergartners are also fascinated by the gargoyles adorning the cathedral of Notre-Dame. The first day, we talk about the gargoyles' body parts, expressions, resemblances to animals, and so on. The second day, the students sketch out in pencil the gargoyle that they will create with cornstarch play-dough prepared by the teacher or a parent volunteer. The students may want to sketch out two or three gargoyles and then choose which one they will make. Before creating the sculptures, the students describe their gargoyles to partners and compare. The third day, the students sculpt their gargoyles. My young students had the assistance of the fourth-grade French students who had been coached by the art teacher on how to help the kindergartners by referring to the selected sketch. I had coached the older students on how to engage with the kindergartners using the target language. After the gargoyles were dry, the students painted them grey and we put them on display for the school to enjoy. We also cut out their paper sketches and put them up high in the room, above the door, around the clock, and beside the bell towers that the teacher designed.

● Activities with Overhead Projectors and Digital Visual Presenters

Using an overhead projector or digital visual presenter, you may project visuals on the screen using a variety of techniques. With the overhead projector you will be using transparencies and with the digital visual presenter you will be able to use the original documents.

- Cover the document with a piece of paper and gradually reveal the entire document.
- Use a "peep show" technique to show only selected parts of the document. Make a mask with "windows" by cutting and hinging doors in an overlay made of stiff paper or card stock. Open the windows to reveal parts of the picture, and allow

the students to guess what the picture is or what story lies behind the picture. As an alternative, make a single hole in an overlay mask and move it around the document at the request of class members, so that they can see various small parts of the picture and come to conclusions as to what the picture is about.

- Use overlays to put together a picture in various stages, or to uncover or reveal various parts of an image in a step-by-step sequence.

- Play "what's missing" games by putting a collection of physical objects or pictures of objects on the machine. Turn off the machine and take away one object at a time; then turn it on again and have the students identify which object is missing.

- Draw simple maps and add paper cutout figures to indicate streets, houses, landmarks, people, and so forth.

- Use the machine to model partner activities. The students serve as one partner and the teacher uses the projector or visual presenter to demonstrate the task of the other partner.

For Overhead Projectors Only:

- Project the outlines of three-dimensional objects by laying them on the glass stage.

- Make shadows on the screen using hand motions. This is especially effective when the projector is placed behind a sheet or translucent screen and the shadow play takes place between the projector and the screen.

- Make silhouette stories by cutting out shapes from stiff paper and moving the shapes around on the projector stage to animate a story or dramatize a point in a lesson.

Summary

- Games and activities are important classroom means by which the communicative goals of the early language program are achieved.

- They involve the students and the teacher in meaningful, motivating situations within which real information is exchanged.

- A game or activity should be enjoyable.

- The use of language must play an important role in the activity.

- All students should be involved or engaged at all times.

For Study and Discussion

1. Choose a game and evaluate it according to the guidelines for games discussed in this chapter.

2. Choose a game from among those described in this chapter that call for little or no spoken

language to be used by the students. Write a
script for the teacher role in introducing and
conducting this game, demonstrating how the
teacher surrounds the activity with language and
provides the class with comprehensible input.

3. Respond to a secondary school language
teacher who complains, "All you do in the elementary school is give them fun and games.
When they get to our program and find out
that really learning languages requires some
work, they are disillusioned and they drop out.
I'd rather just wait and start them out when
they get to high school."

4. Choose a song for a class of young learners that
meets the guidelines suggested in this chapter.

Explain how it might fit into a specific unit of
instruction; describe the vocabulary and concepts it can be used to teach or reinforce; and
discuss the preparation that would take place
before you begin to teach the song. Then
demonstrate actually teaching the song to the
class, using the target language.

5. Plan a lesson in which you use a puppet to
introduce an important concept or a portion of
a common conversational exchange. Refer to
the conversation with the frog in this chapter as
an idea-starter. Demonstrate the lesson to your
class. Caution: Keep it simple!

For Further Reading

The following sources are recommended for additional information about material covered in
this chapter. Chapter citations are documented in Works Cited at the end of this book.

Buttner, Amy. *Activities, Games and Assessment
Strategies for the Foreign Language Classroom.*
Larchmont, NY: Eye on Education, 2007.

Cameron, Lynn. *Teaching Language to Young
Learners.* Cambridge: Cambridge Language
Teaching Library, Cambridge University Press,
2001.

Hamilton, Heidi E., Cori Crane, and Abigail
Bartoshesky. *Doing Foreign Language: Bringing
Concordia Language Villages into Language
Classrooms.* Boston: Pearson Allyn & Bacon,
2005.

Moon, Jayne. *Children Learning English.* Oxford:
Macmillan Heinemann English Language
Teaching, 2000.

Pinter, Anna Maria. *Teaching Young Language
Learners.* Cambridge: Oxford University Press,
2006.

Roth, Genevieve. *Teaching Very Young Children: Pre-
School and Early Primary.* London: Richmond
Publishing, 1998.

Slattery, Mary, and Jane Willis. *English for Primary
Teachers.* Cambridge: Oxford University Press,
2001.

Turnbull, Miles, Jill Sinclair Bell, and Sharon Lapkin.
*From the Classroom: Grounded Activities for
Language Learning.* Toronto: University of
Toronto Press, 2007.

Learners
Teachers
Communication
Programs
Languages & Children
Planning
Resources
Cultures
Content

Chapter 14

Bringing Language to Life with Technology

A Special Resource

Enduring Understanding

- Learning and communication for young learners are closely associated with technology and digital media.

Essential Questions

- What uses of technology tools will best support and enhance language and culture learning?

- How can teachers use digital media in planning, instruction, and assessment?

Technology is a tool. Sometimes the technology resources that early language teachers have at their disposal seem more like a magic carpet or a magic wand, capable of transforming teaching and curriculum in ways that would have been unimaginable even a decade ago. The skilled teacher, like the skilled artisan, matches the tool to the task in order to facilitate and accomplish an important purpose. In this chapter we will examine a number of dimensions of the technology tools we have at our disposal.

At the same time as we consider our own uses for technology, we need to focus on our students and their need for skills to use technology effectively. Technology, especially the Internet, can provide access to authentic sources of language that are simply unavailable any other way. When we integrate technology with our lessons and create opportunities for our students to use technology meaningfully, we are supporting them in the development of two essential tools for lifelong learning in the twenty-first century: skill in the use of another language and the ability to make discerning and effective use of technological tools. For more information on twenty-first–century skills, please see www.21stcentury skills.org/route21/index.php.

As this book goes to print, the catch phrase *Web 2.0* is the label for the way our students view and use technology resources. Whereas we might use the Internet for research, email, and entertainment (the first "version" of technology and the Web), our students use their tools to *create* (Web 2.0, the second generation). The students sitting in today's classrooms have never known a world without cell phones, WiFi, YouTube, and MP3 devices. All of these resources have impacted the way they perceive and function in society. They create videos, add their voice to many different media (YouTube, on-line social networks), blend video game images into their own stories, and create blogs to inform the followers of anything they choose. Keep that in mind. You have a roomful of "techies" to keep you up to date with the latest mainstreamed technological advances!

● National Educational Technology Standards for Students and Teachers

The International Society for Technology in Education has published a set of technology standards for students (2007) and for teachers (2008), in cooperation with the U.S. Department of Education and a number of curriculum organizations, including the American Council on the Teaching of Foreign Languages. These standards can help teachers plan technology components for their lessons to give students experiences with language and cultures that would be unavailable any other way. As students become proficient with the technology tools at their disposal, they can be more independent language learners, pursue their own interests and needs using the target language, and develop skills that will be useful in all dimensions of their education. Technology can bring the cultures, connections, and comparisons goals to life, even as they allow students to use their communication skills to participate in a wider community of speakers of the language they are learning. The standards can be accessed online at www.iste.org/NETS.

New technologies can foster cognitive engagement with content in ways that are well aligned with research on learning and memory. However, the exact same technology can be used for language drill or for meaningful communication, depending on how one approaches the task. Consequently, sound pedagogy is an essential part of successful technology use. Teachers striving to provide technology-infused, standards-based lessons in the target language should ask themselves the following questions posed by Cherice Montgomery (2009):

1. *Purpose:* Will using technology in this lesson allow students to accomplish something that they otherwise could not, or am I using it as just a "bell and whistle"? Am I using the technology primarily for "show and tell," or do my plans include ample opportunities for my *students* to interact and create with it as well?

2. *Task:* Will the technology-based task I have designed develop students' proficiency in the target language? Is the task developmentally appropriate for my students? Have I scheduled enough time for students to successfully complete each individual step of the task?

3. *Tools:* Are the technologies students will use to accomplish the task appropriate, given their needs, skills, and the goals of my lesson?

4. *Process* (i.e., scaffolding):

   ● Product: Are my expectations for what students will do with the technology clear?

   ● Preparation: Have I determined how I will prepare students to accomplish the task (in terms of content, process, and technology skills)?

   ● Process: Have I carefully considered the logistics involved in each segment of the activity and planned accordingly? Have I anticipated at what points students may encounter difficulty and have I developed scaffolding that will enable them to be successful with those portions of the task?

   ● Presentation: Have I thoughtfully planned pedagogically sound ways for students to share their work?

5. *Alignment:* Have I checked to be sure that the purpose, task, tools, and processes involved in my plans are well aligned with my language objectives for students?

● Technology and Planning for the Language Program

When Alisha Dawn Samples presents technology workshops for language teachers, she shares the following technology ideas for enhancing teacher productivity. She suggests that teachers can:

● Create their own roll and record books (especially teachers of young learners since their needs are so different). This makes it much easier to go back another year and make modifications to lessons, activities, and anecdotal notes. It's also easier to share with colleagues this way!

● Create unit frameworks, lessons, and assessments in a word processor to facilitate year-to-year changes and file sharing.

● Create visuals for games using photos and clip art. Teachers may not have to stay up all night coloring if they have access to a color printer—it's a great time saver. You can also make mini-visuals in black and white for students to use in booklets or centers, to take home or for homework, etc. . . . with visuals that look just like the ones they are using in class.

● Include authentic pictures in visuals and materials. This works well if you have digital pictures or images retrieved from the Web. It's a great way to provide authentic culture in games, books, and so forth. Teachers have a responsibility to teach students to use technologies ethically and responsibly. This includes teaching students the importance of honoring copyright restrictions. There are many sites that provide free clip art and quality stock photos that teachers and students can use.

● Create an e-calendar by inserting numbers and photos or clip art into a calendar created in PowerPoint. The clip art can come up as the teacher and/or students count (and click). This works well for sequencing and repeating holiday/thematic vocabulary on a daily basis. You can also print it out for students, or include it as a link on your webpage for viewing from home and for practice away from school!

● Produce newsletters for parents. Include pictures from class, sites to visit at home with students, information about upcoming and completed themes, and so on. The newsletter may be printed out and/or posted on the webpage, where visuals in color will make the newsletter even more enjoyable.

● Create e-games. Use a projector so that everyone can see and participate in whatever activity is being done on the computer. This is a great one for the computer classroom and for teachers who want to do things on the computer with the class as a large group.

  Convert games to an electronic format by using links in PowerPoint. This allows students to take turns as they usually do but also manipulate the mouse and click.

  Create matching games, multiple-choice games, "Jeopardy"-type games, and question-and-answer games. All can be done with PowerPoint slides and links.

● Create e-books using any visuals—clip art, scanned images, or digital photos— and then easily print the visuals that go with the book for games, activities, worksheets, and centers for the whole unit. PowerPoint allows the user to print in "hand-out" mode—different-sized squares that are great for using in games or as manipulatives. Use small photo albums purchased at a dollar store to create "books" for use with activities such as paired reading and in centers. For these books, choose the option of printing two slides to a page, cut them out, and put them into the photo album. The teacher can also print out more slides to a page and run them off so that students have their own books to take home and read to parents—just like the one the teacher made for class. The teacher can read the class book by projecting the PowerPoint for large groups, or print out each slide and make a large book.

  When the teacher creates and presents a digital book, it can include sound effects and music. You can make a book to "read" to students the songs you plan to teach them, so the students learn the meaning and words to a song first by having a literature experience. Then add the music and the students will realize they already know the song.

Teachers have the option to store what they have created on recordable CDs and Flash or USB drives (small-in-size, large-in-capacity storage devices that connect to the computer via USB ports). These storage devices can organize units, student work, and any logs pertaining to a certain class, year, or whatever. Teachers can also use one to share files with other teachers and keep space free on older machines.

To foster collaboration and enrich teaching units, even if you are the only language teacher in the building, you can use several web-based sites to share, communicate, and create with colleagues, students, parents, and/or the community. Participants upload pertinent files to a host site and others are able to edit, comment, and add to original file. A great starting point is a wiki, a server-based software site that allows users to create pages (www.wikispaces.com) . Wikis create an on-line place for document sharing and communication. If you are unfamiliar with this resource, search Wikis in Plain English on youtube.com for an informative video. See the end of the chapter for examples of wikis in the language classroom. Another type of on-line document sharing is Google docs (https://docs.google.com). With any of these resources you can control who can see, edit, or otherwise access what you post. It is a great way to collaborate with fellow teachers across the country.

Podcasts or vodcasts open a world of possibilities to the language teacher. A *podcast* is an audio recording that can be uploaded to the internet or iTunes and instantly shared with a wide audience. A *vodcast* is the same except that it is a video recording saved in a format that can be accessed by a video-capable MP3 device. You can record the audio or video of your lesson and quickly covert it into a format that students and/or parents can access regardless of home computer. Students can even transfer the files to their iPods or other MP3 device to watch on their own. To create a podcast, you will need either Garageband (Mac) or another recording program (PC), such as audacity (http://audacity.source-forge.net/). Rare is the new computer without a built-in microphone, so recording your own material should be simple. Within this type of software, you can record, edit, splice, and add to audio recordings. For additional help in creating your own, access Garageband Help or do a quick Google search. Capturing video is increasingly easy, with digital cameras, camera cell phones, built-in cameras on computers, video game consoles, and of course the dedicated standby, the video camera. Editing video software is readily available, and many computers come equipped with it.

● Technology-Enhanced Learning Environment

There are many tools that language teachers can use in the language classroom. The target culture is no longer a plane trip away! The following are just a few examples of technology working to help students learn another language:

- Computers or laptops with Internet connectivity are the obvious tools. Many uses for these have already been mentioned in this section.
- A digital projector is quickly becoming a "must-have" for language teachers. Websites, PowerPoints, vodcasts, and of course DVDs can easily be displayed for your students.

● A document camera or scanner will enable you to share the color magazine ad you only have one copy of or to show pictures in a children's book as you read to a large class. Either of these tools connect your computer, and the scanner actually creates a digital file of the realia, protecting your original from wear and tear.

● Interactive boards, SmartBoards, Promethean boards, and the like are well suited to the language classroom. Project a website in the target language, and students can tap the board and navigate through an activity. On-line games and teacher-made games, like the ones mentioned in this chapter, actively involve students.

● Student response tools, like clickers and mini-interactive boards, allow teachers to quickly assess student understanding and help to efficiently use class time. These tools allow free response or close-ended response to activities, directed by the teacher. They can tally responses so the teacher can promptly determine if reteaching is necessary.

● Hand-held recording devices, such as a USB voice recorder or a microphone accessory for an MP3 player, allow the teacher to quickly collect speech samples from individuals or pairs of students. Transferring the files to your computer is as simple as connecting the recorder and moving the files.

● Technology-Based Projects and Activities

For teachers who have access to computers, student projects can easily incorporate technology. Depending on the age and language experience of the students, many of the following possibilities can enhance learning in a thematic unit. (Keep in mind that if a specific topic is linked to suggestions listed here, many other topics could also fit well with that particular project or activity.)

● Create a menu using a word-processing or a drawing program.

● Create a greeting card in the target language using clip art with a cultural element.

● Students use digital photos to design a poster with which to introduce themselves to a new student, a student teacher, or parents on Parent Night.

● Create a story, an episode from a story, or a poem, and illustrate with clip art or by using a drawing program. All projects are printed and compiled into a class book.

● Develop a book report by creating a book jacket that includes a front cover designed to reflect book content, flaps to summarize the story, and information about the author on the back cover.

● Create a class newspaper or newsletter.

● Create a brochure about a city or a country in which the target language is spoken—to encourage visits from classmates and their families. Information might come from research on the Internet, and be enhanced with images downloaded from the Web.

● Create an advertisement for a culturally significant product, using images to illustrate the text.

● Develop a personal "picture dictionary" of words (or phrases) in the target language, using images to illustrate the meanings rather than translations into English.

● After researching information about a famous figure from the target culture, using a variety of resources, create a "Who am I?" puzzle, illustrated with images and written in the first person. Place the answer on the back of the page, at the bottom, so it can be folded up to reveal the answer.

● Listen to a podcast—a teacher, student, or authentic one—to enhance a specific topic, or to share/discuss what you learned with classmates.

● Students create a PowerPoint presentation about themselves (or any other topic), using learned vocabulary and following a format provided by the teacher. The students illustrate the presentation with uploaded photos and clip art.

● Students create a digital story to share using Voicethread. This website provides the ability to have text, audio, video, or doodle commentary on each slide by multiple people. It also allows you to upload graphics, photos, and video, and to add text, audio, and/or video commentary. For more information, go to www.voicethread.com. Some examples at www.Voicethread.com are a Chinese story on zodiac animals, a French story on professions, and a story in Spanish about a horse.

● Students create podcasts or vodcasts about local wildlife to share with a class in the target culture. They can add images to illustrate their points and edit their speech sample.

● Students create, contribute, or follow a chat or blog (a *blog* is an on-line journal, commentary, or story written and posted by an individual or specific group) about environmental issues.

● Students exchange opinions about healthy choices in a video conference call with a classmate from the target culture. Skype is a free, on-line phone service using a computer with a microphone and built-in camera (necessary for the video component) that easily supports this activity. Skype is easy to download and use, and it works with most computers. You have the options of a text chat, an audio chat, a video chat, or all of the options at one time. You can record your chats, expand the conversations with extra tools, and more. You also have the option to have group conversations with up to 20 participants. Note: You cannot have video during a conference call. For more information, go to www.skype.com.

● Students infer target culture practices regarding eating habits and health by viewing pertinent information on a school website from the target culture (e.g., cafeteria menu).

● Using Internet Resources

The Internet has placed the target culture within reach of a classroom. Available resources evolve at an incredible speed. Teachers and students alike can access information about the countries where the target language is spoken and learn from and about the people who speak the language. Authentic sources of language are just an Internet connection away. Teachers can use the Web to download pictures, ideas, activities, and units to support their teaching, as well as to initiate and maintain contact with other teachers. The resources available to teachers on the Internet are almost overwhelming, and they make it possible to incorporate cultural information in our lessons in a multitude of ways. It is just short of miraculous to have access to books, teaching activities, virtual greeting cards in the target language, games to print, coloring pages based on famous painters, writing and prewriting activities—the list is endless. One French-language website even provides lined paper in the French style, with a place for the student to write in his or her name and date (see www.momes.net/education/ecriture/modeles/pagevide.html).

Students can access Internet resources, under teacher guidance, to answer questions, research topics of interest, and use their language skills for personal enrichment and enjoyment. Use of the Internet can expand the students' community of target language speakers beyond the classroom and the neighborhood to the world. It is important to remember that although students are inundated by technology, they are not necessarily good consumers of technology-based information. Students of all ages need guidance and skills to filter out the unnecessary in order to glean what is important.

There are growing numbers of sources of ideas for Web-based activities, some of them on listservs such as FLTeach and Ñandu (see "For Further Reading" at the end of the chapter). Teacher idea websites abound, and many of them offer ideas for activities using Internet resources. As teachers consider these ideas for their own classrooms, they may want to access the evaluation form that has been prepared by the California Teachers Project accessible online at http://www.clta.net/lessons/evalform.html, which is helpful in assessing the quality of an activity and its potential for success in their own classrooms.

Many teachers have created their own website or wiki pages (for more information on wikis, search Wikis in Plain English on www.YouTube.com for a five-minute informational video), which they use to provide resources for students and their parents, as well as to share ideas, lessons, and favorite links with colleagues. In some cases, the teacher's page can be a tool for advocacy for early language learning. Some teachers post homework assignments, or links to websites of special interest to students in their classes. Anything and everything the teacher creates in class can be posted to the website for students to review, revisit, or share at home: classroom games, activities, e-books, calendars, collages of student work, or pictures of students in action. If the materials are created electronically, they can be modified to go on the page according to how the teacher wants students to use them. There might even be some things that students did not experience electronically in class, but if they were created electronically they can be shared on the webpage.

This includes newsletters, classroom management rules and procedures, information about the teachers and how to contact them, and program information.

Strategies for the One-Computer Classroom

Although teachers who have access to only one computer for classroom purposes may be limited, there are still a number of ways to take advantage of Internet resources under these circumstances. Teachers can download resources from the Internet to make hard copies for the classroom, or to use in making transparencies that will be visible to the whole class. Of course, there are specific copyright laws that pertain to Internet materials similar to those for other published information. Sometimes teachers download information at a remote site to a USB or flash drive so they can display it in a classroom that doesn't have an Internet connection.

When projection capabilities are available, the teacher or students can use the computer to access webpages that can be seen by the entire class. This is an effective way to use Internet resources to enhance a unit of instruction with authentic documents and pictures. If students have worked individually or in pairs in the computer lab to become familiar with one or more websites that relate to the current class topic, they can demonstrate what they have learned to the entire class.

A single computer in the classroom can also function as a learning station for students working alone or in pairs during a designated study time on Web-based projects or assignments.

WebQuests: A Focused Strategy for Accessing the Internet

The Internet is a rich and wonderful resource—seductive in its color and diversity; unorganized and inconsistent regarding quality; commercialized; uneven in its reliability; and sometimes even dangerous. In short, it is much like the "real world." As teachers, we can send our students to the Web in search of authentic sources of information in the target language, about weather conditions and forecasts, restaurant menus, famous people, online shopping, museums, movies, music videos, real-time broadcasts—the list is almost endless. These kinds of searches among target language websites provide valuable experiences with communication in the interpretive mode, and many opportunities for gaining insights about cultures, as well as making comparisons between the target culture and the student's home culture. Given the nature of the Internet, however, a more focused and carefully designed approach to the Internet can give students more meaningful and memorable learning experiences.

WebQuests have become a widely used tool throughout the country and at every learning level. According to Dodge (1997) and Kuck and Lietz (1998), the WebQuest consists of at least the following components:

1. An *introduction* sets the stage for the activity, provides background for the topic, and engages the learner. The introduction often places the learner in some sort of role-playing situation.

2. A *task* will describe learner expectations and may take the form of a multimedia presentation, a classroom presentation, a written report, or a classroom demonstration, to name a few media.

3. A *description* of the process that students are expected to follow is given in a step-by-step format. The task is described and divided into subtasks, roles, or perspectives for each learner, and learning advice is offered in the form of guided questions and directions. Formats such as time lines, concept maps, or cause-and-effect diagrams may be offered for the students' use.

4. A set of *information resources* is needed to complete the task. Most of these resources will be Internet based, although resources such as books, documents, and personal interviews may also be included. This list of sources helps to discourage aimless "surfing" and directs the learning experience.

5. *Evaluation/Assessment strategies* are described to measure the knowledge gained by the learner. Benchmarks and rubrics are often included here.

6. The *conclusion* summarizes the experience, encourages reflection about the process, and brings closure to the quest.

The WebQuest is usually designed as a group activity, encouraging the development of cooperative skills. WebQuests often assign roles to students (biologist, adventurer, photographer, journalist) and suggest a scenario that reflects a real-world use of the information that will be located in the WebQuest. For example, here is a possible scenario: "You have been hired to do consumer research for a new product about to be introduced in Germany. Your employer wants you to develop an ad campaign that will reflect the values of the new customers and demonstrate qualities that similar products already on the market do not have."

The task is the most important element of the WebQuest, the dimension that raises the cognitive level of the activity and makes it meaningful for the learner. In general a WebQuest involves taking information located through multiple sources—on the Web and elsewhere—and recombining it, organizing or summarizing it in a creative way, or otherwise using the information to achieve a purpose. Some of the task categories identified on the San Diego State University WebQuest website include:

- *Retelling Tasks:* Sharing information in a new form, such as blog entry, not simply cutting and pasting
- *Compilation Tasks:* Creating a cookbook, a time capsule
- *Mystery Tasks:* Wrapping the task in a puzzle or a detective story
- *Persuasion Tasks:* The student taking a position based on research and trying to persuade others to take the same position

These are just a few of the possible tasks that could focus a WebQuest. For a complete introduction to the construction of WebQuests and links to examples from all subject areas, see the resources listed at the end of this chapter.

● Electronic Portfolios

An *electronic portfolio* is a purposeful collection of student work stored digitally on a computer hard drive, on a flash drive, on a DVD, or on the Web. Unlike bulky portfolios stacked in closets or corners, the electronic portfolio takes up little space and provides convenient access to a record of student progress.

As with the portfolios described in Chapter 7, student selection of materials and reflection on their own work are key elements in effective portfolio compilation. Portfolio activities can be used to encourage students to review their own work, analyze their own learning strategies, and assess their collaboration with others. The teacher and the students together can make decisions about what should be included. Students gain valuable technology skills as they create or edit their own portfolios. LinguaFolio, available in an electronic format at casls.uoregon.edu, is an excellent place to begin using portfolios in your classroom, no matter the grade level. With LinguaFolio, students are prompted through goal setting, record keeping, and sample work selection. It is based on a highly successful European model and the Common European Frameworks of Reference, which are the equivalent of foreign-language standards for Europe. The beauty of such a resource is that it is made for you, the language teacher, and your students!

For the most sophisticated portfolio options, the website (www.essdack.org/port/how.html) suggests that the following equipment should be available:

- Computer with video input and output (the more RAM, the better)
- Color flatbed scanner
- Digital camera
- Multimedia software program or a commercial web authoring program

The teacher may choose to set up a template for students to use when entering their information. One of the great advantages of the electronic portfolio is the fact that it can store information using a variety of media, thus reflecting various intelligences and learning styles as well as the whole range of target language applications. Use of electronic portfolios will demonstrate clearly the progress of students as they move from one grade level to another, or from elementary to middle to high school language classes.

● Using Video in Early Language Teaching

Not all applications of technology take place on the Internet or using a computer. Videos have played a role in the classroom for many years, often to supplement classroom instruction. Videos made for children in the target language culture are valuable sources of both language and culture experience, if they are carefully chosen and the class is prepared ahead of time for the viewing experience. This might also be the product of a student project, or the teacher can digitally capture student presentations to share with other classes or with parents.

Alisha Dawn Samples (2002) encourages teachers to video some of their lessons as a way to provide "take-home" lessons for those who are newcomers, and as a method of providing lessons for substitutes or classroom teachers when the language teacher has to be absent. She suggests videoing several generic review lessons every year that pertain to different topics or themes in the curriculum; they can be kept on hand in case of illness or special circumstances. Video lessons work best when the lesson is direct instruction to the camera—not simply teaching a class. Students respond better to lessons that are taught straight into the camera (to them, the audience) rather than watching another class passively. Little children respond to the TV and are much more interactive when the lesson is taught like this. Videoing a class is useful for other purposes—namely, demonstrating teaching for a professional portfolio or using for assessment of student progress. It is important that teachers get written permission from parents and students prior to doing so—especially if the video will be posted on-line.

Video and Television Lessons as Curriculum

Videos and television lessons have been used as part of the language curriculum since the 1960s, often in situations in which a full-time language teacher is not available. With the increasing demand for early language programs, the growing shortage of qualified teachers, and inadequate budgets for these programs, school systems are turning to video-based programs as a possible vehicle to providing instruction to large numbers of students.

Video programs are used in one of four ways (Rhodes and Pufahl, 2004):

1. As the foreign language curriculum by a classroom teacher (or other nonspecialist) who does not speak the language and learns it along with the students

2. As the foreign language curriculum by a classroom teacher who may or may not speak the language, with reinforcement by a foreign language teacher on a weekly basis

3. By a language teacher as a supplement to the foreign language curriculum

4. As the foreign language curriculum by a language teacher (not common)

It is important to remember that the quality of language learning in a technology-based program will be dependent on several important factors. First, the program content must meet a very high standard of quality, making consistent use of the target language in engaging and child-appropriate situations, and the pedagogy must be consistent with current understanding of second-language acquisition. There must be full and informed cooperation by classroom teachers and all assisting personnel involved with the program.

When Wyoming legislators mandated foreign language programs in grades K–2, beginning in the fall of 2002, Ann Tollefson applied for a federal grant to support the development of a video-based Spanish curriculum that could be taught by classroom teachers, most of whom did not speak Spanish. The project was designed to give the teachers sufficient training and support so that they could supplement the videos confidently, using appropriate methodology.

In a FLAP-funded research project comparing student learning in various models of instructional delivery using technology, it was found that, in addition to the regular classroom teacher, having a Spanish speaker in the classroom to support and expand student language learning from videos and CDs resulted in improved student learning.

Although the classroom teacher/language teacher model continues in many Wyoming elementary schools, the Wyoming Legislature has appropriated $1 million per year to hire, train, and support Spanish speakers who serve as paraprofessionals in K–6 classrooms in the state. The paraprofessionals meet weekly via video teleconferencing to customize the program to the classrooms in which they teach. This model has expanded the program through grade 6 for over 9,000 Wyoming students per year. Extensive support materials for the K–2 program can be downloaded at no charge on the Wyoming Department of Education's website, www.k12.wy.us (search for SALSA).

The Georgia Department of Education and Georgia Public Broadcasting, led by Elizabeth Webb, are conducting a pilot project to expand the Wyoming K–2 model by building a full curriculum that relies on the SALSA program supported by both classroom teachers and Spanish-speaking paraprofessionals.

Wyoming's K–6 program has used FLAP funding to develop middle-school materials that are thematically based and follow the principles of backward design. The sixth-grade curriculum and curricular materials have been posted and can be downloaded at no charge at www.Curriki.org (search for Wyoming). The curriculum for seventh and eighth grades will be posted at that site as they emerge from development and piloting.

Rhodes and Pufahl of the Center for Applied Linguistics (2004, p. 5) have identified pros and cons of video-based foreign language teaching, according to teachers:

PROs

- Is cost effective
- Facilitates lesson scheduling
- Can substitute during absence of the foreign language teacher
- Challenges listening comprehension (native speakers and different accents)
- Appeals to students; gets their attention
- Provides ready access for (new) students who have missed part of the program
- Allows students who have missed a lesson to review it
- Creates visual contextualization
- Could incorporate culture not available to local teachers
- Appeals to different learning styles

CONs

- Requires video technology
- May be passive/boring if overused

- Lacks feedback/reinforcement if the teacher does not speak the language
- Lacks interaction among students and among students and teacher
- Lacks control over content and vocabulary

Almost all of the available video-based programs are in Spanish, and it is clear that the quality of the program is the determining factor in student learning and program success. Rhodes and Pufahl (Center for Applied Linguistics, 2002, p. 4) identified characteristics of a good language video for children, based on teacher comments. These characteristics should be met whether the video is intended as the curriculum for the language or as a supplement:

What Makes a Good Language Video for Children?

- Extensive use of the foreign language
- Authentic use of the foreign language
- Clear pronunciation by native speakers
- Catchy tunes
- Lots of repetition
- Humor
- Characters that are fun to watch (puppets, cartoons, and/or people)
- Engaging story line
- Profiles of Spanish-speaking communities (abroad and in United States) from a child's point of view (or profiles of communities that speak the language of the video)
- National/state standards

Using Video or Television Lessons in the Classroom

The effectiveness of any viewing experience in the classroom, whether of a supplementary video, a videotaped lesson, or a television lesson, will be determined in large part by how well the teacher prepares the experience and follows up on it. Alisha Dawn Samples, in her presentation for classroom teachers, makes the following suggestions:

Before Viewing

- Preview and prepare the program(s) prior to classroom viewing.
- Select segments from the video that are most relevant to the lesson topic and specifically target lesson objectives.
- Provide a focus for the students for viewing—what are they looking for?
- Have students sit where they can all see and have access to writing materials and something firm to write on.
- Keep the lights on.

During Viewing (Use the "Pause" button frequently to ...)

● Check comprehension.

● Highlight or underscore a point.

● Invite student inferences or predictions.

● Have students make connections to other topics or "real-world" applications.

● Ask a student to come and point to something on the screen.

● Have students define a word based on contextual clues.

● Decipher a situation or solve a problem.

● Enhance students' observation and memory skills.

● Control the viewing pace and amount of information to be digested.

● Provide students time to reflect on what they have seen.

After Viewing

● Tie the lesson objectives to the video students have just viewed.

● Allow students to respond to the program.

● Recognize the validity of divergent reactions.

● Help students relate the program to their own experiences and feelings.

Material and information from any viewing experience will soon be forgotten if they are not incorporated into later instruction by means of hands-on experiences, related projects or instruction, or by some other means. Video or television instruction holds great promise for presenting language experiences in an interesting and meaningful way, provided that the program is of high quality and meets class objectives. Only if the material is an integrated part of the language curriculum, however, will viewing experiences contribute effectively to the language development of our students.

Summary

● Teachers of young learners have more technology resources at their disposal than at any time in history. These resources are tools that must be matched carefully to the outcomes of instruction and chosen because they are the best means available for reaching a specific goal.

● The National Educational Technology Standards for Students and for Teachers can serve as a guide for us as we choose technology applications for our classrooms.

● Because technology can extend the reach of the language classroom into the world of the target culture, there is tremendous potential for integrating foreign-language curriculum with technology goals and standards.

● The Internet, when it is used well, may be one of the best resources for our students as lifelong learners and users of the language we teach. Therefore, it is our task to help our students use it effectively.

- A number of specific technology applications are highlighted in this chapter. Blogs can provide opportunities for written interpersonal communication that helps students understand the cultures of the language we teach. WebQuests can develop interpretive and presentational skills at the same time as they guide students through useful research processes. Finally, electronic portfolios can help students to gather and reflect on the evidence of their learning during the language class, while they develop and use important skills in technology, such as scanning documents, recording their own speech samples, and using digital media.

- Visual media such DVDs and web-based videos can support language teaching, and can sometimes, under the right circumstances, even provide language instruction when a qualified teacher is not available. These materials, like all other teaching materials, must be carefully evaluated before they are adopted.

- A quick Google search will often yield many ideas and ways teachers are using technology in their classrooms. For example, search for images of families from the target culture to use in class. Many people from other cultures have personal blogs, complete with pictures, that will discuss many things, such as family celebrations and traditions that would not be found in a textbook. New links are added at amazing rates, so if you don't find something today, check again tomorrow!

For Study and Discussion

1. Think of your favorite classroom activity. Could a technology tool enhance it? If so, which one? And how?

2. How can technology help you address the 5 C's of the national foreign language standards?

3. Access several of the WebQuests available on-line from one of the Web pages listed in the "For Further Reading" section. Describe a WebQuest that you would like to design for a thematic unit that you plan to teach in your language class.

4. Go to www.wikispaces.com and sign up for a free site of your own, if you do not already have one. Experiment with the site features, and set up a page for parents to access; it could include your classroom expectations, tips to help their children practice the target language at home, and so on. Search the site for other teachers' examples.

5. View a video that is designed for teaching a foreign language at the elementary or middle school level. Evaluate it using the criteria listed by CAL. Would you use this video? If so, how? If not, why not?

For Further Reading

The following sources are recommended for additional information about material covered in this chapter. Chapter citations are documented in Works Cited at the end of this book.

California Language Teachers Association, California Foreign Language Project. *Internet Activities for Foreign Language Classes.* Available on-line at www.clta.net/lessons/evalform.html.

Green, Anne. "A Beginner's Guide to the Internet in the Foreign Language Classroom with a Focus on the World Wide Web." *Foreign Language Annals* 30:2 (Summer 1997): 253–264.

International Society for Technology in Education (ISTE). *The ISTE National Educational Technology Standards (NETS•S) and Performance Indicators for Students.* 2007. Available on-line at www.iste.org/NETS.

International Society for Technology in Education (ISTE). *The ISTE National Educational Technology Standards (NETS•T) and Performance Indicators for Teachers.* 2008. Availailable on-line at www.iste.org/NETS.

Kost, Claudia R. "Enhancing Communicative Language Skills through Effective Use of the World Wide Web in the Foreign Language Classroom." *Foreign Language Annals* 32:3 (Fall 1999): 309–320.

LeLoup, Jean W., and Robert Ponterio. "Enhancing Authentic Language Learning Experiences through Internet Technology." *ERIC Digest*, 2000. Available on-line at http://www.cal.org/resources/digest/0002enhancing.html.

LeLoup, Jean W., and Robert Ponterio. "Technology and Foreign Language Instruction: Where We Have Been, Where We Are Now, Where We Are Headed," in Audrey Heining-Boynton (Ed.), *Realizing Our Vision of Language for All* (pp. 153–174). Alexandria, VA: ACTFL.

Pacheco, Jean L. "A Successful Keypal Project Using Varied Technologies." *Learning Languages* 7:1 (Fall 2001): 10–14.

Websites of Interest

Internet Resources

Doloff, Deby. "Te Quiero, Tito"—FLES Email Project. *Learning* Languages 4:3 (Spring 1999): 21–23.

Google in the target language: www.google.es (Spanish); www.google.de (German); www.google.fr (French); www.google.ru (Russian); www.google.co.jp (Japanese); www.google.cn (Chinese); www.google.co.kr (Korean); and www.google.com.sa (Arabic).

Intercultural E-Mail Classroom Connections (IECC): www.iecc.org/.

Kendall, Cindy, and Cherice Montgomery. *The Whats, Whys, & Wows of Wikis in the World Language Classroom* (October 6, 2007). Wikispaces. http://worldlanguagewikis.wikispaces.com/.

Kidlink: www.kidlink.org/index.html. A global networking portal for kids around the world.

Lawrence, Geoff. "A Touch of . . . Class!" *The Canadian Modern Language Review* 58:3 (March 2002): 465–472.

Online Netiquette: www.netmatters.com/.

Robb, Thomas N. "E-Mail Keypals for Language Fluency." *Foreign Language Notes* (Foreign Language Educators of New Jersey) 38:3 (Fall 1996): 8–10. Accessed on-line November 2008, at http://www.cc.kyoto-su.ac.jp/~trobb/keypals.html.

Smileys and Emoticons for Effective Communication: www.windweaver.com/emoticon.htm.

WebQuests

San Diego State University WebQuest site:http://webquest.org/index.php.

WebQuests for Learning: http://bestwebquests.com/ and http://tommarch.com/learning/.

Listservs

FLTeach: http://www.cortland.edu/flteach/. Ñandu, Early Language Listserv: www.cal.org/earlylang.

Language Teacher Web/Wiki Pages

Elementary tech teachers: http://elementarytech teachers.ning.com/.

Interpersonal communication use: http://broadcast-Live.com.

K–6 on-line tech projects: http://projectsbyjen.ning.com/.

Toni Theisen, ACTFL 2009 Teacher of the Year: http://tonitheisen.wikispaces.com/.

World language teachers in Michigan: http://miwla connect.ning.com/.

Chapter 15

Making the Case for Early Language Programs

Rationale and Advocacy

Enduring Understanding

- Early language learning plays an important role in the learner's total educational development.

Essential Question

- What information can I use to advocate for early language learning, and how can I go about it?

For world languages, as for any content area seeking a secure place in the school curriculum, offering a convincing rationale holds a high priority. School boards and parent organizations need reasons and evidence before making a commitment of time and resources to a new program, and existing programs can be called into question at any time. Almost every "public" occasion—from class or program coverage by the media to party conversation—holds the potential for the common, recurring question, "Why should children learn new languages in elementary school?"

Perhaps the best response to this question is to rephrase it into a larger and more important one: "Why should foreign languages become a K–12 experience for all students?" This is a question that better reflects the vision of language education expressed in the *Standards for Foreign Language Learning in the 21st Century*. Establishing and maintaining language programs in the elementary school, and then articulating them carefully through middle school and high school, will make it possible to provide all of our citizens with the precious gift of other languages, cultures, and perspectives. Another way to rephrase the "Why?" question might be to ask, "What academic and cognitive benefits are the students missing out on if they do not learn another language?"

A rationale, like a program philosophy, must be developed to meet the needs and priorities of the local school and of the community that it serves. It will address the reasons and goals for language learning, as well as the basis for choice of language(s) to be taught; it may also deal with the methods selected for instruction. The teacher or group developing a rationale can draw from a variety of resources to complete the task. One purpose of this chapter is to give direction to the search for resources and to give guidance for the shaping of a rationale that is both consistent with the national vision and meaningful to the community for which it is developed.

During the surge of popularity for elementary school language programs in the 1960s, it was common for schools to launch programs before setting rationales and goals. As a consequence, many programs gained public support for the wrong reasons: "catching up" with the Russians, taking advantage of government money available, providing a program like that of a neighboring school, trying to produce fluent speakers quickly because learners were thought to be at an optimal age for language learning, and so on. Many administrators, parents, and teachers had unrealistic expectations of student performance. Those who had jumped onto the language bandwagon out of fear or because foreign languages were a fad, or who expected fluency in weeks or months, were bound to suffer disappointment. In their eagerness to expand their offerings into the elementary schools, language teachers sometimes did not discourage such expectations. Disillusionment and lack of clear direction combined to bring an end to programs that had been too hastily begun.

At the beginning of the twenty-first century, there are both a resurgence of interest in early language learning, as a component of the K–12 sequence, and an abundance of information that supports an early start and a long sequence of language study. The resources at the end of this chapter provide rich current evidence of the value of early language learning, as well as links to a growing body of further research and to examples of rationales developed by states, professional organizations, and school districts. All of these resources can help bring clarity of purpose to the development of an effective and enduring program.

● Where to Look for a Rationale for Foreign Languages

Cognitive Science and Brain Research

Parents and teachers often comment that children are much better language learners than adolescents or adults and that we should make the most of this special ability before it is lost. The research of Penfield and Roberts (1959) offered a psychological and physiological basis for starting second-language learning as early as possible, and this research was frequently cited in FLES program rationale in the 1960s. Donoghue (1968, p. 11), in her groundbreaking methods text for elementary school foreign languages, makes this recommendation: "Ideally, the age for beginning the learning of a second language is at birth. But when considering language learning in relation to schooling, the optimum age for beginning the continuous learning of a second language seems to fall within the span of ages four through eight. . . . In this span of ages, the brain apparently has the greatest plasticity and specialized capacity for acquiring speech. This capacity includes the ability to mimic properly all the speech sounds, intonations, and stresses and to learn readily all language patterns."

Some later research evidence suggested that older learners have specific advantages over children in many areas—with a small advantage for children in the area of native-like pronunciation—at least in most classroom settings (Krashen et al., 1982; Harley, 1986; Singleton, 1995). Many of the reasons that children are such successful language learners may lie in other factors, of course, such as the amount of time available for learning the language and the teaching methodology used. The brain research of the 1990s and beyond, however, has tended to support the instincts of parents and teachers, as well as those early research claims.

Since the mid-1990s, there has been a flurry of publication of new information emerging from the study of the brain and cognitive functioning. This research has been made accessible to a wider public through articles in *Newsweek* and *Time*. J. Madeleine Nash, in an often-quoted article (1997, p. 56), pointed out that "the ability to learn a second language is highest between birth and the age of six, then undergoes a steady and inexorable decline." Among the conclusions she draws from the research is this: "What lessons can be drawn from the new findings? Among other things, it is clear that foreign languages should be taught in elementary school, if not before."

Very much the same message was presented in the public radio program "Gray Matters: The Developing Brain." An article in *Learning Languages, Language Learning and the Developing Brain* (Research Notes, 1996, p. 17) summarized some of the key findings from that program. According to Dr. Michael Phelps, chairman of the Department of Molecular and Medical Pharmacology of the UCLA School of Medicine, the child's brain is different from the adult brain in that it is a very dynamic structure that is evolving. A 2-year-old child has twice as many synapses (connections) in the brain as an adult. The young brain must use these connections or lose them.

Thus, failure to learn a skill, such as a foreign language, during a critical or sensitive period, has important significance. The learning experiences of the child determine which connections are developed and which will no longer function. That means that what is easy and natural for a child—learning a language—can become hard work for an older learner.

Another piece of evidence comes from the work of Dr. Susan Curtiss, professor of linguistics at UCLA, also cited in the *Learning Languages* summary (Research Notes, 1996, p. 17). She has found that the 4- or 5-year-old learning a second language is a "perfect model for the idea of the critical period." According to Dr. Curtiss, "The power to learn language is so great in . . . young child[ren] that it doesn't seem to matter how many languages you seem to throw their way. . . . They can learn as many spoken languages as you can allow them to hear systematically and regularly at the same time. Children just have this capacity. Their brain is just ripe to do this . . . there doesn't seem to be any detriment to . . . develop[ing] several languages at the same time."

These conclusions were reinforced by researchers at Dartmouth College, who looked at children who had been exposed to different combinations of languages in both natural and school settings at various ages. As reported in *News in Science* (2002), researcher Laura-Ann Petitto addressed the annual meeting of the Society for Neuroscience on this topic. She reported that children exposed to two languages from a very early age "grow as if there were two monolinguals housed in one brain." She added that there is no contamination of either language by the other. The researchers concluded that "the earlier and more intensively the languages are introduced, the better" (p. 1).

National Reports, Policy Statements, and Studies

Beginning with the appearance of *Strength through Wisdom,* the report of the President's Commission on Foreign Language and International Studies (1979), a series of studies and reports on education have highlighted the need for improvement of opportunities for language study in the schools. The importance of language study has been tied to national security: "A nation's welfare depends in large measure on the intellectual and psychological strengths that are derived from perceptive visions of the world beyond its own boundaries" (p. 2). Language study has been related to the success of the United States in the international marketplace and to the skills required for happy and productive living in a future of increasing global interdependence. The commission specifically recommended that language study begin in the elementary school and continue throughout the student's education. Paul Simon's book, *The Tongue-Tied American: Confronting the Foreign Language Crisis* (1980), provides a wealth of material for the construction of a rationale for language learning.

In *A Nation at Risk,* the Report of the National Commission on Excellence in Education (Gardner, 1983), the study of foreign language and culture was placed alongside the five "basics" of English, mathematics, computer science, social studies, and the natural sciences as a fundamental component of a sound education.

Other commission reports, while focusing on the general decline in the quality of the nation's schools, have also addressed the need for studying foreign languages at the elementary school level. The National Commission on Excellence in Education (Gardner, 1983) maintained that achieving proficiency in a foreign language takes from four to six years of study and suggested that this begin in the elementary grades: "We believe it is desirable that students achieve such proficiency because study of a foreign language introduces students to non-English-speaking cultures, heightens awareness and comprehension of one's native tongue, and serves the nation's needs in commerce, diplomacy, defense, and education" (p. 26).

The National Advisory Board on International Education Programs, in a report to the Secretary of Education ("Critical Needs," 1983, p. 9), stated that language instruction should start as early as possible. In its report, "Critical Needs in International Education: Recommendations for Action," the board recommended that local school districts provide every student with the opportunity to begin the study of foreign language in the earliest years of formal education and to continue study of the same language until a functionally useful level of measured proficiency has been achieved.

These views are reiterated in a study by the College Board (*Academic Preparation for College,* 1983) that emphasized the importance of expanding the concept of basic skills to include foreign-language instruction for all students. More specifically, the report credits knowledge of a foreign language with helping students prepare for careers in commerce, international relations, law, science, and the arts. Furthermore, the report emphasizes that the development and maintenance of foreign language skills is a valuable national resource.

The Goals 2000: Educate America Act includes foreign languages in the list of critical areas for which students should demonstrate competence when leaving grades 4, 8, and 12. In 1996, the American Association of School Administrators listed knowledge of foreign languages as one of the most important skills for K–12 students in the twenty-first century. On September 15, 1999, Secretary of Education Richard W. Riley suggested that foreign language instruction would be a valuable way to raise education standards. He stated, "I believe that in this new economy every high school student should be close to fluent in a foreign language when he or she graduates. We should begin teaching foreign languages in our elementary schools, and then in middle schools and high schools."

Three years later, and under a different administration, U.S. Department of Education Secretary Rod Paige announced new priorities and initiatives for International Education on November 20, 2002. In his news release, Paige wrote, "We are ever mindful of the lessons of Sept. 11—one of which is that all future measures of a rigorous K–12 education must include a solid grounding in other cultures, other languages and other histories." He continued, "In other words, we need to put the 'world' back into 'world-class' education." Among the initiatives included in this announcement was support for international education in K–12 schools, including partnerships with states to provide new resources for high-quality, K–12 programs "that provide international knowledge and skills in our nation's classrooms" (p. 2). Paige also announced plans to honor teachers for outstanding work in helping young learners to understand world issues and other countries, cultures, and languages. These initiatives were announced at the annual meeting of the American Council on the Teaching of Foreign Languages on November 22, 2002.

General Rationale for Teaching Languages

The rationale for elementary and middle school programs is embedded in the rationale for languages generally, but it must also take into account some special characteristics of languages at those levels.

1. One of the most important factors influencing the development of language proficiency is the amount of time spent in working with the language. When language learning begins earlier, it can go on longer and provide more practice and experience, leading ultimately to greater fluency and effectiveness.

2. Every skill and outcome that is important to society is introduced through the elementary school curriculum. The lists of curriculum requirements in almost every state attest to the importance of reading, math, social studies, science, music, art, and physical education. The introduction of computers into nearly every elementary school program clearly reflects the values of our electronic, information age. Not until world languages become a secure part of the elementary school curriculum will language learning begin to meet the needs and challenges of the twenty-first century.

3. The age of 10 is a crucial time in the development of attitudes toward nations and groups perceived as "other," according to the research of Piaget, Lambert, and others (Lambert and Klineberg, 1967). Children are in the process of moving from egocentricity to reciprocity, and information introduced before age 10 is eagerly received. Carpenter and Torney (1974) suggest that exposure to a foreign language serves as a means of helping children move toward intercultural competence. The awareness of a global community can be enhanced when children have the opportunity to experience involvement with another culture through a foreign language.

A Vision for Language Competence in the World of the Twenty-First Century

Organizations for foreign-language professionals and many of our leaders have expressed compelling reasons for language learning. Savignon (1997, p. 169) describes the importance of languages as follows: "Learning to speak another's language means taking one's place in the human community. It means reaching out to others across cultural and linguistic boundaries. Language is far more than a system to be explained. It is our most important link to the world around us. Language is culture in motion. It is people interacting with people."

The National Council of State Supervisors of Foreign Languages (NCSSFL), in a position paper entitled "A Rationale for Foreign Language Education" (2002), endorses "foreign language education in the curriculum for all students, prekindergarten through grade twelve and beyond" (p. 1), and identifies foreign language education as an important part of basic education.

Cloud and Genesee (1998) argue that basic education in the new millennium must include second and third languages if the United States is to cope with the diversity within its borders and compete successfully in the global marketplace. They cite both cognitive and sociocultural benefits of language study. They conclude, "Linguistic and cultural competence will be the mark of the well-educated citizen of the 21st century" (p. 65).

The *Standards for Foreign Language Learning in the 21st Century* make a strong claim for the importance of language in the "Statement of Philosophy" (1999, p. 7):

Language and communication are at the heart of the human experience. The United States must educate students who are equipped linguistically and culturally to communicate successfully in a pluralistic American society and abroad. This imperative envisions a future in which ALL students will develop and maintain proficiency in English and at least one other language, modern or classical. Children who come to school from non-English-speaking backgrounds should also have opportunities to develop further proficiencies in their first language.

In support of these ideas, the philosophy includes three basic assumptions, two of which point directly toward language learning for all learners, beginning in the elementary school:

> All students can be successful language and culture learners, and they

> - must have access to language and culture study that is integrated into the entire school experience;

> Language and culture education is part of the core curriculum.

In May of 2006, the American Council on the Teaching of Foreign Languages (www.actfl.org/i4a/pages/Index.cfm?pageID=4368#early) issued position statements that further support the role of languages in the curriculum and specifically in the elementary and the middle school. The first of these, "General Principles of Language Learning," concludes with the following general principles:

1. All students should learn or maintain at least one language in addition to English.
2. Learning languages should be a central part of the curriculum at all levels of instruction, from young learners through graduate school and adults (Pre-K through 20).
3. Language learning should be offered in extended, well-articulated sequences that develop increasing levels of proficiency at each level of instruction by teachers who are well qualified in language proficiency, cultural knowledge, and teaching skills.

These principles are followed by this statement on early language learning:

> Since research shows that an early language learning experience generally results in the development of native or near-native pronunciation and intonation, it is recommended that students be provided the opportunity to learn a second language as early as possible in school. This early language learning experience not only helps to develop native-like pronunciation but also promotes higher levels of proficiency if the student continues in a well-articulated sequence of language learning. Research corroborates additional benefits including strengthening of literacy in students' first language, raising standardized test scores in other subject areas, and developing comfort with cultural differences. These benefits accrue with instruction that is continuous throughout the school year, connected grade to grade, and more frequent than twice per week, adding

up to at least 90 minutes per week, at both the elementary and middle school levels. (www.actfl.org/i4a/pages/Index.cfm?pageID=4368#early)

Basic Elementary School Skills and Goals

Some of the most powerful sources of rationale for foreign languages in the elementary and middle school are the curriculum guides of the schools themselves. Planners who truly understand both the goals of the elementary school and the potential of foreign languages can demonstrate the value of languages very convincingly by showing the relationship between the two. The local curriculum and philosophy provide the best information about the values and priorities of the school and the community in which the language program will take place.

Among the goals and philosophical positions commonly encountered in local curricula and in references about elementary school curriculum, some of the following themes have particularly high potential for the developer of a rationale for languages:

1. *Basic Skills.* This is certainly not a new concern for elementary school languages. Much of the research done during the banner years of elementary school language programs, the 1960s, was concerned with the relationship of language learning to skills acquisition in English language and mathematics. The concern at that time was almost always to demonstrate that these skills areas had not suffered because of the time "lost" to foreign-language instruction. The evidence was consistent: There was no sacrifice of basic skills when time was given to learning a new language (Donoghue, 1968).

In "Tangible Benefits of the Study of Latin: A Review of Research," Rudolph Masciantonio (1977) published a survey of research that made a stronger case for languages. Latin instruction in the elementary grades had been shown to result in significant and dramatic gains in standardized test performance in basic skills areas. In a similar study, gains were also reported for students of French and Spanish. Studies of immersion programs in Canada and the United States show that students taught by means of a foreign language achieve at similar or higher levels than their peers who are taught only in English, even when testing is done in English. Parents in Chicago, Cincinnati, and Milwaukee, for example, are known to choose metropolitan magnet schools offering languages because of the outstanding record of children in those schools on tests of English basic skills—not always primarily because of the language offerings themselves (Estelle, 1985; Anderson, 1982; Met, 1982). A study in Louisiana (Rafferty, 1986) showed that third-, fourth-, and fifth-graders studying French for 30 minutes a day achieved significantly higher scores on the 1985 Basic Skills Language Arts Test than did a similar group of nonparticipants. In addition, by fifth grade, the math scores of language students were also higher than those of nonlanguage students.

Later studies have confirmed the findings of this research. Armstrong and Rogers (1997), for example, showed that third-graders who were taught Spanish for 30 minutes three times a week showed statistically significant gains on their Metropolitan Achievement Test scores in the areas of math and language after only one semester of study. It is particularly interesting that one class of students in the experimental group had actually received one and a half fewer hours of math instruction per week, and still outperformed the students in control classes in math.

Saunders (1998) examined the performance of third-grade students enrolled in the Georgia Elementary School Foreign Language (ESFL) model program. She compared students who had not received any foreign-language instruction with students one year younger who had received four years of foreign-language instruction, five days each week, for 30 minutes per day. She found that those students in the ESFL program scored significantly higher on the math portion of the Iowa Test of Basic Skills than the older students had scored. They also performed better on the reading portion, but the difference was not statistically significant.

In a longitudinal study of a K–5 Spanish program in Pinellas County, Florida, Taylor, Feyten, Meros, and Nutta (2008) set out to determine the effect of Spanish instruction on native language reading, vocabulary, and language arts. In addition, they researched the effect of the Spanish instruction on their motivation in school generally, their aural/oral Spanish skills, and their cultural awareness of Spanish language culture. As with every previous study of its kind, there were no negative effects on any subgroup of the language study, and the Spanish study in the early grades positively impacted reading comprehension and vocabulary CTBS (California Test of Basic Skills) subtest scores of students with higher stanines.

2. *Communication.* Part of the impact of foreign-language study on basic skills performance can be explained by the greater understanding that students make gains in their own language when they see it from the perspective of a new language. Vygotsky, a significant contributor to contemporary developmental theory, writes in *Thought and Language* (1934/1986, p. 160):

> Goethe clearly saw it [reciprocal dependence] when he wrote that he who knows no
> foreign language does not truly know his own. Experimental studies fully endorse this.
> It has been shown that a child's understanding of his native language is enhanced by
> learning a foreign one. The child becomes more conscious and deliberate in using
> words as tools of his thought and expressive means for his ideas. . . . The child's
> approach to language becomes more abstract and generalized. . . . The acquisition of
> foreign language—in its own peculiar way—liberates him from the dependence on
> concrete linguistic forms and expressions.

Foreign-language study has been shown to enhance listening skills and memory (Ratte, 1968), and the development of second-language skills can contribute a significant additional dimension to the concept of communication.

Anecdotal data in the Taylor and colleagues study (2008) revealed information that supports the findings of Ratte. Teachers noted and commented on children's improved ability to listen, even in their first language. The researchers expressed this very well:

> Perhaps this notion can best be summed up by the idea that *language development is*
> *language development,* regardless of its form or delivery. It is reasonable to state that a
> young mind (flexible and developing as it is), given the opportunity to accommodate

and manipulate varied language constructs and meanings will be encouraged, in the process, to tap into cognitive and metacognitive abilities uniquely cultivated in the foreign language classroom. (p. 36)

Cummins (1990, p. 1) observes, "Research suggests that bilingualism enhances children's understanding of how language itself works and their ability to manipulate language in the service of thinking and problem-solving." The research that Cummins cites is primarily in the field of immersion education. He also indicates that bilingual children learn additional languages much more quickly and efficiently than do monolingual children.

3. *Creativity and Cognitive Development.* Many of the activities common in elementary school language programs—emphasis on movement, imagination, and role-play, for example—stimulate the right hemisphere of the brain, which is often underplayed in the formal school setting. Foreign-language instruction can make a contribution to "whole-brain" education, and one consequence can be enhanced creativity. Elementary school students attending a FLES program were reported to have greater skills in divergent thinking/figural creativity than did those who were monolingual, according to research conducted by Landry (1973).

A number of studies show that people who are competent in more than one language outscore monolinguals on tests of verbal and nonverbal intelligence (Bruck, Lambert, and Tucker, 1974; Hakuta, 1986; Weatherford, 1986). Students learning another language can show greater creativity in complex problem solving, according to Bamford and Mizokawa (1991). Rosenbusch (1995, p. 5) summarizes current research to indicate that "the length of time students study a foreign language relates directly and positively to higher levels of cognitive and metacognitive processing."

Caccavale (2007), in her review of the research, summarizes these benefits clearly:

A review of the literature on early second language learning indicates that bilingual children and monolingual children who begin the study of a second language at an early age and are enrolled in continuous, long-sequence programs can benefit in measurable ways in terms of both mathematical and literacy skill development. . . . It is important to remember that researchers find the highest correlation between second language development and critical thinking, or problem solving skills. While the application of better problem solving skills may result in increased language arts achievement, this correlation may not be entirely direct, and may be the secondary result of increased cognitive ability. (p. 32)

4. *Self-Concept.* Second-language learning in the elementary school, especially in its beginning stages, is less dependent on previous verbal learning than are most other elements of the curriculum. This factor allows some students to succeed who have otherwise experienced repeated failure in school. Evidence from a California study shows language students to have a significantly higher self-concept than do nonlanguage students (Masciantonio, 1977). Students in Cincinnati have also shown such success. In a 1987 study (Holobow et al., 1987) working-class students did just as well in French as middle-class students even though their English skills were not as good. In the study conducted by Taylor and colleagues (2008) teachers observed that certain low-achieving students seemed to express themselves and experience more success in Spanish class than in any other setting during the day.

5. *Societal and Career Benefits.* The rationale white paper published by the National Council of State School Officers of Foreign Languages (NCSSFL) identifies significant societal benefits associated with people who can communicate in at least two languages. As U.S. society becomes ever more diverse, jobs and careers will increasingly require skills in interacting with people who speak languages other than English, and in adapting to a wide range of cultural backgrounds. Managers who know how to deal with a diverse workforce will have an advantage in the growing multiethnic business community. Four out of five new jobs in the United States are created as a result of foreign trade, and the global marketplace has become a reality. Our educational system must provide learners with linguistic and cultural skills that will allow them to function effectively in this new business climate, both at home and around the world.

These new expectations and opportunities will be at every level of employment, not just in positions that require a college education. The needed language skills can only be acquired through extended and intensive language study—that is, an early start and a long sequence. As the NCSSFL (2002) white paper puts it, "The United States must have quality foreign language programs in our schools so that all students will graduate with the ability to interact linguistically and culturally with people from many countries. Students who are competent in at least two languages will dramatically increase the U.S. capabilities in diplomacy, in world trade, and in human understanding" (p. 4). It is also important to note that individuals who already can communicate effectively in two languages are in the best position to learn one or more additional languages quickly and efficiently, when new languages are needed for economic, political, strategic—or personal—purposes.

6. *Integration of All Areas of the Curriculum.* Every area of the curriculum can be reinforced or enriched in the foreign-language classroom, and subject content can be taught through the second language. This kind of integration can foster appreciation of other cultures and can add significant dimensions to the content being taught. With close cooperation between language and classroom teachers, the second-language experience can contribute directly to the mastery of first-language concepts in the curriculum.

7. *Cultural Enrichment.* Most languages taught at the elementary school level can give insight into a variety of cultures, including multicultural elements in the students' own community. The positive impact of cultural information is significantly enhanced when that information is experienced through the foreign language and accompanied by experiences in culturally authentic situations.

Other Sources of Rationale

The Center for Applied Linguistics summarized the benefits of early language learning as follows:

Learning a second language at an early age. . . .

1. Has a positive effect on intellectual growth.
2. Enriches and enhances a child's mental development.
3. Leaves students with more flexibility in thinking, greater sensitivity to language, and a better ear for listening.
4. Improves a child's understanding of his/her native language.
5. Gives a child the ability to communicate with people s/he would otherwise not have the chance to know.
6. Opens the door to other cultures and helps a child understand and appreciate people from other countries.
7. Gives a student a head start in language requirements for college.
8. Increases job opportunities in many careers where knowing another language is a real asset.

Elizabeth Webb, in her summary of research on early language learning (2001), concurs that "many benefits accrue to children who learn a second language." Those include:

1. The ability to speak another language and communicate with people from a different culture.
2. Improved performance in other basic skill areas, as reading and math. (Students of average intelligence seem to make particularly impressive gains in reading skills.)
3. Improved cognitive flexibility, better problem-solving and higher-order thinking skills.
4. Higher SAT and ACT scores.
5. Higher test scores on standardized tests, such as the Iowa Test of Basic Skills, the Metropolitan Achievement Test, and the Louisiana Basic Skills Test, in reading, language arts, math, and social studies.
6. Gains on measures of performance I.Q.
7. Improved communication skills, including better listening skills and a sharper memory.
8. Enhanced career potential.

Many of the resources listed at the end of this chapter will be useful in locating information and evidence to support a rationale. The brochure "Why, How, and When Should My Child Learn a Foreign Language?" (Marcos, 1997) is particularly helpful. In addition, readers are encouraged to examine rationale statements for languages and for elementary school programs available on the Internet. National reports on education often include information that gives strong support to teaching languages at the elementary school level; and reports on international business and trade also make mention of languages and their value. Even popular magazines occasionally publish features that can be valuable sources of rationale statements and that speak clearly to local audiences.

A rationale for teaching foreign languages at the elementary school level will be the result of many resources combined to address the needs and priorities of the local school and its community. The resources are abundant and varied, and serious program planners will find and use the most attractive and appropriate ones for their local situation.

● Advocacy for Early Language Learning

With so much compelling evidence favoring early language learning, it would seem self-evident that foreign languages should be a basic part of the curriculum in the elementary and the middle school. Unfortunately, there are many obstacles to achieving the vision of a K–12 language education for every learner. In the absence of a long tradition of languages for young learners, such as that found in other parts of the world, and given the limited resources available for education at every level, the addition of a "new basic" to the curriculum has not received widespread support. The fact that local control is a significant and valued characteristic of U.S. schools makes it difficult to establish a national language policy like that found in other countries with well-developed early language programs (Rhodes and Branaman 1999). The twenty-first century has brought a new awareness of a need for advocacy for early language learning at the national, state, and local levels.

State and National Advocacy Efforts

The Joint National Committee for Languages and the National Council for Languages and International Studies (JNCL-NCLIS) serves as an important advocacy arm of the foreign-language profession. Based in Washington DC, JNCL-NCLIS serves the profession as the liaison between foreign-language teachers and administrators and the federal government. They lobby for foreign-language goals and inform the profession about dangers and opportunities as they arise. Their website (see "Websites of Interest" at the end of this chapter) is an excellent source of information about pending legislation, funding opportunities, and grants of all types. This group also provides sound advice for foreign-language professionals who wish to make their own advocacy efforts more effective.

The National Network for Early Language Learning (NNELL) has an active Political Action and Advocacy Committee that guides and encourages advocacy efforts for early language learning throughout the country. The advocacy materials on the member portion of the website (www.nnell.org), regularly updated, are an invaluable resource for information about benefits of language learning, resources, and strategies for advocacy efforts.

State Initiatives   Many state associations, including North Carolina, Ohio, Texas, and Wisconsin, have formed political action and advocacy committees to promote language study in their states. In many cases these committees have devoted special attention to the elementary and middle school levels. Advocacy at the state level usually focuses on the state legislators, the governor, and the public at large. Two states, Georgia and North Carolina, will serve as helpful examples of how effective advocacy can take place.

Georgia   Georgia initiated a model programs project in 1992; these state-supported programs began with kindergarten students and added a grade level each year through grade 5. The 15 counties chosen for participation in the program guaranteed that language instruction would take place five days per week, 30 minutes a day, and that teachers would have no more than eight classes per day. Because funding for the program was often in doubt, teachers, parents, and administrators found themselves writing letters and contacting legislators on a regular basis to guarantee support for the coming year. In 2002, a group of concerned educators and other interested individuals formed the Coalition for Language Learning to advocate for foreign-language programs at all levels of instruction. The website for this group still exists, with useful information on the rationale for teaching elementary school languages and excellent materials to assist with advocacy: http://www2.gsu.edu/~wwwgcl/index.htm.

Shortly after the coalition was formed, the group was faced with its first crisis. The governor failed to include funding for the model programs in his budget, and the entire program was threatened. Ironically, the governor's action took place soon after the Center for Applied Linguistics had announced that students in the Georgia Elementary School Foreign Language (ESFL) model programs had scored higher than students in any other program they had tested to date nationwide.

The coalition mobilized and began a campaign of information and advocacy that involved personal visits to legislators and the governor, letter writing by students and parents, and even performances by students at the state capitol. One group of students and parents from a Japanese program folded an origami basket for every legislator. These baskets contained sweet treats and a message— "Save our Japanese program"—written in English and Japanese.

The funding for the program was restored by the legislature and finally approved by the governor. This result would not have been possible without the intensive advocacy efforts of the entire foreign-language community, led by the Georgia Coalition for Language Learning. A visit to the website mentioned above will reveal that funding was ultimately cut for the model programs, and has now been channeled in other directions. The interest generated by the model programs, however, continues to inspire efforts on the part of individual districts to continue or begin early language programs.

North Carolina   The Alliance for Language Learning was established in late 1998 to promote opportunities for learning languages throughout North Carolina. It serves as an advocate and a resource for parents, communities, schools, businesses, and policy makers at state and local levels. The advocacy committee within the Alliance responded to requests for advocacy and made presentations to economic development committees, civic clubs, and others. Decision makers such as legislators and State Board of Education members were regularly provided with information to encourage their support of foreign-language study.

One of the most significant projects undertaken by the Alliance was its Vision 2010, a foreign-language component of the North Carolina goal to have the best education system in the country by the year 2010. The Alliance goal for Vision 2010 was to establish well-developed K–12 model foreign language programs across North Carolina.

North Carolina's first Vision 2010 Model Foreign Language Program was established in the fall of 2002, with 50 kindergarten students who had daily content-related FLES instruction in Spanish, and several additional programs followed. This project planted the seed for long-term foreign-language instruction and articulation. These seeds continue to grow in the even more ambitious project, North Carolina in the World, a globalization project that began in 2005 and goes beyond language to include an international emphasis for all schools. Their Action Plan provides a good model for advocacy at the state level (available at http://ciu.northcarolina.edu/content.php/docs/NCWorld_ActionPlan.pdf).

● The Teacher as Advocate

Once a new program is established, successful, and well regarded, it is tempting to believe that the need for advocacy is over. In fact, the early language teacher needs to be a long-term advocate, if the program is to experience continued success. With a new program there is always a "honeymoon" period of varying length, during which time parents and classroom teachers are amazed at the speed and effectiveness of the language learning. Once this period is over, however, it takes effort on the part of the language teacher to demonstrate what students are learning and to sustain public awareness and support of the program. Each program faces articulation issues, student and parent turnover, and ever-present funding issues, and each of these issues requires a specific advocacy or public relations strategy.

Advocacy begins with the language teacher's day-to-day interactions with the rest of the learning community: school and district administrators; parents; and colleagues such as classroom teachers and teachers of music, physical education and other specials, upper-grade teachers of world languages, guidance counselors, and media specialists. The language teacher can build bridges of cooperation and mutual support that will hold up in the face of budget or scheduling crises. It is also important to help students themselves understand the value of the program and of their opportunity to learn another language, since student attitudes and understandings are the main source of information about the program in many parts of the community. Haxhi (2001) suggests advocacy strategies for use with these groups, as well as with the community at large:

● Keep all "players" informed. Regular newsletters to parents, with copies to administrators, school board members, and classroom teachers, can help all the "players" have realistic expectations of the program and understand what children can be expected to do. Haxhi also uses interactive homework as a means of keeping parents informed about student progress.

● Offer opportunities for involvement, observation, and suggestions.

● Be willing to adapt to changes and to improve.

● Identify the most rewarding (advocacy) activities, and eliminate inefficient activities.

● Get involved!

The language teacher who volunteers to help with the third-grade play, or to usher for the music program, is indirectly advocating for the language program at the same time. The language teacher who offers to help build the class schedule is perceived as a team player and can help to create an effective schedule that is manageable for all the teachers involved.

One of the most effective advocacy activities is a presentation for the local school board, perhaps including students or videotapes that show actual student performance. Virginia Gramer (1999) provided an excellent model for a persuasive school board presentation at a meeting of the ACTFL Delegate Assembly in Chicago. Much of the presentation was devoted to success stories of former students who had begun their language study in the elementary school.

It is important for the language program to be represented at school events, such as parent–teacher meetings, carnivals, and seasonal plays and programs. Sometimes the language classes stage an event themselves, such as a festival, an ethnic dinner, or a classroom presentation for parents. Sometimes the language students develop interesting projects that take the language beyond the classroom, such as writing and reading storybooks in the target language to younger learners, or putting on a play for other classes. In any of these cases, media coverage helps to spread the word about the program and the students involved.

Redmond (1998) suggests some strategies (strategies 4 through 7) for early language specialist teachers to help them become more effective advocates for early language learning, both locally and at the state and national levels. These strategies serve as a summary of the many ways a teacher can advocate for early language learning, both within and beyond the school itself.

Strategy 1: Take every opportunity to inform parents, administrators, and the local community about the foreign-language program and your students' accomplishments.

Strategy 2: Clarify the nature of the foreign-language curriculum and its connectedness to the elementary school classroom.

Strategy 3: Show parents and the community the skills attained and the purposes for the language learned.

Strategy 4: Invite guests to visit your classes to observe the children "in action."

Strategy 5: Assess students' progress both informally and formally and make parents aware of the results.

Strategy 6: Keep politicians, school board members, and other decision makers informed about your program.

Strategy 7: Thank your supporters!

Strategy 8: Change the mindset of those who studied a language unsuccessfully.

Strategy 9: Network with colleagues and unify efforts in grades K–16.

Strategy 10: Establish regular planning sessions with both elementary classroom teachers and K–12 foreign language colleagues.

Strategy 11: Use your state conference to organize advocacy efforts.

Numerous resources are available to assist early language teachers in implementing these strategies, and in developing activities that will highlight both their own programs and the importance of K–12 language learning. The resources listed at the end of this chapter will serve as a helpful starting point. As teachers work together to build and to draw from unified advocacy initiatives, the place of early language learning in U.S. school curricula will become ever more secure.

Summary

- No single rationale for teaching of foreign languages at the elementary school level will be effective for every program in every setting. Those who develop and seek support for such programs will need to tailor their rationale to the priorities and values of the community that the program will serve. An effective rationale will draw from a variety of recognized sources when building the case for early language learning and the K–12 sequence.

- Brain research in the last decade of the twentieth century has given strong support to an early start and a long sequence for language study.

- National reports and studies, both for foreign-language study generally and for elementary school languages in particular give many sound reasons for language learning.

- The level of communication skills in two or more languages that can provide both career benefits and societal benefits can be obtained only through an early start and a long sequence of language study.

- The goals of the elementary school and the philosophy of the school district are additional resources for building a rationale, as they set the context for a holistic education to which foreign language can make a unique and valuable contribution.

- Advocacy for early language learning is an important function of professional organizations at both the state and the national levels.

- It is also the responsibility of elementary and middle school language specialists to serve as advocates for their own programs and for K–12 language learning opportunities for all students.

For Study and Discussion

1. What reasons have you most frequently heard for teaching languages at the elementary school level? Which of these reasons do you feel would be good building blocks for a rationale statement?

2. A parent committee has asked for your assistance in convincing the school board to consider developing a foreign language program at the elementary school level. Write a memo advising the committee how they might go about building their case.

3. The curriculum coordinator in your district has recently discovered research indicating that children may not be better language learners than adults, and that they are in fact less efficient learners of the grammar and structure than are older students. How do you respond to her suggestion that languages should not be taught until grade 9, based on this information?

4. Which of the reasons for teaching languages in the elementary school would be the most convincing for the faculty, administrators, and parents of the school district or school setting with which you are the most familiar?

5. Develop a two-minute advocacy presentation in which you summarize the most important reasons for developing a K–12 foreign-language sequence in your school system.

6. Read at least one reference from the listing below about advocacy for early language learning. Describe one strategy not already mentioned in the chapter that you could use to advocate for your program with each of the following: colleagues, administrators, the community, parents, and students.

For Further Reading

The following sources are recommended for additional information about material covered in this chapter. Chapter citations are documented in Works Cited at the end of this book.

American Association of Teachers of French. "The ABCs of Elementary School Foreign Language Programs: A Guide for Parents." 28:3 (January 2003). http://www.frenchteachers.org/bulletin/articles/fles/ABCs%20for%20parents.pdf.

"The Complete Curriculum: Ensuring a Place for the Arts and Foreign Languages in America's Schools." The National Association of State Boards of Education (NASBE), http://www.nasbe.org/Front_Page/Press_Release.html. To order, call 1-800-220-5183. The cost is $14.00 plus shipping/handling.

Gramer, Virginia. "Advocacy for Early Language Education: A School Board Presentation." *Learning Languages* 4:3 (Spring 1999): 4–8.

Marcos, Kathleen. "Why, How, and When Should My Child Learn a Foreign Language?" Washington DC: ERIC Clearinghouse on Languages and Linguistics, 1997. Available on-line at http://www.cal.org/resources/pubs/whyhowwhen-brochure.pdf (accessed February 9, 2009).

Marcos, Kathleen. "Second Language Learning: Everyone Can Benefit." *The ERIC Review: K–12 Foreign Language Education* 6:1 (Fall 1998): 2–5. http://www.cal.org/earlylang/benefits/marcos.html (accessed February 9, 2009).

Met, Myriam. "Why Language Learning Matters." *Educational Leadership* (October 2001): 36–40.

National Network for Early Language Learning (NNELL) Advocacy Packet. http://nnell.org.

NBC Dateline., Friday, November 28, 1997. Program on the brain and the importance of early language learning. Call 800-777-8398 for a complete transcript of the segment or call 800-420-2626 to determine if video copy is available.

Redmond, Mary Lynn. "ATTENTION! Are You Seeking a Position with Excellent Long-Term Benefits? Be an Advocate!" *Learning Languages* 4:1 (Fall 1998): 4–9.

Robinson, Deborah Wilburn. "The Cognitive, Academic, and Attitudinal Benefits of Early Language Learning." In Myriam Met (Ed.),

Critical Issues in Early Second Language Learning: Building for Our Children's Future (pp. 37–43). Glenview, IL: Scott-Foresman-Addison Wesley, 1998.

Simon, Paul. *The Tongue-Tied American. Confronting the Foreign Language Crisis.* New York: Continuum Publishing, 1980.

Websites of Interest

ACTFL Discover Languages website contains practical advice on how to become a foreign language advocate: www.discoverlanguages.org/i4a/pages/index.cfm?pageid=3656.

ACTFL summary of research in support of language learning and many other useful links and resources: www.discoverlanguages.org.

Association for Supervision and Curriculum Development (ASCD) Advocacy Kit: http://www.ascd.org/advocacykit/.

"Foreign Language Study and the Brain." University of Idaho, Teresa Kennedy. http://www.teresa kennedy.com/.

Joint National Committee for Languages and National Council for Languages and International Studies (Foreign Language Advocacy): http://www.languagepolicy.org.

League of Women Voters: http://www.lwv.org.

Listing of Advocacy Resources: http://www.flanc.org/Involve_Advocacy.html.

Ñandutí Early Language website: http://www.cal.org/earlylang/.

National K–12 Foreign Language Resource Center: http://nflrc.iastate.edu/.

National Network for Early Language Learning (NNELL): http://www.nnell.org.

News in Science. "Bilingual kids not slowed by second tongue." http://www.abc.net.au/science/news/stories/s720173.htm.

North Carolina in the World: www.ncintheworld.org.

"Ten Good Reasons for Learning a Foreign Language": http://www.vistawide.com/languages/why_languages.htm.

Video of Comments by Language Students: https://www.glastonburyus.org/curriculum/foreign language/advocate/Pages/default.aspx.

Chapter 16

Learning from the Past to Enhance the Present and the Future

Enduring Understanding

- Foreign-language program successes and failures of the past are valuable sources of information for planning new programs.

Essential Question

- How can we avoid repeating the mistakes of the past?

Children have been learning new languages in U.S. schools since colonial times, and the presence of these languages in the curriculum has often been the subject of controversy. Many of the concerns raised a century or more ago sound surprisingly like discussions held at contemporary staff and school board meetings at which districts consider the addition or expansion of an elementary school language program. It is important for the advocate of languages for children to understand past successes and problems, especially those of the heyday for early language programs in the 1960s, in order to plan and implement programs that build on the strengths and insights of the past and avoid its failures.

• A Short History of Early Language Learning in the United States

Foreign-language instruction has been fairly common in the United States throughout its history; Latin was often taught in the early years, and German was popular after the great waves of German immigration in 1830 and 1848. French and Spanish schools developed in some areas of the country where there were concentrations of immigrants from French- and Spanish-speaking countries.

Objections to the teaching of German and other languages in the elementary schools were raised by state and territorial officials, often on the grounds that the practice was un-American, and that children in private and parochial schools were being taught by individuals who did not even speak English. However, programs persisted and grew, despite the controversies, until the United States entered World War I. At that time there was a strong reaction against everything German, especially the language, and much elementary school instruction in all languages other than English was eliminated.

New Impetus for Language Instruction

In the 1940s, a concern for improvement of Latin American understanding led to the development of Spanish-language programs in the elementary schools of the American Southwest. In 1957, after the stunning orbit of *Sputnik,* public awareness of the value of foreign-language education was heightened by the jarring information that the United States could have known about the development of the Russian satellite had American scientists been regular readers of Russian journals. As a result, languages were included along with mathematics and science in the generous funding of the National Defense Education Act (NDEA) of 1958. Among other provisions, the act included matching funds for the purchase of instructional equipment and materials, and it provided for the training of teachers in "critical" languages (German, French, Spanish, Russian) at both the elementary and the secondary school levels.

The national sense of urgency explains in part the haste with which many school districts launched language programs at the elementary and the secondary school levels. Years of low priority for languages had failed to produce enough language teachers to meet the new demand, and most of the teachers available had little preparation for the elementary school level. These factors underscored the importance of the training provisions of the NDEA. Institutes were funded throughout the country to prepare teachers in the new aural-oral/audiolingual approach, based on the methods developed for the army during World War II.

These NDEA institutes marked the first time in the United States that there had been a concentrated effort centered on the development of an approach to language teaching. Much of the teaching of modern languages before the 1960s, even at the elementary school level, had been modeled on the teaching of Latin and Greek, and had included an emphasis on reading, translation, and grammatical analysis using the terminology of Latin grammar. That approach may have been intended to earn academic and intellectual respect for modern languages, which had not been valued in a classical education (Grittner, 1977).

In contrast, Emile de Sauze directed a program in Cleveland for selected elementary school students from 1918 until 1949. Under the "Cleveland Plan" all instruction was conducted in the new language, and reading and writing were deferred until the sixth grade (Donoghue, 1968).

At the end of the nineteenth century, some teachers had already begun to break with the Latin-based formula for language teaching, experimenting with the "natural" and the "direct" methods. Each of these methods stressed the spoken word and deemphasized grammar for its own sake, although the direct method approached grammar more systematically and developed more carefully constructed curricula. Both required a teacher who was fluent in the language and who was willing to use the target language almost exclusively (Zeydel, 1961).

Against this background, the audiolingual method of the 1960s represented a dramatic burst of new energy for language teaching. It claimed a basis in the relatively new field of structural linguistics and in behavioral psychology, as it deemphasized the traditional methods of grammar study and focused on language competence developed through habit formation. Elementary school students were viewed as natural candidates for this type of instruction because they were far less resistant to the repetition and drill required by the method. Oral language served as the starting point of all language study, even for those students to whom reading was a primary goal. Inductive grammar and oral drill replaced grammatical analysis in English; listening and speaking practice in the classroom and in the language laboratory replaced reading and translation exercises.

Thousands of teachers were trained or retrained in NDEA institutes, which gave teachers the opportunity to develop skills in the new method and to improve their speaking skills in the language. Except for pockets of resistance or misunderstanding, a whole generation of language teachers began modeling dialogues, conducting pattern drills, and practicing the art of mimicry-memorization.

Short-Lived Gains

There was every reason to be optimistic that the newly attained place for languages in national priorities and the new method, supported with new opportunities for teacher preparation, would lead to a "golden age" for language programs, especially at the elementary school level. But the ambitions and good intentions of school districts often outdistanced genuine planning and the availability of well-trained personnel. The "boom" for languages in the elementary schools lasted barely five years, as programs at this level were in decline after 1964. Many of the reasons for this short period of popularity are described in "A Survey of FLES Practices," a report written for the Modern Language Association in 1961. After visiting 62 communities with reportedly good FLES programs in the spring of 1961, Alkonis and Brophy (1961, pp. 213–217) drew the following conclusions:

1. A majority of the FLES programs that we observed do not fulfill the primary aim of such a program—teaching the four language skills—even when this is clearly stated

as their objective. Sometimes the teacher is weak; just as often the weakness lies beyond the teacher's control, in the materials or the scheduling.

2. Many programs emphasized such aims as "world understanding" or "broadened horizons" to the extent that it is a clear misnomer to call them language programs. We saw no evidence of effective evaluation of the teaching directed toward these objectives. . . .

3. There is such a diversity of linguistic content that a general evaluation of results using a single test or series of tests appears to be impracticable.

4. From the widespread emphasis upon learning lists of words, we conclude that a majority of the FLES teachers think of language as words to be learned in isolation and then strung into "conversation." They showed no awareness of the interacting systems of structure or patterns that are basic to each language.

5. Many programs, started without planning and provision for the materials, the instruction, and the eventual integration with junior- and senior-high school courses, are considered "experimental," but there is no clear statement of the conditions and terms of the experiment and no provision for an evaluation of its results.

6. The most obvious weakness is lack of teachers with sufficient skill in the language and training in methods. (This is no reflection on the sincerity, the enthusiasm, or the good will of the instructors. How many of us, with no knowledge of music and unable to play the piano, could successfully teach a roomful of little children to play that instrument?)

7. In many schools—certainly in the majority of those we visited—FLES is conceived of as merely a preview or prelude to "real" language learning (which will begin in the high school) rather than as a serious, systematic attempt to develop attitudes and skills.

8. Few programs are planned as an unbroken, cumulative sequence from the primary through the junior high school, partly because of the lack of appropriate teaching materials for the junior high school, but more because of the inadequacy of the FLES work itself.

The eight observations made by Alkonis and Brophy effectively summarized the problems that most FLES programs of the 1960s failed to resolve. As budgets tightened and priorities shifted, as promised results failed to materialize, as graduates of FLES programs failed to meet the expectations of junior and senior high school teachers, language programs in the elementary school lost their credibility as well as their value as a status symbol. These programs were among the first to be cut when school systems evaluated their curricula to make room for new trends and emphases.

Although NDEA funding continued through 1968, the last institute designed specifically for elementary school teachers was held in 1965, at which time enthusiasm for the audiolingual method was also beginning to wane. While the combination of structural linguistics and behavioral psychology had focused on the external features of language, a new concern for the internal processing of language was being articulated by the rationalists and the generative grammarians. Emphasis was shifting from the manipulation of patterns that might eventually be used to convey information to the use of language as a means of communication, and from the means by which an idea was expressed to the importance of the idea being communicated.

The decline of interest and support for traditional foreign-language programs in the schools, however, first evidenced by the loss of enthusiasm for elementary school language programs, had become widespread by the early 1970s. Unsettling events at home and abroad led to a period of student apathy and low motivation. The war in Vietnam and student protests at colleges and universities became the focus of public attention. School enrollments began to decline, and enrollments in language classes declined even more rapidly. Critics blamed the tedium and irrelevance of the audiolingual method for declining language enrollments, and universities aggravated the situation by dropping language entrance and exit requirements.

New Challenges and Opportunities

Meanwhile, attempts to understand more about language learning and teaching were being made on behalf of language-minority students. An influx of Spanish-speaking families from Latin American countries and the arrival of refugees from Southeast Asia increased the population of non-English-speaking children in the schools in many areas in the United States and created a need for language instruction for these children.

In dealing with the challenge, teachers of English to speakers of other languages found assistance from linguists and psychologists. This alliance has resulted in a growing body of research that shed new light on how language competence is developed. Abroad, the Council of Europe developed an approach to language teaching and learning that was based on the communication needs of the learner. *The Threshold Level for Modern Language Learning in Schools* (Van Ek, 1991) a resource available for several European languages, identifies functions and vocabulary necessary to interact successfully in a variety of specific situations. Together, these developments reinforced the emerging emphasis on the messages being expressed by language and the process of language acquisition.

In Canada, the desire of English-speaking parents to increase their children's proficiency in French led to the establishment of immersion programs, an innovative educational approach in which the language of the school setting is different from the language of the home, and children learn subject content through the new language. The first French kindergarten class for native speakers of English was offered in September 1965, in St. Lambert, a suburb of Montreal. Public school immersion programs spread throughout Canada and have been thoroughly researched and documented. Immersion has also spread to many parts of the United States, and according to the Center for Applied Linguistics, there were immersion programs in at least 30 cities in the United States by 1987, involving 8,000 school children. By 1999, there were approximately 46,000 children enrolled in 11 languages in 278 immersion schools, more than half of them in Spanish (Center for Applied Linguistics, "Total and Partial Immersion Programs," 2006). In Canada, French immersion programs alone enrolled nearly 50,000 children in 1979, 150,000 in 1985, and over 300,000 by 2000 (Canadian Parents for French, 2006).

Another approach to teaching subject content and language together was developing for the non-English-speaking child in U.S. schools. Beginning with Cuban refugee children in the Dade County schools of Florida in 1963, bilingual programs helped children learn to read and write in their own language as well as introduced them to English. In most such programs subject content material is taught in both languages, with an increasing emphasis on English at each grade level.

Many early bilingual programs also included the opportunity for English-speaking children to learn the second language in the same setting. With this approach, student native speakers serve as language models for one another. These programs, usually called *two-way immersion* or *two-way bilingual programs,* grew in popularity at the turn of the century. By 2000, there were 260 programs in 23 states, most of them in Spanish. This model depends on the presence of a stable population of native speakers in both languages. The growing Spanish population in the United States creates ideal conditions for two-way Spanish immersion programs.

● Renewed Interest in Languages for Young Learners

Twenty years after *Sputnik,* the national interest in languages other than English was again awakened by international events. The rise of multinational corporations, the increasing importance of international trade, and an oil crisis all contributed to a renewed awareness of this country's dependence on global relationships. The 1979 President's Commission on Foreign Language and International Studies was the first of a series of commissions on education to highlight the serious situation created by the lack of language skills among Americans. Its specific recommendations included the urging of language study in the elementary school and the development of imaginative curricula dealing with other countries and cultures. Subsequent national studies and reports about education, such as *A Nation at Risk* (D. Gardner, 1983), amplified the call for a more international vision in the schools and a higher priority for language learning.

The first calls for early language learning were joined by many more voices. Among others, the National Governors Association task force recommended in 1990 that all students should have the opportunity to learn to speak a foreign language in their early years; the Commission on International Education of the American Council on Education expressed support for long sequence programs resulting in proficiency, recommending in 1989 that foreign-language training should begin as early as possible, preferably in elementary school. On September 11, 2001, American awareness was once again jolted into recognition of the importance to national security of citizens who have skills in a variety of languages.

Further impetus for early language learning came from results and interpretation of brain research, brought to popular awareness through reports in *Newsweek* (Begley, 1996) and *Time* (Nash, 1997). J. Madeleine Nash wrote in the *Time* article, "The ability to learn a second language is highest between birth and the age of six, and then undergoes a steady and inexorable decline. . . . What lessons can be drawn from the new findings? Among other things, it is clear that foreign languages should be taught in elementary school, if not before" (p. 56).

Response by the Profession

The professional community responded in several ways to the new public interest in early language programs for children. The National Network for Early Language Learning (NNELL), originally established in 1987 as an informal network of teachers and supervisors, became a formal organization in 1991. Its newsletter, *FLES News,* reached over 500 members three times a year. *FLES News* became a peer-reviewed journal, *Learning Languages,* in 1991, and by 2008, the membership and journal circulation had reached 700. NNELL has grown to include a large board of directors and vigorous state organizations. There are NNELL-sponsored sessions at nearly every national and regional meeting of language teachers, as well as at many state meetings. Advocacy efforts by NNELL have been helpful to teachers and programs throughout the country.

The three largest language-specific teacher organizations have each developed special projects addressing K–8 languages: The American Association of Teachers of German (AATG) has its Kinder lernen Deutsch steering committee, established in 1987, which channels funds from the German government into teacher preparation, materials evaluation and development, and support for program planning and implementation. The American Association of Teachers of French (AATF), long active in support of elementary school programs, has published a series of useful resources through its FLES Commission and sponsors a yearly national contest for young learners. The American Association of Teachers of Spanish and Portuguese (AATSP) supports elementary school programs in a number of ways, most notably through its yearly poster contest for Spanish learners in elementary and middle schools.

Teachers have access to state and national conferences sponsored by these organizations, as well as regional conferences, including the Northeast Conference on the Teaching of Foreign Languages, the Southern Conference on Language Teaching, the Southwest Conference on Language Teaching, and the Central States Conference on the Teaching of Foreign Languages. Most sessions at these conferences focus on curriculum and pedagogy for the K–12 level.

The Center for Applied Linguistics provides research and information about K–12 language learning, and its publications include digests on important educational topics. National Language Resource Centers were created in 1990, under Title VI of the Higher Education Act of the U.S. Department of Education, to serve as resources to improve the nation's capacity to teach and learn foreign languages effectively. As of 2002, there were 14 such resource centers located throughout the United States and Hawai'i. One of these, the K–12 Foreign Language Resource Center at Iowa State University, is focused specifically on issues of curriculum, assessment, and teacher development for K–12 programs, with special emphasis on the K–8 level. The Center for Advanced Research on Language Acquisition, at the University of Minnesota, provides special resources and workshops for immersion education.

Listservs and their archives provide teachers with the opportunity to post questions about programs, materials, or methodology and share their ideas with colleagues from all over the country. Two of the most popular are FLTeach, used especially by middle and high school teachers, and Ñandu, the early language listserv for K–8 teachers.

Responses from States and Local School Systems

State and local responses came in a variety of ways to the call for early language learning and a long sequence of study. A number of states mandated foreign-language study in some form in the elementary school, although not all mandates led to the results envisioned by legislators. In states where there was sufficient financial and professional support for the elementary school initiative, new programs thrived. Where such support was lacking, the mandates led to only a few new programs in districts that could afford to make languages a priority. Other states, such as Georgia and Iowa, offered some types of financial incentives to school districts willing to plan language programs for the elementary school. As budgets tightened and other priorities arose, however, state funding disappeared and so did many of the programs that had depended on it. A 2004 list of state requirements for elementary school programs identifies only 10 states with some form of mandate for world language offerings at the elementary school level. This information, as well as links to state frameworks for world languages and regular information updates, can be accessed at the website of the National Council of State Supervisors of Foreign Languages (NCSSFL): www.ncssfl.org.

The variety of language offerings for young learners also increased. Although Spanish programs outnumbered all others, French, Latin, and German continued to be taught at the elementary school level. Increasing numbers of programs were developed in Chinese, Japanese, Arabic, and Russian, as a reflection of world economic and political realities. Sometimes elementary school language offerings reflected the ethnic background of the community, and the desire to continue with heritage languages. Italian, Portuguese, Hebrew, Czech, Korean, Norwegian, Persian, Greek, and Welsh are examples of such language instruction.

By 1997, there were foreign-language programs in 31 percent of all public and private elementary schools surveyed by the Center for Applied Linguistics, up from 22 percent in 1987. Spanish was taught in 79 percent of the programs, followed by French at 27 percent. Programs in German, Latin, Japanese, and Spanish for Spanish speakers were also well represented (Rhodes and Branaman, 1999). Ten years later, these numbers had shifted again. Preliminary results from the CAL survey completed in June 2008 showed a decrease in public elementary school foreign-language programs, down from 24 percent to 15 percent. Private school offerings declined from 53 percent to 51 percent. Spanish, which continues to be the most frequently taught language, reported in 88 percent of the programs. Both Chinese and Latin showed a marked growth in popularity at the elementary school level, and Arabic programs had also increased.

The decrease in numbers of programs may have many explanations, but two are often cited. With continuing budget cutbacks, early language programs were often regarded as a "frill," especially if they were not well integrated with the whole elementary school program or articulated with the middle and high schools. Another factor has been the No Child Left Behind (NCLB) legislation of 1991, with its strong focus on reading and math and its high-stakes testing. Many language programs were cut back to make room for more time for the tested subject areas.

Federal and Professional Initiatives

Some federal legislation, however, supported the growth of early language programs. The Foreign Language Assistance Program (FLAP) targets foreign-language instruction in elementary and secondary schools. Many existing elementary school language programs owe their existence to the receipt of a FLAP grant. The program began in 1988 when Congress passed the Foreign Language Assistance Act. In 2008 and 2009, these three-year grants were targeted especially at so-called critical foreign languages, including Chinese, Arabic, Russian, Korean, and Hindi.

Another federal initiative, the National Security Language Initiative (NSLI), was developed in 2006 as an interagency effort coordinated by the White House to dramatically increase the number of Americans learning, speaking, and teaching critical need foreign languages. The FLAP grants became an important part of this initiative. Many other innovative programs for critical languages were developed with NSLI funding. For example, the National Foreign Language Center developed the STARTALK program in 2007, an ongoing intensive summer program for students and teachers of Arabic and Chinese.

Contributing to the momentum for language learning, ACTFL launched a successful public relations project, declaring 2005 the "Year of Languages." The organization followed up in 2006 with a "Discover Languages—Discover the World" initiative, a continuing advocacy effort for language learning. Its many activities include a Discover Languages month (February), a student podcast competition, and a website with a wide variety of information for teachers, students, and parents (www.discoverlanguages.org).

The Proficiency Movement and Elementary and Middle School Language Programs

The description of academic expectations, especially at the college and graduate level, and measures of achievement of language goals were based for a long time on grammar as an organizing principle and on the teaching of discrete points as a standard practice. This may have been one reason for poor articulation in the past between communication-based elementary school language programs and the secondary school programs into which they fed.

The Proficiency Guidelines from the American Council on the Teaching of Foreign Languages (ACTFL), first published in 1986, marked a pivotal change in the teaching of new languages in the United States. They refocused language instructional goals from what learners know about language to what they can do with the language they have learned, and at the same time they established a common metric for measuring student performance. Emphasis has shifted from grammar and discrete-item testing to a global evaluation of language competencies. Teachers can permit themselves to assess communication of meaning as well as, though not to the total exclusion of, degree of accuracy, and students can be rewarded for a much broader range of language ability and performance.

The proficiency guidelines describe student performance in listening, speaking, reading, and writing at the novice, intermediate, advanced, and superior levels. They define student language performance in terms of function, content, and accuracy of the message being delivered or received. They were adapted from guidelines developed in U.S. government language schools and have made "proficiency-oriented instruction" a part of the vocabulary of every language teacher. The 1986 guidelines were subsequently reevaluated and revised, beginning with "Speaking" in 1999 (Breiner-Sanders, Lowe, Miles, and Swender, 2000) and "Writing" in 2001 (Breiner-Sanders, Swender, and Terry, 2002).

Elementary school language teachers may find the ACTFL guidelines difficult to apply directly to the curriculum of the elementary school program. Many of the functions and much of the content described are not closely related to the interests and needs of children. Yet the principle of purposeful language use is clearly held in common at all levels of communicative language teaching. The guidelines can serve the elementary school language teacher very well as a guide to the future uses to which the language taught in the elementary school will be put. This can make the ACTFL Proficiency Guidelines useful in bridging the gaps between elementary school, middle school, and high school programs.

The ACTFL guidelines give us an important tool for looking at the outcomes of instruction. This tool can help K–8 language teachers be both more realistic in their goals for instruction and more realistic in their claims for their programs.

● Shaping a K–12 Vision for Language Learning

Perhaps the most significant activity within the language teaching profession has been the movement toward the shared vision of a long sequence of language instruction beginning in the elementary school. "Start Early—Stay Long" was the motto of the initiative established in 1992 by the ACTFL, the umbrella organization for language teachers at all levels. The New American: Project 2017 was a joint project with the National Foreign Language Center to lay the groundwork for sound language programs that progress smoothly from elementary school through the university level. The National Foreign Language Center also sponsored a 1999 National Town Meeting on issues surrounding early language learning entitled "Preparing Young Americans for the 21st Century." The Town Meeting was held in Washington DC and attended by lawmakers and policy makers at the national level, as well as by language professionals.

The Project 2017 initiative was superseded by the challenge and opportunity of the federal Goals 2000 project (later named Educate America 2000). In 1993, the language profession became the seventh and final content area to receive funding from the U.S. Department of Education and the National Endowment for the Humanities to develop a series of content standards—what students should know and be able to do—in foreign-language education. This three-year grant, and the place for foreign languages in the listing of critical subject areas, came after several years of lobbying by professional organizations and the Joint National Committee for Language (JNCL). The ACTFL, together with the AATF, the AATG, and the AATSP, spearheaded the effort to establish goals and standards for language learning, with descriptors and sample progress indicators at grades 4, 8, and 12. The 11-member Standards task force represented a variety of languages, levels of instruction, program models, and geographic regions. The decision to design the Standards for an extended K–12 sequence was made after considerable discussion and significant input from professionals who were already active at the K–6 level.

Standards for Foreign Language Learning in the 21st Century

Just as the proficiency movement spawned a whole new way of thinking about language instruction and assessment, the *Standards for Foreign Language Learning in the 21st Century*, first released in 1996 and revised in 1999, provide a significant new focus for curriculum and program planning. In contrast to earlier curriculum documents, the Standards have created the bold vision of a long sequence of language instruction for all learners, beginning in kindergarten and continuing through grade 12 and beyond. For the first time in the United States, the language teaching profession had made a strong statement about the importance of a long sequence of instruction beginning with the earliest years of schooling. By 1999, the language-specific professional organizations had developed supporting Standards documents describing student progress from kindergarten through the fourth year of college, thus focusing the entire instructional sequence on a unified vision of language education. More languages were added to a third edition in 2006.

Within a short period of time after the appearance of the Standards in 1996, publishers and in-service providers began to focus materials and workshops on the five goals and 11 content standards described in the Standards document. (See the Standards summary on page xxiii.) These content standards describe what students should know and be able to do as a result of instruction, and they are the first step in the process of standards development. Sample performance indicators for grades 4, 8, and 12 provide examples of how students demonstrate progress in meeting a standard. They also point the way toward performance standards that define how students demonstrate competency in a given content standard. The ACTFL Proficiency Guidelines are an example of performance standards, but they were designed to describe language performance of adult or adult-like language users, regardless of where or how that language was acquired.

ACTFL Performance Guidelines for K–12 Learners

An ACTFL Young Learner Task Force drew on the ACTFL Proficiency Guidelines of 1982, the Standards for Foreign Language Learning, and classroom experiences to develop a set of performance standards appropriate for K–12 learners. The ACTFL Performance Guidelines for K–12 Learners, released in November 1997, focuses on students who participate in elementary, middle school, and high school language programs, taking into account the continuous cognitive development of students at these levels and its influence on their ability to perform language tasks. The guidelines also recognize the fact that most K–12 language development takes place in a classroom context, with a curriculum that is articulated from one level to the next (Swender and Duncan, 1998).

The ACTFL Performance Guidelines provide benchmarks for the novice range (end of the K–4 sequence, or grades 5 to 8, or any two years in high school); for the intermediate range (end of the K–8 sequence, or grades 9 to 12, or grades 5 to 12); or for the preadvanced learner range (end of a K–12 sequence). Performance descriptors are grouped into six domains:

Comprehensibility (How well is the student understood?)

Comprehension (How well does the student understand?)

Language Control (How accurate is the student's language?)

Vocabulary Use (How extensive and applicable is the student's vocabulary?)

Communication Strategies (How does the student maintain communication?)

Cultural Awareness (How is the student's cultural knowledge reflected in language use?)

Under each of these domains, student performance is described in terms of the communication modes identified in the Standards: interpersonal (1.1), interpretive (1.2), and presentational (1.3) (see the appendix at the back of this book).

These ACTFL Performance Guidelines for K–12 Learners can assist language teachers in gauging the performance levels of their students. They can also help teachers design effective learning and performance tasks that will guide and assess student progress toward local, state, and national content standards.

In Chapter 17, Figure 17.3 illustrates the anticipated performance outcomes described in the K–12 guidelines and shows their relationship to the ACTFL Proficiency Guidelines. Note that the preadvanced level in the Performance Guidelines is equivalent to the intermediate high level in the Proficiency Guidelines. Once students have attained the preadvanced level, the ACTFL Proficiency Guidelines can be used to describe student progress through the superior level.

Working toward the K–12 Vision

The K–12 vision articulated in the Standards and in the ACTFL Performance Guidelines has infused the language teaching profession in a variety of ways. The National K–12 Foreign Language Resource Center at Iowa State University, together with the ACTFL, launched a New Visions project with a goal of reevaluating and reshaping the profession in the light of the Standards—including the goals of language instruction for every child and appropriate preparation for every language teacher. Many states shifted their licensing for world language teachers from a focus on secondary school students—the 7–12 or 5–12 license—to preparation for the long sequence of instruction: K–12 licensure. This approach to teacher licensing motivates colleges and universities to reexamine and reshape their teacher preparation sequences. More institutions now provide preparation for teachers in K–12, instead of exclusively for middle school (beginning at grade 5, 6, or 7, depending on the state) through grade 12, and this change has become an important factor in moving the K–12 vision forward. Unfortunately, a mandate for K–12 licensure alone cannot ensure that there will be college or university personnel available who understand the elementary school level, and some institutions of higher education find it difficult to create meaningful, appropriately staffed programs. Neither licensing requirements for higher education nor language requirements for elementary schools can ensure quality programs without sufficient funding to institute new programs.

As individual states developed their own standards, in response to the Goals 2000 legislation, most have used the national Standards as their model and described a K–12 sequence of language learning. This has been true even in states with very few existing elementary school programs.

Other efforts to support the K–12 vision have developed through the efforts of foreign-language educators themselves. In North Carolina, for example, the Vision 2010 project of the Alliance for Language Learning seeks to develop at least one model K–12 articulated sequence in every school district in the state by the year 2010. Other states have language alliances that bring language teachers together from prekindergarten through university levels, with a shared goal of advocating for language learning and bridging the gaps in articulation from one school or age level to another.

The K–12 vision challenges the profession to find new ways to communicate across grade levels and new ways to conceptualize curriculum, instruction, and teacher preparation. It will require the involvement of every member of the profession to translate the vision into reality.

Summary

- The challenge for the twenty-first century is to learn from the past, to develop programs strong enough to withstand the shifting winds of enthusiasm and fad, and to realize the vision of the K–12 articulated language sequence.

- Many of the problems that plagued the 1960s still threaten us, especially at the elementary school level: a shortage of qualified teachers, a tendency to establish programs without sufficient planning or careful selection of teachers and materials, a lack of clarity about goals, and a willingness to promise whatever the public wants to hear.

- New tools have emerged to meet the challenges: a solid base of research in psychology and linguistics, extensive experiences in immersion and bilingual education, new insights about communication, improved understanding of first- and second-language acquisition, and new standards for judging proficiency and progress.

- The 1980s and 1990s saw a growing public and professional support for K–8 languages, and the teaching profession has developed numerous initiatives and organizations to assist teachers working at this level.

- Government initiatives have impacted language learning, both positively and negatively.
- The *Standards for Foreign Language Learning in the 21st Century* have established a new vision for language education as a long sequence beginning in the elementary school. The ACTFL Proficiency Guidelines and the Student Performance Guidelines provide new ways to look at student language performance and to describe it across programs and levels.

For Study and Discussion

1. What resources does the curriculum planner for elementary school language programs have available today that will help a school system avoid the pitfalls and problems encountered by earlier programs?

2. Supporting early language learning programs might be considered "getting on another bandwagon," triggered by national reports. What lessons can be learned from the history of language teaching in the United States to help prevent the decline of support for language programs after their "fad value" has worn off?

3. What current national and international events tend to encourage support for language programs at the elementary school level?

4. How might information on the history of foreign language programs be of value when writing a program rationale?

5. What aspects of the history of foreign languages at the elementary school level might have been different if the ACTFL Proficiency Guidelines had been available in the 1960s?

For Further Reading

The following sources are recommended for additional information about material covered in this chapter. Chapter citations are documented in Works Cited at the end of this book.

Birckbichler, Diane W. (Ed.). *Reflecting on the Past to Shape the Future.* The ACTFL Foreign Language Education Series. Lincolnwood, IL: National Textbook, 2000.

Heining-Boynton, Audrey. "Using FLES History to Plan for the Present and the Future." *Foreign Language Annals* 23:4 (1990): 503–509.

Phillips, June K.(Ed.). *Foreign Language Standards: Linking Research, Theories, and Practices.* The ACTFL Foreign Language Education Series. Lincolnwood, IL: National Textbook, 1999.

Chapter 17

Planning, Implementing, and Articulating an Effective Early Language Program

Languages

&

Children

Enduring Understanding

- Quality planning is essential for effective program development and assessment.

- Program goals dictate the choice of a program model, and certain quality characteristics are essential for success.

Essential Questions

- What are the steps in planning effectively for program development and articulation?

- How do we choose a program model to match the goals of our program?

- What are the essential characteristics of a successful early language program?

● Planning Process

Planning is the most crucial element in the success of any early language program, and yet it is often given the least disciplined attention. Programs at this level are frequently initiated because of the enthusiasm of an individual or a group, and in many cases the eagerness to implement the program competes with the need to plan carefully. A thoughtful, thorough planning process that involves all the affected members of the community can build a support system for the program that will help it weather shifting fads and priorities in the curriculum, the school, and the community.

Pressure to implement programs prematurely was a common problem with the short-lived experiments of the 1960s. As Theodore Andersson (1969) pointed out in his thorough account of the history of elementary school foreign-language programs,

> Many communities, enchanted by the promise that a FLES program offers, set out with a minimum of preparation, only to find later that, to endure, a FLES program requires hard work, time, money, and expertise. A minimum commitment—a late start, doubtful continuity, too little class time, overloading the teacher, leaving the teacher to work in isolation—leads to almost certain disenchantment. (p. 138)

At a minimum, a planning group should include parents; elementary, middle school/junior high school, and high school administrators; language teachers from all instructional levels; and classroom teachers at the affected levels. Other valuable participants include a representative from the teacher's union, a special education teacher, and a reading teacher. Participation by a school board member can also be very helpful. The planning group will make recommendations to the superintendent, who ultimately will carry the responsibility for effectively implementing the elementary school foreign-language program and the entire K–12 sequence. The planning group should have a budget that will cover purchase of informational materials, duplication costs, and travel to visit existing programs.

The early language program that begins with planning for the entire language sequence, not just for the initial year, is most likely to succeed. Language teachers from all levels can contribute to planning and program development, and they can work together in staff development activities to facilitate a smooth transition from one grade to the next. All members of the group should be involved in planning from the beginning, so that together they can address these concerns:

- Background and philosophy
- Goals
- Program models
- Program delivery variations
- Scheduling
- Articulation
- Curriculum
- Resources
- Choice of language(s)
- Who should study languages
- Teachers and teacher recruitment
- Budget

- Space allocation
- Support of existing staff
- Program evaluation
- Student assessment
- Building public relations
- Sharing experiences and ideas

● Developing Background

The first step for any planning group is to become as informed as possible about articulated K–12 language programs, with a special emphasis on early language learning. Several options for developing this background include the following:

- Extensive reading
- Visits to existing programs representing a variety of program models
- Consultations with principals, teachers, and program planners from existing programs
- Visits to conferences at which elementary school foreign-language programs are the focus of discussion (American Council on the Teaching of Foreign Languages, and state and regional meetings of language teachers)

Reading and consultations are essential elements of the planning process, but planners need to see programs in action. Although this kind of background development can involve weeks or months, the resulting recommendations and decisions will be based on the best available information. The planning group will be in a position to proceed efficiently and confidently in designing a program best tailored to their local needs.

● Philosophy

The statement of philosophy for the language program must be congruent with the statement of philosophy or mission statement of the school or the district. This statement of philosophy is the starting point for program planning and will shape many of the responses to the planning considerations outlined in this chapter. The philosophy statement from the *Standards for Foreign Language Learning in the 21st Century* (1999, p. 7) provides an excellent model, not only because of its content but also because it served as the basis for the development of the entire Standards document. A portion of this philosophy is reproduced in Chapter 15, on pages 429–430.

The philosophy of Edison Township Public Schools, Edison, New Jersey, provides an excellent example. One full school year was devoted to the development of this department philosophy and the writing of benchmark statements for what students are expected to know and be able to do at the end of elementary, middle, and high school (Smith, 2007):

Departmental Philosophy

1. The study of another language leads to ***communication.*** Our goal is to teach **all** students to communicate beyond their native languages in order to participate effectively in this world. Communication involves the interpretive, presentational, and interpersonal modes.
2. The study of another language leads to ***understanding other cultures.*** Our goal is to recognize what is common to all human experience and to accept that which is different. Students will have experiences with products and practices in order to develop an understanding of the various perspectives of the cultures of the target language.
3. The study of another language leads to ***critical thinking skills.*** Our goal is to enhance the ability to analyze, to compare and contrast, to synthesize, to improvise, and to examine cultures through a language and a perspective other than one's own.
4. The study of another language leads to an ***interdisciplinary view*** of the curriculum. Our goal is to have every student begin language study as early as possible in an interdisciplinary environment.

● Goals

In order to decide which type of program to offer, planners must determine the expected educational outcomes of the program. These goals will flow directly from the philosophy of the program. The broad spectrum of potential outcomes could include, at one end, simply exposing students to foreign-language study in an effort to motivate them to study further, and at the other end, a program in which functional proficiency in listening, speaking, reading, and writing is the goal. The level of language fluency a student will gain in an elementary and middle school foreign-language program is directly related to the amount of time students spend learning the language and on the intensity of that language experience. For example, provided that there is quality teaching, students in a program that meets two or three times a week will not acquire the same level of proficiency as will students who have language instruction five days per week. Students who have language classes for 30 to 40 minutes a day will not attain the same fluency in the language as will their peers in a total immersion program in which they are using the language intensively for the entire school day. Reading and writing the foreign language are realistic goals only for early language programs that provide 120 or more minutes per week of exposure to the language, and for those programs that involve full or partial immersion. If new programs at the elementary or middle school level are to succeed, their positive features and their distinctive goals must be clearly identified and articulated.

Functional language proficiency means that students are able to communicate in the foreign language on any topic appropriate to their age and grade level. Functional language proficiency is a goal that can only be accomplished in programs where there is sufficient time available and sufficient intensity of instruction. It can be accomplished in total and partial immersion programs in which half the school day or more is devoted to second-language learning. This level of proficiency could not be attained in an exploratory program and would be difficult to attain in most other programs for young learners.

The community in which the language program is being planned has a strong influence on the goals that are chosen. For example, it may provide a more favorable climate for one language over another, or community values could very well determine what level of language proficiency is seen as desirable or worthy of support. In some communities, a heavy cultural emphasis might seem very important, whereas in other communities, a heavy career orientation might be seen as important, thus giving other directions to the program.

As program goals emerge, specific program models will suggest themselves. At this point, planners can identify existing programs built on models similar to those they are considering. Planners should correspond with people involved in these programs and try to visit them in order to determine whether the goals they are reaching are comparable to the results they hope to achieve themselves. Study and visits of this type will make it clear that programs must offer languages for a significant amount of time in order to achieve significant goals. School districts should be encouraged to begin programs that will result in as much language learning as possible for the students.

It is vitally important to set realistic program goals and to communicate them to parents, teachers, administrators, the school board, and the community. The language proficiency students attain in any elementary school foreign-language program is a result of the goals of the program, the amount of time students spend in language study, and, most importantly, the guidance of a well-qualified teacher.

Paul Sandrock, former world language specialist for the Wisconsin Department of Public Instruction, has a set of questions he encourages planners to start with as they design a new program:

What makes a quality language learning program?

Three key questions to ask when designing a program:

- Do we want to offer a program to all or some students? Will the program be required of or available to students?
- What are our goals for the program: for students to become increasingly proficient in using the language—or do we really have a Social Studies goal focused on learning about languages and cultures?
- At what grade level can we begin and still sustain the program with quality through twelfth grade: Kindergarten? Third or fourth grade? Sixth grade?

Consider:

- Content connection
  Is the content connected to the grade level curriculum and balanced with language and culture goals?
  vs.—Is the content separate and isolated?
- Frequency of instruction
  Is instruction scheduled at least three times per week?
  Does it continue all year?
  vs.—Are there long lapses between classes? Is instruction spread too far apart (once a week all year or daily for just six weeks)?
- Continuity
  Do students continue to learn the language from grade to grade?
  vs.—Are there gaps during which no language instruction is available?
  Do the same goals continue to be developed throughout the program?
  vs.—Do some grades focus only on cultures, some focus on speaking, and others focus on grammar?
- Access to district's languages
  Is there a careful balance of the district's language offerings?
  Are several world languages being considered?
  vs.—Was only one of the district's language options selected for the first experience (elementary or middle school)?

● Program Models

When planning for language instruction at the elementary school level, school districts are faced with decisions regarding what type of early language program to offer and how to staff that program. Issues of funding, time available in the school day, staffing, and who will study the language all affect the final decision. The most important issue of all is choosing a program model that matches the goals envisioned for students in the program.

Elementary school language programs can be classified along a continuum, with language-focused programs at one end and content-focused immersion and bilingual programs at the other end. These programs vary according to types of emphasis and expected student outcomes (Figure 17.1 shows this continuum and Figure 17.2 gives time allocations and program descriptions of points along the continuum).

The best way to understand the differences among various program models is to visit successful programs in action. Thoughtful and thorough descriptions of effective programs can also offer insight and guidance. Gilzow and Branaman (2000) provide descriptions of seven programs from varying program models, and identify key elements leading to their success. All the programs share four key qualities. First, they have been flexible in the face of fluctuating financial support. Second, there is close teamwork among language professionals, administrators, classroom teachers, and parents. Third, each program has had strong leadership that has been key to program success. Finally, the staff has

● **FIGURE 17.1** Continuum of Intensity and Focus for Early Language Learning Programs Leading to Proficiency

Language, Culture, and Curriculum content are essential elements in every program model. The focus changes as time on task and intensity increase across the continuum, from language-focused programs on the left to content-focused full immersion on the right. A number of variations are possible along the continuum.

Programs with less intensity:
Early language programs that meet less than 30-40 minutes daily, and/or less than three times per week, may not be able to meet the performance goals anticipated by the Standards for Foreign Language Learning and the K–12 Performance Guidelines.

a strong commitment to the program and to the goals of elementary or middle school language education.

Language Focused Programs: The Term *FLES*

FLES (Foreign Language in the Elementary School) is a term that has often been used to label all programs for languages other than English at the elementary school level. However, the term has most appropriately been used to describe a particular type of elementary school language program, one that is taught three to five times a week for class periods of 20 minutes to an hour or more. Many references in the literature continue to use the term *FLES*. In an attempt to firmly place these programs as part of a K–12 sequence, the profession is moving away from the term in favor of more general terms

Content-Focused (Content-Driven) Programs		
Goal:	To become functionally proficient in the new language	
Goal:	To acquire an understanding of and appreciation for other cultures	
Goal:	To master subject content taught in the foreign language	

Program Type	Time Allocations and Descriptions
	Note: Achievement of the goals will vary depending on how much time is allocated for the program.
Total Immersion (Full Immersion) Grades K–6	• 50–100 percent of the school day. • Focus is on learning subject matter taught in FL; language learning per se incorporated as necessary throughout curriculum. • Student population in the United States and Canada is English speakers who are learning a new language. **Description** The second language is used for the entire school day during the first two or three years. In early total immersion programs, reading is taught through the second language. In some programs instruction by means of English is introduced gradually, often in grade 2, and the amount of English is increased until the fifth or sixth grade (the last grade in elementary school), where up to half the day is spent in English and half in the second language. In other programs, once English is introduced (usually at grade 2 or 3) the percentage of time spent in English remains constant throughout the program, at approximately 20 percent. In some other programs the entire day is conducted in the second language for a much greater period of time and English is not introduced until grades 4 or 5.
Two-Way Immersion Grades K–6 (Also called *Two-Way Bilingual, Dual Immersion,* and *Developmental Bilingual Education*)	• At least 50 percent of the school day. • Student population is both native speakers of English and of the target language. **Description** Two-way immersion programs are similar to one-way immersion programs except that the student group includes native speakers of the target language as well as native speakers of English. Thus, all students learn subject matter through their native language as well as through the second language, and both language groups have the benefit of interaction with peers who are native speakers of the language they are learning. The ideal goals of two-way immersion, in addition to subject content mastery, are that the English-speaking students become functionally proficient in the second language and that the second-language speakers become functionally proficient in English. At the same time, all students continue to develop skills and proficiency in their native language.
Partial Immersion Grades K–6	• At least 50 percent (time is spent learning subject matter taught in FL; language learning per se incorporated as necessary throughout curriculum).

	Description All instruction is in the second language for part (at least half) of the school day. The amount of instruction in the foreign language usually remains constant throughout the elementary school program. In early partial immersion programs, students frequently learn to read in both languages at the same time; in some programs, notably Chinese and Japanese partial immersion, literacy skills are taught first in the native language.

Language-Focused (Language-Driven) Programs
Goal: To become functionally proficient in the new language
Goal: To acquire an understanding of and appreciation for other cultures
Goal: To master subject content taught in the foreign language
These goals are the same as for immersion programs.

Program Type	**Time Allocations and Descriptions** *Note:* Achievement of the goals will vary depending on how much time is allocated for the program.
Early Language Learning Programs Grades K–6 (Also known as *Early Start Programs* and *Programs for Young Learners.* Sometimes referred to as *FLES*)	Minimum 30 to 40 minutes per class, at least 3 to 5 days per week. This time allotment should be considered a minimum for an effective nonimmersion early language program. **Description** The focus is on language learning with the integration of culture and content objectives. This presecondary program is articulated vertically throughout the entire program sequence. A student studies a single language throughout the program sequence. (This does not imply that only one language is offered throughout the school district.) Classes meet within the school day, throughout the entire school year. The amount of time allotted to a language-focused program in the elementary school is one of the most important variables in its potential for success. The vision of the Standards calls for an elementary school program that invests the time necessary for students to achieve significant outcomes. In order to achieve the performances described in the ACTFL Performance Guidelines for K–12 Learners, committee members advised that elementary school programs should meet no less than 30 to 40 minutes a day, and no fewer than three to five days per week (Swender and Duncan, 1998).

Underlying every program description is the fact that language proficiency outcomes are related to the amount of time spent by students in meaningful communication in the target language. Met and Rhodes (1990) suggest that the amount of time spent on language learning and the intensity of the learning experience may be among the most important factors determining the rate of language acquisition and the level of proficiency that can be attained in a language program. Planners should seek to design a program that will result in the highest level of proficiency possible, given the resources they have available. Teacher quality, of course, is also an important factor in language outcomes. If the program design includes less time than the stated minimum, planners must be sure to give stakeholders adequate information about the types of student outcomes that may be expected due to the limited nature of the contact time in the program.

such as *early start programs, early language learning programs,* or *programs for young learners,* and we have adopted this practice for this textbook. Note that current best practice for these programs calls for 30 to 40 minutes a day, three to five days per week.

Programs with Less Intensity—Better than Nothing?

Early language programs with less dedicated time and/or less frequent scheduling than three to five days a week are subject to a number of risks. First, learners will not be able to meet the language goals that have been observed in more intensive programs. This will be disappointing to students and parents alike over the long term, even though the program may seem to be dazzling at the beginning because of initial student performance and enthusiasm. The net result may be that these programs are cut when budgets are crunched and results do not live up to expectations. Second, consider the risk to the language teacher, who often has many classes and students to deal with and many students to see in a typical week. Planners are well advised to consider the amount of funding available for a new language program, and to begin that program at whatever grade level will make it possible to develop a language-focused program with greater time and intensity.

The rest of the world is moving ahead with offering strong programs at the primary/elementary school level. The authors believe that here in the United States we must move away from the idea of offering programs that have very little time allotted per week. That is not to say that such programs should be discontinued—far from it! It is urgent to provide support for the programs that are already in existence, but we must also strongly advocate for programs that provide more time.

Exploratory Programs

The goals of exploratory programs are usually limited to introducing students to language and culture, with the intent of arousing interest in further language study. They are set apart from true language programs in that they usually do not have any degree of language proficiency as an outcome, and they are not always part of an articulated sequence. These programs are most common at the middle school level, reflecting an earlier period in which language learning was not introduced into the curriculum until grade 9 or 10. The value of such programs lies in the fact that students are exposed to languages that may be less familiar, or may have become less popular, but are still a viable part of language education for the twenty-first century.

Noncurricular Language Programs

Not all language programs take place within the setting of the school day. Summer camps, immersion weekends, before- and after-school programs, summer day programs, weekend or after-school programs for heritage language speakers, and day schools, among others, all provide opportunities for young learners to be exposed to new languages. When such programs are carefully planned and taught, they can make a positive contribution to early language learning.

A Note about Heritage Speakers by Kim Potowski

Increasingly across the United States, many courses designed to teach "foreign" languages include students who had some exposure to the language at home. These students, referred to as *heritage speakers,* can vary widely in their proficiency in the non-English language based on a number of factors, including age of immigration (theirs or that of their parents), heritage language use patterns in the home, exposure to literacy in the heritage language, and visits to places where the heritage language is widely spoken. Teachers who have received professional preparation to teach "foreign" languages can find themselves understandably at a loss when heritage speakers are concerned, since these students present a unique linguistic and affective profile.

One of the most important traits of effective teachers of heritage speakers is that they *respect* the language these students bring to the classroom, not seeking to criticize or eradicate their ways of communicating (no matter how much they may seem to vary from a formal prestigious variety!) but rather to add to students' communicative repertoires. Heritage speakers with medium to high levels of proficiency may actually benefit more from a native speaker language arts curriculum than from a purely foreign-language–oriented curriculum. Many schools opt to create separate classes for heritage speakers in order to focus on their particular strengths and needs. But all meaning-based, contextualized, and engaging activities can be of benefit to heritage speakers and their foreign-language–learning classmates alike.

Several important resources for teachers of heritage speaker students include the National Heritage Language Resource Center (http://www.international.ucla.edu/languages/nhlrc/) and these recent publications:

Brinton, Donna, Olga Kagan, and Susan Bauckus (Eds.). *Heritage Language Education: A New Field Emerging.* New York: Routledge, 2008. Contains general information as well as specific chapters on Chinese, Japanese, Korean, Spanish, and Russian.

Colombi, Cecilia, and Francisco Alarcon (Eds.). *La Enseñanza del Español a Hispanohablantes: Praxis y Teoría.* Boston: Houghton Mifflin, 1997. Explores issues of "standard" language, culture, and politics; some chapters offer concrete classroom suggestions.

Kondo-Brown, K., and J. D. Brown (Eds.). *Teaching Chinese, Japanese, and Korean Heritage Language Students: Curriculum Needs, Materials, and Assessment.* Mahwah, NJ: Lawrence Erlbaum Associates, 2007.

Potowski, Kim. *Fundamentos en la Enseñanza del Español a Hispanohablantes en los Estados Unidos.* Madrid: Arco Libros, 2005. A "crash course" for teachers, describing the Spanish of heritage speakers and different pedagogical approaches.

Noncurricular programs may be sponsored by the school district, by community groups or parent–teacher organizations, or by tuition-based private education groups. They may be set up in a variety of ways. Some of them have been very successful and have developed sophisticated structures and curricula; others have limited goals and are of relatively short duration. In many communities the interest generated by noncurricular language programs has led to a place for languages within the school curriculum and the school day.

An important strength of noncurricular programs has been their use of community resources that might otherwise remain untapped. In some situations there would be no early language program in the school district without them, and their role as a "foot in the door" is not to be underestimated. Among the most serious weaknesses of many noncurricular programs is the fact that volunteers in such programs often have little or no training, and there is no agency to regulate the goals and the quality of instruction. Even under the best of circumstances, such programs place languages clearly outside the school curriculum and the school day, reinforcing the notion that language learning is "extra" rather than basic.

● Program Delivery Variations

Media-Based Programs

In this model the primary vehicle for teaching the language is some form of media, usually interactive television, DVDs or CDs, and computers. Follow-up and reinforcement are handled in various ways.

Students in U.S. schools are very sophisticated consumers of media products, and they will not likely be engaged with media-based learning materials unless they have meaningful content and high-quality, professional camera work and editing. Media-based programs can present some aspects of culture with great imagination, and media programs can use special effects to lighten and enliven the necessary drill-and-practice sessions. The target language should be the primary means of instruction, just as in classroom-based programs, and the media presentation should be standards-based and proficiency oriented.

The key to success of media-based programs, in addition to the quality of the media product itself, is the quality and intensity of the follow-up. In a successful program, the media will supplement and not replace time spent with a language teacher. Media-based programs in the past that have not adequately provided for classroom interaction with a teacher have been tremendously disappointing in their results. Many have disappeared entirely, leaving behind an extremely negative attitude toward foreign-language instruction.

Limitations

- The success of a media-based program is almost totally dependent on the goodwill of the classroom teacher. Students do not usually have the opportunity to interact with their primary source of instruction, so the attitude of the classroom teacher sets the tone for and establishes the importance of the language sessions.

- Students often feel a detachment from the medium and are adept at shutting it out.

- High-quality media programs for teaching new languages at the elementary school level are difficult to find.

Distance Learning

In an early language program using interactive television as a vehicle for distance learning, the teacher is located at one site (the base site), usually with a group of students, and one or more groups of students are located at a remote site or sites. Remote sites usually are located in another school building some distance away. Video cameras, monitors, and microphones are located at the base and the remote sites so that the teacher and groups of students can see and communicate with each other. Although this model is most frequently used at the high school level, it has been successfully adapted for use with elementary school students when adequate supervision is provided at the remote sites. The National Council of State Supervisors of Foreign Languages (NCSSFL) has published guidelines for distance learning programs available on the Internet.

Small school districts can combine resources to offer a new language at the elementary school level, or even to offer more than one language. A single, talented teacher can reach many more students with this model than would otherwise be physically possible. Some of the limitations of distance learning are:

- It is impossible to engage in as many valuable context-embedded, activity-oriented activities when all of the students and the teacher are not physically in the same place.

- Opportunities for students to produce oral language and teacher evaluation of individual progress are severely limited in this model.

- Teaching on camera requires extensive preparation, skillful planning, and a high level of technical quality. Careful management is required to bring all these factors together. It is critical that the teacher receive adequate preparation time to ensure a quality program.

- Supervision of students at the remote site(s) is an additional cost factor.

Characteristics of Effective Programs

Gilzow and Branaman identified 10 critical program elements in the model programs described in *Lessons Learned: Model Early Foreign Language Programs* (2000). These elements can help to guide program planning, administration, and evaluation:

1. *Implementing National Standards.* All seven of the model programs incorporate the Standards in important and curriculum-shaping ways.
2. *A Focus on Content.* Each program incorporated the general curriculum, using either a content-related or a content-based strategy.
3. *Articulation and Alignment.* The model programs use a number of different approaches to ensure articulation from one language level to another and alignment across each grade level.

4. *Teaching Methods.* Language learning is fun in all the model programs, and teachers use a variety of communicative, interactive, age-appropriate activities.

5. *Technology.* Each of the programs is finding ways to use technology to enhance instruction.

6. *Program Evaluation.* Among the model programs, Glastonbury is notable for the quality and regularity of its program evaluation.

7. *Student Assessment.* This is a key component of effective programs, and several of the model programs have interesting and useful assessment strategies.

8. *Funding.* The model programs typically have benefited from grant funding, especially during the start-up phase, when expenses are particularly high. Secure funding has to be found within the local district for use when grant funding runs out.

9. *Professional Development.* Professional development is critical in the early stages of a language program, and it continues to be important as the program grows and new curriculum and resources are introduced. The model programs use in-service teacher workshops and professional conferences as effective development opportunities.

10. *Advocacy.* In nearly all the model programs, reaching out to the community and achieving visibility within the school and the district have been important. Parent involvement is another key element of effective and enduring programs.

● Scheduling

The way in which the early language program is scheduled may be the determining factor in the ultimate long-term success of the program.

Frequency and Duration of Language Classes   Will the program be offered once a week, every other day, or daily? How much time will be allotted per class? For optimal learning to take place, programs for young learners should meet for a minimum of 30 to 40 minutes a day, five days a week, with as much additional reinforcement of the language throughout the school day as possible. The ACTFL Performance Guidelines for K–12 Learners (Swender and Duncan, 1998) describe student performances for grades 4, 8 and 12 that can be achieved only if students are enrolled "in elementary programs that meet from 3–5 days per week for no less than 30–40 minutes per class; middle school programs that meet daily for no less than 40–50 minutes; and high school programs that equal four units of credit" (p. 482). For Core French programs in Canada (equivalent to FLES programs in the United States), 40 minutes a day is a recommended standard. Programs that do not meet daily will be required to devote a significant proportion of class time to review activity to compensate for the long periods of time between language classes. Figure 17.3 shows sample proficiency outcomes related to length of time in various programs.

Teacher Workload   A second, equally important consideration in scheduling is the number of classes that the language teacher teaches each day. Curtain and Dahlberg (2000,

● **FIGURE 17.3** Visual Representation of Anticipated Performance Outcomes as Described in the ACTFL Performance Guidelines for K–12 Learners

Note: Descriptors are based on information gathered from foreign language professionals representing a variety of program models and articulation sequences. Descriptors are appropriate for languages most commonly taught in the U.S. Descriptors assume a sustained sequence of Standards-based, performance-outcome language instruction. The descriptors on the left refer to the ACTFL Proficiency Guidelines. The descriptors on the right refer to the ACTFL Performance Guidelines for K–12 Learners.

Source: Foreign Language Annals 31, no. 4 (Winter 1998): 484. © ACTFL 1998. Reprinted by permission of ACTFL.

p. 2) highlight teacher workload as one of the major potential pitfalls for an early language program:

Pitfall: Planning Schedules and Workloads that Lead to Teacher Burnout

There is currently a shortage of qualified teachers for early language programs. If we want to rectify this situation, it is imperative that we build programs that are good for children and also good for teachers. With this in mind, the Georgia Department of Education stipulated that FLES teachers in state-supported model programs should teach no more than 8 classes per day, leaving time for the many additional responsibilities of a FLES teacher: interacting with numerous classroom teachers, developing curriculum and materials, communicating with parents and community, and building public relations for the program. Teachers in Bay Point Elementary School (Pinellas County, FL), one of the model programs featured in *Lessons Learned* (2000), also see eight classes per day, and their additional responsibilities are clearly defined (Gilzow and Branaman, 2000, pp. 13, 25–26).

If language teachers work under unfavorable conditions, they are likely to burn out and either leave the profession or opt for regular classrooms. There are dangers in the proliferation of early language programs when attention is not given to the stress factors involved in typical teacher workloads. Elementary school language teachers may find themselves teaching as many as 14 classes in a single day, seeing as many as 600 students in a week, or even more. Their classes are often scheduled back to back, with no time in between. They rarely have their own classroom, typically traveling from classroom to classroom—sometimes from building to building—with all their lessons and materials on a cart. They often lack professional support and opportunities for in-service training. Their schedules rarely allow them time to collaborate with other language teachers or with the classroom teachers in whose rooms they work. Given these difficult conditions, it is not surprising that early language programs have a hard time finding and keeping qualified teachers.

There are other factors that affect the stress level of an early language teacher's schedule. Gilzow and Rhodes (2000) make these recommendations for program staffing (p. 8):

- Do hire at least one foreign language teacher per school so that the teacher is part of the school staff and can communicate and coordinate with regular classroom teachers.
- Do provide adequate workspace. If teachers need to wheel a materials cart from classroom to classroom, ensure that they also have an office or workspace that is their own and that has room for materials, a telephone, and a computer.
- Don't schedule all the language classes back to back. Foreign language teachers need time between classes to gather materials, re-focus on a new group of students, and possibly adapt their lessons to meet a regular classroom teacher's requests.

- Do consider how many students a foreign language teacher will meet with each week. No one teacher can be expected to keep track of—much less really teach—600 students in a week. Fourteen classes in a day is not a reasonable workload; eight 30-minute classes per day is a maximum load.
- Don't expect that the language teacher's number of contact hours will be the same as that of the classroom teachers. Because a language teacher usually meets with a larger number of students and must travel from classroom to classroom, he or she may spend fewer hours per week with students than does a regular elementary classroom teacher.
- Don't require the foreign language teacher to handle multiple grade levels in a single day. Because children's developmental levels are so different in the elementary grades, it is sufficiently challenging for a teacher to work with two grades.
- Do build time in the foreign language teacher's schedule to collaborate with the regular classroom teachers, develop and adapt materials, and participate in meetings and opportunities for professional development.

Scheduling: Finding Time for the Language Program in an Already Crowded School Day

Another important point to consider is how the foreign-language program fits into the total school curriculum. One frequent obstacle to beginning foreign-language programs at the elementary school level is the complaint from classroom teachers and administrators that there is not enough room in the school day for the present curriculum, let alone time to add another subject to it. Here is the answer given by Terry Caccavale from Holliston, Massachusetts:

> I was once asked by a nearby school superintendent how in the world you could add anything such as foreign language to an already full elementary school curriculum. He suggested that it would be quite like trying to add a fifth quart of water to an already full gallon of the same. I replied by saying that when we "add" foreign language to the elementary curriculum, we do not "add" another curricular area, but rather borrow from the existing curricula and teach them in more creative and cognitively engaging ways—kind of like adding food coloring to the water in the full gallon pail—changing its hue, and thus its entire appearance, without adding one ounce to its volume.

Many school districts have addressed this problem by allotting some of the language arts or social studies time for the foreign-language program. Some districts take a little time from each subject area in order to make a place for languages. When going through the difficult process of finding time for an elementary school foreign-language program, it is important to stress the interdisciplinary aspects of foreign-language learning and the well-documented benefits to first-language skills.

Another way to deal with the scheduling problem is to plan a content-related curriculum that interfaces with the basic curriculum at various points and is planned in such a way that many objectives from the basic curriculum are clearly evident in the second-language curriculum. Too often, elementary foreign-language programs state that the program is interdisciplinary or that subject content instruction is included, but in reality these turn out to be only token activities. (For information on effective use of content in the language curriculum, see the discussions in Chapters 6 and 10.)

Middle School Scheduling   Middle school scheduling presents a special challenge because of the variety of scheduling patterns being implemented in schools at this level. Several options have been tried with success, including blocking world languages with the social studies or the language arts component of the curriculum, or building languages into a flexible physical education and arts block. Whatever the solution may be, it is critical that the intensity of the language program be maintained through middle school. Students who have developed meaningful language proficiency in a carefully articulated elementary school program should have the opportunity for real language development during the crucial middle school years.

● Articulation of K–12 Foreign Language Programs

Students leaving the elementary school foreign-language program must have an appropriate course available to them in order to continue their language study. One of the reasons that earlier programs for young learners failed is that the language ability the children had acquired was not taken into account when the students were programmed into middle school or junior high school language courses. Often, elementary school language students were forced to begin the language again when they entered junior high school or high school, because the oral proficiency they had attained was not valued in the grammatically based secondary school program. These experiences discouraged enrollments at the elementary school, discouraged continuation of study at higher levels, and ultimately raised the question of the effectiveness of the programs for young learners themselves.

The middle school program for students continuing from the elementary school must be visibly and substantively different from the program for students who are beginning language study at that level. School districts must either establish a separate track for the continuing elementary school language students, or they must ensure that the content of the middle school courses in which these students are enrolled builds on and is complementary to the background they have already obtained. When full or partial immersion has been implemented at the elementary school level, middle school programs must provide some content instruction in the target language as well as advanced language instruction. As students reach the senior high school with extensive foreign-language background, curriculum at that level must also change in significant, substantive ways.

One reason that expected outcomes differ among language programs at the elementary school, middle school, and high school levels is that the focus at each level is different.

Attempts to describe progress at one level in terms of another level must take into account the differences among programs at each level. Some of these differences are as follows:

1. Elementary school foreign-language programs emphasize listening and speaking skills, whereas an increasing proportion of class time at the middle school and high school is devoted to reading and writing.

2. Elementary school students have very limited experience with grammatical analysis, an area that is addressed more formally at later levels.

3. Language skills at each level are developed to deal with different settings and different interests, in response to the interests and experiences of students at different age levels. The range of vocabulary and situations with which students at various levels can function comfortably will differ accordingly.

Traditionally in U.S. schools the direction of articulation and program development in foreign languages has been determined from the top down. When reform or creative change has developed at the high school level, the expectations of colleges and universities have served as a constraint, even though a minority of the students go on to college study. Junior high and middle school teachers have often experienced criticism from high school teachers who claimed that what incoming students had learned previously was lacking or worse—so middle school teachers often adapt their programs to fit more neatly into the expectations of the teachers who receive their students. It is the challenge of K–12 language programs to turn the traditional articulation pattern on its head—instead of preparing for the next level of the program, planners need to give their attention to designing curriculum and experiences to extend and build on the learning at the preceding level.

The first responsibility of teachers at each level of instruction is to design a program that is congruent with the interests, background, and developmental characteristics of their students. The second responsibility is to design assessment and reporting procedures that are comprehensive and descriptive, so that teachers who receive these students have clear and adequate information on which to base the goals and learning experiences at the next level. Paul Sandrock of the Wisconsin Department of Public Instruction characterizes the desired movement in articulation as being a "rippling up" of information about student attainments at preceding levels, and using that information as the basis for goals and activities at the next level. He contrasts this with the "pointing down" so familiar to language teachers at every level, in which teachers appear to discount the attainments at earlier levels if they do not fit neatly into the expectations and approaches used with the older age group (Sandrock, 1993).

Another important factor related to articulation is the designation of proficiency outcomes for various levels within the K–12 sequence. Figure 17.4a shows an articulation plan (from the Catalina Foothills School District in Tucson, Arizona) with proficiency outcomes for a world language program that starts in elementary school and continues through high school. It is based on the assumption that such a program teaches and tests for proficiency and not for mastery of grammar. The articulation plan shows a possible

● **FIGURE 17.4a**   Sample World Languages Program Articulation Chart

World Languages Program Articulation Chart
Catalina Foothills School District
Tucson, Arizona

Elementary School Program			Middle School Program			High School Program				Targeted Outcomes
						Grade 9 HS1 Novice High	**Grade 10 HS2** Intermediate Low	**Grade 11 HS3** Intermediate Low/Mid	**Grade 12 HS4** Intermediate Mid	Intermediate Mid
			Grade 6 MS1 Novice High	**Grade 7 MS2** Intermediate Low	**Grade 8 MS3** Intermediate Low/Mid	**Grade 9 HS2** Intermediate Mid	**Grade 10 HS3** Intermediate Mid	**Grade 11 HS4** Intermediate Mid/High	**Grade 12 HS5** Intermediate High	Intermediate High
Kindergarten Novice Low	**Grades 1–2** Novice Mid	**Grades 3–5** Novice High	**Grade 6** Novice High to Intermediate Low	**Grade 7** Intermediate Low	**Grade 8** Intermediate Low to Intermediate Mid	**Grade 9** Intermediate Mid	**Grade 10** Intermediate Mid	**Grade 11** Intermediate Mid to Intermediate High	**Grade 12** Intermediate High/ Advanced Low	Intermediate High/ Advanced

To attain the level indicated above for grades K–12 in CFSD, students enrolled in the elementary program meet at least 4 days a week for no less than 30 minutes. Middle school programs meet for 52 minutes per class/5 days a week (260 minutes per week). High school classes meet for 60 minutes per class for 4 days a week (240 minutes per week).

The expected proficiency attainment at the end of each grade level is based on the National and CFSD World Languages Content Standards (Measurement Topics and Benchmarks), ACTFL (American Council on the Teaching of Foreign Languages) Proficiency Guidelines, and the ACTFL Performance Guidelines for K–12 Learners.

Key: HS1 = High School/Level 1; MS1 = Middle School/Level 1 (*Note:* Based on proficiency, students may advance by level not grade.)

proficiency trajectory based on recent results from administration of the ACTFL Oral Proficiency Interview (OPI) and STAMP. (See Chapter 7 for information on the STAMP.) With such an articulation plan in place, schools have clear targets for program outcomes.

Figure 17.4b shows the articulation model that accompanies the Georgia Performance Standards for Modern Languages. The chart shows that there are targeted proficiency levels related to accomplishing certain levels within the Performance Standards. Figures 17.4a and 17.4b clearly show a path to language proficiency. Establishing such goals at the beginning of a language sequence will significantly increase the chances that such goals will be achieved.

Middle School Programs

One of the important philosophical tenets in many middle schools is the concept of exploration. In some cases this concept has been applied to foreign languages by rejecting the possibility of continuing instruction on a daily basis in the same foreign language that students have been studying for several years in elementary school. Exploratory programs are provided, "introducing" learners to the idea of language learning and in several different languages. It has happened that students who have already developed considerable fluency in a language are required to attend introductory classes in that same language, in which they encounter greetings, colors, numbers, and animal names as if for the first time. This is, obviously, a recipe for boredom and frustration, and is likely to discourage later enrollment for that or any other language. But even more serious is the wasted opportunity represented in this situation—students with a solid foundation in one language could be developing a valuable tool during middle school years, which they could apply in learning throughout the curriculum at the senior high school level. It is important to develop

● **FIGURE 17.4b**   K–12 Articulation Model for Georgia Performance Standards for Modern Languages

Time Frame	Instructional Hours Completed	Speaking Proficiency Target	Levels Completed from Curriculum
By the end of 5th grade	540	Novice–High	1, 2
By the end of 8th grade	360 + 540=900	Intermediate–Mid	3, 4, 5
By the end of 12th grade	600 + 900=1,500	Advanced Low	6, 7, 8

Note: Elementary school hours equal 30 minutes a day, five days a week. Middle school hours equal one class period a day for three years. High school hours equal one class period a day for four years. The above trajectories apply to students who begin the foreign-language program early in the elementary grades and who maintain study of that same language through middle and high school.

Source: Reprinted by permission of the Georgia Department of Education.

curriculum for the middle school level that demonstrates the potential for exploration of the world while at the same time building additional fluency, skills, and cultural insight in a single language.

Although some textbook series have been developed or adapted for the middle school level, thematic units can provide the most effective curriculum for the middle school language program. For the continuing language learner, the thematic unit builds on elementary school experiences in a natural way and combines well with the overall integrative nature of the middle school. Beginning language students benefit from integrated thematic units in much the same way, although the language level for the units will be similar to units planned for the elementary school. See Chapter 6 for a complete discussion of thematic planning.

It should be pointed out that graduates of an elementary school program who begin a new language in the middle school will be very different learners from those beginners who have had no previous language experience. They are likely to learn much more quickly, and to approach learning with more sophistication and greater motivation.

One of the most vexing problems for planners is the scheduling of foreign languages in the overcrowded middle school day. One option suggested for Wisconsin schools (Sandrock, 1993) is to make foreign language a part of the interdisciplinary team in the humanities block, together with English, social studies, art, music, physical education, and family and consumer education. The technology block includes science, mathematics, technical education, and computer education. In this plan, English, social studies, foreign language, science, and mathematics meet daily on a flexible schedule planned by teachers in the block; other subjects meet on alternating days. Another option is to schedule the language class in place of the remedial or developmental reading class offered by many middle schools in addition to language arts. Yet another option is to completely reconfigure the time schedule, so that a minimum block of 40 to 45 minutes can be made available daily.

Brown (1995) identifies a number of elements of the long-term success of the foreign language program in Glastonbury, Connecticut, all of which facilitate effective articulation across grade levels:

- Language teachers from all grade levels meet monthly to discuss districtwide events and priorities.
- The curriculum is reviewed with cross-representation from all levels of language instruction, including community members, classroom teachers, and administrators from other disciplines.
- Teachers write collaborative departmental examinations for grades 5 through 12.
- Teachers have created a common scoring mechanism for grading student examinations.
- Teachers exchange students and tapes for oral examinations in order to assess speaking skills and to ensure a common grading standard.

Successful K–12 articulation, and especially the building of a successful middle school link for a program, can be accomplished only with the full participation of teachers from all levels in careful planning and in ongoing, open communication. Adjustments at every level may have to be made as a K–12 program develops, in order to ensure a continuous opportunity for language development. Teachers who understand one another's goals, visit one another's classrooms, and respect one another's professional judgment will be in the best position to build a strong and vital program that provides a positive environment for learning and teaching of foreign languages.

Robert Politzer (1991) developed "Eleven Commandments of Articulation," several of which seem especially pertinent to this discussion.

1. The main principle of articulation is simply a principle of good teaching: Don't (unintentionally) repeat material the student has mastered already; always provide enough new material so that the student is motivated and something new is being learned.
2. Never place students who already know some language in the same class as real beginners.
3. Try and provide a "bridge course" for students who do not fit in an expected level (but do not put them in a beginners' class). . . .
4. If in doubt, follow your experience and instinct concerning good teaching. Remember principle number one. If you feel that you are violating this principle, change and adapt the curriculum. Fight back.

● Curriculum

Once the goals of the program have been set, it is necessary to formulate a curriculum to meet these goals. There are three avenues to approaching curriculum development:

1. *Choosing Curriculum.* The first and easiest approach is to locate already-prepared curriculum that is basically compatible with the program goals and that is suitable for the age level of the students.
2. *Adapting Curriculum.* The second approach is to locate curriculum that is close to what is desired but that needs to be adapted in some way.
3. *Writing Curriculum.* The third avenue, and the most difficult, is to begin from scratch to write curriculum.

Each of these three options is discussed more fully here.

Choosing Curriculum

Sources of curriculum for elementary language programs from outside the district include commercial materials and those developed by other school districts. You may locate commercial materials by contacting publishers, and you may access curriculum documents prepared by other districts on the Internet. A good starting point is the Center for Applied Linguistics' website: www.cal.org.

Other sources of curriculum may include commercial or locally developed materials for ESL and bilingual classes. Many of these materials demonstrate the application of linguistic and psychological research to the language learning process and they can be successfully adapted to a foreign-language format. Materials developed for children in the target culture learning in their native language can be useful resources for the teacher in designing content-related lessons and activities with cultural authenticity, but most of these materials are too difficult for language learners in another setting. An exception might be materials designed for children with special needs or for children learning the target language as a second language, such as non-German speakers learning in a German school, similar to the English language learner in the U.S. context.

Screening Curriculum Sources   Key factors in determining the appropriateness of materials for adoption in the local program include the following:

- *Standards Orientation.* There should be clear evidence that the materials are designed to address all five of the goals of the *Standards for Foreign Language Learning in the 21st Century* (1999) and all 11 Standards.

- *Publication Date.* Most materials with publication dates before 1990 do not reflect the insights gained through research and experience in the last years of the twentieth century. It is important to note, however, that a recent publication date does not guarantee that materials have been developed in harmony with current research and practice.

- *Compatibility with the Philosophy and Goals of the Local Program.* Because goals and circumstances in each local situation differ so markedly, particularly at the elementary school level, the transfer of a curriculum from one setting to another is especially problematic. Publishers find it difficult to produce materials that will meet all the needs of the wide variety of programs being developed.

- *Age Appropriateness.* In some programs, teachers have attempted to solve the problem of materials by adapting high school or college texts, or using texts developed at a much earlier date. We do not recommend the adaptation of high school and college texts because topics and activities covered are inappropriate to the interests of young learners, and there is often a strong grammatical bias even in beginning-level textbooks of this type.

- *Methodology Recommended.* It is important to determine whether the materials reflect an up-to-date approach in learning languages such as that found in the Key Concepts outlined at the beginning of this book (p. xxi), because using materials that do not reflect current pedagogy will detract from the quality of the program being planned. Sometimes the materials themselves may be useful, but teaching recommendations are less compatible with program philosophy. Teachers need to follow their own best instincts and best understanding of effective language teaching, regardless of what suggestions a teacher handbook might offer.

Adapting Curriculum

Whatever curriculum is chosen, be it commercially prepared or developed by another school district, it must be adapted and modified to fit the local situation. For example, a curriculum planned for a daily program would have to be modified to fit the needs of an alternate-day program. A curriculum written for a regular classroom group might have to be modified for use with students in a gifted and talented program, or for a class with a high proportion of students with special needs.

Specific interests and priorities of the local school or community must also be taken into account. Children in a rural community will probably not relate well to a program designed to capitalize on the city environment of the metropolitan school system for which it was created. A school in which many children have realistic expectations of traveling abroad will want to incorporate much more information about life and travel in other countries than might be appropriate in another setting. The background and interests of the teaching staff should also influence which countries and which aspects of culture or of the subject content curriculum will be emphasized in a specific program.

Writing Curriculum

Successful local-curriculum writing requires the talents of a skilled teacher, or preferably a team of teachers who are very familiar with the Standards, foreign-language proficiency, principles of second-language acquisition, communicative language teaching, curriculum development, and child development. In addition, all materials must be screened for linguistic and cultural content and accuracy by at least one native speaker of the language.

Curriculum writers need to examine a wide variety of available materials, both from commercial sources and from other districts, in order to emulate the strengths and avoid the pitfalls represented there. No curriculum will be in its final form until it has been field-tested and revised as a result of student and teacher reaction.

The development of local curriculum is a time-consuming, costly, and rigorous process. It requires strong support from the district and from the administration, through released time and/or summer writing time, and there must be financial recognition of the high degree of skill and dedication involved in the task. The reward for the district can be an exemplary program that meets local needs in a very precise way, based on a curriculum that can also make a contribution to the development of early language programs in other communities.

● **Resources**

Interesting and appropriate instructional materials are an important part of any language program, but up-to-date commercial materials for most program models described here may be difficult to find. Many school systems have developed their own curriculum and materials for programs for young learners, especially in French, German, Spanish, Chinese, and Japanese, and these can serve as a starting point for local materials development.

Some states and other agencies have developed materials that deserve special attention. For example, Ohio has developed a K–4 content-enriched Mandarin Chinese curriculum. The National K–12 Foreign Language Resource Center at Iowa State University has developed K–5 Chinese curriculum, as well as numerous content-related units for the elementary and middle school levels.

Immersion programs in French often draw on resources created for Canadian programs, although these must usually be adapted somewhat for use in the United States. Spanish immersion programs can often make use of some materials developed for bilingual programs, but these materials, too, must be adapted to suit the different language sophistication of the learner. Immersion programs in other languages must rely on locally developed materials and on those developed in already-existing immersion programs. Materials suitable for elementary school children in less commonly taught languages such as Arabic, Chinese, Hebrew, Japanese, and Russian are the most difficult to obtain.

The choice of a program model for which few existing curriculum materials are available requires a commitment to the time and expertise necessary for materials development. Since the goals are so limited, creation of materials for a short-term exploratory program may well be a realistic task for a few teachers working with locally available native speakers during several weeks in the summer. Developing an articulated early language program, however, will require skilled and experienced teachers and the cooperation of native speakers over a significant period of time, probably including regular released time during the school year. The planning time and start-up curriculum costs for an immersion program that has to be developed locally will represent a major investment for the district.

As more school systems make a commitment to languages at the elementary school level, and as more teachers are able to articulate clearly what kinds of materials they need for these programs, publishers are more likely to produce materials that are usable. That development will make planning a program at the elementary or middle school level an easier and more efficient process.

● Choice of Language(s)

Deciding which language(s) to offer is often a difficult and emotional issue at the beginning of the planning process. Community interest, availability of materials and staff, and potential for articulation must all be taken into consideration. When none of these factors plays a determining role, many school districts have chosen to advertise a "foreign-language" position rather than to indicate a specific language. The best available candidate is hired, regardless of the language, and the quality of the resulting program lays a foundation for long-term success. Compelling rationale can be developed for any of the commonly taught or less commonly taught languages, and any language, when well taught, can provide children with the benefits of global awareness, enhanced basic skills, identification with other cultures, self-esteem, and communicative language skills.

If the elementary school program is implemented in only one language, a possible adverse effect on enrollments in other languages at the middle school/junior high school and high school levels must be considered. However, implementing an elementary language program in more than one language may fragment the district's program and compound articulation problems. This is one of the most difficult issues to wrestle with. There is some justification for the fear that students will choose the elementary school language for continuation at the high school level, thus crowding out the other languages. In many districts, however, all languages have benefited from an increased interest in learning languages, and students entering high school will choose to add a third language, or to explore a different language. It is important to provide more than one entry point into the district's language program in order to accommodate students who would like to study an additional language or who were not able to enroll in the elementary language program.

The experience of the Edison Township program may help to ease some of these fears. The introduction of an elementary Spanish program necessitated a redesign of the middle school program, where all students study a foreign language beginning in the sixth grade. The decision was made to maintain the offering of both French and Spanish after the introduction of only Spanish in grades 2 through 5. Students have the option of continuing their study of Spanish or changing to French. The French teachers were concerned that the introduction of only Spanish in the elementary schools would negatively impact enrollments in French, but experience has shown the opposite to be true. French enrollments are stronger than ever and an increase in the French staff at the middle school has occurred. Partly this is because all students are required to choose a language in sixth grade and stay with this language through eighth grade. Also, some students cite a desire to study a different language after 4 years of studying Spanish in elementary school (Smith, 2007).

It is especially desirable to introduce the less commonly taught languages, such as Arabic, Chinese, Japanese, and Russian, into the elementary school because of their critical importance to the national interest. These languages are more difficult for the English speaker and thus require a much longer exposure before competence can be attained than is the case with the more common school offerings. Their introduction early in the curriculum would make it much more likely that students could develop usable communication skills over time. It must be remembered that in order to plan an effective program in one of these languages, teachers and materials are extremely important. If qualified teachers or appropriate materials cannot be found, program planners may have to delay introduction of the less commonly taught language until later in the sequence. Students who have an elementary experience in a commonly taught language can transfer their language learning skills to their new language and will have a head start compared to other students.

● Who Should Study Languages?

The *Standards for Foreign Language Learning in the 21st Century* (1999) provide a clear answer to this question at the beginning of the "Statement of Philosophy" (p. 7):

> The United States must educate students who are equipped linguistically and culturally to communicate successfully in a pluralistic American society and abroad. This

imperative envisions a future in which ALL students will develop and maintain proficiency in English and at least one other language, modern or classical.

The time has arrived to shed the "elitist" image that foreign languages had for most of the last century in the United States. Evidence from the inner-city schools of Philadelphia, Milwaukee, and Cincinnati, among others, supports the idea that foreign-language learning must be for all learners of all levels of ability and background. Students with poor skills may even have the most to gain from the opportunity to study languages (Masciantonio, 1977; Garfinkel and Tabor, 1991). The practice in some schools of reserving foreign-language study for children who are reading at or above grade level stands in direct contradiction to the information obtained from the Masciantonio study. Such practices may be taking away opportunities for foreign-language study from those children who could benefit from it the most.

Boudreaux (1991) identified 16 strategies common to immersion teaching that are especially beneficial to the special education student, suggesting that the foreign-language learning environment could be a hospitable one for students with learning problems. Andrade, Kretschmer, and Kretschmer (1993) offer both reasons and test results to support the offering of foreign languages to all children.

Teachers in Chicago (Estelle, 1985), New York State (Schnitzler, 1986), and in other areas have reported success in teaching foreign languages to students with learning disabilities and to students who are developmentally challenged, especially when they employ an oral, communicative methodology. One special education teacher (Bring, 1986) verified an observation made by many elementary school language teachers when she noted that some of her students in French class were achieving school success and satisfaction for the first time, and that as a result, their overall attitude and performance had improved in other school subjects as well. Results from the Florida study (Taylor, Feyten, Meros, and Nutta, 2008), cited in Chapter 15, support these observations as well.

Gifted and Talented Students

At the other end of the scale, learners who are gifted are often selected first to be given the opportunity to study a language. Language teachers are caught in a conflict regarding programs for these students. Although there is evidence that languages can be of value to every child, and programs offered exclusively to learners who are gifted tend to reinforce an elitist image for languages, it is also true that many language programs that were begun only for the gifted have led to programs for all children because of their success and popularity.

Young people who are gifted are often especially good language learners as a result of certain frequently observed learning characteristics: retentiveness, a high degree of verbal ability, persistent goal-directed behavior, and ability to work independently. For these learners, languages can be a key to unlock new dimensions of learning and new perspectives. With the foreign language as a tool, gifted students have the opportunity to explore a new system of thinking, a new cultural context, and, at advanced levels, even new literary and political perspectives.

The academically talented are among the nation's most precious resources, the pool from which our strongest leaders are likely to come. In an increasingly interdependent global community, these leaders of tomorrow cannot afford to be monolingual. Programs intended specifically for students who are gifted must be designed to meet their specific needs and must capitalize on their particular abilities, and they should be supported by appropriate rationale and curriculum. Coordinators of programs for the gifted, working together with knowledgeable language teachers, can design the best possible program for this group.

● Staffing (Teachers and Teacher Recruitment)

There is no single decision that will affect the success of the language program more than the choice of teachers. School districts will want to ensure that the teachers they select have had training and experience in working with elementary school children, that they have excellent language skills, and that they have had training in the teaching of a foreign language. In states that have a certification category for elementary school language teachers, only licensed/certified teachers should be hired. The best insurance for the success of a language program is the hiring of skilled and talented teachers.

Teacher Skills

Skills and classroom practices commonly found at the secondary school and college levels do not transfer directly into the elementary school classroom. Even teachers who are very successful with older students will require additional background and training before they attempt to work with elementary school children. Successful classroom teachers who are fluent in a foreign language will require some background in foreign-language methodology before they can reach the same high level of effectiveness in foreign-language teaching as they have attained in other subjects. Because so much of the instruction in the elementary school is oral, and because the teacher is the only model for the children most of the time, it is especially important for the teacher to have excellent oral language skills.

Administrators and others sometimes assume that a native speaker of the language is always a better choice to teach in an early language program than is an English speaker who has learned the language. In fact, teachers who have learned the language themselves can be more sensitive to the learning challenges the language presents. They also serve as excellent role models for the learners, who can aspire to be fluent like their teacher but can never become native speakers. Native speakers who were educated in another culture may require considerable orientation and experience before they work comfortably with U.S. students in the American school setting.

A second common assumption is that teachers at beginning levels of instruction do not need to have the same degree of language proficiency as those who teach at more advanced levels. In reality, teachers at all levels need to be fully proficient in the language they teach. Teachers who cannot comfortably use the target language for all classroom purposes will not be able to surround learners with language, an essential component of an effective learning environment in the early language classroom. They will also find it difficult to develop and create curriculum and activities in the target language.

Teacher Availability

The short-term and long-term availability of teachers will influence the selection of both the program model and the language(s) to be taught. An articulated program in Japanese would be a questionable choice in an isolated rural community that finds it difficult to attract new teachers, whereas an option in French, German, or Spanish could be realistic in the same community. Searching for a teacher of Japanese might be very manageable in a large, cosmopolitan urban system where the supply of teachers would be more reliable.

Teachers of any language continue to be in short supply, so the planning team should develop a time line and a recruitment strategy for teachers as early as possible. Human resources personnel are often relatively uninformed about the challenges of recruiting world language teachers for early language classrooms, so close cooperation and advice from the planning team will help to ensure that quality teachers are hired for the program.

Staffing for Content-Focused Programs

Immersion teachers are certified elementary school teachers who are fluent speakers of the target language. Classroom aides who are also fluent in the target language can provide an additional, authentic model for the students as well as helping with individual and small-group instruction throughout the school day. Certainly it is desirable to have special subjects such as music, art, and physical education taught by specialists who are fluent in the target language, but many programs find it difficult to locate staff people who are appropriately trained in these areas, so these subjects are taught either by the classroom teachers or by English-speaking specialists. Partial and two-way immersion programs are usually staffed by two teachers, one a speaker of the immersion language and the other a speaker of English. Many teachers in Spanish immersion programs have been drawn from a background in bilingual education, but some readjustment of attitudes and assumptions is necessary before these teachers adapt smoothly to an immersion approach. (See Chapter 11 for more information.)

Staffing for Language-Focused Programs

Teachers need to have considerable fluency in the target language as well as meaningful living experiences in countries in which the language is spoken. Learners will not be able to achieve fluency greater than that of their teachers. It is also important that these teachers have education and experience in working with elementary school children and that they have an understanding of teaching and learning second languages.

Language Specialist Model   This is the model that has been employed most often in early language programs. The language specialist usually teaches the new language only. The specialist may travel from room to room, or children may come to a special language classroom.

Classroom Teacher Model   In this option, each classroom teacher has the responsibility for teaching the language program. The program is most effective when designed in cooperation with a language specialist, who also coordinates the program, provides in-service assistance for the classroom teacher, and teaches occasional class sessions in individual classrooms. In some cases, there may be media support—audio and/or video—for the classroom teacher and less actual contact with a language specialist.

Program Coordinator   The decision to include a program coordinator in the staffing and budget plan is a major step toward ensuring that planning and implementation of a language program will proceed smoothly. Rosenbusch (1991, p. 308) lists a number of qualities this coordinator should have: " . . . is certified K–12, is experienced in teaching foreign language at all levels, is able to work effectively with other teachers, and is able to communicate well with school administrators, parents, and the community. Most importantly, the coordinator must be committed to the expanded foreign language program and dedicated to maintaining a strong program of excellent quality."

Each of the seven programs described by Gilzow and Branaman (2000), in their overview of model early foreign language programs, has the benefit of some type of coordinator position. The program may be guided by a full- or part-time program coordinator, a district foreign-language supervisor, or another individual with responsibility for program and curriculum development.

It is important to designate at least a half-time professional position to the role of coordinator of the program, whether this position takes the form of a foreign-language supervisor, a lead teacher with released time for supervision and planning, or a resource teacher with administrative responsibility. The coordinator will need time for building the new program; for providing in-service opportunities for language teachers; for developing curriculum, materials, and assessments; and for building school and community support.

Recruitment of Teachers from Abroad

Some school districts have found it necessary to recruit teachers from abroad in order to find staff with adequate background and language skills—and then they have faced the challenge of orienting foreign staff to the realities of the American school and the psyche of the American child. In most cases, this requires intensive preparation for the teachers before they enter their classrooms, and ongoing orientation for a year or more. Although this has been especially the case for immersion teachers, more and more language-focused programs have turned to foreign nationals. Some programs that send teachers from other countries have a built-in limit of the amount of time the teachers can spend in U.S. This can lead to a teacher turnover that challenges the continuity of the program and requires careful advance planning.

● Budget

The level of funding that a school system is willing to commit to a language program will be the final determiner of the shape and scope of a program. It is imperative to plan with budget factors in mind, developing a program that will make the best use of the funds available. The most carefully planned "dream" program will suffer if shortcuts and compromises must be made in order to stretch an inadequate budget. A realistic proposed budget will take the following factors into account.

Start-Up Costs

Language-Focused Programs   Start-up costs include realia, materials, a collection of resource books and sample programs for teacher use, some audiovisual equipment, and other nonconsumable classroom materials. These costs may also include additions to the instructional resource center—such as videos, computer software, CDs, tapes, DVDs, library books, and displays.

Immersion Programs   In an immersion program the start-up costs are significant because target-language materials must be purchased for all elements of classroom instruction and library supplementation, and some may have to be developed locally.

Media-Based Programs   Media-based formats, such as interactive cable programs, will also have relatively high start-up costs for materials and equipment.

Salaries

Language Specialists   Schools choosing a language specialist model will immediately add the expense of salaries for the language teachers. As the program develops, more teachers will be hired to staff new levels and new sections.

Immersion Teachers   Immersion programs have no additional salary costs because the immersion teacher replaces a regular classroom teacher, rather than supplementing that teacher. It should be noted, however, that the most successful immersion models include a native-speaking classroom aide in each classroom, for at least part of each day.

Program Coordinator   The position of program coordinator may be a full-time position, in the case of a large school system, or it may constitute part of the day for a foreign-language classroom teacher. In most cases, this should be at least a half-time position.

Curriculum and Staff Development Time

There are few investments that will yield a greater return than planning time for teachers. If at least some of the initial planning is done by an entire language department, both the commitment to the total program and the chances for smooth articulation are improved.

Schools should budget to fund at least several weeks of planning time before beginning a new program, and regular summer planning time each year thereafter.

Curriculum Development   Although commercial materials are available for some programs for young learners, most schools will find that they need to develop at least some part of the curriculum to meet the particular needs of the local community. There is very little available commercially for exploratory programs or for the less commonly taught languages, so local planning will consume considerable time and energy. Immersion programs require extensive locally developed materials.

Professional Development   Teachers in elementary school foreign-language programs will need regular professional development opportunities, separately and with secondary school language faculty. Especially with the classroom-teacher model, staff development opportunities should not intrude on regular planning time or on what would otherwise be free time.

Attendance at Conferences   Because elementary school language teachers often feel very isolated, some of the best staff development support for teachers comes from attending foreign-language conferences, such as the annual meeting of the American Council on the Teaching of Foreign Languages and various state and regional language conferences. All of these conferences feature workshops and sessions on languages at the elementary school level. A number of states also offer conferences directed specifically at language teaching at the K–8 level. Travel and registration costs for conferences, as well as salary for a substitute teacher, are valuable additions to the language budget.

Materials

After the start-up costs for materials, there will be ongoing expenditures for the following:

Consumable Materials

- Worksheets, workbooks, crafts materials, and food items fall into this category.
- Language teaching in the elementary and middle school/junior high school levels relies heavily on visuals and realia, so costs for realia and visuals needed for each language and each level may well be greater than in other curricular areas.

Import Costs

- Costs of imported materials may be 10 to 20 percent higher than costs of domestic materials.

Textbook Costs

- When texts are available, these costs will increase with each grade level added to the program.

Other Materials Costs

● The costs for photocopying will be proportionally higher in programs for which there is no textbook.

● Hardware and repair costs for all media systems must be included in the budget. Media-based programs will have recurring expenditures in this area.

● Include the cost of videos, CDs, CD-ROMs, and DVDs.

● Include the cost of laminating and other production of visual materials.

Miscellaneous Costs

There will always be various miscellaneous costs to consider:

● Travel between schools for language specialist teachers, when they are assigned to more than one school

● Travel from the base site to the receiving sites in programs that use interactive cable

● Travel for the language coordinator for supervision purposes on the part of the language coordinator

● Delivery costs, when languages are taught by means of interactive cable, for transporting materials and student work from school to school

● Mailing costs for programs that incorporate systematic contacts with schools or children in foreign countries

● Admission fees, speakers' fees, and field trips

● Costs of making connections with language speakers or other representative elements of the target culture (gift shops, restaurants, museums, festivals, art galleries, etc.)

● Food and craft activities

It is sometimes possible for a school system to receive government assistance or a foundation grant for beginning a language program at the elementary school level. Certainly, this eases the impact of the start-up costs and initial planning, but it is critical that there be a school commitment to a realistic level of long-term funding for the program.

● Space Allocation

Early language programs at the elementary school level are usually housed by one of two methods. Either the language teacher has all classes meet in a special language room, which can be used to create a target-language environment for instruction, or the teacher travels from one classroom to another. Teachers have found advantages in either means of organization, although the traveling teacher is severely restricted in terms of extensive use of hands-on materials and realia. When the teacher must travel, it is valuable to have the classroom teacher remain in the room during the language lesson, both to show support and to help ensure that there is no loss of instructional time because of a need to establish behavioral standards. A more extended discussion of these issues is found in Chapter 8.

● Support of Existing District Staff

Support of Elementary School Principals and Teachers

The success of a language program is closely tied to the environment of the school in which it is placed. It is vital that the principal and the teachers in the school be in favor of the program, that they share commitment to its goals, and that they participate in program planning. When planners in a midwestern city developed a new elementary school Spanish program, they began with pilot programs in three schools. All interested schools in the district competed for the opportunity to participate in the pilot project. Only schools in which there was clear and unified support from the entire school community were considered as program sites. As a result, the faculty and administration of the pilot schools felt investment in and support for the new program and were willing to work to help it succeed.

In programs using a language specialist model, classroom teachers who feel accepted as part of the language teaching team can extend the language learning into the regular school day. They may suggest curricular areas for reinforcement or vocabulary development in the language classroom, encourage the use of the foreign language during other school activities, and participate in language classes with the children, thus serving as powerful models of interest and enthusiasm.

In programs using a classroom teacher model, tremendous responsibility for success of the program rests with individual teachers for whom language instruction is only one component in a busy, demanding schedule. Teachers with a commitment to the language program will find ways to use the language communicatively throughout the day and will be in a position to give individual students the special attention they may need in order to succeed to the level of their own potential. Without real commitment to the program, participation may be grudging, and results from the students will be disappointing.

Immersion programs require the coordinated efforts of the principal and all staff to create a second-language environment and to work toward unified goals. When immersion programs are housed in the same building as nonlanguage classrooms, considerable effort may be required to make sure that nonimmersion teachers understand the immersion program and do not resent the special attention that immersion programs often receive, especially when the program is new. Since considerable funding often goes into the start-up of an immersion program, other teachers may perceive immersion teachers and students to be favorites. Problems like these will not disappear unless there is a focused effort to help the entire school work together and to understand the special characteristics and benefits of the immersion program.

Support of Existing Foreign Language Staff

The success of an early language program also depends to a great extent on the support and expertise of the existing foreign-language staff in the school system who will work with the students from the K–8 program after they reach the high school level. If teachers at later levels are unsupportive or ineffective, the program at the elementary school will eventually suffer.

A case in point is a medium-sized Minnesota school that taught three languages at the senior high school; one of the languages, French, had very low enrollments and dissatisfied students. In the 1970s, an elementary school program in French was introduced by a talented and innovative teacher, and junior high enrollments soared when students reached that level. As soon as these students entered the senior high school, however, they dropped French, sometimes after a week or two, or did not ever register, on the basis of the "grapevine" alone.

After a year or two of this type of enrollment pattern, the school board discontinued the entire French program on the grounds that they could not justify continuing a feeder program without the senior high school culmination. The elementary school program was blamed by some for giving children "false" expectations that language learning would be fun, that the work would be meaningful and enjoyable, and that everyone could learn a language. By the mid-1990s, French had been reintroduced in the district, but no languages had returned to the elementary school.

When students leave a middle school program and are told by the receiving teacher that "fun and games were all very well before, but now you will start real language learning," the entire K–8 program is called into question. Language teachers at every level need to understand and affirm the learning that has already taken place and build their own programs on that learning. This is most likely to happen when teachers from all levels of instruction participate in initial program planning and meet regularly to design curriculum and discuss methodology and articulation issues.

Example from Edison Township Public Schools, New Jersey

Preparation of a language department for a new early language program must begin very early and continue regularly as the program grows. The process followed by the Edison Township Public Schools provides an outstanding model for this kind of development.

> The introduction of the study of a world language in the elementary school has had a profound impact on the entire world languages program in the district. This has necessitated a tremendous amount of professional development, curriculum writing and collegial dialogue across all grades levels (2nd through 12th).
>
> All staff has received extensive training in the standards. All curriculum writing and collegial dialogue is informed by working to achieve a well articulated, standards-

based long-sequence world languages program. In addition to numerous workshops on the standards, staff has been trained in the proficiency guidelines. Elementary staff has received training in the SOPA (Student Oral Proficiency Assessment developed by the Center for Applied Linguistics) and middle and high school staff has received training in the MOPI (Modified Oral Proficiency Interview developed by the American Council on the Teaching of Foreign Languages).

. . . One particularly memorable day occurred when all world languages teachers worked in teams to imagine what the theme of family would look like when studied in elementary, middle and high school. This allowed for deep discussion of the different linguistic proficiency levels we expect at each level of the program and the impact of this on curriculum, instruction and assessment.

As the program has been developing, extensive opportunities have been provided for teachers to hear about and see instruction at the various levels. Teachers are provided release time to visit their colleagues in other schools in the district. Starting two years before elementary students were to reach the middle school, all middle school teachers were required to visit the elementary schools. Before middle school students arrived at the high school, teachers from the high school spent a day in the elementary and middle schools. As a preface to these visits, a full day in-service was devoted to having colleagues showcase curricular units from each grade level of instruction.

Curriculum writing has been an on-going, every year process since 1999 when the elementary program was introduced. Many resources (time, money and hard work) have been devoted to the development of curriculum documents. Each curriculum project is a team effort with several representatives from each school assigned to develop specific curricular units. At the high school level, this required school-year curriculum articulation projects where teachers were paid to come together each month to discuss the impact of receiving students from a long-sequence of study and map out the curricular units that would be have to be written to appropriately engage and challenge these students. During this time, the district undertook a district-wide initiative on "backwards-design" and all teachers have been trained in the "backwards-design" model of curriculum development as articulated by Grant Wiggins and Jay McTighe in their book *Understanding by Design*.

Probably the greatest amount of professional development has taken place around the topic of assessment. When the first group of elementary students reached fifth grade, it was decided that an end-of-year benchmark assessment should be implemented to collect data to measure the fifth grade students' linguistic proficiency level. Following the SOPA model, the elementary teachers developed a protocol to interview a sample of students in each school. Each year approximately 25 students per school are interviewed. Using the SOPA rubric, data is analyzed to determine each student's linguistic proficiency level. The interviews are audio and/or video-taped and the teachers review these tapes to reflect upon the results and the interview process. Each interview is conducted by two teachers; one elementary and one middle school teacher. This allows for collegial discussion about how to classify students on the rubric and provides another opportunity for articulation. (Smith, 2007)

● Program Evaluation

Assessment must be an integral part of both program and curriculum design. (See the World/Foreign Language Program Effectiveness Survey in Figure 17.5.) If impact on basic skills, on attitudes, or on performance in other content areas is to be measured, pretests will have to be designed and administered before the beginning of the program. The goals of program assessment should be determined at the outset, so that specific instruments can be developed and a time line for assessment can be built into the school schedule. Types of program assessment include the following:

- Learner language skills performance
- Learner attitudes toward other languages and cultures
- Learner attitudes toward the course
- Learner performance in other content areas
- Teacher performance checklists
- Teacher evaluation of program
- Parent attitudes
- Outside consultant observation
- Teacher-peer observation and review
- Administrator observation and review

The Center for Applied Linguistics has developed the Student Oral Proficiency Assessment (SOPA), appropriate for students in grade 3 and above, and the Early Language Listening and Oral Proficiency Assessment (ELLOPA) for primary school students. These are designed for assessing overall student performance using randomly selected students, and not for individual student assessment.

Instruments for assessing several of the other areas of program effectiveness have been developed by Heining-Boynton (1991) for use with early language learning programs in North Carolina. These resources are shared in her article in *Foreign Language Annals* and they can be adapted very successfully for local program use.

● Student Assessment and Grading

Assessment of student performance can be a valuable indicator of program success, and it also provides teachers with essential information about the effectiveness of instruction and the needs of individual students. Meaningful assessment will reflect the goals of the program and the nature of instruction; that is, it will be based on student performance in

● FIGURE 17.5   World/Foreign Language Program Effectiveness Survey

4 Strongly Agree 3 Agree 2 Disagree 1 Strongly Disagree	4	3	2	1	NA
Program Delivery					
There is sufficient contact time for World/Foreign Language Program.					
Elementary School					
Middle School					
High School					
There are adequate facilities for language classes.					
There are adequate resources for student learning.					
Teachers are qualified and hold language certification or advanced degrees.					
Programs for heritage learners are in place.					
There is support for the language program by school administrators.					
Curriculum					
There is a clearly stated curriculum known by the teachers.					
The curriculum is used in planning and implementing the lessons. The curriculum rather than the textbook drives instruction.					
A variety of instructional materials such as thematic units, modern media, and textbooks are being used.					
The curriculum is aligned with local, state, and national standards.					
The curriculum is aligned and articulated horizontally within the school.					
The curriculum is aligned and articulated vertically within elementary, middle, and high schools.					
The curriculum is adjusted based on formal and informal student performance data (e.g., oral and written quizzes, tests, student work, and anecdotal records).					
The foreign/world language curriculum integrates language, content, and culture.					
The curriculum demonstrates attention to the individual needs of all students through a differentiated curriculum (e.g., learning styles, developmental variations).					
The curriculum reflects multicultural perspectives.					

4 Strongly Agree 3 Agree 2 Disagree 1 Strongly Disagree	4	3	2	1	NA
Assessment					
Program outcomes are documented with external assessment instruments.					
Students meet performance and content expectations.					
Assessment tasks are varied and consistent with research-based instructional practices.					
Teachers use various forms of documentation to report student progress, achievement, and participation.					
Teachers monitor student performance, provide meaningful feedback in a timely fashion, and adjust language instruction accordingly.					
Students have an opportunity to assess their own progress.					
Assessment tasks are designed to evaluate speaking, writing, listening, and reading skills within the interpersonal, interpretive, and presentational modes of communication as they relate to comprehensibility, comprehension, language control, vocabulary, cultural awareness, and communication strategies.					
Scoring guides and rubrics for foreign/world language assessments, including identified criteria, are developed, distributed to students, and consistently followed.					
Instruction					
Teachers use a variety of instructional strategies depending on the students, the content, and the objectives of the lesson.					
Teachers use a variety of pairs, small groups, and large groups during instruction.					
Technology is integrated into foreign/world language instruction.					
Teachers have adequate time to plan within their department and to collaborate with others.					
Professional Development					
Teachers are involved in a sustained program of professional development.					

Source: Adapted from Helena Curtain, "World Language Program Effectiveness Survey, How Far Have We Come? Where Do We Want to Go?" and "Program Effectiveness Review for Kentucky Schools World Languages," 2007. http://www.education.ky.gov/KDE/Instructional+Resources/High+School/Language+Learning/Other+World+Languages/Kentucky+Framework+for+World+Language+Learning.htm.

meaningful, communicative language tasks. Just as traditional paper-and-pencil methods of testing are giving way to performance evaluation and portfolio development across the rest of the curriculum, so, too, will assessment of student performance in foreign-language instruction require a variety of nontraditional measures.

Although some school districts have chosen to give students in early language classes a pass/fail grade, or no grade at all, a program that seeks parity with other courses in the curriculum should be treated like other content areas in terms of grading. Both students and parents tend to perceive classes for which grades are not given as less important, as peripheral to the basic curriculum. The basis for assessing student progress and for awarding grades must be compatible with the goals and the philosophy of the program. That is, if oral skills are emphasized, assessment will be based on listening and speaking performance, even though reading and writing skills might be easier to measure objectively. Specific suggestions for effective assessment, evaluation, and reporting of student performance are provided in Chapter 7.

● Building Public Relations

Planning the foreign-language program must involve parents, the community, the staff, and the school board in every step of the process. The support of these people will be the decisive factor in the later success of the program. Once the program is in progress, spending the time and effort necessary to develop a broad support base in the school and the community will prove to be very rewarding.

The planning committee for the new program can continue to play an important role after the program has been established. Such a committee has the expertise necessary to help the community understand and appreciate the value of language learning, and it can form the core of broader community support. In the event that the new program is threatened in some way, such as a cutback in staffing or in scheduling, there is a strong advocacy team immediately available. Finally, as Tucker and Donato (1999) point out, this committee can continue to guide the program and to plan for its expansion.

Leadership from a foreign-language program coordinator can be especially helpful in ensuring ongoing and consistent activity to build public support. Some of the activities that can contribute to this support include the following:

● Making use of the media to provide publicity

● Taking field trips

● Inviting parents and others to visit classes

● Recording classes and specific class projects to share with parent groups and administrators

● Reporting class activities to parents, the principal, and other teachers

- Sending out a monthly newsletter
- Taking part in school programs
- Putting on a special program for parents and/or the community
- Sending second-language invitations and greeting cards as a class writing activity

These activities give the program visibility and communicate the activities and accomplishments of the elementary school foreign-language program. They also serve as an effective recruitment tool for languages at all levels. Additional information about public relations and advocacy is found in Chapter 15.

● Sharing Experiences and Ideas—Networking

Sharing the experiences and good ideas that you have gained from developing an effective K–12 program will enable others interested in starting a program to build on what has already been done. Your experiences can help prevent them from making the same discoveries and the same mistakes in isolation. Materials that have been painstakingly developed should be shared on the Internet or in other ways, so that others may take advantage of what has been done. They might also be shared with the state foreign-language consultant and with the state foreign-language organization. Presentations at local, regional, and national conferences, newsletter articles, and contacts with professional associations are also effective ways of giving program experiences and ideas an impact beyond the local setting.

Summary

- School districts and program planners must choose among program models according to the language proficiency outcomes they desire and the budgetary and staffing circumstances in which they find themselves. Planners should seek to design the best possible program, in terms of language proficiency, that they have the resources to implement.

- There is no factor in the program that will be more crucial to its success than a careful and thorough plan that addresses the key areas of program philosophy and goals, program model, time allocation, budget, staffing, materials, articulation, evaluation, and staff and community involvement and support.

- A successful plan requires a significant investment of planning time and the unqualified support of the administration and school board.

- The following checklist provides useful guidelines for applying the principles of this chapter.

Early Language Program Planning Checklist

1. _____ Hold districtwide planning meetings

   _____ Involve community

   _____ Involve classroom and language teachers, administrators, union representatives

2. _____ Complete mission statement, program philosophy

3. _____ Select program model and goals

   _____ Identify students

   _____ Plan for amount of instructional time: days per week, hours per day, years

   _____ Plan for a reasonable teacher workload (eight 30-minute classes per day is optimal)

   _____ Develop patterns of organization for staffing

   _____ Allocate budget for staff, materials, in-service, and miscellaneous costs

4. _____ Identify teachers

5. _____ Select language(s)

6. _____ Develop budget

7. _____ Develop curriculum

   _____ Locate and adapt materials

   _____ Plan scope and sequence, classroom activities

8. _____ Plan articulation with secondary school programs

9. _____ Develop an evaluation plan

10. _____ Design public relations activities

11. _____ Disseminate program information

For Study and Discussion

1. Describe an elementary school-level early language program that you know in the greatest detail. Explain how it fits into the categories of this chapter, and identify its strengths and its limitations. What particular aspects of the model account for the program's strengths? What changes in the model might bring about improvements in the program?

2. Your school district has had a very successful program for young learners for several years; it is staffed by several traveling specialist teachers, and follow-up programs at the middle school and at the high school are well designed and effective. Many parents and teachers would like to make an even stronger commitment to languages in the elementary school. What options and suggestions would you offer to the parent planning committee?

3. Because there are a number of international companies located in your community, as well as a college with a large population of international students, there is a strong interest in early languages and cultures throughout the district. How might you tap the international resources of the community to provide language learning experiences for elementary school children?

4. Which program-planning considerations might weigh most heavily in each of the following settings?
   - An isolated rural community
   - A community with a rapidly expanding suburban population
   - A small town near a medium-sized city in the American Southwest
   - An urban district with many elementary and secondary schools
   - A medium-sized city near the Canadian border
   - A private school
   - A K–12 school housed in a single building

5. You are a middle school foreign-language teacher in a system with a strong secondary school program in your language and reasonably successful programs in three other foreign languages, including Latin. You have just been asked to chair a committee to plan an elementary school foreign-language program. You may choose your own committee and set your own agenda. How will you proceed?

6. An elementary school curriculum coordinator has agreed to support a new foreign-language program but he believes strongly that the elementary school day is already too fragmented. He asks you to design a program that will require the minimum time out of the school day. How will you respond to his request?

7. The curriculum planners in your school district are simultaneously designing a K–12 foreign-language program and a new middle school to replace an existing junior high school. You have the opportunity to serve on both committees. What can you do in your role on both committees to help build the best possible K–12 language program and the most effective possible middle school experience for early adolescent learners?

8. One of the elementary school classroom teachers with whom you work comes to you privately and complains that your workload of eight 30-minute world language classes per day is unfair, since she has to teach a full six hours per day. How might you respond?

For Further Reading

The following sources are recommended for additional information about material covered in this chapter. Chapter citations are documented in Works Cited at the end of this book.

Brown, Christine. "A Case for Foreign Languages: The Glastonbury Language Program." *Perspective, Council for Basic Education* 7:2 (1995). Available on-line at http://www.foreignlanguage.org/advocacy/case.htm.

Christian, Donna, et al. *Profiles in Two-Way Immersion Education.* McHenry, IL: Center for Applied Linguistics and Delta Systems, 1997.

Curtain, Helena, and Carol Ann Dahlberg. *Planning for Success: Common Pitfalls in the Planning of Early Foreign Language Programs.* Washington, DC: Center for Applied Linguistics, ERIC Digest, December 2000. Available on-line at http://www.ericdigests.org/2001-3/common.htm.

Donato, Richard, G., Richard Tucker, Jirada Wudthayagorn, and Kanae Igarashi. "Converging Evidence: Attitudes, Achievements, and Instruction in the Later Years of FLES." *Foreign Language Annals* 33:4 (July/August 2000): 377–393.

Duncan, Gregory. "Administrators and Counselors: Essential Partners to FLES." *FLES News* 2:2 (1988–1989): 1, 6.

Gilzow, Douglas F., and Lucinda E. Branaman. *Lessons Learned: Model Early Foreign Language Programs.* McHenry, IL: Delta Systems, 2000.

Gilzow, Douglas F., and Nancy C. Rhodes. *Establishing High-Quality Foreign Language Programs in Elementary Schools.* Northeast and Islands Regional Educational Laboratory at Brown University. *Perspectives on Policy and Practice* (December 2000). Available on-line at www.alliance.brown.edu/pubs/perspectives/PerspCal.pdf.

Lipton, Gladys C. *Practical Handbook for Elementary Language Programs* (4th ed.). Available from Blueprints for Learning, PO Box 2632, Kensington, MD 20891.

Met, Myriam. "Decisions, Decisions, Decisions!" *Foreign Language Annals* 18:6 (December 1985): 469–473.

Met, Myriam. "Which Foreign Language Should Students Learn?" *Educational Leadership* 7:1 (1989): 54–58.

Met, Myriam. *Middle Schools and Foreign Languages: A View for the Future.* Washington DC: Center for Applied Linguistics. *ERIC Digest* (February 1996). Available on-line at http://www.cal.org/resources/digest/met00002.html.

Met, Myriam (Ed.). *Critical Issues in Early Second Language Learning: Building for Our Children's Future.* Glenview, IL: Scott Foresman-Addison Wesley, 1998.

National Council of State Supervisors of Foreign Languages and the American Council on the Teaching of Foreign Languages. "NCSSFL/ACTFL Statement on the Study of Foreign Languages in Elementary School." *ACTFL Newsletter* 3:3 (1990). Available on-line at http://ncssfl.org/papers/index.php?elementary.

National K–12 Foreign Language Resource Center: http://www.nflrc.iastate.edu/.

North Carolina Department of Public Instruction. *Scheduling Foreign Languages on the Block.* Washington, DC: Center for Applied Linguistics. *ERIC Digest* (October 1988). Available on-line at http://www.cal.org/resources/digest/blockdigest.html.

Ohio K–4 Mandarin Chinese curriculum: http://www.ode.state.oh.us/GD/Templates/Pages/ODE/ODEDetail.aspx?Page=3&TopicRelationID=1701&Content=63068.

Pesola, Carol Ann. "Articulation for Elementary School Foreign Language Programs: Challenges and Opportunities." In John F. Lalande II (Ed.). *Shaping the Future of Foreign Language Education: FLES, Articulation, and Proficiency* (pp. 1–10). Report of Central States Conference on the Teaching of Foreign Languages. Lincolnwood, IL: National Textbook Co., 1988. Available for download at eric.ed.gov/ERICWebPortal/recordDetail?accno=ED292332.

Rieken, Elizabeth, et al. "Building Better Bridges: Middle School to High School Articulation in Foreign Language Programs." *Foreign Language Annals* 29: 4 (1996): 562–570.

Rosenbusch, Marcia H. "Elementary School Foreign Language: The Establishment and Maintenance of Strong Programs." *Foreign Language Annals* 24:4 (1991): 297–314.

Rosenbusch, Marcia H. *Guidelines for Starting an Elementary School Foreign Language Program.* Washington DC: Center for Applied Linguistics. *ERIC Digest* (June 1995). Available on-line at http://www.cal.org/resources/digest/rosenb01.htm.

Short, Deborah J., and Karen F. Willetts. *Implementing Middle School Foreign Language Programs.* Washington DC: Center for Applied Linguistics. *ERIC Digest* (June 1991). Available on-line at www.ericdigests.org/pre-9220/middle.htm.

Tucker, G. Richard, and Richard Donato. "Designing and Implementing an Innovative Foreign Language Program: Reflections from a School District-University Partnership." *Learning Languages* 4:2 (Winter 1999): 4–12.

Tucker, G. Richard, and Richard Donato. *Implementing a District-Wide Foreign Language Program.* Washington DC: Center for Applied Linguistics. *ERIC Digest* (September 2001). Available on-line at http://www.cal.org/resources/digest/0103implement.html.

Willets, Karen A., and Deborah J. Short. *Planning Middle School Foreign Language Programs.* Washington DC: Center for Applied Linguistics. *ERIC Digest* (November 1990). Available on-line at http://findarticles.com/p/articles/mi_pric/is_199106/ai_580074822.

Wilson, Jo Anne. *Foreign Language Program Articulation: Building Bridges from Elementary to Secondary School.* Washington DC: Center for Applied Linguistics. *ERIC Digest* (November 1988). Available on-line at http://www.ericdigests.org/pre-929/bridges.htm.

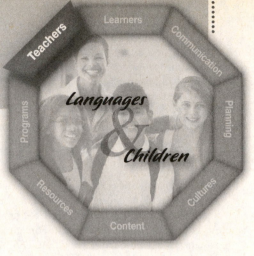

Chapter 18

Developing Professional Teachers for Early Language Programs

Enduring Understanding

- Students are active constructors of meaning in meaningful, communicative contexts.

Essential Question

- How can I create meaningful contexts for everything I teach?

Teachers for elementary and middle school language classrooms of the twenty-first century require a combination of competencies and background that may be unprecedented in the preparation of language teachers. The emphasis on target language use for all classroom purposes calls for strong language skills, and especially for fluent oral language that provides a good model for the learner. In the absence of a textbook as the core of the curriculum, thematic planning demands flexible language and a strong vocabulary base, allowing the teacher to respond to student interests and take advantage of opportunities that arise in the development of a theme. Teachers who do not rely on a textbook need an excellent background in children's literature and in the target culture, so that they can draw these elements into unit and daily lesson plans. Integrative, thematic planning also depends on solid understanding of the general curriculum, in order to relate language

502

instruction effectively with mathematics, science, health, social studies, music, art, language arts, and physical education.

The preparation of language teachers has traditionally taken place in the context of a language and literature major, with education as a secondary emphasis. The typical content of literature classes often does not provide the background most useful for elementary and middle school teachers, and in many cases the culture and language addressed in programs for language majors are not well suited to the future roles of these teachers.

Preparation of teachers for the K–8 language classroom must address four basic areas:

1. Language skills and understanding of the culture, especially the culture of children and young adolescents, within which the language is used

2. Methodology for and experiences with teaching languages to young learners

3. Understanding and application of the *Standards for Foreign Language Learning in the 21st Century* and ACTFL Performance Guidelines for K–12 Learners, as well as their implications for curriculum, instruction, and assessment

4. Background in the curriculum and philosophy of the elementary and the middle school

Clients for this preparation come from three basic groups: in-service and preservice K–8 teachers who have language background; in-service and preservice secondary school language teachers who have interest in working with K–8 learners; and native speakers of the language whose education and teacher preparation have taken place outside the United States. Although each group of clients requires a somewhat different pattern of emphasis in their preparation, they can work together very effectively in the same program, each sharing their particular areas of expertise with their colleagues.

The short-term need in teacher preparation is for programs that can facilitate the recertification or relicensure of in-service teachers to staff-emerging elementary and middle school programs. A number of intensive summer workshops around the country, including programs in such widespread locations as New York City, Minnesota, Georgia, Florida, and Texas, have been designed to meet this challenge. Some local districts provide intensive in-service programs for their own staff, such as the immersion teacher education program developed in Montgomery County, Maryland. More intensive recertification workshops are needed to meet the growing immediate need for teachers, together with the development of licensure programs in colleges and universities nationwide.

For the long term, programs in higher education are needed that will encourage the development of teachers who have dual certification: teachers of language who are fluent language users and are also licensed elementary school generalists or middle school teachers of another content area. Teachers with this kind of background will be able to work successfully with both foreign-language immersion programs and intensive, language-focused programs. They will be in the best position to provide successful experiences with new languages for young learners of all backgrounds.

The American Council on the Teaching of Foreign Languages (1988, p. 78) recommended the following guidelines for the preparation of teachers at the elementary school level. These characteristics are listed in addition to those expected of foreign-language teachers at other levels.

Programs provide information about and experience in the elementary educational system to include:

1. an understanding of first language development and its relation to second language learning in childhood;
2. knowledge of instructional methods appropriate to second language instruction in the elementary school;
3. the ability to teach reading and writing as developmental skills to learners acquiring literacy skills in their first language;
4. familiarity with aspects of the target culture appropriate to the developmental needs and interests of students, including children's literature appropriate to the target culture;
5. knowledge of the elementary school curriculum, the relationship among the content areas, and ability to teach or reinforce elementary school curricula through or in a foreign language;
6. knowledge of elementary school principles and practices, and the ability to apply such knowledge to creating an affective and physical environment conducive to foreign language learning.

● Preparation of Teachers

The strongest influence on the quality of foreign-language teaching in K–12 classrooms is the quality of the teacher preparation programs in which new teachers develop both the skills and the vision for language teaching. Until the fall of 2002, when ACTFL released new teacher standards, the teacher situation for early languages had changed remarkably little since the 1960s: Demand has continued to overwhelm supply, and many programs continue to be staffed by teachers without specific preparation in teaching world languages to children, by native speakers without any qualification other than language skill, and sometimes even by teachers who have limited language skills themselves. Few states had addressed the issue of special licensure or certification for foreign-language teachers at the elementary school level, so there had been little by way of a standard for schools to use in evaluating and employing a potential teacher. Relatively few institutions of higher education have had staff and programs in place to prepare teachers for this emerging field.

Much of the burden of elementary school foreign-language teacher preparation has been laid on workshops, summer institutes, and teacher in-service work. Although this "bandage" approach cannot be expected to replace a professionwide commitment to quality teacher preparation, a number of priorities in teacher background and skills have begun to emerge.

ACTFL Program Standards for the Preparation of Foreign Language Teachers (Initial Level—Undergraduate and Graduate)(For K–12 and Secondary Certification Programs)

Before the fall of 2002, there was little uniformity among states and institutions of higher education regarding standards for teachers entering the profession by way of a teacher licensure program. In August 2002, the ACTFL Foreign Language Teacher Standards Writing Team completed a draft of program standards that was subsequently approved by the National Council for Accreditation of Teacher Education (NCATE), the most widely supported accreditation process for teacher preparation institutions.

The ACTFL/NCATE standards include content standards, supporting standards, supporting explanations, and rubrics for each of the supporting standards. They represent the final step in the process of unifying classroom instruction, teacher preparation, and professional development around carefully designed standards and performances. A careful reading of the entire document will give a clear picture of well-prepared foreign-language teachers as they enter the profession. The standards can be accessed on-line at http://www.actfl.org/i4a/pages/Index.cfm?pageid=3384.

Georgia Model Programs Guidelines for Teachers of Young Learners

In Georgia, teachers in the statewide model programs developed and endorsed the following set of guidelines for teachers of young learners (Georgia Department of Education):

Georgia Model Programs Statements of Understanding

As a Georgia model program teacher, I demonstrate support for the philosophy of the program when I

- Teach 98–100 percent of the time in the target language.
- Use the target language for classroom management as well as for instruction.
- Avoid using translation as a tool for clarifying meaning.
- Help learners to clarify meaning and express understanding without translation.
- Provide learners with a rich target language environment that includes extended listening opportunities such as narration, descriptions, and explanations.
- Provide learners with meaningful concrete experiences, making extensive use of visuals, props, realia, and hands-on activities.
- Present vocabulary in chunks and in context rather than as isolated words or lists.
- Plan and teach around a theme.
- Seek ways to include meaningful culture content in every lesson and every unit.
- Seek to integrate concepts from the general elementary school curriculum in every lesson and every unit.
- Use songs and rhymes to reinforce meaning and practice language.

- Choose authentic songs, games, stories, and rhymes in preference to translations whenever possible.
- Incorporate communicative use of reading and writing from early stages of instruction.
- Plan lessons to include a variety of activities, student groupings, and types of interaction that will appeal to differing learner interests and learning styles.
- Provide opportunities for learners to express personal meaning from the earliest stages of the program.
- Encourage growing independence and independent language use on the part of learners, moving them toward increased expression of individual ideas and opinions.
- Assess learner progress frequently and regularly, using a variety of types of assessment.
- Use a variety of strategies to maintain frequent and regular contact with parents.
- Communicate regularly with classroom teachers about student progress and program goals and content.
- Work closely with other teachers in the program to plan curriculum and resolve issues.
- Seek frequent opportunities for professional and language development.
- Maintain open communication about the program and student progress among teachers, administrators, and the general public.

● The K–8 Language Teacher as a Growing Professional

The opportunities for professional growth as a language teacher have never been greater, particularly at the K–8 level. In some states, early language teachers have banded together to offer special meetings and conferences to support one another with in-service opportunities.

Professional Organizations and Resources

One of the first and most important steps toward becoming a growing professional is active participation in one or more of the organizations that support and unite language teachers. A combined voice is always more effective than a lone voice, and the combined resources of the profession enrich every teacher's classroom.

The founding of the National Network for Early Language Learning (NNELL) in 1987 was a landmark for teachers in K–8 classrooms. The organization provides many opportunities for teachers to become active both locally and nationally, and its journal, *Learning Languages,* connects early language teachers all over the country. At the NNELL website (www.nnell.org) teachers can access articles from the journal, and members have additional access to many useful resources. An early language website at the Center for Applied Linguistics (www.cal.org/earlylang/), called Ñanduti, is dedicated to foreign-language learning in grades pre-K to 8. The site hosts a very active early language listserv, Ñandu, where teachers in all languages ask and answer questions and share curriculum, program, and teaching ideas and experiences. Additional resources and information are available from the website for the National K–12 Foreign Language Resource Center (http://nflrc.iastate.edu/), which has hosted institutes, conducted research, and developed materials of direct interest to K–8 language teachers.

The American Council on the Teaching of Foreign Languages (ACTFL) is the umbrella organization for all language teachers, and a leader in the movement of the profession toward proficiency-oriented, standards-based language learning. The organization has a special interest group dedicated to early language learning. Annual conferences, publications, workshops, and many other services make ACTFL a powerful force for change and for uniting teachers of all languages, at all levels.

Each of the languages commonly taught in early language programs has a national organization, and many have state chapters: American Association of Teachers of German (AATG), American Association of Teachers of French (AATF), American Association of Teachers of Spanish and Portuguese (AATSP), Chinese Language Teachers Association (CLTA), Chinese Language Association of Secondary-Elementary Schools (CLASS), American Classical League (ACL), American Association of Teachers of Italian (AATI), National Council of Japanese Language Teachers (NCJLT), American Council of Teachers of Russian (ACTR), and American Association of Teachers of Arabic (AATA). Membership in these organizations brings teachers of young learners together with other teachers who share many of the same language and culture issues in their classrooms. These groups also offer important cultural resources, websites, and contacts that are unavailable any other way. Several of these groups also have national contests, exchange programs, and materials designed for early language learners.

Asia Society, from its New York headquarters, has become a powerful resource and advocate for the teaching of Asian languages. From its education website (www.asiasociety.org/education/) teachers can access a world of information. Specific cultural information on 30 countries is available at www.askasia.org, and they have a presence on Facebook, Flickr, and Twitter, as well as a channel on YouTube (http://www.youtube.com/user/asiasociety).

Membership in organizations mentioned; attendance at state, regional, and national conferences; and regular reading of professional journals such as *Learning Languages, Modern Language Journal,* and *Foreign Language Annals* as well as language-specific journals connects the language teacher with the wider profession and supports the quality of instruction in every classroom. As teachers grow in their experience with conferences and professional journals, they will be in a position to propose and present sessions and to author articles themselves.

Action Research

As teachers grow in their experience with early language curriculum, classrooms, and learners, they begin to have questions that are not satisfied in conversations with colleagues or articles in professional journals. No one else's answers speak adequately to the issues of this classroom or this particular group of students. A growing number of teachers are turning to classroom-based action research as a means of answering their own questions about teaching and learning, and also contributing to the professional body of understanding about early language learning.

Briefly stated, research involves identifying a question the teacher would like to have answered, refining that question to make it manageable, collecting and analyzing data or information that may answer the question, and interpreting the information collected. Action research is conducted by teachers, and it may result in changes in curriculum, in teaching practices, or in other aspects of the teaching and learning context.

Chamot (1994, p. 6) suggests several possible research questions as examples of possibilities for action research in an early language classroom:

- What themes or content topics are most interesting to children at particular grade levels?
- What interlanguage features characterize children's L2 [second language] at different points in instructional time?
- What differences exist between successful and less successful language learners in these area(s)? Select one or two only: (a) attitudes toward the target language and culture; (b) access to/use of L2 outside of school (e.g., parents, community, television); (c) use of appropriate language learning strategies; (d) level of achievement in L1 [first language] language arts; (e) transfer of knowledge, skills, or strategies from L1; (f) level of self-confidence in own language learning ability.
- What are students' reactions to/acceptance of particular instructional techniques (e.g., cooperative learning, information gap activities, instruction in learning strategies, grammar explanation and practice, Total Physical Response, teaching to different learning styles)?
- What types of assessment measures (e.g., oral interviews, role plays, multiple choice, cloze exercises, writing samples, portfolios) are best suited for assessing children's language proficiency in a particular area or in general?

Some of the methods used for collecting information include diaries, think-aloud interviews, stimulated recall, structured interviews, questionnaires, and classroom observation. All of the suggested topics are researchable by classroom teachers, and the information this research could yield would be a valuable contribution to our understanding of the early language classroom.

Jeannette Borich provides an excellent description of this research process in her article, "Learning through Dialogue Journal Writing: A Cultural Thematic Unit" (2001).

National Board Certification

The National Board of Professional Teaching Standards was established in 1987 as a result of a key recommendation by the Carnegie Task Force on Teaching as a Profession in its 1986 report, "A Nation Prepared: Teachers for the 21st Century." The board issued its policy statement in 1989, "What Teachers Should Know and Be Able to Do," which has served as a guide for schools, states, and teacher preparation institutions in establishing a vision for teacher preparation and teacher development.

This policy statement also serves as the foundation for National Board Certification, a voluntary system for certifying teachers who have met a set of advanced standards representing accomplished practice. National Board Certification is a symbol of professional teaching excellence, designed to recognize and reward the excellent teachers who are already at work in the schools. Only teachers who have had at least three years of experience at the designated age level are eligible for certification. Teachers who apply for certification go through a rigorous process; they construct a portfolio that represents an analysis of their classroom work, and then undergo testing and a variety of other activities that allow them to demonstrate their knowledge, dispositions, and professional judgment.

A number of states and individual school districts have set up reward systems for teachers who receive National Board Certification, sometimes including yearly salary increments. Some districts and some states offer to pay the costs of registration for the process for a limited number of teachers who apply. Teachers who have completed the process praise its rigor and the quality of the experience. World language teachers were participants for the first time in the 2001–2002 school year, in one of two categories: early and middle childhood or early adolescence through young adulthood. Although the early and middle childhood has since been discontinued, except for renewal, the other category is still available to Spanish and French teachers of students aged 11 to 18 (and over).

The preparation and licensure of teachers for elementary school foreign-language programs is of the highest priority if foreign-language programs are to become an important part of the elementary and middle school curriculum. An early language teacher needs to have the qualities of both an excellent foreign language teacher and an excellent elementary or middle school teacher. As these qualities are now becoming clearly identified and defined, programs can be developed to prepare the best possible teachers for these classrooms.

Guidelines for teacher preparation are now available from ACTFL and NCATE, the most widely used independent certification organization for college and university teacher education. These guidelines describe the teacher candidate in a standards- and performance-based context. The National Board of Professional Teaching Standards (NBPTS) has described standards for the accomplished world language teacher that can guide the professional development of the career teacher. The number of states offering or requiring K–12 foreign-language teacher licensure encourages the development of college and university programs to prepare teachers for the growing number of elementary and middle school programs.

As early language programs emerge to play an important role in the education of every child, the challenges of defining goals clearly and of preparing teachers effectively take on considerable significance. There is strong evidence that these challenges are being met and that early language programs will continue to develop as a secure and well-grounded part of the curriculum, unshaken by fad and respected throughout the education community.

For Study and Discussion

1. Why is it important that states develop licensure standards for teachers of foreign languages at the elementary school level?

2. What special skills and background do K–8 teachers need that might not be provided in a methods program designed primarily for secondary school teachers?

3. Download a copy of the ACTFL/NCATE Standards for the Preparation of Foreign Language Teachers

(http://www.actfl.org/i4a/pages/Index.cfm?page id=3384). Using the rubrics that appear in the document, evaluate your own progress toward meeting the standards and supporting standards for teachers in K–12 foreign-language programs.

4. How can National Board Certification contribute to the effectiveness of K–8 foreign-language teachers and to the credibility of the foreign language teaching profession?

For Further Reading

The following sources are recommended for additional information about material covered in this chapter. Chapter citations are documented in Works Cited at the end of this book.

ACTFL/NCATE Standards for the Preparation of Foreign Language Teachers. Available on-line at http://www.actfl.org/i4a/pages/Index.cfm?pageid =3384. Accessed February 8, 2009.

Chamot, Anna Uhl. "The Teacher's Voice: Action Research in Your Classroom." *FLES News* 8:1 (Fall 1994): 1, 6–8.

National Board of Professional Teaching Standards (NBPTS). "Standards for World Languages Other than English." Available on-line at http://www .nbpts.org/the_standards. Accessed February 8, 2009.

National Board of Professional Teaching Standards (NBPTS). "What Teachers Should Know and Be Able to Do." Available on-line at www.nbpts.org/ UserFiles/File/what_teachers.pdf. Accessed February 8, 2009.

a p p e n d i x

....

ACTFL Performance Guidelines
for K–12 Learners

● Comprehensibility: How Well Are They Understood?

....

Novice Learner Range: Grade K–4 or Grade 5–8 or Grade 9–10

Interpersonal

- Rely primarily on memorized phrases and short sentences during highly predictable interactions on very familiar topics;
- Are understood primarily by those very accustomed to interacting with language learners;
- Imitate modeled words and phrases using intonation and pronunciation similar to that of the model;
- May show evidence of false starts, prolonged and unexpectedly placed pauses, and recourse to their native language as topics expand beyond the scope of immediate needs;
- Are able to meet limited practical writing needs, such as short messages and notes, by recombining learned vocabulary and structures to form simple sentences on very familiar topics.

Presentational

- Use short, memorized phrases and sentences in oral and written presentations;
- Are understood primarily by those who are very accustomed to interacting with language learners;
- Demonstrate some accuracy in pronunciation and intonation when presenting well-rehearsed material on familiar topics;
- May show evidence of false starts, prolonged and unexpectedly placed pauses, and recourse to their native language as topics expand beyond the scope of immediate needs;
- Show abilities in writing by reproducing familiar material;
- Rely heavily on visuals to enhance comprehensibility in both oral and written presentations.

Intermediate Learner: Grade K–8 or Grade 7–12

Interpersonal

- Express their own thoughts using sentences and strings of sentences when interacting on familiar topics in present time, are understood by those accustomed to interacting with language learners;
- Use pronunciation and intonation patterns which can be understood by a native speaker accustomed to interacting with language learners;

ACTFL Performance Guidelines for K–12 Learners. Reprinted by permission of ACTFL.

511

- Make false starts and pause frequently to search for words when interacting with others;
- Are able to meet practical writing needs such as short letters and notes, by recombining learned vocabulary and structures demonstrating full control of other time frames.

Presentational

- Express their own thoughts, describe and narrate, using sentences and strings of sentences, in oral and written presentations on familiar topics;
- Use pronunciation and intonation patterns that can be understood by those accustomed to interacting with language learners;
- Make false starts and pause frequently to search for words when interacting with others;
- Communicate oral and written information about familiar topics with sufficient accuracy that listeners and readers understand most of what is presented.

Pre-Advanced Learner: Grade K–12

Interpersonal

- Narrate and describe using connected sentences and paragraphs in present and other time frames when interacting on topics of personal, school, and community interest;
- Are understood by those with whom they interact, although there may still be a range of linguistic inaccuracies, and on occasion the communication partner may need to make a special effort to understand the message;
- Use pronunciation and intonation patterns that are understandable to a native speaker unaccustomed to interacting with language learners;
- Use language confidently and with ease, with few pauses;
- Are able to meet practical writing needs such as letters and summaries by writing descriptions and narrations of paragraph length and organization, showing sustained control of basic structures and partial control of more complex structures and time frames.

Presentational

- Report, narrate and describe, using connected sentences, paragraph length and longer forms of discourse, in oral and written presentations on topics of personal, school, and community interest;
- Use pronunciation and intonation patterns that are understood by native users of the language, although the listener/reader may on occasion need to make a special effort to understand the message;
- Use language confidently and with ease, with few pauses;
- Communication with a fairly high degree of facility when making oral and written presentations about familiar and well-researched topics.

● Comprehension: How Well Do They Understand?

Novice Learner Range: Grade K–4 or Grade 5–8 or Grade 9–10

Interpersonal

- Comprehend general information and vocabulary when the communication partner uses objects, visuals, and gestures in speaking or writing;
- Generally need contextual clues, redundancy, paraphrase or restatement in order to understand the message.

Interpretive
- Understand short, simple conversations and narratives (live or recorded material), within highly predictable and familiar contexts;
- Rely on personal background experience to assist in comprehension;
- Exhibit increased comprehension when constructing meaning through recognition of key words or phrases embedded in familiar contexts;
- Comprehend written and spoken language better when content has been previously presented in an oral and/or visual context;
- Determine meaning by recognition of cognates, prefixes, and thematic vocabulary.

Intermediate Learner: Grade K–8 or Grade 7–12

Interpersonal
- Comprehend general concepts and messages about familiar and occasionally unfamiliar topics;
- May not comprehend details when dealing with unfamiliar topics;
- May have difficulty comprehending language not supported by situational context.

Interpretive
- Understand longer, more complex conversations and narratives as well as recorded material in unfamiliar contexts;
- Use background knowledge to comprehend simple stories, personal correspondence, and other contextualized print;
- Identify main ideas and some specific information on a limited number of topics found in the products of the target culture such as those presented on TV, radio, video, or live and computer-generated presentations, although comprehension may be uneven;
- Determine meaning by using contextual clues;
- Are aided by the use of redundancy, paraphrase, and restatement in order to understand the message.

Pre-Advanced Learner: Grade K–12

Interpersonal
- Comprehend main ideas and most details on a variety of topics beyond the immediate situation;
- Occasionally do not comprehend but usually are able to clarify details by asking questions;
- May encounter difficulty comprehending language dealing with abstract topics.

Interpretive
- Use knowledge acquired in other settings and from other curricular areas to comprehend both spoken and written messages;
- Understand main ideas and significant details on a variety of topics found in the products of the target culture such as those presented on TV, radio, video, or live and computer-generated presentations, although comprehension may be uneven;
- Develop an awareness of tone, style, and author perspective;
- Demonstrate a growing independence as a reader or listener and generally comprehend what they read and hear without relying solely on formally learned vocabulary.

● Language Control: How Accurate Is Their Language?

Novice Learner Range: Grade K–4 or Grade 5–8 or Grade 9–10

Interpersonal
- Comprehend messages that include predominantly familiar grammatical structures;
- Are most accurate when communicating about very familiar topics using memorized oral and written phrases;
- Exhibit decreased accuracy when attempting to create with the language;
- Write with accuracy when copying written language but may use invented spelling when writing words or producing characters on their own;
- May exhibit frequent errors in capitalization and punctuation when target language differs from native language in these areas.

Interpretive
- Recognize structural patterns in target language narratives and derive meaning from these structures within familiar contexts;
- Sometimes recognize previously learned structures when presented in new contexts.

Presentational
- Demonstrate some accuracy in oral and written presentations when reproducing memorized words, phrases and sentences in the target language;
- Formulate oral and written presentations using a limited range of simple phrases and expressions based on very familiar topics;
- Show inaccuracies and/or interference from the native language when attempting to communicate information which goes beyond the memorized or pre-fabricated;
- May exhibit frequent errors in capitalization and/or punctuation and/or production of characters when the writing system of the target language differs from the native language.

Intermediate Learner: Grade K–8 or Grade 7–12

Interpersonal
- Comprehend messages that include some unfamiliar grammatical structures;
- Are most accurate when creating with the language about familiar topics in present time using simple sentences and/or strings of sentences;
- Exhibit a decline in grammatical accuracy as creativity in language production increases;
- Begin to apply familiar structures to new situations;
- Evidence awareness of capitalization and/or punctuation when writing in the target language;
- Recognize some of their own spelling or character production errors and make appropriate adjustments.

Interpretive
- Derive meaning by comparing target language structures with those of the native language;
- Recognize parallels between new and familiar structures in the target language;
- Understand high-frequency idiomatic expressions.

Presentational

- Formulate oral and written presentations on familiar topics, using a range of sentences and strings of sentences primarily in present time but also, with preparation, in past and future time;
- May show inaccuracies as well as some interference from the native language when attempting to present less familiar material;
- Exhibit fairly good accuracy in capitalization and punctuation (or production of characters) when target language differs from native language in these areas.

Pre-Advanced Learner: Grade K–12

Interpersonal

- Comprehend messages that include unfamiliar grammatical structures;
- Are most accurate when narrating and describing in connected sentences and paragraphs in present time with decreasing accuracy in past and future times;
- May continue to exhibit inaccuracies as the amount and complexity of language increases; communicate successfully by applying familiar structures to new situations;
- Rarely make errors in capitalization and in punctuation; are generally accurate in spelling or production of characters.

Interpretive

- Deduce meaning in unfamiliar language passages by classifying words or concepts according to word order or grammatical use;
- Apply rules of language to construct meaning from oral and written texts;
- Understand idiomatic expressions;
- Move beyond literal comprehension toward more critical reading and listening.

Presentational

- Accurately formulate paragraph-length and longer oral and written presentations in present time, on topics of personal, school, community and global interest;
- May show some inaccuracies and/or interference from the native language when presentations deal with multiple time frames and/or other complex structures;
- Successfully communicate personal meaning by applying familiar structures to new situations and less familiar topics, and by integrating information from audio, visual, and written sources;
- Exhibit awareness of need for accuracy in capitalization and/or punctuation (or production of characters) when target language differs from native language in these areas.

● Vocabulary Use: How Extensive and Applicable Is Their Vocabulary?

Novice Learner Range: Grade K–4 or Grade 5–8 or Grade 9–10

Interpersonal

- Comprehend and produce vocabulary that is related to everyday objects and actions on a limited number of familiar topics;
- Use words and phrases primarily as lexical items without awareness of grammatical structure;

- Recognize and use vocabulary from a variety of topics including those related to other curricular areas;
- May often rely on words and phrases from their native language when attempting to communicate beyond the word and/or gesture level.

Interpretive

- Recognize a variety of vocabulary words and expressions related to familiar topics embedded within relevant curricular areas;
- Demonstrate increased comprehension of vocabulary in spoken passages when these are enhanced by pantomime, props, and/or visuals;
- Demonstrate increased comprehension of written passages when accompanied by illustrations and other contextual clues.

Presentational

- Use a limited number of words and phrases for common objects and actions in familiar categories;
- Supplement their basic vocabulary with expressions acquired from sources such as the teacher or picture dictionaries;
- Rely on native language and phrases when expressing personal meaning in less familiar categories.

Intermediate Learner: Grade K–8 or Grade 7–12

Interpersonal

- Use vocabulary from a variety of thematic word groups;
- Recognize and use vocabulary from a variety of topics including those related to other curricular areas;
- Show some understanding and use of common idiomatic expressions;
- May use false cognates or resort to their native language when attempting to communicate beyond the scope of familiar topics.

Interpretive

- Comprehend an expanded range of vocabulary;
- Frequently derive meaning of unknown words by using contextual clues;
- Demonstrate enhanced comprehension when listening to or reading content which has a recognizable format.

Presentational

- Demonstrate control of an expanding number of familiar words and phrases and of a limited number of idiomatic expressions;
- Supplement their basic vocabulary, for both oral and written presentations, with expressions acquired from other sources such as dictionaries;
- In speech and writing, may sometimes use false cognates and incorrectly applied terms, and show only partial control of newly-acquired expressions.

Pre-Advanced Learner: Grade K–12

Interpersonal

- Understand and often use idiomatic and culturally authentic expressions;

- Recognize and use vocabulary from a variety of topics related to other curricular areas;
- Use more specialized and precise vocabulary terms within a limited number of topics.

Interpretive
- Comprehend a wide range of vocabulary in both concrete and abstract contexts;
- Infer meaning of both oral and written texts by recognizing familiar words and phrases in new contexts;
- Use context to deduce meaning of unfamiliar vocabulary;
- Recognize and understand the cultural context of many words and phrases.

Presentational
- Demonstrate control of an extensive vocabulary, including a number of idiomatic and culturally authentic expressions, from a variety of topics;
- Supplement their basic vocabulary by using resources such as textbooks and dictionaries;
- May use more specialized and precise terms when dealing with specific topics that have been researched.

● Communication Strategies: How Do They Maintain Communication?

Novice Learner Range: Grade K–4 or Grade 5–8 or Grade 9–10

Interpersonal
- Attempt to clarify meaning by repeating words and occasionally selecting substitute words to convey their message;
- Primarily use facial expressions and gesture to indicate problems with comprehension.

Interpretive
- Use background experience to anticipate story direction in highly predictable oral or written texts;
- Rely heavily on visuals and familiar language to assist in comprehension.

Presentational
- Make corrections by repeating or rewriting when appropriate forms are routinely modeled by the teacher;
- Rely heavily on repetition, non-verbal expression (gestures, facial expressions), and visuals to communicate their message.

Intermediate Learner: Grade K–8 or Grade 7–12

Interpersonal
- May use paraphrasing, question-asking, circumlocution, and other strategies to avoid a breakdown in communication;
- Attempt to self-correct primarily for meaning when communication breaks down.

Interpretive
- Identify the main idea of a written text by using reading strategies such as gleaning information from the first and last paragraphs;

- Infer meaning of many unfamiliar words that are necessary in order to understand the gist of an oral or written text;
- Use contextual clues to assist in comprehension.

Presentational
- Make occasional use of reference sources and efforts at self-correction to avoid errors likely to interfere with communication;
- Use circumlocution when faced with difficult syntactic structures;
- Problematic spelling, or unfamiliar vocabulary;
- Make use of memory-aids (such as notes and visuals) to facilitate presentations.

Pre-Advanced Learner: Grade K–12

Interpersonal
- Are able to sustain an interaction with a native speaker by using a variety of strategies when discussion topics relate to personal experience or immediate needs;
- Show evidence of attention to mechanical errors even when these may not interfere with communication.

Interpretive
- Use background knowledge to deduce meaning and to understand complex information in oral or written texts;
- Identify the organizing principle(s) in oral or written texts;
- Infer and interpret the intent of the writer.

Presentational
- Demonstrate conscious efforts at correct formulation and self-correction by use of self-editing and of reference sources;
- Sustain length and continuity of presentations by appropriate use of strategies such as simplification, reformation, and circumlocution;
- Make use of a variety of resource materials and presentation methods to enhance presentations.

● Cultural Awareness: How Is Their Cultural Understanding Reflected in Their Communication?

Novice Learner Range: Grade K–4 or Grade 5–8 or Grade 9–10

Interpersonal
- Imitate culturally appropriate vocabulary and idiomatic expressions;
- Use gestures and body language that are generally those of the student's own culture, unless they are incorporated in to memorized responses.

Interpretive
- Understand both oral and written language that reflects a cultural background similar to their own;
- Predict a story line or event when it reflects a cultural background similar to their own.

Presentational
- Imitate the use of culturally appropriate vocabulary, idiomatic expressions and non-verbal behaviors modeled by the teacher.

Intermediate Learner: Grade K–8 or Grade 7–12

Interpersonal
- Use some culturally appropriate vocabulary and idiomatic expressions;
- Use some gestures and body language of the target culture.

Interpretive
- Use knowledge of their own culture and that of the target culture(s) to interpret oral or written texts more accurately;
- Recognize target culture influences in the products and practices of their own culture;
- Recognize differences and similarities in the perspectives of the target culture and their own.

Presentational
- Use some culturally appropriate vocabulary; idiomatic expressions and non-verbal behaviors;
- Demonstrate some cultural knowledge in oral and written presentations.

Pre-Advanced Learner: Grade K–12

Interpersonal
- Use culturally appropriate vocabulary and idioms;
- Use appropriate gestures and body language of the target culture.

Interpretive
- Apply understanding of the target culture to enhance comprehension or oral and written texts;
- Recognize the reflections of practices, products, and/or perspectives of the target culture(s) in oral and written texts;
- Analyze and evaluate cultural stereotypes encountered in oral and written texts.

Presentational
- Demonstrate increased use of culturally appropriate vocabulary, idiomatic expressions and non-verbal behaviors;
- Use language increasingly reflective of authentic cultural practices and perspectives.

works cited

....

For Further Reading at the end of each chapter lists additional reference books and articles that may be of interest for specific topics.

Many of the resources listed are identified by an ERIC (Educational Resources Information Center) Document number (e.g., ED 208 653). These documents can be read on microfiche at libraries with an ERIC collection, or ordered in paper copy from the ERIC Document Reproduction Service (EDRS), DynEDRS, Inc., 7420 Fullerton Road, Suite 110, Springfield, VA 22153-2852, Toll-free: (800) 443-ERIC (3742), email: service@edrs.com, URL: http://www.edrs.com.

For the location of an ERIC collection nearest you, write to ERIC Clearinghouse on Languages and Linguistics, Center for Applied Linguistics, 4646 40th Street NW, Washington DC 20016-1859, email: info@cal.org.

Academic Preparation for College: What Students Need to Know and Be Able to Do. New York: The College Board, 1983.

Alkonis, Nancy V., and Mary A. Brophy. "A Survey of FLES Practices." *Reports of Surveys and Studies in the Teaching of Modern Foreign Languages, 1959–1961.* New York: The Modern Language Association of America, 1961.

Alvis, Vicki Welch. "Let's Assess in FLES: Reaching Beyond the Customary Borders of Evaluation." Presentation at ACTFL Annual Meeting, Salt Lake City, November 23, 2002.

American Council on the Teaching of Foreign Languages. *ACTFL Teacher Education Guidelines.* Hastings-on-Hudson, NY: ACTFL, 1988.

American Council on the Teaching of Foreign Languages. *ACTFL Performance Guidelines for K-12 Learners.* Yonkers, NY, 1998.

American Council on the Teaching of Foreign Languages. *Standards for Foreign Language Learning in the 21st Century.* Yonkers, NY: ACTFL, 1999.

American Council on the Teaching of Foreign Languages. *Program Standards for the Preparation of Foreign Language Teachers.* Yonkers, NY: ACTFL, 2002. Available on-line: www.actfl.org.

Anderson, Helena. Personal communication, 1980 and 1982.

Anderson, Lorin W., and David R. Krathwohl, Eds. *A Taxonomy of Learning, Teaching, and Assessment: A Revision of Bloom's Taxonomy of Educational Objectives.* New York: Longman, 2001.

Andersson, Theodore. *Foreign Languages in the Elementary School: A Struggle against Mediocrity.* Austin: University of Texas Press, 1969.

Andrade, Carolyn, and Julie Benthouse Banner. "The Writing Process: From Single Words to Student-Authored Books." Presentation at Central States Conference on the Teaching of Foreign Languages, Des Moines, IA, March 27, 1993.

Andrade, Carolyn, Richard R. Kretschmer, and Laura W. Kretschmer. (1993). "Two Languages for All Children: Expanding to Low Achievers and the Handicapped." In John W. Oller (Ed.), *Methods That Work: Ideas for Literacy and Language Teachers* (pp. 99–112). Boston: Heinle and Heinle.

Armstrong, Penny W., and J. D. Rogers. "Basic Skills Revisited: The Effects of Foreign Language Instruction on Reading, Math and Language Arts." *Learning Languages* 2:3 (Spring 1997): 20–31.

Armstrong, Thomas. *Seven Kinds of Smart: Identifying and Developing Your Many Intelligences.* New York: Penguin Books, 1993.

Armstrong, Thomas. *Multiple Intelligences in the Classroom.* Alexandria, VA: Association for Supervision and Curriculum Development, 1994.

Armstrong, Thomas. "Utopian Schools." *Mothering* (Winter 1996). Available on-line: http://www.thomasarmstrong.com/articles/utopian_schools.htm.

Asher, James J. *Learning Another Language through Actions: The Complete Teacher's Guidebook* (6th ed.). Los Gatos, CA: Sky Oaks Publications, 2000.

Ashton-Warner, Sylvia. *Teacher.* New York: Simon & Schuster, 1963.

Bamford, K. W., and D. T. Mizokawa. "Additive-Bilingual (Immersion) Education: Cognitive and Language Development." *Language Learning* 41:3 (1991): 413–429.

Barnum, Nancy. "E-Mail in FL Instruction." Handout for presentation "*Das Bild der Anderen, ein 'Kochbuch' für Email Anfänger DaF.*" Presented at ACTFL annual meeting, Washington DC, November 17, 2001.

Barron, A., C. Feyten, M. Venable, A. Hibelink, K. Hogarty, J. Kromrey, and T. Lang, "Laptop Computers in Teacher Preparation: Lessons Learned from the University of South Florida Implementation." *Journal of Computing in Higher Education* (2007): 1–23.

Begley, Sharon. "Your Child's Brain." *Newsweek,* February 19, 1996.

Bloom, Benjamin S., et al. (Eds.). *Taxonomy of Educational Objectives: The Classification of Educational Goals, by a committee of college and university examiners.* New York: McKay, 1956–1964.

Borich, Jeanette Marie Bowman. "Learning through Dialogue Journal Writing: A Cultural Thematic Unit." *Learning Languages* 6:3 (Spring 2001): 4–19.

Boudreaux, Ellen. "Strategies of Immersion Teaching and Special Education." Unpublished handout for presentation at Advocates for Language Learning Conference, October 1991.

Breiner-Sanders, Karen E., Pardee Lowe, Jr., John Miles, and Elvira Swender. "ACTFL Proficiency Guidelines—Speaking. Revised 1999." *Foreign Language Annals* 33 (2000):13–18.

Breiner-Sanders, Karen E., Elvira Swender, and Robert M. Terry. "Preliminary Proficiency Guidelines—Writing. Revised 2001." *Foreign Language Annals* 35 (2002): 9–15.

Bring, Sandra. Personal communication, 1986.

Brown, Christine. "A Case for Foreign Languages: The Glastonbury Language Program." *Perspective, Council for Basic Education* 7:2 (1995).

Brown, H. Douglas. "TESOL at Twenty-Five: What Are the Issues?" *TESOL Quarterly* 25:2 (Summer 1991): 256–257.

Brown, Jeff. *Flat Stanley.* Steve Björkman, Illustrator. New York: Harper Trophy, 1996.

Bruck, M., W. E. Lambert, and R. Tucker. "Bilingual Schooling through the Elementary Grades: The St. Lambert Project at Grade Seven." *Language Learning* 24:2 (1974): 183–204.

Bruner, Jerome. *Acts of Meaning.* Cambridge, MA: Harvard University Press, 1990.

Bruner, Jerome. *The Culture of Education.* Cambridge, MA: Harvard University Press, 1996.

Caccavale, Therese. "The Correlation between Early Second Language Learning and Native Language Skill Development." *Learning Languages* 13:1 (Fall 2007): 30–32.

Caine, Renate Nummela, and Geoffrey Caine. *Making Connections: Teaching and the Human Brain.* Alexandria, VA: Association for Supervision and Curriculum Development, 1991.

Caine, Renate Nummela, and Geoffrey Caine. *Education on the Edge of Possibility.* Alexandria, VA: Association for Supervision and Curriculum Development, 1997.

CAL: Center for Applied Linguistics. Total and Partial Immersion Programs. 2006. Available on-line: http://www.cal.org/resources/immersion.

CAL: Center for Applied Linguistics. Directory of Foreign Language Immersion Programs in U.S. Schools. July 2006. Available online at http://www.cal.org/resources/immersion/.

CAL: Center for Applied Linguistics. Directory of Two-Way Bilingual Immersion Programs, 2008. Available on-line: http://www.cal.org/twi/directory/.

Campbell, Russell N. "The Immersion Approach to Foreign Language Teaching." *Studies on Immersion Education: A Collection for United States Educators.* Sacramento: California State Department of Education, 1984, pp. 114–143.

Campbell, Russell N., Tracy C. Gray, Nancy C. Rhodes, and Marguerite Ann Snow. "Foreign

Language Learning in the Elementary Schools: A Comparison of Three Language Programs." *The Modern Language Journal* 69:1 (Spring 1985): 44–54.

Canadian Parents for French. *The State of French Second-Language Education in Canada.* 2006. Available on-line: http://www.cpf.ca/eng/resources-reports-fsl-2006.html.

Canale, Michael, and Merrill Swain. *Communicative Approaches to Second Language Teaching and Testing.* Toronto: The Ministry of Education, 1979.

CARLA: Center for Advanced Research on Second Language Acquisition. University of Minnesota, Minneapolis. http://carla.acad.umn.edu/.

Carpenter, John A, and Judith V. Torney. "Beyond the Melting Pot." In Patricia Maloney Markun (Ed.), *Childhood and Intercultural Education: Overview and Research.* Washington DC: Association for Childhood Education International, 1974, pp. 14–23.

Chamot, Anna Uhl. "The Teacher's Voice: Action Research in Your Classroom." *FLES News* 8:1 (Fall 1994): 1, 6–8.

Chamot, Anna Uhl, and J. Michael O'Malley. *A Cognitive Academic Language Learning Approach: An ESL Content-Based Curriculum.* Rosslyn, VA: National Clearinghouse for Bilingual Education, 1986.

Clark, Barbara. *Growing up Gifted: Developing the Potential of Children at Home and at School.* Upper Saddle River, NJ: Merrill Prentice-Hall, 2002.

Cloud, Nancy, and Fred Genesee. "Multilingualism *Is* Basic." *Educational Leadership* 55:6 (March 1998): 62–65.

Cloud, Nancy, Fred Genesee, and Else Hamayan. *Dual Language Instruction. A Handbook for Enriched Education.* Boston: Heinle & Heinle, 2000.

Cohen, Andrew D. "The Culver City Spanish Immersion Program: The First Two Years." *The Modern Language Journal* 58:3 (1974): 95–103.

"Critical Needs in International Education: Recommendations for Action." A Report to the Secretary of Education by the National Advisory Board on International Education Programs.

Washington DC: U.S. Government Printing Office, 1983.

Cummins, James. "The Role of Primary Language Development in Promoting Educational Success for Language Minority Students." *Schooling and Language Minority Students: A Theoretical Framework.* Los Angeles: Evaluation, Dissemination, and Assessment Center, California State University, 1981.

Cummins, James. "The Academic, Intellectual, and Linguistic Benefits of Bilingualism." *So You Want Your Child to Learn French* (2nd rev. ed.). Ottawa: Canadian Parents for French, 1990.

Curtain, Helena. Immersion Education and the Teaching of Subject Content: A Qualitative Research Project. Unpublished manuscript. 1994.

Curtain, Helena, and Carol Ann Dahlberg. *Planning for Success: Common Pitfalls in the Planning of Early Foreign Language Programs.* Washington DC: Center for Applied Linguistics, ERIC Digest. Available on-line: www.cal.org/ericcll/digst/0011planning.html. Accessed April 15, 2003.

Day, Elaine M., and Stanley M. Shapson. "Assessment of Oral Communicative Skills in Early French Immersion Programmes." *Journal of Multilingual and Multicultural Development* 8:3 (1987): 237–260.

Day, Elaine M., and Stanley M. Shapson. *Studies in Immersion Education.* Clevedon, UK: Multi-lingual Matters, 1996.

Dodge, Bernie. "Some Thoughts about WebQuests." San Diego State University, 1997. Available on-line: http://webquest.sdsu.edu/aboutwebquests.html.

Doloff, Deby. "*Te Quiero, Tito*"—FLES Email Project. *Learning Languages* 4:3 (Spring 1999): 21–23.

Donoghue, Mildred R. *Foreign Languages and the Elementary School Child.* Dubuque, IA: William C. Brown, 1968.

Dulay, Heidi, Marina Burt, and Stephen Krashen. *Language Two.* New York: Oxford University Press, 1982.

Dyer, Haley Bell, Margita Haberlen, Kathy Farris Hadidi, Jennifer Roth, Carolyn Smith, and Azusa Uchihara. "Classroom Management: What Every FLES Teacher Needs to Know." Handout prepared for model program training, 1997.

Echevarria, Jana, and Anne Graves. *Sheltered Content Instruction: Teaching English Language Learners with Diverse Abilities* (3rd ed.). Boston: Pearson Allyn and Bacon, 2007.

Echevarria, Jana, MaryEllen Vogt, and Deborah Short. *Making Content Comprehensible for Elementary English Learners: The SIOP Model.* Boston: Pearson Allyn and Bacon, 2010.

Echevarria, Jana, MaryEllen Vogt, and Deborah Short. *Making Content Comprehensible for Secondary English Learners: The SIOP Model.* Boston: Pearson Allyn and Bacon, 2010.

Egan, Kieran. *Educational Development.* New York: Oxford University Press, 1979.

Egan, Kieran. *Teaching as Story Telling.* Chicago: University of Chicago Press, 1986.

Egan, Kieran. *Primary Understanding.* New York: Routledge, 1988.

Egan, Kieran. *Imagination in Teaching and Learning: The Middle School Years.* Chicago: University of Chicago Press, 1992.

Egan, Kieran. *The Educated Mind: How Cognitive Tools Shape Our Understanding.* Chicago: University of Chicago Press, 1997.

Ellis, Rod. "Principles of Instructed Second Language Acquisition." *CAL Digest.* Center for Applied Linguistics (December 2008). Available on-line: http://www.cal.org/resources/digest/instructed2ndlang.html.

Emberley, Ed. *Go Away, Big Green Monster!* Boston: Little, Brown, 1992.

Estelle, Emelda. Personal communication, 1985.

Fluegelman, Andrew (Ed.). *The New Games Book.* Garden City, NY: Dolphin Books, Doubleday, 1976.

Fortune, Tara, and Helen Jorstad. "US Immersion Programs: A National Survey." *Foreign Language Annals* 29:2 (1996): 163–190.

Fortune, Tara Williams, and Diane J. Tedick. "One-Way, Two-Way and Indigenous Immersion: A Call for Cross-Fertilization." In Tara Williams Fortune and Diane J. Tedick (Eds.), *Pathways to Multilingualism: Evolving Perspectives on Immersion Education* (pp. 3–21). Clevedon, UK: Multilingual Matters, 2008.

Foss, Nancy. Foreign Language and Style: A Guide for the Application of Style Sensitive Instruction in the Foreign Language Classroom. Unpublished manuscript, 1994.

Foss, Nancy. Personal communication, November 2002.

Gardner, David P. (Ed.). *A Nation at Risk: The Imperative for Educational Reform.* Washington DC: U.S. Department of Education, 1983. Available on-line: www.cids.ie/A_Nation_at_Risk_1983.pdf.

Gardner, Howard. *Frames of Mind: The Theory of Multiple Intelligences.* New York: Basic Books, 1983.

Gardner, Howard. *Multiple Intelligences: The Theory in Practice.* New York: Basic Books, 1993.

Gardner, Howard. *Intelligence Reframed: Multiple Intelligences for the 21st Century.* New York: Basic Books, 1999.

Garfinkel, Alan, and Kenneth E. Tabor. "Elementary School Foreign Languages and English Reading Achievement: A New View of the Relationship." *Foreign Language Annals* 24:5 (October 1991): 375–382.

Genesee, Fred. *Learning through Two Languages: Studies of Immersion and Bilingual Education.* Cambridge, MA: Newbury House, 1987.

Genesee, Fred. "Second Language Learning in School Settings: Lessons from Immersion." Paper presented at the Conference on Bilingualism, Multiculturalism and Second Language Learning in honor of Wallace Lambert, Esterel, Quebec, May 1989.

Genesee, Fred. "Brain Research: Implications for Second Language Learning." *ERIC Digest.* December 2000. Available on-line: http://www.cal.org/ericcll:digest/0012brain.html and http://www.cal.org/resources/digest/0012brain.html.

Gilzow, Douglas F., and Lucinda E. Branaman. *Lessons Learned: Model Early Foreign Language Programs.* McHenry, IL: Center for Applied Linguistics and Delta Systems, 2000.

Gilzow, Douglas F., and Nancy C. Rhodes. *Establishing High-Quality Foreign Language Programs in Elementary Schools.* Northeast and Islands Regional Educational Laboratory at Brown University: Perspectives on Policy and Practice. December 2000.

Ginott, Haim G. *Teacher and Child: A Book for Parents and Teachers.* New York: Macmillan, 1972.

Goals 2000: Educate America Act. H.R. 1804. Available on-line: http://www.ed.gov/legislation/GOALS2000/TheAct/.

Goleman, Daniel. *Emotional Intelligence.* New York: Bantam Books, 1995.

Good, Thomas, and Jere Brophy. *Looking in Classrooms* (10th ed.). Boston: Pearson Allyn and Bacon, 2007.

Grady, Michael P. *Teaching and Brain Research: Guidelines for the Classroom.* New York: Longman, 1984.

Gramer, Virginia. "Advocacy for Early Language Education: A School Board Presentation." *Learning Languages* 4:3 (Spring 1999): 4–8.

Grittner, Frank. *Teaching Foreign Languages.* New York: Harper and Row, 1977.

Hadley, Alice Omaggio. *Teaching Language in Context* (3rd ed.). Boston: Heinle & Heinle, 2001.

Hakuta, Kenji. *Cognitive Development of Bilingual Children.* Los Angeles: University of California, Center for Language Education and Research, 1986. EDRS ED 278 260.

Hans, Patricia Ryerson. "Story Telling and Children's Literature." Presentation at Concordia College, Moorhead, MN, June 30, 1999.

Hans, Patricia Ryerson. Personal communication, 2002.

Harley, Birgit. *Age in Second Language Acquisition.* Clevedon, UK: Multilingual Matters, 1986.

Harley, Birgit. "The Outcomes of Early and Later Language Learning." In Myriam Met (Ed.), *Critical Issues in Early Language Learning: Building for Our Children's Future.* Glenview, IL: Scott Foresman–Addison Wesley, 1998, pp. 26–31.

Harley, Birgit, P. Allen, James Cummins, and Merrill Swain. *The Development of Second Language Proficiency.* Cambridge, UK: Cambridge University Press, 1991.

Haxhi, Jessica Lee. "Long-Term Advocacy: Keeping the Magic of a Japanese Program Alive." Presentation and handout at the Northeast Conference on the Teaching of Foreign Languages, March 31, 2001.

Heining-Boynton, Audrey L. "The FLES Program Evaluation Inventory (FPEI)." *Foreign Language Annals* 24:3 (1991): 193–2002.

Holobow, Naomi, F. Genesee, W. E. Lambert, M. Met, and J. Gasright. "Effectiveness of Partial French Immersion for Children from Different Social Class and Ethnic Backgrounds." *Psycholinguistics* 8:2 (June 1987): 137–151.

International Society for Technology in Education (ISTE). The ISTE National Educational Technology Standards (NETS•S) and Performance Indicators for Students. 2007. Available on-line: www.iste.org/NETS.

International Society for Technology in Education (ISTE). The ISTE National Educational Technology Standards (NETS•T) and Performance Indicators for Teachers. 2008. Available on-line: www.iste.org/NETS.

"Internet Activities for Foreign Language Classes." California Language Teachers Association, California Foreign Language Project. Available on-line: http://www.clta.net/lessons/.

Irujo, Suzanne. Differentiated Instruction: We Can No Longer Just Aim Down the Middle. *ELL Outlook™.* Available on-line: http://www.coursecrafters.com/ELL-Outlook/2004/sept_oct/ELLOutlookITIArticle2.htm. Retrieved June 18, 2008.

Jackson, Claire W. (Ed.). *A Challenge to Change: The Language Learning Continuum.* New York: College Entrance Examination Board, 1999.

Jensen, Eric. "Brain-Based Learning: A Reality Check." *Educational Leadership* 57:5 (April 2000): 76–79.

Jensen, Eric. *Teaching with the Brain in Mind* (2nd ed.). Alexandria, VA: Association for Supervision and Curriculum Development, 2005.

Johnson, David W., Robert T. Johnson, and Edythe Johnson Holubec. *Cooperative Learning in the Classroom.* Alexandria, VA: Association for Supervision and Curriculum Development, 1994.

Johnson, David W., and Robert T. Johnson. *Learning Together and Alone* (5th ed.). Boston: Allyn & Bacon, 2005.

Johnson, Robert Keith, and Merrill Swain. *Immersion Education International Perspectives.* Cambridge, UK: Cambridge University Press, 1997.

Kagan, Spencer, and Miguel Kagan. *Kagan Cooperative Learning.* San Clemente, CA: Kagan, 2008.

Kennedy, Teresa J. "Language Learning and Its Impact on the Brain: Connecting Language Learning with the Mind through Content-Based Instruction." *Foreign Language Annals* 39:3 (Fall 2006): 471.

Knop, Constance K. Various workshop presentations at Wisconsin Association for Language Teachers conference, 1985–1988.

Kohn, Alfie. (1994). "The Risks of Rewards." *Eric Digest* EDO-PS-94-14. ERIC Clearinghouse on Elementary and Early Childhood Education, December 1994.

Krashen, Stephen D. *Second Language Acquisition and Second Language Learning.* New York: Pergamon Press, 1981. Available on-line: www.sdkrashen .com/SL_Acquisition_and_Learning/index/html.

Krashen, Stephen D., Robin C. Scarcella, and Michael H. Long (Eds.). *Child-Adult Differences in Second Language Acquisition.* Rowley, MA: Newbury House, 1982.

Krashen, Stephen D., and Tracy Terrell. *The Natural Approach: Language Acquisition in the Classroom.* Hayward, CA: Alemany Press, 1983.

Krashen, Stephen D., and Tracy Terrell. *The Natural Approach: Language Acquisition in the Classroom* (rev. ed.). Englewood Cliffs, NJ: Prentice-Hall, 1996.

Kretschmer, Richard R., and Laura W. Kretschmer. "What Special Challenge Do Learners with Disabilities Bring to the Foreign Language Classroom?" In Myriam Met (Ed.), *Critical Issues in Early Second Language Learning* (pp. 65–68). Glenview, IL: Scott, Foresman–Addison Wesley, 1998.

Kuck, Pam, and Kaye Lietz. *Taming the Wild, Wild Web: WebQuests.* PowerPoint presentation, 1998. Available on-line: http://www.keyknox.com/ bwit/webquest/Default.htm.

Lambert, Wallace E. "An Overview of Issues in Immersion Education." In *Studies on Immersion Education: A Collection for United States Educators* (pp. 8–30). Sacramento: California State Department of Education, 1984.

Lambert, Wallace E., and Otto Klineberg. *Children's Views of Foreign People.* New York: Appleton-Century-Crofts, 1967.

Lambert, Wallace E., and G. Richard Tucker. *Bilingual Education of Children: The St. Lambert Experiment.* Rowley, MA: Newbury House, 1972.

Landry, Richard G. "The Enhancement of Figural Creativity through Second Language Learning at the Elementary School Level." *Foreign Language Annals* 7:1 (October 1973).

Lange, Dale L. "Planning for and Using the New National Culture Standards." In June K. Phillips (Ed.), *Foreign Language Standards: Linking Research, Theories, and Practices* (pp. 57–135). The ACTFL Foreign Language Education Series. Lincolnwood, IL: National Textbook Company, 1999.

Lapkin, Sharon, Merrill Swain, and Stanley M. Shapson. "French Immersion Research Agenda for the 90's." *Canadian Modern Language Review* 46 (1990): 638–674.

Lawrence, Geoff. "A Touch of…Class!" *The Canadian Modern Language Review* 58:3 (March 2002): 465–472.

Linse, Caroline. *The Children's Response: TPR and Beyond—Toward Writing.* San Francisco, CA: Alemany Press, 1983.

Long, M. H. Native Speaker/Non-Native Speaker Conversation in the Second Language Classroom. In M. Clark, and J. Handscombe (Eds.), *On TESOL '82. Pacific Perspectives on Language Learning* (pp. 207–225). Washington DC: TESOL, 1983. Reprinted in M. H. Long and J. C. Richards (Eds.), *Methodology in TESOL. A Book of Readings* (pp. 339–354). New York: Newbury House/Harper and Row, 1987.

Lyster, Roy. "Immersion Pedagogy and Implications for Language Teaching." In Jasone Cenoz and Fred Genesee (Eds.), *Beyond Bilingualism: Multilingualism and Multilingual Education.* Clevendon: Multilingual Matters, 1999.

Lyster, Roy. *Learning and Teaching Languages through Content: A Counterbalanced Approach.* Philadelphia: John Benjamins.

Marcos, Kathleen. Why, How, and When Should My Child Learn a Foreign Language? Washington DC: ERIC Clearinghouse on Languages and Linguistics, N.D. Available on-line: http://www .cal.org/resources/pubs/whyhowwhen_brochure .pdf.

Marcos, Kathleeen M. "Second Language Learning: Everyone Can Benefit." *The ERIC Review* 6:1

(Fall 1998): *K-12 Foreign Language Education*, 2-5. Available on-line: http://www.cal.org/early-lang/benefits/marcos.htm.

Marzano, Robert J., Debra J. Pickering, and Jane E. Pollock. *Classroom Instruction That Works: Research-Based Strategies for Increasing Student Achievement.* Alexandria, VA: Association for Supervision and Curriculum Development, 2001.

Masciantonio, Rudolph. "Tangible Benefits of the Study of Latin: A Review of Research." *Foreign Language Annals* 10:4 (September 1977).

McLaughlin, Barry. "Second-Language Development in Immersion Contexts." In E. B. Lorenz and M. Met (Eds.), *Second Language Acquisition.* Montgomery County Public Schools, 1989.

Met, Myriam. Personal communication, 1982.

Met, Myriam. Making Connections. In June K. Phillips (Ed.), *Foreign Language Standards: Linking Research, Theories, and Practices* (pp. 137–164). The ACTFL Foreign Language Education Series. Lincolnwood, IL: National Textbook Company, 1999.

Met, Myriam. "Elementary School Immersion in Less Commonly Taught Languages." In R. D. Lambert and E. Shohamy (Eds.), *Language Policy and Pedagogy.* Philadelphia: John Benjamins, 2000.

Met, Myriam. "Paying Attention to Language." In T. Fortune and D. J. Tedick(Eds.), *Pathways to Multilingualism: Evolving Perspectives on Immersion Education.* Clevedon, England: Multilingual Matters, Ltd., 2007.

Met, Myriam, and Eileen Lorenz. *What It Means to Be an Immersion Teacher.* Rockville, MD: Montgomery County Public Schools, 1988.

Met, Myriam, and Eileen Lorenz (Eds.). *Culture Scope and Sequence Kindergarten through Grade 8.* Draft 2. Rockville, MD: Montgomery County Public Schools, 1993.

Met, Myriam, and Eileen Lorenz. "Lessons from U.S. Immersion Programs: Two Decades of Experience." In R. K. Johnson and S. Merrill (Eds.), *Immersion Education: International Perspectives* (pp. 343–364). Cambridge, UK: Cambridge University Press, 1997.

Met, Myriam, and Nancy Rhodes. "Elementary School Foreign Language Instruction: Priorities for the 1990s." *Foreign Language Annals* 23:5 (October 1990): 433–443.

Middle School Task Force of the Wisconsin Association of Foreign Language Teachers. "Foreign Languages in the Middle Level School: Guiding Principles." Madison, WI, November 15, 1991.

Milwaukee Public Schools. *Rising High with Thinking Skills.* Milwaukee: Milwaukee Public Schools, 1985.

Mohan, Bernard. *Language and Content.* Reading, MA: Addison-Wesley, 1986.

Montgomery, Cherice. Personal communication, 2009.

Morrow, Keith. "Principles of Communicative Methodology." In Keith Johnson and Keith Morrow (Eds.), *Communication in the Classroom.* Burnt Mill, Harlow, Essex, UK: Longman, 1981.

Nash, J. Madeleine. February 3, 1997. "Fertile Minds." *Time* 149:5 (1997, February 3): 49–56. Available on-line: http://www.burchschool.com/fertmind.html.

National Board of Professional Teaching Standards (NBPTS). Standards for World Languages Other than English. Available on-line: http://www.nbpts.org/the_standards.

National Board of Professional Teaching Standards (NBPTS). What Teachers Should Know and Be Able to Do. Available on-line: http://www.nbpts.org/UserFiles/File/what_teachers.pdf.

National Council of State Supervisors of Foreign Languages (NCSSFL). A Rationale for Foreign Language Education. Available on-line: http://www.ncssfl.org/papers/index.php?rationale. Accessed September 7, 2008.

Nerenz, Ann, and Constance Knop. "The Effect of Group Size on Student's Opportunity to Learn in the Second Language." In Alan Garfinkel (Ed.), *ESL and the Foreign Language Teacher.* Skokie, IL: National Textbook Company, 1982.

News in Science. "Bilingual Kids Not Slowed by Second Tongue." July 11, 2002. Available on-line: http://www.abc.net.au/science/news/stories/s720173.htm. Accessed December 30, 2002.

North Carolina Department of Public Instruction. *Building Bridges: A Guide to Second Languages in the Middle Grades.* Raleigh, NC: North Carolina

Department of Public Instruction, 1991. ED 343 428.

Olsen, Roger, E. Winn-Bell, and Spencer Kagan. "About Cooperative Learning." In Carolyn Kessler (Ed.), *Cooperative Language Learning: A Teacher's Resource Book* (pp. 1–30). Englewood Cliffs, NJ: Prentice-Hall, 1992.

Pacheco, Jean L. "A Successful Keypal Project Using Varied Technologies." *Learning Languages* 7:1 (Fall 2001): 10–14.

"Paige Outlines New International Education Priorities." Press Release from Office of Public Affiars, U.S. Department of Education for release on November 20, 2002. Available on-line: http://www.ed.gov/news/pressreleases/2002/11/11202002.html. Accessed December 2008.

Pappas, Christine C., Barbara Z. Kierer, and Linda S. Levstik. *An Integrated Language Perspective in the Elementary School* (4th ed.). Boston: Allyn & Bacon, 2005.

Penfield, Wilder, and Laram Roberts. *Speech and Brain-Mechanisms.* Princeton, NJ: Princeton University Press, 1959.

Pesola, Carol Ann. "Culture in the Elementary School Foreign Language Classroom." *Foreign Language Annals* 24:4 (September 1991): 331–346.

Pesola, Carol Ann Bjornstad. Background, Design and Evaluation of a Conceptual Framework for FLES Curriculum. Unpublished dissertation, University of Minnesota, 1995.

Peyton, Joy Kreeft. "Dialogue Journals: Interactive Writing to Develop Language and Literacy." *ERIC Digest.* April 1993. Available on-line: http://www.cal.org/resources/Digest/peyton01.html.

Phillips, June K. "Practical Implications of Recent Research in Reading." *Foreign Language Annals* 17:4 (1984): 285–296.

Piaget, Jean. *The Language and Thought of the Child.* New York: W. W. Norton, 1963.

Pink, Daniel H. *A Whole New Mind: Why Right Brainers Will Rule the Future.* New York: Riverhead Books Penguin Group, 2006.

Politzer, Robert L. Speech and handout provided at conference on Articulation, University of Wisconsin–Milwaukee, March 1991.

President's Commission on Foreign Language and International Studies. *Strength through Wisdom: A Critique of U.S. Capability.* Washington DC: United States Government Printing Office, 1979.

Rafferty, Eileen A. *Second Language Study and Basic Skills in Louisiana.* Baton Rouge: Louisiana Department of Education, 1986.

Ratte, E. H. "Foreign Language and the Elementary School Language Arts Program." *The French Review* 42 (1968).

Redmond, Mary Lynn. "ATTENTION! Are You Seeking a Position with Excellent Long-Term Benefits? Be an Advocate!" *Learning Languages* 4:1 (Fall 1998): 4–9.

"Research Notes: Language Learning and the Developing Brain." *Learning Languages* 1:2 (Winter 1996): 17.

Rhodes, Nancy C., and Lucinda E. Branaman. *Foreign Language Instruction in the United States: A National Survey of Elementary and Secondary Schools.* Washington DC and McHenry, IL: Center for Applied Linguistics and Delta Systems, 1999.

Rhodes, Nancy C., and Ingrid Pufahl. *Language by Video: An Overview of Foreign Language Instructional Videos for Children* (Professional Practice Series No. 4). Washington DC: Center for Applied Linguistics and Delta Systems, 2004.

Rieken, Elizabeth, et al. "Building Better Bridges: Middle School to High School Articulation in Foreign Language Programs." *Foreign Language Annals* 29:4 (1996): 562–570.

Riley, Richard W. "Changing the American High School to Fit Modern Times." The National Press Club, September 15, 1999. Available on-line: http://www.ed.gov/Speeches/09-1999/990915.html.

Rivers, Wilga M. "Comprehension and Production in Interactive Language Teaching." *The Modern Language Journal* 70:1 (1986): 1–7.

Robb, Thomas N. "E-Mail Keypals for Language Fluency." *Foreign Language Notes* (Foreign Language Educators of New Jersey) 38:3 (Fall 1996): 8–10. Available on-line: http://www.cc.kyoto-su.ac.jp/~trobb/keypals.html. Accessed November 30, 2008.

Roberts, Deborah Fernald. "Group Work: Practicing Language in Context." Presentation at ACTFL Annual Meeting, Salt Lake City, November 3, 2002.

Romijn, E., and C. Seely. *Live Action English*. Elmsford, NY: Pergamon Press, 1983.

Rosenbusch, Marcia. "Elementary School Foreign Language: The Establishment and Maintenance of Strong Programs." *Foreign Language Annals* 24:4 (September 1991): 297–314.

Rosenbusch, Marcia. *Colloquium on Foreign Languages in the Elementary School Curriculum. Proceedings 1991*. Munich: Goethe Institut, 1992a. (Available from AATG, 112 Haddontowne Court, No. 112, Cherry Hill, NJ 08034.)

Rosenbusch, Marcia. "Is Knowledge of Cultural Diversity Enough? Global Education in the Elementary School Foreign Language Program." *Foreign Language Annals* 25:2 (April 1992b): 129–136.

Rosenbusch, Marcia. "Language Learners in the Elementary School: Investing in the Future." In R. Donato and R. Terry (Eds.), *Foreign Language Learning: The Journey of a Lifetime*. Lincolnwood, IL: National Textbook Company, 1995.

Samples, Alisha Dawn. Personal communication, December 12, 2002.

Sandrock, Paul. Presentation to Wisconsin FLES Fest, March 1993.

Sandrock, Paul. Personal communication, November 4, 2002.

Saunders, Carol M. The Effect of the Study of a Foreign Language in the Elementary School on Scores on the Iowa Test of Basic Skills and an Analysis of Student-Participant Attitudes and Abilities. Unpublished dissertation, University of Georgia, 1998.

Savignon, Sandra J. *Communicative Competence. Theory and Classroom Practice: Texts and Contexts in Second Language Learning* (2nd ed.). New York: McGraw-Hill, 1997.

Schinke-Llano, Linda. *Foreign Language in the Elementary School: State of the Art*. Washington DC: Center for Applied Linguistics, 1985.

Schnitzler, Wolfgang. Personal communication, 1986.

Seelye, H. Ned. *Teaching Culture: Strategies for Intercultural Communication* (3rd ed.). Lincolnwood, IL: National Textbook Company, 1993.

Segal, Berty. *Teaching English through Actions*. Brea, CA: Berty Segal, Inc., n.d. (Available from Berty Segal, Inc., 1749 Eucalyptus St., Brea, CA 92621.)

Short, Deborah J. *How to Integrate Language and Content Instruction: A Training Manual* (2nd ed.). Washington DC: Center for Applied Linguistics, 1991.

Simon, Paul. *The Tongue-Tied American: Confronting the Foreign Language Crisis*. New York: Continuum Publishing, 1980.

Singleton, David M. "A Critical Look at the Critical Period Hypothesis on Second Language Acquisition Research." In D. Singleton and Z. Lengyel (Eds.), *The Age Factor in Second Language Acquisition*. Clevedon, UK: Multilingual Matters, 1995.

Smith, Frank. *Joining the Literacy Club: Further Essays into Education*. Portsmouth, NH: Heineman, 1988.

Smith, Frank. Speech given at California Association of Bilingual Education (CABE), February 2, 1994.

Smith, Frank. *Reading without Nonsense* (4th ed.). New York: Teachers College Press, 2006.

Smith, Martin. Personal communications, 2008, 2009.

Snow, Marguerite Ann, Myriam Met, and Fred Genesee. "A Conceptual Framework for the Integration of Language and Content in Second/Foreign Language Instruction." *TESOL Quarterly* 23:2 (1989): 201–217.

Sprenger, Marilee. *Learning & Memory: The Brain in Action*. Alexandria, VA: Association for Supervision and Curriculum Development, 1999.

Standards for Foreign Language Learning in the 21st Century. Yonkers, NY: National Standards in Foreign Language Education Project, 1999.

Strength through Wisdom: A Critique of U.S. Capability. Washington DC: U.S. Government Printing Office, 1979.

Swain, Merrill. "What Does Research Say about Immersion Education?" In Beth Mlacak and Elaine Isabelle (Eds.), *So You Want Your Child to Learn French*. Ottawa, Canada: Canadian Parents for French, 1979.

Swain, Merrill. "A Review of Immersion Education in Canada: Research and Evaluation Studies." In *Studies on Immersion: A Collection for United States Educators* (pp. 87–112). Sacramento, CA: California State Department of Education, 1984.

Swain, Merrill. "Communicative Competence: Some

Roles of Comprehensible Input and Comprehensible Output in Its Development." In Susan M. Gass and Carolyn G. Madden (Eds.), *Input in Second Language Acquisition* (pp. 235–253). Series in Second Language Research. Rowley, MA: Newbury House, 1985.

Swain, Merrill. "Manipulating and Complementing Content Teaching to Maximize Second Language Learning." *TESL Canada Journal* 6 (1988): 68–83.

Swain, Merrill, and Sharon Lapkin. "Immersion French in Secondary Schools: 'The Goods' and 'The Bads.'" *Contact* 5:3 (1986): 2–9.

Swender, Elvira, and Greg Duncan. "ACTFL Performance Guidelines for K-12 Learners." *Foreign Language Annals* 31:4 (Winter 1998): 479–491.

Sylwester, Robert. *A Celebration of Neurons: An Educator's Guide to the Human Brain.* Alexandria, VA: Association for Supervision and Curriculum Development, 1995.

Tardif, Claudette, and Sandra Weber. "French Immersion Research: A Call for New Perspectives." *Canadian Modern Language Review* 44:1 (1987): 67–77.

Taylor, Gregory, Carine Feyten, John Meros, and Joyce W. Nutta. "Effects of FLES on Reading Comprehension and Vocabulary Achievement: A Multi-Method Longitudinal Study." *Learning Languages* 13:2 (2008): 30–37.

Teacher Partnership Institute. "Relevant and Essential Background for the K–6 Foreign Language Teacher." Iowa State University: National K–12 Foreign Language Resource Center, 1994.

Tomlinson, Carol Ann. *How to Differentiate Instruction in Mixed-Ability Classrooms* (2nd ed.). Alexandria, VA: Association for Supervision and Curriculum Development, 2001.

Tucker, G. Richard, and Richard Donato. "Designing and Implementing an Innovative Foreign Language Program: Reflections from a School District–University Partnership." *Learning Languages* 4:2 (Winter 1999): 4–12.

Van Ek, J. A. *The Threshold Level for Modern Language Learning in Schools.* Strasbourg: The Council of Europe, 1991.

Vygotsky, Lev S. *Thought and Language.* Cambridge, MA: MIT Press, 1934/1986.

Wajnryb, Ruth. "Story-Telling and Language Learning." *Babel* 21:2 (August 1986): 17–24.

Weatherford, H. J. "Personal Benefits of Foreign Language Study." *ERIC Digest.* Washington DC: ERIC Clearinghouse on Languages and Linguistics, 1986. EDRS 276 305.

Webb, Elisabeth L. The Effect of Second Language Learning on Test Scores, Intelligence and Achievement: An Annotated Bibliography. Retrieved from http://www.doe,K12.ga.us/DMGetDocument.aspx/AnnBiblio.pdf?p=BE1EECF99CD364EA5554055463F1FBB0B70FECF5942E123FE4810FFF53501CAAE8CB82838C0A540749FE3E915&Type=D. Accessed February 15, 2009.

Wiggins, Grant. "Creating Tests Worth Taking." *Educational Leadership* 49:8 (May 1992): 26–33.

Wiggins, Grant, and Jay McTighe. *Understanding by Design* (2nd ed.). Alexandria, VA: Association for Supervision and Curriculum Development, 2005.

Wolfe, Patricia. *Brain Matters: Translating Research into Classroom Practice.* Alexandria, VA: Association for Supervision and Curriculum Development, 2001.

Wong, Harry K., and Rosemary T. Wong. *The First Days of School: How to Be an Effective Teacher.* Mountain View, CA: Harry K. Wong Publications, 1998.

Wong-Fillmore, Lily. "The Language Learner as an Individual: Implications of Research on Individual Differences for the ESL Teacher." In M. A. Clark and J. Handscombe (Eds.), *On TESOL '82: Pacific Perspectives on Language Learning and Teaching.* Washington DC: TESOL, 1983.

Wong-Fillmore, Lily. "When Does Teacher Talk Work as Input?" In Susan M. Gass and Carolyn G. Madden (Eds.), *Input in Second Language Acquisition* (pp. 17–50). Rowley, MA: Newbury House, 1985.

Zeydel, Edwin H. "The Teaching of German in the United States from Colonial Times to the Present." *Reports of Surveys and Studies in the Teaching of Modern Foreign Languages, 1959–1961.* New York: The Modern Language Association of America, 1961.

name index

subject index